THE **CB** SOLUTION

Print + Online

CB⁸ delivers all the key terms and core concepts for the **Consumer Behavior** course.

CB Online provides the complete narrative from the printed text with additional interactive media and the unique functionality of **StudyBits**—all available on nearly any device!

What is a StudyBit™? Created through a deep investigation of students' challenges and workflows, the StudyBit™ functionality of **CB Online** enables students of different generations and learning styles to study more effectively by allowing them to learn their way. Here's how they work:

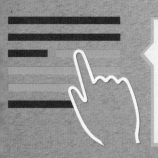

COLLECT WHAT'S IMPORTANT
Create StudyBits as you highlight text, images or take notes!

WEAK

FAIR

STRONG

UNASSIGNED

RATE AND ORGANIZE STUDYBITS
Rate your understanding and use the color-coding to quickly organize your study time and personalize your flashcards and quizzes.

StudyBit™

CORRECT

INCORRECT

INCORRECT

INCORRECT

TRACK/MONITOR PROGRESS
Use Concept Tracker to decide how you'll spend study time and study YOUR way!

85%

PERSONALIZE QUIZZES
Filter by your StudyBits to personalize quizzes or just take chapter quizzes off-the-shelf.

CB8
Barry J. Babin, Eric J. Harris

Sr. Vice President, General Manager:
  Balraj Kalsi

Product Manager: Laura Redden

Content/Media Developer: Tricia Hempel

Product Assistant: Eli Lewis

Marketing Manager: Katie Jergens

Marketing Coordinator: Audrey Jacobs

Content Project Manager: Darrell E. Frye

Manufacturing Planner: Ron Montgomery

Production Service: MPS Limited

Sr. Art Director: Bethany Casey

Internal Designer: Joe Devine, Red Hangar

Cover Designer: Lisa Kuhn, Curio Press,
  LLC/Trish & Ted Knapke, Ke Design

Cover Image: © RossHelen

Special Page Images: Computer and tablet
  illustration: ©iStockphoto.com/furtaev;
  Smart phone Illustration: ©iStockphoto.
  com/dashadima; Feedback image:
  Rawpixel.com/Shutterstockcom

Intellectual Property Analyst: Diane Garrity

Intellectual Property Project Manager:
  Carly Belcher

For product information and technology assistance, contact us at
Cengage Learning Customer & Sales Support, 1-800-354-9706

For permission to use material from this text or product,
submit all requests online at **www.cengage.com/permissions**
Further permissions questions can be emailed to
permissionrequest@cengage.com

Library of Congress Control Number: 2016959310

Student Edition ISBN: 978-1-305-57724-4

Student Edition with Online ISBN: 978-1-305-57714-5

Cengage Learning
20 Channel Center Street
Boston, MA 02210
USA

Cengage Learning is a leading provider of customized learning solutions with employees residing in nearly 40 different countries and sales in more than 125 countries around the world. Find your local representative at **www.cengage.com**

Cengage Learning products are represented in Canada by Nelson Education, Ltd.

To learn more about Cengage Learning Solutions, visit **www.cengage.com**

Purchase any of our products at your local college store or at our preferred online store **www.cengagebrain.com**

Printed in the United States of America
Print Number: 02   Print Year: 2017

BABIN / HARRIS
CB⁸

BRIEF CONTENTS

MyWallet   BUY

Purchase
Cab Fare: $14.20

© RossHelen

CONTENTS

Part 1
INTRODUCTION

Juice Images/Getty Images

Donald Miralle/Getty Images

Part 3
EXTERNAL INFLUENCES

Part 4
SITUATIONS AND DECISION MAKING

Larry Dale Gordon/Getty Images

Part 5
CONSUMPTION AND BEYOND

michaeljung/Shutterstock.com

14 Consumption to Satisfaction 286

15 Beyond Consumer Relationships 304

CB8
ONLINE

ACCESS TEXTBOOK CONTENT ONLINE—
INCLUDING ON SMARTPHONES!

Includes Videos & Other
Interactive Resources!

1 | What Is CB and Why Should I Care?

LEARNING OBJECTIVES

After studying this chapter, the student should be able to:

1-1 Understand the meaning of *consumption* and *consumer behavior*.

1-2 Describe how competitive marketing environments lead to better outcomes for consumers.

1-3 Explain the role of consumer behavior in today's business and society.

1-4 Be familiar with basic approaches to studying consumer behavior.

1-5 Appreciate how dynamic the field of consumer behavior continues to be, particularly as CB is shaped by technological advances including big data analytics, the "internet of things" and the sharing economy.

Juice Images/Getty Images

Remember to visit **PAGE 23** for additional **STUDY TOOLS**

INTRODUCTION

Students rarely feel like an expert when they begin a new college class. However, a consumer behavior (CB) course is an exception. Everyone reading this book has years of experience spending and consuming! As we will see, spending means that something is being used, perhaps, time and/or money, are being used toward a value-producing activity, meaning consumption takes place. In fact, we act as consumers every day and every waking hour. That's correct: Every day you have been alive you have been a consumer. As a result, you begin this book with a degree of expertise that makes the subject come alive with relevance.

The human experience is made up largely of consumption-relevant episodes. We wake, we drink, we eat, we clean, we dress, we ride, we shop, we play, we read, we choose, we watch, we Instagram, we Tweet, and on and on. Practically everything we do involves consumer behavior in some way. Take a look at Pinterest and it becomes obvious that many of the posts call attention to things to buy, places to go, things to do, and

how they should be done. Websites like Pinterest mimic real discussions where one consumer tells others about the things that bring value to their lives. Certainly, the sharing of preferences and information about what to do helps consumer make decisions. The desire to share such information has driven Pinterest to one of the top websites in the United States.[1]

Consumer decisions are sometimes simple, involving few resources, and other times complex, involving large amounts of resources. When consumers make decisions, they set in place a chain of reactions that change their lives, the lives of those around them, and the lives of people they don't even know. How can even simple decisions be so important to society? The answer to this question is one of the key points of this subject.

A consumer makes a decision with the intention of improving his or her life—that is, doing something of value. But, the value creation doesn't stop here. Businesses survive by offering value propositions that tell consumers how they can maintain or make life better by engaging with some good, service, or experience. As long as consumers continue shopping, buying, and consuming, opportunity exists for business. The process

of making a purchase starts a chain reaction of value-creating actions.

Much of the news reported in the media focuses on the economy. Various aspects of the economy cause great concern. Why so? Consider the labor participation rate, which has slid every year since 2007.[2] As a result, analysts become concerned about what is being sold, particularly housing sales. When consumers stop buying houses, many industries and people downstream are affected. Fewer home sales means fewer appliance and furniture purchases, less demand for architects, builders, and building supplies, and in turn, fewer jobs for people in those industries. Jobs provide resources for consumers to enhance their lives by acquiring value-providing goods and services. Those that are unemployed or underemployed are less likely to be able to make major purchases like a home. Thus, when consumers stop buying, bad things can take place.

Now, what happens when consumers buy things? Have you adopted some type of smartwatch yet? Three out of four smartwatch adopters express satisfaction with the device. Although owners are aggravated by some aspects such as short battery life, overall sales are growing. When someone buys a smartwatch, a chain reaction occurs. Not only does the owner receive value, but value is created for others as the store must restock its inventory, meaning the manufacturer produces more products. To do this, the manufacturer purchases raw materials, parts, and services from suppliers. Companies like UPS or FedEx ship raw materials and finished products, providing even more jobs. The consumer also will enhance the product by adding appropriate apps. Apps that track fitness can even change lifestyles: some consumers report changing their lifestyles and exercising because they don't want their Fitbit or other exercise tracking app to register 0 at the end of a day.[3] Thus, what seems to be even a simple purchase sets in place a chain reaction of value-enhancing activities that improve individual lives and lives for those who work to provide those products.

Marketers are challenged to continue to provide innovations that offer relative value advantages. While Apple turns its attention toward an autonomous electric car, others are looking at transportation alternatives that don't involve cars at all. In fact, imagine climbing inside a tube that is propelled through a hyperloop at 500 miles per hour using technology commonly seen at bank drive-throughs for decades.[4] Will innovations like these offer value for consumers?

Imagine climbing inside a tube that is propelled through a hyperloop at 500 miles per hour using technology seen at bank drive-throughs for decades. . . .

Although some may call a course like this one "buyer behavior," consuming involves more than just *buying*. Certainly, businesses are interested in getting someone to buy something. But consumption goes on long after purchase, and this consumption story ultimately determines how much value results.

As you can see, our behavior as consumers is critically important, not just to ourselves, but to many other people. This is why so many people, not just marketing people, are interested in learning about CB. True, the marketer who understands consumers will be able to design products with greater value potential and thus a greater chance of enhancing the well-being of stakeholders, including the company and customers. Policy makers also show interest in CB because the knowledge allows them to make more effective public policy decisions. Last but not least, consumers who understand CB can make better decisions concerning how they allocate scarce resources—that is, they become better consumers. Thus, an understanding of CB can mean better business for companies, better public policy for governments, and a better life for individuals and households.

> Consumers who understand CB can make better decisions concerning how they allocate scarce resources— that is, they become better consumers.

consumer behavior set of value-seeking activities that take place as people go about addressing their real needs

1-1 CONSUMPTION AND CONSUMER BEHAVIOR

We consider CB from two unique perspectives:

1. The actual human thoughts, feelings, and actions involved in consumption experiences, and/or
2. A field of study (human inquiry) that is developing an accumulated body of knowledge about human consumption experiences.

If we think of a consumer considering the purchase of a smartwatch, CB captures the thoughts, feelings, reactions, and consequences that take place as the consumer goes through a decision-making process, ownership, and usage of a product, in this case a smartwatch. Alternatively, we consider the body of knowledge that researchers accumulate as they attempt to explain these thoughts, feelings, actions, reactions, and consequences as the field of study known as consumer behavior. Thus, rather than choosing between the two alternative approaches, the best appreciation of CB requires consideration of both perspectives.

1-1a Consumer Behavior as Human Behavior

Consumer behavior is the set of value-seeking activities that take place as people go about addressing and attempting to address real needs. In other words, when a consumer is motivated by a need, a process kicks in as the consumer sets out to find desirable ways to fill this need. The process involves multiple psychological events, including thinking, feeling, and behaving, and the entire process culminates in value. If it's successful, the process creates sufficient value to address the need that began the process.

THE BASIC CB PROCESS

Exhibit 1.1 illustrates the basic consumption process. We discuss each step in detail in later chapters. However, we briefly illustrate the process here, using a consumer who just got a new smartwatch. At some point, the consumer realized a need to more conveniently access outside media, such as Snapchat, Viber, and email,

Exhibit 1.1

The Basic Consumption Process

Need → Want → Exchange → Costs and Benefits → Reaction → Value

via the Internet. The realization of this need may be motivated by a desire to do better on the job, to have better access to friends and family, to more quickly post news about personal activities, or some combination of reasons. The realization of a need creates a want. A *want* is a specific *desire* that spells out a way a consumer can go about addressing a recognized need. A consumer feels a need to stay in touch, belong, socialize, or feel good about him or herself, and this need manifests itself in the want for better media access devices.

Realizing the need, our consumer decides to visit the new Buckhead HH Gregg store (consumer electronics

koya979/Shutterstock.com

Devices create customers for apps.
Consumers drive the economy.

and appliances retailer). After looking at several alternative devices and talking it over with a salesperson, the consumer selects the Samsung Gear S2 smartwatch. Having made a choice, the consumer completes an exchange in which he gives up resources in return for ownership and the potential to use the product. An **exchange** is the acting out of a decision to give something up in return for something perceived to be of greater value. Here, the consumer decides the watch will be worth at least the price of the product plus any apps and subscriptions that may be needed to fully use the device.

The consumer then uses the product and experiences all the associated benefits and costs associated with consumption. **Costs** are the negative results of consumption experiences. The costs involve more than just the monetary price of the product. Consumers spend time both shopping for and learning how to use a device. Physical effort also takes place as consumers visit retail stores and browse web resources during the process. The time, money, and effort spent acquiring a product comes at the expense of other activities, resulting in high opportunity costs for the consumer. Also, compatibility often is an issue for so-called smart devices. Health-conscious, budget-minded consumers like the Fitbit Blaze? Consumers need to check compatibility with Windows, Android, and OSX before making the purchase. An incompatible phone or PC means the smartwatch's value is limited. In fact, even if a consumer might prefer a Samsung Gear S2, he/she may end up with an iWatch, especially if he/she already owns an iPhone or MacBook.[5]

Benefits are positive results of consumption experiences. The benefits are multifaceted, ranging from potentially better job performance, easier text, email, and social network access, and benefits from other smartwatch apps that do things like monitor heart rate and calories consumed. Other tacit benefits may exist for some consumers who like the fact that other consumers notice and admire the smartwatch. Benefits like these potentially enhance the perceived self-esteem of the consumer.

Over time, the consumer evaluates the costs and benefits and reacts

want a specific desire representing a way a consumer may go about addressing a recognized need

exchange acting out of the decision to give something up in return for something perceived to be of greater value

costs negative results of consumption experiences

benefits positive results of consumption experiences

to the purchase in some way. These reactions involve thoughts and feelings. The thoughts may involve reactions to features such as the ease of use. The feelings may sometimes include frustration if the features do not work correctly or conveniently. Ultimately, the process results in a perception of value. We will discuss value in more detail in Chapter 2.

CONSUMPTION

Another way to look at the basic consumer behavior process is to consider the steps that occur when consumption takes place. Obviously, a consumer consumes. Interestingly, very few consumer behavior books define consumption itself. **Consumption** represents the process by which consumers use goods, services, or ideas and transform the experience into value. Thus, the actions involved in acquiring and using a technological device like a smartwatch create value for a consumer. Consumption is a value-producing process in which the marketer and the consumer interact to produce value. When the consumer fails to realize value from the process, something has broken down in the process; perhaps a bad performance from the marketer or perhaps a bad decision by the customer. Thinking about the result of all of these interactions considered together, one easily sees that consumption outcomes affect consumer well-being by affecting quality of life.

1-1b Consumer Behavior as a Field of Study

Consumer behavior as a field of study represents the study of consumers as they go through the consumption process. In this sense, consumer behavior is the science of studying how consumers seek value in an effort to address real needs. This book represents a collection of knowledge resulting as consumer behavior researchers go about studying consumers.

Consumer behavior, as a field of study, is a very young field. The first books focusing on consumer or buyer behavior date from the 1960s.[6] Thus, compared with older disciplines, researchers have had less time to develop the body of knowledge. Therefore, each decade the accumulated body of knowledge grows significantly. Clearly, however, much uncertainty

consumption process by which consumers use and transform goods, services, or ideas into value

consumer behavior as a field of study study of consumers as they go about the consumption process; the science of studying how consumers seek value in an effort to address real needs

economics study of production and consumption

Exhibit 1.2

Relationships of CB with Other Disciplines

Source: Based on D. J. MacInnis and V. S. Folkes, "The Disciplinary Status of Consumer Behavior: A Sociology of Science Perspective on Key Controversies," *Journal of Consumer Research* 36 (April 2010): 899–914.

remains, and consequently, the body of accepted theory and rules of practice remains small. This is one reason consumer behavior is so exciting to study. CB researchers continue to expand the knowledge base at a fast pace compared to more mature disciplines.

Like other fields of study, CB has family ties with other disciplines. Exhibit 1.2 displays the relationship between CB and other disciplines. Research in various disciplines produced relevant knowledge for marketers seeking to understand consumers. The genesis of the CB field lies in business and the growing body of academic research produced by business schools in the late 20th and early 21st century.[7] The exhibit displays the overlapping nature of CB and marketing; other fields that sometimes contribute to and to which CB sometimes contributes are also shown. A few of these disciplines share a special bond with CB, as we discuss below. CB shares particularly strong interdisciplinary connections with economics, psychology (particularly social psychology), marketing, and anthropology.[8]

ECONOMICS AND CONSUMER BEHAVIOR

Economics often is defined as the study of production and consumption. A free enterprise system allows individuals to participate freely in the market.[9] Accordingly, it is easy to see that marketing has origins in economics, particularly with respect to the production and distribution of goods. As the definition implies, economics also involves consumption. Therefore, consumer behavior and economics have a lot in common. However, the economist's focus on consumer behavior is generally a broad or macro perspective bounded by broad assumptions. Economic studies often involve things like commodity consumption of nations over time. This may even involve tracking changes in consumption with dif-

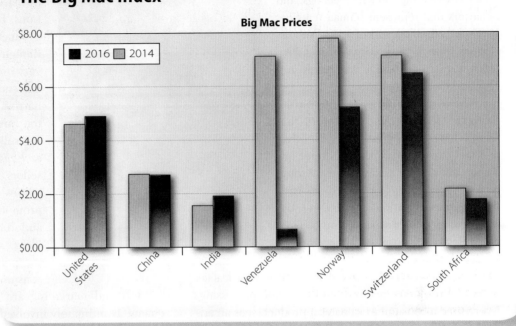

Exhibit 1.3

The Big Mac Index

Big Mac Prices

ferent price levels, enabling price elasticity to be determined. The economist finds data for a study like this in historical sales records. This type of study does not require data describing individual consumers that may reveal the thoughts, feelings, and behaviors associated with consumption.

Economists' inclination to track and compare overall consumption of a specific phenomenon illustrates a macro perspective. For instance, *The Economist* journal tracks prices of Big Macs globally.[10] The Big Mac Index compares the relative price of hamburgers country by country. The idea was to show relative purchasing power, but economists now realize the Big Mac Index actually predicts currency fluctuations with some accuracy. A relatively low price indicates an undervalued currency. The prices represent aggregate prices paid by thousands of anonymous consumers within each country. Exhibit 1.3 displays the Big Mac Index prices for several countries for both 2014 and 2016. Large differences in the prices indicate less stable currencies. In this case, Venezuela and Norway show the biggest changes in two years. The fluctuation is likely tied to the fact that oil prices have dropped from well over $100 per barrel in 2014 to well under $50 a barrel in 2016.[11] Both Norway's and Venezuela's economies rely heavily on oil.

In contrast, consumer behavior researchers generally study CB at much more of a micro level, often focusing on individual consumers rather than countries. The Big Mac Index assumes equal liking for Big Macs and does not take into account individual difference characteristics or even cultural variables that might influence the value of a Big Mac. Most Indian consumers for instance, would not pay a penny for a Big Mac because eating beef would run counter to Hindu beliefs. CB research relaxes many assumptions of economics including rationality to better understand why consumer preferences vary so much. For instance, consumer researchers study how consumers' desires for fast food are influenced by various health claims or even by the relative body shape of other individuals in the fast-food restaurant.[12] These results suggest, among other things, that a consumer who buys a "healthy" burger is likely to indulge in more side orders than a consumer buying a burger that makes no health claims.

> **Consumption is a value-producing process in which the marketer and the consumer interact to produce value.**

PSYCHOLOGY

Psychology is the study of human reactions to their environment.[13] Psychologists seek to explain the thoughts, feelings, and behaviors that represent human reaction. Psychology itself consists of several subdisciplines. Social psychology and cognitive psychology, in particular, are highly relevant to consumer behavior.[14]

Social psychology focuses on the thoughts, feelings, and behaviors that people have as they interact with other people (group behavior). Consumer behavior most often takes place in some type of social setting or sometimes with the specific intention of affecting the way others view the self. Thus, social psychology and consumer behavior overlap significantly.

beornbjorn/Shutterstock.com

Cognitive psychology deals with the intricacies of mental reactions involved in information processing. Every time a consumer evaluates a product, sees an advertisement, or reacts to product consumption, information is processed. Thus, cognitive psychology is also very relevant to consumer behavior and a prominent topic throughout the text.

Today the study of cognitive psychology is assisted by developments in neuroscience. **Neuroscience**, the study of the central nervous system including brain mechanisms associated with emotion, offers potential for understanding CB by charting a consumer's physicological brain functions during the consumption process. Neuroscience researchers use sophisticated brain imaging equipment to monitor brain activity. One finding suggests that when consumers think about enjoying some of their favorite foods their brains become more active than when they actually eat the food.[15] Is thinking about consuming as good as actually consuming? Neuroscience applications addressing such questions continue to increase in number.

psychology study of human reactions to their environment

social psychology study that focuses on the thoughts, feelings, and behaviors that people have as they interact with other people

cognitive psychology study of the intricacies of mental reactions involved in information processing

neuroscience the study of the central nervous system including brain mechanisms associated with emotion

marketing multitude of value-producing seller activities that facilitate *exchanges* between buyers and sellers, including production, pricing, promotion, distribution, and retailing

MARKETING

One doesn't have to look very hard to find different definitions of marketing. Many older definitions focus heavily on physical products and profitability. Even though products and profits are very important aspects of marketing, such definitions are relatively narrow.[16] **Marketing** consists of the multitude of value-producing seller activities that facilitate *exchanges* between buyers and sellers. The value-producing activities include the production, promotion, pricing, distribution, and retailing of goods, services, ideas, and experiences, all with the potential to create value for consumers and other stakeholders.

CB and marketing are very closely related. Exchange is intimately involved in marketing and, as can be seen from Exhibit 1.1, exchange also is central to CB. In fact, in some ways, CB involves "inverse" marketing as consumers operate at the other end of the exchange. Marketing actions are targeted at and affect consumers, while consumer actions affect marketers. A marketer without customers won't be a marketer very long. In fact, without consumers, marketing is unnecessary.

Some researchers view the CB discipline as separate and distinct from marketing. Others view CB as a subdiscipline within marketing.[17] The details of the argument are beyond the scope of this text; however, the very fact that such an argument exists illustrates the close bond between the two. Marketing and CB share considerable relevance, and both are essential inputs to organizational success.

CONSUMER BEHAVIOR AND OTHER DISCIPLINES

Commerce increased tremendously with the industrial revolution and the coinciding political changes that fostered economic freedom in many countries. Businesses looked to the new field of marketing for practical advice initially about distribution and later about pricing, packaging, advertising, and communication. Thus, although marketing may have originally shared more in common with economics, the turn toward consumer research brought numerous psychologists into the field. Many of these psychologists became the first consumer researchers.

CB research and marketing research overlap with each other more than they do with any other discipline, as illustrated by the overlapping shapes in Exhibit 1.2. Beyond this, CB research shares much in common with psychological research, particularly in terms of shared research approaches and shared theories. Consumer research is based largely on psychology, and to some extent psychology draws from consumer behavior research.

Disciplines beyond economics, psychology, and marketing also intersect with consumer behavior. Sociology focuses on the study of groups of people within a society. Sociology's relevance for CB lies in the fact that consumption often takes place within group settings or is in one way or another affected by group dynamics. Consumers take value from sharing experiences with others not only because it is enjoyable, but because shared experiences can build social capital. [18]

Anthropology has contributed to consumer behavior research by allowing researchers to interpret the relationships between consumers and the things they purchase, the products they own, and the activities in which they participate. Anthropological consumer research often features the symbolic meanings behind our possessions. One interesting study looks at the role of gift-giving among victims held in Nazi concentration camps and links both giving and possessing to self-identity.[19] Other disciplines, such as geography and the medical sciences, overlap with consumer behavior in that they draw from some of the same theories and/or research approaches.

1-2 THE WAYS IN WHICH CONSUMERS ARE TREATED

Is the customer always "king"? Look at this list of familiar service environments:

- A typical Department of Motor Vehicles (DMV) office
- The registrar's office at a state university
- A bank lobby
- A university health clinic
- A Veterans' Administration (VA) Clinic
- A sports bar
- A New York City fine dining establishment
- A Honolulu resort

Think about the following questions. Does a consumer receive the same degree of service at each of these

ROBYN BECK/Getty Images

Compared to a restaurant, what motivation does the DMV have to provide a high-value waiting experience?

places? What is the waiting environment like at each one? Is there a clean, comfortable waiting area with pleasant music? How dedicated are the employees to delivering a high-quality service experience? How likely are employees to view the customer as a nuisance? If you don't see the point of these questions yet, contrast the waiting area at a driver's license bureau with the elaborate lobby where you wait for check-in service (probably not very long) at a Miami Beach resort.

Some organizations can survive while treating customers badly, while others need to pamper customers just to have a chance of surviving. Consider these two questions in trying to understand why this is so:

1. How competitive is the marketing environment?

2. How dependent is the marketer on repeat business?

1-2a Competition and Consumer Orientation

Where do consumers go if they don't like the service at the DMV? If the choice comes down to visiting the bureau or not driving, nearly all consumers will put up with the less-than-immaculate surroundings, long waits, and poor service that all too typically go along with getting a driver's license. Put yourself into the shoes of the service providers at the

sociology the study of groups of people within a society, with relevance for consumer behavior because a great deal of consumption takes place within group settings or is affected by group behavior

anthropology field of study involving interpretation of relationships between consumers and the things they purchase, the products they own, and the activities in which they participate

Competitive pressures motivate marketers to provide good service.

bureau. Is there any concern about doing something that would make a customer not want to return to do business again? Is there any real incentive to provide a pleasant and valuable experience?

FEW COMPETITIVE PRESSURES?

In essence, the DMV typifies a service organization that operates in a market with practically no competitive pressure and a captive audience. In a government service like this, the answers to the two questions above are (1) not at all competitive and (2) not at all dependent on keeping customers. No matter how poor the service is, they know consumers will return to do more business when the term on their license expires or they need to register a vehicle. The incentive for better customer service remains relatively small.

Unlike a restaurant, DMV management may not be compelled to adjust workloads to demand. DMV *customers* in many places face long lines and even wait times counted in hours, not minutes. Even after state officials in Colorado introduced the "Wait Less" program, designed

consumer (customer) orientation way of doing business in which the actions and decision making of the institution prioritize consumer value and satisfaction above all other concerns

to cut wait times to 15 minutes, many Colorado drivers still face waits of 2 to 3 hours.[20] Veterans waiting for care from a VA health facility sometimes wait months or years to receive care. The excessive wait times did much to fuel the recent VA scandal.[21] Imagine a bank touting wait times of less than two hours or a sports bar saying "Come back next year!" A few states have turned to combinations of technology and private outsourcing to improve service. Some states have outsourced DMV offices to private companies. The private companies generally provide consumers with better service, and the DMV ends up with better and more accurate information about drivers.[22] Why does the private company improve service? They are the marketer, and the city, county, or state is the customer. Just like the sports bar customer, if the public officials are unhappy with the service, they'll find another company to do the job.

MANY COMPETITIVE PRESSURES?

Now consider the customer dining in New York City. A consumer can choose from thousands of options including over 1,000 Italian restaurants alone. A diner doesn't have to put up with poor treatment. The consumer can simply go next door. While the consumer without a reservation may wait for a table at the establishments with a loyal clientele, many provide a comfortable lounge area to enjoy a drink, some music, and conversation while waiting. Here the consumer deals with firms operating in a highly competitive market dependent on repeat business. Thus, firms are oriented toward value creation, and consumers typically receive better treatment.

Governments sometimes realize that competition in the marketplace serves to protect consumers. In the United States, many federal laws oversee commerce with an eye toward ensuring business competition. The Robinson-Patman Act, the Sherman Act, and the Clayton Act are examples of such legislation. They attempt to restrict practices such as price fixing, secret rebates, and customer coercion. European officials are debating consumer privacy acts under the name of a "right to be forgotten" as part of the European Agenda for Security intended to prohibit companies, including Google, Amazon, and Facebook, from divulging consumer information without permission.[23]

FIRM ORIENTATIONS AND CONSUMERS

Competition eventually drives companies toward a high degree of consumer orientation. **Consumer (customer) orientation** is a way of doing business in which the actions and decision making of the institution prioritize consumer value and satisfaction above all other concerns. A consumer orientation is a key component of a firm with a market-oriented culture. **Market orientation** is an organizational culture that embodies the importance of creating value for customers among all employees. In addition to understanding customers, a market orientation stresses the need to monitor and understand competitor actions in the marketplace and the need to communicate information about customers and competitors throughout the organization.[24] Market-oriented firms develop effective ways of listening to consumers, and these skills usually, but not always, lead to better performance.[25]

A market orientation represents a less narrow focus than a strategic orientation that focuses more solely on production. However, an even broader orientation comes when firms adapt **stakeholder marketing**. Under this orientation, firms recognize that more than just the buyer and seller are involved in the marketing process.[26] In fact, primary stakeholders include customers, employees, owners (or shareholders), suppliers, and regulating agencies; secondary stakeholders include the mass media, communities, and trade organizations. Stakeholder marketing orientation recognizes that all stakeholders are involved in and/or are affected by the firm's marketing in some way. This means that even secondary stakeholders can alter the value equation and have relevance for marketing strategies.

1-2b Relationship Marketing and Consumer Behavior

Let's go back to the list of service environments. Certainly, banks and restaurants are generally in very intense competition with rival businesses. Competitive pressures challenge businesses to get customers to repeatedly purchase the goods or services they offer. Even in a city with a population as great as New York, without repeat business each restaurant would have fewer than ten customers per night. In addition, virtually all firms see repeat customers as less costly to serve.[27] For instance, business managers often need to buy a lot of advertising for new customers to learn about a restaurant, whereas old customers already know the place.

Thus, **relationship marketing** means the firm's marketing activities aim to increase repeat business as a route to strong firm performance. Relationship marketing recognizes that customer desires are recurring and that a single purchase act may be only one touchpoint in an ongoing series of interactions with a customer. **Touchpoints** are direct contacts between the firm and

David Pereiras/Shutterstock.com

This consumer is encountering a touchpoint with her stylist. Are there other touchpoints taking place at the same time?

a customer. Increasingly, multiple channels or ways of making this contact exist, including phone, email, text messaging, online social networking, and especially face-to-face contact.[28] Every touchpoint, no matter the channel, should be considered as an opportunity to create value for the customer. Like any type of relationship, a customer–marketer relationship will continue only as long as both parties see the partnership as valuable.

Marketers are increasingly realizing the value of relationship marketing. Wait staff sometimes provide business cards to customers. These customers can use the card to ask for this waiter again on the next visit or to recommend the restaurant and server to a friend. Notice that with relationship marketing, the firm and its employees are very motivated to provide an outstanding overall experience. In sum, both a competitive marketplace and a relationship marketing orientation create exchange environments where firms truly treat customers as "king."

market orientation organizational culture that embodies the importance of creating value for customers among all employees

stakeholder marketing an orientation in which firms recognize that more than just the buyer and seller are involved in the marketing process, and a host of primary and secondary entities affect and are affected by the value creation process

relationship marketing activities based on the belief that the firm's performance is enhanced through repeat business

touchpoints direct contacts between the firm and a customer

1-3 THE CB FIELD'S ROLE IN BUSINESS, SOCIETY, AND FOR CONSUMERS

As mentioned earlier, multiple reasons for studying consumer behavior exist. Each perspective provides unique and interesting opportunities for study. CB is important in at least three ways:

1. CB provides an input to business/marketing strategy.
2. CB provides a force that shapes society.
3. CB provides an input to making responsible decisions as a consumer.

1-3a Consumer Behavior and Marketing Strategy

What companies do you think of as successful? The ultimate hallmark of success for a business is long-term survival. One hundred years is a blink of an eye in the course of history. But how many companies survive at least 100 years? Exhibit 1.4 lists some famous international companies, their core business, and their age.

None of these companies are even 100 years old. Even though we may think about big famous companies as lasting forever, chances are some of these giants will not be around 100, 50, or perhaps even 20 years from now. So, surviving is not a trivial goal, and the companies that do survive long term do so by finding ways to continuously obtain resources from consumers in return for the value they offer. This is a basic tenet of **resource-advantage theory**, a prominent theory that explains why companies succeed or fail.[29] Companies succeed by acquiring more resources from consumers and in turn using those resources to gain advantages in physical and intellectual capital. Consumer research is needed to understand what makes a consumer give up scarce resources. Ultimately, consumers give up resources in the pursuit of value.

In contrast to the companies listed in Exhibit 1.4, many companies that were thought of as innovative and can't miss never make it out of infancy. Amazon.com,

resource-advantage theory theory that explains why companies succeed or fail; the firm goes about obtaining resources from consumers in return for the value the resources create

attribute a part, or tangible feature, of a product that potentially delivers a benefit of consumption

Chris Hondros/Getty Images

The Pets.com sock puppet. The San Francisco-based pet products company, known for its commercials with the sock-puppet dog and the slogan "Because pets can't drive," closed in late 2000 after failing to find a financial backer or buyer.

founded in 1994 and now synonymous with online retailing, is ancient in terms of ".com" firms. Remember Pets.com? Probably not! This online pet supply retailer spent vastly more on Super Bowl advertising than it made in revenue and never saw its first birthday. Similarly, flooz.com, intended to provide online currency to replace credit card payments, and quirky.com, an invention platform allowing consumers to vote on their favorite new things, failed to create sufficient value and didn't make it to adolescence.[30]

One company that has survived over 100 years is Abercrombie and Fitch (A&F). They were founded in the early 1890s as a store providing high-quality gear for the active hunter or fisherman. Not what you think about when you think of A&F today? Well, this illustrates how the companies that survive long term cannot be complacent or think that consumers do not change.

WHAT DO PEOPLE BUY?

When consumers buy something, they give up resources in the form of time, money, and energy in return for whatever is being sold. Consider a customer who purchases a Toyota Prius. What does she really get? Well, the tangibles include an engine, high-powered batteries, plastic, integrated circuitry, seats, wheels, and so on. These parts, or **attributes**, make up the product. No reasonable

Exhibit 1.4

The Short Life Span of Success?

Company	Core business	Birthdate	Place of birth
Tesco	Food Retailing	1919	London, England
Toyota	Motor Vehicles	1937	Tokyo, Japan
Target	Discount Retailing	1962	Ohio
Samsung	Electronic Equipment	1969	Seoul, South Korea
Microsoft	Computer Software and Systems (originally operating systems)	1975	New Mexico
Amazon.com	Retailing	1994	Washington State
Home Depot	Retail and Contractor Building Supply	1976	Georgia
FedEx	Express Package Shipping—Originally founded as Federal Express in 1973	2000	Tennessee
Facebook	Online Social Networking	2004	Massachusetts
Apple Inc.	Media devices and peripheries—Originally founded as Apple Computers in 1976	2007	California

consumer would pay around $30,000 for a pile of these parts. Consumers don't really pay for the physical attributes of a product. So what do consumers pay for? The attributes do function to enable the consumer to enjoy benefits such as transportation and comfort. Also, the product's image, in this case a Prius, creates a feeling within the owner. Outcomes like these are valuable and represent what the customer is ultimately buying.

Marketing firms often implement poor strategies when they don't fully understand what a product truly is. A **product** is not a collection of attributes but rather a potentially valuable bundle of benefits. Theodore Levitt, one of the most famous marketing researchers, understood this by saying that a customer who buys a drill is really buying holes in the wall. He emphasized the importance of the value a customer receives from a product, rather than the product itself.

INNOVATION

Ultimately, companies need to understand why people buy their products to recognize which other current and future products represent competitive threats. Let's look at the companies that produced slide rules (rulers used to do calculations) such as Accu-Rule. They did not go out of business because their products were flawed. Accu-Rule made great slide rules. They went out of business because they failed to innovate.

Newness alone does not make an innovation. An innovation has to produce value for consumers to be successful. Over time, successful innovations exhibit all or some of these characteristics:

1. **Relative Advantage**—makes things better than before
2. **Simplicity**—all things equal, a simpler innovation is better than a complex innovation
3. **Observable**—things that are observable tend to get adopted faster
4. **Trialability**—things that can be tried with little or no risk get adopted faster
5. **Consistency**—consumers are more likely to adopt things that are congruent with existing values and knowledge

> The companies that survive long term cannot be complacent or think that consumers do not change.

Consider our consumer with the new smartwatch from the beginning of the chapter. His liking of the new device will depend on these characteristics, but more importantly for those involved in marketing these

product potentially valuable bundle of benefits

Exhibit 1.5

Different Ways of Doing Business

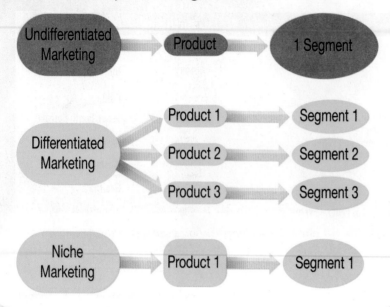

WAYS OF DOING BUSINESS

Each company adopts a way of doing business that is epitomized in its corporate culture. Corporate cultures fall roughly into one of several categories representing different ways of doing business. Exhibit 1.5 summarizes different ways of doing business. Each way of marketing coincides with a varying degree of consumer orientation, which, as we indicated earlier, is a basic component of a market or stakeholder orientation. The ways of doing business often guide a firm's marketing practices.

In **undifferentiated marketing**, the same basic product is offered to all customers. Mass merchandisers typify undifferentiated marketers in that they rely on selling a high volume to be successful. As such, they focus on serving

undifferentiated marketing
plan wherein the same basic product is offered to all customers

production orientation
approach where innovation is geared primarily toward making the production process as efficient and economic as possible

differentiated marketers firms that serve multiple market segments, each with a unique product offering

one-to-one marketing
plan wherein a different product is offered for each individual customer so that each customer is treated as a segment of one

devices, these characteristics will ultimately determine if the category represents a successful innovation.

very large segments in which consumers do not have specific desires (are not picky). Undifferentiated marketers generally adopt a **production orientation**, wherein innovation is geared primarily toward making the production process as efficient and economical as possible. In other words, the emphasis is on serving customers while incurring minimum costs. Walmart typifies this approach with their Supercenters and their state-of-the-art distribution network, which ships massive quantities of products to stores around the world at the lowest possible cost. The need for consumer orientation and consumer research is minimal because all consumers are treated the same.

Differentiated marketers serve multiple market segments, each with a unique product offering. A market orientation usually serves a differentiated marketer well. The emphasis here is on matching a product with a segment.

Many people are aware that Budweiser and Ultra are two of several Anheuser-Busch beer brands. Each brand has unique characteristics appealing to a different market segment. However, companies in other industries also create different brands to appeal to different market segments. In much the same way, Prada represents a prestige name in designer accessories (shoes, handbags, etc.), appealing to the luxury segment. Prada also operates the Miu Miu brand. Prada aims Miu Miu at women who are design- and fashion-conscious, but who may be slightly more price sensitive than the Prada shopper. Prada also offers footwear under the Church's brand (English-style shoes for men), and the Car Shoe brand, the ultimate driver's shoe (for the male driver).

Marketers can take differentiated marketing to the extreme with a practice known as **one-to-one marketing**. Here, the company offers a unique product to each individual customer and thereby treats each customer as a segment of one. A custom home builder practices one-to-one marketing. Computer-aided information processing, design, and production have helped make this a reality on a large scale. Many media sources use consumer preferences and past browsing history to create an experience tailored specifically to that individual. The *Wall Street Journal* and other news sources feed to each unique online user stories that match user profile characteristics and the type of stories read previously.

Firms that specialize in serving one market segment with particularly unique demand characteristics practice

CONSUMERS AND TECHNOLOGY

What a Gas

The Volkswagen emissions debacle illustrates how policy, company, and consumers all play relevant roles in CB. U.S. government policy includes auto emission standards as part of the Clean Air Act. One downside of emissions-choking devices is reduced auto performance. Cleverly, some Volkswagen engineers installed technology on diesel-powered cars that could actually detect when an emissions test was being conducted, and activate the emissions-choking mechanisms. In normal driving, the emissions devices automatically shut down so drivers enjoy improved power and fuel economy. Volkswagen went into 2015 poised to challenge Toyota as the world's top auto seller. In 2016, sales of Volkswagen-branded cars dropped substantially worldwide. Volkswagen now faces reduced sales and enormous fines, and consumers feel less confident about the

radub85/123RF

brand. Interestingly, Audi, a separate brand of Volkswagen, is enjoying increased sales through the period and the industry is highly anticipating Audi's 2018 models.

Boston, W. (2016), "Sales Slide at VW Continues Globally," Wall Street Journal, (January 9), B3. Fry, E. (2015), "VW Fooled Everyone. Was it the Only One?" Fortune, 172 (11/1), 18.

niche marketing. Niche marketers may be consumer oriented. However, some niche marketers are product oriented and produce a product that has unique appeal within a segment. For example, many companies serve the golf market one way or another, and some of them are huge differentiated marketers like Taylormade or Callaway, offering many products aimed at multiple markets. However, the Bobby Grace company specializes in one product: the putter. They only make putters and have a very small product offering of accessories beyond that. Bobby Grace markets their putters as highly advanced technologically because all of the company's attention is dedicated to just one club, the putter.

1-3b Consumer Behavior and Society

The things that people buy and consume end up determining the type of society in which we live. Things like customs, manners, and rituals all involve consumption—value-producing activities. Certainly, not every society around the world is the same. Just think about the ways we eat and the types of food consumed around the world. Additionally, when governments create laws that govern the way we buy and consume products, consumer behavior is involved. Thus, consumer behavior creates the society in which we live and serves as an important source of input to public policy in a free society.

For example, how does U.S. society treat smoking? Cigarette advertisements made up a large chunk of all TV advertising before a federal ban took effect on January 2, 1971. Popular culture glamorized smoking as a valued behavior. In the movies, cigarette smoking certainly did not harm James Bond's image. On the stage, famous performers like Sammy Davis Jr. and Frank Sinatra often smoked during their acts. At home, practically every room in the house included at least one ashtray. No Smoking sections did not exist in stores, restaurants, offices, or planes. In fact, flight attendants (then stewardesses) on those planes walked the aisles, offering passengers "coffee, tea, or cigarettes."

My, how things have changed! Smoking has become nearly taboo in the United States. Smoking inside any public building is practically impossible either due to laws restricting smoking or rules created by building owners prohibiting smoking. Smoking is not allowed throughout most U.S. restaurants and in many parts of Europe. Increasingly, consumers look upon smoking as a non–value-producing activity. Furthermore, politicians realize political advantage in creating more restrictions as consumer opinion continues to turn against the behavior. Policy makers should make such

niche marketing plan wherein a firm specializes in serving one market segment with particularly unique demand characteristics

Consumers and Their Phones

As discussed in the chapter, smartphone technology represents a discontinuous innovation. Discontinuous innovations change and create behaviors. In this case, the change may be best reflected by the term "smombie," or smartphone zombie. Are you a smombie?

We love our phones, but they also are a source of aggravation—particularly to others. Restrictions on the use of phones in cars are being enacted as a matter of public safety. Some restaurants now frown on or even prohibit phone usage. Consider the following list. In your opinion, do any of these behaviors violate acceptable mobile phone etiquette?

Andresr/Shutterstock.com

1. Using the smartphone (texting, browsing, etc.) while involved in a face-to-face conversation with others—a phenomenon that's come to be known as "phubbing"

2. Using a smartphone (to text, browse, or social network) when dining with others

3. Having a phone conversation at the table while dining in a nice restaurant

4. Texting, browsing, accessing social networks, or playing games under the table in class

5. Using profanity on the phone when others can overhear the conversation

6. Using the phone in any manner in a movie theater

7. Having a phone conversation in a public bathroom toilet stall

8. Texting while using the bathroom

9. Speaking so loudly that your phone conversation is easily heard by others around you

10. Texting, emailing, browsing, social networking, etc. while driving

11. Texting, emailing, browsing, social networking while walking in public or riding a bicycle

12. Using the phone while in the checkout line at the store

The majority of Americans believe using a phone in a restaurant, at the movies, or in a meeting is inappropriate. And about using the phone in any manner in the bathroom . . . well, studies show that your phone is probably the dirtiest product most people own!

Sources: Dewey, C. (2015), "When It Is and Isn't Okay to Be on Your Smartphone: The Conclusive Guide," *Washington Post*, https://www.washingtonpost.com/news/the-intersect/wp/2015/08/26/when-it-is-and-isnt-okay-to-be-on-your-smartphone-the-conclusive-guide/, accessed February 7, 2016; Piro L. (206), "Is Your Phone Dirtier than a Toilet Seat?", http://www.goodhousekeeping.com/home/cleaning/videos/a27005/phone-dirtier-than-toilet/.

pimpic/Shutterstock.com

decisions with a thorough understanding of the CB issues involved.

Another current public policy issue concerns the use of mobile phones. Consider how much consumers' widespread adoption of the mobile phone has changed, and continues to change, society. Over 92 percent of American adults own a cellphone; nearly 2 of 3 of those phones are smartphones. Nearly 50 percent own a tablet computer, and while 40 percent own game consoles, that percentage is no longer growing. Worldwide, more consumers (6 billion) have access to a phone than to a toilet (4.5 billion). Out of those 6 billion phones, nearly 1 in 3 are smartphones.[31] Clearly, "smart" phone technologies represent a discontinuous innovation by altering our behaviors and communications in many ways.

1-3c Consumer Behavior and Personal Growth

We face many important decisions as consumers. Among these are choices that will affect our professional careers, our quality of life, and the very fiber of our families. By this point in your life, you have already experienced many of these decisions. Some decisions are good; some are not. All consumers make dumb decisions occasionally.

Consider modern consumers' decisions to take on debt. Credit can be a good thing, but it has its limits. Americans owe about $1 trillion in consumer credit card debt. Some consumers carry no credit card debt, however, so the average amount of debt for those households carrying balances is just over $15,000. Americans also owe over $1 trillion in student loan debts (an average of $45,000 per household in student debt).[32] College students are prime targets for credit cards, and as can be seen on many college campuses, students are quite willing to apply for cards in exchange for something as mundane as a new t-shirt. Thus, one can easily see why many consumers continue to have negative net worth years into their professional life because of the debt accumulated in early adulthood.

The culture of debt also exists in many governments. Total U.S. debt exceeds $19.5 trillion, which comes to over $159,000 per taxpayer.[33] This amount has doubled since 2006. Surely, U.S. consumers and most Western nations' governments know how to spend. Eventually, though, debt becomes problematic, and drastic changes are needed to the national budgets.

For individuals, decisions that lead to high levels of debt do not seem to be wise, as bankruptcy, financial stress, and lower self-esteem often result. Although often overlooked, decisions about household budget allocation are very relevant aspects of CB. However, budget decisions are not the only way one can choose unwisely when acting as a consumer.

Thus, when consumers learn CB, they should be able to apply that knowledge by making better consumer decisions. Several topics can be particularly helpful in enlightening consumers, including:

1. Consequences associated with poor budget allocation
2. The role of emotions in consumer decision making
3. Avenues for seeking redress for unsatisfactory purchases
4. Social influences on decision making, including peer pressure
5. The effect of the environment on consumer behavior

1-4 DIFFERENT APPROACHES TO STUDYING CONSUMER BEHAVIOR

Consumer researchers have many tools and approaches with which to study CB, and researchers don't always agree on which approach is best. In reality, the consumer researcher should realize that no single best way of studying CB exists. Rather, different types of research settings may call for different approaches and the use of different tools. Thus, we provide a brief overview of two basic approaches for studying CB. The purpose is to provide the reader with an idea of how the knowledge found in this book was obtained. For a more detailed view of the different research approaches, the reader is referred elsewhere.[34]

1-4a Interpretive Research

One consumer's music is just noise to another consumer. What creates value in the musical experience? What does music mean and how much does the meaning shape the value of an experience? These are questions that evoke very abstract comments and thoughts from consumers. They are questions that lend themselves well to interpretive research, especially when environmental factors like culture shape behaviors.[35] **Interpretive research** seeks to explain the inner meanings and motivations associated with specific consumption experiences. Consumer researchers interpret these meanings through the words that consumers use to describe events or through observation of social interactions. With this approach, researchers interpret meaning rather than analyze data.

Interpretive research generally falls into the broader category of qualitative research. **Qualitative research tools** include things such as case analyses, clinical interviews, focus group interviews, and other means by which data are gathered in a relatively unstructured way. In other words, consumer respondents are usually free to respond in their own words or simply through their own behavior. Data of this type requires that the researcher interpret its meaning.

interpretive research approach that seeks to explain the inner meanings and motivations associated with specific consumption experiences

qualitative research tools means for gathering data in a relatively unstructured way, including case analysis, clinical interviews, and focus group interviews

Different types of consumer situations call for different types of research approaches.

© d3images/Shutterstock.com

Such results are considered **researcher dependent**, because the interpretation is a matter of opinion until corroborated by other findings.

The roots of interpretive consumer research go back over 50 years to the earliest days of consumer research. The focus was on identifying the motivations that lie behind all manner of consumer behavior, including mundane things such as coffee drinking or taking an aspirin, to more elaborate issues such as what "drives" one to buy a Ford versus a Chevy.[36] The motivational research era in consumer research, which lasted through the early 1960s, generally proved disappointing in providing satisfying explanations for consumer behavior on a large scale. Unfortunately, many interpretive research tools were scarcely applied for years afterwards. However, these approaches have made a recent comeback and are now commonly applied to many aspects of the field.

Interpretive researchers adopt one of several orientations. Two common interpretative orientations are phenomenology and ethnography. **Phenomenology** represents the study of consumption as a "lived experience." The phenomenological researcher relies on casual interviews with consumers from whom the researcher has won confidence and trust. This may be supplemented with various other ways that the consumer can tell a story. **Ethnography** has roots in anthropology and often involves analyzing the artifacts associated with consumption. An ethnographer may decide to go through trash or ask to see the inside of a consumer's refrigerator in an effort to learn about the consumer. These approaches represent viable options for consumer researchers. More recently, ethnographic CB research takes a twist, brought on by the prominence of social networking in everyday life. **Netnography** applies ethnographic tools to study the behavior of online cultures and communities.[37] While the field is new, researchers believe results will help explore the interplay between brands, products, and belonging based on the virtual relationships played out on Facebook and other social networking sites.

1-4b Quantitative Consumer Research

Which consumer group is most likely to listen to rap music? Statistical models can be applied to retail sales data to identify clusters of consumers who are more likely to be in the market for specific types of products. Sometimes, the results are so spot-on they become controversial. For instance, researchers working for Target stores used patterns of purchases to predict which customers are highly likely to be pregnant.[38] Using this data, the consumers who fall into those groups coincidentally (or not) begin receiving promotions from the store for baby strollers, diapers, and other maternity-related items. One teen's father went to a Target store to complain when his teenage daughter began receiving the maternity-related promotions only to have to apologize when his daughter broke the news to him. The fact that individual customer purchases can be recorded and stored by loyalty or credit card numbers makes this type of quantitative modeling possible.

Other types of quantitative research exist as well. Researchers employ multivariate statistical analysis, which involves examining relationships among many variables, to predict individual consumers' profitability, the likelihood of purchasing name brands or private labels, the likelihood of trying a new product, what type of media a consumer will respond to, and much more. For instance, statistical analytics can group consumers into categories based on whether they tend to buy products in many products in only a few categories or a few products in

researcher dependent
subjective data that requires a researcher to interpret the meaning

phenomenology
qualitative approach to studying consumers that relies on interpretation of the lived experience associated with some aspect of consumption

ethnography qualitative approach to studying consumers that relies on interpretation of artifacts to draw conclusions about consumption

netnography a branch of ethnography that studies the behavior of online cultures and communities

NEW VALUE OF USING THINGS

The Internet of Things is a term that refers to connection of everyday things electronically to the web, allowing the transfer of real-time data between a consumer and a services provider. Even everyday things like clothing and light bulbs can be connected with small chips so that the data about when the products are used and for how long are automatically recorded and shared through the web. What does it mean for consumers? When companies express the benefits of connection in terms of services, such as Uber providing an Internet service rather than a connection of automobiles, they communicate value to consumers. For companies, the data provided by the patterns of usage likewise prove a valuable community. Some companies may even pay consumers to use services in exchange for the data that is provided. An automatic record of all the media used by a consumer could prove an extremely valuable asset for companies looking to offer bundles of benefits consistent with patterns of media usage. Imagine getting paid for using—rather than paying for—a smartphone. It could happen.

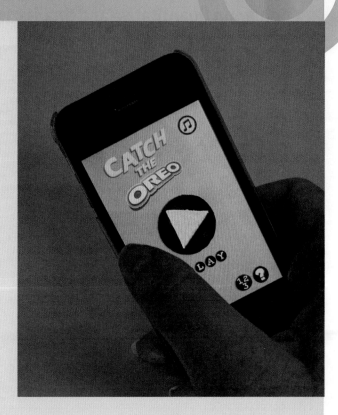

Sources: http://www.wsj.com/articles/the-internet-of-things-is-here-and-it-isnt-a-thing-1471799999. http://www.businessinsider.com/what-is-the-internet-of-things-definition-2016-8.

many categories.[39] Data can also be correlated with outside influences such as the time of the day, temperature, chance of rain, and so forth to suggest changes in merchandising that can affect the bottom line. Researchers also employ quantitative measurement through surveys and very often use surveys to capture responses to some experiment that may manipulate some characteristic of an ad or product. For instance, survey responses allow numerical representation of consumers' attitudes. Using an experimental approach, research suggests that consumers often express a more favorable attitude for a product promoted with an "amount off" discount as opposed to a percentage discount, particularly for higher-priced products.[40]

These studies typify quantitative research. **Quantitative research** addresses questions about consumer behavior using numerical measurement and analysis tools. The measurement is usually structured, meaning that the consumer will simply choose a response from among alternatives supplied by the researcher. In other words, structured questionnaires typically involve multiple-choice questions. Alternatively, quantitative research might analyze sales data tracked via the Internet or with point-of-sale scanners.

Unlike qualitative research, the data are not researcher dependent to the extent that the numbers are the same no matter who the researcher may be. Typically, quantitative research better enables researchers to test hypotheses as compared to interpretive research. Similarly, quantitative research is more likely to stand on its own and does not require deep interpretation. For example, if consumers have an average willingness-to-pay score of $50 for brand A and $75 for brand B, we can objectively say that consumers will pay more for brand B. Exhibit 1.6 illustrates characteristics of qualitative and quantitative research.

quantitative research approach that addresses questions about consumer behavior using numerical measurement and analysis tools

Exhibit 1.6

Comparing Quantitative and Qualitative Research

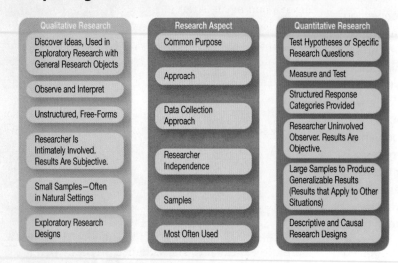

Qualitative Research	Research Aspect	Quantitative Research
Discover Ideas, Used in Exploratory Research with General Research Objects	Common Purpose	Test Hypotheses or Specific Research Questions
Observe and Interpret	Approach	Measure and Test
Unstructured, Free-Forms	Data Collection Approach	Structured Response Categories Provided
Researcher Is Intimately Involved. Results Are Subjective.	Researcher Independence	Researcher Uninvolved Observer. Results Are Objective.
Small Samples—Often in Natural Settings	Samples	Large Samples to Produce Generalizable Results (Results that Apply to Other Situations)
Exploratory Research Designs	Most Often Used	Descriptive and Causal Research Designs

1-5 CONSUMER BEHAVIOR IS DYNAMIC

All one has to do is examine the differences in standards of living between today's American consumers and those living in the years 1875, 1925, 1985, and 2005 to gain an appreciation of how CB has changed over time. As an overall statement, we can say that consumers are never completely satisfied. Actually, this is a good thing, because as companies strive to meet consumer demands, increasingly innovative products are offered, and companies grow in response to increased sales. As a result, they hire more people and raise income levels throughout the economy.

The way marketers respond to consumers is changing dramatically. Marketers have historically used advances in technology to provide consumers with greater opportunities to communicate with companies. Today, billions of consumers around the world have 24-hour, seven-day-a-week access to markets via the Internet. Consumers do not need to wait to go to a retail store to purchase music. They can download their favorite new tunes, movies, books, games, and apps while walking down the street. Here are some of the trends that are shaping the value received by consumers today.

1-5a Internationalization

When Starbucks opened its first store in 1971, the thought may not have occurred that the concept could spread to other parts of the state of Washington or even other parts of the United States. In 1996, Starbucks opened its first store outside the United States in Tokyo, Japan. Today, consumers around the world can order up a latte at one of about 20,000 Starbucks locations in over 65 countries.[41] Whether you are on business in Guadalajara, Mexico; Seoul, South Korea; London, England; Shanghai, China; Nantes, France; or Ruston, Louisiana, you can relax at a Starbucks. Almost anywhere the modern consumer travels, he or she can find a familiar place to eat or drink. A Subway, a Pizza Hut, or a McDonald's never seems far away.

Although these chains can be found worldwide, consumers are not alike everywhere these firms operate. An Outback Steakhouse in Seoul will offer *kimchi* (fermented cabbage) on the menu, something neither American nor Australian. Companies must therefore deal with geographical distances as well as cultural distances. The international focus of today's modern company places a greater demand on CB research. Every culture's people will interpret products and behaviors differently. The meanings these consumers perceive will determine the success or failure of the product being offered.

1-5b Technological Changes

We live in an age where technological advances seem to be coming at an ever-increasing rate. Upon closer reflection, we may realize that technology has influenced business practices ever since the advent of industry. Certainly, many retailers felt threatened by mail order technology that was practiced through the Sears Roebuck catalog and the telephone. In 1895, the Sears catalog contained 532 pages of products that enabled rural consumers to obtain things that would have been otherwise difficult to get.[42] Why would people go to a store when they could simply telephone and have products delivered to their door?

What do the Sears Catalog from 1895 and an online shopping cart have in common?

In the mid-20th century, television revolutionized consumer behavior. Not only did TV change advertising forever, but true home shopping became a possibility. Now, the consumer could actually see a product in use on television and then make a purchase either by picking up the phone or punching buttons on a cable device. Why would someone go to a store?

A consumer now has 24/7 access to purchasing almost any type of product. The Internet has made geographical distance almost a nonissue. Additionally, the consumer can truly shop on his or her own schedule, not on a schedule determined by store hours. Communication technology has also advanced tremendously. The entire world is now truly the market for consumers in free countries. With all of this advancing technology, e-commerce accounts for around 8% of total U.S. retailing as of 2016.[43] That's still about $380 billion out of a total of $4.8 trillion U.S. sales excluding autos.

Shopping online can be a valuable experience, but are virtual shopping and "real" shopping gratifying in the same way? Amazon.com's worldwide sales topped $100 billion in 2015. Perhaps surprisingly, Amazon's growth plans include physical stores in major shopping centers. Part of the enticement may be the fact that in-store shoppers buy 50 percent more than online shoppers.[44]

CHANGING COMMUNICATIONS

As technology changes, so do the ways that people communicate with each other. Once upon a time, consumers' predominant form of communication was face-to-face.

Interestingly, many surveys of preferred communication methods don't even list face-to-face communication. Among other sources, email appears far from dead. Consumers can easily access their email from any smart device, and email is the most widely tracked source of data analytics among marketers.[45]

Google, Facebook, Twitter, and Pinterest remain good sources of digital media for reaching consumers. Marketers are experimenting with newer media tools including Twitter's Periscope.com. Periscope allows anyone with the app to live-stream video. Brands can use spokespeople on short live videos, have experts present content, present live news, and perhaps most important of all, use Periscope to promote other media including the brand website.[46]

BIG DATA

Back in the days of small general stores in small towns, store owners came to know their customers extremely well. They could sometimes predict when a customer would show up, and they could fill their order from memory. The business and the customer had an intimate connection. As electronic storage becomes simpler and cheaper, and as more real-time electronic devices are used to record information, the amount of data available for analysis grows exponentially. By the time a university sophomore today finishes college, more data will have been collected than in all eternity before that time.

The term big data has come to be used to represent the massive amounts of data available to companies, which can potentially be used to predict customer behaviors. The data include internal records of customer behavior like scanner purchase data, survey responses, and web traffic records, as well as data from social network interactions and even things like GPS tracking.[47] Researchers apply statistical tools to try to discover patterns in the data that will allow better prediction. The application of these statistical tools sometimes is referred to as predictive analytics. Although the application of big data in this sense is still in its infancy, one can get an idea about how this works when purchasing something online and getting shown products that consumers "who bought this product also

big data term used to represent the massive amounts of data available to companies, which can potentially be used to predict customer behaviors

predictive analytics the application of statistical tools in an effort to discover patterns in data that allow prediction of consumer behavior

Collaborative consumption in the sharing economy is fast approaching annual transactions of $100 billion globally with little sign of the growth slowing

purchased." This is certainly a technological trend that will affect how companies study their customers. The term **internet of things** refers to the fact that everyday products themselves allow data to be gathered and stored for analysis through the use of technologies like near-field communication. In fact, the data provided by some products may prove more valuable to some companies than the reveneu generated by the product that will send the data.

1-5c Changing Demographics

In most of the Western world, notable demographic trends have shaped consumer behavior patterns greatly over the past quarter century or so. First, households increasingly include two primary income providers. In contrast to the stereotypical working dad and stay-at-home mom, families today often include two parents with career orientations. Second, family size is decreasing throughout most of Western culture. European

Internet of things the automatic recording of data from everyday products that signal consumers patterns of behavior

families are averaging less than one child per family. As a result, the relative importance of cultures as consumer markets is changing. Marketers around the world find it hard to ignore the nearly 2 billion consumers in China or the 1 billion in India. We'll discuss demographic trends in a later chapter.

1-5d Changing and Sharing Economy

Recent years have seen a downturn in the economy in much of the developed world. A smaller percentage of the U.S. population is working today than since 1978.[48] Today, under 62 percent have a job or are actively seeking work. Many college students are deciding to stay in school longer, given limited prospects in the workforce. Mature workers are more apt to retire, given the decreased opportunity to work at an acceptable wage. These factors contribute to stagnant income. Moreover, economic, political, and social turmoil around the world contributes to a picture that leaves many consumers uneasy. As a result, U.S. consumer spending has changed in several ways. Consumers are more cautious about spending money and react

Exhibit 1.7

Global Consumer Trends

▶ Selling "Shares"—not just Uber, but all manner of sharing services including sharing what you wear as in "Girl Meets Dress."

▶ International Shopping—malls, particularly in emerging economies, offer consumers access to far-away experiences

▶ Consumers as Marketers—many consumers become vloggers spreading videos that include their brand likes and dislikes

▶ Green and Healthy—consumers will pay for options they see as good for the Earth and body, but it's not so simple

▶ Easy over Size—consumers now see convenience as a nearby albeit smaller option for food and staples

Source: Kasriel-Alexander, K. (2015), Top 10 Global Trends for 2015, Euromonitor International.

more favorably to price-cutting policies. Private label brands (such as retail store brands like Walmart's Sam's Choice) become more attractive alternatives as a way of saving money.

Globally, including the United States, consumers display several signs of the times. Two related global consumer trends include the continued desire for greater convenience and the increased acceptability of temporary use in the form of sharing as an alternative to owning. The term **sharing economy** is used to capture the market activity involving temporary usage for hire (rentals) as a replacement for traditional ownership. When the rental transaction activity is consumer to consumer (peer to peer), the term **collaborative consumption** is often applied. Many new businesses exist to put consumer and consumer together for things other than dates! Airbnb, Uber, Getaround, and girlmeetsdress offer rooms, rides, cars, and dresses for temporary use on a consumer to consumer basis. The sharing economy is fast approaching annual transactions of $100 billion globally with little sign of the growth slowing. Later chapters will address various reasons for the trend away from ownership, although clearly one big motivator is convenience. Green marketing continues to trend, satisfying consumers' desire to save the Earth. In addition, vlogging (video blogging) is growing quickly as a means of communicating with and by consumers. Exhibit 1.7 summarizes a few global trends.

sharing economy the global consumer trend toward rental (temporary usage for hire) rather than ownership

collaborative consumption the term used for a rental transaction activity that is consumer to consumer, rather than business to consumer or business to business

STUDY TOOLS 1

LOCATED AT BACK OF THE TEXTBOOK

☐ Tear out Chapter Review Card

LOCATED AT WWW.CENGAGE.COM/LOGIN

☐ Review Key Term flashcards and create your own cards

☐ Track your knowledge and understanding of key concepts in consumer behavior

☐ Complete practice quizzes to prepare for tests

☐ Complete interactive content within CB Online

☐ Review the Chapter Highlight boxes for CB Online

2 | Value and the Consumer Behavior Framework

LEARNING OBJECTIVES

After studying this chapter, the student should be able to:

2-1 Describe the consumer value framework, including its basic components.

2-2 Define consumer value and compare and contrast two key types of value.

2-3 Apply the concepts of marketing strategy and marketing tactics to describe the way firms go about creating value for consumers.

2-4 Explain the way market characteristics like market segmentation and product differentiation affect marketing strategy.

2-5 Analyze consumer markets using elementary perceptual maps.

2-6 Justify consumers' lifetime value as an effective focus for long-term business success.

Dimitri Otis/Getty Images

Remember to visit **PAGE 43** for additional **STUDY TOOLS**

INTRODUCTION

When two people meet for the first time, one of the fastest ways to get to know one another is to share information about each other's favorite things. You might ask, What is your favorite thing to do? What are your favorite brands? What are your favorite things to eat and to drink? And the person may answer, playing poker with friends, Urban Outfitters, shrimp, and craft beer. Now you know something about that person.

Online dating has become commonplace. Just under half of single consumers in America report visiting an online dating site. The choices have grown beyond match.com and eHarmony.com to more targeted sites such farmersonly.com, christianmingle.com, outime.com, and blackpeoplemeet.com, just to mention a few. All the dating sites involve personal descriptions that include physical appearance, occupation, and, as mentioned above, favorite things. Can users believe what they see in an online profile? Research suggests that

lying is common in these sites. In particular, consumers like to lie about what they own and what they do, in addition to embellishing their personal appearance. Common lies often involve activities like traveling, as people try to portray themselves as living a certain lifestyle.[1] People also choose which hobbies to list based more on how they believe this will appeal to others than on the way they actually spend time. The fact that those seeking dates commonly stretch the truth about the things they spend time and money on demonstrates how important consumer choices are in shaping individual identity.

Many consumers who use dating sites seek a relationship. Likewise, consumers and businesses often benefit from relationships. These relationships begin with consumer preference. Consumer preference can be varied and fickle. For example, one consumer likes sauerkraut while another can't even go near it. This book sheds light on why the things that provide so much value to certain consumers in certain times

or certain situations don't really do anything for other consumers or even the same consumer at a different time or in a different situation. This chapter introduces the Consumer Value Framework and some of the core concepts that tie all of CB together and make it actionable in marketing.

2-1 THE CONSUMER VALUE FRAMEWORK AND ITS COMPONENTS

Consumer behavior is multifaceted. Not only does the study of consumer behavior involve multiple disciplines, but anyone who has ever made a major purchase like a house, an automobile, or an apartment knows that many factors can affect both the purchase decision and the way one feels after the purchase. This book tries to explain these sorts of phenomena and in doing so provide clues as to how consumers can be better served.

2-1a The Consumer Value Framework

Given the potential complexity involved in explaining consumption, a framework for studying consumer behavior is useful. Exhibit 2.1 displays the framework used in this book. The Consumer Value Framework (CVF) represents consumer behavior theory, illustrating factors that shape consumption-related behaviors and ultimately determine the value associated with consumption. The different components shown with different colors roughly correspond to the different parts of this book. However, the student of consumer behavior must recognize and accept the fact that each aspect of the CVF is related in some way to other components of the model. The arrows connecting the different components typify these connections.

2-1b Value and the CVF Components

Value is at the heart of experiencing and understanding consumer behavior. Thus, we will never get too far

Consumer Value Framework (CVF) consumer behavior theory that illustrates factors that shape consumption-related behaviors and ultimately determine the value associated with consumption

Exhibit 2.1

Consumer Value Framework (CVF)

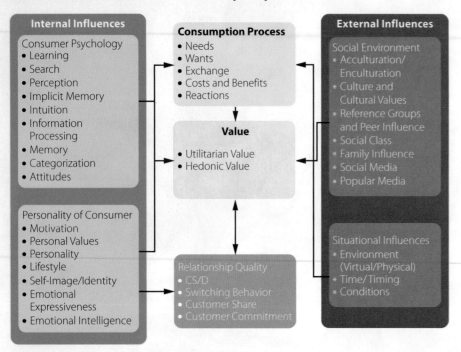

Internal Influences

Consumer Psychology
- Learning
- Search
- Perception
- Implicit Memory
- Intuition
- Information Processing
- Memory
- Categorization
- Attitudes

Personality of Consumer
- Motivation
- Personal Values
- Personality
- Lifestyle
- Self-Image/Identity
- Emotional Expressiveness
- Emotional Intelligence

Consumption Process
- Needs
- Wants
- Exchange
- Costs and Benefits
- Reactions

Value
- Utilitarian Value
- Hedonic Value

Relationship Quality
- CS/D
- Switching Behavior
- Customer Share
- Customer Commitment

External Influences

Social Environment
* Acculturation/ Enculturation
* Culture and Cultural Values
* Reference Groups and Peer Influence
* Social Class
* Family Influence
* Social Media
* Popular Media

Situational Influences
* Environment (Virtual/Physical)
* Time/ Timing
* Conditions

from value in any chapter of this book. We'll expand more on value later in this chapter and throughout the book. In the rest of this section, we present the basic components of the CVF that either contribute to or are outcomes of value.

RELATIONSHIP QUALITY

Over the past two decades or so, **Customer Relationship Management (CRM)** has become a popular catchphrase, not just in marketing but in all of business. A basic CRM premise is that customers form relationships with companies as opposed to companies conducting individual transactions with customers. A CRM system tracks detailed information about customers so marketers can make more customer-oriented decisions that hopefully lead to longer-lasting relationships.

CRM means each customer represents a potential stream of resources rather than just a single sale. **Relationship quality** reflects the connectedness between a consumer and a retailer, brand, or service provider.[2] In practice, a high-quality relationship is typified by a consumer who feels like he or she should buy the same brand each time a need for that product arises. When relationship quality is strong between customer and company, customers are highly receptive to brand extensions and thus the brand enjoys a near ready market for new products.[3] Loyal customers are more profitable than customers who consider switching brand or providers each time they make a purchase.

A customer who experiences high value from service realizes that relationship quality is high. Over time, the consistent value delivery builds customer loyalty. Salesforce.com has grown into one of the leading Fortune 500 firms overall and one of the top 10 firms to work for, all based on the idea that systems that build customer relationships provide win-win exchanges where both customer and business benefit. Their products include analytics tools that push valuable information to a salesforce, so that salespersons can enter any meeting with a client armed with key information that points toward the types of products clients are most likely to need or desire.

CONSUMPTION PROCESS

Consumers must decide to do something before they can receive value. The consumption process involves deciding what is needed, what the options for exchange might be, and the inevitable reaction to consumption. The consumption process can involve a great deal of decision making and thus represents a consumer decision-making process and the results of service. **Service** can be thought of as the organization's efforts and resources applied toward value creation. Many factors influence this process, and these factors can be divided into different categories, such as internal and external influences.

A Tech Firm Has to Know Its Limitations

When we think about technology firms, we have expectations that they all will develop the next big thing! So much so that Samsung latched on to "the next big thing" as its slogan. Inevitably, firms want to grow. But, how should they grow? Very often, when a tech firm builds lots of resources, they attempt to build a product at the next layer of technology. Eventually, the next big thing is something more technologically complex.

The term "stack fallacy" refers to the mistaken belief that success lies in creating the next, more complicated, layer of technology. However, history shows that success often comes from moving down the technology stack, not up. Google tried moving up to social networking with less than outstanding results (Google +). However, its move down to create its own servers has allowed it to better provide value through

its core service—facilitating search! A firm has to know its limitations to create value for customers.

Sources: Mims, C. (2016), "Why Companies Are Being Disrupted," *Wall Street Journal* (January 25), B4. Limer, C. (2015), "Samsung Galaxy 6: Not the Next Big Thing, Just a Great Phone," http://gizmodo.com/samsung-galaxy-s6-review-not-the-next-big-thing-just-1695061015, accessed February 10, 2016.

INTERNAL INFLUENCES: THE PSYCHOLOGY AND PERSONALITY OF THE CONSUMER

The Psychology of the Consumer. Most consumers can think of a place they try hard to avoid solely because of the irritating music played there. Consumers fear they may develop an *earworm*, a term that refers to the real phenomenon of a song that "gets stuck in my head." Is getting a song stuck in someone's head a good idea if you want to sell something? Repetitive rhythms provide a mechanism that facilitates learning.[4] But the effect can also be irritating, as evidenced by the fact that songs like Single Ladies (Beyoncé), Ice Ice Baby (Vanilla Ice), and, perhaps the top example, It's a Small World (Disney), drive many consumers up the wall. Questions like this involve the psychology of the consumer. In other words, the mechanisms that create such effects are **internal influences**, things that go on inside the consumer's mind and heart or that are indeed truly a part of the consumer.

The psychology of the consumer involves both cognitive and affective processes. The term **cognition** refers to the thinking or mental processes that go on as we process and store things that can become knowledge. A child hears parents talk about smoking as a *nasty* thing to do. Smoking becomes associated with nastiness, and the

child may develop a dislike of smoking. **Affect** refers to the feelings experienced during consumption activities or feelings associated with specific objects. If the child continues to receive negative information about smoking, the belief that it's nasty may result in feelings of disgust.

Many people think of these types of things when they think of CB. Certainly, our perceptions help shape the desirability of products, which can influence decision processes and the value perceived from consuming something. Recall that value is a subjective assessment. Therefore, value is very much a matter of perception.

The Personality of the Consumer. Every consumer has certain characteristics and traits that help define him or her as an individual. We refer to these traits generally as **individual differences**. Individual differences that tangibly make one person

internal influences things that go on inside the mind and heart of the consumer or that are truly a part of the consumer psychologically

cognition thinking or mental processes that go on as we process and store things that can become knowledge

affect feelings associated with objects or activities

individual differences characteristic traits of individuals, including demographics, personality, and lifestyle distinct from another, which include personality and lifestyle, help determine consumer behavior. Consumer researchers focus increasingly on the self-identity of consumers. The increased attention may be driven in part by the theory that today's teens and young adults are more self-absorbed than previous generations. This belief is built largely on the fact that narcissism scores, a personality trait capturing self-absorption, are higher among these consumers than those from previous generations.[5] What do you think? If this is so, how would it influence marketing?

Companies have spent vast amounts of money and time trying to harness individual differences in a way that allows consumer choice to be predicted. They do so because individual differences like these include basic motivations, which trigger consumer desires. Also, individual differences shape the value experienced by consumers and the reaction consumers have to consumption.

EXTERNAL INFLUENCES

Every consumer contains a storehouse of information internally, but in many cases some external influence triggers the consumption process or provides information necessary for a consumer to make a decision. Pam, a 20-year-old student at an urban university, decides to move to a university apartment complex with a roommate she's known since high school. The complex is typical, and they have a ground-floor flat with two reserved parking spots in the back, about 40 yards from their apartment door. They like the quiet location facing the rear of the complex. Both are content and excited about their new place. One day, Pam is surfing Slideshare.net as she has a bite to eat near her place. She takes a look at a slideshow called "What they didn't tell me." The slides contain a list of "mistakes" made by the author, a young woman with whom Pam can relate. Several slides talk about the horror of break-ins in her ground-floor flat and warn viewers that ground-floor apartments are not safe and to always get an apartment with a door in plain view (not rear-facing), or better, to choose an apartment complex with interior apartment access only via a 24-hour doorman.

The next day, while Pam is buying a textbook online using her smartphone, she notices a link to a blog about apartment safety. She clicks through and finds a link to a video of a new eight-floor apartment building two miles from campus. The video provides a virtual visit and clearly displays the friendly doorman (in a security uniform) providing entry to the building and pointing the way to the elevator. She talks about her fears with her roommate, friends, and parents. Her parents agree to pay to break the lease and tell her to find a safer place. Now she goes back to the Web and searches for the address of the high-rise apartment complex and checks for other apartment buildings nearby. At this moment, Pam experiences what some call the "zero moment of truth." That's the point when a passive shopper becomes an active shopper and actively seeks out exchange alternatives.[6]

In this example, numerous external influences have come together to change the value equation for Pam, change the relationship with her current apartment complex, activate a need, and trigger the desire for a better place to live. External influences include social, cultural, media, environmental, and temporal factors, among others. They are critical to understanding CB.

Social Environment. The social environment includes people and groups who help shape a consumer's everyday experiences. Some influence is personal, meaning the consumer actually knows the people; some is impersonal, coming from unknown people like celebrities; and still other influence is virtual, coming from unknown sources online or in social networks.

Consumer researchers focus increasingly on the self-identity of consumers, based on the theory that today's teens and young adults are more self-absorbed than previous generations were.

external influences
social and cultural aspects of life as a consumer

social environment
elements that specifically deal with the way other people influence consumer decision making and value

zero moment of truth The point when a shopper moves from passive to active and seeks out exchange alternatives.

NESPRESSO: SO EMOTIONAL

In economics, we typically think lower prices lead to greater demand. Is that the case? Think of the strongest brands that you associate with coffee. Do they sell for the lowest price? In fact, no brand in coffee has gained more strength recently than Nespresso, which sells for over $50 per pound. But looking at the CVF, one has to consider the entire model to understand the Nespresso appeal.

The coffee makers were originally useful in creating customers for pods. However, coffee is a mere vehicle to provide customers with an emotional experience. Nespresso boutiques provide retail theater epitomizing the hedonic value experience that allows Nespresso to build and reinforce relationships with its customers. Nespresso's huge success lies not in a low price, but in emotional design delivering a total value experience—not just a cup of coffee.

Sorbis/Shutterstock.com

Sources: Foster, J., and McLelland, M. A. (2015). "Retail Atmospherics: The Impact of a Brand-Dictated Theme," *Journal of Retailing and Consumer Services*, 22, 195–205. Wrigley, C. and R. Ramsey (2016), "Emotional Food Design: From Designing Food Products to Designing Food Systems," *International Journal of Food Design*, 1, 11–29.

In addition, any time a consumer chooses to do something, at least in part, to please or appeal to another consumer, the social environment plays a role in that process. Group influence is one mechanism through which social influences work. Simple decisions ranging from what breakfast foods to buy to complicated things like attending a university all are shaped by subtle influences like acculturation, the sometimes not-so-subtle influence of family and friends.

Situational Influences. External influences also include situational influences. **Situational influences** are temporary factors unique to a time or place that can change the value seen in a decision and received from consumption. Situational influences include the effect that the physical environment has on consumer behavior. For example, the presence of music in an environment may shape consumer behavior and even change buying patterns. Timing also plays an important role. Research suggests that for a short time following the purchase of a lottery ticket, consumers are more likely to participate in impulsive shopping.[7] More enduring temporal factors, such as the economic condition at any given time, also affect the value of things. Exhibit 2.2 shows some of the external influences on one consumer.

The Customer Value Framework (CVF) helps organize the remainder of

Exhibit 2.2

External Influences Shape Consumers' Decisions

situational influences
things unique to a time or place that can affect consumer decision making and the value received from consumption

this book. The CVF should be a valuable study aid, particularly given that the different theoretical areas of CB are so closely related to each other. Additionally, the CVF is a good analysis tool for solving consumer behavior business problems. Lastly, the CVF is a valuable tool for businesses that are trying to understand the way consumers respond to their product offerings. Thus, the CVF is useful in developing and implementing marketing strategy.

shutteratakan/Shutterstock.com

2-2 VALUE AND ITS TWO BASIC TYPES

The heart of the Consumer Value Framework, and *the* core concept of CB, is value. **Value** is a personal assessment of the *net worth* a consumer obtains from an activity. From a marketing perspective, the firm serves consumers well when consumers realize value from activities involving interactions with the firm or its products. Value is what consumers ultimately pursue, because valuable actions address motivations that manifest themselves in needs and desires. In this sense, value captures how much gratification a consumer receives from consumption. In return, the firm receives value from consumers as they make purchases.

Most consumers would not list a convenience store as their favorite place to shop. Consumers see the selection as small, the prices high, and the service minimal. Yet consumers return repeatedly because, as their name implies, convenience is the key to value in this setting. Consumers will actually repeat behavior for which they have previously experienced low satisfaction. Walmart stores do not have a relatively high consumer satisfaction index, yet many customers repeatedly visit Walmart. Walmart delivers value, as we will see in

value a personal assessment of the net worth obtained from an activity

a later chapter. In contrast to these examples, contriving a situation where consumers are not seeking value is virtually impossible. In fact, everything we do in life we do in pursuit of value.

2-2a The Value Equation

Exhibit 2.3 reflects some components of value and how a consumer might put these together to determine the overall worth of something—or its value. Worth to a consumer is actually a function of much more than price. Value can be modeled by playing the "what you get" from dealing with a company against the "what you have to give" to get the product. The "what you get" includes all sorts of benefits or positive consequences of consumption. The "what you give" includes sacrifices or the negative consequences of consumption. Opportunity costs play a role. For instance, if a student goes to the movies on a weeknight, he may be giving up the opportunity to attend a class. In major decisions, like where to attend college, purchasing a smartphone, or buying a home, one can easily see that the entire CVF is involved. However, even in simpler situations, all the components of the CVF are subtly in play. Thinking back to the chapter opening: when someone lies on an online

---

Exhibit 2.3

The Value Equation

Value	=	What you get	−	What you give

What you get

Benefits such as:

Quality

Convenience

Emotions

Prestige

Experience

Other factors like:

Scarcity

Nostalgia

What you give

Sacrifice of:

Time

Money

Effort

Opportunity

Emotions

Image

---

dating site, they are attempting to distort the value equation from reality.

Later in the book, a chapter is devoted to further describing value and other related concepts, including expectations, satisfaction, and quality. However, because value is an essential part of consumer behavior, a basic overview is provided in this chapter. While theoretically one could probably break down value into many very specific types, a very useful value typology can be developed using only two types. Thus, we distinguish *utilitarian* value from *hedonic* value.

2-2b Utilitarian Value

Activities and objects that lead to high utilitarian value do so because they help the consumer accomplish some task. **Utilitarian value** is gratification derived from something that helps the consumer solve problems or accomplish tasks that are a part of being a consumer. When consumers buy something in pursuit of utilitarian value, they can typically provide a clearly rational explanation for the purchase. For instance, when a consumer calls a plumber, she undoubtedly has a problem like a stopped-up toilet. The consumer purchases the plumbing services because they accomplish something. In this case, the services accomplish the end of getting a toilet working. Actions that provide utilitarian value are worthwhile because they provide a means to an end.[8] The actions provide value because the object or activity allows something

Going to the movies? What are the gets and gives that determine value from the movie experience?

else good to happen or be accomplished. Search engines provide value as a means of providing the end of finding potentially useful information.

2-2c Hedonic Value

The second type of value is referred to in CB as hedonic value. **Hedonic value** is the immediate gratification that comes from experiencing some activity. Seldom does one go to a horror film or play Face Swap Online in an effort to get a job done. With hedonic value, the value is provided entirely by the actual experience and emotions associated with consumption, not because some other end is or will be accomplished.

Conceptually, hedonic value differs from utilitarian value in several ways. First, hedonic value is an end in and of itself rather than a means to an end. Second, hedonic value is very emotional and subjective in nature. Third, when a consumer does something to obtain hedonic value, the action can sometimes be very difficult to explain objectively.

Rather than being viewed as opposites, the two types of value are not mutually exclusive. In other words, the same act of consumption can provide both utilitarian value and hedonic value. Dining in a place like the Hard Rock Café is an event. One doesn't have to go to Hard Rock to eat, but dining there is a lot of fun—an experience. However, the Hard Rock consumer also accomplishes the task of having something to eat—getting nourished. In fact, the very best consumer experiences are those that provide both high utilitarian value and high hedonic value.

What are your favorite movies of all time? Exhibit 2.4 shows the top 10 grossing movies of all time.[9] Is anything surprising about the list? All are rated G, PG, or PG-13. Not even a single R rating appears among the top 10, even though Hollywood produces more R-rated movies than any other rating. Maybe Hollywood doesn't understand all the ways a movie provides value. With a family film, parents can take the kids to the movie and accomplish the job of keeping the kids happy while at the same time enjoying the movie themselves. In this way, movies like these provide high value and the value translates into business success for the studios.

Exhibit 2.5 illustrates the value propositions of example brands. Marketers can do well by concentrating on providing one type

utilitarian value gratification derived because something helps a consumer solve a problem or accomplish some task

hedonic value value derived from the immediate gratification that comes from some activity

Exhibit 2.4

All Time-Box Office Sales Leaders

Rank	Movie	Year released	Total sales ($millions)	Domestic sales ($millions)
1	Avatar	2009	$2,788.00	$760.50
2	Titanic	1997	$2,186.80	$658.70
3	Star Wars: The Force Awakens	2015	$2,026.60	$914.80
4	Jurassic World	2015	$1,670.40	$652.30
5	Marvel's The Avengers	2012	$1,519.60	$623.40
6	Furious 7	2015	$1,516.00	$353.00
7	Avengers: Age of Ultron	2015	$1,405.40	$459.00
8	Harry Potter and the Deathly Hallows Part 2	2011	$1,341.50	$381.00
9	Frozen	2013	$1,276.50	$400.70
10	Iron Man 3	2013	$1,215.40	$409.00

Source: http://www.boxofficemojo.com/alltime/world/, accessed October 17, 2016.

imagination and cap off a tantalizing hedonic experience for the targeted segment of the population.

It's easy to start thinking about utilitarian and hedonic value as opposites, but one does not exclude the other. In fact, some brands and experiences offer high or low levels of both. Many may find their smart devices typify high utilitarian and high hedonic value. The Woodhouse may not be high-tech, but it clearly offers high levels of both types of value through an indulgent day spa experience that is also good for clients' minds and bodies. The day spa business is fast growing in the United States; in fact, some hospital brands are opening medical spas to enhance customers' physical and emotional well-being. The decision of just how to deliver value becomes an important marketing strategy question.

of value or the other. In the best-case scenario, they provide high levels of both. Walmart epitomizes a brand that does well by concentrating providing utilitarian value its customers find by shopping in a Walmart store or at Walmart online. Twin Peaks is a fast-growing but controversial restaurant chain. The Twin Peaks experience includes a mountain lodge atmosphere and a reasonably priced bar food menu featuring typical items like chicken wings, quesadillas, and cold beer. So what's controversial? Well, Twin Peaks servers' uniforms leave little to the

High utilitarian and high hedonic value help build brand success.

Exhibit 2.5

Value Propositions Involve Combinations of Value

		Utilitarian Value	
		Low	High
Hedonic Value	Low	Kodak	Walmart
	High	Twin Peaks	Woodhouse

Firms that offer low utilitarian and low hedonic value typically are failing. Kodak, once lauded for its marketing genius, has struggled mightily in the digital era. Currently, most traditional Kodak products, like traditional cameras, offer little usefulness and little experience beyond nostalgia. Thus, Kodak is in the unfortunate position of offering low levels of both utilitarian and hedonic value.

2-3 MARKETING STRATEGY AND CONSUMER VALUE

One way that a company can enhance the chance of long-run survival is to have an effective marketing strategy. To an army general, a strategy provides a way of winning a military conflict. Generally, a strategy is a planned way of doing something to accomplish some goal.

2-3a Marketing Strategy

If strategy is a way of doing something, given the purpose of business, a marketing strategy is the way a company goes about creating value for customers. The strategy also should provide an effective way of dealing with both competition and eventual technological obsolescence, by making sure the firm's offerings deliver value in a way that competitors cannot duplicate easily and in a way not defined only in terms of the tangible product offered.

A complete understanding of the value consumers seek is needed to effectively develop and implement a strategy. The market is filled with competing Internet service providers (ISPs). CenturyLink, Comcast, Cox, and AT&T are major ISP players. While they obviously compete with each other, each also competes less obviously with relatively unknown companies working toward a solution that bypasses ISPs. One such firm is working on a satellite-based solution that beams free Internet communication directly to consumers' devices through an inexpensive plug-and-play receiver coupled to a satellite dish.[10] If the Outernet becomes even easier to access, why would one need an ISP? Couple this with the fact that Skype provides free real-time voice and video communication, and more and more consumers rely on YouTube and Netflix for entertainment; some of these ISPs, cable companies, or phone companies could be in their final years. Each firm needs to understand what benefit they truly provide. A communication company may be better than an ISP or a phone company.

> The company that focuses on value creation builds innovative solutions around consumer needs and wants, not the physical product.

When companies define themselves in terms of products like phones, cable, or even the Internet, they often fail to realize how they truly serve customers. When firms fail to realize how their products provide value, they run the risk of developing marketing myopia, defined as a condition in which a company views itself competing in a product business rather than in a value- or benefits-producing business.[11] Thus, when technology makes a good or service obsolete, the myopic business goes out of business. In contrast, the company that focuses on value creation builds innovative solutions around consumer needs and wants, not the physical product. It's interesting to contemplate what business famous brands like Apple, Google, and Facebook are really in. Do they know? Eharmony might easily define itself only as a dating site, but the company views itself as being more in the compatibility business, and is experimenting with job placement—matching employees with compatible jobs.

Strategies exist at several different levels. Exhibit 2.6 demonstrates this point. Basically, corporate strategy deals with how the firm will be defined and sets general goals. This strategy is usually associated with a specific corporate culture, which provides an operating orientation for the company. Marketing strategy then follows. Different business units within the firm may have different marketing strategies. In describing how value is created, the strategies tell why customers will choose to buy things from the company.

Strategies must eventually be implemented. Implementation deals with operational management.

strategy a planned way of doing something to accomplish some goal

marketing strategy way a company goes about creating value for customers

marketing myopia a common condition in which a shortsighted company views itself in a product business rather than in a value- or benefits-producing business

corporate strategy way a firm is defined and its general goals

Exhibit 2.6

Business Strategy Exists at Different Levels

Corporate Culture

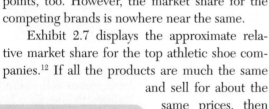

CORPORATE STRATEGY

↓

MARKETING STRATEGY

↓

TACTICS

In marketing, this level includes activities known as tactics. **Marketing tactics**, which involve price, promotion, product, and distribution decisions, are ways marketing management is implemented. Together, marketing strategy and marketing tactics should maximize the total value received by a company's customers.

2-3b Total Value Concept

Products are multifaceted and can provide value in many ways. Consider the market for athletic shoes. Different brands of athletic shoes appear very similar. A running shoe from Nike appears to be made from much the same materials and in much the same manner as a running shoe from Adidas or New Balance. Take a look at the prices and one finds that they have shoes at the same price points, too. However, the market share for the competing brands is nowhere near the same.

Exhibit 2.7 displays the approximate relative market share for the top athletic shoe companies.[12] If all the products are much the same and sell for about the same prices, then they should have comparable market share. Yet that's not nearly the case. Nike dominates

> **marketing tactics** ways marketing management is implemented; involves price, promotion, product, and distribution decisions

with about half the total market. Adidas has less than half the share of Nike, and Reebok, which was purchased by Adidas in 2006, has only a small share. Puma, New Balance, and newcomer to the footwear market, Under Armour, lag far behind. Nike is more than a rubber sole with leather and nylon uppers and laces: the swoosh matters. A couple of interesting facts that may be more than coincidental:

- ▸ Nike's advertising budget is twice the size of its nearest competitor.
- ▸ Nike's revenue is boosted by premium shoes tied to famous athletes like the "Lebron"—a basketball shoe that retails for around $250.
- ▸ Among consumers who run more than ten miles per week, New Balance has a share comparable to Nike.

Do these facts shed some light on the way these brands' shoes provide value to the consumer? Probably so. Is the Nike image, fueled by massive amounts of advertising and celebrity tie-ins, as important to the serious runner as it is to the mass market?

While we associate airlines with transportation, they have other ways of providing value. While discount airlines may charge for all sorts of extras, many full-service airlines still offer things like complimentary food and drink and individual electronic entertainment

Exhibit 2.7

Market Share for Athletic Shoes

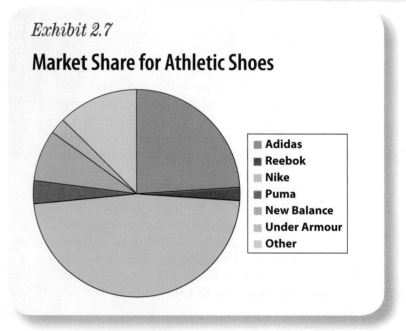

- ■ Adidas
- ■ Reebok
- ■ Nike
- ■ Puma
- ■ New Balance
- ■ Under Armour
- ■ Other

systems for playing games, watching movies, or creating a playlist. Airlines also offer their preferred customers perks like flight lounges, with comfortable work spaces, food, drinks, and sometimes even a place to shower. The term **augmented product** means the original product plus the extra things needed to increase the value from consumption.

> ## Nike is more than a rubber sole with leather and nylon uppers and laces: the swoosh matters.

Thus, every product's value proposition is made up of the basic benefits, plus the augmented product, plus the "feel" benefits. A company must try to understand all the ways a product offers value to its customers. The **total value concept** is practiced when companies operate with the understanding that products provide value in multiple ways. Many products and brands, for instance, provide some benefits that produce utilitarian value and some that provide hedonic value. This value, in turn, helps instill a brand's meaning in the consumer psyche.

2-3c The Total Value Concept Illustrated

Let's consider a consumer who purchases a 2017 Ferrari 458 Speciale. Does the consumer buy the car for its near 600 horsepower V-8 engine, carbon-filament doors, bright red color, or dual-clutch seven-speed gear box? No, the consumer buys the car because of the total value offered. What does the Ferrari 458 Speciale value proposition offer?

1. **Transportation.** In other words, the Ferrari solves the job of getting a consumer from point A to point B. This is one way the Ferrari provides value—utilitarian value in this case.

2. **The Ferrari service plan.** A Ferrari needs TLC. Ferrari offers a three-year warranty, which means for at least three years, the problem of repairing the Ferrari is solved—utilitarian value is added.

3. **The feelings associated with driving the car.** The car can go from 0 to 60 mph in three seconds flat. At a top speed of over 200 mph, the car can exceed the speed limit, but we know consumers always obey the speed limit—right? The excitement that is the Ferrari driving experience provides hedonic value.

4. **The positive feelings that go along with ownership.** The Ferrari owner will certainly take pride in the car. He may also believe that social status comes from being seen as a Ferrari owner. He can even impress friends with a drive on the Pacific Coast Highway.

5. **The feelings of status and pride that come with ownership.** A Ferrari jacket and cap help make the statement, "I'm a Ferrari owner." The realization of ownership provides a hedonic value.

6. **The negative feelings that go along with ownership.** Hopefully, our Ferrari owner is independently wealthy. At a price tag of about US$300,000, the car loan could be the size of a modest mortgage—not including insurance. If the Ferrari is a financial strain, then worry will result when the owner thinks about the car. Friends may have also suggested that Ferraris are unreliable. All of these feelings may detract from the hedonic value offered by the car.

> ## The total value proposition includes the basic benefits, the augmented product, plus the feel benefits.

Altogether, most readers would certainly like to drive the Ferrari but probably would not care to pay the high price. Thus, the Ferrari does not offer enough benefits for us to make the necessary sacrifice. If the idea of a

augmented product actual physical product purchased plus any services such as installation and warranties necessary to use the product and obtain its benefits

total value concept business practice wherein companies operate with the understanding that products provide value in multiple ways

How does the Ferrari provide value? If you understand this, you understand the total value concept.

driverless car (like the one Alphabet now is working on commercializing) is appealing to you, then you are looking for a different value proposition than the one offered by Ferrari.[13]

2-3d Value Is Co-Created

Alone, a marketer can only propose a way of creating value to consumers. In other words, the marketer cannot create value alone.[14] Rather, consumers add resources in the form of knowledge and skills to do their own part in the consumption process. The marketer's offering does not create value directly, but rather consumption involves value co-creation. The marketer serves its customer by making potentially beneficial outcomes of consumption available, but the customer plays a role in whether or not the offering's attributes actually do prove beneficial, and therefore valuable. The consumer and marketer, as a true service provider, are active in turning the offer into value. For example, a 24-hour fitness center serves customers by making workout facilities available any time of day. However, the consumer can only realize value from the offer by paying for this service and applying diligence, skill, and effort to a workout regime. In many instances, a bad consumption experience is not entirely the fault of the business. The consumer plays a role in the value equation as well.

value co-creation the realization that a consumer is necessary and must play a part in order to produce value

marketing mix combination of product, pricing, promotion, and distribution strategies used to implement a marketing strategy

target market identified segment or segments of a market that a company serves

market segmentation separation of a market into groups based on the different demand curves associated with each group

2-4 MARKET CHARACTERISTICS: MARKET SEGMENTS AND PRODUCT DIFFERENTIATION

Marketing management involves managing the marketing mix and deciding to whom the effort will be directed. The marketing mix is simply the combination of product, pricing, promotion, and distribution strategies used to position some product offering or brand in the marketplace. The marketing mix represents the way a marketing strategy is implemented within a given market or exchange environment. Marketers often use the term target market to signify which market segment a company will serve with a specific marketing mix. Thus, target marketing requires that managers identify and understand market segments. But what exactly is market segmentation?

2-4a Market Segmentation

Market segmentation is the separation of a market into groups based on the different demand curves associated with each group. Market segmentation is a marketplace condition; numerous segments exist in some markets, but very few segments may exist in others. We can think of the total quantity of a product sold as a simple mathematical function (f) like this:[15]

$$Q = f(p, w, x, \ldots z)$$

where Q = total quantity sold, p = price, and w, x, and z are other characteristics of the particular product. The function means that as price and the other characteristics are varied, the quantity demanded changes.

For example, as the price of tablet computers decreases, the quantity sold increases; in other words, there is a negative relationship between price and quantity sold. Negative relationships occur when as one variable increases the other decreases. This type of relationship represents the typical price-quantity relationship commonly depicted in basic economics courses. As the length of the warranty increases (w in this case), more tablets are sold. Thus, if we limit the demand equation to two characteristics (price p and warranty w in this case), the equation representing demand for tablets overall might be:

$$Q = -3p + 2w$$

The numbers, or coefficients, preceding p and w, respectively, for each group represent the sensitivity of each segment to each characteristic. The greater the magnitude (absolute value) of the number, the more sensitive that group is to a change in that characteristic. In economics, *elasticity* is a term used to represent market sensitivity to changes in price or other characteristics.[16] This equation suggests that consumers are more sensitive to price than warranty, as indicated in this case by the respective coefficients, -3 for price and $+2$ for warranty.

However, this overall demand "curve" may not accurately reflect any particular consumer. Instead, the market may really consist of two groups of consumers that produce this particular demand curve when aggregated. In other words, the two groups may be of equal size and be represented by equations that look something like this:

$$q_1 = 21p + 3w$$

$$q_2 = 25p + 1w$$

In this case, q_1 and q_2 represent the quantity that would be sold in groups one and two, respectively. Group one is more sensitive to the warranty ($|3| > |1|$), and group two is more sensitive to price ($|25| > |21|$). If we put all the segments together, we get total demand once again:

$$Q = q_1 + q_2$$

Thus, a market for any product is really the sum of the demand existing in individual groups or segments of consumers. The fast-food market may consist of many segments including a group most interested in low price, a group most interested in food quality, a group most interested in convenience, and perhaps a group that is not extremely sensitive to any of these characteristics. In this sense, market segmentation is not really a marketing tactic because the segments are created by consumers through their unique preferences. Market segmentation is critically important to effective marketing, though, and the marketing researcher's job becomes identifying segments and describing the segments' members based on characteristics such as age, income, geography, and lifestyle.

Exhibit 2.8 depicts the market segmentation process. For simplicity, we consider the quantity sold as a function of price alone. The frame on the left depicts overall quantity demanded. Typically, as price goes up (moves right on the *x*-axis), the quantity sold goes down, meaning

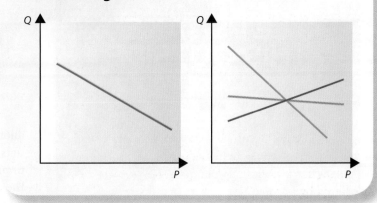

Exhibit 2.8

Total Market Sales and Sales within Market Segments

price is negatively related to quantity. The frame on the right breaks this market into three segments:

1. **The orange line depicts a segment that is highly sensitive to price. Changes in price correspond to relatively large changes in sales. In this particular case, price increases reduce the quantity demanded.**

2. **The green line represents a segment also sensitive to price, so that higher prices are demanded less, but this segment is not nearly as sensitive as the first segment. Changes in price are not associated with as large of a change in quantity sold.**

3. **The violet line turns out to be perhaps most interesting. Here, when price goes up, the quantity sold actually goes up, too. Thus, the group is sensitive to price but actually buys more at a higher price than at a lower price.**

Actually, although a positive relationship between price and quantity may seem unusual, *backward sloping demand,* a term used in economics to refer to this situation, is hardly rare. When one considers product category demand, a market segment for many products will feature a positive price-to-quantity demanded relationship. For instance, how much perfume with a brand name of Très Cher could be sold in a gallon container for $2? Probably not very much. However, Chanel No. 5 is highly demanded at about $325 an ounce.

Earlier, we discussed the athletic shoe market in the context of the total value concept, and how higher-priced brands were the best sellers. If we think of a change in price as the difference in price between the bargain

elasticity reflects how sensitive a consumer is to changes in some product characteristic

Nike's long-term market dominance illustrates that their value proposition goes beyond footwear.

brands and Nike, most consumers seem to prefer higher-priced shoes. At the very least, athletic shoe consumers appear insensitive to price. Although this may seem inconsistent with "rational" economics, consumer behavior theory offers an explanation. Name-brand products like Nike are indeed worth more, meaning they are more valuable, than bargain-brand shoes. The added value comes not just from the tangible characteristics of the shoes, but also from the feelings that come along with knowledge of the brand.

Market segments are associated with unique value equations just as they are associated with unique demand equations. Thus, if each segment is offered a product that closely matches its particular sensitivities, all segments can receive high value. This brings us to product differentiation.

2-4b Product Differentiation

product differentiation
marketplace condition in which consumers do not view all competing products as identical to one another

Product differentiation is a marketplace condition in which consumers do not view all competing products as identical to one

> Added value comes not just from the tangible characteristics of offerings, but also from the feelings that come with knowledge of the brand.

another. We refer to commodities very often as products that are indistinguishable across brands and/or manufacturers—that is, no matter who produced them or where they were produced. Regular gasoline approaches a commodity status, but even here, a few consumers will regard certain brands as unique. In contrast, consumers looking for companionship do not see all online dating sites as the same. While all of the sites offer potential utilitarian value in the form of putting users together, they differ in terms of how they do so, pricing, and in how potential dates communicate with each other. Some offer to narrow the market based on offering services ostensibly to those only of a certain age group, ethnicity, religion, or lifestyle. Thus, farmersonly.com brings together farmers. Narrowing the market adds utilitarian value. Others make the communication process more interesting by offering online flirting or winking. Naturally, certain segments, each aligned with various demographic and or lifestyle profiles, gravitate toward the online dating site most suited to them. In the same way, most markets are characterized by product differentiation and market segmentation.

2-5 ANALYZING MARKETS WITH PERCEPTUAL MAPS

Product differentiation becomes the basis for **product positioning**. Positioning refers to the way a product is perceived by a consumer and can be represented by the number and types of characteristics that consumers perceive. A standard marketing tool is a perceptual map.

2-5a Perceptual Maps

Marketing analysts use **perceptual maps** to depict graphically the positioning of competing products. When marketing analysts examine perceptual maps, they can identify competitors, identify opportunities for doing more business, and diagnose potential problems in the marketing mix. For instance, the analyst may realize that by changing the amount of some product characteristic, they can move closer to some segment's ideal point, and thus increase the competitiveness of the product. Alternatively, a new business may choose to position a product in a way that leaves it facing little direct competition. This can be done by "locating" the product as far away from other brands as possible.

Cirque de Soleil followed a marketing strategy that positioned its offering far away from other circuses by eliminating tents and circus animals (moving into arenas and auditoriums), raising prices (a ticket far above the normal circus ticket), reducing the number of acts, and creating themes for acrobatic shows. In doing so, they created what marketing analysts refer to as a blue ocean.[17] A **blue ocean strategy** seeks to position a firm so far away from competitors that, when successful, the firm creates an industry of its own by finding an uncontested market space where, at least for a time, it isolates itself from competitors.

2-5b Illustrating a Perceptual Map

Exhibit 2.9 illustrates a perceptual map. Perceptual mapping is used throughout this book as a way to link differences in consumer behavior to changes in marketing strategy or tactics. In this case, the perceptual map depicts consumer beliefs about tourist attractions in New Orleans, Louisiana. Each attraction is listed in a small rectangle.

The researcher identified and collected consumer perceptions of the ten tourist destinations and of the **ideal points**, meaning the combination of tourist destination characteristics providing the most value among the five most prominent consumer segments: Adventure Seekers, Culture Explorers, Relaxers, Knowledge Seekers, and Thrill Seekers.[18] Colored ovals indicate these segments centered on each segment's ideal point. The x- and y-axes of this plane represent important

Exhibit 2.9

A Perceptual Map for Alternative Tourist Attractions

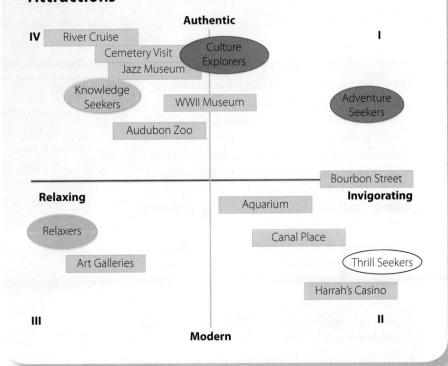

product positioning
way a product is perceived by a consumer

perceptual map
tool used to depict graphically the positioning of competing products

blue ocean strategy positioning a firm far away from competitors' positions so that it creates an industry of its own and, at least for a time, isolates itself from competitors

ideal point combination of product characteristics that provide the most value to an individual consumer or market segment

dimensions that consumers use to separate competitors on specific characteristics. Here, the *x*-axis identifies product offerings based on how relaxing to invigorating consumers view each. The *y*-axis separates product offerings based on how relatively modern versus authentic consumers view each. The perceptual map allows several key observations.

1. **The competition among attractions viewed as highly authentic and relaxing is intense. Consumers regard the Mississippi River Cruises, a visit to the Jazz Heritage Museum, a cemetery visit, and the Audubon Zoo as possessing these characteristics as shown in quadrant IV of the perceptual map. The World War II Museum also competes with these attractions, viewed as a moderately authentic, moderately invigorating attraction.**

2. **Two segments, Culture Explorers and Knowledge Seekers, possess ideal points near the five segments mentioned above.**

3. **Harrah's Casino offers an option for the thrill-seeking market with its position as highly exciting, highly modern.**

4. **The city's numerous art galleries offer the Relaxer segment an attractive option.**

5. **The Adventure Seeker segment appears underserved, with no option prominent in quadrant I.**

The marketing analyst draws several conclusions based on these observations:

1. **The highest demand positioning is in quadrant IV (highly authentic, relaxing). The city's overall image as rich in heritage and relatively laid-back—"The Big Easy" being one of the many nicknames—helps attract consumers looking for these types of experiences. An entrepreneur wishing to open another major tourist attraction positioned in this way may see the large number of potential customers desiring this positioning as an opportunity. However, the downside to this positioning is the large number of entrenched competitors. In general, competing directly with large, entrenched competitors usually requires a large amount of resources.**

2. **An opportunity may exist in quadrant I. Here, major competition for the adventure-seeking market appears absent. The advantage of positioning a new business away from the competitors is that it takes**

fewer resources to get started because the major competitors are not likely to see the new offering as a threat. Here, the opportunity for rustic, overnight stays in the swamplands that surround New Orleans may provide an attractive offering for this segment. The success of such an offering depends on a steady stream of Adventure Seekers coming to New Orleans.

Perceptual maps are widely used to plot the way consumers view competitors in an industry. As illustrated in the example, they are very useful for spotting opportunities in the marketplace, allowing a business to better understand exactly whom they compete with, and identifying what-if situations by examining what would happen if they changed an offering by raising or lowering characteristics. Very commonly, brands analyze themselves on a perceptual map with price and quality as the dimensions. If a firm lowers price or raises quality, their competition may well change in response. Perceptual mapping is used in practically every competitive industry, including the nonprofit sector.[21] The simple two-dimensional graphics give the user an easy way to analyze a market.

> Businesses are constantly using consumer behavior to make better strategic and operational decisions.

2-5c Using Consumer Behavior Theory in Marketing Strategy

Businesses are constantly using consumer behavior to make better strategic and operational marketing decisions. We will focus considerably on using consumer behavior in business decision making throughout this book. Students, and practicing managers for that matter, sometimes struggle with the application aspect of CB. In other words, how do we translate knowledge of the CVF into more effective analyses and decision making? Checklists can be a powerful aid to decision making as a way to develop more creative, thoughtful, and logically sound marketing strategy and tactics. Exhibit 2.10 displays a checklist inspired by the CVF framework—the CB idea checklist.

Exhibit 2.10

The CB Idea Checklist

Question	Idea
What specific consumer needs and desires are involved?	
▶ Is a specific product(s) involved in this situation?	
▶ Can something else provide the same value or address the same need or desire?	
How is the product positioned (types and amounts of value intended)?	
▶ How is our position superior to competitors?	
▶ How can we get closer to desirable ideal points?	
▶ How is our position inferior to competitors?	
▶ How can we isolate ourselves from competition?	
How does the consumer actually receive value from this company?	
▶ In the current situation, has value been diminished? can value be enhanced?	
▶ Can the product be modified to enhance value?	
▶ Can the company introduce a new product to enhance value?	
▶ Can the company add services to improve value for consumers?	
▶ Can communication be improved?	
▶ Is a competitor in a better position to provide superior value?	
▶ If so, how?	
Where is this product consumed?	
▶ Can value be enhanced by changing the consumption setting?	
▶ When do consumers avoid consuming this product?	
▶ Can new uses be discovered in different settings?	
Who . . .	
▶ Is buying the product?	
1. Individual consumers	
2. Groups of consumers (families)	
3. Business consumers	
▶ Is not buying the product?	
Why should a consumer . . .	
▶ Buy this product?	
▶ Avoid this product?	
When do consumers . . .	
▶ Find the product most valuable?	
▶ Find the product least valuable?	
What are the key CVF elements involved in understanding the consumption process in this case?	
Is additional consumer research needed?	
▶ Will the information be worth what it would cost to obtain it?	
▶ What type of research would be required?	

WHAT'S IN THE APPLE?

Everyone with an iPhone knows that the Apple logo has a bite out of it. But what's going on inside? The latest iPhone and iPad releases have underperformed based on sales growth statistics; their phone business may be showing signs of maturity. Is Apple trying to avoid marketing myopia? Well, several things are in the works inside Apple. In the near term, Apple is working to reposition the iPad as being higher in utilitarian value. The company is working with app firms specializing in professional fields like accounting and medicine to make the iPad more useful as a work tool. Apple has also been refining Apple TV, and, in what seems a drastic departure from their core business, an Apple Titan test automobile has been spotted on the streets near San Francisco. A key marketing strategy question is whether or not there is any consistency behind these potential innovations.

Hadrian/Shutterstock.com

Sources: Wakabayashi, D. (2016), "Apple's Sales Growth Slows," *Wall Street Journal* (January 27), B1–B5. Ovide, S. and D. Wakabayashi (2015), "With iPad Sales Cooling, Apple Leans on Partners," *Wall Street Journal* (August 13) B1–B4.

2-6 VALUE TODAY AND TOMORROW—CUSTOMER LIFETIME VALUE

Earlier, we defined marketing as value-producing activities that facilitate exchange. In other words, marketing makes exchange more likely. Exchange is far from a one-way street. Consumers enter an exchange seeking value, and so do marketers. The value the company receives from exchange may be slightly easier to explain than is the value that a consumer receives. Obviously, when a consumer spends money for a product, the company receives economic resources in the form of revenue that the company then uses to pay employees, cover costs, and help the firm grow. The company may also receive additional benefits if the consumer becomes a loyal customer who is an advocate for the firm's products.

Customer Lifetime Value (CLV) approximate worth of a customer to a company in economic terms; overall profitability of an individual consumer

Thus, not every customer is equally valuable to a firm. Firms increasingly want to know the customer lifetime value associated with a customer or customer segment.[19] **Customer Lifetime Value (CLV)** represents the approximate worth of a customer to a company in economic terms. Put another way, CLV is the overall, long-term profitability of an individual consumer. Although there is no generally accepted formula for the CLV, the basic idea is simple:

$$CLV = npv \text{ (sales} - \text{costs)} + npv \text{ (equity)}$$

The customer lifetime value then is equal to the net present value (npv) of the stream of profits over a customer's lifetime, plus the worth attributed to the equity a good customer can bring in the form of positive referrals and word of mouth. Consider a consumer shopping twice weekly at IKEA (see www.ikea.com). On average, this IKEA customer spends $200 per week, or $10,400 per year. If we assume a 5% operating margin, he yields IKEA a *net* $520 per year. Even if any potential positive word-of-mouth is not considered, the consumer is worth about $9,000 to IKEA today, assuming a 30-year life span and a 4% annual interest rate.

Interestingly, until recently IKEA did not record customer-level data. Thus, out of over 500 terabytes of data, they had no data on CLV.[20] In contrast, other firms, from convenience stores to Harrah's Casinos, have elaborate systems for tracking individual customer behavior and targeting these consumers with individualized promotions and products. This allows them to practice one-to-one marketing in a real sense and to identify segments of consumers containing a high proportion of very valuable customers. For instance, one retailer found that high CLV customers tend to have the following characteristics:[21]

- ▶ Female
- ▶ 30–50 years of age
- ▶ Married
- ▶ $90,000 income
- ▶ Loyalty card holder

In contrast, the low CLV customers tended to have quite different characteristics:

- ▶ Male
- ▶ 24–44 years of age
- ▶ Single
- ▶ Less than $70,000 income
- ▶ Single channel shopper (meaning only Internet or only stores)

Thus, marketers can maximize the value they receive from exchange by concentrating their marketing efforts on consumers with high CLVs. Recently, bargain-conscious consumers have latched on to online closeout retailers like Rue La La. When a consumer names Rue La La as a favorite thing, that consumer is worth a lot to the retailer.

STUDY TOOLS 2

LOCATED AT BACK OF THE TEXTBOOK
☐ Tear out Chapter Review Card

LOCATED AT WWW.CENGAGE.COM/LOGIN
☐ Review Key Term flashcards and create your own cards
☐ Track your knowledge and understanding of key concepts in consumer behavior
☐ Complete practice quizzes to prepare for tests
☐ Complete interactive content within CB Online
☐ Review the Chapter Highlight boxes for CB Online

CASES

IDEO: Consumer-Focused Innovation

Written by Professor Vicky Szerko, Dominican College

A great example of how companies make use of consumer behavior data is the enormously innovative and influential product design firm, IDEO (www.ideo.com). It has developed products for many of the world's most successful and exciting companies, from technology leader Apple to the venerable consumer packaged goods giant, Procter & Gamble.

While the name IDEO obviously draws from the word *idea*, it is Thomas A. Edison's famous observation regarding genius as being "1% inspiration and 99% perspiration" that actually guides the firm's product development process. Preceding every "flash of genius" is a painstaking and disciplined approach that focuses intently on the consumer experience.

Whenever IDEO is asked by a client to design a new product, it turns to a highly effective form of idea generation called the "deep dive."[1] The "deep dive" consists of a total immersion in the customer experience, requiring IDEO's team of developers and designers to place themselves in the actual situation for which the product is ultimately intended.

For example, a commission to design a better wheelchair would mean living as a disabled person to learn what it's like to be dependent on a wheelchair for tasks most of us take for granted. Besides the physical aspects of navigating the wheelchair, developers have to ask themselves: How does being in a wheelchair make you feel? Does the wheelchair provide a sense of empowerment or frustration? What things about the wheelchair are positive or negative? Once the team has been able to experience the wheelchair from a disabled person's perspective, it can much better address the features and benefits that will be most valuable to the user.

Research tells us that people relate to products from multiple perspectives. Why does someone prefer Brand X to Brand Y—although they both do, essentially, the same thing? It may be because Brand X enhances the person's status (as in a designer bag), or reassures him that he is receiving high quality (as in an expensive appliance). Simply put, people prefer products that don't just do the job (utilitarian value) but also affect the way they feel (hedonic value). Well-designed wheelchairs must not only get people around but make them feel good about using them, too.

To illustrate how IDEO takes both utilitarian and hedonic considerations in designing products, consider a recent commission: the redesign of the classroom desk. IDEO was asked by Steelcase, a global company in the office furniture industry, to help them break into the education market. Could IDEO transform the traditional tablet-arm desk?

IDEO's team began by using the desks and observing them in the classroom setting. They saw that the desks were uncomfortable for larger individuals (Americans have been increasing in weight), that the word "tablet" now meant not just spiral notebooks but increasingly referred to digital devices, and that moving and rearranging the desks in the classroom was noisy, cumbersome, and annoying. Also, with many more individuals going to school and class sizes getting larger, the traditional desks produced a sense of overcrowding, an unpleasant feeling for most individuals.

IDEO created a series of prototypes based on their developers' experience in the classroom. They then invited students and faculty to test each prototype in the classroom and provide direct feedback. As feedback was received and considered in light of the desk's role in the classroom experience, the tablet-arm desk was completely redesigned. It was dubbed the Node chair.

"The details betray a remarkable thoughtfulness," wrote Cliff Kuang in *Fast Company*. "The seat is a generously sized bucket, so that students can shift around and adapt their posture to whatever's going on: the seat also swivels, so that students can, for example, swing around to look at other students making class presentations; and a rolling base allows the chairs to move quickly between lecture-based seating and group activities. In group activities, the proportions are such that the chairs and integrated desktops combine into something like a conference table."[2] Clearly, the whole experience of sitting in a classroom had been substantially improved.

In a recent TED Talk, IDEO's founder and president David Kelley discussed how "human-centered design," or looking at things from the user's point of view, can solve what may seem to be insurmountable problems. He used Pittsburgh Children's Hospital's experience with CT scanning of children to illustrate his point.

The problem had to do with the CT scanners themselves. Although the scanners were remarkably accurate and scientifically advanced, they produced a traumatic experience in young children; as many as 80% of children had to be sedated before the scans could take place.

While the scanners delivered a high degree of utility from a medical standpoint, they were woefully lacking in providing a good, or even acceptable, experience for young patients. Doug Dietz, principal designer for GE Global Design, which had developed and produced the scanners, set out to see what could be done to improve the children's experience.

"We did simple things that got overlooked. I mean, some of the most effective insights came from kneeling down and looking at a room from the height of a child," recalled Dietz.[3] The huge machines in the impersonal, utilitarian rooms frightened the children. Dietz's solution was to divert the children's attention from the machine itself by placing it in the context of an exciting fantasy adventure.

The newly redesigned rooms were dubbed the GE Adventure Series™. The rooms and scanners were specially outfitted to resemble a child's fantasy adventure— a pirate ship, a jungle, an underwater journey. Sights, sounds, and even smells (such as the piña colada scent in the pirate ship adventure) engaged the child's attention and turned the scanner into an integral part of the fantasy experience.

The impact of the redesign was dramatic: The number of children having to be sedated dropped from 80% to just around 10%. What better testament to the importance of the hedonic, or experiential, dimension in product design? Before the redesign, the scanners were just highly sophisticated medical devices; afterward, they provided a delightful experience to children and even simplified the job experience of the medical technicians involved.

Moral of the story? The best products not only get the job done, but make doing the job a pleasure.

QUESTIONS

1 Where does IDEO get inspiration for its product designs?

2 What kind of value do you think successful products deliver to consumers?

3 Why do you think having a product that simply works doesn't always translate to consumer acceptance?

4 What is the relative importance of the utilitarian versus the hedonic value of products, as suggested by the work of IDEO?

5 Do you agree with Edison's observation that "genius is 1% inspiration and 99% perspiration"? Explain your answer.

CASE 1-2

Born or Reinvented in the "Foreign" Land? Examining Brands and Their Country of Origin

Written by Aditi Grover, Plymouth State University

Consumers make choices while considering the expected value they would derive from products and services. Companies likewise seek to enhance the value of their product offering while considering a variety of factors that might guide consumer decision making.

Among the various factors known to play a role in consumer decision making, country of origin—where a certain product or brand was manufactured—is seen to play an important role at least in some circumstances. Research has shown consumers might choose brands manufactured in their own country over the same brands manufactured elsewhere. This preference towards products manufactured within one's own country, called *consumer ethnocentrism*, may be strong enough to persist regardless of price and quality.[1] Furthermore, this phenomenon has been observed not only within the United States but across the globe—in Africa, France, and China, among other regions. Diverse factors may drive people's consumer ethnocentrism. For example,

CASES

in 2011 the *ABC World News with Diane Sawyer* series "Made in America" tried to promote products made 100% within the United States. According to ABC News, "Economists say that if every one of us spent an extra $3.33 on U.S.-made goods every year, it would create nearly 10,000 new jobs in this country."[2] Note, however, the preference towards products from one's home country does *not* automatically mean animosity towards products from other countries.

Even though data suggests that some consumers might show a preference—overt or covert—towards products manufactured in their country of origin, the question arises whether consumers possess the accurate knowledge of where a product or brand is manufactured, or where the brand originated. For example, consider the famous chocolate hazelnut spread Nutella. Did the brand originate in the United States? No, the Nutella spread was born in the 1940s in northwest Italy. How about L'Oreal? How many of us know that Black-Berry is a Canadian company? These examples demonstrate that even though individuals might prefer brands manufactured in their country of birth, consumers might not possess the knowledge to identify a brand's country of origin accurately. Researchers have defined consumers' ability to correctly identify the countries of origin of well-known brands as Brand Origin Knowledge, or BoK.[3]

Table 1 lists top growing brands from "2016 Ranking of Top 100 Brands," developed by Interbrand—the world's leading brand consultancy—alongside the brand's country of origin. Examine the table to test your BoK (or lack thereof). Visit Interbrand's website for a complete list of the top brands (www.interbrand.com/).

As consumer behavior students, it would be helpful to further understand how BoK might vary from consumer to consumer, especially if such information makes a difference in consumers' decision making: Would BoK be higher for people who are more educated (versus less educated)? Could BoK vary depending on the demographic factors such as age and gender? Could the extent to which a consumer has traveled across the globe or been exposed to diverse brands be yet another factor? Consider Ms. Sandler, a citizen of the United States and a top executive at SAP, the German firm. She drives a Ferrari and shops only at Cartier for her jewelry and Armani for her clothing, while carrying her cash in her favorite Louis Vuitton bag. She likes to party with friends while sharing a drink of Corona before a final drink of Nestlé's instant coffee. Would such a consumer be more likely to have higher or lower BoK?

Table 1. Test Your BoK

2011 Rank	Brand	Country	Sector
1	Facebook	USA	Social Network
2	Amazon	USA	Internet Technology
3	LEGO	Denmark	Toys
4	Nissan	Japan	Autos
5	Adobe	USA	Software
6	Starbucks	USA	Coffee Experience
7	Zara	Spain	Affordable Fashion
8	MINI	U.K.	Auto
9	Porsche	Italy	Auto
10	Mercedes-Benz	Gernamy	Auto
11	Huawei	China	Telcom
12	Hermes	France	High Fashion
13	Adidas GP	Germany	Fitness
14	Paypal	USA	Payment Services
15	Audi	Germany	Auto
16	AXA	France	Insurance
17	Samsung	S. Korea	Electronics
18	Visa	USA	Credit Services

Source: 2016 Ranking of the Top 100 Brands (http://interbrand.com/best-brands/best-global-brands/2016/, accessed October 17, 2016).

While the level of knowledge about the origin of a brand might be attributed to several factors, an important one could be the length of time a "foreign" brand has existed within the United States. This might significantly alter the extent to which it is considered foreign. For example, if we trace the history of Adidas, the German sporting goods company founded in 1948, we learn that the company has had an interesting story as it traversed from Germany into other countries of the world. Even though companies such as Adidas can successfully and seamlessly surpass the preference of products manufactured in one's own country (also known as the country-of-origin effect), it might not always be the case.

Characteristics of certain products might be so inextricably mapped onto a consumer's country that it might be hard to ignore the brand's country of origin while making a consumption decision. For example, consider wine: do people generally prefer to buy wine from France or from the United States? France's history of wine-making is at least as old as the Roman Empire, and France has almost always held the title of the world's largest producer of wine. In a related vein, the United States is known for its edge in Internet services and electronics, for it gave rise to global powerhouses such as Alphabet's Google, Apple, and Amazon. Within the realm of brand and its country of origin, when consumers demonstrate preference for products that map onto the competitiveness of the country in which they originate, it may be referred to as "product ethnicity." Therefore, when product ethnicity is taken into account, consumers might choose to ignore their ethnocentric values while making consumption decisions.

Furthermore, it will be important to see how one brand might be showcased differently in various countries of the brand's presence. For example, a KFC that one sees in the United States has a much different menu offering than does a KFC in China. As another example, consider Wrigley's, the chewing gum. Examining how this brand might be marketed differently in the United States versus in Europe would highlight how the same brand might employ different marketing strategies. Companies analyze varied dimensions (such as culture and corporate regulations) of a country before launching a product in foreign locations. However, the core fundamental lesson of consumer behavior remains consistent around the globe: To be successful, companies need to ensure that the product offering meshes well with consumers' needs and with what they value.

QUESTIONS

1 Examine further the "2016 Ranking of Top 100 Brands." Classify these brands while considering the product category or sector and the country of origin. Can you detect a pattern? For example, do you see that strong players in the automotive sector emerge largely in Western Europe?

2 List all the brands that you have in your home. Then research to find the country of origin of all the brands on your list. What do you find? How can marketing professionals make use of the information that you have analyzed?

3 Use the "2016 Ranking of Top 100 Brands" table to test the level of BoK of at least five people (excluding yourself). Examine and write a short reflection on how the extent of their knowledge varies with their lifestyles.

4 Your textbook refers to the concept of perceptual maps. Construct a perceptual map using the following two dimensions: (i) product ethnicity (low vs. high), and (ii) level of BoK (low vs. high). Choose at least ten brands or product categories to represent on the map. You may use the list of brands/categories available at the Interbrand website to populate a list for the map. Use the information from question 3 to identify the average level of knowledge of product ethnicity and extent of BoK.

5 Using the information in question 3, how do you think a company can enhance its understanding of market segmentation so as to efficiently target a marketing message to its potential and existing consumers?

CASES

DemandTec®: Using Collaborative Analytics in a Fragmented Latin American Market

Written by Kristine Pray, Muskingum University

In February 2012, headlines across America alerted consumers that mass-market retailer Target had discovered a way to predict the gestational state of their female shoppers, even before family members were aware of the pregnancy.[1] With this predictive ability, Target would be able to capitalize on the life-altering events of their customers. Imagine anticipating the changing needs of individual consumers with such accuracy that developing the associated marketing mix brings implementing the marketing concept to a whole other level. Sending targeted promotions to highly segmented markets while the rest of the competition remains unaware offers a strategic advantage to marketers competing in the 21st century.

The accuracy of these predictions is based on models that identify changes in the behavior of consumers. In the case of Target, changes in the purchase behavior of female shoppers, such as increased spending on supplements important to neonatal development, as well as unscented soaps and lotions, were a strong indication of pregnancy.[2] This is, of course, an oversimplification. Aggregating vast amounts of consumer behavior data and creating predictive models to strategically target individual consumers is only made possible by the use of very powerful software, software which has been developed to further the emergent practice known as collaborative analytics.

Although collaborative analytics and cloud-based software company DemandTec made the news recently when it was acquired by IBM for $440 million, it is not likely that anyone outside of the industry is familiar with the San Mateo, California-based company.[3] In the field of collaborative analytics, however, DemandTec is well established, with a client list of over 500 retailers and consumer products companies, including ConAgra Foods, General Mills, Home Depot, PETCO, Sara Lee, Walmart, and, of course, Target.[4] With increased global competition and price-conscious consumers, companies know how important it is to properly segment the market and create the right marketing mix for each of those consumer segments. DemandTec provides companies with the tools they need to optimize those decisions.

American companies, however, are not the only ones faced with increased global competition. Emerging markets in countries like Argentina, Peru, India, and China are appealing to multinational companies. Domestic as well as foreign corporations can also benefit from the services of companies like DemandTec.

In Sao Paulo, Brazil, the largest market in Latin America, Companhia Brasileira de Distribuicao Grupo Pao de Acucar (GPA), referred to as the "Walmart of Latin America," is striving to hold on to the majority share of the grocery market.[5] French-owned supermarket giant Carrefour maintains a close second place, followed by global retail behemoth Walmart, which plans to invest heavily in the region to edge out the competition for market leader.[6] If that does not make circumstances difficult enough for GPA, the Brazilian market itself is very fragmented. With heterogeneous consumer segments coming from diverse socioeconomic backgrounds and different geographic areas, determining the appropriate marketing strategy becomes even more complex. Enter DemandTec.[7]

Using "everyday price optimization software-as-a-service" from DemandTec, GPA can optimize their pricing strategy at the local level.[8] GPA segments their market using geographic segmentation variables (region); demographic segmentation variables (income and social class); psychographic segmentation variables (lifestyle); and behavioristic segmentation variables (price sensitivity), resulting in 12 distinct target segments.[9] In addition to managing all of the consumer segmentation information, GPA must also integrate stock-keeping unit (SKU) information. Usually in the form of a machine-readable bar code, SKU numbers are assigned to individual items in inventory to help monitor inventory, sales, pricing, transactions, and consumer spending patterns.[10] With 99 variants for each SKU across each of GPA's regions, the amount of data to be processed would be overwhelming without the use of DemandTec's price optimization software.[11]

DemandTec's powerful modeling software collectively analyzes regional competitor prices and then aggregates consumer demand for items, vendor costs, customer characteristics, and consumer segments to arrive at optimal prices for all products across all SKU variants.[12] Collaborative analytics not only helps GPA to optimize prices but also helps them to optimize the price perception of items which have the most elastic demand; in other words, products for which consumers exhibit the most price sensitivity.[13]

The idea of using "loss leaders" as a form of sales promotion is not new to the grocery industry. Consumers tend to be more sensitive to the prices of certain items like bread or milk, so retailers offer these products at a price at or below cost to draw consumers into the store, with the hopes that the consumers will purchase additional, more profitable items. Without the proper intelligence, this promotional strategy can backfire, as consumer price perception of other items in the store discourages value-conscious consumers from buying those items with higher margins, cutting into the profitability of retailers. Collaborative analytics allows marketing managers to process volumes of data to make optimal decisions.

In an era of social media and mobile technology, today's consumers have access to an infinite amount of marketing information in real time. Armed with smart phones and unlimited apps, they can locate product, promotion, and pricing information by typing in a product name or scanning a bar code as they stand in the aisle of their local retailers. In order to meet the needs of these technology-savvy and price-conscious consumers, marketers must arm themselves with the next generation of marketing tools, collaborative analytics.

QUESTIONS

1 Predictive models used by Target identified in female shoppers changes in their purchase behavior that indicated they might be pregnant, including increased spending on supplements important to neonatal development as well as unscented soaps and lotions. What other changes in purchase behavior might indicate that a female shopper is expecting?

2 How does the use of collaborative analytics provide value to the consumer and help to facilitate exchanges between buyers and sellers?

3 Based on collaborative analytics, Target created targeted sales promotions for newly expectant mothers, such as mailing coupons to them for purchasing diapers or baby bottles. GPA, in Brazil, uses collaborative analytics to optimize prices for their various customer segments. These are only two of the four marketing mix variables. Can you think of other ways that companies might use collaborative analytics to fine-tune the other marketing mix variables?

4 GPA uses collaborative analytics to look at the shopping behavior of their customers. The next time you purchase food items (groceries), make a list of every item you purchased. Try to organize the items in a meaningful way. Imagine that a researcher was using ethnographic methods to analyze your grocery list. What insights might they have about you based on your purchases?

5 Choose a local retailer that is not part of a national or regional chain. Assume they have decided to expand their efforts internationally and have therefore enlisted the help of DemandTec. How will the use of collaborative analytics help them to better understand consumers in this new market?

CASES

Sears: A Dying Company?

Written by Dr. Venessa Funches, Auburn University, Montgomery

Ashley is on her way to her local mall. She pulls up to the mall and finds a great parking spot close to the Sears entrance. She walks briskly through tools, lawn and garden, as well as kids apparel, noticing nothing. In fact, no one seems to notice her either. She is not approached or greeted by any salespeople. What a relief! The store seems empty. Ashley is a little concerned. She came to hang out with friends, but this place seems pretty dead. Just as she rounds the corner through the women's department, a shirt catches her attention. As she glances at the price tag, she decides she can get it cheaper elsewhere. Just then her cell phone rings. It's her friend; everyone is waiting for her at Aéropostale near the food court. She picks up the pace as she rushes through men's apparel, jewelry, and finally bedding. She is relieved as she catches a glimpse of her friends through the crowd in the interior of the mall. She is looking forward to a good time shopping with her friends. As she nears the food court, she is distracted by all the cool outfits displayed in the windows of stores like American Eagle, Abercrombie & Fitch, and Buckle.

Ashley represents many of today's shoppers, who hurry on about their business—shunning department stores like Sears and its competitors. The entire department store category has been experiencing decline in recent years.

Sears has a rich history spanning over 100 years. In the past, Sears was a retail force to be reckoned with. According to the Sears Archives website (www.searsarchives.com), from the 1950s to the 1980s Sears was the largest U.S. retailer. The Sears catalog could be found in virtually every home in America.

Sears has been serving the American consumer since the turn of the century. The firm began in 1886 as a watch company, founded by Richard W. Sears. At that time most Americans lived as farmers in rural areas with limited access to the products they needed. As a result, the local general store served as the farmers' primary retail establishment. Due to the limited availability of products, price gouging was rampant. Richard W. Sears and Alvah Roebuck teamed up to form their own mail order company. They began by selling only jewelry and watches but quickly added other products in order to meet the need in the marketplace. The catalog business flourished and grew quickly.

It was not until the 1920s that the firm's management saw the need to alter their business model. The country was changing, and many people were now moving to city centers. As a result, new chain retailers were gaining popularity. Sears joined the fray by opening their own retail locations and expanding vigorously. Sears experienced great success and kept on expanding well into the 1970s. In 1973, Sears built a new headquarters located in Chicago called Sears Tower. At that time it was the tallest building in the world. By the 1980s Sears was not only expanding but also diversifying into different businesses like Allstate car insurance, Dean Witter financial services, and Discover credit cards.

Today, Sears offers a broad array of products and services. Its offerings include appliances, consumer electronics, tools, sporting goods, outdoor living, lawn and garden equipment, certain automotive services and products, home fashion products, as well as apparel, footwear, jewelry, and accessories for the whole family. Sears offers proprietary brands like Kenmore, Craftsman, DieHard, Lands' End, Covington, Apostrophe, and Canyon River Blues. These brands are important to the company because they signify quality and drive consumer traffic. Despite the strong brands, many consumers find Sears' selection bland, unattractive, or too costly. Instead they opt for specialty stores like Home Depot, Best Buy, or discounters like Target or Walmart.

The tide has shifted and Sears is struggling. Over the past two decades, Sears has ended its catalog services and closed numerous store locations.[1] In addition, the company has gone through multiple restructurings and divestitures of Dean Witter and Allstate in an effort to refocus and strengthen the business.

In 2005, Kmart bought Sears. The newly formed company became the nation's third largest retailer behind Walmart and Home Depot. The hope was that the combined firm would allow for greater cost savings and result in lower prices to consumers. Many questioned the deal, and a lot of the proposed benefits never fully materialized and the K-mart division is deeply troubled.

Sears asked the Kardashian sisters, Kim, Kourtney, and Khloé, to develop their own product line. Sears management hoped to use the Kardashians' success and popularity to create excitement, especially among younger consumers. The advertising campaign has tried to capitalize on the sexy Kardashian image. The ad campaign has showcased Kim, Kourtney, and Khloé in seductive lingerie and topless in a denim jean ad. The product line, which includes denim jeans, dresses, shoes, jewelry, handbags, intimates, belts, and sunglasses, has thus far been disappointing and unsuccessful. Despite management's efforts, sales continue to plummet.

Sears has been generally unprofitable for years. The causes of Sears' problems are multifaceted. Sears' business model has failed to keep step with changing consumer tastes. Many of its locations are out of date and need remodeling. Competitors have outspent Sears in terms of modernizing their locations by a wide margin. Second, many of its stores are located in malls that are decreasing in popularity and expensive to rent. Third, today's consumer has a vast number of shopping options. Many consumers are opting for convenient one-stop shopping at open-air shopping centers rather than enclosed malls, or avoiding them altogether for discount retailers. Finally, Sears' traditional mid-range pricing strategy has left them stranded, unable to compete with the low prices of discount stores or the broad selections of specialty stores.

Sears is down but not out of the game. The remaining stores and brands are still valuable assets. The company's management has a daunting task ahead. Can Sears refocus and find a new way to deliver value to its customers?

QUESTIONS

1 Describe how some of the trends mentioned in the textbook are affecting Sears.

2 Describe the external and situational influences that steer shoppers like Ashley away from Sears.

3 Compare and contrast the total value concept for Sears and your favorite retailer.

4 What types of utilitarian and hedonic value does Sears presently provide to its customers?

5 Can Sears be revived? If so what should their new value equation be? If not, explain.

PART 2

3 | Consumer Learning Starts Here: Perception

LEARNING OBJECTIVES

After studying this chapter, the student should be able to:

3-1 Define learning and perception and how the two are connected.

3-2 List and define phases of the consumer perception process.

3-3 Apply the concept of the just noticeable difference.

3-4 Contrast the concepts of implicit and explicit memory.

3-5 Know ways to help get consumers' attention in a crowded information environment.

3-6 Understand key differences between intentional and unintentional learning.

Tony Shi Photography/Getty Images

Remember to visit **PAGE 69** for additional **STUDY TOOLS**

INTRODUCTION

Marketing strategy describes the way a firm goes about creating value—value that comes in two distinct forms: utilitarian and hedonic. Among all the symbolic aspects of a brand's strategy, its logo embodies and signals brand meaning more than any other. A study by Adweek points to elements that are used to help create a successful logo: unique fonts, shapes, and colors.[1]

tanuha2001/Shutterstock.com

Take a look at the FedEx logo, for example. Notice the effective use of all elements. In particular, do you see the arrow signaling FedEx as a brand that moves forward? The shape of the arrow appears creatively between the last e and the x.

Consumers learn from all stimuli that they encounter. Every day, consumers are exposed to hundreds, if not thousands, of logos. Subtle changes in a logo can change

learning change in behavior resulting from some interaction between a person and a stimulus

what consumers perceive about a brand. For instance, just changing the logo's color can shape a brand's meaning. These days, green is a positive color due to associations with cleanliness and ecological friendliness. What happens when a brand includes green in their logo? Well, research suggests that the green logo inoculates the brand against consumer criticism of potentially unethical actions.[2] Green carries a meaning that affects what consumers learn about a brand. Learning begins with the simple act of perception.

3-1 DEFINING LEARNING AND PERCEPTION

Marketers cannot help create value for consumers unless they can effectively communicate the value proposition to consumers in a way that they perceive and learn about the potential benefits. Learning refers to a change in behavior resulting from the interaction between a person

and a stimulus. Perception refers to a consumer's awareness and interpretation of reality. Accordingly, perception serves as a foundation upon which consumer learning takes place. Stated simply, value involves learning, and consumer perception plays a key role in learning because consumers change behavior based on what they perceive. Sometimes, consumers set out to *intentionally* learn marketing-related information. Other times, consumers learn *unintentionally* (or incidentally) by simply being exposed to stimuli and by forming some kind of response to it. Both types of learning rely, to greater or lesser degrees, on perceptual processes.

This chapter focuses on issues relating to the learning process as it applies to consumers. Specifically, the chapter details the earliest phases of perception along with a number of issues related to unintentional learning. The chapter closes with a discussion of *conditioning*, which represents a well-known approach to unintentional learning. Intentional learning and the associated cognitive processes are discussed in a later chapter.

3-1a Consumer Perception

Are perception and reality two different things? With some thought, this question can stimulate deep, philosophical thinking. Perhaps more importantly for CB, the key question is, "What's more important, perception or reality?" Consumer researchers expend a great deal of effort trying to understand consumer perception, because one way or another, consumer perception shapes learning and thus behavior.

Perception and reality are distinct concepts because the perceptions that consumers develop do not always match the real world. For example, someone who sings in the shower does not really perceive the actual quality of the music. The singer's perceptual system protects her from that but not somebody else who happens to hear the typical consumer singing to herself. Perception simply doesn't always match reality. Perception can also be ambiguous. Exhibit 3.1 illustrates this point.

We treat perception as a consumer's awareness and interpretation of reality. Perception represents a *subjective* reality, whereas what actually exists in the environment determines objective reality. For example, at a restaurant, the objective reality is that a certain amount of food is served on a plate and a certain amount of beverage is poured into a glass. Restaurants often control proportions by weighing food and measuring drink portions as a means of cost

perception consumer's awareness and interpretation of reality

Exhibit 3.1

What Is the Reality in the Image Below?

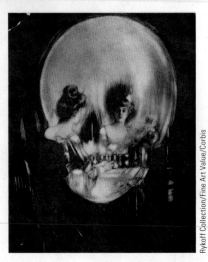

Rykoff Collection/Fine Art Value/Corbis

control. However, consumers may not always view the proportions as equally satisfying. How can this be? The answer to this question illustrates the concept of subjective reality. In this case, subjective and objective reality may differ because things like the size of the plate, glass, or container affect the amount of food and drink perceived.

Research demonstrates several ways in which the type of food container influences consumer perceptions in a way that distorts reality. For example, consumers will perceive a taller, thinner wine glass as containing more wine, but will drink more from a rounder glass.[3] Similarly, the same amount of food can leave a consumer wanting more when it is placed on a large rather than small plate. Consumers also judge tea that is physically the same temperature as not as cold or icy when served in a paper cup versus a glass container.[4]

Brands in numerous food categories have found success by making servings smaller rather than larger. Sales of 7.5-ounce bottles Coke and Pepsi have helped curb a decline in sales stemming from consumers' increasing perceptions that

exposure process of bringing some stimulus within proximity of a consumer so that the consumer can sense it with one of the five human senses

sensation consumer's immediate response to a stimulus

sensory marketing actively seeking to engage customers' senses as the primary aspect of the value proposition

sugary sodas are unhealthy. Consumers show a tendency to eat or drink until a package is empty. Small packages influence how much is consumed, but package size also influences liking, as consumers tend to perceive the very same product as being of better quality when it is in a smaller package.[5] In addition, consumers expect to pay more per ounce when the package is small. Thus, size shapes perception in many ways.

3-1b Exposure, Attention, and Comprehension

During the perceptual process, consumers are *exposed* to stimuli, devote *attention* to stimuli, and attempt to *comprehend* stimuli. Exposure refers to the process of bringing some stimulus within the proximity of a consumer so that it can be sensed by one of the five human senses (sight, smell, taste, touch, or sound). The term sensation describes a consumer's immediate response to this information.

Touch may not be the first sense that comes to mind as a marketing tool. But that doesn't diminish its importance. iPad and many other tablet sales have not lived up to sales expectations in recent years. One reason may lie in their feel. A tablet, no matter how powerful it really is, does not feel as substantial as does even a small laptop computer. The Microsoft Surface Pro series builds in a number of characteristics that make it feel more comfortable and more substantial than a traditional tablet computer. Increasingly, marketers practice sensory marketing by actively seeking to engage consumers' senses as the primary aspect of the value proposition.[6]

Exhibit 3.2

Will the Type of Cup Affect the Coffee's Warmth?

©Robert Neumann/Shutterstock.com
Mega Pixel/Shutterstock.com

Marketers expose consumers to many messages, but that does not guarantee that consumers will pay attention. **Attention** is the purposeful allocation of information-processing capacity toward developing an understanding of some stimulus. Many times, consumers simply cannot pay attention to all the stimuli to which they are exposed. This is probably now more true than ever given all the communication channels available, including countless social media outlets. Consumers report consulting more sources now than in the past, but they also feel "imprisoned" by the overwhelming amount of information presented.[7] As such, consumers are increasingly selective in the information to which they pay attention. Quite simply, there is just too much stimulation in the environment for consumers to pay attention to everything.

Comprehension occurs when consumers attempt to derive meaning from information they receive. Of course, marketers hope that consumers comprehend and interpret information in the intended way, but this is not always the case. As a simple example, a receptionist tells patients there will be a *short* wait. Will all patients think the wait is short? For example, two consumers who wait 20 minutes may perceive the wait differently. What is short to one may not be so short to another. A professional taking an hour away from her busy day may react differently than a retired person without a hectic daily schedule. Furthermore, can something be done to change perceptions of the wait time? A receptionist might update a patient every few minutes, explaining what is going on and why the wait is continuing. Alternatively, pleasant music can be played in the waiting room. In either case, the patient may either perceive a shorter wait or react more negatively to the wait than if left quietly alone. Even subtle perceptions like the color of a web page can alter the comprehension of waiting time.[8]

3-2 CONSUMER PERCEPTION PROCESS

If a friend were to ask, "Do I look good in this outfit?" you would immediately draw upon your perceptions to determine how to respond to the question. (Whether or not you voice your true opinion is an entirely different subject!) As we have stated, in its most basic form, perception describes how consumers become aware of and interpret the environment. Accordingly, we can view consumer perception as including three phases. These phases, *sensing, organizing,* and *reacting,* are shown in Exhibit 3.3.

Notice that the phases of perception overlap with the concepts of exposure, attention, and comprehension. That is, we sense the many stimuli to which we are exposed, we organize the stimuli as we attend and comprehend them, then we react to various stimuli by developing responses.

3-2a Sensing

Consumers sense stimuli to which they are exposed. Sensing is an *immediate* response to stimuli that have come into contact with one of the consumer's five senses (sight, smell, touch, taste, or sound). Thus, when a consumer touches his phone, enters a store, browses on Amazon, reads a Tweet, tastes food, looks at an advertisement, or tries on clothes, the perceptual process goes into action.

When consumers go by a billboard, they are provided with an opportunity to pay attention to the message.

George Rose/Getty Images

attention purposeful allocation of information-processing capacity toward developing an understanding of some stimulus

Tell-a-Taste

Want to know what steak tartare, the classic French dish of raw chopped steak and eggs, tastes like, but can't find the courage to try it? Well, technology may make that possible! Scientists now can use electronic stimulation of the tongue to allow consumers to experience taste sensations like tartness, bitterness, saltiness, and even sweetness. The technology may potentially benefit diabetic consumers by allowing them the sensation of tasting something sweet without the detrimental side effects. Online game designers also may use the technology to help train gamers by associating successful actions with a sensation of mint or other good taste. In the future, if you want to tell your friends what something tastes like, maybe you'll be able to send it as an attachment! Scientists also warn, though, that the virtual taste is not a replacement for either the utilitarian or hedonic value of eating. Eating involves more than taste, including both the smell and texture sensations as well as the nutrition.

Sources: https://www.sciencedaily.com/releases/2014/01/140102114807.htm, accessed March 11, 2016; http://www.fastcompany.com/3024198/reverse-engineered/this-new-tech-brings-virtual-reality-to-taste-buds, accessed March 11, 2016.

Dario Lo Presti/Shutterstock.com

Exhibit 3.3

Sensing, Organizing, and Reacting

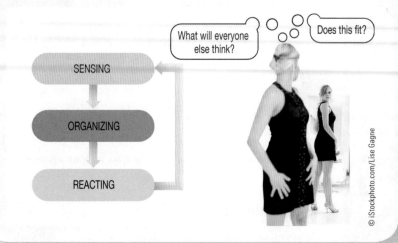

© iStockphoto.com/Lise Gagne

Grounded cognition
theory that suggests that bodily sensations influence thoughts and meaning independent of effortful thinking

However, sensing alone does not allow a consumer to make *sense* out of something. This leads to the second stage of the perceptual process.

Sensing also influences comprehension in less direct ways. The notion of **grounded cognition** suggests that bodily sensations influence thoughts and meaning independent of effortful thinking. If someone senses a warm cup of tea, then the person who serves it may be thought of as warm. A consumer standing may also take a more global evaluation of a product than a consumer in a sitting position.[9] Thus, our senses provide the basis for the meanings we construe.

3-2b Organizing

Sometimes, things just don't make sense. Our smartphones are supposed to help us communicate but sometimes even the best technology lets us down. The auto-correct feature tries to organize what we've typed into a coherent message, but sometimes it lets us down, leading to miscomprehension or even nonsense. Here a few examples of texts that are at least near nonsense:

▸ **put cursed oreos in bowl**
▸ **pick up some human beef**
▸ **happy birthday to my dead husband (see the endnote for intended messages)[10]**

When we speak of **cognitive organization**, we refer to the process by which the human brain assembles the sensory evidence into something recognizable. The organization that takes place in your brain is analogous to someone performing a sorting task—such as sorting mail. When an object is first handled, the sorter hasn't a clue what slot the object belongs in. However, information allows the sorter to place the object into progressively more specific categories.

When someone tries to decide if an outfit looks right, the perceptual process goes to work. Consider the clothing pictured in Exhibit 3.3. Is this outfit appropriate for Emilia, a professional consultant? At first, we perceive that the outfit is obviously a woman's dress. However, does the outfit represent proper business attire? If Emilia's brain organizes the outfit into this category, then she becomes likely to buy it and wear it to work as a consultant. Her clients may perceive the outfit differently, and this may interfere with their ability to see her as a professional consultant. Again, we see the subjectivity of perception.

As consumers' brains organize perceptions, some comprehension takes place in the form of an interpretation. This interpretation provides an initial cognitive and affective meaning. The term *cognitive* refers to a mental or thinking process. A reader of this book almost instantly converts a word into meaning as long as the word on the page matches a known English-language word. Sometimes marketers need to know how consumers will react to unknown words when creating the name for a new product or new company. In fact, the actual sound of a name (that is otherwise nonsense) can evoke different meanings and feelings. Consider the following two sounds (say them each aloud):

Sepfut

Sepsop

Exhibit 3.4

"Organizing" Morning Beverages

©George Dolgikh/Shutterstock.com

©weedezign/Shutterstock.com

©Wollertz/Shutterstock.com

Assimilation—Product Characteristics Fit Category Easily

Accommodation—An Adjustment Allows Product to Fit Category—Coffee Can Be Served on the Rocks

Contrast—The Product Characteristics Are Too Different to Fit Category

Which would make a better name for a new ice cream brand? Actually, when consumers sampled the same new ice cream described with one of these two names, Sepsop was preferred. The researchers theorized that consumers evaluate sounds with a repetitive pattern (like sep-sop) more favorably.[11]

Consumers cannot organize everything they sense so easily. When a consumer encounters a stimulus that is difficult to categorize, the brain instinctively continues processing as a way of reconciling inconsistencies. When even this extra effort leaves a consumer uncertain, he or she will generally avoid the stimulus.

In general, depending on the extent to which a stimulus can be categorized, the following reactions may occur (see Exhibit 3.4 for illustration).

cognitive organization process by which the human brain assembles sensory evidence into something recognizable

assimilation state that results when a stimulus has characteristics such that consumers readily recognize it as belonging to some specific category

1. **Assimilation.** Assimilation occurs when a stimulus has characteristics such that individuals readily recognize it as an example of a specific category. A hot, brown coffee served in a ceramic mug fits the "morning beverage" category easily.

2. **Accommodation.** Accommodation occurs when a stimulus shares some, but not all, of the characteristics that allow it to fit neatly in an existing category. At this point, the consumer will begin processing, which allows exceptions to rules about the category. An iced coffee may require some adjustment for a consumer used to hot coffee as a morning beverage. In this case, the consumer may relax the category rule that the coffee must be hot to accommodate iced coffee in the category. Mild incongruence is not a bad thing when selling products. New products that are mildly incongruent with expectations can sometimes be preferred to perfect matches.[12]

3. **Contrast.** Contrast occurs when a stimulus does not share enough in common with existing categories to allow categorization. An icy, bright red, alcoholic, sweet beverage served in a salt-rimmed glass shares very little in common with the "morning beverage" category. The differences are so great that the consumer cannot even force a fit through accommodation. As a result, the product contrasts with the relevant category.

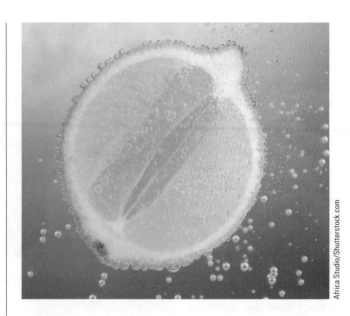

Africa Studio/Shutterstock.com

If all stimuli were consciously processed, our minds would truly be overloaded.

3-2c Reacting

The perceptual process ends with a reaction. If an object is successfully recognized, chances are some nearly automatic reaction takes place. For example, when a driver notices that the car in front of him has its brake lights on, the learned response is to apply brakes as well. Here, the reaction occurs as a response or behavior. Note that reactions can include both physical and mental responses to the stimuli encountered.

APPLICATIONS TO CONSUMER BEHAVIOR

The perceptual process has many implications for consumer behavior. For example, just what is it that leads consumers to think some service environment, like a restaurant, hospital, or hotel is clean? Colors and lighting can help change perceptions of cleanliness. For instances, consumers associate bright blue colors and citrus scents with cleanliness. When signs of cleanliness are absent, consumers tend to be dissatisfied with a service environment.[13]

Even subtle cues influence perception. Take a look at an advertisement for a watch. Chances are, time stands still in watch advertisements. The watch almost certainly had a time of about 10 past 10. Why? A watch with that time appears to be smiling at the consumer, and this subtle difference can cause a watch to be preferred over a frowning watch that says 20 past 8.[14] The term **anthropomorphism** refers to a design that gives humanlike characteristics to inanimate objects. Consumers who attribute humanlike characteristics to their automobiles also have been shown to trust them more and even be less likely to blame them for an accident![15]

3-2d Selective Perception

Consumers encounter thousands of stimuli each day. If all stimuli were consciously processed, our minds would truly be overloaded. Rather than processing all stimuli,

accommodation state that results when a stimulus shares some but not all of the characteristics that would lead it to fit neatly in an existing category, and consumers must process exceptions to rules about the category

contrast state that results when a stimulus does not share enough in common with existing categories to allow categorization

anthropomorphism giving humanlike characteristics to inanimate objects

consumers practice selective perception. *Selective perception* includes selective exposure, selective attention, and selective distortion. That is, consumers are selective in what they expose themselves to, what they attend to, and what (and how) they comprehend. **Selective exposure** involves screening out most stimuli and exposing oneself to only a small portion of stimuli. **Selective attention** involves paying attention to only certain stimuli.

Consider a tourist walking through downtown Tokyo, Japan. How can she possibly pay attention to all of this information? Marketers use the term *clutter* to describe the idea that the environment often bombards consumers with too much information in their daily lives. Consumers can't possibly pay attention to all of this. Instead, they will choose something that stands out, or is personally relevant, and devote attention to that object.

Selective distortion is a process by which consumers interpret information in ways that are biased by their previously held beliefs. This process can be the result of either a conscious or unconscious effort. For example, consumers with strong beliefs about a brand tend to comprehend messages about the brand either positively or negatively, depending on their pre-existing attitudes. Sports fans provide good examples of selective distortion. Fans from one team may be enraged when a "bad call" goes against their team. Fans for the other team are unlikely to comprehend the controversial play in the same way. Both groups

Sean Locke Photography/Shutterstock.com

With selective distortion, different consumers can see the same thing but react very differently.

of fans observe the same thing but comprehend and react differently.

EXPOSURE

Exposure occurs when some stimulus is brought within the proximity of a consumer so that it can be sensed. Obviously, marketers who want to inform consumers about their products must first expose them to information. As such, exposure represents a first and necessary step to learning. In fact, exposure is a vital component of both intentional and unintentional learning.

3-2e Subliminal Processing

Subliminal processing refers to the way in which the human brain senses low-strength stimuli, that is, stimuli that occur below the level of conscious awareness. Such stimuli have a strength that is lower than the **absolute threshold** of perception, the minimum strength needed for a consumer to perceive a stimulus. This type of "learning" is unintentional, because the stimuli fall below the absolute threshold.

To illustrate effects below the absolute threshold, consider what often happens when a mosquito lands on one's arm. Chances are the mosquito is so small that you will not be consciously aware of the sensation without seeing it. Likewise, sounds often occur that are below the threshold. Images also can be displayed for such a short period of time, or at such a low level of intensity, that the brain cannot organize the image and develop a meaning.

selective exposure process of screening out certain stimuli and purposely exposing oneself to other stimuli

selective attention process of paying attention to only certain stimuli

selective distortion process by which consumers interpret information in ways that are biased by their previously held beliefs

subliminal processing way that the human brain deals with very low-strength stimuli, so low that the person has no conscious awareness

absolute threshold minimum strength of a stimulus that can be perceived

Subliminal persuasion is behavior change induced or brought about based on subliminally processing a message. Popular conceptions about subliminal persuasion have fueled interest in it for many years. For instance, many people believe that:

▶ Marketers can somehow induce consumers to purchase brands by using subliminal advertising.

▶ Marketers can subliminally alter products or packages to make them more appealing to consumers.

▶ Sexual imagery can be hidden in a product itself, the product packaging, or in product advertising.

▶ People's sense of well-being can be enhanced by listening to subliminally embedded tapes of nature sounds and/or music.[16]

The belief is that communication can influence consumers through mere exposure to subliminal stimuli. The most famous example of subliminal persuasion involves a researcher for an ad firm who claimed that he had embedded subliminal frames within the movie *Picnic* in a New Jersey movie theater in 1957. Exhibit 3.5 illustrates the way this process reportedly took place. Very brief embeds of the phrases "Drink Coke" and "Eat Popcorn" were supposedly placed in the movie. The researcher claimed that popcorn sales rose nearly 60% as a result and that Coke sales rose nearly 20%. This experiment is often called the "Vicary experiment."

This story grew in such popularity that researchers attempted to replicate the study. Interestingly, these scientific replications failed to produce any increase in desire for Coke or popcorn. Consumer researchers also conducted experiments testing the effectiveness of sexual embeds involving airbrushed genitalia, the word *sex*, or provocative nudity in advertisements. Results of these experiments generally indicate that these practices do little to nothing that would directly make a consumer more likely to buy the advertised product.[17]

As a general statement, the research examining subliminal processing suggests that subliminal persuasion is ineffective as a marketing

---

Exhibit 3.5

The Vicary Subliminal Persuasion "Study"

The motion picture *Picnic* is run with a standard projector.

A frame is replaced displaying a subliminal message for 1/2000 second.

The movie *Picnic* continues while the audience flocks to concession stand.

---

tool.[18] This is not to dismiss subliminal processing as having no impact whatsoever on what consumers might learn or how they might behave. But any effects are small in power and far from straightforward.[19]

Despite evidence to the contrary, many consumers are willing to believe that subliminal persuasion is a powerful and influential tool.[20] Estimates suggest that over 60% of Americans believe that advertisers can exert subliminal influences strong enough to cause unwanted purchase behavior.[21] Over the years, books have fueled the controversy by promoting the idea that advertisers know about, and use, certain "hidden persuaders" to create an irresistible urge to buy.[22] Consumers are often willing to attribute their own behavior to some kind of "uncontrollable influence," especially when the consumption involves products like cigarettes or alcoholic beverages.[23] Consumers' willingness to believe that subliminal persuasion tricks them into buying these products may simply be an attempt to downplay their own role in decision making.

The truth is that the Vicary experiment was a *hoax*. Vicary himself never conducted the experiment. Rather, he fabricated the story in an effort to create positive publicity for the advertising firm.[24] Marketers sometimes make light of subliminal persuasion by presenting images in advertisements that they know consumers will see.

3-3 APPLYING THE JND CONCEPT

We discussed the concept of the absolute threshold as representing a level of strength a stimulus must have or surpass to activate the perceptual process. A closely related concept deals with changes in the *strength* of stimuli. The JND (just noticeable difference) represents how much stronger one stimulus has to be relative to another so that someone can notice that the two are not the same.

---

subliminal persuasion behavior change induced by subliminal processing

JND just noticeable difference; condition in which one stimulus is sufficiently stronger than another so that someone can actually notice that the two are not the same

The JND concept may be best explained in terms of a physical example. How do people pick out one sound over another? For example, for consumers to be able to physically discern two sounds that originate from the same source, the two sounds must be separated by at least 0.3 second. Separating the sounds by only 0.1 second is likely to produce the perception of one sound. Separating them by 0.3 second or more likely produces the perception of two different sounds.[25]

In general, the ability to detect differences between two levels of a stimulus is affected by the original intensity of the stimulus. This is known as **Weber's Law**. The law states that as the intensity of the initial stimulus increases, a consumer's ability to detect differences between two levels of the stimulus decreases.[26] For example, if the decibel level at a rock concert decreases from 120 to 115 dB, the change likely won't be noticeable. Marketers need to understand that change made a little at a time may be unnoticed by a consumer; change a lot at once and it will be noticed. The JND has numerous implications for marketers who attempt to provide value for consumers, including:

▶ **Pricing.** Consumers do not perceive very small differences in price as truly different.[27] A price of $29.49 is generally not perceived as being different from a price of $29.99. Thus, marketers may consider increasing prices in small increments to avoid a negative backlash from consumers. Conversely, a price reduction needs to be large enough so that consumers truly perceive the new price as representing significant savings.[28]

▶ **Quantity.** Small differences in quantity are often not perceived as being different. For instance, if a pack of computer paper changes from 485 sheets to 495 sheets, most consumers won't notice.

▶ **Quality.** Small improvements in quality may not have any impact on consumers. Thus, if Internet speed changes by a fraction of a second, most consumers will not notice.

▶ **Add-on Purchases.** A small additional purchase tacked onto a large purchase may not create the perception of increased spending. For instance, a consumer buying a $365 overcoat may be receptive to the suggestion of adding a plaid scarf priced at $45 to the order. The total for the coat is not perceived as being really different than the total for the coat and scarf together.

▶ **Change in Product Design.** Small changes in product design also are not likely to be noticed. For instances, small changes in the flavoring or viscosity of beverages are not likely to produce differences in liking.[29]

In general, these examples highlight an important idea: When marketers make a "positive" change, they should make sure the

Weber's law law that states that a consumer's ability to detect differences between two levels of a stimulus decreases as the intensity of the initial stimulus increases

difference is large enough to be perceived by consumers. Conversely, when they make a "negative" change, they should think about implementing the change in small increments so that each difference is not distinguished from what existed previously. However, marketers should make sure that changes are not perceived as being deceptive. Deliberately deceptive actions are unethical.

3-3a Just Meaningful Difference

A topic closely related to the JND is the JMD (just meaningful difference). The JMD represents the smallest amount of change in a stimulus that would influence consumer consumption and choice. For instance, how much of a change in price is really needed to *influence* consumer behavior and learning? A consumer can surely "notice" an advertisement stating a price drop of a Rolex from $19,999 to $19,499. Clearly, this is a $500 difference. However, is this price drop really meaningful? Retailers generally follow a rule that states that an effective price drop needs to be at least 20%.[30]

3-4 IMPLICIT AND EXPLICIT MEMORY

Normally, we associate learning with educational experiences. When we think about learning, we think of people studying and paying close attention, like when you read this book. The knowledge one obtains from this type of experience is stored in **explicit memory**, that is, memory for information one is exposed to, attends to, and applies effort to remember. However, this is not the only kind of memory we develop. **Implicit memory** represents stored information concerning stimuli one is exposed to but does not pay attention to. Implicit memory creates **preattentive effects**, learning that is developed in the absence of attention. The following example illustrates the contrast between implicit and explicit memory.

Consider the case of online banner ads. Do you pay any attention to most of those ads? Since 2010, the average click-through rate (CTR) is 0.1%. That means that only 1 exposure in 1,000 produces a page view for the advertised offer. The rate can be a little higher (1.5%) if the advertising is marked clearly as paid advertising showing in the results from an intentional online search or as a promoted post on Facebook (0.8%). Interestingly, an animated ad actually produces an even lower CTR on initial exposures.[31] Obviously, only explicit memory is at play and produces intentional learning in a very small portion of exposures. What about the vast majority of exposures that go unnoticed by consumers? This is where the role of implicit memory may come into play. A brand image processed in implicit memory, meaning no attention was given to the image, can lead to greater liking. And interestingly, learning through implicit memory actually gets stronger as the consumer is more distracted from paying attention.

3-4a Mere Exposure Effect

The **mere exposure effect** represents another way that consumers can learn unintentionally.[32] The mere exposure effect is the idea that consumers will prefer stimuli they have been previously exposed to over stimuli they have not seen before. This effect occurs even when there is no recall of the previous stimulus.

Exhibit 3.6 illustrates a classical approach to studying the mere exposure effect. Experiments in mere exposure effect expose subjects to something they do not know. In this case, a group of consumers were shown a list of words that were potential names for a new dining establishment. Some of the words even contained letters that did not exist in the English alphabet.

On August 30, the beginning of the semester, student subjects were exposed to the list of words on the left. Then, on December 1, at the end of the semester, the researcher exposed the same subjects to the list on the right. If you look closely, you'll notice that one word is

JMD just meaningful difference; smallest amount of change in a stimulus that would influence consumer consumption and choice

explicit memory memory that develops when a person is exposed to, attends, and tries to remember information

implicit memory memory for things that a person did not try to remember

preattentive effects learning that occurs without attention

mere exposure effect effect that leads consumers to prefer a stimulus to which they've previously been exposed

Exhibit 3.6

The Mere Exposure Effect Illustrated

August 30	December 1
Billécourt	Bernardus
Satturi	Orvôl
Yonsusan	Billécourt
Reinsstressa	Keilenspat
Mer soleil	Monopole
Les Crayers	Jimané
Jeroboams	Apostager

can't "remember" seeing the stimuli, some degree of familiarity is created by the mere exposure.

FAMILIARITY

All things equal, consumers prefer the familiar to the unfamiliar. Once exposed to an object, a consumer exhibits a preference for the familiar object over something unfamiliar. An interesting application involves marketing of music. People generally like to hear songs that they have heard before, but what happens when we hear a song for the first time? Research suggests that songs with greater repetitiveness end up being liked better. While the effect can occur due to music and lyrics, more repetitive songs are popular.[33]

The research on mere exposure and music suggests that many, but not all, effects of familiarity work through implicit memory. Several relevant points can be made about the mere exposure effect.

▶ The mere exposure effect is created in the absence of attention. For this reason, the effect is considered preattentive.

▶ Preferences associated with the mere exposure effect are easy to elicit. Thus, marketers can use this effect to improve attitudes marginally.

▶ The mere exposure effect has the greatest effect on novel (previously unfamiliar) objects.

▶ The size of the effect (increased liking) is not very strong relative to an effect created by a strong cohesive argument. For example, a Notre Dame football fan might develop a preference for a face to which he's repeatedly been exposed, but if he finds that the face belongs to an Alabama fan, the preference will likely go away based on the strong information.

on both the August 30 and December 1 lists. That word was rated more favorably than the other potential names.

The results of this type of experiment generally show that the "familiar" words will be preferred even though subjects cannot recall ever having seen them before. Consumers not only develop preferences for words, but they learn them as well. In fact, the learning process facilitates positive feelings that become associated with the stimuli. The mere exposure effect therefore has applications in both consumer learning and attitude formation.

Theoretically, an explanation for the increased preference involves familiarity. Even though consumers

▶ The mere exposure effect works best when the consumer has a low involvement in processing the object, and indeed when a consumer is distracted from processing the focal stimulus. For example, if a small brand logo is displayed on a magazine page across from an involving story, a greater increase in liking would be found than if the consumer were less distracted from the stimulus.

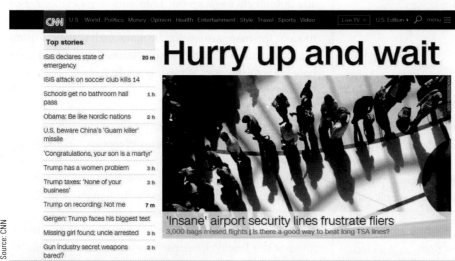

Source: CNN

Nearly every commercial web page presents an opportunity for consumers to learn through explicit and implicit memory.

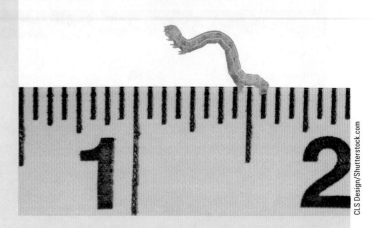

"Two and two are four, four and four are eight . . ." Maybe you remember this little rhyme from childhood easily—even if you do not wish to ever hear it again. Psychologists refer to spontaneous musical "sounds" that pop into our heads as earworms. *"Just a small-town girl . . ."* We don't fully understand earworms. Research suggests that "stickiness" plays a big role. Stickiness refers to repetition that creates familiarity even if a consumer is not actively processing the information. Think of Taylor Swift's "Shake it Off!" Earworms are more likely to occur during downtimes like when you're in the shower, are less welcome by consumers with higher IQs, and can be driven out, at least temporarily, by listening to the actual song all the way through or by chewing gum (another repetitive activity).

Sources: Beck, M. (2015), "The Science of Why a Song Sticks in Your Head," *Wall Street Journal* (October 27), D1–D2. Jakubowski, K., Farrugia, N., Halpern, A. R., Sankarpandi, S. K., & Stewart, L. (2015), "The Speed of Our mental Soundtracks: Tracking the Tempo of Involuntary Musical Imagery in Everyday Life," *Memory & Cognition*, 43, 1229–1242.

NOTE ON SUBLIMINAL AND MERE EXPOSURE EFFECTS

Before moving on, we should distinguish the mere exposure effect from subliminal effects. A subliminal message is one presented below the threshold of perception. In other words, if you are aware of the stimulus or message, then the process is not subliminal. With the mere exposure effect, the stimulus is evident and people could pay attention to it if they wanted to. No attempt is made to keep people from seeing the stimuli, as they are presented with a strength above the threshold of perception.

MERE ASSOCIATION

Sometimes, consumers' judgments are influenced by mechanisms that have little to do with reasoning. One effect closely related to mere exposure is the **mere association effect**. This effect occurs when meaning transfers between two unrelated stimuli that a consumer gets exposed to simultaneously. The mere exposure effect deals specifically with transfers between objects that are dissimilar other than an accidental proximity. An example makes this clearer. A study dealing with the topic demonstrated how a consumer simultaneously exposed to the concept "Mayo Clinic," a famous healthcare institution, and mayonnaise ends up transferring meaning.[34] The exposure to the name "Mayo" activates concepts about hospitals and because the phonics are the same, the same concepts become more active for mayo. In this case, consumers' attitudes toward mayonnaise became less positive when exposed to the Mayo Clinic. For brand managers, the mere exposure effect means care should be taken to avoid any potentially negative but unintended associations. For instance, if Ford announces a safety recall on Ford Fusion models, the mere association by name with Gillette Fusion razors may inadvertently cause consumers to reduce their beliefs about the razor providing a safe shave.

PRODUCT PLACEMENTS

An interesting application of implicit memory and mere exposure involves brand placements in movies, videos, online games and social networks. Gaming can be very captivating. The person playing a game is unlikely to pay attention to things like embedded brand logos. In a manner similar to the way banner ads are processed, implicit memory is created when the logos appear within a game, and an attitude towards the brand develops.[35] As with other preattentive effects, the effect is stronger as the game is more involving.

Product placements are intentional insertions of branded products within media content not otherwise

mere association effect the transfer of meaning between objects that are similar only by accidental association

product placements intentional insertions of branded products within media content not otherwise seen as advertising

seen as advertising. Originally, product placements drew attention for having brands play roles in motion pictures. Even if consumers pay no attention to a placement, it still can affect consumer learning. Research generally supports product placements as an effective means of enhancing consumer attitudes. In fact, product placements also may enhance how much consumers like movies they are placed in, unless placements become too frequent and too noticeable. One website even gives an "Oscar" of sorts in the form of the Annual Brand Cameo Award. Apple was the winner recently based on how frequently their products appeared on screen.[36] Advertisers use all sorts of media for product placements these days, from books to apps.

3-4b Attention

From the discussion above, it's clear that attention plays a key role in distinguishing implicit and explicit memory. Attention is the purposeful allocation of cognitive capacity toward understanding some stimulus. Intentional learning depends on attentive consumers. However, we don't pay attention only to things we wish to. **Involuntary attention** is autonomic, meaning that it is beyond the conscious control of the consumer and occurs as the result of exposure to surprising or novel stimuli. For example, if you were to cut your finger, you would automatically direct attention to the injury due to its pain. When attention is devoted to a stimulus in this way, an orientation reflex occurs. An **orientation reflex** is a natural response to a threat from the environment. In this way, the orientation reflex represents a protective behavior.

 3-5 ENHANCING CONSUMERS' ATTENTION

Consumers face a difficult challenge in penetrating the clutter to pay attention to an intended message. As mentioned earlier, the enormous array of information available electronically creates clutter that can frustrate consumers. Getting a consumer's attention directed toward specific information, voluntarily or involuntarily, is increasingly difficult, but that's a goal of effective marketing communication.

These factors can help create attention:

▶ **Intensity of Stimuli.** All things equal, a consumer is more likely to pay attention to stronger stimuli than to weaker stimuli. For example, vivid colors can be used to capture a consumer's attention. Loud sounds, like a loud advertisement, capture more attention than quieter sounds and can create an orientation reflex.

▶ **Contrast.** Contrasting stimuli are extremely effective in getting attention. Contrast occurs in several ways. In days past, a color photo in a newspaper was extremely effective in getting attention. However, today's newspapers are often filled with color, so a color advertisement is less prominent. A black-and-white image in a magazine filled with color, however, can stand out. Nonconformity can also create attention because of the contrast with social norms.[37] Marketers often show people standing out from the crowd as a means of capturing attention for an ad.

▶ **Movement.** With electronic billboards, electronic retail shelf tags and animated web ads, marketers attempt to capture consumer attention by the principle of movement. Items in movement simply gain attention. Flashing lights and "pointing" signage are particularly effective tools for gaining consumer attention.

▶ **Surprising Stimuli.** Unexpected stimuli gain consumers' attention. Occasionally, retailers replace mannequins with human models. This surprise usually attracts attention.

▶ **Size of Stimuli.** All else equal, larger items garner more attention than smaller ones. Marketers therefore often attempt to have brands appear large in advertisements. This is a reason advertising copy usually features large headlines.

▶ **Involvement.** Involvement refers to the personal relevance a consumer feels towards a particular product. In general, the more personally relevant (and thus more involving) an object, the greater the chance that the object will be attended to. We discuss involvement and comprehension in more detail in the cognitive learning chapter.

Gaining consumer attention is an important task for any marketer. Of course, paying attention can be beneficial for consumers as well. Attention is particularly beneficial when consumers actively try to learn about a value proposition.

involuntary attention attention that is autonomic, meaning beyond the conscious control of a consumer

orientation reflex natural reflex that occurs as a response to something threatening

involvement the personal relevance toward, or interest in, a particular product

Surprising stimuli can get attention.

3-6a Behaviorism and Cognitive Learning Theories

Recall that perception and learning are closely related topics. As the preeminent behavioral psychologist B. F. Skinner once wrote: "In order to respond effectively to the world around us, we must see, hear, smell, taste and feel it."[38]

Psychologists generally follow one of two basic theories of learning. One theory focuses on changes in behavior occurring as conditioned responses to stimuli, without concern for the cognitive mechanics of the process. The other theory focuses on how changes in thought and knowledge precipitate behavior modification. Those in the first camp follow a **behaviorist approach to learning** (also referred to as the behavioral learning perspective). This approach suggests that because the brain is a "black box," the focus of inquiry should be on the behavior itself. In fact, Skinner argued that no description of what happens inside the human body can adequately explain human behavior.[39] With the behaviorist approach, the brain is a black box, and we needn't look inside.

> **Advertisers use all sorts of media for product placements these days, from books to apps.**

From the behaviorist perspective, consumers are exposed to stimuli and directly respond in some way. Thus, the argument is that the marketing focus should be on *stimulus and response*. Behaviorists do not deny the existence of mental processes; rather, they consider these processes to be behaviors themselves. For example, thinking is an activity in the same way as walking; psychological processes are viewed as actions.[39] Note that the term *conditioning* is used in behavioral learning, as behavior becomes conditioned in some way by the external environment.

3-6 THE DIFFERENCE BETWEEN INTENTIONAL AND UNINTENTIONAL LEARNING

Before moving on to cognitive learning and information processing, let's detail the distinction between the two types of consumer learning—intentional and unintentional learning. Both types of learning concern what cognitive psychologists refer to as perceptual processes; however, with **unintentional learning**, consumers simply sense and react (or respond) to the environment. Here, consumers "learn" without trying to learn. They do not attempt to comprehend the information presented. They are exposed to stimuli and respond in some way. With **intentional learning**, consumers set out to specifically learn information devoted to a certain subject. To better explain intentional and unintentional learning, we examine two major theories in the psychology of learning.

unintentional learning learning that occurs when behavior is modified through a consumer-stimulus interaction without any effortful allocation of cognitive processing capacity toward that stimulus

intentional learning process by which consumers set out to specifically learn information devoted to a certain subject

behaviorist approach to learning theory of learning that focuses on changes in behavior due to association without great concern for the cognitive mechanics of the learning process

The second theory of learning involves an **information processing (or cognitive) perspective**. With this approach, the focus is on the cognitive processes associated with comprehension, including those leading to consumer learning. The information processing perspective considers the mind as acting much like a computer. Bits of knowledge are processed electronically to form meaning. With this approach, we must look to see what goes on inside the human brain.

Traditionally, the behavioral learning and cognitive perspectives have competed against one another for theoretical dominance. However, we avoid such debate, because on closer inspection the two theories really share much in common. At the very least, both perspectives focus on changes in behavior as people interact with their environment. We adopt an orientation more directly applicable to consumer learning by separating learning mechanisms into the intentional and unintentional groups that we have presented. The next section discusses unintentional learning and how consumers respond to stimuli they are exposed to.

3-6b Unintentional Learning

Unintentional learning occurs when behavior is modified through a consumer-stimulus interaction without a cognitive effort to understand a stimulus. With this type of learning, consumers respond to stimuli to which they are exposed without thinking about the information. The focus is on *reacting*, not on cognitive processing. Unintentional learning can be approached from two behavioral learning theory perspectives: *classical conditioning* and *instrumental conditioning*.

CLASSICAL CONDITIONING

Classical conditioning refers to a change in behavior that occurs simply through associating some stimulus with another stimulus that naturally causes a reaction. The most famous classical conditioning experiment was performed by the behavioral psychologist Ivan Pavlov. Pavlov conducted experiments using dogs, meat powder (an **unconditioned stimulus** that naturally led to a salivation response), and a bell (a **conditioned stimulus** that did not lead to the response before it was paired with the powder).[41] The experiment reveals that the bell eventually evoked the same behavior that the meat powder naturally caused.

In the experiment, Pavlov began ringing the bell every time meat powder was provided to the dogs. Thus, the bell became associated with the meat powder. Eventually, Pavlov rang the bell without providing the meat powder. As predicted, the bell proved enough to increase the amount of saliva the dogs produced. Originally, the dogs would salivate from being exposed to the unconditioned stimulus. The salivation was called an **unconditioned response**, which occurred naturally as a result of exposure to the unconditioned stimulus (the meat powder). The dogs eventually would respond in the same way to the exposure to the bell. This response became known as a **conditioned response**. The response became conditioned by the consistent pairing of the unconditioned and conditioned stimuli. Dogs do not cognitively process in the way we usually think that humans do. So the dogs learned this response without trying to do so.

To be effective, the conditioned stimulus is presented to people before the unconditioned stimuli, and the pairing of the two should be done consistently (and with repetition). Typical unconditioned stimuli include images of animals that can condition the meaning of soft or warmth and sexy images that portray excitement and vitality.

INSTRUMENTAL CONDITIONING

Much of what we know about instrumental (or operant) conditioning comes from the work of Skinner. With **instrumental conditioning**, behavior is conditioned through reinforcement. Reinforcers are stimuli that strengthen a desired response. The focus is on behavior and behavioral change—not on mental processes that lead to learning. With instrumental conditioning, the likelihood that a behavior will increase is influenced by the reinforcers

information processing (or cognitive) perspective learning perspective that focuses on the cognitive processes associated with comprehension and how these precipitate behavioral changes

classical conditioning change in behavior that occurs simply through associating some stimulus with another stimulus that naturally causes some reaction; a type of unintentional learning

unconditioned stimulus stimulus with which a behavioral response is already associated

conditioned stimulus object or event that does not cause the desired response naturally but that can be conditioned to do so by pairing with an unconditioned stimulus

unconditioned response response that occurs naturally as a result of exposure to an unconditioned stimulus

conditioned response response that results from exposure to a conditioned stimulus that was originally associated with the unconditioned stimulus

instrumental conditioning type of learning in which a behavioral response can be conditioned through reinforcement—either punishment or rewards associated with undesirable or desirable behavior

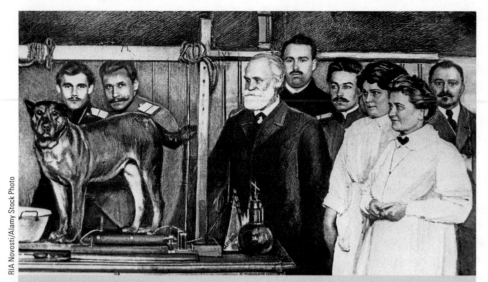
RIA Novosti/Alamy Stock Photo

Pavlov, shown here (center) with one of the dogs used in his experiments, conducted one of the most well known studies of classical conditioning.

(consequences) of the behavior. The reinforcers are presented after the initial behavior occurs.

As an example of instrumental conditioning, consider child development. When parents are "potty training" a child, they are more concerned with getting the desired result than with teaching the child the benefits of using a toilet over a diaper. All parents know that it is very difficult to rationalize with young children. Therefore, attempting to get them to think about the various reasons to become trained is almost useless. The focus is on changing the behavior through reinforcement. When a child performs the desired behavior, he or she receives rewards in the form of hugs, kisses, toys, and so on. These rewards reinforce the desired behavior.

Positive reinforcers come in many forms in the consumer environment and often take the form of some type of reward. The effects can be seen in marketing efforts that encourage repeat purchase behavior. For example, many casinos have players' cards that accumulate points the more a customer plays. The casino keeps track of these points. As the points accumulate, various offers are provided to the consumer, including free hotel rooms, meals, and other things that could otherwise be expensive. In this case, the points are used to elicit a desired response—repeat purchase behavior.

Discriminative Stimuli, Reinforcement, and Shaping. **Discriminative stimuli** differentiate one stimulus from other stimuli because they signal the presence of a reinforcer. These stimuli essentially signal that a type of reward will occur if the consumer performs a specific behavior. Advertisements that feature special promotions represent marketing examples of discriminative stimuli. Here the ad informs consumers that they will receive some type of reward (for example, 10% off a purchase) if they perform the desirable behavior (for example, shop at a store). The stimulus serves as a signal presented before the behavior occurs, and the behavior must occur in order for the reinforcement to be delivered. Brand names can be discriminative stimuli because they signal potential customer satisfaction and value. For example, consumers realize that by using FedEx, they can receive overnight delivery with outstanding quality. The reinforcer occurs after the behavior has been performed. Again we see the importance of exposure to the discriminative stimuli, further highlighting the relationship between perception and behavioral learning.

SHAPING BEHAVIOR

Shaping is a process through which the desired behavior is altered over time, in small increments. Here, the focus is on rewarding small behaviors that lead to the big behavior ultimately desired. For example, universities invite prospective employers to participate in "career day" events. The employers hope that students who come by their booth will pick up some free promotional goods and have a good time interacting with company representatives. The small rewards along the way help shape the desired

positive reinforcers reinforcers that take the form of a reward

discriminative stimuli stimuli that occur solely in the presence of a reinforcer

shaping process through which a desired behavior is altered over time, in small increments

behavior—which is getting the students interested in a career.

Not all reinforcement is positive. **Punishers** represent stimuli that decrease the likelihood that a behavior will occur again. When children misbehave, they get punished. The hope is that the behavior will not occur again. In the same way, when consumers make poor decisions and purchase products that deliver less value than expected, they are punished. Chances are they won't buy those same products again.

Behaviors often cease when reinforcers are no longer present. This represents the concept of **extinction**. For example, consumers may become accustomed to receiving free tea and cookies at a local nail salon every time they get their nails done. If the salon decides to stop offering the free food and drink, the consumers may take their business elsewhere.

FINAL THOUGHT ON BEHAVIORAL CONDITIONING

Conditioning effects do modify behavior and thus represent learning. These effects can be subtly transferred. Researchers demonstrate that even casual association between morally repugnant behavior and a product can reduce consumption. For instance, subjects exposed to a movie portraying an incestuous relationship drank smaller amounts of chocolate milk than subjects watching a movie portraying a normal relationship.[41] The reduction in consumption occurred without any thought about the product, that is, it occurred unintentionally.

Conditioning represents a type of learning because it focuses on behavioral change that occurs through a consumer's interaction with the environment. For behaviorists, perception itself is an activity, not a mental process. Through the behavioral approach, consumers are exposed to stimuli and react in some way. Consumer learning through behavioral conditioning occurs without a conscious attempt to learn anything new.

punishers stimuli that decrease the likelihood that a behavior will persist

extinction process through which behaviors cease due to lack of reinforcement

STUDY TOOLS 3

LOCATED AT BACK OF THE TEXTBOOK

☐ Tear out Chapter Review Card

LOCATED AT WWW.CENGAGE.COM/LOGIN

☐ Review Key Term flashcards and create your own cards

☐ Track your knowledge and understanding of key concepts in consumer behavior

☐ Complete practice quizzes to prepare for tests

☐ Complete interactive content within CB Online

☐ Review the Chapter Highlight boxes for CB Online

4 | Comprehension, Memory, and Cognitive Learning

LEARNING OBJECTIVES

After studying this chapter, the student should be able to:

4-1 Identify factors that influence consumer comprehension.

4-2 Explain how knowledge, meaning, and value are inseparable, using the multiple stores memory theory.

4-3 Understand how the mental associations consumers develop are a key to learning.

4-4 Use the concept of associative networks to map relevant consumer knowledge.

4-5 Apply the cognitive schema concept in understanding how consumers react to products, brands, and marketing agents.

STRINGER/Getty Images

Remember to visit **PAGE 91** for additional **STUDY TOOLS**

INTRODUCTION

In the previous chapter, we defined consumer learning as a change in behavior resulting from some interaction between a consumer and a stimulus. We learned about a behaviorist approach to learning, which focuses on behaviors rather than inner mental processes, and we introduced human perception as the basis for cognitive learning. Cognitive learning focuses on mental processes occurring as consumers comprehend, elaborate, and act upon information. The cognitive perspective views learning as an active mental process in which a consumer processes information, forms associations between concepts, and gains knowledge.

Exhibit 4.1 shows the basic components of information processing. We have already discussed several of the concepts presented, including exposure, attention, and comprehension. In the current chapter, we look more closely at

comprehension the way people cognitively assign meaning to (i.e., understand) things they encounter

comprehension and other issues related to cognitive learning, including memory and elaboration.

Any student knows how difficult intentional learning can be even when desire for a good GPA should provide a strong motivation. As sometimes happens with students, consumers often lack a strong motivation to learn and thus, despite a near constant bombardment of marketing communications via radio, television, social networking sites, printed media, signage, flyers, and more, marketers face a difficult task in creating the learning that they intend to create. Even if one can get over the difficulty in gaining attention, there is no guarantee that any message will be meaningfully encoded and comprehended as intended.

4-1 WHAT INFLUENCES COMPREHENSION?

Consumers can't realize value without an ability to assign meaning to the things consumed. **Comprehension** refers to the interpretation or understanding a consumer develops about some attended

stimulus based on the way meaning is assigned. What happens when a consumer sees a "some assembly required" sticker on a product? Of course, this means that the consumer will likely have to master a set of detailed instructions before consumption can begin. An easy-to-comprehend set of instructions would certainly contribute to the total value equation for the product. Police have even had to respond to a call of potential "domestic violence" due to banging and screaming noises coming out of an apartment where a couple was trying to assemble some IKEA furniture.[1] We all know how frustrating assembly instructions can be. In this and many other ways, marketers must teach us things so that we realize the most value from consumption.

Other products contain warning labels that signal specific associated risks. Consider a typical cigarette package. Consumers don't always comprehend messages as intended. A consumer might even see a cigarette warning label as authoritarian and end up mocking the ad, with the end result being that the ad makes smoking more appealing by reinforcing "rebellion" as a benefit.

Exhibit 4.1

The Components of Consumer Information Processing

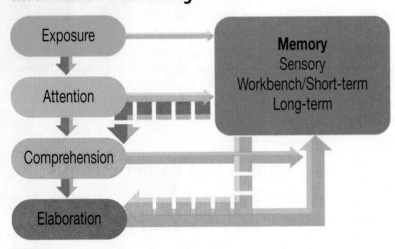

Other times, consumers may actually overestimate the dangers associated with smoking when they read a warning of "rare" side effects.[2] Research suggests that traditional cigarette warning labels actually have only a small effect on consumer behavior.[3] As a result, policy makers have sought to use graphic images to convey meaning more strongly. Some research signaled that consumers may see less value in cigarettes with the graphic warnings; an experiment demonstrated that adult consumers were willing to pay less for a pack of cigarettes with a photographic warning than they would for a pack with a conventional written label.[4] Neurological studies suggest that extremely graphic warning labels create more brain activity than do traditional verbal warnings and this activity is associated with greater reported avoidance of smoking.[5]

Thus, brain activity and comprehension are connected. The following points summarize three factors related to consumer comprehension:

1. **Internal factors within the consumer powerfully influence the comprehension process. Recall from a previous chapter that factors influencing consumer behavior often interact with each other. Numerous components in the Consumer Value Framework alter comprehension.**

2. **Comprehension includes both *cognitive* and *affective* elements. That is, the process of comprehension involves both thoughts and feelings. As such, comprehension applies not only to consumer learning but also to consumers' attitudes. A number of topics in this chapter apply equally to consumer attitude formation and persuasion (a later chapter is devoted to these topics).**

3. **Every message sends signals. Signal theory tells us that communications provide information in ways beyond the explicit or obvious content. A retailer promises to match competitors' prices (PMG or a price-matching guarantee) as a signal to consumers that prices are indeed low.[6] Consumers don't always comprehend messages or get the desired signal, and to this extent, consumer comprehension is not always "correct." Quite simply, consumers sometimes just don't get *it*; however, they act on what they do get.**

signal theory explains ways in which communications convey meaning beyond the explicit or obvious interpretation

PMG price matching guarantee

In this case, do consumers learn more from pictures or words?

4-1a Factors Affecting Consumer Comprehension

Meaning and value are inseparable, and consumers must comprehend marketing messages to learn the intended value of a product. As marketers attempt to communicate value, many factors influence what a consumer comprehends in a given situation. These factors can be divided into three categories:

1. Characteristics of the message
2. Characteristics of the message receiver
3. Characteristics of the communication environment

4-1b Characteristics of the Message

Marketers believe that they can affect consumer learning by carefully planning the execution of marketing communications. As you browse practically any website, you can see advertisements within the source or in browser frames, and chances are, these ads use many different styles. Exhibit 4.2 summarizes some of the ways the message characteristics might influence comprehension about the city of Barcelona. We discuss these below.

Consumers sometimes just don't get it; however, they act on what they do get.

Exhibit 4.2

Message Characteristics Impact Consumer Learning

Message Congruity
- Is image consistent with copy meaning (inspiring business)?

Figure and Ground
- What in the ad is the focal image and what is the background?

Message Source
- Is the source seen as credible and trustworthy?

Physical Characteristics
- Intensity—slogan moves into image on line—break in Barcelona below encourages processing
- Background color influences quality perceptions
- Font signals meaning
- Shape—Golden Section?

Simplicity–Complexity
- Is the image and copy combination easy to process?

Source: www.behance.net

PHYSICAL CHARACTERISTICS

The **physical characteristics** of a message refer to the elements of a message that one senses directly. These parts come together to execute a communication of some type. While these elements affect comprehension, you may note that some of these characteristics also affect the likelihood that consumers pay attention. Here are just a few physical characteristics that can contribute to effective communication.

Intensity. Generally speaking, the greater the movement, the larger the picture, or the louder the sound, the more likely a consumer is to attend and comprehend something from a message. Large numbers or letters appear to shout. In fact, prices that are written in big numerals signal low prices but perhaps not the best quality.

Color. Color affects the likelihood of gaining a consumer's attention, but it can also have an impact on comprehension. Gold signals quality. Similarly, blue is associated with higher quality and higher price expectations. Warm colors like red and orange get attention but also may lower quality perceptions relative to cool colors. For fresh produce, colors that blend in with the actual fruit (red mesh for red apples) also can enhance quality perceptions.[7] Green signals environmental friendliness today. The mere presence of a green package increases "green"

beliefs, although the actual question of what is environmentally friendly is much more complicated.[8]

Font. Consumers derive meaning from both the actual text of a message and the visual presentation of the message. Font styles send meaningful signals. The same brand or store name presented in a block font such as Courier may take on a different meaning if presented in a script font. For instance, research suggests that different fonts signal the personality of a brand. In particular, the more natural a font appears, the more positive the personality.[9] Fonts can also signal masculinity, femininity, or strength, among other brand characteristics. Consider the two examples below:

ACME BRICK COMPANY

ACME BRICK COMPANY

Which sends the better message for a brick company? One can easily see that the signal the font sends should be consistent with the type of service offered.[10]

Numbers. Many brand managers rely on alphanumeric names, combining letters and numbers, when creating names for

physical characteristics tangible elements or the parts of a message that can be sensed

new products, brands, or models. Examples of alphanumeric names include 7-Up, A-1, and Rue 21. Technologically meaningful brands often employ such names. HTC One (M8) smartphone provides an example of an alphanumeric name free to take on a meaning unhindered by a real concept, because combinations of numbers and letters have little specific meaning. This gives marketers a better opportunity to shape the intended meaning of brands and products. In contrast, Galaxy, Sprint, and Focus have real meanings. Alphanumeric names also tend to convey subtly meanings through an association with incremental improvement and advanced technology.

Spacing. All types of communicators, from salespeople to advertisers to teachers, repeat messages as a way of increasing comprehension. If a communicator is going to repeat a message multiple times, is it better to repeat it in sequence or to break up the repetition? Actually, consumers display greater recall of an intended message when information is presented in intervals rather than in sequence.[11] For instance, in media advertising, three 30-second ads spread over three hours achieve better consumer recall of information than a single 90-second advertisement.

Shape. Product designers influence the comprehension of products through many factors but perhaps the shape that they choose is the most basic. Consumers prefer objects that are consistent with the **golden section**. The golden section refers to a ratio of dimensions of about 1.62. Thus, objects that fit into a rectangle of 1.62 × 1.00 (inches, meters, feet, . . .) will be preferred. Photographs depicting images arranged in proportions that match the golden section are perceived as more beautiful than other images.[12]

SIMPLICITY VERSUS COMPLEXITY

Generally speaking, the simpler the message, the more likely a consumer develops meaningful comprehension, which, of course, relies on a consumer's ability to process information. The Federal Food and Drug Administration (FDA) is rightly concerned about how consumers comprehend nutrition and health information on product labels. A large amount of research points to the fact that simplicity is the key. The simpler health information can be presented, the more accurately consumers will understand the

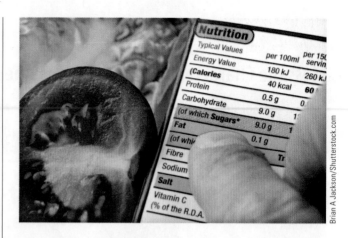

Brian A Jackson/Shutterstock.com

consequences. Thus, terms like *fat-free* are better understood than numeric breakdowns.[13]

MESSAGE CONGRUITY

Message congruity represents the extent to which a message is internally consistent and fits surrounding information.

The conventional wisdom is that congruent content would lead to improved comprehension. However, this may not always be the case. Moderate levels of incongruity motivate deeper processing than when everything in a string of messages is highly congruent. The result can be improved comprehension. However, incongruence can have drawbacks. Celebrity spokespeople endorse many brands, some of them congruent with their personas and some not. Odell Beckham, Jr. plays football. Thus, his meaning is consistent with sports-related products like energy drinks or athletic shoes, but inconsistent with products like personal computers or heart medicine. When consumers pay attention to an ad, an incongruent endorser can hurt the product's image.[14] Similarly, a hedonic ad produces more favorable attitudes for a hedonic brand. Thus, if the primary goal is to create a favorable attitude rather than increased comprehension, then marketers should minimize incongruity. If comprehension is the goal, a little incongruity can be appropriate.

The incongruity of a message with surrounding messages works in much the same way.[15] In fact, consumers will comprehend and remember more from an ad that is presented with incongruent material surrounding it. Consider a brand like L'Oréal Preference hair care products. The consumer will comprehend and remember more when presented with only one hair care message in any three-message sequence (see Exhibit 4.3). In this case, frame B offers better comprehension for the L'Oréal Preference brand.

golden section a preferred ratio of objects, equal to 1.62 to 1.00

message congruity extent to which a message is internally consistent and fits surrounding information

FIGURE AND GROUND

Every message is presented within a background, but sometimes the background becomes the message. A photographer usually concentrates on capturing a focal image in a photo frame. The focal image, or the object intended to capture a person's attention, is much the same as a **figure** in a message. In a message, everything besides the figure should be less important and simply represent the **ground** (or background) relative to the central message. The contrast between the two represents the psychological **figure-ground distinction**.

Look at the simple message in Exhibit 4.4. What would a consumer comprehend? Well, most consumers would easily see the English word *here*. However, look more closely and concentrate on the *T*-shaped image at the left. Most consumers place that in the background. However, if that becomes the figure, then the message may easily become "there" and not "here."

TYPE OF LANGUAGE

The choice of language can influence the meaning of products. Consumers are exposed to and often themselves use figurative rather than literal language. **Figurative language** involves expressions that send a nonliteral meaning. DirectTV advertisements portray a family of "settlers." The family doesn't need DirectTV because they "settle" for cable. In addition, they settle

---

Exhibit 4.4

The Figure and Ground Distinction

HERE

---

for faceless dolls, homemade haircuts, and drab clothing. The ads effectively send the signal that cable is technologically inferior to DirectTV. Consumers themselves use figurative language when describing brands that compete well on hedonic value, while they use literal language when describing brands competing on utilitarian value.[16]

MESSAGE SOURCE

The source of a message also can influence comprehension. Message sources include a famous celebrity in an advertisement, a salesperson in a sales context, a family member giving advice, a Facebook friend, or even a computer-animated avatar. A source influences comprehension to varying degrees based upon characteristics like the following:[17]

1. **Likeability**
2. **Attractiveness**
3. **Expertise**
4. **Trustworthiness**
5. **Congruence**

A likeable source can change the interpretation of a stimulus. Celebrities like Jennifer Lawrence may convey a sense of likability and trustworthiness for Dior. Geico's image is shaped largely by

figure object that is intended to capture a person's attention, the focal part of any message

ground background in a message

figure-ground distinction notion that each message can be separated into the focal point (figure) and the background (ground)

Figurative language use of expressions that send a nonliteral meaning

---

Exhibit 4.3

Congruent or Incongruent Message Sequences?

Congruent Messages

Head and Shoulders Shampoo   L'Oréal Preference   PM Kids Shampoo

Consumer comprehends less about L'Oréal

Incongruent Messages

The Sak   L'Oréal Preference   Lipton Tea & Honey

Consumer comprehends more about L'Oréal

The Settlers DIRECTV Commercial: Neighbors

DIRECTV

Subscribe 42,222

157,555 views

Add to   Share   ••• More   64   2

DirectTV ads effectively send the signal that cable is technologically inferior to their product.

spokescharacters. Caleb the Camel, with over 20 million hits on Youtube, Maxwell the Piggy, the Caveman, and last but not least, the Geico Gecko, all create likability for the brand. As a sign of Geico's advertising effectiveness, 98% of consumers correctly associate the ads with the brand. A source's attractiveness functions in much the same way as likability.

Expertise refers to the amount of knowledge that a source is perceived to have about a subject. **Trustworthiness** refers to how honest and unbiased a source is perceived to be. Consumers associate expertise and trustworthiness with **credibility**. Like likeability, credible sources tend to lower the chances that consumers will develop **counterarguments** toward a message. Counterarguments are thoughts that contradict a message. **Support arguments** are thoughts that further support a message. Brand managers should especially rely on a likable, attractive, and credible source. At times, brands will even use celebrity spokespeople to communicate key facts with media. In such a case, it's best to avoid a controversial celebrity like Alec Baldwin, who would be unlikely to generate any support arguments based on his public persona.

In summary, we can say that desirable source characteristics can help to convey the desired message through cognitive

expertise amount of knowledge that a source is perceived to have about a subject

trustworthiness how honest and unbiased the source is perceived to be

credibility extent to which a source is considered to be both an expert in a given area and trustworthy

counterarguments thoughts that contradict a message

support arguments thoughts that further support a message

processes. However, sources can influence consumers in other more subtle ways. In a later chapter, we focus on how sources influence persuasion.

4-1c Message Receiver Characteristics

INTELLIGENCE/ABILITY

As a general statement, intelligent, well-educated consumers are more likely to accurately comprehend a message than are less intelligent or less educated consumers. With this being said, we offer two caveats. First, a great deal of knowledge is specific to particular product categories. Therefore, a consumer who does not have a high IQ may be able to comprehend certain product information more readily than another consumer with a high IQ. Second, even a highly intelligent consumer would understand a simpler message better than a more complex message. Marketers should communicate information pertaining to product warnings, usage instructions, or assembly directions in a way that those with relatively low intelligence can understand.[18]

PRIOR KNOWLEDGE

The human brain matches incoming information with preexisting knowledge. This preexisting or prior knowledge provides resources or a way through which other stimuli can be comprehended. Even consumers of very high intelligence may lack prior knowledge to comprehend certain consumer messages. Even young kids have more knowledge of handheld electronic devices than many adults—particularly college professors. Consumers display a preference for things that are consistent with their prior knowledge.

Guess what Geico ads do? Create likability!

SIMPLE, SIMPLER OR SIMPLEST?

When it comes to nutrition labels, the simplest seems best. When consumers are processing information about purchases, simplest seems to win also. Researchers use the term "stickiness" to refer to the fact that a consumer actually carries through on a purchase intention. Decision simplicity, meaning how easy it is to process reliable information and compare alternatives, contributes most to stickiness. Is simplest always best? When it comes to slogans that get people to think, maybe simple is better than simplest. A slogan that is too simple both in sound and content fails to create a lot of additional information processing that may lead to deeper comprehension. On the other hand, a slogan with just a touch of complexity in sound and content encourages consumers to think

a little harder and, as a result, creates deeper meaning. "Nothing Says Lovin' Like Something from the Oven" beats "Believe in Something Better."

Sources: Miller, D.W. and M. Toman (2015), "An Analysis of the Syntactic Complexity in Service Corporation Brand Slogans," *Services Marketing Quarterly*, 36, 37–50. Spenner, P. and K. Freeman (2012), "To Keep Your Customers, Keep It Simple," *Harvard Business Review*, 90 (May), 108–114. Hoidas, A. (2016), "Top 10 Effective and Ineffective Advertising Slogans," *Brandingbeat*, https://www.qualitylogoproducts.com/blog/10-effective-ineffective-advertising-slogans/, accessed March 16, 2016.

Consider the role that superstition can play in comprehending value propositions. Do you believe it's good luck to find a penny or that the number 7 is lucky and 13 is unlucky? You aren't alone if you do. One in three Americans believes finding a penny is good luck; nearly one in four believe in lucky numbers. Not everybody is equally superstitious, though. The same research suggests that younger consumers tend to be more superstitious and that Democrats tend to be a bit more superstitious than Republicans.[19] Even marketers who are not superstitious would be wise to acknowledge the meanings that such prior knowledge among a segment of consumers might convey to products. Thus, take care putting 13 in a brand name!

INVOLVEMENT

Consumers are not equally involved with every message sent their way. As discussed in Chapter 3, highly involved consumers tend to pay more attention to messages. They also exert more effort in comprehending messages.[20] As a result, these consumers show better recall than consumers with lower levels of involvement.[21] Consider the consumer who views a website describing a new product. The highly involved consumer will click through more hyperlinks, explore more pages, and comprehend more information than a less involved consumer.

Today's technology offers the highly involved consumer lots of opportunities to engage with brands.

Near-field technologies allow advertising to be pushed to consumers through their smart devices. Highly involved consumers comprehend not only the content of the ads better because they are better able to process that information, but they also are more open to ads that the less involved consumer finds intrusive.[22]

FAMILIARITY/HABITUATION

Consumers tend to like the familiar. However, in terms of comprehension, familiarity can *lower* a consumer's motivation to process a message. While some degree of familiarity may improve consumer attitude, high levels of familiarity may actually change or reduce comprehension.[23] Few humorous ads are as enjoyable after ten exposures as they were on the first viewing, so a consumer may tune the message out.

Habituation is the process by which continuous exposure to a stimulus affects the comprehension of and response to some stimulus. Consider the following psychological experiment. Subjects in one treatment group immerse their arms in extremely cold water (2°C) for 60 seconds. Obviously, this is an unpleasant task. Another group of subjects is asked to do the very same thing, except after the first immersion,

> **habituation** process by which continuous exposure to a stimulus affects the comprehension of, and response to, the stimulus

WRITING'S ON THE WALL!

"It's only *weird* if it doesn't work!" That's the tagline for a Bud Light campaign built around consumers and their superstitions. Superstitions can affect the meaning of messages and activities. Superstitions, omens, or the perception of foresight allow consumers to feel they have a role in future events even when the outcome is totally beyond their influence. Do you know someone with a "lucky" shirt that they have to wear on game day, even if it hasn't been washed in years? Baseball fans know what a *rally cap* does. When a shop sells a winning lotto ticket it can expect to sell a lot more tickets as the news gets out. Marketers can benefit from having their products associated with good outcomes, which is the attempt of the superstition campaign. However, it could be that playing along with a superstition adds hedonic value by creating a little fun.

At right, Bryce Harper, shown in the photo at the right, of the Washington Nationals wears a rally cap during a 2016 game against the Minnesota Twins. And yes, the Nationals won . . .

Sources: Hanks, L., L. Zhang and S. McGinley (2015), "Unconditioned Superstition and Sports Bar Fans," *Journal of Hospitality Marketing & Management*, 1–19. Yang, A.X. and O. Uminsky (2015), "The Foresight Effect: Local Optimism Motivates Consistency and Local Pessimism Motivates Variety," *Journal of Consumer Research*, 42, 361–377.

Patrick McDermott/Getty Images

they are asked to immediately immerse their arms into slightly less frigid (6°C) water for 30 additional seconds. At the end of the procedure, both groups rated the task hedonically. Surprisingly, the group that immersed their arms for 90 seconds rated the task more favorably than did the group that immersed their arms for only 60 seconds.

Habituation theory explains this result. The first 60 seconds of exposure to the extremely cold water habituated the subjects and created an **adaptation level**. As a result, when the second group was exposed to water that was still unpleasant but slightly less frigid than the first, a more favorable evaluation was obtained because the entire experience was framed by the relatively more valuable (less painful) last 30 seconds.

On a global level, consider that consumers in the United States, Canada, Australia, and throughout Western Europe expect fairly pleasant shopping experiences in which many goods and services are readily available in a comfortable setting. This hardly compares with many parts of the developing world, where shopping as we know it hardly exists. A decade after the breakup of the Soviet Union, consumer researchers measured the hedonic and utilitarian shopping value Russian consumers experienced trying to obtain everyday goods and services.[24] The capitalist reforms had been slow to spread throughout Russia, and these consumers still faced shops with empty shelves and long lines to buy things like boots or jackets. A Russian word to describe this experience is *dostats*, which roughly means "acquiring things with great difficulty." The surprising result of the research was that the Russian consumers reported similar amounts of shopping value compared to American shoppers. What is the explanation for this outcome? Even though shopping in Russia was certainly worse than shopping in America, shopping was still framed by their life experiences beyond the familiar reality

adaptation level level of a stimulus to which a consumer has become accustomed

of *dostats*. These life experiences provided a frame of reference in which shopping was *less* unpleasant than were many other routine activities. Over time and improvements to the marketing infrastructure, the mere availability of product selection may cause a different hedonic response.

EXPECTATIONS

Expectations are beliefs about what will happen in a future situation. They play an important role in many consumer behavior settings and can impact comprehension. We discuss expectations in more detail later when satisfaction becomes the focus. For now, note that what consumers expect to experience has an impact on their comprehension of the environment.

To illustrate, consider how packaging influences consumers' comprehension of products. Beverage marketers have realized for decades that packaging plays a major role in how beverages are perceived. In fact, studies indicate that consumers cannot even identify their "favorite" brand of beer without the label.[25] Removing the label affects consumers' expectations, which affects their comprehension by blocking brand-specific thoughts.

PHYSICAL LIMITS

A consumer's physical limitations can also influence comprehension. For example, we all have limits in our abilities to hear, see, smell, taste, and think. Obviously, someone who can't hear an audio message can't comprehend information in it. Also, consumers who are color blind will have difficulty comprehending information related to color. For instance, if a caution or warning label is colored red to signal risk, a color-blind consumer will not likely comprehend this aspect of the message.[26]

BRAIN DOMINANCE

Brain dominance refers to the phenomenon of *hemispheric lateralization*. Some people tend to be either right brain– or left brain–dominant. This, of course, does not mean that some consumers use *only* the left or right parts of their brains. Right brain–dominant consumers tend to be visual processors (tend to favor images for communication), whereas left brain– dominant consumers tend to deal better with verbal processing (words).

Hemispheric lateralization influences metaphor comprehension, among other things. Advertisements use metaphors regularly; despite the slogan "you're in good

Making writing fashionable again. ✐ **PILOT**
Jacksonville Fashion Week 2012 | | PILOTPEN.US

Metaphoric messages like this one for Pilot Pens presented at Jacksonville Fashion Week are particularly effective among right brain–dominant consumers.

hands with Allstate," one isn't really in someone's hands. A **metaphor** communicates a message figuratively rather than literally. Metaphors can increase one's ability to remember an ad message, and they particularly affect consumers when the metaphor is processed in the right brain hemisphere.[27] Thus, consumers who are right-brain dominant may respond particularly well to metaphors. Metaphors are not limited to words, as images often depict animate objects as products and vice versa.

expectations beliefs about what will happen in some future situation

brain dominance refers to the phenomenon of *hemispheric lateralization*. Some people tend to be either right brain– or left brain–dominant

metaphor in a consumer context, an ad claim that is not literally true but figuratively communicates a message

4-1d Environmental Characteristics

INFORMATION INTENSITY

Information intensity refers to the amount of information available for a consumer to process within a given environment. When consumers are overloaded, the overload not only affects their attention but also their comprehension and eventual reaction. One of the drawbacks of frequent online social networking is burnout in the form of SNS (social networking services) fatigue. The intensity of information (too much, too fast) plays a role in reducing communication effectiveness.

FRAMING

Framing is a phenomenon in which the meaning of something is influenced (perceived differently) by the information environment. Thus, the same event can produce multiple meanings depending on how the information is presented. Framing and the consumer adaptation level (habituation) often work together to affect comprehension. Would you like an ice cream sundae? Most consumers probably would. However, if a consumer has just finished two ice cream sundaes, that will probably frame the third so that it doesn't seem so tasty.

Prospect theory hypothesizes that the way in which information is *framed* differentially affects risk assessments and associated consumer decisions. To illustrate prospect theory, consider what you have likely heard about risks associated with prolonged exposure to the sun. The following are two methods of presenting information about those risks:[28]

> ▶ **Failing to use sunscreen leaves one vulnerable to skin cancer.**
>
> ▶ **Using sunscreen helps avoid skin cancer.**

The first statement frames the behavior negatively: Don't use the product and *you'll get skin cancer*. The second statement frames the behavior positively: Use this product and *you'll stay healthy*!

The frame within which consumers receive information causes concepts associated with it to become available for processing. **Priming** is the term that refers to this cognitive process in which active concepts activate other closely associated concepts, thereby affecting both value perceptions and meaning. Negatively framed information primes losses, which consumers wish to avoid, and encourages consumers to be more willing to take a chance on a product. Generally, negatively framed information creates a relatively strong impact on consumers compared to positively framed information, and so the perceived value of the sunscreen in the above example may increase by presenting a negative information frame.

Exhibit 4.5 further illustrates this aspect of framing. Most consumers faced with the first choice set in the exhibit will choose option 2. Notice that the frame is negative ("losing").[29] In the second choice set, where the frame is positive, priming gains and consumers tend to choose option 1. The differing pattern of choices happens even though the expected value ($E(v)$) for each choice is the same ($200). Presenting a negative frame primes thoughts that lead to a consumer being more willing to take risks. In terms of prospect theory, we say that losses weigh more heavily than gains. Losing $200 is certainly a loss and hurts hedonic value more than winning $200 helps create hedonic value.[30] As such, consumers more willingly take on a risk when faced with the first choice.

Priming occurs in many subtle ways beyond positive and negative frames. Brand names and logos can

information intensity amount of information available for a consumer to process within a given environment

framing a phenomenon in which the meaning of something is influenced (perceived differently) by the information environment

prospect theory theory that suggests that a decision, or argument, can be framed in different ways and that the framing affects risk assessments consumers make

priming cognitive process in which context or environment activates concepts and frames thoughts and therefore affects both value and meaning

Exhibit 4.5

An Illustration of Framing—What Would You Do?

Choose one of the two options below:
1. You lose $200.
2. You have a 20% chance of losing $1,000 and an 80% chance of losing nothing.

barang/Shutterstock.com

Choose one of the two options below:
1. You win $200.
2. You have a 20% chance of winning $1,000 and an 80% chance of winning nothing.

Yuri_Arcurs/Shutterstock.com

serve as primes. The shopping environment can prime bargain expectations. For instance, a consumer may think $200 is a good price for a watch in a counter filled with watches selling for $1,000 or more. Conversely, the same watch at $200 may not seem like a good deal when it is the most expensive watch in the case.[31] Consumers also possess naïve theories about marketing.[32] At times, these naïve theories are primed and influence subsequent reactions. Imagine a consumer reading about how important purchasing expensive flooring is to the resale value of a home while waiting to order in a restaurant. This story primes the theory that higher priced options are better. As a result, the consumer is more likely to select a relatively expensive option than if she had not read the story. Thus, previous events prime subsequent events.

MESSAGE MEDIA

These days, marketers can't always control the type of media by which consumers encounter a message. Do consumers process information the same way on paper as they would on a PC or on a smartphone? The answer seems to be no. In terms of intentional learning, some studies suggest that we comprehend more and better when reading from a message printed on paper than from a digital message.[33] Differences also exist among digital sources. One interesting study suggests that consumers process an advertised message in a more detailed way when exposed on a smartphone versus a desktop computer screen.[34] The explanation involves the proximity of one's hands to the information being processed. If so, ads designed to convey detailed information should perhaps be better designed for viewing on a smartphone as opposed to a larger screen.

CONSTRUAL LEVEL THEORY

The information environment can sometimes cause us to think about, or construe, things in different ways. **Construal level** refers to whether we are thinking about something using a concrete or an abstract mindset. One might construe a foreign destination at an abstract level and think of a trip to Europe. Alternatively, he could construe the destination at a concrete level and think of a trip to Chimay, Belgium. The more concrete the mindset, the closer the event tends to seem in both time and distance. Although we all know the old adage "time is money," consumers tend to view money resources as concrete relative to time resources.[35] Thus a concrete request like "give $10" is more likely to yield a concrete response ("here is $10") than an abstract request ("please volunteer").

TIMING

Timing also affects comprehension. For our purposes, timing refers to both the *amount of time* a consumer has to process a message and the *point in time* at which the consumer receives the message. For example, consumers who have only a couple of seconds to process a message, such as when driving by a billboard advertisement, cannot possibly comprehend a message in as much depth as a consumer who is not facing a timing issue.

The time of day can also affect the meaning and value of a product. For many consumers, coffee is a morning beverage. Consumers comprehend an advertisement for a brand of coffee quite differently based on the time of day. Most consumers will respond to a coffee advertisement in the morning far more enthusiastically than the same ad shown before bedtime, due to habituation effects associating hot coffee with morning consumption. The way time or age influences the interpretation of things is sometimes called *zeitgeist*.

4-2 MULTIPLE STORE THEORY OF ACQUIRING, STORING, AND USING KNOWLEDGE

Memory is the psychological process through which people record and store knowledge. As shown in Exhibit 4.1, all elements of information processing interrelate with memory. In our chapter on perception, we discussed the topics of implicit and explicit memory. Here, we discuss memory from the cognitive learning perspective—the multiple store theory of memory.

4-2a Multiple Store Theory of Memory

The **multiple store theory of memory** views the memory process as utilizing three different storage areas within the human brain. The three areas are sensory memory, workbench (or short-term) memory, and long-term memory. Exhibit 4.6 illustrates this approach.

> **Construal level** whether or not we are thinking about something using a concrete or an abstract mindset
>
> **memory** psychological process by which knowledge is recorded
>
> **multiple store theory of memory** theory that explains memory as utilizing three different storage areas within the human brain: sensory, workbench, and long-term

Exhibit 4.6

The Multiple Store Approach to Memory

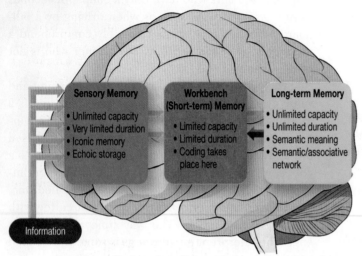

Sensory Memory	Workbench (Short-term) Memory	Long-term Memory
• Unlimited capacity • Very limited duration • Iconic memory • Echoic storage	• Limited capacity • Limited duration • Coding takes place here	• Unlimited capacity • Unlimited duration • Semantic meaning • Semantic/associative network

Information

Meaningful encoding takes place with the transfer from workbench to long-term memory.

SENSORY MEMORY

Sensory memory is the area in memory where we store what we encounter with our five human senses. When we hear something, sensory memory is responsible for storing the sounds. The consumer walking through an airport terminal encounters many sounds, smells, and sights. Sensory memory picks these things out and stores them even though the consumer has not yet allocated attention to any sensations. This portion of memory is considered to be preattentive.

Sensory memory is truly remarkable. For one thing, it has unlimited capacity. Sensory memory stores everything one is exposed to, taking an exact record of what is encountered. Our sensory memory uses multiple distinctive mechanisms. **Iconic storage** is the storage of visual information as an exact representation of the scene.

sensory memory area in memory where a consumer stores things exposed to one of the five senses

iconic storage storage of visual information in sensory memory and the idea that things are stored with a one-to-one representation with reality

echoic storage storage of auditory information in sensory memory

haptic perception interpretations created by the way some object feels

Echoic storage is the storage of auditory information as an exact representation of the sound. All sights, sounds, smells, tactile sensations, and tastes are recorded as exact replicas in the mind of the consumer.

If this is the case, then why can we recall only a fraction of what we encounter? Another remarkable aspect of sensory memory concerns duration. Sensory memory is very perishable and lasts only a very short time. In most cases, sensory memory begins to fade immediately after the sensation and typically lasts less than a second. Thus, the strength of sensory memory is capacity, but the weakness is duration.

Sensory memory can easily be illustrated. Take a quick look at an object and then close your eyes. What happens in the fractions of a second immediately after you shut your eyes? In most instances, your brain will hold the image immediately after you close your eyes—that is, you will be able to see the image mentally. However, very quickly things will start to fall out of the mental picture until eventually all that is left is the most central feature. If you are familiar with a strobe light, you may have noticed that when the light speeds up, images look continuous. This is because sensory memory is able to "hold" the image through the dark portion of the strobe—that is, until the next image is physically sensed.

Sensory memory effects are essential for cognitive learning. However, sensory memory alone creates little opportunity for intentional learning because of the short duration. The last images held in sensory memory get transferred to the next storage mechanism, where a sensory input like the touch of a package helps create meaning.[36] The term **haptic perception** refers specifically to interpretations created by the way some object feels.[37] Footjoy recently marketed one of its gloves packaged in a black felt container. Inevitably, consumers who picked up the package believed the glove was more expensive than consumers who did not touch the package. Many put the package down immediately without even checking the price. The feel of the package translated into an image evoking an expensive product. Sensory memory works in conjunction with other memory functions in this way.

WORKBENCH MEMORY

Workbench, or working, memory is the storage area in the memory system where information is stored and encoded for placement in long-term memory and eventually retrieved for future use. As we will see, workbench memory works very closely with long-term memory. **Encoding** is the process by which information is transferred from workbench memory to long-term memory for permanent storage. **Retrieval** is the process by which information is transferred back into workbench memory for additional processing when needed.

To illustrate workbench memory, imagine a consumer who is walking the aisles of Central Market. The consumer places several items into the cart, including some Camembert, Morbier, Speculoos, and multiple household items including paper towels, storage bags, bleach, and toilet tissue. How much do you think all of this is going to cost the consumer? If he doesn't physically write down each item's cost, can we expect that he will be able to know what the total bill will be? To some extent, his accuracy will depend on his ability to hold prices in memory long enough to be able to compute a total upon checkout.

Let's consider a single item. He picks up the bleach, checks the price, and puts the item in the cart. The price quickly enters his sensory memory and then moves on to his workbench memory because he is trying to pay attention to the price. The relevancy of duration, capacity, and involvement quickly come into play.

▸ **Duration.** The term *short-term* is often used when describing workbench memory because this memory storage area, like sensory memory, has limited duration. The duration is not nearly as limited as sensory memory, but stimuli that enter short-term memory may stay there approximately 30 seconds or so without some intervention. Therefore, our consumer can hardly be expected to remember the prices for all items in his cart by the time he reaches the checkout counter.

▸ **Capacity.** Unlike sensory memory, workbench memory has limited capacity. Generally, the capacity limit for workbench memory is between three and seven units of information. This fact is sometimes known as Miller's Law. Think of a physical workbench. If the bench is almost full, we cannot expect to put additional items on it. Some items must be removed first. Thus, we cannot expect our consumer to remember all the prices, especially if he is buying several products. In fact, working memory is taxed even further if the prices contain more syllables. A price of $13.47 is harder to remember than $12.10 because it contains more sounds, and more syllables contributes to a meaning of more expensive.[38]

▸ **Involvement.** The capacity of workbench memory expands and contracts based on the level of a consumer's involvement. The more involved a consumer is with a message, the greater will be the capacity of his workbench memory. When involvement is very low, workbench memory capacity contracts to a minimum.

To test your own workbench memory, try to do the following: Without looking back, name all the items purchased by our Central Market customer. How many can you remember? Don't feel bad if you can't remember them all. In fact, most people would not be able to correctly recall more than a couple of items. Many may recall that toilet tissue was one item. Unless a consumer has some knowledge of French cheeses, though, he or she is unlikely to recall Camembert and/or Morbier. We recall things better when we can make meaningful associations.

4-3 MAKING ASSOCIATIONS WITH MEANING AS A KEY WAY TO LEARN

So, what kind of work goes on in workbench memory? The task of a consumer may be to recall things, both over a short time period and over a long time period. When we use the expression "remember something," we really mean that we can recall some information or make it active in our minds intentionally.

4-3a Mental Processes

Four mental processes help consumers remember things:

1. **Repetition** is a process in which a thought is held in short-term memory by mentally repeating the thought.

2. **Dual Coding** is a process in which two different sensory "traces" are available to remember

---

workbench, or working, memory storage area in the memory system where information is stored while it is being processed and encoded for later recall

encoding process by which information is transferred from workbench memory to long-term memory for permanent storage

retrieval process by which information is transferred back into workbench memory for additional processing when needed

repetition simple mechanism in which a thought is kept alive in short-term memory by mentally repeating the thought

dual coding coding that occurs when two different sensory traces are available to remember something

something. As we shall see, a *trace* is a mental path by which some thought becomes active.

3. **Meaningful Encoding** is a process that occurs when preexisting knowledge is used to assist in storing new information.

4. **Chunking** is a process of grouping stimuli by meaning so that multiple stimuli can become a single memory unit.

Meaningful encoding and chunking rely heavily on making associations between new information and meaning that is stored in long-term memory.

Repetition. Repetition is a commonly employed way of trying to remember something. Picture someone trying to remember this license plate number:

TT 867-53-09

One way to remember this number is by thinking it repeatedly. This process is known as *rehearsal*. However, one major problem with this approach is **cognitive interference**. Cognitive interference simply means that other things are vying for processing capacity when a consumer rehearses information. To illustrate, try to count backwards from 1,000 by 3. This seems like an easy task. But if you try to do this while someone is calling out random numbers at the same time, the task becomes much more difficult. All things equal, repetition is the weakest form of learning.

Dual Coding. Dual coding occurs when two different sensory traces are available to remember something. Marketing messages often combine an image with a description in attempt to promote dual coding.[39] Researchers tested the extent to which product feature recall might improve through dual encoding using scents. Consumers in the experiment showed greater recall for product features, even for a product as innocuous as a pencil, when the product gave off an identifiable scent. In a similar way, associating products with rhythm helps consumers remember information. Why is this? A consumer is able to retrieve the information in two ways—by the content of the message and by the rhythmic sound that makes up music. Consumers recall brand names that give a rhythmic sound, like Coca-Cola, when pronounced more easily than other names.[40]

Some foods can be difficult to spell; does pepperoni have two *R*s? But, generations of Americans have no problem spelling another type of Italian sausage in part due to an Oscar Mayer jingle that finishes like this:

"… 'cause Oscar Mayer has a way with B – O – L – O – G – N – A!"

Chick-fil-A employs a logo that turns the C into a chicken. Thus, consumers can easily remember Chick-fil-A and the types of products it sells. A logo enriched with imagery can enhance recall.

Meaningful Encoding. Meaningful encoding involves the association of active information in short-term memory with other information recalled from long-term memory. By this process, new information is coded with meaning.

To illustrate meaningful encoding, let's return to the license plate example. Consumers often find it difficult to associate anything meaningful with a number. However, a fan of 1980s pop rock would recognize the sequence of digits as the title of a famous hit by the rock artist Tommy Tutone. (The letters *TT* on the plate support this.) A consumer who can retrieve the memory of this song and attach it to the license plate can remember the plate's number much more easily. In a way, this example involves both dual and meaningful encoding, because the music (also stored in memory) serves as a

White Castle's castle-shaped logo makes it a more effective image, an example of dual coding.

meaningful encoding
coding that occurs when information from long-term memory is placed on the workbench and attached to the information on the workbench in a way that the information can be recalled and used later

chunking process of grouping stimuli by meaning so that multiple stimuli can become one memory unit

cognitive interference
notion that everything else that the consumer is exposed to while trying to remember something is also vying for processing capacity and thus interfering with memory and comprehension

memory aid itself. For a consumer who knows 1980s music, the numbers *867-5309* can only mean Tommy Tutone. (If you know the song, it's probably created an earworm now.)

Chunking. Chunking is the process of grouping stimuli by *meaning* so that multiple stimuli can become one memory unit. Remember that the capacity of workbench memory is rarely more than seven chunks of information. A **chunk** is a single memory unit. Here's a simple experiment that helps demonstrate what is meant by a chunk of memory. Show someone the following list of numbers for only a few seconds:

1 4 9 2 1 7 7 6 1 9 4 5

After taking the list away, engage them in conversation for a couple of minutes. Then, ask the person to recall the list. Why is this task so difficult? When someone treats each numeral as a distinct chunk of information, his or her memory capacity is exceeded. After all, 12 numerals, or chunks, are included in the list.

Now look at the list in this way:

1 4 9 2 – 1 7 7 6 – 1 9 4 5

If the person did well in American history class, the task should be considerably easier. A history student should recognize that these are all important dates in U.S. history. The set of 12 numbers can now be stored and recalled as only three pieces of information instead of 12.

Retrieval and Working Memory. As we have discussed, a task of workbench memory is the scanning and retrieval of information from long-term memory. When a consumer retrieves information from long-term memory, the retrieved information once again ends up on the workbench memory. Through a process of **response generation**, consumers

reconstruct memory traces into a formed representation of the thing they are trying to remember or process. See Exhibit 4.7.

> **Remember that the capacity of workbench memory is rarely more than seven chunks.**

Meaning and knowledge are the keys to effective coding and cognitive learning. To illustrate, consider the following list of words:

▶ **Weep**

▶ **Sheep**

▶ **Deep**

▶ **Keep**

▶ **Peep**

Suppose a consumer looked at this list one day and the next day had to guess if the word *sleep* was on the list.

Now consider another list:

▶ **Night**

▶ **Rest**

▶ **Awake**

Exhibit 4.7

The Workbench Is Where Meaning Happens

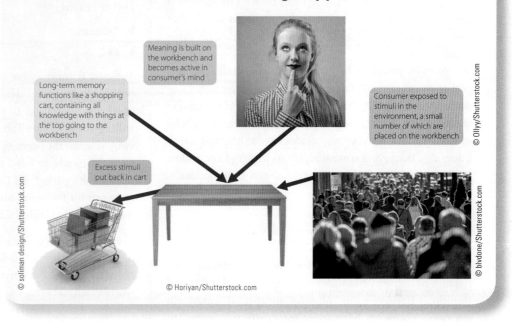

Meaning is built on the workbench and becomes active in consumer's mind

Long-term memory functions like a shopping cart, containing all knowledge with things at the top going to the workbench

Consumer exposed to stimuli in the environment, a small number of which are placed on the workbench

Excess stimuli put back in cart

© soliman design/Shutterstock.com

© Horiyan/Shutterstock.com

© Ollyy/Shutterstock.com

© blvdone/Shutterstock.com

chunk single memory unit

response generation reconstruction of memory traces into a formed representation of what they are trying to remember or process

- ▶ **Tired**
- ▶ **Dream**

Would this list produce fewer false memories when the consumer tries to guess if *sleep* was on it? The answer is yes. The key is that the second list contains words that are easier to apply meaning to and thus they produce better memory.[41]

Marketers can help with meaningful coding by exposing consumers to concepts with shared meaning. Consumers are more likely to recall a web address containing meaning like 26thstreetgym than a shorter term without meaning: 26SG. Another way marketers can help is through integrated marketing communications that try to provide a unified promotional message across all consumer media.

LONG-TERM MEMORY

A consumer's long-term memory plays a very important role in learning. **Long-term memory** is a repository for all information that a person has encountered. This portion of memory has unlimited capacity and unlimited duration. Barring some physical incapacity, long-term memory represents permanent information storage. Information stored in long-term memory is coded with **semantic coding**, which means the stimuli are converted to meaning that can be expressed verbally.

Why can't consumers always recall information when needed if storage is permanent? The problem is not a storage issue as much as it is a retrieval issue. To illustrate, consider that even things consumers process at very low levels leave some memory trace. A **memory trace** is the mental path by which some thought becomes active. For example, in the United States, childhood Easter memories generally include rabbits, eggs, and candy. Memory traces from *Easter* for many consumers also spread to specific brands like Russell Stover and Cadbury (chocolates) and of course, no Easter memory is complete without Peeps.

Psychologically, a memory trace shows how cognitive activation spreads from one concept to another. This process is known as **spreading activation**. Marketers want their brand names to cause cognitive activation to spread to favorable, rather than unfavorable, thoughts. For example, consider the following brands:

- ▶ **Tabasco**
- ▶ **KFC**

Tabasco is most often associated with "hot." Generally, hot things are good. Hot music is good, hot fashions are good, and hot food is good. Therefore, consumers are willing to purchase Tabasco brand clothing (ties, shirts, etc.). From the concept of KFC, activation may still spread quickly to *fried* chicken and perhaps the notion of unhealthy food. KFC introduced grilled chicken and at many outlets emphasized the fact by proclaiming it was Kentucky Grilled Chicken—not KFC.

Mental Tagging. Let's look again at Exhibit 4.1. In psychological terms, a **tag** is a small piece of coded data that helps us get that particular piece of knowledge onto the workbench. The tags function much like the bar-coded information on checked luggage. When everything works right, the information on the tag allows the luggage to be located and directed toward the correct destination. However, we all realize that not everything always goes right and luggage sometimes ends up in the wrong place. Similarly, if consumers do not tag information in a meaningful way, the encoding process results in errors.

As adults, most people have recalled some innocuous childhood memory for seemingly no apparent reason. These types of memories illustrate how long-term memory is permanent and how events that were poorly tagged during encoding can emerge at practically any time. Stimuli that consumers pay attention to but do not really comprehend or elaborate upon tend to be poorly tagged.

Rumination. **Rumination** refers to unintentional, spontaneous, recurrent memory of past and sometimes long-ago events that are not necessarily triggered by anything in the environment.[42] These thoughts frequently include consumption-related activities. Psychologists tend to think of frequent rumination as unhealthy and at times symptomatic of depression. Consumers who have had a bad experience with a brand ruminate about the bad experience. The rumination can culminate in attempts to sabotage the brand through malicious online behavior or intentional acts aimed at harming the brand.[43] Brands that get activated during negative ruminations may become disliked over time.

Not all rumination is bad, however, and nostalgic rumination may include positive associations with brands.

long-term memory repository for all information that a person has encountered

semantic coding type of coding wherein stimuli are converted to meaning that can be expressed verbally

memory trace mental path by which some thought becomes active

spreading activation way cognitive activation spreads from one concept (or node) to another

tag small piece of coded information that helps with the retrieval of knowledge

rumination unintentional but recurrent memory of long-ago events that are spontaneously (not evoked by the environment) triggered

Nostalgia, a mental yearning to relive the past, produces emotions of longing. Often product and brand associations can generate nostalgia. For example, Cracker Barrel stores sell products like Mallo Cups, Moon Pies, and Pixie Sticks, which seem to assimilate well with memories of childhood and childhood vacations. The products help consumers revisit the past.

Louella938/Shutterstock.com

Nostalgia can motivate product purchases as consumers attempt to relive the pleasant feelings of the past. Consumers become more willing to make purchases when a nostalgic ad evokes or recaptures a childhood mood. Music, toys, magazines, home products, and movies are products that consumers commonly report buying in association with feelings of nostalgia.[44] The large number of advertisements that include popular "oldies" songs also illustrates attempts at evoking nostalgic feelings. Nostalgia can create melancholy feelings that can be made more positive by some artifact linking the present with the past.

ELABORATION

The multiple stores theory of memory is an active process of association. **Elaboration** refers to the extent to which a person continues processing a message even after she develops an initial understanding in the comprehension stage.[45] With elaboration, increased information is retrieved from long-term memory and attached to the new information and understanding. This means more and richer tags and a better chance of recall. In particular, **personal elaboration**, in which people imagine themselves associating with a stimulus being processed, provides the deepest comprehension and greatest chance of accurate recall.

In Exhibit 4.1, notice the information processing steps linked to memory get more pronounced from exposure through elaboration. The darker and more pronounced lines linking comprehension and elaboration to memory represent the strength with which incoming information is tagged. Remember, our brains tag information so that we can understand it. Consumers who reach the elaboration stage are most likely to meaningfully encode information so that intentional retrieval is possible later. In a marketing context, therefore, appeals to a consumer to associate aspects of their own lives are likely to lead to deeper comprehension and better recall.[46] When an advertisement says, "Have you ever been in this situation?" or, "Imagine yourself on a deserted island," these primes can trigger personal elaboration in a consumer, resulting in better recall. For anyone trying to

gain knowledge on purpose, personal elaboration provides the strongest link to meaningfully encoding information so that it can be useful in decision making.

4-4

ASSOCIATIVE NETWORKS AND CONSUMER KNOWLEDGE

4-4a Associative Networks

Knowledge in long-term memory is stored in an associative network. An **associative network**, sometimes referred to as a semantic network, is a network of mental pathways linking all knowledge within memory. These networks are similar to family trees, as some family members are obviously related, but other family members, while still linked together, are not so obviously related. Do you know your sixth cousins? Some say that on average, a stranger sitting next to you is a sixth cousin.

Exhibit 4.8 shows how we depict portions of a consumer's associative network. In this case, the portion of the network depicts meanings evoked from the concept of "Champagne." Normally, we think of brands as companies. But some regions are synonymous with products. In those cases, as with Champagne, regional brands emerge. The exhibit shows a typical American consumer's flow of associations from the concept of Champagne. These associations provide cues for how concepts become active from long-term memory. When someone thinks of Champagne, they very likely also activate thoughts about holiday celebrations.

4-4b Declarative Knowledge

Declarative knowledge is a term used in psychology to refer to cognitive components that represent facts. Declarative knowledge is

nostalgia a yearning to relive the past that can produce lingering emotions

elaboration extent to which a consumer continues processing a message even after an initial understanding is achieved

personal elaboration process by which people imagine themselves somehow associating with a stimulus that is being processed

associative network network of mental pathways linking knowledge within memory; sometimes referred to as a semantic network

declarative knowledge cognitive components that represent facts

Exhibit 4.8

Schema for "Champagne" as a Brand

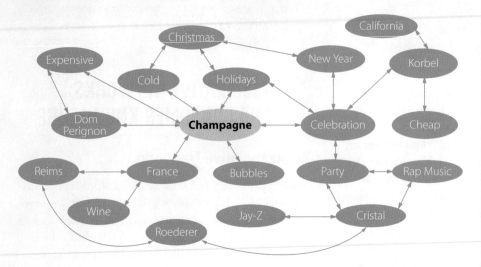

represented in an associative network by two nodes linked together by a path. **Nodes** simply represent concepts in the network, while **paths** represent association between nodes. Consumers' declarative knowledge may not always be correct, but consumers do act upon the beliefs this knowledge represents. The following are examples of declarative knowledge based on the associative network in Exhibit 4.8:

> *Champagne is bubbly and is something for celebrating, particularly during the holidays. Dom Perignon is a brand of Champagne. Parties go well with Champagne. Jay Z pours champagne in his rap videos . . .*

In everyday experiences, a consumer compares all of these bits of knowledge with reality. Every time a consumer encounters a supportive instance of declarative knowledge, that knowledge becomes stronger. Consider: "Champagne is wine with bubbles." Although consumers typically use the term "Champagne" for any wine with bubbles, true Champagne can only come

Igor Lateci/Shutterstock.com

nodes concepts found in an associative network

paths representations of the association between nodes in an associative network

schema a portion of an associative network that represents a specific entity and thereby provides it with meaning

from the Champagne region of France. But every time a consumer encounters someone calling any bubbly wine Champagne, that false rule is reinforced and becomes stronger. In this way, the associations represent rules that determine consumer reactions. When an intermediary node like peanuts comes between the brand and another concept, like "stinks," the indirect association still affects the brand's meaning.

Amazingly, every concept within a consumer's associative network is linked to every other concept. Consider the following request:

List at least 10 snack foods in 60 seconds or less.

A typical consumer would list things like potato chips, an energy bar, a Twinkie, and a candy bar. Few would argue that these are indeed snack foods. All are linked to the snack concept and distinct from other food categories—like dinner entrees. A glass of milk may also be a snack, but the association between milk and snack food must first pass through several nodes. By that time, the association is weak. Selling milk as a snack, therefore, is difficult. However, if a dairy packages milk in a small container reminiscent of a snack food's plastic wrapper, the likelihood that consumers would view milk as a snack will increase, and the rule that milk could be a snack will subsequently increase in strength.

4-5 PRODUCT AND BRAND SCHEMAS

Consumers' knowledge for a brand or product is contained in a **schema**. A schema is a portion of an associative network that represents a specific entity and thereby provides it with meaning. Exhibit 4.8 illustrates a brand schema for Champagne as a regional brand, while Exhibit 4.9 illustrates a product schema for snack food. A brand schema is the smaller part within one's total associative network responsible for defining a particular marketing

Exhibit 4.9

Consumer Knowledge for Snack Foods

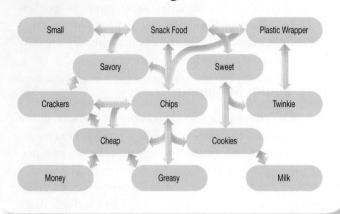

Exhibit 4.10

Category Exemplars

Product category	Exemplar
MLB (Major League Baseball) Team	New York Yankees
Laundry Detergent	Tide
Online Retailer	Amazon.com
Golf Ball	Titleist Pro V1
Social Network Site	Facebook
Smartphone	iPhone
Search Engine	Google
Coffee Shop	Starbucks

entity. Similarly, product schemas function in much the same way. Each time a consumer encounters something that could be a snack food, the mind quickly compares all the associations in the schema to see if indeed the thought is correct. Several types of *schemata* (plural for schema) exist.

4-5a Exemplars

An **exemplar** is a concept within a schema that is the single best representative of some category. Exemplars can differ from one person to another based on their unique experiences. In a snack food schema, potato chips

Laurie Blue Adkins is better known as Adele.

Featureflash Photo Agency/Shutterstock.com

may be the exemplar. Who is Laurie Blue Adkins? Well, by her stage name, Adele, she may be the category exemplar for female pop star.

The exemplar provides consumers with a basis of comparison for judging whether something belongs to a category. When a consumer encounters a carrot, the association with chips as the exemplar of a snack food may not be close. But, if a retailer offers small bite-sized carrots packaged in a small plastic bag, the carrots share more in common with chips and may well fit into the snack food category. Exhibit 4.10 illustrates other possible category exemplars.

4-5b Prototypes

Some categories are not well represented by an exemplar. For instance, a "pharmaceutical sales rep" category likely does not evoke a specific person who best represents that category. However, an image is associated in one's mind with the category. That image contains the characteristics most associated with a pharma rep. Several characteristics may come to mind and they are active in your own mind at this moment. This type of schema is known as a **prototype**. Whether represented by a prototype or an exemplar, consumers compare new and unknown examples to the standard by comparing features with those found in the schema. If interviewing for a pharma rep job, one probably wants to evoke assimilation with that category.

exemplar concept within a schema that is the single best representative of some category; schema for something that really exists

prototype schema that is the best representative of some category but that is not represented by an existing entity; conglomeration of the most associated characteristics of a category

4-5c Reaction to New Products/Brands

When consumers encounter new products or brands, they react to them by comparing them to the existing schema. Sometimes new products fail because they are too different or just way ahead of their time. Tablet computer–type devices first appeared in the 1990s but didn't catch on. Today, Google Glass remains controversial, perhaps in much the same way. Are we ready for heads-up web display and real-time recording of all activities? One way that new products can ease their way into a market is through cobranding. TGI Fridays, for instance, cobrands with Jack Daniels (JD) as a way of introducing menu items infused with JD flavor. Google is currently exploring cobranding opportunities for Glass. Rayban and Oakley, both high-end eyewear brands, are partnering with Google to offer more stylish Glass versions.[47]

4-5d Script

A *script* is a schema representing an event. Consumers derive expectations for service encounters from these scripts. For instance, when a consumer dines in a fine Italian restaurant, the script probably contains things such as valet parking, a greeting by a well-dressed maître d', a linen-covered table, and perhaps music by Dean Martin. Since the script is positive (Italian fine dining is a good experience), restaurant managers try to not vary too much from expectations or risk confusing, and even frustrating, consumers.

Similarly, salespeople employ scripts in performing their jobs. For instance, salespeople who work for charitable appeals use scripts that consists of sequences of actions known to increase consumer compliance.[48] The salesperson develops these scripts over time, facilitating an ability to predict what will happen next.

4-5e Episodic Memory

Closely related to the concept of a script is *episodic memory*. Episodic memory refers to the memory for past events, or episodes, in one's life. A consumer may have fond memories of childhood holiday celebrations. Another consumer may remember graduating from college or getting a first job. Both of these are episodes, and they involve products and brands. Brands associated with positive events stored in episodic memory receive something of a halo and

tend to be preferred by consumers.[49] Episodic memories and scripts both can include knowledge necessary for consumers to use products. Younger consumers' memories likely are much better developed than older consumers when it comes to finding and posting important marketing information of Facebook and Twitter. On the other hand, older consumers possess better episodic memory for how to take prescription medicine.

4-5f Social Schemata

A *social schema* (or *social stereotype*) is the cognitive representation that gives a specific type of person meaning. A stereotype captures the role expectations of a person of a specific type. Consumers generally like when a service provider matches an existing stereotype. Consumers are comforted by a surgeon who looks and acts like a surgeon. In fact, a service provider who does not fit the social schema for that category can alter behavior. A nonconforming server who is too over- or underweight, may cause consumers to eat more or less than they might otherwise.[50]

A social schema can be based on practically any characteristic that can describe a person, including occupation, age, sex, ethnicity, religion, and even product ownership. What kind of person do you think drives a

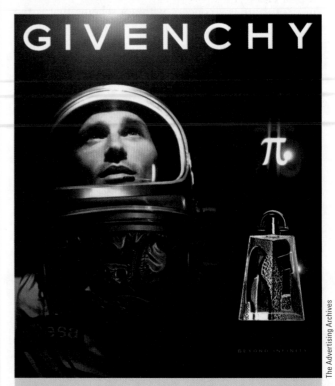

Givenchy hopes to benefit from the associations that make up the astronaut social stereotype.

script schema representing an event

episodic memory memory for past events in one's life

social schema cognitive representation that gives a specific type of person meaning

social stereotype another word for social schema

Have You Got the Point?

The printed word can be provided to consumers through many technologies. Some technologies, like ink on paper, are centuries old. Others date back only decades or less. If you want a consumer to remember a message, does the media technology affect comprehension? Researchers in several fields, including education, consumer behavior, and advertising, among others, are keenly interested in the question. While the matter is far from settled, research points to some interesting findings. Paper still seems to be best, but, for short messages, consumers also comprehend detail well when reading from a smartphone screen. We don't know exactly why. Some believe it's because we tend to touch the information with our fingers when reading a phone. Others believe we are socialized to focus better on what is on our phone.

Andrey_Popov/Shutterstock.com

Sources: Mangen, A., B. R. Walgermo, and K. Bronnick (2013), "Reading Linear Texts on Paper Versus Computer Screen: Effects on Reading Comprehension," *International Journal of Educational Research*, 58, 61–68. Coulter, K. S. (2016), "How Hand Proximity Impacts Consumer Responses to a Persuasive Communication," *Psychology & Marketing*, 33, 135–149.

Toyota Prius? A team of researchers sought to identify if drivers were more or less courteous based on what make and model of car they drive. The researchers were surprised, in contrast to their preconceived stereotype, to find that Prius drivers were the least courteous drivers.[51]

Consumers also realize that, as consumers, they belong to certain categories of person types. This phenomenon falls under the general heading of social identity, the idea that individual identity is defined in part by the groups to which one belongs. Many consumers will try to match the characteristics associated with a desired stereotype. We will return to this in a later chapter about reference group behavior.

Also, attempts to "demarket" a product can be implemented by stigmatizing consumption with a negative stereotype. Perhaps no better example exists than the stigmatization of smoking. A *smoker*, as opposed to a non-smoker, is more likely to be attributed with the following characteristics: *energetic, interesting, disgusting, offending,* and *unkempt.* Additionally, a person described as a smoker is liked less than a similar person described as a nonsmoker, and interestingly, even smokers are more likely to describe a fellow smoker as disgusting and offensive.[52] Thus, the stereotype seems pervasive. Obviously, a product associated with increasing the belief that a consumer is disgusting and offensive is more difficult to sell. To the extent that anti-smoking public policy messages have tried to stigmatize smokers, the messages have been effective.

> **social identity** the idea that one's individual identity is defined in part by the social groups to which one belongs

STUDY TOOLS 4

LOCATED AT BACK OF THE TEXTBOOK
☐ Tear out Chapter Review Card

LOCATED AT WWW.CENGAGE.COM/LOGIN
☐ Review Key Term flashcards and create your own cards
☐ Track your knowledge and understanding of key concepts in consumer behavior
☐ Complete practice quizzes to prepare for tests
☐ Complete interactive content within CB Online
☐ Review the Chapter Highlight boxes for CB Online

5 | Motivation and Emotion: Driving Consumer Behavior

LEARNING OBJECTIVES

After studying this chapter, the student should be able to:

5-1 Understand what initiates human behavior.

5-2 Classify basic consumer motivations.

5-3 Describe consumer emotions and demonstrate how they help shape value.

5-4 Apply different approaches to measuring consumer emotions.

5-5 Understand how different consumers express emotions in different ways.

5-6 Define and apply the concepts of schema-based affect and emotional contagion.

Fuse/Getty Images

Remember to visit **PAGE 111** for additional **STUDY TOOLS**

INTRODUCTION

Seeing is not always believing. At times, consumers are very difficult to read. Why does someone who chooses Guinness in public buy Bud Light at home? What do our behaviors really mean? Marketing researchers are picking up on ways they can try to judge consumer feelings based on posts to Twitter or other social networking sites. **Sentiment analysis** has met big data. The researchers use programs that try to match sentences or phrases to consumer feelings and then apply data mining procedures to search social networks for the sentences. Tweets about celebrity hairstyles during the Golden Globe awards get coded, automatically triggering reports to executives at L'Oréal that they should push out advertising tying their products to information showing how to accomplish the look.[1] True meaning and true feelings are driven by human motivations.

5-1 WHAT DRIVES HUMAN BEHAVIOR?

The basic consumption process (recall from Chapter 1) is a central component of the Consumer Value Framework (CVF) that starts with consumer needs. Consumer needs start the process because they kick-start or *motivate* subsequent thoughts, feelings, and behavior. Simply put, **motivations** are the inner reasons or driving forces behind human actions that drive consumers to address real needs. As the CVF indicates, motivations do not completely determine behavior. Other sources, including situational factors like the physical environment, influence behavior. However,

sentiment analysis
sometimes called conversation analysis; automatic procedures that search social networking sites like Twitter for phrases/sentences that are coded for emotional meaning

motivations inner reasons or driving forces behind human actions that drive consumers to address real needs

motivations do much to provide the intended reason for a consumer's actions.

5-1a Homeostasis

Human motivations are oriented around two key groups of behavior. The first is behavior aimed at maintaining one in a current acceptable state. Homeostasis refers to the fact that the body naturally reacts in a way to maintain a constant, normal bloodstream. Shivering motivates consumers to wear coats to keep their blood from becoming too cold. When one's blood sugar falls below an acceptable state, the physiological reaction is hunger. Hunger then motivates a consumer to eat, such as a Snickers bar, and restore the body to an acceptable state. Thus, consumers act to maintain things the way they are, and their wants are a function of the need driven by homeostasis.

Homeostasis applies to things other than hunger. A consumer shivering in the cold feels the need for a coat or to go inside to restore the body to normal. Bad weather also causes drops in brain chemicals such as dopamine or serotonin that can motivate consumption, particularly of hedonically rewarding products.[2] The

consumption might involve tobacco or alcohol or just drive self-gift purchases as a way of restoring a healthy level of happiness.

5-1b Self-Improvement

The second group of behavior results from self-improvement motivation. These behaviors are aimed at changing one's current state to a level that is more ideal—not simply maintaining the current state of existence. Consider why one exercises. Beyond some level, consumers exercise not to maintain themselves but to improve their health and well-being. In much the same way, when a consumer upgrades from a Touch-Ups handbag to a Prada handbag, she is not acting out a decision to maintain herself, but she sees Prada as a way of improving her status in life. Self-improvement leads

homeostasis state of equilibrium wherein the body naturally reacts in a way so as to maintain a constant, normal bloodstream

self-improvement motivation motivations aimed at changing the current state to a level that is more ideal, not at simply maintaining the current state

Regulatory focus theory explains that even simple acts like hair brushing are driven either by a prevention (maintenance) or promotion (self-improvement) orientation.

consumers to perform acts that cause emotions that help create hedonic value.

5-1c Regulatory Focus

Consumer researchers try to capture the manner through which motivation orients consumers through various theories about how we try to control our behaviors. **Regulatory focus theory**, following closely from the contrast between homeostasis and self-improvement, puts forward the notion that consumers orient their behavior either through a prevention focus or a promotion focus. A prevention focus orients consumers toward avoiding negative consequences, while a promotion focus orients consumers toward the opportunistic pursuit of aspirations or ideals.[3] The prevention terminology captures the motivation to maintain homeostasis, and the promotion focus shares similarity with self-improvement goals. Consider the following two toothpaste brands:

regulatory focus theory puts forward the notion that consumers orient their behavior either through a prevention or promotion focus

Maslow's hierarchy of needs a theory of human motivation that describes consumers as addressing a finite set of prioritized needs

1. **White-Bright:** White-Bright gives you an appealing white smile.
2. **Drill-Not:** Drill-Not is the leader in preventing tooth decay.

White-Bright appeals fit more with a promotion focus and achieving the ideal of a sexy, white smile. Drill-Not fits better with a prevention focus and trying to avoid the pain, discomfort, and inconvenience of tooth decay and related diseases.

Theories like self-regulatory focus try to describe the different motivational approaches that orient us as consumers. We turn now to two related classification schemes—one a classic, general motivational classification and another aimed more specifically at CB and value creation.

5-2 GENERAL HIERARCHY OF MOTIVATION

Perhaps the most popular theory of human motivation in consumer and organizational behavior is **Maslow's hierarchy of needs**. This theory describes consumers as addressing a finite set of prioritized needs. The following list displays the set of needs, starting with the most basic.

▸ **Physiological.** Basic survival (food, drink, shelter, etc.)

▸ **Safety and security.** The need to be secure and protected

▸ **Belongingness and love.** The need to feel like a member of a family or community

▸ **Esteem.** The need to be recognized as a person of worth

▸ **Self-actualization.** The need for personal fulfillment

According to Maslow's theory, people first seek value by satisfying the most basic needs. Thus, a starving consumer will risk safety to get something to eat. A consumer whose survival is in doubt would find little value in things that might provide esteem or self-actualization. In contrast, when successful businesspeople retire, they may indeed find the most value in things that do not bring esteem, love, or safety, but instead provide self-fulfillment. Several financial firms run advertisements showing retirees leaving high-paying careers to travel to far-off places or go off and work in a mission. This appeal typifies how CB can provide value by addressing the self-actualization need.

Further, consider how Maslow's hierarchy may operate differently around the world. In war-torn areas of the world, consumers may indeed risk their lives to buy basic necessities. Clearly, this type of shopping is providing only utilitarian value. In the United States, consumers may find esteem through performing well on the job and owning a large house. In Japan, however, space is so scarce that very few people own large homes. Therefore, esteem may manifest itself more in owning a nice car or in one's manner of dress.

Similarly, the things that address self-actualization needs are likely to vary in different places around the world. Motivations can determine the type and amounts of value consumers seek. Generally, the most basic needs are addressed with utilitarian value, and as needs become more elaborate, hedonic value is often needed to satiate the need state. Exhibit 5.1 illustrates the hierarchical aspect of needs and includes an example of a consumer behavior that goes with each need.

5-2a Simpler Classification of Consumer Motivations

The preceding discussion suggests an even simpler classification of consumer motivations. Not surprisingly, the types of motivations match up with the types of needs. A simple but very useful way to understand CB is to classify motives based on whether some need creates wants associated with predominantly utilitarian or hedonic value.[4]

UTILITARIAN MOTIVATION

Utilitarian motivation is a drive to acquire products that consumers can use to accomplish things. Utilitarian motivation bears much in common with the idea of maintaining behavior. When a consumer runs out of toothpaste, there will be a strong motivation to do something about this problem and acquire more toothpaste. He may want to buy some Crest toothpaste. In the sense that utilitarian motivation helps a consumer maintain his or her state, these motivations work much like homeostasis.

HEDONIC MOTIVATION

Hedonic motivation involves a drive to experience something personally gratifying. These behaviors are usually emotionally satisfying. Interestingly, although sales via the Internet continue to grow, they account for just 8% of all retailing. Perhaps part of the reason is that the process itself is not very rewarding. For people who really love to shop, the Internet may not provide the multisensory experience that a rich shopping environment can deliver. For these consumers, the Internet may be fine for acquiring things but disappointing as a rewarding shopping experience. Exhibit 5.2 illustrates some typical behaviors that are motivated by utilitarian or hedonic shopping motives.

5-2b Consumer Involvement

CB researchers use the word involvement a great deal. Perhaps one of your family members can't let go of his phone and constantly pauses to check in when visiting restaurants, coffee shops, tourist attractions, and so on. Another hardly takes his phone out of his pocket. In rare instances, a

gresei/Shutterstock.com

utilitarian motivation drive to acquire products that can be used to accomplish something

hedonic motivation drive to experience something emotionally gratifying

---

Exhibit 5.1

An Illustration of Consumer Motivations According to Maslow's Hierarchy

Self-actualization — Pursuing a degree during retirement

Esteem — Posting achievements in online gaming

Belongingness and love — Fitting in with college group

Safety and Security — Gated apartment complex

Physiological Needs — Dining on ramen noodles in the dorm

Hedonic Value

Utilitarian Value

Exhibit 5.2

Utilitarian and Hedonic Motivations Lead to Consumer Behaviors

Utilitarian motivations lead to . . .	Hedonic motivations lead to . . .
Joining LinkedIn to network professionally	Downloading Snapchat to show friends cool selfies
Visiting the health clinic because of a high fever	Going to a health club to have fun playing racquetball with friends
Choosing to shop with retailers that are seen as useful and easy to use	Choosing to shop with retailers that are seen as fun and exciting
Using air freshener to cover up a strange smell in the apartment	Using air freshener because one really enjoys the smell
Going gift shopping out of a sense of obligation to give a gift	Giving a gift to enjoy the giving process and the joy the recipient experiences when opening the gift

relative may not even have a phone. What makes them all so different?

Involvement is synonymous with motivation. A highly involved consumer is strongly motivated to expend resources in a particular consumption activity.[5] **Consumer involvement** represents the degree of personal relevance a consumer finds in pursuing value from a given category of consumption. Thus, when a consumer is highly involved, there is a greater chance of achieving relatively high value, as long as things go as expected. The person just mentioned who is highly involved in social networking via a smartphone thus gets more value

consumer involvement
degree of personal relevance a consumer finds in pursuing value from a particular category of consumption

moderating variable
variable that changes the nature of the relationship between two other variables

from the activities than the other family members.

CONSUMER INVOLVEMENT AS A MODERATOR

Consumer researchers often consider involvement a key moderating variable. A **moderating variable** is one that changes the nature of a relationship between two other variables. For example, consider the relationship between the number of alternative brands of a product, perhaps running shoes, and the amount of time and effort a consumer spends choosing a pair of shoes. Logically, one might expect that the larger the selection, the greater the time needed to make a decision. However, would this be the case for all consumers? Exhibit 5.3 illustrates the way a moderating variable works.

Highly involved consumers are likely to take more time because they recognize a greater number of attractive alternatives. A willing (motivated) consumer spends time evaluating multiple pairs of shoes, trying them on, and comparing their attributes. Value comes only from making the right choice. On the other hand, a large

Exhibit 5.3

Involvement Acts as a Moderator of the Selection–Time Relationship

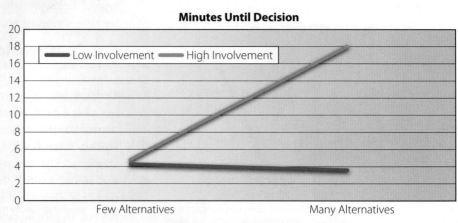

selection quickly overwhelms a consumer lacking motivation to study shoes. This other consumer falls back to some simple choice decision like "pick the cutest." A consumer needs some degree of involvement to have an ability to evaluate multiple brands effectively. A consumer with low involvement will not spend more time just because there are more types of shoes. A consumer with high involvement, though, will be motivated to give a larger number of alternatives consideration.

DIFFERENT TYPES OF INVOLVEMENT

Involvement can mean different things to different people. However, one way to bring different perspectives together is to realize that there are different types of involvement. In each case, high involvement still means high personal relevance and the importance of receiving high value. Here are some key types of consumer involvement:

▶ **Product involvement** means that some product category has personal relevance. **Product enthusiasts** are consumers with very high involvement in some category. A relatively large segment of product enthusiasts find fashion highly relevant. These consumers find great value in learning about fashions, shopping for fashions, and wearing fashionable clothes and accessories. Some product categories are much more involving than others. Handbags and computers tend to be high involvement, while band-aids and bananas tend to be low involvement for most consumers.

▶ **Shopping involvement** represents the personal relevance of shopping activities. This relevance enhances personal shopping value. From a utilitarian value perspective, highly involved shoppers are more likely to process information about deals and are more likely to react to price reductions and limited offers that create better deals.[6]

▶ **Situational involvement** represents the temporary involvement associated with some imminent purchase situation. Situational involvement often comes about when consumers are shopping for something that they have little interest in but that comes with a relatively high price. Things like household and kitchen appliances often qualify as evoking situation involvement. For instance, few consumers are highly involved with their home heating systems. However, when a consumer is about to purchase a water heater, he may temporarily learn a lot about water heaters to avoid paying too much or choosing an inappropriate unit.

▶ **Enduring involvement** is not temporary but rather represents a continuing interest in some product or

© AntonioDiaz/Shutterstock.com

Enduring involvement is emotional. Consumers often show passion for activities in which they are enduringly involved.

activity. The consumer is always searching for opportunities to consume the product or participate in the activity. Enduring involvement is associated with hedonic value, because learning about, shopping for, or consuming a product for which a consumer has high enduring involvement are all personally gratifying. Consumers with high enduring involvement typically find hedonic value in learning more about that particular product or activity.

▶ **Emotional involvement** represents how emotional a consumer gets during some *specific* consumption activity. Emotional involvement shares much in common with enduring involvement because the things that consumers care most about will eventually create highly emotional responses. Sports fans typify consumers with high emotional involvement, and as we know, sports fans can be rowdy and do wild and crazy things.

product involvement
the personal relevance of a particular product category

product enthusiasts
consumers with very high involvement in some product category

shopping involvement
personal relevance of shopping activities

situational involvement
temporary interest in some imminent purchase situation

enduring involvement
ongoing interest in some product or opportunity

emotional involvement
type of deep personal interest that evokes strongly felt feelings simply from the thoughts or behavior associated with some object or activity

5-3 CONSUMER EMOTIONS AND VALUE

5-3a Emotion

What is *emotion*? Emotion is a difficult term to define. In fact, some refer to emotion as a "fuzzy" concept, believing that no exact definition exists. According to this view, the best that one can do is list examples of emotions. Love, for example, is a primary example of an emotion, and all readers can relate to the experience of love. Yet, how is *love* defined?

Ask someone to put love into words, and people will usually provide examples or types of love, such as romantic love, brotherly love, maternal love, or love for one's school. Although quite different from love, anger is also a typical emotion and shares something in common with love. Both love and anger are controlling emotions, in that they tend to shape one's behavior strongly.

While emotions seem a bit "fuzzy," we can offer a straightforward definition. **Emotions** are specific psychobiological reactions to appraisals. When a consumer is contemplating a vacation, she appraises different sites and thinks about the total vacation experience.[7] A consumer reacts differently to Maui, Hawaii, than to Branson, Missouri. Emotions are **psychobiological** because they involve both psychological processing and physical responses.[8] Indeed, emotions create **visceral responses**, meaning that certain feeling states coincide with certain behaviors in a very direct way. Exhibit 5.4 lists some typical visceral responses to emotions.

Emotions are extremely important to CB and marketing because consumers react most immediately to their feelings. Notice that the word *motivation* and the word *emotion* both contain "motion" as a root. The fact that emotions are hardwired to behavior has been explained as follows:

[Emotions are] fuels for drives, for all motion, every performance, and any behavioral act.[9]

Emotions create visceral responses—such as a smile.

Monkey Business Images/Shutterstock.com

Behaviors are closely tied to emotion, creating close links between emotions, CB, and value. Thus, marketing success is determined by emotions, because actions bring value to a consumer to the extent that desirable emotional states can be created.[10] Urban designers try to create aesthetically pleasing downtown shopping areas because research demonstrates the ability of such an environment to create more feelings of pleasure and arousal among shoppers.[11] In turn, these emotions determine spending. Consumer emotions also influence how marketing messages are processed. An ad depicting an angry spokesperson can produce favorable attitudes if the angry person is providing strong arguments.[12]

5-3b Cognitive Appraisal Theory

What gives rise to consumer emotions? Psychologists have debated the different sources of emotions for decades, but **cognitive appraisal theory** represents an increasingly popular school of thought. Cognitive appraisal theory describes how specific types of thoughts can serve as a basis for specific emotions. When consumers make an appraisal, they are assessing some past, present, or future situation. Four types of cognitive appraisals are especially relevant for consumer behavior.[13]

1. **Anticipation appraisal.** Focuses on the future and can elicit anticipatory emotions like hopefulness or anxiety

---

emotion a specific psychobiological reaction to a human appraisal

psychobiological a response involving both psychological and physical human responses

visceral responses certain feeling states that are tied to physical reactions/behavior in a very direct way

cognitive appraisal theory school of thought proposing that specific types of appraisal thoughts can be linked to specific types of emotions

anticipation appraisal appraisal focusing on the future that can elicit anticipatory emotions like hopefulness or anxiety

Exhibit 5.4

Visceral Responses to Emotions by Consumers

Type of appraisal/situation	Emotion	Behavioral reaction
Anticipation appraisal—Consumer waits while doctor examines X-rays	Worry	Grim face with turned-down eyebrows and mouths. Hands likely near face. Consumer would rather avoid situation.
Outcome appraisal—Consumer wins a contest	Joy	Genuine smile including turned-up mouths and eyebrows and open hands. The consumer approaches the situation.
Equity appraisal—Consumer sees a customer receive faster and better service than he or she receives	Anger	Turned-down mouths and eyebrows with clenched fists and hunched back. The consumer seeks to approach an agent of the company.
Agency appraisal—An advertisement shows an animal choking on a plastic shopping bag	Shame	Pinched facial expression and turned head. The body naturally withdraws from (avoids) the situation.
Outcome appraisal—Consumer shows up at an important party inappropriately dressed	Embarrassment	Face flushes (turns red and feels hot), head cowers, and a strong desire to flee is experienced.

2. Agency appraisal. Reviews responsibility for events and can evoke consequential emotions like gratefulness, frustration, guilt, or sadness

3. Equity appraisal. Considers how fair some event is and can evoke emotions like warmth or anger

4. Outcomes appraisal. Considers how something turned out relative to one's goals and can evoke emotions like joyfulness, satisfaction, sadness, or pride

Exhibit 5.4 illustrates each of these appraisal types. A basic behavioral response is to either approach or avoid. Marketers generally benefit from approach responses; thus, they would like to create appraisals leading to emotions that evoke approach behaviors, and avoid appraisals and emotions that evoke avoidance.

Appraisals are often complicated enough to involve more than one type of appraisal and sometimes conflicting behavioral responses. Anticipatory appraisals can involve suspenseful emotions such as hope. A consumer may appraise an ad for a charitable cause in a manner that evokes hope and become more willing to consider donating to that cause. However, the same ad could cause a consumer to feel guilty if he makes an agency appraisal and ends up feeling a sense of responsibility for the problem that the charity addresses. Guilt may be

less effective than hope in gaining compliance with an appeal.[14] Consumers also make equity appraisals such as the perception of very unfair treatment. They end up feeling angry and may cope with the anger by seeking revenge.[15] Health services often create situations involving both anticipation and outcome appraisals. A consumer visiting the dentist may be worried about having cavities but feel joyful when the dentist provides a clean bill of health. Cognitive appraisal theory emphasizes the fact that emotions result from appraisals.

Specific types of thoughts serve as a basis for specific emotions.

5-3c Emotion Terminology

MOOD

Moods can be distinguished from the broader concept of emotion based on specificity and time. Consumer **mood** represents a transient (temporary and changing) and general feeling state often

agency appraisal reviewing responsibility for events; can evoke consequential emotions like gratefulness, frustration, guilt, or sadness

equity appraisal considering how fair some event is; can evoke emotions like warmth or anger

outcomes appraisal considering how something turned out relative to one's goals; can evoke emotions like joyfulness, satisfaction, sadness, or pride

mood transient and general affective state

characterized with simple descriptors such as a "good mood," "bad mood," or even a "funky mood." Moods are generally considered less intense than many other emotional experiences; nevertheless, moods can influence CB. Consumers in good moods tend to make decisions faster and to outspend their bad-mood counterparts. In addition, consumer mood affects satisfaction, with a bad mood being particularly detrimental to consumer satisfaction.[16] In this sense, marketers do not have complete control of the satisfaction they deliver.

Employees' moods can also affect consumption outcomes as they interact with consumer mood. Perhaps curiously, consumers who enter a situation in a bad mood react better to service providers who are also in a bad mood than they do to service providers in a good mood. Consumers seem to be most receptive to an employee with a matching mood rather than to an employee who always has a positive mood.[17]

A consumer's mood can serve as a type of frame that can transfer into product value judgments. For instance, consumers in a happy mood are more receptive to new products because they tend to discount risks associated with the unknown.[18] In doing so, consumers make **mood-congruent judgments**, an evaluation in which they judge the value of a target in a mood-consistent way. As a result, retailers should prefer that consumers shop in their stores when they are in a good mood. Many cues can make a consumer's mood more positive, including music, smells, and even exposure to lucky numbers.[19] Conversely, things that lower one's mood make consumers less likely to trust market information.[20] Environmental cues that can affect mood significantly influence the value consumers get from shopping and service experiences, as we will see later.

Moods, feelings, and the manner in which a person thinks about him-/herself also affects consumer decision-making in general. In a variation of construal-level theory, introduced earlier, **consumer self-construal**, which represents whether a consumer is thinking about the self as an independent person or construing the self as an interdependent person within a network of others, determines how much mood influences consumer choice.[21] When a person construes him-/herself independently, thinking about self rather than others, mood plays a bigger role in decisions. In fact, an independent mindset allows feelings to play a bigger role in decisions relative to cognition. Thus, advertisements that focus on independence from rather dependence on others may do better when they make an emotional appeal rather than a cognitive appeal.

Sometimes, a consumer intentionally goes about some action as a way of altering mood. Consumers may purchase a gift for themselves, for instance, as a way of improving their mood. In much the same way, research shows that consumers who are in bad moods may be more likely to be generous to others. Generosity can unlock a better mood and prove hedonically rewarding.[22]

AFFECT

Affect is another term used to represent the feelings a consumer experiences during the consumption process. At times, people use affect as a general term encompassing both emotion and mood. However, in CB, **consumer affect** is often used to represent the general feelings a consumer has about a particular product or activity expressed as tone or liking.[23] Thus, when a consumer likes Dairy Queen (DQ) more than KFC, she is expressing her affect toward the DQ brand. Exhibit 5.5 contrasts the notions of emotion, consumer mood, and consumer affect and illustrates how they create value. The process begins with sensations caused by some stimulus or the environment itself. These shape perceptions that drive some type of feeling-based reaction. Those reactions shape the experience that produces value. While feelings are strongly associated with hedonic value, the fact is that feelings also influence our performance and thus can affect utilitarian value, too.

 5-4 ## MEASURING EMOTION

Marketing and consumer researchers place a great deal of emphasis on properly measuring consumer emotion, because emotions play such a key role in shaping value. The CB researcher has multiple options and technologies for measuring emotions. Some tools measure physical reactions of consumers, from which the researcher infers emotions. Other tools require the respondent to self-assess his/her emotional state. Each approach has advantages and disadvantages.

---

mood-congruent judgments evaluations in which the value of a target is influenced in a consistent way by one's mood

consumer self-construal the manner in which a consumer thinks about him/herself as either an independent person or an interdependent self within a network of others

consumer affect feelings a consumer has about a particular product or activity, often expressed as tone or liking

Exhibit 5.5

Affect, Mood, Emotion, and Value

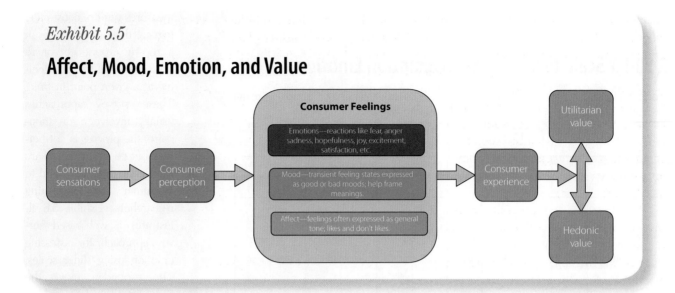

Consumer Feelings

Consumer sensations → Consumer perception →

Emotions—reactions like fear, anger, sadness, hopefulness, joy, excitement, satisfaction, etc.

Mood—transient feeling states expressed as good or bad moods; help frame meanings.

Affect—feelings often expressed as general tone; likes and don't likes.

→ Consumer experience → Utilitarian value / Hedonic value

5-4a Autonomic Measures

Autonomic measures automatically record visceral body reactions or neurological (brain) activity. Autonomic emotion measures monitor things like facial reactions, physiological responses such as sweating in a galvanic skin response, heart rate, pupil dilation, and electrical activity in areas of the brain responsible for certain specific emotions, which can be documented via brain imaging.[24] Consumer researchers use fMRI (functional magnetic resonance imaging) machines, identical to those used to identify brain disorders, to examine consumers' brain activity when exposed to advertising messages including cigarette ads and anti-smoking ads.

Autonomic measures assess emotional activity without requiring a volitional response from the consumer. This advantage comes with the drawback of greater intrusiveness. Autonomic measures usually require the attachment of some type of device to the consumer. A consumer in an fMRI machine must lay completely still for periods of time of an hour or more. During this time, the researcher exposes them to the advertisements or other emotion-inducing stimuli. The research subject is normally told to relax and react normally to the stimuli. Consumers do not typically view ads strapped into a machine or with electrodes attached to their skin. Interestingly, however, research suggests that these autonomic responses generally correspond fairly well to introspective self-reports of emotional experience, suggesting to some extent[25] that consumers do know how they feel.

Eye-tracking technologies are increasingly popular because they are relatively inexpensive and not as intrusive as most neurological measurements. **Eye-tracking technology** combines hardware and software that can measure precisely where a consumer's gaze is directed and also assess pupil dilation. Our pupils dilate when we are experiencing a visceral reaction to emotion. Retailers benefit from knowing how consumers react to merchandising. For example, do consumers ever gaze at the bottom shelf? Package designers benefit from knowing how consumers react to differences in logo appearance, colors, and other design elements. A few

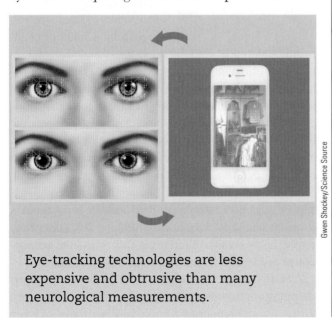

Gwen Shockey/Science Source

Eye-tracking technologies are less expensive and obtrusive than many neurological measurements.

autonomic measures
means of recording responses based on either automatic visceral reactions or neurological brain activity

Eye-tracking technology
combination of hardware and software that measures precisely where one's pupils are gazing and assesses amount of pupil dilation. Eye-tracking technologies automatically record consumers' gazes.

Exhibit 5.6

A Slider Scale to Measure Consumption Emotion

Thank you for your recent visit to our service center. Please use the slider scales below to rate the extent to which you felt each emotion listed during your service experience.

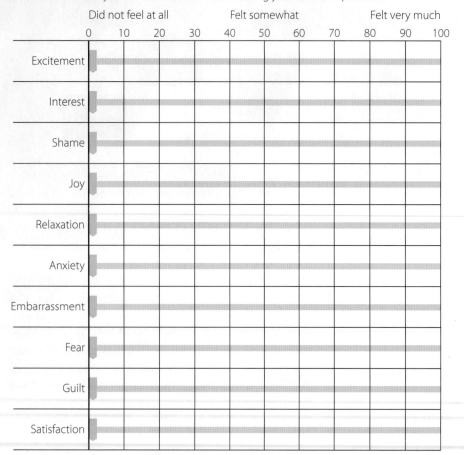

measures require consumers to recall their affect state from a recent experience, or to state the affect they are feeling at a given point in time. These survey approaches usually involve a questionnaire; the process is not perfect, but generally results are valid enough to be useful to consumer and marketing researchers. Exhibit 5.6 illustrates a web-based survey approach for assessing emotion using slider scales. The respondent moves the slider from 0 to 100 until the scale indicates how much they feel a certain emotion. Many different options exist for applying self-report measures, with each option usually based on a somewhat different perspective of emotion theory.

PAD

PAD is an acronym that stands for pleasure–arousal–dominance, three dimensions proposed to represent emotional experiences. A PAD scaling approach asks consumers to rate their feelings using a number of semantic differential (bipolar opposites) items that capture emotions experienced in an environment. The theory behind PAD is that pleasure—the evaluative dimension of emotion—is bipolar, meaning that if one feels joyful, one cannot also experience sadness.[27] Arousal represents the degree to which one feels energized, excited, or interested. Arousal also is bipolar, in that a consumer is either aroused or bored, as is dominance, the degree that one feels in control of the environment. Researchers have combined applied adjectives taken from PAD scales and put them in a format similar to that shown in Exhibit 5.6, rather than relying on a semantic differential. This relaxes the assumption of predefined opposites for each emotion item.

milliseconds extra in gaze accompanied by an arousing reaction translates into millions in potential sales for a new product. Researchers demonstrate that emotions are evoked even in trivial choice situations,[26] such as choosing between yogurts, and that gaze and positive reactions go together.

5-4b Self-Report Measures

Self-report measures are less obtrusive than biological measures, because they don't involve physical contraptions like imaging machines or lie detectors. Self-report affect

Many researchers use a PAD approach to study shopping environment atmospherics. These studies capture consumer emotions across many environment types

PAD pleasure–arousal–dominance; a self-report measure that asks respondents to rate feelings using semantic differential items

bipolar situation wherein if one feels joy he or she cannot also experience sadness

100 Virtual Bottles of Beer on the Wall

Consumers have lots of feelings about beer. But advanced technology may eventually help us produce the perfect beer—or at least the perfect beer bottle. A digital marketing agency sponsored a limited trial release of a bottle of beer called 0101, which was "brewed by data." The firm used marketing analytics to design the beer to embody the emotions of a new year. But how can a beer be tested without the expense of a trial run? Here is where imaging and eye-tracking come into play. Using eye-tracking, consumer reactions to images of a beer bottle were analyzed to see if they were the same as those of consumers viewing the actual beer bottle. The results? Well, virtual beer is not as good as real beer—yet. It seems that consumer reactions vary

because virtual images cannot match all the nuanced ways in which consumers view the real thing.

Sources: Noyes, K. (2016), "If You Didn't Love Analytics Before, You Will Now," *Network World*, http://www.networkworld.com/article/3031208/analytics/data-science-achieves-the-ultimate-roi-a-craft-beer.html, accessed April 3, 2016. Rojas, J.C., M. Contero, N. Bartomeu, and J. Guixeres (2015), "Using Combined Bipolar Semantic Scales and Eye-Tracking Metrics to Compare Consumer Perception of Real and Virtual Bottles," *Packaging Technology and Science*, 28, 1047–1056.

beyond traditional stores, including museums, parks, tourist destinations and even advertising contexts.[28] Because the scale captures arousal separately, the approach is advantageous when the degree of activation or excitement is of particular interest. For example, when consumers go to a movie, they may feel pleased but not excited. Often, the combination of pleasure and arousal builds consumer loyalty. The PAD approach allows a separate accounting for feelings of dominance, sometimes known as control. When consumers feel lower control, situational influences play a greater role in shaping their behavior.

PANAS

PANAS stands for positive-affect-negative-affect scale and allows respondents to self-report the extent to which they feel one of 20 emotional adjectives.

Researchers generally apply the PANAS to capture the relative amount of positive and negative emotion experienced by a consumer at a given point in time. However, this raises several questions about the nature of emotion, including whether or not positive and negative emotions can coexist.

Every PANAS item represents either a good or a bad feeling. Thus, one might wonder why "inspired" and "upset" would both need to be measured. If a new product

inspired a consumer, it would seem that the consumer could not be upset at the same time. If feeling good excludes feeling bad, then wouldn't a researcher need only measure positive terms or negative terms to account for a consumer's feelings?

The issue is theoretically interesting but also has practical implications. For instance, do consumers react differently to equal amounts of positive and negative emotions? Does a mad consumer or a glad consumer react more strongly? Considerable attention in psychology and marketing research addresses this question, and the evidence isn't crystal clear. The best we can say in addressing whether feeling bad is more influential than feeling good is "sometimes." Consider the following situations:

▸ A consumer rating the feelings experienced when a pop-up box appears while playing an online game

▸ A consumer rating the feelings experienced when planning a wedding

▸ A student expressing how he feels about his college experience on his graduation day.

The first situation is quite simple. In situations like these, positive and negative emotions tend to be opposites. If people have bad feelings in the time the pop-up is blocking the view of the game, they are unlikely to have any good feelings until it is gone. The second and third situations are more complex and extend over a longer period. In situations such as these, bad and good feelings do not cancel each other out completely, and people can indeed experience some levels of both good and bad emotions.

Thus, when consumer researchers are studying highly complex situations, a scale like the PANAS allows them to capture both positive and negative dimensions of emotional experience. The possibility exists that each dimension might explain somewhat unique experiences. Positive affect is highly related to consumer spending, but negative emotion is not. The more good feelings consumers have, the more they buy. A consumer experiencing negative emotions, on the other hand, often still completes the shopping task but also may look for another place to shop next time.

Is it rational to spend more on a tailgate motorhome than one's house?

> ## Does a mad consumer or a glad consumer react more strongly?

5-5 DIFFERENCES IN EMOTIONAL BEHAVIOR

Two consumers receive the same poor service from a service provider. Will they react the same way? Probably not. Different consumers react with differing emotions.[29] One might complain furiously to store management, while the other simply walks away to find a quieter shopping environment. Emotions are tied deeply to individual differences such as motivations and traits. Thus, personality characteristics can affect the way consumers experience or demonstrate their emotions.

Neuroticism is a basic human personality trait that affects emotional reactions. Highly neurotic consumers, for example, tend to be less affected by emotionally restorative effects that can calm a consumer who is low in neuroticism.[30] Highly neurotic consumers also report more negative emotion when playing online games, but those negative emotions actually lead to increased hedonic value perceptions.[31] Marketers benefit from consumer research describing how individual differences relate to emotional experience.

5-5a Emotional Involvement

The things that tap our deepest emotions have the ability to evoke the greatest value. This brings us to emotional involvement, meaning the type of deep personal interest that evokes strongly felt feelings associated with some object or activity. Emotional involvement drives one to consume generally through repeated experiences of relatively strong hedonic motivations. Often, emotional involvement can make a consumer appear irrational. Consider the amount of money and time a college alumnus and football fan will spend following his team. Some spend hundreds of thousands of dollars on motor homes used only on football weekends for tailgating. The consumer is deeply and emotionally involved with the team and in many ways becomes one with the team.

Emotional involvement increases when the consumer receives something extra with products purchased. For instance, if someone buys a nice leather backpack, the company might consider adding a premium, such as a phone holster, calculator, or gift certificate to a local pub. The brands that do a little something extra get paid back in customers with higher emotional involvement.

FLOW

All consumers can probably relate to the experience of enjoying a good book or movie so much that one loses awareness of time passing. When this occurs, a consumer

> ## Highly involved consumers sometimes obtain a flow experience.

has achieved a state of **flow**, meaning extremely high emotional involvement in which a consumer is engrossed in an activity.

Computer-related activities are common contributors to flow. For instance, consumers can become so involved that they have little physical awareness of their surroundings.[32] When consumers are in a texting or gaming frenzy, they may have no conscious awareness of someone trying to speak to them in person. YouTube is replete with videos of "smombies" (smartphone zombies) doing dumb things. One consumer was caught on a mall security camera stumbling right into the mall's fountain all while continuing to text. Consumer addiction to social networking is epidemic. Here are some signs that might indicate social networking addiction:[33]

▸ Ignoring work to continue surfing social media sites

▸ Feeling like dinner is incomplete if you don't send an Instagram of a restaurant dinner entrée before eating it

▸ A need to continually refresh your Facebook news page

▸ Feeling more attached to your group of virtual friends than the real kind

▸ Replacing sleep with online social networking

▸ Checking as soon as waking to see how many people commented on the "witty" Tweet you left the night before

▸ Interacting with social media while using the bathroom

▸ Becoming nervous or depressed when facing an extended period away from online social networking (more than a day)

▸ Saying "lol" instead of laughing

▸ Getting irritated when a real friend interrupts your use of Facebook

▸ Checking Facebook, Twitter, Instagram, Snapchat, etc. while driving or walking across a street

Highly involved shoppers sometimes achieve a flow experience. When this occurs, the consumer is likely to spend more time browsing, spend more money, make repeat purchases, and be more prone to impulse purchasing.[34] Online consumers can pursue a flow state while shopping; however, interruptions in Internet service, poor navigational clues, or slow page load times can inhibit the

The state of flow is value enhancing, but can it cause an addiction—such as Facebook addiction?

flow experience and lower both utilitarian and hedonic shopping value.[35] If the consumer achieves hedonic value, positive outcomes can result for both the consumer and the marketer. However, the consumer must be able to maintain control of the situation to avoid compulsive or addictive behaviors.

5-5b Emotional Expressiveness

Not all consumers express their emotions as obviously as others do. **Emotional expressiveness** represents the extent to which a consumer shows outward behavioral signs and otherwise reacts obviously to emotional experiences. The consumer with relatively high emotional expressiveness is likely to react in some way to outcomes that are unexpected. A bad poker player, for example, is unable to hide emotions from other players, so his reaction displays high emotional expressiveness.

Many who study emotions ask whether women are more emotionally expressive than men. Researchers do not provide a clear answer to this question. For instance, psychologists interested in studying the human experience of, and reaction to, disgust have conducted experiments in which subjects are exposed to films depicting either an actual amputation or a man being swarmed by

flow extremely high emotional involvement in which a consumer is engrossed in an activity

emotional expressiveness extent to which a consumer shows outward behavioral signs and otherwise reacts obviously to emotional experiences

cockroaches.[36] Male and female subjects report on average the same level of disgust while viewing the films. However, female respondents are more likely than males to react to the disgusting experience by leaving the room before the film is finished. Beyond disgust, research shows that women display greater emotional expressiveness for other emotions too.[37] Research suggests that when male and female consumers react with similar emotions, women express the emotions more noticeably. Negative emotions decrease value and loyalty more strongly among female than male consumers.[38] Because of this, to the extent that a marketer can judge a consumer's emotional reaction, female consumers may prove more valuable in signaling poor or outstanding service than would male consumers.

5-5c Emotional Intelligence

Emotions can be useful in determining the most appropriate reaction to events. **Emotional intelligence** is a term used to capture one's awareness of the emotions experienced in a situation, and an ability to control reactions to these emotions. This includes awareness of the emotions experienced by the individual as well as an awareness and sympathy for the emotions experienced by others. Emotional intelligence (EI) is a multifaceted concept; Exhibit 5.7 illustrates EI components. High EI consumers are able to use awareness of emotions in decision making and are better able to manage their own emotions and exhibit self-control.[39] High EI also enables consumers who have difficulty controlling consumption, such as overeating, to associate bad habits with unpleasant emotions as a way of potentially enhancing control.[40]

In a marketing context, salespeople and service providers with high emotional intelligence often are considered more effective. High EI service employees in hospitality and health care industries tend to create more valuable experiences for customers. Although most research points to higher sales from employees with high EI, some research points to a mechanism by which emotional

emotional intelligence awareness of the emotions experienced in a given situation and the ability to control reactions to these emotions

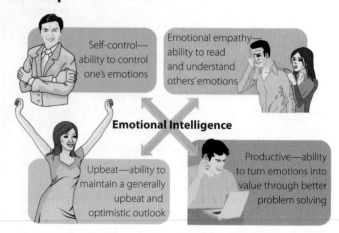

Exhibit 5.7
Emotional Intelligence Consists of Multiple Elements

Self-control—ability to control one's emotions

Emotional empathy—ability to read and understand others' emotions

Emotional Intelligence

Upbeat—ability to maintain a generally upbeat and optimistic outlook

Productive—ability to turn emotions into value through better problem solving

regulation can inhibit salesperson creativity as a possible limiting factor.[41]

5-5d What's Funny

Laughter is almost always a positive experience and can add a lot of value to one's life. Marketers often try to evoke laughter as a way of getting attention or

Dear Kitten: The Forbidden Water Bowl

Purina Friskies

Subscribe 140,785

1,240,385 views

Humorous ads like this one for Friskies can create schema-based affect, which helps shape a brand's meaning.

creating positive affect that may become associated with a brand. What makes something funny? Funny things usually present some mental incongruity that our brain naturally tries to resolve. "I just shot an elephant in my pajamas." The contrasting concepts challenge our brain to try to resolve inconsistencies. "How he got in my pajamas I'll never know!"[42] The punch line resolves the inconsistency and presents a humorous surprise. Humor creates value-added experiences through hedonic value and can serve more utilitarian functions such as reducing stress.

 ## 5-6 EMOTION, MEANING, AND SCHEMA-BASED AFFECT

What is the relation between cognition and emotion? Intuitively, emotion and cognition seem so different that one might easily presume the two are completely independent. However, emotion and cognition are actually closely related. One can easily see the close relationship in the role that affect, mood, and emotion can play in signaling and developing meaning. This section focuses on the interplay between emotion and cognitive learning.

5-6a Semantic Wiring

In the previous chapter, we learned that in our memory, a network connects all concepts to other concepts. A concept such as a "toaster" is closely linked with a concept like "breakfast" but very remotely linked with another concept like "zoo." A consumer's ability to remember things about brands and products can be explained using theory developed around the principles of *semantic* or *associative* networks. Remember, all concepts are linked to all other concepts, but some are linked strongly and others very weakly. It's difficult to put weak concepts together.

Although the term *semantic* refers to cognitive thought processes, the active processing and storage of knowledge depends on emotions in several ways. The general expression "**emotional effect on memory**" refers to relatively superior recall for information presented with mild affective content compared to similar information presented in an affectively neutral way.[43]

The implications for marketing are fairly direct. Marketing communications that present product information in a way that evokes mild levels of emotions will tend to be more effective in producing recall than communications

Exhibit 5.8

Illustration of Emotion Aiding Learning

that are affectively neutral.[44] Caution is needed in executing such communications, because intense emotions are more complicated to deal with and can sometimes even distract consumers from the task of actually processing information. But Exhibit 5.8 illustrates the way that emotion shapes the meaning of a brand.

5-6b Mood-Congruent Recall

Many consumers can remember their first day of school, first airplane trip, or first visit to a theme park. In each case, products and brands are associated with the experience. Likewise, in each case, each event is associated with a fairly specific mood. For many consumers, the first day of school is filled with apprehension, the first airplane ride may be a blend of fear and excitement, and a visit to a theme park is associated with joy.

Autobiographical memories are memories of previous meaningful events in one's life. Consumers are more likely to recall autobiographical memories characterized by specific moods when the same mood occurs again in the future.[45] Simply put, moods tend to match memories.

emotional effect on memory relatively superior recall for information presented with mild affective content compared to similar information presented in an affectively neutral way

autobiographical memories cognitive representation of meaningful events in one's life

Exhibit 5.9

Examples of Schema-Based Affect

Schema	Relevant affect type (emotion)	Typical consumer reaction
Apple	Confidence, pride	Apple consumers feel a sense of superiority that comes along with the products.
Individual countries	Consumers may have slightly different affect associated with each country	Consumers are less favorable toward products manufactured in countries for which that consumer's schema evokes negative affect.
Dentist	Anxiety	Consumers avoid scheduling an appointment and cringe in anticipation.
Puppies	Tenderness, warmth	Products depicted with puppies benefit from the warm feelings that are created.
Champagne	Anticipation, excitement	The product is associated with parties, celebrations, rituals, and joyful good times.
Stereotypes	Each stereotype evokes slightly different affect	The affect associated with the stereotype can cause consumers to be more or less willing to approach and may alter information processing.

Mood-congruent recall means that to the extent that a consumer's mood can be controlled, his or her memories and evaluations can be influenced. Music is one tool useful in inducing moods. When music sets a mood, consumers will recall products associated with that mood more readily. In addition, consumers in good moods tend to evaluate products positively compared to consumers in bad moods, and vice versa.[46] When students have a fun spring break, the products associated with it may experience increased favorability over a short time period.[47]

5-6c Schema-Based Affect

As we know from consumer information processing theory, knowledge of familiar things becomes organized in a cognitive unit of meaning known as a *schema*. A schema contains the knowledge of a brand, a product, or any concept. However, a schema is not a purely cognitive entity. Schemata are developed and reinforced through actual experience. For instance, we come to perceive what a car salesperson truly is based on our total experience with that category. Experience involves more than cognition. When we encounter a car salesperson or hear stories that involve car salespeople, we also experience some type of affect or emotion. These emotions become part of the meaning for a category in the form of schema-based affect.

Schema-based affect helps provide meaning and thus provides another example of how emotion and cognition work together. However, a consumer can actually experience a feeling once a schema becomes active. For example, a consumer who fears going to a dentist can actually experience true nervousness and apprehension simply by thinking about a visit to the dentist. This makes the dentist visit script active. Social schemata, or stereotypes, are characterized by specific schema-based affect. A politician schema usually evokes suspicion or skepticism. A seasoned airline pilot may create a sense of calm. Exhibit 5.9 displays examples of schema-based affect that can influence consumers' reactions to consumption experiences. Although the term is schema-based "affect," the use of specific emotion terms means it could easily be thought of as schema-based emotion as well.

mood-congruent recall consumers will remember information better when the mood they are currently in matches the mood they were in when originally exposed to the information

schema-based affect emotions that become stored as part of the meaning for a category (a schema)

"THE HAPPY PLACE"

Where are consumers in the best mood? Maybe in the happy place! Where are the happiest places on Earth? Well, survey-based consumer research points to 10 places as the happiest countries on Earth. While weather can affect mood, researchers were surprised to note that most of the happiest places have some of the worst weather: Denmark, Norway, the Netherlands, Switzerland, and Sweden are the five happiest places, according to this research. What makes the people happy? Well, these nations tend to have high GDP, highly rated restaurants, and famous parks, like Tivoli Gardens in Denmark. Interestingly, Australia, coming in at number 10, is the only nation not characterized by a cold climate. So do parks and restaurants help make consumers happy more than weather does? Well, in the United States, one place claims to be the "Happiest Place on Earth": Walt Disney World. Obviously, Disney has parks, and in recent years, Disney has also become known for fine dining. Good times and good food makes for happy consumers.

Sources: Hetter, G. (2015), "Get Happy in the World's Happiest Countries," http://www.cnn.com/2014/03/20/travel/happiest-countries-to-visit/index.html, accessed April 5, 2016. http://national.deseretnews.com/article/1368/is-walt-disney-world-really-the-happiest-place-on-earth.html, accessed April 5, 2016.

AESTHETIC LABOR

Aesthetic labor deals specifically with employees who most carefully manage their own personal appearance as a requisite to performing their job well, and fitting what managers see as the stereotype for their particular company's service. Many service employees—including cosmetic representatives and fashion models for companies like L'Oréal and Victoria's Secret, flight attendants, and table servers for such companies as Korean Air and Hooters—perform aesthetic labor. The belief is that a specific appearance generates the appropriate emotional reaction in the consumer. These emotions promote behavior that can ultimately create value and potentially lead to loyalty.

From a marketing standpoint, aesthetic labor helps set the mood for an effective service environment. A&F uses strict aesthetic labor practices to create a uniform look and a feeling of excitement and sex appeal. Thus, by creating a known and identifiable look, the company can affect the feelings of its customers, which in turn, drives value.[48] In this sense, aesthetic labor is a

> **aesthetic labor** effort put forth by employees in carefully managing their appearance as a requisite for performing their job well

JUST SELLING SOAP

When one thinks of products with strong emotional meaning, hand soap may not spring to mind. But even a simple everyday product can enhance its value proposition with emotional meaning. That's just what Lifebuoy soap has accomplished. Lifebuoy launched a campaign called "Help a Child Reach 5" in India. The campaign featured emotional videos of rituals performed by families celebrating a child's fifth birthday. In India, where childhood mortality claims around 2 million children a year under the age of 5, the fifth birthday is a meaningful milestone. But the campaign involves more than ads. For example, Lifebuoy works with preschool children to teach them jingles that make washing for at least 20 seconds fun. The end result is a lot of positive emotion attached to the Lifebuoy brand, emotions that translate into a strong brand positioning.

Thanamat Somwan/Shutterstock.com

Sources: Aaker, D. (2016), "Lessons from Lifebuoy," *Marketing News* (January), 16–17. http://www.lifebuoy.com/socialmission/help-childreach5/, accessed April 6, 2016.

form of **emotional labor**, meaning that part of the job of many service providers is to manage the emotions of the customers.[49] In many service situations where consumers may be nervous, such as on an airplane or in a health-related circumstance, emotional labor can be a big part of the way the services create value.

5-6d Self-Conscious Emotions

Getting laughed at can be painful. Marketers sometimes execute communications designed to take advantage of consumers' natural tendency to avoid ridicule. Brands emphasize how embarrassed one should feel for having less than pearly white teeth, body odor (BO), bad hair, a bad figure, and on and on. Others tend to shame consumers who smoke, text while driving, or don't recycle. Appeals like these are often effective because the emotions they evoke relate closely to one's self-concept.[50] Self-conscious emotions result from some evaluation or reflection of one's own behavior—which can include both actions and failures to act. **Self-conscious emotions** include pride, embarrassment, guilt, regret, shame, and hope. Consumers experiencing negative self-conscious emotions can perceive not only the need to rectify some problem, but also the need to restore their self-esteem.

The feeling of guilt can play a role in CB in many ways. Consumers may feel guilty for the way they treat a service provider. For instance, a consumer using the same hair stylist for several years may feel guilty for saving a few dollars and going to a different person to get a haircut. Consumers sometimes feel self-conscious when they see consumers who are not as wealthy and lack buying power. In all these instances, a consumer may perform some counterbalancing behavior, such as recommending the old service provider to others or making a charitable contribution.

5-6e Emotional Contagion

Are emotions contagious? This is the idea behind **emotional contagion**, which represents the extent to which an emotional display by one person influences the emotional state of a bystander. Consumers who perceive other consumers or employees around them as either happy or sad may experience a corresponding change in actual happiness or sadness themselves. Emotional contagion means marketing managers who have a mantra of "service with a smile" may have a good reason to do so.

emotional labor effort put forth by service workers who have to overtly manage their own emotional displays as part of the requirements of the job

self-conscious emotions specific emotions that result from some evaluation or reflection of one's own behavior, including pride, shame, guilt, and embarrassment

emotional contagion extent to which an emotional display by one person influences the emotional state of a bystander

Imagine a service provider promoting a brand. When a consumer encounters that service provider in a photo or in person, he or she takes on some of that emotion and uses the emotion as information to signal behavior. When the emotion is positive, consumers become more favorable toward purchasing and enjoy the experience more, particularly in first-time encounters with a person.[51]

PRODUCT CONTAMINATION

Picture this. A consumer sees a price reduction on a shirt he has wanted for a long time. He buys it, but when he gets home and begins to put it on, he realizes it no longer has the pins and cardboard backing that should come with a new shirt. "Has somebody already purchased this and returned it?" he asks himself. All of a sudden, the value in wearing the new shirt is diminished because the idea that someone else may have worn the shirt creates uneasiness. **Product contamination** refers to the fact that consumers feel uneasy about buying things that others have previously touched. Supermarket consumers can be seen searching the back of the shelf for an untouched package or avoiding produce that they have seen others handling. Even subtle cues of others touching products such as disorganized shelving can lead to perceived contamination.[52] However, in an interesting twist, research shows

Many supermarket consumers can be seen reaching to the back of the shelf for an untouched package.

that through a type of emotional contagion process, a product's value can actually increase after a consumer sees the product handled by an attractive member of the opposite sex.[53] Instead of avoiding that product, the consumer will actually seek it out.

product contamination refers to the diminished positive feelings someone has about a product because another consumer has handled the product

---

STUDY TOOLS 5

LOCATED AT BACK OF THE TEXTBOOK

☐ Tear out Chapter Review Card

LOCATED AT WWW.CENGAGE.COM/LOGIN

☐ Review Key Term flashcards and create your own cards

☐ Track your knowledge and understanding of key concepts in consumer behavior

☐ Complete practice quizzes to prepare for tests

☐ Complete interactive content within CB Online

☐ Review the Chapter Highlight boxes for CB Online

6 | Personality, Lifestyles, and the Self-Concept

LEARNING OBJECTIVES

After studying this chapter, the student should be able to:

6-1 Define personality and understand how various approaches to studying personality can be applied to consumer behavior.

6-2 Discuss major traits that have been examined in consumer research.

6-3 Understand why lifestyles, psychographics, and demographics are important to the study of consumer behavior.

6-4 Comprehend the role of the self-concept in consumer behavior.

6-5 Understand the concept of self-congruency and how it applies to consumer behavior issues.

Lighthunter/Shutterstock.com

Remember to visit **PAGE 129** for additional **STUDY TOOLS**

INTRODUCTION

If you were to describe yourself on a popular dating app, how would you do it? Are you quiet? Reserved? The life of the party? Do your selfies say something about who you are? Or how you feel about yourself? And what exactly is the "self," anyway? Most consumers probably don't think about those questions, but consumer researchers do. Understanding the ways in which consumers differ from each other is an important part of determining why consumers value different things.

The current chapter focuses on consumer personality, lifestyles, and the self-concept. These concepts are often referred to as **individual difference variables**, which are descriptions of how individual consumers differ according

individual difference variables descriptions of how individual consumers differ according to specific trait patterns of behavior

personality totality of thoughts, emotions, intentions, tendencies, and behaviors that a person exhibits consistently as he or she adapts to the environment

to specific traits or patterns of behavior.[1] These variables have several applications in consumer research and marketing practice. Marketing managers are especially interested in identifying consumer characteristics that are associated with the likelihood of purchasing products. Concepts like personality, lifestyle, and self-concept help to describe these likelihoods. Demographics are also important, and we include this concept in our discussion. Identifying and using these variables has become easier thanks to one-to-one marketing technologies like the internet and smartphone apps.

6-1 PERSONALITY AND CONSUMER BEHAVIOR

Personality has been studied for many years in both psychology and consumer behavior. It therefore shouldn't be surprising that there have been many different definitions for the concept. We define **personality** as the totality of thoughts, emotions, intentions, tendencies, and

behaviors that a person exhibits consistently as he or she adapts to the environment.[2] This definition highlights the *cognitive* (thoughts), *affective* (emotions), *motivational* (intentions), and *behavioral* (behaviors) aspects that are central to personality. Personality is but one characteristic that helps explain why a particular behavior, for example attending sporting events at a college, provides great value for one consumer but none to another.

Personality exhibits a number of distinct qualities, including:

1. **Personality is unique to an individual.** Personality helps distinguish consumers based on the specific characteristics each exhibits. Consumers differ in personalities, although some characteristics, or traits, may be shared across individuals.

2. **Personality can be conceptualized as a combination of specific traits or characteristics.** Like all consumers, your overall personality is really a combination of many stable characteristics, or traits. In fact, for many psychologists, personality psychology deals exclusively with the study of human traits.[3]

3. **Personality traits are relatively stable and interact with situations to influence behavior.** Personality traits are expected to remain consistent across situations. However, consumer researchers realize the importance of situational influencers, and the combined influence of situations and traits greatly influences specific behaviors (this is referred to as an *interaction* between the person and the situation).[4] To illustrate, imagine how an unstable person might act when she has to wait a long time at a restaurant.

4. **Specific behaviors can vary across time.** Simply knowing a consumer possesses a specific trait does not allow us to predict a particular behavior. For example, knowing that a consumer is "materialistic" does not allow us to predict the exact type of product the person may buy. For this reason, personality researchers often a[dopt] an **aggregation approach** in which behaviors and tendencies are measured over time.

As we have mentioned, marketing managers are particularly interested in how consumers differ according to their personalities. Consistent patterns of thoughts, emotions, intentions, and behaviors can signal the need for individualized marketing campaigns, and today's marketers are quite adept at individualizing messages, especially by utilizing social media. Technological advances, like smartphone apps for example, have made it much easier for companies to communicate one-on-one with their customers. Companies have also realized that they can learn about consumer personalities by researching social media postings and tweets. The "digital self" continues to get a lot of marketing attention.

There are many ways to discuss the concept of personality. Here we focus on two popular approaches: the psychoanalytic approach and the trait approach.

Sigmund Freud (1856–1939), in 1885, when he was training as a psychiatrist at General Hospital in Vienna.

EVERETT COLLECTION, INC.

6-1a Psychoanalytic Approach to Personality

According to the famous psychologist Sigmund Freud, human behavior is influenced by an inner struggle between various systems within the personality system.[5] His approach, commonly referred to as the **psychoanalytic approach to personality**, is applicable to both motivation and personality inquiry. Freud's approach highlights the importance of unconscious mental processes in influencing behavior. The idea is that deep-seated motivations lead people to act in various ways.

For Freud, the human personality consists of three important components: the *id*, the *superego*, and the *ego*. The **id** focuses on pleasure-seeking and immediate gratification. It operates on a **pleasure principle** that motivates a person to focus on maximizing pleasure and minimizing pain. One's id, therefore, focuses on hedonic value. Indeed, a key concept in the id is the *libido*. The libido represents a drive for sexual pleasure, although some researchers view it in slightly different ways. The **superego** works against the id by motivating behavior that matches societal norms and expectations, much like the consumer's conscience. The **ego** focuses on resolving the conflicts between the id and the superego. The ego works largely in accordance with the **reality principle**. Under this principle, the ego seeks to satisfy the id within the constraints of society. As such, the ego attempts to balance the desires of the id with the constraints of, and expectations found in, the superego.

PSYCHOANALYTIC APPROACH AND MOTIVATION RESEARCH

In the early days of consumer research, researchers applied psychoanalytic tools to try to identify explanations for behavior. This was known as the **motivational research era**. Consumer researchers in this era utilized tools such as *depth interviews* and *focus groups* to improve their understanding of inner motives and needs.[6] Depth interviews explored deepseated motivations by asking consumers a series of probing questions.

Suppose a researcher is studying a consumer who posts a lot of videos to an app like *SnapChat*. The researcher might ask the following probing questions:

▶ "Do the videos you post say anything about how you see yourself?"
▶ "Why do you post the types of videos that you do?"
▶ "Why is this important to you?"
▶ "Why do you think you enjoy it so much?"

psychoanalytic approach to personality approach to personality research, advocated by Sigmund Freud, that suggests personality results from a struggle between inner motives and societal pressures to follow rules and expectations

id the personality component in psychoanalytic theory that focuses on pleasure-seeking motives and immediate gratification

pleasure principle principle found in psychoanalytic theory that describes the factor that motivates pleasure-seeking behavior within the id

superego component in psychoanalytic theory that works against the id by motivating behavior that matches the expectations and norms of society

ego component in psychoanalytic theory that attempts to balance the struggle between the superego and the id

reality principle the principle in psychoanalytic theory under which the ego attempts to satisfy the id within societal constraints

motivational research in consumer research based heavily on psychoanalytic approaches

A Snapchat user might reveal that posting videos is a way to have fun and relieve stress. Having fun is necessary to combat the stresses of everyday life. Participating in experiences that offer fantasy and escape, as many apps do, provides consumers with hedonic value. From this example we can see how motivational research can uncover a number of consumer behaviors related to fantasy, escape, and release.

In general, the motivational research era proved disappointing because it did not spawn any compelling, practical consumer behavior theories or guidelines for marketing actions. Although deeply seated motivations could be uncovered, they often seemed removed from specific marketing tactics. Nevertheless, Freud clearly influenced the study of personality and consumer behavior, and researchers remain interested in deep-seated motivations.[7] In fact, the saying "Sex sells" may be tied to the Freudian and motivational approaches.

6-1b Trait Approach to Personality

While the psychoanalytic approach helped set the groundwork for much of consumer personality research, the **trait approach to personality** has received significant attention over the past few decades, and many consumer researchers focus on this approach today. A **trait** is

> ## Today's marketers are quite adept at individualizing messages.

defined as a distinguishable characteristic that describes one's tendency to act in a relatively consistent manner.

Not surprisingly, there are multiple approaches available for consumer researchers. Here, we discuss the differences between nomothetic and idiographic approaches, and between single- and multi-trait approaches.

NOMOTHETIC VERSUS IDIOGRAPHIC APPROACHES

The nomothetic perspective and the idiographic perspective can be distinguished as follows.[8] The **nomothetic perspective** is a "variable-centered" approach that focuses on particular variables, or traits, that exist across a number of consumers. The goal of this perspective is to find common personality traits that can be studied across people.

An example helps to explain the nomothetic approach. Consider Scott. Scott's friends notice that he tends to complain about lots of things on Twitter. He tweets about every bad thing that comes to mind, and his friends think it is a bit much. Of course, there are a lot of people that are this way. Here, researchers would say he is complaint prone, and they use this label to describe a lot of consumers like Scott. Complaint-prone consumers usually take their complaints straight to a company, but sometimes they complain to other people and tweet about their unhappiness. The focus here would be on the complaint proneness trait and how it describes a lot of consumers. Assessing personality traits through posts to Twitter and other social media is now a standard practice for employers, and research indicates that the practice can be considered valid.[9]

The **idiographic perspective** focuses on the total person and the uniqueness of his psychological makeup. Attention is not placed on individual traits or how they can be studied across multiple consumers. Rather, the focus is on understanding the complexity of each individual consumer. Some

Do you use Snapchat?

Jane Smith/Shutterstock.com

trait approach to personality approaches in personality research that focus on specific consumer traits as motivators of various consumer behaviors

trait distinguishable characteristic that describes one's tendency to act in a relatively consistent manner

nomothetic perspective variable-centered approach to personality that focuses on particular traits that exist across a number of people

idiographic perspective approach to personality that focuses on understanding the complexity of each individual consumer

Personality can be studied in many ways.

Jane Smith/Shutterstock.com

researchers today focus on what is referred to as consumer introspections and how they explain behavior. *Consumer Introspection Theory* views the consumer herself as the research instrument and examines how her introspections can explain things like product involvement and choice.[10] Introspections can reveal much about the inner motivations and psychology of consumers. Although this approach has been around for several years, it has recently gained significant research attention.

The trait approach takes a nomothetic approach to personality. That is, the trait approach assumes that the human personality can be described as a combination of traits that can be studied across consumers. From this perspective, individuals can be described by using various trait descriptors.

SINGLE-TRAIT AND MULTIPLE-TRAIT APPROACHES

We can further distinguish between single-trait and multiple-trait approaches to consumer research. With the single-trait approach, the focus of the researcher is on one particular trait. Here, researchers can learn more about the trait and how it

affects behavior. For example, a researcher may want to investigate how a consumer's tendency to be productive affects his leisure activities, such as what he does on a family vacation.[11]

With the **multiple-trait approach**, combinations of traits are examined and the total effect of the collection of traits is considered. Here, the researcher is interested in trait scores on numerous traits as potential predictors of consumer behavior. The prediction of individual behavior tends to be stronger with the multiple-trait approach.[12] However, both the single- and multiple-trait approaches have been used extensively in consumer research.

 ## MAJOR TRAITS EXAMINED IN CONSUMER RESEARCH

One of the main challenges facing consumer researchers who want to study traits is that there are so many traits that apply to consumer behavior. As far back as 1936, researchers Gordon Allport and Henry Odbert identified nearly 18,000 names for human characteristics found in Webster's Dictionary.[13] Imagine how many have been identified since then. Many traits are essentially descriptions that we use in everyday life, and we often call them labels. For example, we commonly use terms like "talkative" or "mean" to describe people. Some labels come and go. For example, years ago people used the word "persnickety" to describe someone who focuses too much on unnecessary details. We don't hear that term much anymore. The traits that are used in consumer research are usually very specific and tend to be studied for relatively long periods of time.

6-2a Many Traits Examined in CB

When there are thousands of ways to describe people, it obviously becomes difficult to know exactly what trait should be examined. Although numerous traits have received research attention, we will discuss only a handful of traits found in consumer research because there just isn't enough space in this text to describe them all. We discuss value consciousness, materialism, innovativeness, need for cognition, competitiveness, and productivity orientation.

VALUE CONSCIOUSNESS

As we have stated throughout this text, value is at the heart of consumer behavior. Although all consumers ultimately seek value, some consumers are more highly focused on value than are others. As such, value consciousness is often studied as a trait. **Value consciousness** represents the tendency for consumers to focus on maximizing what is received from a transaction as compared to what is given.

Research reveals that value consciousness is an important concept in consumer behavior. For example, value consciousness underlies tendencies to perform behaviors like redeeming coupons.[14] Value-conscious consumers can be expected to pay close attention to the resources that they devote to transactions and to the benefits that they receive. In today's turbulent economy, value consciousness is an important trait to study.

MATERIALISM

Materialism refers to the extent to which material goods are important in a consumer's life. Most Western cultures are generally thought of as being relatively materialistic. However, within each culture, the degree to which each individual is materialistic varies. Studying this trait has been very popular among consumer researchers, and numerous studies have examined the impact of materialism on various consumer behaviors.

Materialism is seen as consisting of three separate dimensions:[15]

▸ *Possessiveness.* A tendency to retain control and ownership over possessions

▸ *Nongenerosity.* An unwillingness to share with others

▸ *Envy.* Resentment that arises as a result of another's belongings and a desire to acquire similar possessions

Giuseppe Costantino/Shutterstock.com

Highly materialistic consumers tend to be possessive, nongenerous, and envious of other's possessions. These consumers view possessions as a means of achieving happiness, and they may hold onto possessions as long as possible.[16] Research even indicates that materialistic people establish strong bonds with products in order to ease fears regarding their own mortality.[17] Products can be a real source of comfort for materialistic consumers. Given that materialism can have both positive and negative effects, marketers are advised to use caution when promoting a link between possessions and happiness.[18]

Interestingly, consumers today commonly bring many of their favorite material possessions into the workplace. Personal possessions in the workplace can produce calm feelings and stabilize an employee's sense of

self.[19] In this way, material possessions play an important part in self-expression. That is, material possessions help consumers express who they think they are, and even who they would like to be.[20]

Materialism tends to differ among generations, with lower materialism scores typically found among older consumers.[21] Indeed, younger consumers have long been thought of as relatively materialistic. A change in the prevalence of materialism does appear to be occurring, however. Although the U.S. culture is widely viewed as materialistic, research suggests that consumers are beginning to "downshift." Downshifting refers to a conscious decision to reduce one's material consumption. This may be a positive development as high levels of materialism can adversely affect debt levels and personal relationships.[22] The "great recession," which began in late 2007, also contributed to a growth in consumer *frugality*, or the extent to which consumers exhibit restraint when purchasing and using material goods.[23]

INNOVATIVENESS

Consumer **innovativeness** refers to the degree to which a consumer is open to new ideas and quick to adopt, buying new products, services, or experiences soon after they are introduced. Innovative consumers are also generally dynamic and curious, and they are often young, educated, and relatively affluent.[24] Because of how quickly new products are adopted worldwide in the era of social media, it is important to recognize the importance of innovativeness across cultures.[25] Obviously, consumer innovativeness is an important trait for marketers to consider when introducing new products.

Although researchers do not necessarily agree on the extent to which innovativeness is exhibited across product categories, a consumer with a strong degree of innovativeness may be expected to be innovative in a number of situations. For example, innovativeness has been shown to relate to a number of behaviors, including new product adoption, novelty seeking, information seeking, and online shopping.[26]

value consciousness the extent to which consumers tend to maximize what they receive from a transaction as compared to what they give

materialism extent to which material goods have importance in a consumer's life

innovativeness degree to which an individual is open to new ideas and tends to be relatively early in adopting new products, services, or experiences

PUT ME IN, COACH

You can take the dog out of a fight, but you can't take the fight out of a dog. That's an old saying, but it's true. And the saying comes to life each year for the thousands of sports fans who join fantasy camps in which they temporarily "become" professional football, baseball, or basketball players. Whether its attending a New York Yankees camp, a Kansas City Chiefs camp, or the 2017 Notre Dame football Fantasy Camp, there are dozens of opportunities to live out sports dreams.

Fantasy camp attendees can range in age from early adults to the elderly, and they often dish out thousands of dollars to play alongside the biggest names in the game. Even though their prime years are often long gone, the fire of competition still burns inside these consumers. Of course, many consumers join these fantasy camps just for fun. Who wouldn't want to play football against NFL talent? To other consumers, these camps represent competition at its best. It's a time to compete not only against other fans, but also against the best in the business. Competition is competition, and it doesn't matter if it's real or for fun. For highly competitive sports fans, the price of admission is well worth it, and the memories of competing against the world's best live on for a lifetime.

Vanessa Belfiore/Shutterstock.com

Sources: Pabst, Paul (2016), "The Best Mancation Fantasy Camps," www.travelchannel.com, online content retrieved at http://www.travelchannel.com/interests/mancations/articles/the-best-mancation-fantasy-camps, accessed February 8, 2016; Jessop, Alicia (2013), "Fantasy Basketball Camps Provide Millionaire Businessmen the Opportunity to Live the Life of College Basketball Players," Forbes.com, online content retrieved at http://www.forbes.com/sites/aliciajessop/2013/10/30/fantasy-basketball-camps-provide-millionaire-businessmen-the-opportunity-to-live-the-life-of-college-basketball-players/, accessed February 8, 2016; Ronca, Debra (2009), "How Sports Fantasy Camps Work," Howstuffworks.com, online content retrieved at http://adventure.howstuffworks.com/sports-fantasy-camp.htm, accessed February 8, 2016.

NEED FOR COGNITION

Need for cognition refers to the degree to which consumers tend to engage in effortful cognitive information processing.[27] Consumers who have a high degree of this trait tend to think carefully about products, problems, and even marketing messages. For example, research has shown that consumers with a high need for cognition tend to be influenced heavily by the quality of the arguments in an advertisement. Conversely, consumers with a low need for cognition tend to be influenced by things like an endorser's attractiveness and cues that are not central to a message.[28] Need for cognition also impacts how consumers react to event sponsorships, with high need for cognition consumers thinking more deeply about sponsorship fit.[29]

Research also indicates that the effect of humorous advertising is impacted by the need for cognition. Humorous ads tend to lead to more positive consumer attitudes and purchase intentions for consumers who have a low degree of need for cognition. Studies also indicate that the need for cognition trait influences consumers' reactions to ads with sexual content. For example, consumers with a low degree of need for cognition have exhibited more positive attitudes and purchase intentions toward brands that are advertised using sexual imagery than consumers with a high degree of need for cognition.[30]

COMPETITIVENESS

The **competitiveness** trait may be defined as an enduring tendency to strive to be better than others. The predominance of competitiveness in consumer society is easy to see, and the use of competitive themes in marketing messages is widespread.

need for cognition
refers to the degree to which consumers enjoy engaging in effortful cognitive information processing

competitiveness
enduring tendency to strive to be better than others

A competitive person is generally easy to identify; research reveals that the trait often emerges in the following ways:[31]

▶ **When a consumer is directly competing with others.** Online gaming has grown so rapidly that it is now featured on X Games and has its own professional league, Major League Gaming.

▶ **When a consumer enjoys winning vicariously through the efforts of others** (as when we enjoy seeing our team win). Sports fans often *bask in reflected glory* (BIRG) when their team wins. This means that they will wear team apparel and display team merchandise when their team is successful (As researchers point out, you hardly ever hear them say things like "They're number one!"[32]) Interestingly, fans may also CORF. That is, they *cut off reflected failure* by hiding their association with losing teams.

▶ **When a consumer attempts to display superiority over others by openly flaunting exclusive products,** especially publicly visible products. The term *conspicuous consumption* describes a tendency of the wealthy to flaunt their material possessions as a way of displaying their social class. Products ranging from automobiles to jewelry help to signal a consumer's status and can be used to convey images of consumer "superiority."

Source: MLG.TV

Online gaming is now featured on X Games and has its own professional league.

PRODUCTIVITY ORIENTATION

Productivity Orientation represents the tendency for consumers to focus on being productive, making progress, and accomplishing more in less time.[33] The pressure on consumers to be productive in their everyday life seems to be ever increasing. Consumers with a high degree of productivity orientation are able to be productive even when pursuing leisure activities. For example, researchers have found that this trait influences the tendency for consumers to pursue collectable experiences before

Exhibit 6.1

Examples of Other Traits in Consumer Research

Frugality	The tendency of a consumer to exhibit restraint when facing purchases and using resources
Trait Superstition	A tendency to follow superstitions and superstitious beliefs
Trait Impulsivity	A tendency to buy products and engage in experiences on impulse
Bargaining Proneness	The tendency for a consumer to engage in bargaining behaviors when making purchases
Trait Vanity	The tendency for consumers to take excessive pride in themselves, including their appearance and accomplishments

dying such as pursuing a list of places to visit or sampling a list of food or beers from around the world.[34] Having a strong productivity orientation affects one's bucket list!

OTHER TRAITS FOUND IN CONSUMER RESEARCH

It should be emphasized that the preceding traits represent only a small fraction of the many traits that have been investigated in consumer research. Exhibit 6.1 highlights other traits that are often studied. There are many, many more!

THE FIVE-FACTOR MODEL APPROACH

One of the most popular multiple-trait approaches found in both personality psychology and consumer research is the **five-factor model** (FFM) approach.[35] Numerous studies have examined the influence of the traits in the FFM on a wide range of behaviors, both inside and outside the field of consumer research. The FFM proposes that five

productivity orientation represents the tendency for consumers to focus on being productive, making progress, and accomplishing more in less time

five-factor model multiple-trait perspective that proposes that the human personality consists of five traits: agreeableness, extroversion, openness to experience (or creativity), conscientiousness, and neuroticism (or stability)

Exhibit 6.2

Five-Factor Model

Personality trait	Description
Extroversion	Talkative, outgoing
Agreeableness	Kindhearted, sympathetic
Openness to Experience	Creative, open to new ideas, imaginative
Stability	Even-keeled, avoids mood swings
Conscientiousness	Precise, efficient, organized

Source: Based on R. R. McCrae and P. T. Costa, *Personality in Adulthood: A Five-Factor Theory Perspective*, 2nd ed. (New York: Guilford, 2005).

dominant traits are found in the human personality, including:

1. Extroversion

2. Agreeableness

3. Openness to Experience (also referred to as *creativity*)

4. Stability (or Instability; sometimes referred to clinically as *neuroticism*)

5. Conscientiousness

Extroverted consumers are outgoing and talkative with others. Agreeable consumers are kindhearted to others and sympathetic. Creative consumers are imaginative and enjoy new ideas. Stable consumers tend to be able to control their emotions and avoid mood swings. Conscientious consumers are careful, orderly, and precise. These traits are presented in Exhibit 6.2.

As we have stated, the FFM approach is a multiple-trait approach, meaning that a consumer's personality is conceptualized as a *combination* of these traits and that each consumer will vary on the respective traits. For example, Joey might possess relatively strong degrees of extroversion, agreeableness, and openness, but he may not be very stable or conscientious. By examining consumers across the five dimensions of the FFM, we gain an expanded view of how multiple traits influence specific consumer behaviors.

The FFM approach is indeed popular with consumer researchers, and the traits found in the FFM have been shown to impact consumer behaviors such as complaining, bargaining,

hierarchical approaches to personality approaches to personality inquiry that assume that personality traits exist at varying levels of abstraction

banking, compulsive shopping, mass media consumption, and commitment to buying environmentally friendly products.

Even though the FFM has proved useful for presenting an integrative approach to personality, the model is not universally accepted by all researchers. In fact, there have been some lively debates regarding its usefulness.

HIERARCHICAL APPROACHES TO PERSONALITY TRAITS

If you are beginning to think that there are so many different approaches to trait psychology theory that it is hard to keep them all straight, you are not alone. Organizing all of these traits is one of the goals of what are known as **hierarchical approaches to personality**.

Hierarchical approaches begin with the assumption that personality traits exist at varying levels of abstraction. That is, some traits are specific (bargaining proneness), and others are more broad (extroversion). Specific traits refer to tendencies to behave in very well-defined situations. For example, a bargaining-prone consumer will bargain when shopping for products. Here, the situation is very specific. Broad traits refer to tendencies to behave across many different situations. For example, an extroverted consumer may be very outgoing when with friends, when in a restaurant, or when discussing a group project with classmates. As a general statement, specific traits tend to be better predictors of individual behaviors than broad traits. A number of researchers have argued for the existence of these hierarchies, with many suggesting that abstract traits influence more specific traits in a hierarchical fashion.[36]

FINAL THOUGHTS ON THE TRAIT APPROACH

The trait approach in consumer research is very popular today in large part due to its ability to objectively assign a personality trait score, from a survey for example, to a consumer. In this way, the approach has an advantage over the psychoanalytic approach, in which personality dimensions are assigned based on the psychologist's subjective interpretation. As mentioned earlier, marketers have gained the ability to interact one-on-one with consumers thanks to internet and smartphone technologies. This development has made it even more worthwhile for companies to understand individual difference variables like traits. We should emphasize, however, that the trait approach is not without criticism. Exhibit 6.3 reveals a number of criticisms that have been leveled against trait research.[37]

Exhibit 6.3

Criticisms of the Trait Approach

▶ Personality traits traditionally have not been shown to be strong predictors of consumer behavior relative to other explanatory variables.

▶ So many personality traits exist that researchers often select traits for study without any logical theoretical basis.

▶ Personality traits are sometimes hard to measure, and researchers often use measures with questionable validity.

▶ Personality inventories used to measure traits are often meant for use on specific populations, but they are frequently applied to practically any consumer group.

▶ Researchers often measure and use traits in ways not originally intended.

▶ Consumer traits generally do not predict specific brand selections.

PERSONOLOGY

We discussed previously that personality and motivation are closely related topics. A relatively new approach to researching consumers, which combines personality theory and motivation, is the "personology" approach. This approach allows consumer researchers to better understand the uniqueness of the individual consumer by combining information on traits, goals, and even consumer life stories.[38]

As you can see, many ways to view the human personality exist, and several different approaches to exploring the influence of personality on consumer behavior have been used. Personality inquiry, while controversial and not without limitations, continues to be a fruitful avenue of research for consumer researchers.

Exhibit 6.4

Brand Personality Dimensions

Personality trait	Description	Example
Competence	Responsible, reliable, dependable	Maytag—"Depend on Us"
Excitement	Daring, spirited	Monster Energy —"Unleash the Beast"
Ruggedness	Tough, strong	Ford Trucks—"Built Ford Tough"
Sincerity	Honest, genuine	Wrangler Jeans—"Genuine. Wrangler"
Sophistication	Glamorous, charming	Cartier jewelry—"Brilliance, Elegance, Exuberance"

Source: Based on Jennifer Aaker, "Dimensions of Brand Personality," *Journal of Marketing Research* (August 1997): 347–56.

6-2b Brand Personality

Do brands have personalities? This question may sound a bit strange at first, but upon reflection, consumers do describe brands with human-like qualities. How would you describe the personality of Fox News? How is Spencer's different from JCP?

Marketing managers and consumer researchers alike are very interested in the "personalities" of products. Brand personality refers to human characteristics that can be associated with a brand.[39] Brand personalities can be described across five dimensions including competence, excitement, ruggedness, sincerity, and sophistication. These dimensions are described in Exhibit 6.4.

Brand personalities represent opportunities for companies to differentiate their products. Accordingly, a brand's personality may be viewed as a part of its overall image.[40] Brand personalities also provide marketers with opportunities to build strong brand relationships with consumers, especially when they have an understanding of their customer's personality.[41] A well-known Old Spice campaign says "Smell Like a Man, Man," signifying how the products relate to this overall image. Hallmark cards may be seen as sincere and trustworthy. Guess is considered to be sophisticated clothing, and Mercedes-Benz is a sophisticated automobile. Recent research indicates that the brand personality concept applies to sports teams as well.[42]

FORMATION OF BRAND PERSONALITY

Many factors contribute to the development of a brand's personality.[43] You can infer certain qualities from a product's category. For example, if you hear

brand personality collection of human characteristics that can be associated with a brand

Personality Apps

Given that there are now apps for practically everything, it is probably not too surprising that dozens of personality apps have popped up. Consumers today can download these apps and gain recommendations for daily living based on their personality profiles.

From learning how to excel at work (e.g., Talenttoday Personality Test) to how to manage finances (e.g., Money Personality Test) to how to select a dream city to live in (e.g., What's Your City Personality?), dozens of apps that match personality profiles to consumer decisions are now widely available. And the apps appear to be very popular. It seems that consumers are more than willing to have their personalities analyzed by answering a very few personality-related questions in the hope of making better marketplace decisions. This is especially true for Millennials. These consumers are,

Melpomene/Shutterstock.com

after all, often looking for ways to excel in their careers, to manage money, and to select their dream locales. Millennials also tend to seek the products, services, and jobs that best match their own unique qualities. Time will tell if these apps continue to gain popularity, but for now, matching personality to important decisions can be as simple as a quick app download.

---

the name *Sampson, Whitten, and Taylor* and find out that it is a law firm, you may develop an idea that the firm is serious, professional, and competent. In order for the perceived personality to match the intended personality that is promoted, managers should be sure to present a strong concept, differentiate the product well, create credible messages about the brand, involve the consumer to a high degree, and generate a positive attitude toward the brand.[44]

BRAND PERSONALITY APPEAL

The brand personality concept has proven to be valuable for both consumer researchers and marketers alike. However, current research reveals that understanding a brand's personality is not enough. Rather, the appeal of the brand's personality should be considered. **Brand personality appeal** refers to a brand's ability to appeal to consumers based on the human characteristics associated with it.[45] A brand's personality should be perceived as having strong degrees of *favorability*, *originality*, and *clarity*. When consumers view a brand's personality

brand personality appeal a product's ability to appeal to consumers based on the human characteristics associated with it

in these terms, they are more likely to purchase the brand in question.

PERSONALITY AND BRAND RELATIONSHIPS

The brand personality concept is especially important when one considers that consumers, to a certain extent, have relationships with brands, and that personality traits are important in the formation and maintenance of these relationships.[46] To illustrate, Coca-Cola's sincere and traditional personality enables the Coca-Cola Company to easily remind consumers that the brand always has been and always will be a part of their lives. In fact, "Always Coca-Cola" is one of Coke's best-known advertising campaigns. A clearly defined brand personality and a strong brand personality appeal help with consumer–brand relationship formation.

The concept of consumer–brand relationships has received considerable research attention. Several factors help indicate the level of relationship between a consumer and a brand. Consumer researcher Susan Fournier proposes that the overall quality of such relationships can be explained by:

▶ **Love and Passion.** A consumer may have such strong feelings about a brand that they actually describe

A brand's personality is an important part of its image.

it with the term *love*. A consumer may say, "I love my Fitbit" or "I love 'Very Sexy' cologne." Service employees play a part in the formation of brand love.[47]

▸ **Self-Connection.** Brands may help to express some central component of a consumer's identity. Research indicates that the correct match between consumer and brand personality leads to higher overall satisfaction.[48]

▸ **Commitment.** In a strong consumer–brand relationship, consumers are very committed to their brands and feel very loyal to them. Miss Me clothing owners are well-known for their commitment to the brand.

▸ **Interdependence.** Consumer–brand relationships may be marked by interdependence between the product and consumer. This can be described in terms of the frequency of use, the diversity of brand-related situations, and the intensity of usage. Consumers are often reminded that "Like a good neighbor, State Farm is there."

▸ **Intimacy.** Strong relationships between consumers and brands can be described as intimate. Deep-seated needs and desires of consumers can be tied directly to specific brands. For example, a need for intimacy and passion can be directly tied to a specific brand of perfume or Victoria's Secret apparel.

▸ **Brand Partner Quality.** In general, brands that are perceived to be of high quality contribute to the formation of consumer–brand relationships. In this sense, consumers develop feelings of trust regarding specific brands, and these feelings of trust foster consumer–brand relationships. Brand personality traits also affect relationship quality when service problems occur, with sincere brands suffering more than exciting brands.[49]

6-3 CONSUMER LIFESTYLES, PSYCHOGRAPHICS, AND DEMOGRAPHICS

Consumer lifestyles, psychographics, and demographics are all important variables that highlight differences between consumers. Many consumer research companies focus nearly exclusively on these variables because they give very good information regarding consumer behavior. Each of the concepts is discussed below.

6-3a Lifestyles

The term *lifestyle* is used commonly in everyday life. For example, we often speak of healthy lifestyles, unhealthy lifestyles, alternative lifestyles, and even dangerous lifestyles. The word has also been used in many ways in consumer research. Stated simply, **lifestyles** refer to the ways consumers live and spend their time and money.

Personality and lifestyles are closely related topics. In fact, lifestyles may be referred to as context-specific personality traits. This has implications for how the concepts are measured. That is, instead of asking a consumer if she is an "outdoor type," a lifestyle approach will ask the consumer about the amount of time she spends outdoors and what she does when she is outdoors. Importantly, lifestyles aren't completely determined by personality. Instead, they emerge from the influence of culture, groups, and individual processes, including personality.[50] Not surprisingly, consumer lifestyles vary considerably across cultures.

Lifestyles have proved extremely valuable to marketers and others interested in predicting behavior. Purchase patterns are often influenced by consumer lifestyles, and numerous lifestyle categories can be identified. It shouldn't be surprising, therefore, that marketers often target consumers based on lifestyles. For example, "Beats by Dr. Dre" has been aimed at active, young consumers, and "Body by Vi" appeals to the health-conscious market. Because lifestyle can be directly tied to product purchase and consumption, consumer lifestyles are considered an important manifestation of social stratification.[51] In other words, they are very useful in identifying viable market segments. Appealing to a consumer's lifestyle is so important that it's not uncommon to see advertisements focusing as much on lifestyle as on the actual product or service itself.

lifestyles distinctive modes of living, including how people spend their time and money

6-3b Psychographics

The term **psychographics** refers to the way consumer lifestyles are measured. Psychographic techniques use quantitative methods that can be used in developing lifestyle profiles. Psychographic research has been used to investigate lifestyles for many years, and advances in technology have helped psychographics become very popular with consumer researchers. Psychographic analysis involves surveying consumers using **AIO statements** to gain an understanding of consumers' activities, interests, and opinions. These measurements can be narrowly defined (as relating to a specific product or category) or broadly defined (as pertaining to activities that the consumer enjoys).

Consumer segments very often contain consumers with similar lifestyles. Although the categorization of segments is rarely based on consumer behavior theory, the process can be very helpful in identifying marketing opportunities. As an example, one effort to identify segments in the European tourism industry resulted in the following lifestyle segment profiles:[52]

▶ **Home Loving.** Fundamentally focused on the family, this segment values product quality. These consumers enjoy cultural activities such as visiting art exhibits and monuments. The home-loving group takes the greatest number of long, family-oriented travel vacations.

▶ **Idealistic.** These responsible consumers believe that the road to success is based on bettering the world. They enjoy classical music and theater and travel to destinations that include rural locations and country villages.

▶ **Autonomous.** These independent-thinking consumers strive to be upwardly mobile. They enjoy the nightlife and read few newspapers. This segment enjoys weekend travel.

▶ **Hedonistic.** The hedonistic segment values human relationships and work. They are interested in new product offerings and enjoy listening to music. These consumers enjoy visiting large cities.

psychographics
quantitative investigation of consumer lifestyles

AIO statements activity, interest, and opinion statements that are used in lifestyle studies

▶ **Conservative.** Like the home-loving segment, this segment focuses largely on the family. These consumers tend to view success simply in terms of their work careers. This group dislikes nightlife and modern music and instead focuses on issues related to religion, law, and order.

Psychographic profiles of various other consumer groups have resulted in lifestyle segments such as: Harley-Davidson owners (including "cocky misfits" and "classy capitalists"), wine drinkers (including "conservatives," "experimenters," and "image oriented"), Porsche owners (including "top guns," "elitists," and "fantasists"), and health, wellness, and sustainability focused consumers (including "lifestyle of health and sustainability").[53] There are numerous ways in which to segment consumers based on lifestyles.

SPECIFICITY OF LIFESTYLE SEGMENTS

The lifestyle approaches that we have discussed here can be categorized in terms of specificity—either narrowly defined or more broadly defined. Generally, lifestyles are very specific. The magazine industry is particularly efficient at identifying consumer lifestyles and targeting advertising messages at them. For example, "recessionistas" are women who don't let hard economic times get in the way of fashion. In fact, recessionistas often pride themselves on thrifty fashion.

Paul Matthew Photography/Shutterstock.com

Recessionistas don't let hard times get in the way of fashion.

VALS

When using lifestyle segmentation, marketers can either identify their own segments or use established methods that are already available. One popular method in consumer research is the VALS™ approach.[54] Developed and marketed by Strategic Business Insights, VALS is a very successful segmentation approach that has been adopted by several companies. VALS stands for "Values and Lifestyles." VALS classifies consumers into eight distinct segments based on resources available to the consumer (including financial, educational, and intellectual resources), as well as three primary motivations (ideals motivation, achievement motivation, and self-expression motivation). The VALS segments are presented in Exhibit 6.5.

Exhibit 6.5

VALS Segments

▸ **Innovators.** Innovators are successful, sophisticated people who have high self-esteem. They are motivated by achievement, ideals, and self-expression. Image is important to these consumers.

▸ **Thinkers.** Thinkers are ideal motivated. They are mature, reflective people who value order and knowledge. They have relatively high incomes and are conservative, practical consumers.

▸ **Achievers.** Achievers have an achievement motivation and are politically conservative. Their lives largely center around church, family, and career. Image is important to this group, and they prefer to purchase prestige products.

▸ **Experiencers.** Experiencers are self-expressive consumers who tend to be young, impulsive, and enthusiastic. These consumers value novelty and excitement.

▸ **Believers.** In some ways, believers are like thinkers. They are ideal motivated and conservative. They follow routines, and their lives largely center around home, family, and church. They do not have the amount of resources that thinkers have, however.

▸ **Strivers.** Strivers are achievement motivated, but they do not have the amount of resources that are available to achievers. For strivers, shopping is a way to demonstrate to others their ability to buy.

▸ **Makers.** Makers are like experiencers in that they are motivated by self-expression. They have fewer resources than experiencers. They tend to express themselves through their activities, such as raising children, fixing cars, and building houses.

▸ **Survivors.** Survivors are very low on resources and are constricted by this lack of resources. They tend to be elderly consumers who are concerned with health issues and who believe that the world is changing too quickly. They are not active in the marketplace, as their primary concerns center around safety, family, and security.

PRIZM

Another popular tool for lifestyle analysis is a geodemographic procedure known as PRIZM®.[55] **Geodemographic techniques** combine data on consumer expenditures and socioeconomic variables with geographic information in order to identify commonalities in consumption patterns of households in various regions. PRIZM is a popular lifestyle analysis technique that is marketed by Nielsen Claritas. PRIZM, which stands for Potential Ratings Index by ZIP Market, is based on the premise that people with similar backgrounds and means tend to live close to one another and emulate each other's behaviors and lifestyles.

PRIZM combines demographic and behavioral information in a manner that enables marketers to better understand and target their customers. The technique uses 66 different segments as descriptors of individual households, which are ranked according to socioeconomic variables. Segments found using the PRIZM technique include "Movers and Shakers," "Money and Brains," "Red, White and Blues," and "Back Country Folks." There are other geodemographic techniques available as well, including ESRI's GIS and Mapping Software.

6-3c Demographics

Demographics refer to observable, statistical aspects of populations, including such factors as age, gender, or income. Notice that this is very different from either lifestyles or psychographics. The study of demographics is known as *demography*. Demographic variables include age, ethnicity, family size, occupation, and sometimes income.

Age. Age is important not only because of its descriptive nature, but also because consumers who experience significant life events at approximately the same age are influenced greatly by the events. This is the "cohort effect." Groups such as "Generation Y" or "Millennials" (born between 1981 and 1995), "Generation X" (born between 1965 and 1980), "Baby Boomers" (born between 1946 and 1964), and "The Greatest Generation" (born prior to

VALS popular psychographic method in consumer research that divides consumers into groups based on resources and consumer behavior motivations

geodemographic techniques techniques that combine data on consumer expenditures and socioeconomic variables with geographic information in order to identify commonalities in consumption patterns of households in various regions

PRIZM popular geodemographic technique that stands for Potential Ratings Index by ZIP Market

demographics observable, statistical aspects of populations such as age, gender, or income

Demographics are important, but they don't always tell the whole story.

© spotmatik/Shutterstock.com

1946) are identifiable segments. Baby Boomers receive a lot of attention because of the group's size and spending power. Gen Z consumers, born between 1996 and 2010, are gaining the attention of marketers, as this group shows distinct differences from their predecessors.

Ethnicity. Diversity is growing in the United States. Minority groups (such as Hispanics, African Americans, and Asian Americans) are expected to grow considerably in the years to come. In fact, projections reveal that by 2050, the "minority" segment will exceed more than half of the total population.

Income. Income is another important variable. Although it is often discussed in terms of socioeconomic variables, we include it here because it is often present in several popular demographic publications such as the U.S. Census. Income obviously affects consumer behavior in numerous ways. Engel's Law states that as income increases, a smaller percentage of expenditure is devoted to food, and the percentage devoted to consumption rises slower than the rise in income.

Demographics can be used in conjunction with psychographic analysis. In fact, demographics can be used to help locate and understand lifestyle segments. Failing to consider psychographic measures leads to the trap of assuming that all consumers of a certain demographic have the exact same tastes. An example is

self-concept totality of thoughts and feelings that an individual has about himself or herself

symbolic interactionism perspective that proposes that consumers live in a symbolic environment and interpret the myriad of symbols around them, and that members of a society agree on the meanings of symbols

semiotics study of symbols and their meanings

found in the concept of "psychological age." A person's actual age and his or her psychological age can be very different. As some have said, "today's sixty is yesterday's forty."

DEMOGRAPHICS AND THE ONLINE WORLD

Changes in perspectives on demographic segmentation are often attributed to the world of social media. For example, researchers are beginning to note that traditional strategies based on demographic segmentation may not be useful when consumers around the world have easy access to new information and products. This is similar in some ways to the concept of psychological age. Consumers from many different age groups can try products and enjoy experiences that may not follow traditional ideas about their age or demographic group. This is not to say that demographic analysis is not important; rather, the point is that traditional views about how to segment on demographics may be changing. This issue is discussed in more detail in another chapter.[56]

 6-4

THE ROLE OF SELF-CONCEPT IN CONSUMER BEHAVIOR

The self-concept is another important topic in consumer behavior. The term **self-concept** refers to the totality of thoughts and feelings that an individual has about him- or herself. Self-concept can also be thought of as the way a person defines or gives meaning to his or her own identity, as in a type of self-schema.

Consumers are motivated to act in accordance with their self-concepts. As such, consumers often use products as ways of revealing their self-concepts to others. According to a **symbolic interactionism** perspective, consumers agree on the shared meaning of products and symbols.[57] These symbols can become part of the self-concept if the consumer identifies with them strongly.

An important field of study that relates to the symbolic interactionism approach is semiotics. **Semiotics** refers to the study of symbols and their meanings. As we have stated, consumers use products as symbols to convey their self-concepts to others. In this sense, products are an essential part of self-expression.[58] Popular websites like Pinterest, Instagram, and Twitter give consumers easy ways of expressing themselves.[59]

Let's first explore various dimensions of the self before examining how a consumer's self-concept influences various behaviors. First, we note that a consumer will have a number of "concepts" about himself that may emerge over time and surface in different social situations.[60] A few of the different self-concepts that may emerge include the actual self, the ideal self, the social self, the ideal social self, the possible self, and the extended self.[61]

The *actual self* refers to how consumers currently perceives themselves (that is, who I am). The *ideal self* refers to how consumers would like to perceive themselves (that is, who I would like to be in the future). The *social self* refers to the beliefs that consumers have about how they are seen by others. The social self is also called the "looking-glass" self because it denotes the image that a consumer has when she looks into the mirror and imagines how others see her. The *ideal social self* represents the image that a consumer would like others to have about her. The *possible self*, much like the ideal self, presents an image of what the consumer could become, whereas the *extended self* represents the various possessions that a consumer owns that help him form perceptions about himself. The virtual world has given consumers more options for expressing themselves. This is discussed in the "It's Just a Selfie" box feature.

The relationship between consumer self-concept and product consumption is a two-way street. That is, consumers express their self-concepts by purchasing and displaying various products, while products help to define how they see themselves.[62] Note that the relationship between the self-concept and consumption is not limited to adult consumers only, as consumer–brand connections have been shown to form as early as childhood.[63]

6-4a Self-Concept and Body Presentation

The issue of self-concept in consumer behavior has several practical implications. For example, the cosmetics and weight-loss industries are well-known for offering products that purportedly help improve one's self-image. The term **self-esteem** refers to the positivity of an individual's self-concept. The effect of advertising on consumers' self-esteem is an important consumer research topic and one that has often been overlooked.[64]

The fashion industry is often criticized for promoting overly thin models and body types. Research confirms that consumers compare their bodies with those of models in advertisements, and that these comparisons can have harmful effects. This is particularly the case for young females.[65] **Body esteem** refers to the positivity with which people hold their body image.[66] Low body esteem can result in a number of negative behaviors and attitudes.

In response to growing public concern regarding this issue, the Council of Fashion Designers of America (CFDA) updated guidelines to encourage healthy eating habits and to discourage the use of overly thin models in advertisements. "The fashion business should be sensitive

Unrealistic body images affect consumers' self-esteem.

to the fact that we do have a responsibility in affecting young girls and their self-image," CFDA president Diane von Furstenberg commented.[67] The problem is not solely for women, however, as evidence suggests that male consumers are also affected by unrealistic body imagery in advertising.[68] Although the industry has received much negative publicity, not all model effects are negative. Consumers can feel better about themselves when they find similarities between their bodies and those of models.[69]

Unilever Corp. addressed the issue of unrealistic body types with their Real Beauty campaign for the brand Dove. The campaign seeks to provide more realistic views of beauty and to improve the self-esteem of both women and young girls.

COSMETIC SURGERY AND BODY MODIFICATION

Because of the many ways consumers compare themselves to others, it is easy to understand why many medical procedures that promise to improve consumers' perceptions of their bodies are now available. According to the American Society for Aesthetic Plastic surgery, there were over 15.9 million cosmetic procedures performed in the United States in 2015, and there was an upward trend in the percentage of procedures performed. In fact, there was a 2% increase in procedures during 2015 over the previous year. Consumers spend billions each year on cosmetic procedures, with popular procedures including

self-esteem positivity of the self-concept that one holds

body esteem positivity with which people hold their body image

It goes without saying that consumers are constantly posting photos and videos to popular apps like Instagram, Vine, and Snapchat. Facebook also remains popular, though its popularity with young consumers has decreased somewhat. Selfies have become quite the rage with consumers, as evidenced by the word *selfie* being named the Oxford Word of the Year in 2013. Consumer researchers often refer to the virtual aspect of the self as the "digital self."

What's wrong with posting some selfies? Well, usually, there's really nothing wrong. However, researchers are starting to uncover some darker sides to the selfie phenomenon. For example, studies have indicated that posting numerous selfies is related to high levels of narcissism and psychopathy. Furthermore, the popularity of selfies has led to an increase in the number of people seeking plastic and cosmetic surgery in order to look

better online. Also, people have been killed taking dangerous selfies, such as when they are standing in front of trains or even on cliffs. Suicide rates are also beginning to be attributed to social media postings, including selfies, by young people. It seems that consumers can become so fixated on the "likes" of other people that their own sense of self gets lost between the real and the virtual world.

9george/Shutterstock.com

Sources: Anonymous (2016)," New 2015 Stats: Face of Plastic Surgery Goes Younger Due to Growing Social Media and Reality TV Influence on Millennials (Press Release)," *American Academy of Facial Plastic and Reconstructive Surgery, Inc.,* https://www.aafprs.org/media/press-release/20160114.html; Fox, J., and Rooney, M.C. (2015), "The Dark Triad and Trait Self-Objectification as Predictors of Men's Use and Self-Presentation Behaviors on Social Networking Sites," *Personality & Individual Differences,* 76, 161–165; Basu, Tanya (2016), "How Selfie-Related Deaths Happen," *CNN.com,* February 11, 2016, online content retrieved at http://www.cnn.com/2016/02/11/health/death-by-selfie/, accessed February 15, 2016.

---

liposuction, breast augmentation, abdominoplasty, eyelid surgery, and face lifts. A relatively new trend is the increase in the popularity of buttock augmentation. Women tend to have more procedures than men, but more and more men are opting for cosmetic surgery. Most procedures tend to be performed on consumers aged 35–54.[70]

BODY PIERCINGS AND TATTOOS

Body piercings and other forms of body decorations, such as tattoos, represent other methods of promoting one's self-concept. Estimates vary widely, with one study revealing that as many as 51% of teenagers and young adults have some form of body piercing. The same estimates reveal that up to 14% of the general population have body piercings. Interestingly, piercings tend to be more popular with female consumers than with male consumers.[71] The growth in body art suggests that new attitudes about the body's role in self-presentation are emerging.[72]

While body piercings are popular forms of self-expression and are frequently used as innocent methods of self-expression, research also indicates that the use of piercings can sometimes be associated with increased levels of drug and alcohol use, unprotected sexual activity, trait anxiety,

self-congruency theory
theory that proposes that much of consumer behavior can be explained by the congruence of a consumer's self-concept with the image of typical users of a focal product

and depression.[73] Consumers also form impressions of employees who have tattoos and piercings, and these perceptions may impact how they view organizations with such employees.[74] For consumers, body piercings and tattoos have become more popular than ever.

6-5 SELF-CONGRUENCY THEORY AND CONSUMER BEHAVIOR

Reference group members share symbolic meanings. This is an assumption of **self-congruency theory**, which proposes that behavior can be explained by the congruence (match) between a consumer's self-concept and the image of typical users of a focal product.[75] For example, one study found that store loyalty is influenced by the congruency between self-image and store image.[76] Another study found that passengers on a cruise ship rated their experience based on the congruence between their self-image and their images of other passengers.[77]

6-5a Segmentation and Self-Congruency

Marketers can use congruency theory by segmenting markets into groups of consumers who perceive high self-concept congruence with product-user image. Imagine a consumer who sees himself as being a stylish person. If he believes that people who drive Corvettes are stylish, then he will be motivated to drive a Corvette. In this way, brands become vehicles for self-expression.

As discussed earlier, there are several types of self-concepts, and different products may relate to each concept. That is, one product may relate quite well to the actual self-concept, but not as strongly to the ideal self-concept. One study found that the purchase of privately consumable items (such as frozen dinners or suntan lotion) is heavily influenced by the actual self-concept, while the purchase of publicly visible products (like clothing) is more strongly related to the ideal self-concept.[78]

A popular advertising campaign for Ford trucks illustrates the role of self-congruency theory in marketing. The successful ad campaign, which centers on the "Built Ford Tough" theme, sends the message that if you are a hardworking man you need a hardworking truck like Ford. Rolex watches are well-known for being watches for people who have arrived or who soon will be "arriving."

CONSUMER IDENTITY AND PRODUCT OWNERSHIP

Beyond consumer–product congruity, some consumers view brands much more intensely. Given the many ways in which consumers use and display brands, some researchers suggest that brands are used to express and validate *consumer identity*. For these consumers, the task of self-expression through product ownership is one of identity maintenance and communication. This occurs when the consumer believes that the brand expresses his or her identity. The classic "I'm a Pepper" advertising slogan for Dr. Pepper is a good example. Research indicates that consumers also consider the match between their values and a brand's values. When there is congruency between a consumer's values and the values of a brand, consumer identification is strengthened. This finding highlights how congruency theory plays a role in consumer identification.[79]

A Green Bay fan shows his Packers tattoo before an NFL game.

ORGANIZATIONAL IDENTIFICATION

Consumers also form close associations with companies and organizations. When consumers feel very close to organizations, *organizational identification* is said to be present.[80] For consumers, the organization becomes a vehicle for self-expression, and for organizations, consumer loyalty and commitment become quite strong. Identifying with an organization also helps consumers to forge stronger social identities.[81] Consumer and organizational identification illustrate the important role that products and organizations can play in the expression of the self. Extending our discussions of tattoos, some consumers become so closely identified with organizations and their brands that they tattoo themselves with brand names and logos.

FINAL THOUGHT ON PERSONALITY, LIFESTYLES, AND THE SELF-CONCEPT

Personality, lifestyles, and the self-concept are all important topics in the study of consumer behavior. Consumers differ across each of these concepts, and these differences help signal the need for targeted marketing communications. As technological advancements continue to develop, it can be expected that consumer researchers and marketing managers alike will continue to be interested in these topics.

STUDY TOOLS 6

LOCATED AT BACK OF THE TEXTBOOK
☐ Tear out Chapter Review Card

LOCATED AT WWW.CENGAGE.COM/LOGIN
☐ Review Key Term flashcards and create your own cards
☐ Track your knowledge and understanding of key concepts in consumer behavior
☐ Complete practice quizzes to prepare for tests
☐ Complete interactive content within CB Online
☐ Review the Chapter Highlight boxes for CB Online

7 | Attitudes and Attitude Change

LEARNING OBJECTIVES

After studying this chapter, the student should be able to:

7-1 Define attitudes and describe attitude components.

7-2 Describe the functions of attitudes.

7-3 Understand how the hierarchy of effects concept applies to attitude theory.

7-4 Comprehend the major consumer attitude models.

7-5 Describe attitude change theories and their role in persuasion.

7-6 Understand how message and source effects influence persuasion.

Cakes and Cupcakes Mumbai

Remember to visit **PAGE 151** for additional **STUDY TOOLS**

INTRODUCTION

So, do you still "like" Facebook? That seems to be the question these days as studies show that Facebook has lost popularity among both Millennial and Gen Z consumers.[1] What about Twitter? Do you send a lot of tweets? Or is Twitter getting old? What about Instagram? Do you like to use it? Is it fun to send photos on Snapchat?

Of course, there are tons of other sites and apps out there. Some of those apps you might like and some of them you might not like at all. If you like them, you probably use them. If you don't like them, you probably don't use them.

Getting consumers to feel positively about products and services is something that marketers constantly try to achieve. When consumers have positive attitudes toward products, they often promote them to others. Have you ever told a friend about a new app? Chances are that you have. This is a win-win situation for both a customer and a company. Conversely,

negative attitudes can have a profound impact as well. Some people become so upset with a company and its products that they boycott everything the company sells—and tell others that they should do the same.

Consumers tend to have strong attitudes and opinions about social issues and trends as well. Do you like vaping? Or do you hate it when people vape? Are you in favor of increased gun control or opposed to it? Do you believe in capitalism or socialism? Of course, the first question doesn't seem like a big deal, but the last two have political implications.

Understanding the factors that influence consumer attitudes is very important for marketers. This may seem obvious for companies, but consumer attitudes are important in nontraditional settings as well. For example, politicians want to know how voters *feel* about candidates and issues. City managers want to know if citizens *believe* that a new construction project is a good idea. Policy makers want consumers to stop the dangerous behavior of texting and driving. Consumer attitudes are important in

each of these examples as they highlight three important components of attitudes: feelings, beliefs, and behaviors.

7-1 ATTITUDES AND ATTITUDE COMPONENTS

The term *attitude* has been used in many ways. **Attitudes** are relatively enduring overall evaluations of objects, products, services, issues, or people.[2] Attitudes play a critical role in consumer behavior. They are particularly important because they motivate people to behave in relatively consistent ways. It shouldn't be surprising that attitudes are among the most researched topics in the entire field of consumer research, and in fact, in all of the social sciences.

Attitudes and value are closely related. In general, consumers have positive attitudes toward products that deliver value. Likewise, when products deliver poor value, consumer attitudes are usually negative. In order to understand how attitudes influence consumer behavior,

Do you like vaping or do you hate it?

we need to distinguish between the components of attitudes and the functions that attitudes perform.

attitudes relatively enduring overall evaluations of objects, products, services, issues, or people

7-1a Components of Attitude

According to the **ABC approach to attitudes**, attitudes possess three components: *affect*, *behavior*, and *cognitions*. *Affect* refers to feelings about an object and *cognitions*, as used here, refer to beliefs that the consumer has about the object. *Behavior* refers to the overt behavior that consumers exhibit as well as their intentions to behave. To understand these components, consider the following statements:

- ▶ "I like Snapchat."
- ▶ "I always look at Snapchats my friends send me."
- ▶ "Sending Snapchat videos is a good way for me to stay connected with friends."

These statements reflect the three components of a consumer's attitude found in the ABC approach. "I like Snapchat" is a statement of affect because it describes the feelings, or affection, a consumer has about the app. "I always look at Snapchats my friends send me" refers to one's behavior regarding the app. "Sending Snapchat videos is a good way for me to stay connected with friends" is a cognitive statement that expresses the belief that the app helps one connect with friends.

7-2 FUNCTIONS OF ATTITUDES

Knowing that attitudes represent relatively enduring evaluations of products, and that attitudes can be broken into three components, is valuable. But what do attitudes do for the consumer? That might sound like a strange question, but understanding the functions of attitudes gives marketers an opportunity to develop better promotional messages.

According to the **functional theory of attitudes**, attitudes perform four functions.[3] The four functions are the *utilitarian* function, the *knowledge* function, the *value-expressive* function, and the *ego-defensive* function. These functions are summarized in Exhibit 7.1.

7-2a Utilitarian Function

The **utilitarian function of attitudes** is based on the concept of reward and punishment. This means that consumers learn to use attitudes as ways to maximize rewards and minimize punishment. Buying a product because it delivers a specific benefit is one example of the utilitarian function of attitudes. The consumer is rewarded through a desired product benefit. For example, many high school boys pay a lot of attention to the brands of clothing they wear. By wearing the right clothes, they are able to feel as though they fit in with the expectations of others. Consumers can reap social rewards through expressing attitudes, and they often express their attitudes as an attempt to develop or maintain relationships. A study of college sports fans presents an example. In the study, football fans revealed that one of the many reasons they wear their team's apparel is to fit in and make connections with new friends.[4]

ABC approach to attitudes approach that suggests that attitudes encompass one's affect, behavior, and cognitions (or beliefs) toward an object

functional theory of attitudes theory of attitudes that suggests that attitudes perform four basic functions

utilitarian function of attitudes function of attitudes in which consumers use attitudes as ways to maximize rewards and minimize punishment

---

Exhibit 7.1

Functions of Consumer Attitudes

Attitude function	Description	Example
Utilitarian	Attitudes are used as a method to obtain rewards and to minimize punishment.	High school boys wear cool brands so they fit in.
Knowledge	The knowledge function of attitudes allows consumers to simplify their decision-making processes.	A consumer is very loyal to Apple products and believes that they are best, thereby simplifying their search efforts.
Value-expressive	This function of attitudes enables consumers to express their core values, self-concept, and beliefs to others.	A consumer supports Greenpeace because he places much value on environmentalism.
Ego-defensive	The ego-defensive function of attitudes works as a defense mechanism for consumers to avoid facts or to defend themselves from their own low self-concept.	Smokers discount information that suggests that smoking is bad for their health.

7-2b Knowledge Function

The **knowledge function of attitudes** allows consumers to simplify decision-making processes. For example, consumers may not like credit card offers because they want to stay out of debt. The decision to shred the offers would then be easy. Attitudes perform the important function of helping consumers avoid undesirable situations and approach more desirable situations. They also help consumers select objects that they do like. Brand loyalty is important here. It is usually much easier to repurchase a product that you know you like than it is to try a new one. Attitude components become stored in the associated network in consumers' long-term memory and become linked together to form rules that guide behavior. Here, we can see again that attitudes are linked to comprehension and knowledge.

7-2c Value-Expressive Function

The **value-expressive function of attitudes** is found in a number of consumer settings. This function enables consumers to express their core values, self-concept, and beliefs to others. Accordingly, this function of attitude provides a positive expression of the type of person a consumer perceives herself to be and the values that she holds. For example, consumers who believe in the protection of the environment might support a group like Greenpeace. It is easy to learn about consumers' values by looking at the bumper stickers they place on their cars, the posters that place in their apartments, and the types of T-shirts they wear.

7-2d Ego-Defensive Function

The **ego-defensive function of attitudes** works as a defense mechanism for consumers. There are a couple of ways in which this function works. First, the ego-defensive function enables consumers to protect themselves from information that may be threatening. For example, people who like to smoke may discount evidence that smoking is bad for their health. In this case, the attitude works as a defense mechanism that protects the individual from the reality that smoking isn't healthy.

Another example of the ego-defensive function is when consumers develop positive attitudes toward products that enhance their self-image. Many college-aged male students wear athletic apparel to enhance their image of being in shape and active. This function also works as a protection mechanism. For some consumers this behavior compensates for a general feeling

Brand loyalty is associated with the knowledge function of attitudes.

of being out of shape, thereby protecting the ego and self-image.

 ## 7-3 HIERARCHY OF EFFECTS

Research indicates that the three components of attitudes may be formed in a sequential pattern. This process is known as the **hierarchy of effects**.[5] According to this approach, affect, behavior, and cognitions (beliefs) form by following one of four hierarchies:

1. **High-involvement (or "standard learning") hierarchy**
2. **Low-involvement hierarchy**
3. **Experiential hierarchy**
4. **Behavioral influence hierarchy**

These hierarchies are discussed in the next section and presented in Exhibit 7.2.

knowledge function of attitudes function of attitudes whereby attitudes allow consumers to simplify decision-making processes

value-expressive function of attitudes function of attitudes whereby attitudes allow consumers to express their core values, self-concept, and beliefs to others

ego-defensive function of attitudes function of attitudes whereby attitudes work as a defense mechanism for consumers

hierarchy of effects attitude approach that suggests that affect, behavior, and cognitions form in a sequential order

Exhibit 7.2

Hierarchy of Effects

Purchase context	Hierarchy of effects
High involvement	Cognition—affect—behavior
Low involvement	Cognition—behavior—affect
Experiential	Affect—behavior—cognition
Behavioral influence	Behavior—cognition—affect

7-3a High-Involvement Hierarchy

The high-involvement, or standard learning, hierarchy of effects occurs when a consumer faces a high-involvement decision or addresses a significant problem. High-involvement decisions are important to a consumer and often contain significant risk. In this hierarchy, beliefs about products are formed first. The consumer carefully considers various product features and develops beliefs and thoughts about each feature. Next, feelings or evaluations about the product are formed. The consumer may begin to think the product is good and will suit his needs based on the beliefs that have been formed. Finally, after beliefs and feelings are formed, the consumer decides to act in some way toward the product. Here, a purchase decision is made. The consumer decides to either buy the product or not.

Imagine the process that Andre went through when he bought a new television. He knew that it would be a significant purchase, and he was careful about his selection. He first considered the various attributes of each TV and began to develop favorable evaluations toward a few of the brands. Realizing that he felt best about the Samsung, he decided that this would be the one to buy.

7-3b Low-Involvement Hierarchy

The standard learning approach was once considered the best approach to explain consumer attitude formation. Marketers began to realize, however, that many consumer purchases and problems are not very risky or even significant. In fact, many purchases are routine and boring.[6]

When low-involvement purchases are made, consumers often have some basic beliefs about products without necessarily having strong feelings toward them.

Gabriel, a serious photography hobbyist, may not care much about a mundane product like printer paper. In fact, he probably doesn't think much about printer paper at all. He may just think, "Staples is a popular brand, so I'll buy it." Only after he buys and uses it will he develop any type of feeling about the paper. Even when he does, those feelings are probably relatively mild. At first, he thinks "Staples is popular" (belief) and he decides to buy it (behavior). Only later does he say "I like it" (affect). Of course, he'd think very carefully about photography equipment and probably follow the standard learning hierarchy. It is easy to see that the purchase of an expensive camera is much more involving for Gabriel than a $6 ream of paper.

7-3c Experiential Hierarchy

Many purchases are based on feelings, and consumers often purchase products or try experiences simply because they "feel good" or "feel right." For example, when a student decides to visit a new dance club, she makes the decision simply because it sounds like a fun thing to do.

Impulse purchases can be explained from the experiential perspective. These purchases are often motivated by feelings. Impulse purchasing means that a consumer buys a product spontaneously and with little concern for consequences. Dessert items are often purchased on impulse. When a waiter brings a tray by, the chocoholic feels strongly about one of the desserts and simply buys it on impulse. Here, she feels strongly and acts on those feelings. A great deal of research focuses on the experiential hierarchy.[7]

7-3d Behavioral Influence Hierarchy

The behavioral influence hierarchy suggests that some behaviors occur without either beliefs or affect being strongly formed beforehand. Strong environmental pressures lead to behaviors without belief or affect formation. An example of this may be found when a consumer eats at a restaurant playing soft, slow music. Restaurant managers know that one way to get people to relax and order more drinks is to play soft, soothing music. Retail store managers know that by placing a product display in appropriate locations, consumers can be propelled to buy a product seemingly with very little or no thought at all. Behavior is influenced by environmental cues. This means that there are times when behaviors may be performed in the absence of strong beliefs or feelings.

CONSUMER ATTITUDE MODELS

As you can see, understanding consumer attitudes is very important for understanding consumer behavior. This leads to the question of how to measure attitudes. In this section we review a major approach to measuring attitudes developed by Martin Fishbein and Icek Ajzen, the attitude-toward-the-object model.[8] This model is known as a **multiattribute attitude model** because it combines information about a number of beliefs and evaluations pertaining to an object's attributes.

7-4a Attitude-Toward-the-Object Model

The **attitude-toward-the-object (ATO) model** (sometimes simply referred to as the *Fishbein model*) proposes that three key elements must be assessed to understand and predict a consumer's attitude. The first element consists of the *salient beliefs* that a person has about the attributes of an object. The second element is the *strength of the belief* that a certain object under consideration does indeed have the attribute. The third element is an *evaluation of the attribute* in question. These elements are combined to form the overall attitude toward the object (referred to as A_o, or attitude toward the object). The formula for predicting attitudes with this approach is

$$A_o = \sum_{I=1}^{N} (b_i)(e_i)$$

where A_o = attitude toward the object in question (or A_{brand}), b_i = strength of belief that the object possesses attribute i, e_i = evaluation of the attractiveness or goodness of attribute i, and N = number of attributes and beliefs.

The formula states that belief (b) and evaluative ratings (e) for product attributes are combined (multiplied), and the resulting product terms are added together to give a numerical expression of a consumer's attitude toward a product. This model can be used both for predicting a consumer's attitude and for understanding how beliefs, strength of beliefs, and evaluations influence attitude formation.

USING THE ATO APPROACH

To understand this model, first consider how the various elements are measured. To begin, note that belief ratings (b) can be measured on a 10-point scale such as:

> *How likely is it that the Sony television will give you a clear picture?*
>
> *1 2 3 4 5 6 7 8 9 10*
>
> *Extremely unlikely   Extremely likely*

The evaluative (e) rating can then be measured on a -3 to $+3$ scale such as:

> *How bad/good is it that a television has a clear picture?*
>
> *−3   −2   −1   0   +1   +2   +3*
>
> *Very bad   Very good*

The consumer would rate the Sony television and any other brand being considered on each relevant attribute. They would also consider their evaluations of the attributes, and ultimately combine the information.

An example may help to clarify the use of this formula. Think of the situation that Jamal faces selecting a new apartment. Jamal recently graduated from college and received a job offer in a large city. He is now considering three different apartment complexes that currently have vacancies. How could we predict his attitude toward each one? This information is presented in Exhibit 7.3.

Jamal is evaluating the following three complexes: *City Pointe, Crown View,* and *Kings Landing.* He first thinks of the attributes, or features, that come to mind when he thinks of apartment complexes. He decides that the following attributes are relevant: location, high rent/fees, security, fitness center, and pet friendliness. It is important to emphasize that the attributes need to really be relevant to the product under consideration. After identifying the relevant attributes, Jamal thinks of how likely it is that each apartment will perform well on the various attributes, or how likely it is that the complexes have these attributes. Jamal would be answering questions such as:

> *How likely is it that City Pointe is pet-friendly?*
>
> *1   2   3   4   5   6   7   8   9   10*
>
> *Extremely unlikely   Extremely likely*

Jamal rates each apartment across all relevant attributes. His belief (b) ratings for the apartments are shown in Exhibit 7.3. From his belief ratings, we can see that he thinks that Kings Landing is most pet-friendly. This complex allows dogs of any size. City Pointe allows dogs under fifty pounds with a large damage deposit, and Crown View does not allow any pet over 20 pounds.

multiattribute attitude model a model that combines a number of pieces of information about belief and evaluations of attributes of an object

attitude-toward-the-object (ATO) model attitude model that considers three key elements: beliefs consumers have about salient attributes, the strength of the belief that an object possesses the attribute, and evaluation of the particular attribute

Exhibit 7.3

Attitude-Toward-the-Object Model Applied to Apartment Complexes

Attribute	e	City pointe b	City pointe (b)(e)	Crown view b	Crown view (b)(e)	Kings landing b	Kings landing (b)(e)
Location	3	7	21	9	27	6	18
High rent/fees	−2	8	−16	9	−18	7	−14
Security	3	7	21	8	24	6	18
Fitness center	1	5	5	7	7	10	10
Pet friendliness	−3	5	−15	2	−6	9	−27
A_o			16		34		5

Note: e = evaluative ratings. These ratings are generally scaled from −3 to +3, with −3 being very negative and +3 being very positive. b = strength of belief that the object possesses the attribute in question. Beliefs are generally scaled from 1 to 10, with 1 meaning "highly unlikely" and 10 meaning "highly likely." $(b)(e)$ is the product term that is derived by multiplying the evaluative ratings (e) by belief strength (b). A_o is the overall attitude toward the object. This is determined by adding the $(b)(e)$ product terms for each object.

Next, Jamal considers how he *feels* about the relevant attributes, or how good (or bad) the attributes are. An example from the model would be:

How good/bad is it that an apartment complex is pet-friendly?

$$-3 \quad -2 \quad -1 \quad 0 \quad +1 \quad +2 \quad +3$$

Very bad   *Very good*

Jamal has a number of pet allergies and would prefer to stay away from complexes that he considers to be overly pet-friendly $(e = -3)$. Unfortunately, all three complexes that have vacancies allow pets. Most complexes require some fee for pets, and they also limit the size of pets that are allowed. He evaluates the other attributes as well. He highly values a location that is close to the downtown entertainment district $(e = +3)$ and a complex with its own security force $(e = +3)$. Jamal knows that the fees and limitations can vary greatly, and he really doesn't want to have problems with his allergies. He also values a fitness center but realizes that these centers usually raise the overall costs associated with a lease $(e = +1)$. He would naturally like to pay as little as possible in rent. He does believe, however, in the old adage "you get what you pay for," so he thinks that higher rent probably signals higher quality $(e = -2)$. As such, he doesn't view higher rent as a completely bad thing. *It is important to emphasize that the evaluative ratings (e) do not vary across the brands under consideration, while the belief ratings do.* That is, consumers know what attributes they like regardless of which product they are considering.

Using this model, Jamal's attitude would be calculated by multiplying each belief rating (b) by the corresponding evaluation (e). For example, the belief rating of 7 for City Pointe (security) would be multiplied by the evaluation of 3 to arrive at 21. Similarly, the belief rating of 2 for Crown View (pet friendliness) would be multiplied by the evaluation of −6. This is performed for all belief ratings and evaluations. Finally, the product terms are added together to arrive at a predicted attitude score.

Attitudes play an important role in searching for an apartment.

Poor ratings on one attribute can be compensated for by higher ratings on another.

From Exhibit 7.3, we see that his most positive attitude is toward Crown View ($A_o = 34$), followed by City Pointe ($A_o = 16$), and finally Kings Landing ($A_o = 5$).

What was it that led to the higher attitude toward Crown View versus the other complexes? An examination of Exhibit 7.3 reveals that Crown View was rated higher than the other two complexes on the two highly valued attributes, location and security. Kings Landing has an excellent fitness center, but it is also the most pet-friendly of the three complexes, with practically no limitations on pets. He also views City Pointe as relatively pet-friendly. Notice that Crown View was considered to be the most expensive complex ($b = 9$), but this is still the complex to which Jamal holds the most positive attitude. How could this be? The higher ratings on other attributes compensated for the belief that Crown View would be the most expensive complex. Accordingly, the ATO approach is known as a **compensatory model**. With compensatory models, attitudes are formed holistically across a number of attributes, with poor ratings on one attribute being compensated for by higher ratings on another attribute.

IMPLICATIONS OF THE ATO APPROACH

Information obtained from this model has important marketing implications. First, we note that attitude research is most often performed on entire market segments rather than on individuals. Marketing researchers would generally want to understand how an entire segment of consumers feel about apartment complexes. Information would be gathered from a sample of several consumers in the segment.

An equally important issue for managers would be learning if consumers believe that products offer relevant attributes. Does the target segment know that Crown View offers excellent security? Do they know that Kings Landing offers a high-quality fitness center? If targeted segments do not know these things, then they could be emphasized in advertising campaigns. This would particularly be the case if the attribute was highly valued by the consumers. Therefore, both belief (b) and evaluative (e) ratings have important implications.

Consumers know what they like and what they don't like.

As a general statement, it would be easier for managers to convince a targeted segment that they do offer a specific feature (like an excellent fitness center) than it would be to attempt to change how consumers evaluate the attribute (in other words, how people feel about fitness centers). This is why marketers need to perform extensive research up front to gain clear understanding of attributes that are highly valued, and then develop their products and services around these features.

A couple of questions commonly arise regarding this approach. "Do consumers really form attitudes in this way?" Most consumer researchers would respond "Yes." Think of a person considering the purchase of a new cell phone. Chances are that they will first think of the features that are relevant. Next, they will rate each brand on how well it performs on those features. They will also consider how they feel about each of the features. Finally, they will combine their beliefs with the evaluations and make a decision. Granted, *they probably won't write down the formula when they evaluate different cell phones*, but consumers think about relevant features of products, how much they value the features, and how each product rates on the features.

compensatory model
attitudinal model wherein low ratings for one attribute are compensated for by higher ratings on another

The next question that is commonly asked is, "Do consumer researchers really do this?" Again, the answer is yes. Researchers are very interested in how attitudes are formed, and the approach presented here can easily be performed through consumer surveys. The resultant information can have a significant impact on marketing strategy. As the apartment example reveals, this type of research can affect both product development and promotional strategy. For example, managers could decide that they should improve features that are desired by the targeted segment. Or they could focus on improving customer awareness that a complex actually does have the features that the targeted consumers want. Managers could also do both of these things.

Overall, the attitude-toward-the-object model has value from both an academic and a practical viewpoint. We do note, however, that one difficulty with the model is that the weights that are associated with the various attributes do not necessarily remain constant over time, and the list of relevant attributes may indeed change. For this reason, managers should try to stay current on these issues.

DO ATTITUDES ALWAYS PREDICT BEHAVIOR?

Marketing managers and researchers alike realize that just because a consumer has a positive attitude toward a product doesn't mean that he will always purchase the product. In fact, there would be little need for sales promotion if this were the case. **Attitude—behavior consistency** refers to the extent to which a strong relationship exists between attitudes and actual behavior. A number of situations may keep consumers from selecting products they hold positive attitudes toward.[9] In general, attitudes are stronger predictors of behavior when the decision to be made is classified as high involvement, when situational factors do not impede the product selection (for example, the product is out of stock or the consumer doesn't have enough money), and when the attitude is held quite strongly. Because attitudes don't always predict behavior, other approaches, including the behavioral intentions model, have been developed to improve upon the ATO approach.

attitude–behavior consistency extent to which a strong relationship exists between attitudes and actual behavior

behavioral intentions model model developed to improve on the ATO model, focusing on behavioral intentions, subjective norms, and attitude toward a particular behavior

7-4b Behavioral Intentions Model

The **behavioral intentions model**, sometimes referred to as the *theory of reasoned action*, has been offered as an improvement over the attitude-toward-the-object model. This model differs from the attitude-toward-the-object model in a number of important ways.[10] First, rather than focusing explicitly on attitudes, the model focuses on intentions to act in some way. Second, the model adds a component that assesses the consumer's perceptions of what other people think they should do. This is referred to as the *subjective norm*. Finally, the model explicitly focuses on the consumer's attitude toward the behavior of buying rather than the attitude toward the object.

The formula for the behavioral intentions model is as follows:[11]

$$B \approx BI = w_1(A_{behavior}) + w_2(SN)$$

where B = behavior, BI = behavioral intention, $A_{behavior}$ = attitude toward performing the behavior (or A_{act}), SN = subjective norm, and w_1, w_2 = empirical weights.

This model states that a consumer's behavior is influenced by the intention to perform that behavior (BI), and that this intention is determined by the attitude toward performing the behavior ($A_{behavior}$) and *subjective norms* (SN).

From our apartment complex example, the $A_{behavior}$ component includes the belief that the behavior will lead to a consequence (for example, "If I rent from Crown View, I'll be safe") and an evaluation of the consequence (for example: "Being safe is a good thing"). The SN component includes a consumer's belief that a reference group thinks that he or she should (or should not) perform the behavior (for example, Jamal's friends think he should choose Kings Landing because of its excellent fitness center) and the extent to which the consumer wants to comply with the suggestions of others (for example, will Jamal follow his friends' recommendations?).

The aspects of the behavioral intentions model are presented in Exhibit 7.4.

The behavioral intentions model was introduced as an improvement to the ATO model. Again, two major differences are found in the attitude toward the behavior and subjective norm components. For marketers, a clear understanding of the perceived consequences of product selection is crucial. Researchers must determine the consequences that are highly valued by their targeted consumer segments. Consumers don't always select products for the most predictable reason. Renters don't always choose an apartment based on rent or location. They may rent based largely on pet policies.

Marketing managers should also pay close attention to the subjective norm component of the model. Word-of-mouth communications are becoming critical for

Exhibit 7.4

Behavioral Intentions Model (a.k.a. The Theory of Reasoned Action)

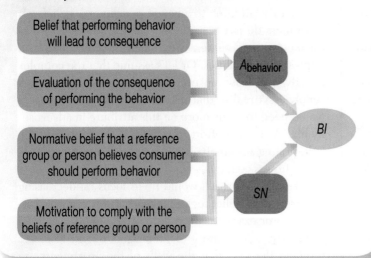

marketers. What do referent others think that the consumer should do? To what extent are they motivated to comply with the input of these people? The answers to these questions are quite valuable.

FACTORS THAT WEAKEN THE ATTITUDE–BEHAVIOR RELATIONSHIP

Although consumer attitude models are very popular in consumer research, researchers note that a number of factors can weaken the attitude–behavior relationship. Of course, simply liking a product doesn't mean that we will buy it. Maybe we don't have enough money to buy what we want. That's very common, of course. Other factors weaken the relationship. For example, as the length of time between attitude measurement and overt behavior grows, the predictive ability of attitudinal models weakens. The specificity with which attitudes are measured also has an impact on accuracy. For example, measuring the intentions of buying a new Sony television would be more appropriate for Sony managers than would measuring one's intentions to buy any new television in the next month. Strong environmental pressures can also keep consumers from performing intended behaviors. For example, when consumers feel rushed, decisions are often made in haste. Finally, attitude–behavior models tend not to perform very well in impulse-buying situations. Impulse purchases are sometimes hard to explain.

ALTERNATIVE APPROACHES TO ATTITUDE

One small variation of this theory is the **theory of planned action**, which expands upon the behavioral intentions model by including a *perceived control* component. This component assesses the difficulty involved in performing the behavior and the extent to which the consumers perceive that they are in control of the product selection.[12] Products can be difficult to purchase, especially if they are in short supply.

EXPANDING THE ATTITUDE OBJECT

The definition of attitudes presented earlier states that attitudes are relatively enduring evaluations of objects, products, services, issues, or people. For this reason, consumer researchers often study attitudes toward several different entities, not just brands or products.

One area that has received considerable consumer research attention is *attitude toward the advertisement*. Research has shown that there is generally a positive relationship between a consumer's attitude toward an advertisement and her attitude toward a particular product.[13] We note, however, that several factors have been shown to affect this relationship, including the overall liking of the television program in which the ad is embedded, the vividness of the imagery in the ad, the ad context, and the mood of the consumer.[14]

A growing area of research interest has also focused on attitude toward the company. What consumers know or believe about a company (sometimes referred to as *corporate associations*) can influence the attitude they have toward its products.[15] The study of consumer beliefs toward companies is therefore gaining considerable attention from consumer researchers. Of particular importance for many consumers is the question of how responsible companies are with their business practices. In general, consumers who feel positively about a company's business practices are likely to react more favorably toward the brands that the company markets.[16]

ATTITUDE TRACKING

Assessing one's attitude toward a specific product, brand, purchase act, advertisement, or company at only one specific point in time can also limit the accuracy of attitudinal models. Researchers therefore track how attitudes change over

theory of planned action attitudinal measurement approach that expands upon the behavioral intentions model by including a perceived control component

time. Because attitudes toward a brand can be influenced by several things, including attitude toward advertisements and companies, it is especially important to study changes in consumer attitudes. Attitude tracking refers to the extent to which a company actively monitors its customers' attitudes over time. What is important to understand is that even though attitudes are relatively enduring evaluations of objects, products, services, issues, or people, these attitudes should be monitored over time to gauge changes that may occur.

A great example is found in attitude studies about teens' perceptions of Facebook. Evidence is mounting that the phenomenally popular social networking site is not seen as cool anymore with young consumers.[17] Marketers can also monitor attitudes through watching Twitter trends or monitoring popular stories on sites like Reddit.com.

7-5 ATTITUDE CHANGE THEORIES AND PERSUASION

An important issue in the study of consumer behavior is how attitudes are changed. Politicians want to persuade people in order to win their votes, and organizations want to convince people to join. Advertising plays a major role in all of these issues, and today social media plays a major role as well. The term persuasion refers to specific attempts to change attitudes. Usually, the hope is that by changing beliefs or feelings, marketers can also change behavior.

There are many different persuasive techniques, and the following discussion presents the theoretical mechanisms through which persuasion may occur. These include the ATO approach, the behavioral influence approach, the schema-based affect approach, the elaboration likelihood model, the balance theory approach, and the social judgment theory approach.

7-5a Attitude-Toward-the-Object Approach

According to the ATO model, both beliefs about product attributes and evaluations of those attributes play important roles in attitude formation. By focusing on these components, the ATO approach presents marketers with a number of alternatives for changing consumer attitudes. To change attitudes according to this

attitude tracking effort of a marketer or researcher to track changes in consumer attitudes over time

persuasion attempt to change attitudes

approach, marketers can attempt to change beliefs, create new beliefs about product features, or change evaluations of product attributes.

CHANGING BELIEFS

As discussed in our apartment complex example, marketers may attempt to change consumers' beliefs. If consumers do not believe that Crown Pointe offers an excellent fitness center, then managers could focus on improving its facilities. Or let's assume that the complex already does have an excellent center, but consumers simply don't realize that they do. In this case, managers would need to focus more on this attribute in advertisements. With each effort, the focus is on improving the belief rating for an attribute that is evaluated positively (here, fitness center).

Another approach would be to focus on decreasing the strength of belief regarding a negatively evaluated attribute. For example, since pet friendliness is evaluated negatively in this case (−3), managers might decide to promote the idea that the walls of the apartments are quite thick and pet allergies shouldn't be a problem in their apartments. Here, the focus is on decreasing the belief rating of a negatively evaluated attribute. As we have discussed throughout this text, communicating value is an important marketing task. A good example of changing beliefs about a product is orange juice manufacturers attempting to convince consumers that the juice can be consumed all day instead of just in the morning. It's not just for breakfast!

ADDING BELIEFS ABOUT NEW ATTRIBUTES

Another strategy for changing attitudes under the ATO approach is adding a salient attribute to the product or service. Like the changing beliefs approach, this may require a physical change to the product itself. For example, an apartment complex might add basic DIRECTV service to all units. Here, a new attribute that is likely to be evaluated positively by consumers is added. When a valued attribute that was not previously considered is added, the overall attitude toward the complex may be improved.

At other times, the new beliefs may not be tied to an actual new attribute. Rather, they may simply emphasize something that consumers had previously not considered. To illustrate, consider what has happened with the marketing of red wine. In the 1980s, Robert Mondavi Winery added labeling to its wines that referred to the health benefits of drinking wine. Initially, the FDA stopped this practice, based on the notion that the label was misleading and detrimental to consumers. However, after years of research, the health-giving properties of

HOT BUTTONS

The study of attitude and attitude change often falls outside of traditional marketing boundaries. In fact, many of the major issues that consumers face in everyday life pertain to social issues and politics. Of course, politicians use marketing techniques constantly. Politicians and political parties expend much effort trying to win votes.

Few political issues are as divisive as gun control. This was certainly a big theme of the 2016 presidential election. Pro–gun control consumers feel that more restrictions should be placed on the sale of various types of guns. In the extreme, some consumers feel that all guns should be outlawed. Anti–gun control consumers, on the other hand, believe that owning a firearm is a protected right under the Second Amendment to the Constitution. These consumers believe that buying and possessing firearms should remain a basic consumer right if the purchaser is legally able to buy and possess a gun. Somewhere in the middle of the arguments is the level of background checks that should be required.

The issue highlights one central theme in attitude research: when a consumer holds a belief with much conviction, it is more difficult to change their attitude. This is illustrated by Social Judgment Theory, which suggests that when an attitude is very strong, a consumer's latitude of acceptance will be small and their latitude of rejection will be large. Regardless of the theory, the issue of gun control is a very hot button in society today.

---

wine are widely accepted. Red wine is associated with a reduced risk of heart disease and cancer, and this information has now been widely promoted. Thus, although the health-related benefits of red wine are nothing new, only in the last few years has the belief become prominently known and accepted. By adding a new belief, wine marketers have increased the market share of wine relative to beer and spirits. Recently, the advantages of apple cider vinegar have been promoted. Several health experts suggest consuming the vinegar daily, since it reportedly leads to many health advantages. The vinegar purportedly helps the body break down fats, decrease bad cholesterol, and improve blood pressure.[18]

CHANGING EVALUATIONS

As noted earlier, marketers may also attempt to change the evaluation of an attribute. Here, the marketer tries to convince consumers that an attribute is not as positive (or negative) as they may think. For example, an apartment complex may attempt to persuade consumers that a downtown location is not necessarily a good thing and that living in the suburbs is better. As discussed previously, changing evaluations of an attribute is usually more difficult than changing the strength of a belief regarding that attribute. Quite simply, consumers know what they like, and they make selections accordingly.

À votre santé! The belief that wine is healthy can lead people to like it even more.

7-5b Behavioral Influence Approach

Another strategy commonly applied by marketers follows the Behavioral Influence hierarchy. You may remember that this hierarchy proposes that behavior precedes cognition and affect. Marketers may use this approach in many ways. Changing a retail store's design or atmospherics can have a direct influence on behavior. In fact, that's what the scented marketing industry is based on.

> ## Changing a retail store's design or atmospherics can have a direct influence on behavior.

You may also remember from our discussion on conditioning in an earlier chapter that behavioral conditioning can be very effective. Consumers respond to marketing stimuli in certain ways, and behaviors frequently result without either beliefs or affect changing first.

7-5c Changing Schema-Based Affect

We introduced the notion of schema-based affect in a previous chapter. From an attitude perspective, schema-based affect refers to the idea that schemas contain affective and emotional meanings. If the affect found in a schema can be changed, then the attitude toward a brand or product will change as well.

To illustrate, consider what happened when Domino's first entered Japan. Initially, the company had to deal with commonly held beliefs that tomatoes

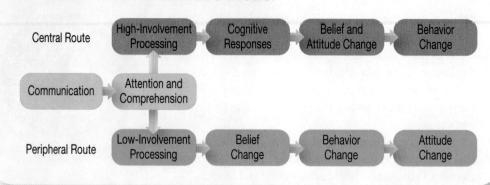

Exhibit 7.5

The Elaboration Likelihood Model

were unhealthy and that delivery food was not clean. Rather than trying to change these beliefs directly, Domino's created funny delivery carts and advertisements that attempted to attach positive feelings to the product schema and their brand. Thus, a positive attitude was shaped by this feeling found within the schema. This attitude-change technique can be effective if performed properly.

7-5d The Elaboration Likelihood Model

Another popular approach for conceptualizing attitude change is found in the **elaboration likelihood model**.[19] The elaboration likelihood model (ELM) illustrates how attitudes are changed based on differing levels of consumer involvement. Numerous research studies have examined the usefulness of the ELM in explaining the attitude change process. This model is shown in Exhibit 7.5.

According to the ELM, a consumer begins to process a message as soon as it is received. Depending on the level of involvement and a consumer's ability and motivation to process a message, the persuasion process then follows one of two routes: a *central route* or a *peripheral route*.[20]

THE CENTRAL ROUTE

If consumers find that the incoming message is particularly relevant to their situation (and thus highly involved), they will likely expend considerable effort in comprehending the message. In this case, high-involvement processing occurs, and the **central route to persuasion** is activated. Here, the consumer develops a number of thoughts (or cognitive responses) regarding the incoming message that may either support or contradict the information. Contradicting

"They said what?"

You will notice that many theories of attitude measurement require you to rate a product or issue based on your feelings, beliefs, and behaviors. Another major issue in this chapter is that you tend to spread the word about products and issues that you either like or don't like. Understanding why consumers hold certain attitudes towards products has been an important marketing issue for decades.

Today, however, companies are beginning to rate and spread the word about customers. This has become much more widespread in today's social media world. Companies from Uber to Airbnb to eBay either directly rate and review customers, or allow sellers to do so. This has shifted the dynamic in ratings from being a "one-way" street to a "two-way" street. A low rating from a service may mean that it's harder for a customer to get future services when needs arise. In other words, if you're a bad customer, you will likely find it harder to catch a ride or find a place to sleep.

The moral of the story is that "the customer is always right" may no longer be the case. Whereas consumers have always shared their attitudes with other

consumers, now the tables are turning and companies can do the same thing. It seems like it's more important than ever to get a company to like you and believe that you're a good customer!

Sources: Streitfeld, David (2015), "Ratings Now Cut Both Ways, So Don't Sass Your Uber Driver," *New York Times (online edition)*, January 30, 2015, http://www.nytimes.com/2015/01/31/technology/companies-are-rating-customers.html; Dzieza, Josh (2015), "The Rating Game: How Uber and Its Peers Turned Us into Horrible Bosses, *The Verge* (online), October 28, 2015, http://www.theverge.com/2015/10/28/9625968/rating-system-on-demand-economy-uber-olive-garden; Weed, Julie (2014), "For Uber, Airbnb and Other Companies, Customer Ratings Go Both Ways," *New York Times* (online), December 1, 2014, http://www.nytimes.com/2014/12/02/business/for-uber-airbnb-and-other-companies-customer-ratings-go-both-ways.html?_r=0.

thoughts are known as counterarguments. Thoughts that support the main argument presented are known as support arguments.

In the central route, the consumer relies on **central cues**. Central cues refer specifically to information found in the message that pertains directly to the product, its attributes, its advantages, or the consequences of its use.

To illustrate this process, consider an experienced photographer who sees an advertisement for Sony cameras. Because he knows a lot about cameras and is highly interested in them, he will likely think carefully about the message he sees and the arguments presented as to why Sony cameras are the best cameras on the market. The arguments presented in the ad are critical. The photographer will consider the arguments and compare them to his current beliefs. He may even form counterarguments against the ad. For example, he may think "Canons are better." Or, he may think "Sony cameras really are better than Canons after all." (It is important to note that responses can be either negative or positive.)

If the consumer's beliefs are changed as a result of message exposure, attitude and behavior change will follow. Because the consumer is highly involved, and because he has made an effort to carefully attend to the message, it is likely that the attitude change will be relatively enduring. This is an important aspect of the central route to persuasion: *Attitude change tends to be relatively enduring when it occurs in the central route.*

THE PERIPHERAL ROUTE

If consumers are not involved with a message or lack either the motivation or ability to process information, the **peripheral route to persuasion** will be followed. In this route, consumers are unlikely to develop cognitive responses to the message (either supporting arguments or counterarguments), and

central cues information presented in a message about the product itself, its attributes, or the consequences of its use

peripheral route to persuasion path to persuasion found in ELM where the consumer has low involvement, motivation, and/or ability to process a message

are more likely to pay attention to things like the attractiveness of the person delivering the message, the number of arguments presented, the expertise of the spokesperson, and the imagery or music presented along with the message. These elements of the message (that is, nonproduct-related information) are referred to as **peripheral cues**.

Many products, ranging from beer to cologne to clothing, use peripheral cues in their advertisements. If the consumer is influenced more by peripheral cues than central cues, any resulting belief or attitude change will likely be only temporary. That is, because the consumer is not highly engaged in the process, it is unlikely that attitude change will be enduring.

LOW-INVOLVEMENT PROCESSING IN THE CONSUMER ENVIRONMENT

It is important to note that the vast majority of advertisements to which consumers are exposed are processed with low-involvement processing. Consumers are simply not motivated to carefully attend to the thousands of ads that they are exposed to each day. Therefore, advertisers tend to rely heavily on the use of peripheral cues—attractive models, enticing imagery, upbeat music—when developing advertisements.

7-5e Balance Theory

Another way to conceptualize attitude change processes is through balance theory. The **balance theory** approach was introduced by social psychologist Fritz Heider.[21] The basic premise of balance theory is that consumers are motivated to maintain perceived consistency in the relations found in mental systems. Accordingly, this approach is based on the **consistency principle**. This principle states that human beings prefer consistency among their beliefs, attitudes, and behaviors.

Balance theory focuses on the associations, or relations, that are perceived between a person (or observer), another person,

peripheral cues
nonproduct-related information presented in a message

balance theory theory that states that consumers are motivated to maintain perceived consistency in the relations found in a system

consistency principle
principle that states that human beings prefer consistency among their beliefs, attitudes, and behaviors

Exhibit 7.6
Balance Theory

and an attitudinal object. The relations between these elements may be perceived as being either positive or negative. An example is shown in Exhibit 7.6.

Note that the system (composed of observer, person, and object) is referred to as a *triad* because it consists of a set of three elements. The relations between the elements are referred to either as sentiment relations or as unit relations. *Sentiment relations* are the relations between the observer (consumer) and the other elements in the system. In Exhibit 7.6, the observer-person relation and the observer-object relation are referred to as sentiment relations. The object-person relation is referred to as a *unit relation*. Unit relations are based on the idea that two elements are in some way connected to one another.

Again, the basic premise of balance theory is that consumers are motivated to maintain perceived consistency in the relations found in the triad. Importantly, the perceived relations between the cognitive elements in the balance theory system may be changed when inconsistency occurs.

To illustrate, look carefully at Exhibit 7.6. Assume that Isaiah, a quarterback on the local college team, is a fan of Peyton Manning. Here, there would be a positive (+) sentiment connection between Isaiah and Peyton. Isaiah notices that Peyton endorses Papa John's pizza. He sees advertisements for Papa John's during many NFL games on television. Isaiah's never felt strongly about Papa John's, but he really likes Peyton. Isaiah would perceive a positive unit relation (+) between Peyton and

An attractive model represents a peripheral cue.

Papa John's. That is, Isaiah assumes the star endorses the product because he really likes it. How would Isaiah feel about the product? Well, in order to maintain balance in this triad, he would develop positive feelings toward Papa John's, resulting in a positive sentiment connection between himself and the brand.

This example illustrates a key premise of balance theory: *Consistency in the triad is maintained when the multiplication of the signs in the sentiment and unit relations results in a positive value.* When the resulting value is negative, consumers are motivated to change the signs (feelings) associated with one of the relations.

Suppose Isaiah doesn't like Peyton Manning. That is, suppose there is a negative ($-$) sentiment relation between Isaiah and the star. Because he perceives a positive unit relation between Peyton and Papa John's, he will be motivated to form a negative sentiment relation between himself and the brand (note that $[-] \times [+] \times [-] = +$). According to the theory, weak perceived relations are generally changed, while stronger relations remain unchanged. Here, Isaiah would be turned off by the advertisement and would develop a negative sentiment relation between himself and the brand. We note that while balance theory is often used to explain endorser effectiveness, the theory has also been applied in several other contexts, including product placements in television shows, goal-oriented behavior, consumer–brand relationships, and sports fan/team identification.[22, 23]

It should also be noted that marketers who rely on this approach should be careful to monitor any changes that occur in how a target market perceives an endorser. As we have seen, public attitudes toward celebrities can change nearly overnight. In this case, the sentiment connection between the endorser and the consumer can become negative, leading to trouble for the brand advertised!

7-5f Social Judgment Theory

Social judgment theory is yet another theory for explaining attitude change.[24] This theory proposes that consumers compare incoming information to their existing attitudes about a particular object or issue. The initial attitude acts as a frame of reference, or standard, against which the incoming message is compared. Around these initial reference points are *latitudes of acceptance* and *latitudes of rejection.* For a message to fall within the latitude of acceptance, the information presented must be perceived as being close to the original attitude position. A message that is perceived as being far away from, or opposed to, the original attitude position will fall within the latitude of rejection. These aspects of the theory are presented in Exhibit 7.7.

According to the theory, when an incoming message falls within the latitude of acceptance, *assimilation* occurs. This means that the message is viewed as being congruent with the initial attitudinal position, and the message is received favorably. In fact, the message may be viewed as being even more congruent with the initial attitudinal position than it really is. As a result, the consumer is likely to agree with the content of a message falling within the latitude of acceptance, and the attitude would change in the direction of the message.

If the message is perceived as falling in the latitude of rejection, an opposite effect occurs. In fact, the message will be viewed as being even more opposed to the original attitude than it really is, and the message will be rejected. In this way, a *contrast effect* is said to occur.

social judgment theory theory that proposes that consumers compare incoming information to their existing attitudes about a particular object or issue and that attitude change depends upon how consistent the information is with the initial attitude

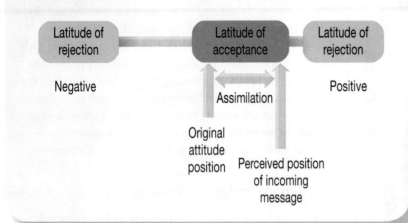

Exhibit 7.7

Social Judgment Theory

Latitude of rejection — Latitude of acceptance — Latitude of rejection

Negative

Positive

Assimilation

Original attitude position

Perceived position of incoming message

The implication for marketers is that messages should be constructed so that they fall within the latitude of acceptance of the targeted consumer. An important finding in this line of research is that when the original attitude is held with much conviction (either positive or negative), the latitude of acceptance is quite small and the latitude of rejection is large. On the contrary, when the original attitude is weak (either positive or negative), the latitude of acceptance is large and the latitude of rejection is small. This finding helps to explain why it is difficult to change a person's attitude when his or her attitude is very strong. Anyone who has tried to change a friend's mind will understand!

7-6 MESSAGE AND SOURCE EFFECTS AND PERSUASION

An important part of understanding persuasion is comprehending how communication occurs. As we have discussed, consumers are exposed to thousands of messages every day and attention spans are decreasing. In response, some marketers are making their messages very brief. In fact, some marketers are using radio ads called "blips" that are only one or two seconds long![25]

message effects how the appeal of a message and its construction affect persuasiveness

source effects characteristics of a source that influence the persuasiveness of a message

Communicating in such a short time span is obviously difficult. Ads this short are generally well-edited sound bits. Regardless of attention spans, both the message being sent and the source of the message affect persuasion.

The term **message effects** is used to describe how the appeal of a message and its construction affect persuasion. **Source effects** refer to the characteristics of the person or character delivering a message that influence persuasion. To understand how message and source effects work, we must begin by introducing a simple communication model. A basic communication model is shown in Exhibit 7.8.

According to this model, a source encodes a message and delivers the message through some medium. The medium could be personal (for example, when a salesperson speaks with a customer) or impersonal (for example, when a company places an ad on television, on Facebook, or in an app). The receiver (consumer) decodes the message and responds to it in some way. Feedback consists of the responses that the receiver sends back to the source. For example, a consumer might voice an objection to a sales pitch or decide to call a toll-free number to receive additional product information.

The *noise* concept is very important to this model. Noise represents all the stimuli in the environment that disrupt the communication process. In today's environment, noise comes in many different forms. For example, the popularity of online pop-up blockers is evidence of the number of distractions found on the Web. From a traditional advertising perspective, the basic

Exhibit 7.8

Basic Communication Model

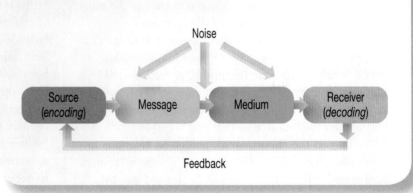

Noise

Source (encoding) — Message — Medium — Receiver (decoding)

Feedback

communication model is referred to as a "one-to-many" approach, because it illustrates how a marketer may attempt to communicate with numerous consumers.[26]

7-6a Interactive Communications

The one-to-many communications model works well when examining personal communications or traditional advertising media such as television, newspapers, or radio. However, interactive communications have radically changed the communication paradigm. In fact, recent estimates reveal that 3.2 billion consumers used the Internet as of year-end 2015. Eighty percent of households in developed countries have Internet access as compared to only 34% in developing countries.[27] Due to the continued proliferation of the Internet and smartphone technologies, we must consider its effect on the communication process.

Importantly, information flow is no longer considered a "one-way street," in which consumers passively receive messages from marketers. Rather, communication is seen as an interactive process that enables a flow of information among consumers and/or firms in what might be referred to as a many-to-many approach.[28] In this evolving context, marketers essentially lose control of messages in many circumstances and they attempt to latch on to positive messages that users send to other users. Senders can place content (web pages, blogs, interactive TV ads) into a medium and communicate directly with receivers through social networking sites, apps, and text messages. Satellite and cable television programming has also become much more interactive. This dramatically changes the communication model, with a newer conceptualization being presented in Exhibit 7.9. You will notice that even though this model was developed over two decades ago, it still holds true today, particularly when it comes to social media. Research confirms that social media significantly influence consumer loyalty and WOM today.[29]

As we have discussed, both the message itself and the person delivering the message have an impact on the overall effectiveness of an advertisement. For this reason, marketers must consider both elements when developing communication strategies. This section discusses a number of findings regarding message and source effects. As you may remember, some of these topics were first introduced in our chapter on comprehension.

Exhibit 7.9

Communication in a Computer-Mediated Environment

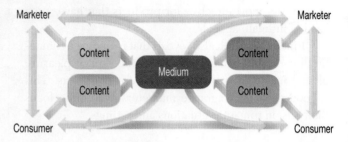

Source: Adapted from Hoffman, Donna L., and Thomas P. Novak (1996), "Marketing in Hypermedia Computer-Mediated Environments: Conceptual Foundations," *Journal of Marketing* 60, no. 3, 50–68.

7-6b Message Appeal

There are several ways to conceptualize how a message may impact the persuasiveness of an advertisement. Here, we focus on the appeal (or general content) of an advertisement. A number of appeals are used by advertisers, including sex appeals, humor appeals, and fear appeals. Much of the research in this area has been conducted using traditional marketing messages and advertising, but many ideas apply to social media content as well.

SEX APPEALS

A popular saying in marketing is that "sex sells!" Using sexual imagery in advertisements certainly is popular in many parts of the world. In fact, European media usually contain stronger and more explicit sexual appeals than do American media. As we discussed in another chapter, the rationale for this approach is found within the psychoanalytic approach, and these appeals are often used as peripheral cues in the elaboration likelihood model (ELM).

Interestingly, consumers often find sexually appealing ads to be persuasive, even when they consider them to be exploitative or offensive![30] However, consumers' reactions to the strategy depend on a number of factors. Moderate levels of nudity appear to be most preferred, as highly explicit content tends to direct attention away from the product. Also, highly sexual ads tend to outperform non-sexual ads when they have highly arousing content.[31]

Gender plays a role in advertising effectiveness regarding nudity. For example, one study found that women react negatively to the use of female nudity in advertising, but that men respond favorably toward the practice.[32] Conversely, a later study revealed men react negatively toward the use of male nudity in ads, and that women responded favorably. The type of product being advertised also plays an important role. That is, the use of nudity is most effective for products that have some level of intimate appeal.[33]

Finally, research also reveals that including a romantic theme (rather than focusing on the explicit pleasure of sex) may have positive benefits for marketers. This is good news for fragrance marketers, who often focus their ads on romantic situations and settings.[34]

HUMOR APPEALS

Marketers also frequently use humorous ads. In today's age of intense advertising clutter, ads that are humorous can be effective. Advertisers tend to use humor in their ads intermittently because they know that humor can get old after a while and no longer cut through the clutter. Super Bowl commercials often use humor in order to stand out. The 2016 Super Bowl saw an increase in the use of humor once again, with many advertisers choosing to develop funny ads.[35] One recent study confirmed that humorous ads can attract attention, create a positive mood, and enhance both attitude toward a brand and purchase intentions. However, humor appeals can also decrease the credibility of a message source.[36] Research also suggests that the use of humor should relate to the product being advertised.[37]

The overall effectiveness of a humorous ad depends, in part, on the characteristics of both the individual consumer and the advertisement. Recent research reveals that male consumers evaluate satirical humor more positively than do female consumers, who tend to prefer sentimental humor.[38] As discussed in another chapter, research also indicates that humor is more effective when a consumer's need for cognition is low rather than high,[39] and also when a consumer has a high need for humor.[40] Furthermore, the initial attitude that a consumer has regarding the product plays an important role, as humorous ads appear to be most effective when the consumer's attitudes are initially positive rather than negative.[41]

The amount of humor to place in an advertisement is another issue. High levels of humor can cause consumers to fail to pay attention to the product being advertised, and high levels can also limit information processing.[42] Obviously, marketers don't want to spend millions of dollars on ad campaigns simply for entertainment purposes.

In today's economy, consumers make their own marketing messages.

FEAR APPEALS

In addition to using sexual and humor appeals, advertisers also frequently attempt to evoke some level of fear in their target audiences as a means of changing attitudes and behaviors. These ads often rely on the relationship between a threat (an undesirable consequence of behavior) and fear (an emotional response).[43] The product being advertised is often promoted as a type of a solution that will remove the threat.

For example, an insurance company might try to evoke fear in consumers by suggesting that their loved ones may fall into financial hardship if the consumer doesn't carry enough life insurance. Public service announcements may attempt to evoke fear in consumers by highlighting the tragic consequences of unsafe sexual practices (for example, HIV). Security monitoring services may use fear appeals to draw attention to the frightening consequences of home invasions.

Numerous research studies have addressed the effectiveness of fear appeals in marketing. As a general statement, research suggests that the use of fear appeals can be effective. However, the level of fear that results is very important. Overly high levels of fear may lead consumers to focus on the threat so much that they lose focus on the proposed solution.[44] Paradoxically, if fear arousal is not strong enough consumers may either discount the message or develop more positive attitudes towards the behavior that is being discouraged.[45] Also, different consumers are likely to react in different ways to the exact same fear appeal, complicating the issue further.[46] As a result, it is very difficult to predict how an individual consumer will react to any fear appeal. The context in which fear appeals are placed can also influence their effectiveness. For example, attitudes toward a fear-inducing ad have been found to be less positive when the ad is embedded in a sad television program than when the ad is placed in a happy (comedic) program.[47]

As an overall statement, fear appeals appear to be effective when they (1) introduce the severity of a threat, (2) present the probability of occurrence, (3) explain the effectiveness of a coping strategy, and (4) show how easy it is to implement the desired response.[48]

Although the use of fear appeals is popular among advertisers, it is important to note that there is an ethical question regarding their use. Critics often argue that the use of fear appeals in advertising is essentially a means of unfair manipulation.[49]

VIOLENCE APPEALS

One trend that has been growing over the last few decades is the use of violent scenes in advertisements. There is much variety in violent themes, from the seemingly innocent to the downright shocking. The effects on viewers often go beyond marketing-related reactions. For  example, children who view violent ads are more likely to develop aggressive thoughts, which can eventually lead to aggressive behavior.[50] Evidence has also shown that women are less receptive to violence in advertisements regardless of the level of severity of the violence, and that younger consumers are generally more receptive to violence in advertising.[51] It is interesting to note that many violent ads also use elements of humor, seemingly in an attempt to lessen the degree to which the ad is disturbing. In fact, many popular commercials have a combination of violence and humor, and a recent study found that the most popular Super Bowl ads include both humor and violence.[52] Though research in this area remains relatively new, early evidence suggests that men find comedic violence to be more humorous than do women.[53] This area is likely to continue to gain research attention in CB.

age fotostock/Alamy Stock Photo

7-6c Message Construction

The way that the message is constructed also impacts its persuasiveness. Advertisers must consider a number of issues when constructing a message. Here, we present a number of questions that marketers must answer.

▶ *Should an ad present a conclusion or should the consumer be allowed to reach his own conclusion?*

Advertisements that allow consumers to arrive at their own conclusions tend to be more persuasive when the audience has a high level of involvement with the product. Conversely, when the audience is not engaged with the message, it is generally better to draw the conclusion for consumers.[54]

▶ *Should comparative ads that directly compare one brand against another be developed?*

Advertisers generally have three alternatives when developing an ad. First, they can promote their brands without mentioning competing brands. Second, advertisers can promote their brands and compare them generically to "the competition." Third, they can actively compare their products against specific competitors by explicitly naming the competing brands in the advertisement.

Directly comparing one brand against specific competitors can be effective—especially when the brand being promoted is not already the market leader.[55] Promoting a brand as being "superior to all competition" can also be very persuasive when a firm hopes to court users away from all competing brands.[56]

▶ *Where should important information be placed?*

The placement of information in a specific message at the beginning, middle, or end of the message impacts the recall of the information. This is a basic tenet of what is known as the serial position effect.[57] When material presented early in a message is most influential, a primacy effect is said to occur. When material presented later in the message has the most impact, a recency effect is said to occur.[58]

Research suggests that primacy effects are likely to occur when the audience is highly engaged (highly involved) and when verbal (versus pictorial) content is present.[59] If marketers are attempting to reach a highly involved audience, important information

serial position effect occurs when the placement of information in a message impacts recall of the information

primacy effect occurs when the information placed early in a message has the most impact

recency effect occurs when the information placed late in a message has the most impact

should be placed early in the message. Marketers can also attempt to gain the consumer's attention as early as possible and encourage careful processing of information by using statements such as "an important message" or "listen carefully." For audiences with lower levels of involvement, important information can be placed late in the message. These effects also occur in series of messages, and can impact the recall of commercials placed in any particular block of commercials. For example, research has revealed that primacy effects prevail for the recall of Super Bowl commercials. That is, commercials placed at the beginning of a block resulted in higher levels of consumer recall.[60] Interestingly, it has also been demonstrated that a consumer's mind-set, which is affect by a particular type of television program such as a political debate, can affect how consumers react to ads.[61]

▶ *Should the message be straightforward and simple, or complex?*

Advertisers must consider both message and source effects. In general, complex ads take more effort on the part of the consumer and require deep information processing. Overly complex messages can cause frustration within consumers and lead to unfavorable reactions. As noted earlier in the section on the ELM, the number of arguments presented in an ad is considered a peripheral cue. Highly involved consumers are more motivated to attend to a larger number of arguments than are less motivated consumers.

7-6d Source Effects

Another important issue in the study of persuasion is how the source of a message (a spokesperson or model, for example) influences consumers' attitudes. Source effects include issues such as credibility, attractiveness, likeability, and meaningfulness. You may notice that some of these effects were presented as peripheral cues in the ELM.

SOURCE CREDIBILITY

Source credibility plays an important role in advertising effectiveness. In general, credible sources tend to be more persuasive than less credible sources. This effect tends to be highest when consumers lack the ability or motivation to expend effort attending to the details of an ad (low involvement).[62] However, credible sources also influence highly involved consumers, especially if their credentials are clearly communicated early in a message.[63] The credibility of sources also impacts the certainty with which consumer attitudes are held, with lower levels of credibility leading to higher levels of certainty.[64]

© iStockphoto.com/GYI NSEA

Source credibility is important in advertising. Awareness of this led to Nike ending its arrangement with cyclist Lance Armstrong.

As we discussed in our comprehension chapter, credibility consists of two elements: expertise and trustworthiness. *Expertise* refers to the amount of knowledge that a spokesperson is perceived to have about the product or issue in question. You may remember from our presentation on the ELM that source expertise represents a peripheral cue in advertising. Expertise can be an important quality for a spokesperson to possess. In fact, a major review of source effects has revealed that source expertise has the biggest influence of all source effects on consumer responses to advertisements.[65]

Trustworthiness refers to a perception of the extent to which a spokesperson is presenting a message that he or she truly believes, with no reason to present false information. Interestingly, expertise and trustworthiness can independently influence persuasion. That is, trustworthy sources can be persuasive even if they're not experts, and expert sources can be persuasive even if they're perceived as being untrustworthy.[66]

Finally, we note that source credibility, although generally conceptualized as pertaining to a spokesperson or model, also applies to the sponsoring company. In fact, research reveals that the credibility of both the spokesperson and the company influences the effectiveness of an advertisement, with the credibility of the spokesperson having a stronger influence than the credibility of the company.[67]

SOURCE ATTRACTIVENESS

Source attractiveness is another quality that has received a great deal of attention. Attractive models are often thought to possess desirable qualities and personalities. They also tend to be more persuasive than unattractive spokespeople.[68] However, the type of product plays an important role in the process. Much like the research regarding the use of sex appeals, research into attractiveness reveals that attractive models are more effective when promoting products that have an intimate appeal, whereas unattractive models are more effective when promoting products that have no intimate appeal.[69] This is particularly the case when consumers have the ability and motivation to process the message being presented and elaboration likelihood is high.[70]

SOURCE LIKEABILITY

Source likeability also affects a spokesperson's effectiveness. Likeable sources tend to be persuasive. Of course, individuals differ in terms of which celebrities they like and dislike, and marketers are very interested in finding the best possible spokesperson for a given market segment. The advertising industry relies heavily on a Q-score rating provided by Marketing Evaluations, Inc. as an indication of the overall appeal of celebrities.[71] Interestingly, it has been found that source likeability affects persuasion more for consumers with low need for cognition than for those with a high degree of this trait. This again highlights the importance of individual difference variables in persuasion.[72]

SOURCE MEANINGFULNESS

Celebrities have images and cultural meanings that resonate with consumers. For example, a famous athlete like Dwayne Wade embodies the image of hard work and success. Pairing Dwayne with athletic apparel or footwear simply makes sense. You should recall that research on the use of sexual imagery and source attractiveness suggests that these characteristics should be matched with the type of product being advertised. This is true for source meaningfulness as well. That is, the dominant characteristics of a source should match the characteristics of the product. This is a key concept that is found in the **matchup hypothesis**, which states that a source feature is most effective when it is matched with relevant products.[73]As such, we should expect NBA star Dwayne Wade to be an effective spokesperson for footwear and less effective when promoting a product that has no athletic qualities at all.

As you can see, marketers face a number of decisions when constructing campaigns that are aimed at changing consumer attitudes.

> **matchup hypothesis**
> hypothesis that states that a source feature is most effective when it is matched with relevant products

---

STUDY TOOLS 7

LOCATED AT BACK OF THE TEXTBOOK
☐ Tear out Chapter Review Card

LOCATED AT WWW.CENGAGE.COM/LOGIN
☐ Review Key Term flashcards and create your own cards
☐ Track your knowledge and understanding of key concepts in consumer behavior
☐ Complete practice quizzes to prepare for tests
☐ Complete interactive content within CB Online
☐ Review the Chapter Highlight boxes for CB Online

CASES

Climbing To The Top!

Written by Dr. David Matthews, SUNY Adirondack; students Sandra Dickinson and Christina Green, SUNY Adirondack

Where can one go and relax while having a thrill-seeking adventure? Ever heard of vertical yoga? Would you, could you, imagine being 30 feet off the ground in a tranquil state of mind, knowing you have just reached a new high? Tom Rosecrans began an adventure of a lifetime when he bought out two partners of Rock Sport Indoor Rock Climbing (www.rocksportny.com). A small-scale facility with varying degrees of difficulty ranging from beginner to advanced bouldering, the setting may be small in square footage but it sure fills the desires of experienced climbers. Never having owned his own business, this high school teacher powdered his hands and held on tight, taking his venture to new levels ten years later. With over 36 years of rock climbing experience, Tom has experienced destinations on a global scale, including two expeditions to the Himalayas.

Running a business of passion could be overwhelming, so Tom kept things relatively manageable, never really trying to outdo or grow the business beyond modest proportions, satisfied to own a part-time "hobby" business. However, the situation has changed and Tom has decided now is the time for adjustment, and with good reason. A few months ago a newer, bigger, brassier indoor rock climbing gym opened just 20 minutes away and is drawing excitement from Rock Sport's current customer base as well as the public. With few choices and immediate need, Tom must use market research to determine how to increase Rock Sport's target market and client base through innovated new programs.

Outdoor rock climbing, or mountaineering, began in Europe in the early 1800s, though the first mountaineering club wasn't started until 1857. Rock climbing for recreation came much later in the 20th century, when styles, grading, and equipment were all brought together and turned the adventure into a sport.[1] In the 1980s alternatives were made for busy climbers; indoor facilities that took less time to manage were designed to have different degrees of difficulty and to allow realistic experiences for the sport enthusiast.[2]

Climbing is both physically challenging and psychologically rewarding. For example, major progress can be made in improving one's cardiovascular health, muscle tone, and weight loss. But one of the great benefits of rock climbing is the thrill and joy it brings, as well as a pure sense of achievement. Children love the challenge in a risky environment, while parents enjoy the safety features in today's indoor gyms. Having fun with family, friends, or finally reaching one's personal "trail" goal is satisfying. A simple focus group conducted at a gym even revealed customers speaking of "peak performances and experiences," conditions indicative of the intrinsically satisfying "flow" state of motivation.

However, there are some negative perceptions in society today regarding rock climbing, many stemming from cautious Baby Boomers. Survey research revealed the following possible obstacles: fear of falling, fear of heights, low self-image while climbing (embarrassment), and even the fear of failure. All were cited as reasons why adult participation in rock climbing has declined over the years. On top of this, cost and time limitations were also mentioned by survey respondents. Tom's biggest challenge is drawing in new people or markets to try rock climbing. He is convinced the sport can be viewed as another "soft recreation" alternative similar to kayaking and bicycling. In fact, he has made it a personal mission to get more Baby Boomers like himself to try the sport. The children's market is not the problem. Hundreds of Generation-Y parents are bringing their kids to the facility for birthday parties and non-competitive meets. In addition, students from the local community college are also regular customers who share their experiences on social media like Facebook. No, the younger demographic segments are not the issue. As such, Tom is now challenged to change this negative attitude among the Generation-X and Baby Boomer market segments.

Other indoor gyms have grown their businesses by making the needed changes in facility offerings and programs. In the past, strong athletic men were the avid climbers; today the average climber is in his or her mid-20s, with the number of children right behind and growing rapidly.[3] There are stories of toddlers climbing indoor rock walls in just diapers, and even five- and six-year-olds on open mountain ranges

CASES

climbing better than most adults, which shows how they will become the new generation of the sport. Women have slowly gained interest in the sport mainly due to themed nights and special events. Many believe that rock climbing is for the 130-pound, athletic, outgoing type and miss that rock climbing can fit anyone who is willing to try. There has even been a national marketing campaign introduced to stress the safety of climbing.

Currently, most of Rock Sport's customers are the children of Generation Xers in the athletic programs and some college students. Tom would like to encourage Baby Boomers and parents of the children that use his facility to give indoor climbing a try. Convincing the older generations of the health benefits and the fun and exciting adventures is tricky in today's society. Their opinion of adventurers is young and fit, not parents and grandparents. Changing the views of these age groups is challenging and can cost quite a bit of money and time if not done correctly.

Soon Tom will pass the business off to his daughter, but not without leaving her a strategy that ensures sustainable growth forward. Ideas include moving into a larger facility, revamping the website, increasing social media use, and bringing in yoga and Pilates instructors to lead classes. Creating large competitive events that showcase the facility and spread awareness are other possible ideas. As such, Tom is challenged by what the future holds and eager to turn ideas into action plans.

QUESTIONS

1 What types of programs or tactics would you suggest the owner institute to reduce Baby Boomers' fear of and change their attitudes toward rock climbing?

2 What do you think motivates one to rock climb or try this sport? Is the value provided utilitarian or hedonic? If you never tried rock climbing, would you now consider it? If so, what would be your motivation?

3 Explain how the intrinsic motivation state of flow might occur in rock climbing.

4 Using the multiple trait approach to consumer behavior, analyze which specific consumer traits would explain one's motivation to rock climb. For example, the Five Factor Model of personality traits is one framework that can be used.

5 Using the ABC approach to attitudes, explain why a Baby Boomer might feel that rock climbing is a "young person's sport." Then, create a program for Rock Sport that attempts to change this negative attitude and invites Baby Boomers to try indoor rock climbing.

CASE 2-2

Plasma, LCD, LED, Ultra HD TVs—Much Ado About Nothing?

Written by Rob Rouwenhorst, Ph.D., University of Iowa

There are numerous factors consumers need to consider as they upgrade their televisions to newer high-definition (HD) sets. Bulky cathode ray tubes, weighing sometimes hundreds of pounds, are dead and rear-projection TVs are dying, leaving three distinct types of HDTVs: plasma, liquid crystal displays (LCD) backlit with cold cathode fluorescent lights (CCFL), and LCDs backlit with light-emitting diodes (LED). There is also a new "Ultra HD" technology that is available, and some marketers have offered curved screens to improve the viewing experience. As technology is constantly evolving and improving, audio-video enthusiasts debate which technology is best and provides the most value. Can consumers really tell the difference, and what are ways marketers can influence viewers' perceptions of HDTVs?

When HDTVs first came on the scene, the only real choice was plasma. The phosphors that make a plasma television's image light up themselves and do not require backlighting. Because they do not require backlighting, plasma provides dark blacks and great picture quality. On the down side, they literally can be hot to the touch and are power-hungry. In general, they consume two to three times the power consumed by an LCD TV.[1]

Gradually, thinner, energy-efficient LCDs lit with CCFL backlighting became less expensive and began gaining ground on plasma TVs. The liquid crystal screen does not light up itself, so a backlight is required. CCFL were in many of the first LCDs produced and are still used in more inexpensive sets available today. CCFLs are similar to the fluorescent lights you may use in an overhead

CASES

fixture. Because of the need for a backlight, CCFL LCDs are worse in picture quality compared to plasma TVs.

Today, LED-backlit LCDs are increasingly popular. With their ability to backlight portions of the screen that you want lit up (e.g., a character talking), and stay off in other parts that should remain black (e.g., a night sky or black bars), LED technology promises the best of both worlds: picture quality to match plasma sets, with the energy efficiency and thinness of LCDs.

To further complicate television buying, a TV's resolution has become another statistic. Terms such as 720i, 720p, 1080i, and 1080p are used to describe the HD signal being shown. The number represents the number of lines being displayed from the top to the bottom of the screen. To put this in perspective, older standard-definition televisions and DVDs had only 480 lines. While more lines lead to a better image, it is difficult to tell the difference between 720 and 1080 lines on a small screen (those less than 32 inches).

Several years ago, when sets that topped out at 720p cost less than 1080p sets, there was a large debate about whether the average consumer would notice the difference. However, the debate has been ruled largely academic, as most large (40 inches and more) HDTVs nowadays are capable of displaying a 1080p signal. However, smaller screens (those less than 32 inches) come in both 720 and 1080 flavors.

HD signals are denoted with an *i* for interlaced and a *p* for progressive. Interlaced signals mean the screen is divided into even and odd lines that are alternately refreshed or redrawn, meaning there is a slight delay between odd and even line refreshes, which can cause some jaggedness. This occurs because half of the lines are keeping up with a moving image while the other half are waiting to be refreshed. Progressive signals mean that every line on the screen is redrawn or refreshed. The distinction is nuanced, but progressive signals look better. However, the progressive signals also come with the drawback of having to carry more information, so many cable and satellite providers only provide interlaced signals to decrease their bandwidth costs. Ultra HD technology adds to the debate, and most consumers can clearly see the benefits of Ultra.

Refresh rates get a lot of talk in the marketing of TV sets. Saying that more frames shown per second leads to a smoother look sounds great, but in practice there is not much of a difference. Television can be thought of as 30 pictures shown each second. Those pictures or *frames* are interlaced to 60 frames per second to match the 60Hz refresh rate of the majority of LCD TVs you can buy today. Movies are shot at 24 frames per second, and to make the footage look as close to the film as possible, Blu-ray players display 24 frames per second. When HDTVs were in their infancy, they would suffer from blurriness during very fast movement (e.g., sports). But technology has progressed such that motion blur has mostly been eliminated. So if you are considering a backlit LCD/LED with 120Hz or 240Hz or a plasma with 600Hz, know that the various technologies that increase refresh rate on HDTVs do not actually add any detail to the video and are another way to market TVs that will not be that discernable from one another.

Finally, there is the consideration of size and price. Do not assume that bigger is always better. Much like with a computer monitor, if you sit too close to the TV, images will become jagged and pixelated. For instance, do not get a 60-inch TV if you will be sitting within six feet of the screen.[2]

All of us have walked down the TV aisle of a large discount or electronics store and seen the wall of televisions. While comparing two TVs may seem easy as they are next to one another, you must consider the motivations of the store. There are a myriad of settings that can be adjusted on each TV. For instance, the brightness can be controlled to make one television brighter than the other. Is the store displaying the ideal, calibrated settings? Or are they displaying the settings out of the box? Are they making one TV that has a higher margin for the retailer look especially good?

Buying a television is not an easy thing to do. There are so many alternatives and emerging technologies available. As Ultra High Definition becomes more widely adopted, these alternatives will only continue to expand. Also, features like curved screens will be continued to be added. Given that most televisions costs several hundred dollars or more, the TV buying experience will continue to be studied by consumer researchers.

CASES

QUESTIONS

1 In what ways are TV manufacturers practicing the total value concept? What features are consumers coming to expect in a modern TV?

2 Say you manage the electronics department at your local Best Buy. Would you tweak the TV settings so each TV displays an ideal picture or would you leave them as they are out of the box? How would your decision influence returns and customer satisfaction?

3 Apple has made a case for the "retina" display on the latest iPhone and iPad, saying the pixels are so small the human eye cannot detect them. This gets away from official statistics like 2048-by-1536 screen resolution. In what ways is this positive or negative for consumers?

4 Say you are the product manager for a line of plasma televisions. What features would you emphasize the most with customers? Why?

5 Given what you now know about HDTVs, in what ways does marketing influence consumers' perceptions of products such as TVs?

CASE 2-3

Virtually Free!

Written by Barry J. Babin, Louisiana Tech University

An old marketing adage puts forward the importance of creating customers. In times gone by, companies like Kodak were heralded for using inexpensive cameras like the Kodak 110 to create customers for film and film services. Kodak's success lay in film, not in cameras.

Perhaps the connection between Kodak and video games isn't so obvious, but success in gaming is all about creating customers. Before the widespread adoption of online gaming, companies like Nintendo used game consoles as loss leaders to create customers for games. The online gaming companies don't even have to manufacture or sell consoles as loss leaders.

Zynga is one of the major players in online gaming. While Zynga's original marketing strategy was to provide games free to users and generate revenue from advertisers, they've morphed into a revenue model strongly driven by Facebook users. Zynga games like Castleville, Cityville, Farmville, Fishville, and Zynga Poker have become a social networking phenomenon in recent years. Zynga and other online gamers now use the "freemium" as the primary tool to create customers. The term *freemium* refers to the free games that companies offer to consumers as a tool to sell virtual products that help freemium customers succeed in their game play. Zynga grew on this business model to revenues topping $600 million in 2010 (from $1 million in 2008).[1] Zynga went public with an initial stock offering in late 2011. Initially shares sold for $10 and showed a decline to about $5 by the middle of 2012.[2]

Zynga's hope is to create more *whales*, a term referring to heavy consumers of virtual products. However, Zynga faces a lot more competition today than it did in 2011, as consumers find many more options for online games.[3] Take for example TinyCo, makers of Tiny Zoo, available as an app in iTunes or for Android systems through Google. After playing Tiny Zoo for only 60 seconds, new users receive a message saying "looks like you need more Coins to buy a Chickity Puff." The idea behind the game is to amass a prized collection of virtual (not real) animals to display in the virtual (not real) zoo. Perhaps with more than a touch of irony, one of the prized animals is known as the Cash Cow! In case you haven't guessed by now, TinyCo sells Tiny Zoo virtual coins for real money. One market segment for virtual products is children. One eight-year-old spent two months' allowance ($50) when Tiny Zoo released a new batch of animals. These kids are not playing the games on computers but on their parents' smartphones and tablets—or on their own tablets and iPods. Many parents willingly allow their kids to use payment apps to buy virtual products as a sort of babysitting device. After all, parents have always given in to kids in toy stores. Trouble is, unlike a real toy store, the app store is open 24-7 and the kid is in the store any time the smartphone is in their hands.[4] Industry analysts expect the mobile gaming business to grow fivefold to nearly $20 billion per year by 2015.[5]

CASES

The growth may seem like good news for Zynga, but many questions linger. Among these questions are the following:

▶ Zynga games are predominantly played on PCs through Facebook. Consumer trends seem to be moving toward gaming on mobile devices. Zynga would be a latecomer to this market. Will consumers continue to play games like Farmville on Facebook or will consumers substitute gaming on mobile devices at the expense of Zynga?

▶ Zynga is closely tied to Facebook. Is this risky?

▶ Apple's new operating system will facilitate social networking simultaneously with the use of many online games. Will this make Zynga's typical distribution outdated?

▶ Can Zynga continue to develop new and creative freemiums given the large number of app designers entering the gaming market?

With these issues in mind, Zynga may need to rethink their marketing strategy. Consumer behavior knowledge may be useful to them in better understanding their customers.

QUESTIONS

1 Consumers, whether adults are children, have to learn how to play online games like Tiny Zoo or Castleville. In this part of the book, learning is described as being either intentional or unintentional. Explain your opinion on whether these games are learned more by intentional or unintentional learning mechanisms.

2 Brand loyalty is an important marketing concept. Define the concept of schema. How important is the brand schema in consumer decisions to play these games? Do you think consumers think of the company (Zynga), the game (Cityville), or the host (Facebook) when playing the games?

3 All consumer behavior is motivated by something. What motivations underlie online gaming and purchasing of online games? In the case of parents paying for virtual goods used by their kids, what value is involved in the consumption?

4 Do consumer attitudes play a role in online gaming?

CB8
ONLINE
STUDY YOUR WAY
WITH STUDYBITS!

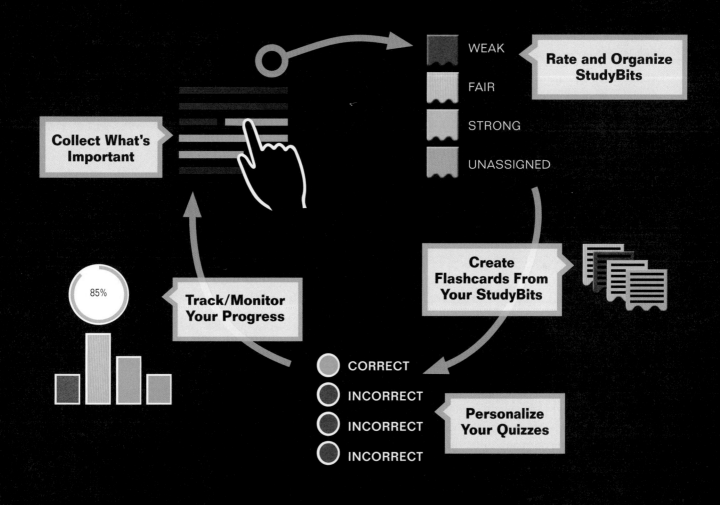

WEAK

FAIR

STRONG

UNASSIGNED

Rate and Organize StudyBits

Collect What's Important

Create Flashcards From Your StudyBits

CORRECT

INCORRECT

INCORRECT

INCORRECT

Track/Monitor Your Progress

85%

Personalize Your Quizzes

4LTR PRESS

Access CB8 ONLINE at www.cengagebrain.com

8 | Group and Interpersonal Influence

LEARNING OBJECTIVES

After studying this chapter, the student should be able to:

8-1 Understand the different types of reference groups that influence consumers and how reference groups influence value perceptions.

8-2 Describe the various types of social power that reference groups exert on members.

8-3 Comprehend the difference between informational, utilitarian, and value-expressive reference group influence.

8-4 Understand social media's role in consumer behavior.

8-5 Understand the importance of word-of-mouth in influencing consumer behavior.

8-6 Comprehend the role of household influence in consumer behavior.

Remember to visit **PAGE 179** for additional **STUDY TOOLS**

INTRODUCTION

Nearly everything that a consumer does is in one way or another influenced by other people, groups, or organizations. This is because an important human need is the need to belong. Human beings are social creatures who desire contact and affiliation with others. In fact, one of Maslow's primary motivations is the need to belong. Consuming products, services, or ideas helps consumers satisfy this need.

Consumers belong to many different groups, and these groups exert significant influence on behavior. It's not only groups, however. Consumers are also influenced by other individuals. This is especially true with social media. The popular website Pinterest allows consumers to influence others by recommending things like crafts, recipes, and clothing.

In this chapter, we discuss a number of issues relating to the concept of group and interpersonal influence and how these concepts apply to value. We begin by discussing the various types of reference groups that influence CB.

8-1 REFERENCE GROUPS

A **reference group** is a group of individuals who have significant relevance for a consumer and who have an impact on the consumer's evaluations, aspirations, and behavior.[1] This influence affects the ways that consumers seek and receive value from consumption. Most people don't realize all the ways that reference groups influence their behavior. However, we can start to understand this better when we think of all the groups that we belong to. Consumers become members of many groups that either meet physically or, thanks to the Internet, meet in cyberspace. Social media has greatly impacted interpersonal influence. How many Facebook groups do you "like"? How many people or companies do you follow on Twitter? Have you discovered any new music from Spotify or

reference group individuals who have significant relevance for a consumer and who have an impact on the consumer's evaluations, aspirations, and behavior

learned about a new hobby on Pinterest? Do you get a lot of Snapchat photos or Vine video clips?

To begin our discussion of interpersonal influence, we begin by discussing topics related to groups.

8-1a Group Influence

Group influence refers to ways in which group members influence attitudes, opinions, and behaviors of others within the group. Groups are an important part of social life, and they profoundly affect consumer behavior by changing the perceived value of products. In fact, gaining acceptance into a group provides value for consumers directly by satisfying the need for belonging discussed previously. Consider the following aspects of group life:

▶ *Group members share common goals and interests.* For example, members of Mother's Against Drunk Drivers have the goal of stopping the dangerous and illegal act of drinking and driving.

▶ *Group members communicate with and influence one another.* For example, members of a school's alumni group meet regularly and influence one another.

▶ *Group members share a set of expectations, rules, and roles.* For example, a volleyball team has specific rules for its team members.

▶ *Group members view themselves as members of a common social unit.*[2] For example, current and ex-military members proudly display their affiliation with their branch of service.

Sociologically speaking, consumers think in terms of *ingroups* and *outgroups*. From a social identity perspective, an ingroup is a group that a person identifies with as a member. An outgroup is a group with which a person does not identify. Members of an ingroup are generally viewed as having cohesion and exhibiting similar attitudes and behavior. Value perceptions are also influenced in large part by ingroups.

> **group influence** ways in which group members influence attitudes, behaviors, and opinions of others within the group
>
> **ingroup** a group that a person identifies with as a member
>
> **outgroup** a group with which a person does not identify

PRIMARY/SECONDARY GROUPS

A **primary group** is a group that includes members who have frequent, direct contact with one another. Primary reference groups generally have the most influence on their members, and *social ties* for these groups are very strong. A social tie is a measure of the strength of connection between group members. An example of a primary reference group is the family unit. Family members generally have much influence on one another, and many times it directly affects behavior in the marketplace. For example, studies reveal that parental influence on children's shopping and saving behavior can be quite strong.[3] Parents who openly discuss financial matters, such as developing savings accounts, can greatly influence these behaviors.

In a **secondary group**, interaction within the group is much less frequent than in a primary group. Professional organizations and social clubs are examples of secondary groups. Usually, the influence of these groups on members is not as strong as the influence of primary groups on their members. Furthermore, social ties are not as strong in secondary groups as in primary groups.

One special type of secondary group is a **brand community**. Brand communities are groups of consumers who develop relationships based on shared interests or product usage.[4] A popular example of a brand community is the KISS Army. The KISS Army is a group of fans of the legendary rock group who form close bonds with each other and who regularly attend band conventions that may be referred to as *brandfests*. Brandfests have become very popular today. Country music brandfests are especially popular.

In general, personal connections originating in brand communities lead to positive outcomes for consumers and companies. Consumers learn more about the products they enjoy, and they develop bonds with other users. Companies reap the rewards of positive consumer commitment, which they can build by sponsoring the events.[5] The commitment members share helps them

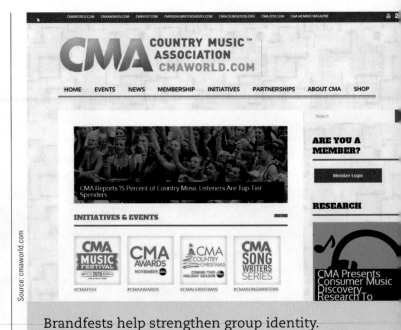

Brandfests help strengthen group identity.

form tight bonds.[6] When fans attend music festivals, they strengthen their bonds with their favorite artists.

FORMAL/INFORMAL GROUPS

A **formal group** is a group in which a consumer formally becomes a member. For example, a consumer becomes a formal member of a church congregation. Formal groups generally have a set of stated rules, accepted values, and codes of conduct that members are expected to adhere to.

An **informal group** is a group that has no membership or application requirements, and codes of conduct may be nonexistent. Examples of informal groups include groups that meet regularly to exercise, have coffee, or go to sporting events. Although informal group influence may not be as strong as formal group influence, these groups can have an impact on consumer behavior.

ASPIRATIONAL/DISSOCIATIVE GROUPS

An **aspirational group** is a group in which a consumer desires to become a member. Aspirational group membership often appeals to the consumer's *ideal* self. The ideal self is an important part of the consumer's self-concept, and consumers often visualize themselves as belonging to certain groups. For example, a business student may desire to become a member of a professional business association once he earns his degree. Consumers frequently emulate the members of aspirational groups and perform behaviors that they believe

primary group group that includes members who have frequent, direct contact with one another

secondary group group to which a consumer belongs, with less frequent contact and weaker influence than that found in a primary group

brand community group of consumers who develop relationships based on shared interests or product usage

formal group group in which a consumer formally becomes a member

informal group group that has no membership or application requirements and that may have no code of conduct

aspirational group group in which a consumer desires to become a member

will lead to formal acceptance into the group. Getting a first job would be the first step for joining a business organization.

A **dissociative group** is a group to which a consumer does not want to belong. A dissociative group is generally considered a type of outgroup for a consumer. For example, a Republican might want to avoid being perceived as belonging to a Democratic group (and vice versa). Recent college graduates may want to disassociate themselves from groups from their past as they take the next step into adulthood.

8-1b Conformity and Authority

Two important topics in the study of group and interpersonal influence are conformity and authority. **Conformity** occurs when an individual yields to the attitudes and behaviors of other consumers. Conformity is similar in some ways to the concept of persuasion. The key difference between persuasion and conformity is that with conformity, the other party does not necessarily defend its position. That is, a group may give no reason for why it expects its group members to act or think a certain way. Persuasion, on the other hand, relies on one party defending its position in an attempt to change behavior.[7] **Authority** refers to the ability of a person or group to enforce the obedience of others. Some groups, such as governments and municipalities, have legal authority over consumers.

PEER PRESSURE

Peer pressure is closely related to conformity. **Peer pressure**, the pressure an individual feels to behave in accordance with group expectations, can greatly influence behavior. In fact, peer pressure is often the strongest type of influence a consumer experiences in daily life.

Consumers of all ages feel peer pressure. In fact, very young children often desire to wear the types of clothing and brands that will allow them to feel accepted. One study found that children as young as ten prefer to wear brand-name footwear (e.g., Nike) so that they will fit in with their peers.[8]

> # Consumers of all ages feel peer pressure.

Peer pressure and conformity share some similarities. Both are based on behaviors that are in line with what others expect. With peer pressure, there is usually some type of sanction that is threatened if the consumer does not go along with the group. With conformity, behavioral choices are generally more strongly based on internal desires to belong, even when the threat of sanction is not present.

NEGATIVE PEER PRESSURE

Peer pressure to wear a certain brand of clothing is not necessarily a bad thing. Unfortunately, negative consumer behaviors are often heavily influenced by peer pressure. Consumers sometimes succumb to group pressures that subtly or not so subtly encourage counterproductive or unethical—perhaps illegal—behaviors.

Experts frequently cite peer pressure as particularly persuasive among young consumers. The media direct a lot of attention to peer pressure and illegal alcohol or tobacco consumption. Binge drinking among underage consumers is a serious societal problem that can have disastrous, and sometimes fatal, effects. Peer pressure often plays a large role in this behavior. Even virtual group pressure, such as is exerted through social networking sites, is sometimes blamed for encouraging underage smoking.[9] Although this form of peer pressure is negative, marketers can harness the power of peer pressure in positive ways. For example, advertisements that encourage young consumers to abstain from negative behaviors (like underage drinking) can be effective when peer group members deliver the message.[10] And consumers who stick together can change together, as illustrated by a Facebook group that encourages friending among those who want to stop smoking.

Adolescents are particularly susceptible to peer pressure and are often compelled to rebel against their families in favor of behaviors that win acceptance from their peers. Teens commonly go against family expectations and parental rules. At this stage in social development, friends begin to take on additional importance and exert greater influence in teens' lives. This can be considered a natural part of a child's development; nevertheless, negative influences, including conflict within the family, can result.

Adults also feel and yield to peer pressure, and sometimes the pressure is

dissociative group group to which a consumer does not want to belong

conformity result of group influence in which an individual yields to the attitudes and behaviors of others

authority the ability of a person or group to enforce the obedience of others

peer pressure extent to which group members feel pressure to behave in accordance with group expectations

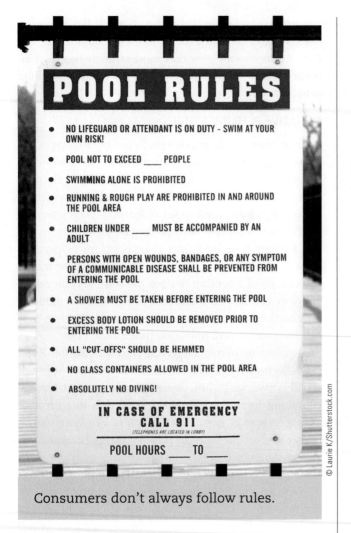

POOL RULES

- NO LIFEGUARD OR ATTENDANT IS ON DUTY - SWIM AT YOUR OWN RISK!
- POOL NOT TO EXCEED ____ PEOPLE
- SWIMMING ALONE IS PROHIBITED
- RUNNING & ROUGH PLAY ARE PROHIBITED IN AND AROUND THE POOL AREA
- CHILDREN UNDER ____ MUST BE ACCOMPANIED BY AN ADULT
- PERSONS WITH OPEN WOUNDS, BANDAGES, OR ANY SYMPTOM OF A COMMUNICABLE DISEASE SHALL BE PREVENTED FROM ENTERING THE POOL
- A SHOWER MUST BE TAKEN BEFORE ENTERING THE POOL
- EXCESS BODY LOTION SHOULD BE REMOVED PRIOR TO ENTERING THE POOL
- ALL "CUT-OFFS" SHOULD BE HEMMED
- NO GLASS CONTAINERS ALLOWED IN THE POOL AREA
- ABSOLUTELY NO DIVING!

IN CASE OF EMERGENCY CALL 911
(TELEPHONES ARE LOCATED IN LOBBY)

POOL HOURS ____ TO ____

Consumers don't always follow rules.

© Laurie K./Shutterstock.com

directed toward negative behaviors. In fact, one study of adult consumers reveals that respondents reported a greater likelihood to buy an illicit product (counterfeit or stolen merchandise) if their friends did the same.[11] As with influence on children, this form of peer pressure is negative and can affect consumers, marketers, and society as a whole.

8-2 SOCIAL POWER

Another important topic in the study of reference groups and group influence is social power. **Social power** refers to the ability of an individual or a group to alter the actions of others.[12] Consumers often believe that others hold a great deal of power over their own behavior. As a result, social

social power ability of an individual or a group to alter the actions of others

power can greatly influence the types of products that consumers buy, the attitudes they hold, and the activities in which they participate.

8-2a Types of Social Power

Social power can be classified into five categories.[13] These categories include *referent power*, *legitimate power*, *expert power*, *reward power*, and *coercive power*. These forms of power can be exerted both by referent groups and by other individuals. These power bases are presented in Exhibit 8.1 and then discussed in more detail.

REFERENT POWER

Consumers often imitate the behaviors and attitudes of groups as a means of identifying with the group. For example, a new resident of a city might desire to join the local Rotary Club, or perhaps a country club. In these cases, it is likely that the behaviors of other group members will be imitated. Belonging to such groups often allows consumers to feel as though they are fitting in.

LEGITIMATE POWER

In many situations, social arrangements dictate that differing levels of power are dependent upon one's position in a group. Legitimate power is used to describe this type of power, and it is associated with authority. For example, bosses have legitimate power and authority over their employee, including the authority to fire their employees. Notice that employees are usually very limited in any power that they can exert over a boss.

EXPERT POWER

An important motivation in CB is the motivation to understand the environment. Expert power refers to the ability of a group or individual to influence a consumer due to the group's or individual's knowledge of, or experience with, a specific subject matter. For example, consumers often find advice on health issues by consulting groups such as the American Heart Association or American Diabetes Association. Medical patients also often consult various online discussion groups for information. By consulting these groups for advice and direction relating to specific medical issues, consumers can alter their behaviors based on the perceived expertise of the source of information.

Exhibit 8.1

Types of Social Power

Type of power	Description	Example
Referent Power	A consumer admires the qualities of a group and emulates their behavior.	A student joins Enactus and emulates that group's behaviors.
Legitimate Power	Specific agreements are made regarding membership, and the punishment for nonconformity is understood.	A neighborhood association has the power to annually increase membership fees.
Expert Power	Groups possess knowledge that members, prospective members, or other consumers seek.	Consumers seek out medical information from groups such as the American Dental Association.
Reward Power	Groups have the power to reward members for various behaviors.	Weight loss clubs give out prizes for weight loss goals.
Coercive Power	Groups have the power to sanction group members for breaking rules or failing to follow expectations.	A member of a professional association is excused for breaking a code of conduct.

REWARD POWER

Groups frequently have the power to reward members for compliance with expectations. For example, at season's end, sports teams often distribute "most valuable player" awards based on performance. The desirability of the rewards is very important. If the reward isn't valued by the group members, then the motivation to perform the desired behavior is not overly strong.

COERCIVE POWER

Groups may also exert coercive power over their members. When consumers fail to give in to group expectations or rules, disapproval can be harsh and may even result in loss of membership. For example, college athletes can be kicked off sports teams for using illegal substances like steroids. As mentioned earlier, groups may sanction members based on their legitimate power to do so, or they may revoke the membership of group members who do not comply with group rules.

How does social power originate? Social power depends upon a member's agreement to, or acceptance of, the fact that the power bases do indeed exist. That is, members must (a) *be aware that the power base exists* and (b) *desire to maintain or establish membership in the group* in order for the power base to be effective. For example, if you don't value your membership in a particular club or relationship, you won't be motivated

to follow the stated rules. In sociological terms, this is where *deviance* might begin. If someone doesn't value the rules of society, they may begin to act out with defiance or deviance.

8-3 REFERENCE GROUP INFLUENCE

The study of reference groups requires an understanding of group influence processes. Reference group influence generally falls into one of three categories: *informational influence*, *utilitarian influence*, and *value-expressive influence*. These categories of influence are discussed next.[14]

8-3a Informational Influence

The **informational influence** of groups refers to the ways in which consumers use the behaviors and attitudes of reference groups as information for making their own decisions. Reference groups often provide members with product- or issue-related information, and consumers often consider group-related information when purchasing products or services. Consumers desire to make informed decisions,

> **informational influence**
> ways in which a consumer uses the behaviors and attitudes of reference groups as information for making his or her own decisions

and reference groups are often perceived as being effective sources of information.[15] Groups can be very influential in this way. Informational influence can be a result of explicit searching behavior. For example, when a consumer is seeking a doctor, friends may influence the choice by saying, "This doctor is very good."

Informational influence is also present even when the consumer is *not* explicitly searching for product-related information, but rather observing others' behaviors. For example, a consumer may simply see another person drinking a new soft drink and decide to try one.[16]

Informational influence helps to explain why word-of-mouth communication is so persuasive. Consumers share all kinds of information about products, services, and experiences, and this information can have a significant impact on consumer behavior. Internet discussion groups, in particular, have rapidly become important sources of information for group members.

The informational influence of a group is particularly strong if the group is seen as being credible. Credibility is often associated with expertise. Professional groups are often perceived as being very credible, and for this reason, they can exert significant informational influence even if a consumer is not a member of the group. For example, a consumer may be persuaded by a message that proclaims that "four of five dentists recommend brand X." This same information obtained from the American Dental Association can affect a dentist's decisions as well, as informational influence is directly related to expert power.

8-3b Utilitarian Influence

The **utilitarian influence** occurs when consumers conform to group expectations to receive a reward or avoid punishment (this is sometimes referred to as "normative" influence). This is similar in many ways to the utilitarian function of attitudes. Compliance with group expectations often leads to valued rewards.

As discussed earlier, young consumers often think they need to buy the correct brand of shoes or clothing to fit in. By wearing apparel approved by the reference group, a child feels accepted (the reward). If the wrong clothing is selected, the child may feel shunned by the group (a punishment). When the group is perceived as being able to give rewards and punishment based on compliance, then this influence is quite strong.

Utilitarian influence of groups is not limited to any age group or demographic profile. Adult consumers often perceive a great deal of utilitarian influence from reference groups. Driving the right car, living in the right neighborhood, and belonging to the right clubs can make adults feel accepted. Here, we can see that utilitarian influence is related to reward power.

8-3c Value-Expressive Influence

Consumers often desire to seek membership in groups that hold values that are similar to their own. They also choose to adopt the values that are held by the desirable group. The **value-expressive influence** of groups refers to the ways in which consumers internalize a group's values or the extent to which consumers join groups to express their own closely held values and beliefs. This influence is related to referent power.

Consumers may also use group membership as a way to project their own self-image. Importantly, the self-image of the individual is influenced by the group, and group membership helps the individual project the desired image. For example, a consumer may choose to join Mothers Against Drunk Driving because she feels strongly about the drunk driving issue. Once she has joined, she can project the values of the group as well. This is also similar to the value-expressive function of attitudes.

8-3d Value and Reference Groups

External influences have a direct impact on the value of many activities. Reference groups and value are related in various ways.

From a utilitarian value perspective, joining a campus organization like Students in Free Enterprise can be quite a valuable experience. The benefits associated with membership (networking, work experience, accomplishment) may be greater than the work

utilitarian influence ways in which a consumer conforms to group expectations in order to receive a reward or avoid punishment

value-expressive influence ways in which a consumer internalizes a group's values or the extent to which consumers join groups in order to express their own closely held values and beliefs

Dreams Come True/Shutterstock.com

SHARE AND SHARE ALIKE

Share and share alike. Many of us grew up with that saying. In today's economy, it takes on a whole new meaning, as consumers often choose to share products in one way or another rather than buying them and permanently owning them. As discussed elsewhere, the terms *sharing economy* and *collaborative consumption* have been used to describe this rapidly growing consumer movement.

The sharing economy is directly related to consumer group behavior. That is, consumers look to other consumers to help address wants and needs that they have, and they often form groups who choose to share product ownership. In fact, some consumers have organized swap parties to help exchange and share items such as clothing. Other consumer groups form to share ownership of vehicles. Still others use social media to rent items such as lawn equipment out to others.

Although borrowing, swapping, and renting arrangements have been around for hundreds of years, the movement toward group sharing has skyrocketed recently. Ultimately, the issue is how consumers seek value in products. Today, it appears that more and more consumers are finding value not in ownership, but

rather in sharing. Consumers can satisfy both utilitarian value needs (by solving problems) and hedonic value needs (by belonging to a sharing group) through the new sharing economy. This is likely to continue into 2017 and beyond.

Sources: Matlzer, Kurt, Viktoria Veider, and Wolfgang Kathan (2015), "Adapting to the Sharing Economy," *MIT Sloan Management Review*, 56 (2): 71–77; Bardhi, F. and G.M. Eckhardt (2012), "Access-Based Consumption: The Case of Car Sharing," *Journal of Consumer Research*, 39 (4): 881–898; Marx, P. "The Borrowers: Why Buy When You Can Rent?", *The New Yorker*, January 31, 2011, online content retrieved at http://www.newyorker.com/magazine/2011/01/31/the -borrowers, accessed April 4, 2016.

---

that is put into the organization (work performed to complete a project, hours devoted to planning and meetings). In this way, utilitarian value is derived from belonging to the group, and membership becomes a means to a valued end state. Group membership also involves hedonic value perceptions. Value can be derived from simply enjoying group meetings and activities. Here, value is an end in itself. Members of the KISS Army receive both utilitarian and hedonic value from membership. They are able to enjoy interacting with other fans while also obtaining special deals on concert tickets and other memorabilia from the band.

Reference group influences affect value perceptions in other ways. Because consumers learn about products and services from referent others, the information that is obtained from groups directly affects consumer expectations about product benefits such as quality and convenience. If you hear from your friends that a product is good, you'll probably believe it. These expectations, in turn, affect value perceptions and satisfaction.

8-3e Reference Group Influence on Product Selection

A number of things affect how much influence reference groups have on product selection. First, the situation in which the product is consumed must be considered. "Public" products (for example, a watch) are easily seen by others. "Private" products (for example, socks) usually are not. Second, the extent to which the product is considered to be a necessity or a luxury affects the level of reference group influence.[17] We really do need some products (for example, a bed). Others aren't really necessary (for example, an espresso maker). Third, reference group influence differs depending on whether a type of

Exhibit 8.2

Reference Group Influence on Product Selection

Product Necessity

Consumption Setting	Necessity	Luxury
Public	**Public Necessity (1)** (e.g., shoes, automobile) *Weak group influence for product selection; strong group influence for brand selection.*	**Public Luxury (2)** (e.g., jewelry, country club membership) *Strong group influence for product selection; strong group influence for brand selection.*
Private	**Private Necessity (3)** (e.g., microwave oven, socks) *Weak group influence for product selection; weak group influence for brand selection.*	**Private Luxury (4)** (e.g., pinball machine, espresso maker) *Strong group influence for product selection; weak group influence for brand selection.*

Source: Adapted from William O. Bearden and Michael J. Etzel, "Reference Group Influences on Product and Brand Purchase Decisions," *Journal of Consumer Research*, 9, no. 2 (1982): 183–194.

product or a particular brand is being selected. Obviously, a watch is a product. Rolex is a very expensive brand of watch. These elements are presented in Exhibit 8.2. Keep in mind that the meaning of necessity and luxury vary by consumer.

For necessities, reference group influence is weak for product selection (boxes #1 and #3). Reference groups rarely influence the decision to buy shoes, in general. With public necessities, however, the influence of reference groups on brand selection is strong (for example, "You should get some Sperry's"; box #1). For luxuries, reference group influence is strong for *product* selection (boxes #2 and #4). However, group influence on *brand* selection is only strong for public luxuries (for example, "You need to join *our* country club!"). A careful look at the exhibit reveals that group influence on brand selection is strong for all publicly

social media media through which communication occurs

social networks consumers connecting with one another based on common interests, associations, or goals

social networking website website that facilitates online social networking

apps mobile application software that runs on devices like smartphones, tablets, and other computer-based tools

viewed products. This highlights the importance that brands play in the everyday life of consumers.

8-4 SOCIAL MEDIA'S ROLE IN GROUP AND INTERPERSONAL INFLUENCE

To say that social media and the Internet have radically changed consumer behavior and group influence would be an understatement. Social media and social networking now play big roles in CB, as current estimates reveal that nearly 21% of Americans go online "almost constantly."[18] As discussed previously, consumers get both hedonic and utilitarian value from interacting through social networking. Because some of these sites revolve specifically around causes, interests, and activities, they also directly impact behavior in different ways. Few groups ever meet physically, making most of them informal and secondary for group members. However, their importance shouldn't be overlooked. Even when the physical proximity of other people is close, many consumers choose to connect through social media rather than face to face. One study found that 20% of adults in the United States use digital tools to "talk" with neighbors.[19]

8-4a Social Media and Consumer Behavior

It is important to distinguish among several concepts that pertain to social media and online behavior. **Social media** refers to media through which communication occurs. **Social networks** are networks of consumers that are formed based on common interest, associations, or goals. In sociology, a social network is viewed as a group of individuals who share information and experiences. **Social networking websites** (sometimes referred to as "online social network sites") are websites that facilitate online social networking. Networking has taken on a new meaning in the digital age and has almost become synonymous with social media. The term **apps**, or mobile applications, refers to specific types of software that run on various devices like smartphones, tablets, and other computer-based tools.

Interestingly, social networking has primarily become a mobile activity, as friends stay in virtual touch with others through smartphones, tablets, laptops, and other devices. The majority of social media and Internet usage now originates from mobile devices instead of other types of devices.[20] Furthermore, consumers have quickly switched to apps over traditional website browsing as the preferred method of communication.

POPULARITY OF SOCIAL NETWORKING WEBSITES AND APPS

It is hard to overstate the impact of social media on consumers' lives today. Current estimates reveal that 62% of the U.S. adult population is currently on Facebook, compared to 26% on Pinterest, 24% on Instagram, and 20% on Twitter. These percentages change daily.[21] Two websites in particular highlight the role that the social media plays in consumer behavior: Facebook and Twitter. Facebook continues to be one of the most popular websites in the world. Although statistics change daily, Facebook reported more than 1.7 billion active monthly users as of late 2016. To put that in perspective, if Facebook were a country, it'd be the third largest country in the world! The worldwide dominance of Facebook is reflected in the fact that the site is available in more than 70 languages, and that more than 85% of users reside outside of the United States.[22] The majority of users check Facebook frequently throughout the day and post daily as well.

There's no question that Facebook has been *the* major player in online social networking. Facebook applies well to our discussion of groups because of all of the groups that consumers can join or "like." While Facebook is currently the dominant social networking site, evidence suggests that it is losing popularity among young consumers, though it is too early to make strong predictions.[23]

Twitter continues to be very popular. Twitter's own statistics reveal that there were more than 320 million users as of 2016 and approximately 500 million tweets per day.[24] Twitter appears to be more popular with men than with women, especially compared to Facebook. In today's information age, Twitter has become an important part of information flow, with many news stories breaking on Twitter before they are covered on network news stations. As mentioned, Pinterest and Instagram also play a big role in consumer behavior, with over 300 million users currently on Instagram and more than 170 million on Pinterest.

It is important to emphasize that the motivation to join social networking groups goes beyond a simple need to communicate. For many consumers, it's about connection. In this way, social networking helps to fulfill the need to belong. Of course, there are countless other websites and apps that are popular, with each one attempting

Connecting with others is just a click away.

to satisfy a unique niche. For example, YouTube, and Snapchat allow users to share video content. Sharing visual content has become a very big business, as evidenced by the fact that Facebook acquired Instagram for approximately $1 billion in 2012.[25] While this deal was huge, it pales in comparison to the $19 billion purchase of WhatsApp in 2014.[26] Other sites that are based on special interests such as LinkedIn, Classmates, Tagged, Meetup, Friendster, Ning, Bebo, and Ourtime continue to grow in popularity.

VALUE AND SOCIAL MEDIA

Recall from an earlier discussion that consumers derive both utilitarian and hedonic value from group membership. This pertains to social media as well. To illustrate, consider the website Stylehive. Stylehive is a social shopping community where people share fashion ideas and products. The site allows consumers to organize their shopping activities, learn about other consumers with similar fashion styles, and connect with popular fashion retailers. Users are also able to learn about special deals (a utilitarian benefit) and enjoy connections with other consumers (a hedonic benefit). Foursquare, a popular social networking application website that centers around geolocation and mobile technologies, not only allows users to inform friends of their location, but also allows users to earn rewards, to leave tips about particular destinations, and to collect coupons for various retailers.[27]

Pinterest allows users to organize and share their interests with others, attracting their millions of unique visitors each month. The site is most popular with women, who regularly post images of their favorite fashions, foods, and other interests.[28] By pinning on categorized boards, consumers can follow others with similar interests. They can even repin content onto their own boards. This way content can be spread quickly from consumer to consumer.

Social gaming apps like Bike Race, Ruzzle, and Doodle Jump also allow consumers to enjoy playing games with one another. These apps have become very big business as they provide hedonic value for consumers who play the games.

SOCIAL BUYING AND COUPONING

Social buying refers to consumer buying behavior that takes place on social networking sites. Social couponing is a closely related topic. *Social couponing* refers to a type of buying where consumers receive a coupon, or deal, by joining a special social networking website. In some cases, the coupons become valid after a certain number of consumers choose to take advantage of the offer.

There are a number of popular social buying and social couponing websites. One of the most popular is Groupon. Groupon allows members to take advantage of several deals daily when enough consumers join in for a specified deal. One of the advantages to consumers and businesses alike is that consumers are often persuaded to try new things that they might not have otherwise tried. Similar sites like Livingsocial, Yipit, and Scoutmob have also gained in popularity.

Social media sites like the ones discussed in this section have dramatically influenced consumer behavior. Consumers receive

both utilitarian and hedonic value from these sites, and there is little reason to believe that the popularity of the sites will wane in the foreseeable future.

8-4b Individual Differences in Susceptibility to Group Influence

Although group influence plays an important role in influencing consumer behavior, not all consumers conform to group expectations equally. Individual difference variables play an important role in the extent to which consumers conform to the expectations of others. They also influence how one behaves in the presence of others. Three important variables are susceptibility to interpersonal influence, attention to social comparison information, and separateness-connectedness.

SUSCEPTIBILITY TO INTERPERSONAL INFLUENCE

One individual difference variable, *susceptibility to interpersonal influence*, assesses an individual's need to enhance the image others hold of him or her by acquiring and using products, conforming to the expectations of others, and learning about products by observing others.[29]

Studies reveal that consumers who are particularly susceptible to interpersonal influence are more likely to value conspicuous items (that is, highly valued items like luxury automobiles or jewelry).[30] In the value equation (value = what you get − what you give), the benefits of quality and image would be weighted heavily in their perception of value.

Seeking approval of others through product ownership is very important to these consumers. Consumers who score high on the susceptibility to interpersonal influence scale are also more likely to desire avoiding negative impressions in public settings.[31] For example, wearing "uncool" clothes in a shopping mall would be much more distressing to a consumer who is highly susceptible to interpersonal influence than to other consumers.

ATTENTION TO SOCIAL COMPARISON INFORMATION

Another individual difference variable that affects consumer behavior related to group influence is *attention to social comparison information (ATSCI)*. Consumers who score high on this measure are concerned about how other people react to their behavior.[32] The trait is closely related to susceptibility to interpersonal influence. Sample items from this scale are presented in Exhibit 8.3.

The ATSCI trait often emerges when a consumer is shopping, as consumers with a strong degree of the

---

social gaming online or app-based game played on a social media platform

social buying consumer buying behavior that takes place on social networking sites

social couponing type of buying where consumers receive a coupon, or deal, by joining a special social networking website

susceptibility to interpersonal influence individual difference variable that assesses a consumer's need to enhance the image others hold of him or her by acquiring and using products, conforming to the expectations of others, and learning about products by observing others

attention to social comparison information (ATSCI) individual difference variable that assesses the extent to which consumers are concerned about how other people react to their behavior

Exhibit 8.3

Sample Items from Attention to Social Comparison Information Scale

It's important to me to fit into the group I'm with.
At parties I usually try to behave in a manner that makes me fit in.
I tend to pay attention to what others are wearing.
I actively avoid wearing clothes that are not in style.
My behavior often depends on how I feel others wish me to behave.

Source: Adapted from William O. Bearden and Randall L. Rose, "Attention to Social Comparison Information: An Individual Difference Factor Affecting Consumer Conformity," *Journal of Consumer Research*, 16 (March 1990): 461–471.

trait tend to modify their purchasing behaviors when they are shopping with others. For example, a consumer who has a strong degree of ATSCI might buy an imported beer when he is shopping with others but a less expensive beer when he is shopping alone. Paying attention to what others think is likely to lead consumers to conform to others' expectations, and studies have shown that consumers with a strong degree of ATSCI are more likely to conform to the expectations of others.[33]

Social gaming provides hedonic value.

SEPARATENESS-CONNECTEDNESS

Consumers differ in their feelings of "connectedness" to other consumers. A consumer with a **separated self-schema** perceives himself as distinct and separate from others, while a consumer with a **connected self-schema** sees herself as an integral part of a group.[34] Marketers are well aware of the differences in how people view their relationships with groups, and marketing messages are often based on "connected" or "separated" themes. One study found that consumers who feel connected respond more favorably to advertisements that promote group belonging and cohesion.[35] Another study found that consumers with a high need for connection respond quite favorably to salespeople with whom they share some degree of similarity.[36]

Culture plays an important role in how separated or connected consumers feel. For example, consumers in Eastern cultures tend to feel more connected to others, while consumers in Western cultures tend to feel more separate and distinct. Advertising themes in a collectivist culture (a culture that focuses heavily on the interdependence of citizens) therefore often promote connected themes, while advertisements in the United States tend to emphasize separate themes.[37]

SOCIAL PRESENCE AND EMBARRASSMENT

The influence of other people on consumer behavior is strongest when consumers know they are being observed. In some cases, the presence of others in a specific situation (referred to as *social presence*) can make one feel uncomfortable.[38] This is especially the case when consumers are consuming or buying personal products. Consumers can even feel embarrassed by the presence of others when purchasing these items. One study revealed that college students were particularly embarrassed with the purchase of condoms when other consumers were present.[39] This influence was affected, however, by the amount of experience the students had with buying condoms. Consumers who were familiar with the act of buying the product did not feel significantly

separated self-schema self-conceptualization of the extent to which a consumer perceives himself or herself as distinct and separate from others

connected self-schema self-conceptualization of the extent to which a consumer perceives himself or herself as being an integral part of a group

high levels of embarrassment if others were present during the purchase. Many consumers are uncomfortable working out in a gym for fear of how they appear to others.

Social presence can also have positive effects. One recent study concluded that the presence of others in a service setting can make a customer feel more satisfied with a positive experience than they would be if they were alone when the positive experience occurred. Importantly, the same study concluded that consumers can be even more dissatisfied with a bad experience when other consumers are present.[40] It seems that social presence intensifies feelings of satisfaction and dissatisfaction.

8-5 WORD-OF-MOUTH AND CONSUMER BEHAVIOR

Another important concept in the study of interpersonal influence is word-of-mouth behavior. **Word-of-mouth (WOM)** is information about products, services, and experiences that is transmitted from consumer to consumer. WOM includes all kinds of information that can be spread about various consumer behaviors. Although word-of-mouth processes have been important in marketing for years, they've taken on even more importance in the digital age.

Two types of WOM influences can be distinguished: *organic* and *amplified*. The distinction between the concepts is highlighted by the Word of Mouth Marketing Association (WOMMA). According to WOMMA, organic WOM occurs naturally when consumers truly enjoy a product or service and they want to share their experiences with others. Amplified WOM occurs when marketers attempt to accelerate WOM in existing customer circles, or when they develop entirely new forums for WOM, like blogs or web pages.[41]

Consumers are heavily influenced by WOM, and its power is impressive. Consumers tell each other about products, services, and experiences all day long. If a movie is really good, moviegoers tell others. It's no wonder that word-of-mouth influences the vast majority of consumer product sales! WOM is influential because in general consumers tend to believe other consumers more than they believe advertisements and explicit marketing messages from companies.

word-of-mouth (WOM)
information about products, services, and experiences that is transmitted from consumer to consumer

8-5a Positive and Negative WOM

The more satisfied consumers are with a company or product, the more likely they are to spread positive WOM. If consumers believe strongly in a company and its products, they are more likely to talk to others about it.[42] Terms such as *brand advocate* or *brand ambassador* describe consumers who believe strongly in a brand and tell others about it. Consumers are also more likely to spread WOM when a product is particularly relevant to their own self-concept and when they are highly involved with the product category.[43] For example, a drummer is more likely to spread WOM about musical products than a consumer who doesn't play any instruments.

Marketers realize that negative WOM can be extremely damaging. The reason why negative WOM is so damaging to a company is that this form of WOM is especially influential. In general, negative word-of-mouth is more influential than positive word-of-mouth.[44] Hearing that the food at a restaurant is terrible is much more influential than hearing that it is good. Consumers also tend to tell more people about unsatisfactory experiences than pleasing ones.

VALUE AND WORD-OF-MOUTH

As noted earlier, group influence processes are closely related to consumer perceptions of value. Similarly, WOM is affected in large part by the perceived value that consumers receive from products and services. One study, performed in a South Korean service setting, found that both utilitarian and hedonic value positively influence WOM intentions.[45] Customers who believed the restaurant allowed them to efficiently address their hunger received utilitarian value, and those who enjoyed the experience beyond addressing hunger received hedonic value. When this value was perceived as being particularly high, consumers were motivated to encourage their families and friends to go to that restaurant as well. The more value that consumers receive, the more likely they are to tell others about their experiences with products and services.

WORD-OF-MOUTH, SOCIAL MEDIA, AND SOCIAL MEDIA MARKETING

It's clear that the digital world has had a drastic effect on consumer word-of-mouth. Consumers seek out other

> **Eighty percent of Internet users have sought online advice for health issues.**

online users for advice on all kinds of issues, ranging from what types of products to buy, to input into health, personal, and financial decisions. In fact, estimates reveal that 80% of Internet users have sought online advice for health issues.[46] Consumers also regularly spread WOM through text messaging and tweets. Consider that one in three teens sends more than 100 texts per day, and it's easy to see how this can impact WOM.[47] And that's just teens!

Many websites encourage the spread of information from consumer to consumer. These sites play an important role in social media marketing. **Social media marketing** refers to the practice of using social media to generate consumer interest in a product, service, or idea. Some sites are even dedicated specifically to WOM and social media marketing, like BzzAgent and Yelp.[48] BzzAgent only allows consumers to spread WOM and also to share web content. By becoming a "bzza-gent," consumers are able to participate in a popular online WOM network. Yelp.com allows consumers to learn about places to eat, shop, and relax based on the opinions of knowledgeable locals.

iQoncept/Shutterstock.com

Many companies actively encourage WOM by including discussion boards on their own websites. This also allows companies to assist in the development and maintenance of brand communities. Although marketers can encourage the spread of positive WOM, they must also be mindful of the spread of negative WOM in the online world. Because negative WOM is so influential, it is important for companies to monitor the content that is posted on various websites. It is becoming quite common to see what can be called *anti-brand communities*, or *anti–fan clubs*. These are communities in which members spread negative information about companies and products to other users. Marketers should pay close attention to these communities.

MEASURING ONLINE WOM

Given the importance of online WOM and how it influences CB, consumer researchers and marketers alike must gather valid information on WOM statistics. Many services offer web traffic analytic and effectiveness services, including Quantcast, Alexa, and Comscore. Some web traffic services allow users to focus on specific topics or trends, as would be the case with WOM. Services

such as Tweetreach, Whatthetrend, and of course Twitter focus specifically on tweets and trending issues. Popular trends generally include tweets about products, movies, celebrities, and news events. Search engine trends are also monitored. Google Trends, for example, monitors the popularity of search terms on its search engine. All of these services can be quite valuable for understanding popular online topics, trends, and WOM.

8-5b Buzz Marketing

One marketing tactic that continues to evolve is called **buzz marketing**. Buzz marketing includes marketing efforts that focus on generating excitement (or buzz) that is spread among market segments. Quite often, this type of marketing utilizes some form of WOM, as is found with the BzzAgent website. Successful buzz marketing can be a powerful tool for marketers, as information about products and services can spread quickly. Buzz marketing is one form of what is called **guerrilla marketing**, or the marketing of a product using unconventional means.

Although marketers have attempted to create a buzz about their products for years, buzz marketing is currently becoming popular in large part as a response to mass media fragmentation and advertising clutter. The techniques can be quite clever. For example, automobile companies can give customers automobiles to simply ride around and be seen in. This was a tactic the Ford Motor Company utilized when it gave a handful of consumers Ford Fiesta automobiles to drive around while performing activities assigned by the company. By having consumers see the new automobile in use and receive WOM from others, Ford was able to take advantage of the power of buzz marketing.[49]

The spreading of WOM online through social networking sites can

Social media marketing the practice of using social media to generate consumer interest in a product, service, or idea

buzz marketing marketing efforts that focus on generating excitement among consumers and that are spread from consumer to consumer

guerrilla marketing marketing of a product using unconventional means

CONSUMERS AND TECHNOLOGY

Maybe Talk Isn't Cheap

Marketers are excited about the many opportunities that are available in cyberspace. One valuable opportunity can be found in blogging (a term formed from the words "web logging"). Blogging allows consumers to voice their opinions on a number of different topics, products, and services. Blogging has become so popular that the practice is now a part of the marketing mix for many companies.

A number of websites now allow companies to hire bloggers to write blogs about their products and services. Sites such as Sponsoredreviews.com have grown in popularity. Although the requirements for each site vary, the basic idea is that bloggers are given the opportunity to blog about products or companies for pay. Advertisers tell bloggers what products or services they want included in the blog, and the blogger agrees to write about it. The arrangement can be a win-win

Ivelin Radkov/Shutterstock.com

situation for both the blogger and advertiser. Of course, this practice may be considered to be unethical by some. Nevertheless, this form of promotion has rapidly becoming an important component of buzz marketing, and it is likely that it will continue to grow in popularity.

---

be considered another form of buzz marketing. In fact, buzz marketing uses social media tools and websites regularly. As we have discussed, companies sometimes hire consumers to spread such messages. One buzz marketing tactic that relates directly to WOM is termed viral marketing. **Viral marketing** uses online technologies to facilitate WOM by having consumers spread marketing messages through their online connections. A great example of viral marketing was when Columbia Records and Legacy Recordings developed a viral campaign to promote a Bob Dylan greatest hits collection. Consumers were able to superimpose personalized notes over the famous rock video for the song "Subterranean Homesick Blues" and then send the video to friends. Hundreds of thousands of consumers joined in on the fun, making the campaign a success. Companies sometimes attach their own viral messages to messages that are sent by consumers. For example, HTC and Sprint use viral marketing by including the message "Sent from my HTC on the Now Network from Sprint!" on text messages sent from the popular phone.

Although buzz marketing may be facilitated through online message boards and networking sites, this type of marketing is not limited to online content. The term *buzz marketing* is used much more broadly than that, with messages being delivered in many different ways to create buzz.

8-5c Stealth Marketing

Another more controversial form of marketing that uses WOM is stealth marketing. **Stealth marketing** is a guerrilla marketing tactic that is similar to buzz marketing; however, a key difference is that with stealth marketing consumers are completely unaware that they are being marketed to (hence the term *stealth*). As an example of stealth marketing, imagine a camera marketer who has employees pose as tourists. These "tourists" then ask others to take their pictures with a new camera. Of course, the picture takers don't realize that the tourists are employed by the company and that they are being targeted by a marketing message.[50] A movie titled *The Joneses*, starring Demi

viral marketing marketing method that uses online technologies to facilitate WOM by having consumers spread messages through their online conversations

stealth marketing guerrilla marketing tactic in which consumers do not realize that they are being targeted for a marketing message

Jurassic World - Official Trailer (HD)

Universal Pictures

Subscribe 754,860

80,606,863 views

306,122   15,431

Add to   Share   More

Product placements in movies have become quite common. Samsung and Mercedes-Benz were prominent in 2015's *Jurassic World*.

Moore, presents an entertaining, albeit exaggerated example of stealth marketing. Some consider *product placements* in television shows and movies to be a type of stealth marketing, because consumers generally don't realize that companies pay for these placements. Soap operas, such as *Days of Our Lives*, have turned to product placements as a marketing tool.[51] Research suggests that female consumers have more positive attitudes toward product placements than do male consumers.[52] Product placements were once considered to be unique, but in today's environment they are becoming commonplace. Marketers often use the terms *brand content*, *advertainment*, or *infotainment* when using these strategies.

The use of stealth marketing techniques, though growing, is considered questionable or unethical by many marketing professional organizations such as WOMMA. The following tactics are generally viewed negatively by many professionals in the industry:

▶ *Stealth marketing.* Deceiving consumers about the involvement of marketers in a communication

▶ *Shilling.* Compensating consumers to talk about or promote products without disclosing that they are working for the company

▶ *Infiltrating.* Using fake identities in online discussions to promote a product

8-5d Opinion Leaders

Buzz marketing techniques are especially effective when opinion leaders are used. **Opinion leaders** are consumers who have great influence on the behavior of others relating to product adoption and purchase. Opinion leaders are knowledgeable about specific products or services and have a high level of involvement with those products. Characteristics of opinion leaders depend largely on the type of product under consideration, but in general, opinion leaders are socially active and self-confident.

With online social networking and media sites, it's easy to find a few key posters that other users tend to listen to. With Twitter, you can even track the number of followers for each user. The Ford Motor Company included influential women bloggers in their "What Women Want" campaign. Popular bloggers were invited to test new Ford products and interact with company executives. Inviting the bloggers was a good way of ensuring some online buzz.[53] As with the Ford Fiesta example, it appears the company is becoming quite adept with buzz marketing campaigns.

MARKET MAVENS AND SURROGATE CONSUMERS

Opinion leaders are not the only influential consumers that have been identified. Market mavens and surrogate consumers also exert much influence on others. A **market maven** is a consumer who spreads information about all types of products and services that are available in the marketplace. The key difference between an opinion leader and a market maven is that the market maven's influence is not category specific. That is, market mavens spread information about numerous products and services.

Consumers can also be heavily influenced by what are termed surrogate consumers. A **surrogate consumer** is a consumer who is hired by another to provide input into a purchase decision. Interior decorators, travel consultants, and stockbrokers

opinion leader consumer who has a great deal of influence on the behavior of others relating to product adoption and purchase

market maven consumer who spreads information about all types of products and services that are available in the marketplace

surrogate consumer consumer who is hired by another to provide input into a purchase decision

Exhibit 8.4

Adopter Categories

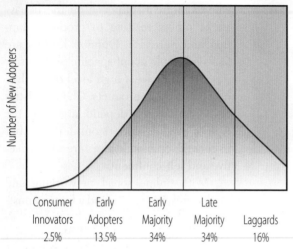

Consumer Innovators	Early Adopters	Early Majority	Late Majority	Laggards
2.5%	13.5%	34%	34%	16%

Adapted from Rogers, Everett M. *Diffusion of Innovation*, 4th ed., New York: The Free Press, 1995.

can all be considered surrogate consumers. Surrogate consumers can be very influential, and marketers should carefully consider the level of influence of these individuals.[54] Because of their extensive product expertise, surrogate consumers can often help others derive the maximum amount of value out of their transactions by maximizing the benefits associated with product purchase.

8-5e Diffusion Processes

One area of interest in the study of group processes is the diffusion process. The **diffusion process** refers to the way in which new products are adopted and spread throughout a marketplace. Researchers have learned that different groups of consumers tend to adopt new products at different rates. One group may adopt a new product (for example, a hybrid automobile) very early in the product's life cycle, while another group may be very slow to adopt the product, if it adopts the product at all. A product life cycle is a description of the life of a product from the time it is introduced to the time it dies off.

diffusion process way in which new products are adopted and spread throughout a marketplace

household decision making process by which decisions are made in household units

family household at least two people who are related by blood or marriage who occupy a housing unit

In all, five categories of consumers have been identified. They include innovators, early adopters, early majority, late majority, and laggards. These groups are presented in Exhibit 8.4.[55]

What makes group influence relevant to the diffusion process is that each group learns about new products not only from seeing marketing messages, but also from talking with other consumers and observing their behavior. Group influence processes therefore apply to these categories.

Innovators and early adopter consumers tend to be influential when discussing products and services with members of other groups. As such, they tend to be opinion leaders for specific product categories. Innovators are often risk takers and financially well-off. Early adopter consumers are generally young and well educated. Members of other groups, including late majority consumers and laggards, tend to be more cautious about buying new products and wait significantly longer to buy the latest innovations. These consumers also tend to be somewhat older, with lower levels of education and spending power.

8-6 HOUSEHOLD DECISION MAKING AND CONSUMER BEHAVIOR

As we discussed previously, the family unit is an important primary reference group for consumers. Family members typically have a great deal of influence over one another's attitudes, thoughts, and behaviors. Consider the many ways that the family has an impact on consumer behavior. **Household decision making** is the process by which household units choose between alternative courses of action. One interesting finding relates to what has been termed the *consumer doppelganger effect*.[56] Research reveals that mothers often mimic their daughters' identities through clothing and fashion choice. Some might realize that this is similar to mothers living vicariously through their children, but it more strongly emphasizes the fact that parents can be influenced by their children just as easily as children can be influenced by their parents. To begin our discussion of household decision making, we first discuss the various conceptualizations of the term *household*.

8-6a Traditional Family Structure

The ways in which society views the family unit have changed dramatically in recent decades. Traditionally, the **family household** has been viewed as at least two

Family members greatly influence one another.

people who are related by blood or marriage and who occupy a housing unit. In fact, this is how the U.S. Census Bureau defines a family unit. Other traditional family definitions include the *nuclear* family and the *extended* family.

The **nuclear family** consists of a mother, a father, and a set of siblings. The **extended family** consists of three or more generations of family members, including grandparents, parents, children, and grandchildren. In individualistic cultures like the United States, emphasis is placed on the nuclear family. However, in collectivist cultures, more focus is placed on the extended family, and it is not uncommon to see households made up of extended family members living together. With this being said, the growth in multigenerational households in the United States (an individualistic culture) has been significant in recent years, with the greatest growth coming in the economically turbulent years of 2007–2009.[57]

EMERGING TRENDS IN FAMILY STRUCTURE

As mentioned previously, the traditional views of the family have changed over time. Today, many nontraditional household arrangements exist throughout the United States. Societal trends toward people of opposite sex sharing living quarters (termed POSSLQ or cohabitation) and homosexual households have altered the way in which family households are conceptualized. According to the most recent estimates, 34% of households are defined as nonfamily households (that is, consumers sharing the same living quarters who are not related by

blood or marriage).[58] Nonfamily households grew twice as fast as traditional households from 2000 to 2010.[59]

Divorce rates tend to be quite high in the United States. It is widely quoted that nearly 50% of all marriages in the United States end in divorce, but the exact number is really unknown and many consider this 50% figure to be a myth.[60] Regardless, even higher rates are seen in second and third marriages, as estimates reveal that 67% of second marriages and 74% of third marriages end this way.[61] Divorces have clearly altered the composition of the American family, and they have led to *blended families*. Blended families consist of previously married spouses and their children. While divorces began to dip during the great recession, hitting a low point of approximately 3.6 per 1,000 people, the years immediately following saw a gradual increase. It has been estimated that when the unemployment rate rises 1%, the divorce rate drops 1%. Many consumers could not afford to divorce in the shaky economy, but rates increased to a total of 2.4 million divorces in 2012.[62] A sluggish economy also explains the relatively low birth rates during those years. Data reveal a 2016 U.S. birth rate of 59 births per thousand women.[63] That was the lowest in 100 years!

Many people simply decide never to marry. And many other people delay marriage. In 2014, the marriage rate in the United States was 6.8 per 1,000 consumers.[64] The median age of first marriages for men is 28.7 and 26.5 for women. This has been increasing since the 1960s, when the median ages were in the early 20s.[65] Also, more American women are living without a husband than with one.[66] As a result of this trend and the divorce rate, single-parent households have increased. Approximately 27% of U.S. children lived with only one parent in the year 2016,[67] and approximately 40% of births are to unmarried women.[68] Of course, not all women have children. It has been reported that 48% of women aged 15–44 have never had children as of 2014, compared to 46% in 2012. In 2013, there were just 62.9 births per 1,000 women, the lowest rate ever recorded.[69] Yet another trend is that single men are adopting children at a record rate.[70]

Finally, the meaning of the term *nonfamily* is open to debate and interpretation. For many, the term itself is plagued by personal beliefs and biases, and it has evolved based on societal changes. One topic of current interest is same-sex marriages. Same-sex marriages are becoming increasingly common and as a result, it is becoming

nuclear family a mother, a father, and a set of siblings

extended family three or more generations of family members

more common for marketers to target same-sex couples in many of their advertisements.

Despite widespread attention to nontraditional households, census data reveal that the largest portion of American consumers still live in something resembling a "traditional" household, consisting of a married couple who either have yet to have children, have children living under the same roof, or have already raised children who no longer live at home. Also, the data reveal that the majority of American children reside in a traditional household, as is shown in Exhibit 8.5.

8-6b Household Life Cycle

An important concept in the study of the family unit is the **household life cycle (HLC)**. The HLC represents a segmentation technique that acknowledges that changes in family composition and income alter household demand for products and services.

The traditional HLC segments families into a number of groups based on the number of adults present and the age of the head of household. This conceptualization is presented in Exhibit 8.6. Based on this conceptualization, a number of segments are present, including consumers who never marry (Bachelor 1, 2, and 3); two-adult, childless households (Young Couple, Childless Couple, and Older Couple); two adults with children (Full Nest 1, 2, and 3 and Delayed Full Nest); and one adult with children (Single Parent 1, 2, and 3).

The categorization of the household is important for consumer researchers.[71] Product expenditures vary greatly by stage in the HLC, and at each stage consumers often try to obtain the most value that they can from their purchases. For example, Full Nest 1 consumers often face costly expenses related to raising young children, including the cost of baby clothes, furniture, and day care. These young consumers often have to search for new living accommodations in the form of larger apartments or a starter home when children are born. Single parents face the same challenges as two-adult families, but they must face these challenges alone. A great strain is therefore placed on the income of single parents. Older, childless couples have more disposable income to spend on their own needs. They are much more likely to enjoy

household life cycle (HLC) segmentation technique that acknowledges that changes in family composition and income alter household demand for products and services

boomerang kids young adults between the ages of 18 and 34 who move back home with their parents after they graduate from college

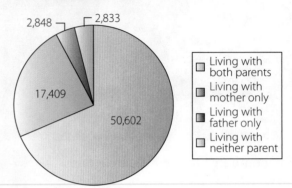
luxuries such as vacation homes, financial investments, and upscale automobiles. Couples older than 64 often enjoy their retirement years, or choose to remain employed beyond retirement age.

The categories and assumptions in the HLC are representative of general patterns of spending behavior. Not every consumer will fall neatly into one specific category. Rather, the categories help to explain the living situations and expenditures of many consumers. Obviously, consumers face their own situations.

BOOMERANG KIDS AND THE SANDWICH GENERATION

Two important groups that are of interest to researchers are boomerang kids and members of the sandwich generation. **Boomerang kids** are young adults, ages 18 to 34, who graduate from college and move back home with their parents. Quite often, the motivation is to reduce debt that has accumulated in the college years. Some have suggested the term *adultolescence* to describe this stage. The trend is growing, and a recent report estimated that nearly 53% of college graduates planned to move back home with their parents.[72]

The economy plays a big role in influencing boomerang kids. A 2012 report revealed that nearly 30% of adults aged 25–34 lived with their parents due to the shaky economy.[73] Another study found that 78% of

Exhibit 8.6

Traditional Household Life Cycle Categories

	Under 35 years	35–64 years	Older than 64 years
One-adult household	Bachelor 1	Bachelor 2	Bachelor 3
Two-adult household	Young Couple	Childless Couple	Older Couple
Two adults + children	Full Nest 1 (children < 6 years old) Full Nest 2 (children > 6 years old)	Delayed Full Nest (children < 6 years old) Full Nest 3 (children > 6 years old) Empty Nest	Empty Nest
One adult + children	Single Parent 1 (children < 6 years old) Single Parent 2 (children > 6 years old)	Single Parent 3 Empty Nest	

Source: Adapted from M. C. Gilly and B. M. Enis, "Recycling the Family Lifecycle: A Proposal for Redefinition," in *Advances in Consumer Research*, Vol. 9, ed. Andrew A. Mitchell, 271–276 (Ann Arbor, MI: Association for Consumer Research, 1982).

consumers in this segment stated they couldn't afford to live on their own.[74] More interestingly, however, is a recent study that found that in 2015 26% of Millennials lived with their parents despite an improved job market. It seems that attitudes toward older children in the home are changing.[75] This trend challenges the traditional HLC, and it impacts how middle-aged consumers spend their money. A humorous view of adult children at home can be found in the movie *Failure to Launch*, starring Matthew McConaughey. The issue, however, is not a laughing matter. In fact, it has been estimated that boomerang kids cost their parents $5,000 per year in disposable income.[76] It's not just boomerang kids, however. Another trend is "doubling up," where additional adults live together who are in no way related. While "roommates" have been around for decades, it's now not uncommon for families to house an extra, unrelated adult. In fact, in 2015, 48% of millennials reported doubling up in some way, either through having a roommate or having a friend live with parents.[77]

Financial and emotional strains on middle-aged consumers also come from belonging to the sandwich generation. The **sandwich generation** consists of those consumers who must take care of both their own children and their aging parents. It is now estimated that nearly half of American consumers aged 40–50 are considered sandwiched consumers.[78] This number is expected to increase dramatically over the next decade, as millions of Baby Boomers continue to reach their retirement years. Taking care of both children and parents obviously affects the behavior of these consumers, as income is devoted to the needs of others. In fact, the average cost of caring for others aged 50-plus is nearly $6,000 per year. For consumers who must care for others long distance, the cost is nearly $9,000 per year.[79] Caregivers also lose much time at work, and they lose income and benefits as a result. These losses can be substantial and average over $300,000 over the lifetime of the caregiver. Businesses also lose money in the amount of as much as $34 billion per year, due to sandwich generation employees missing work.[80]

gresei/Shutterstock.com

sandwich generation
consumers who must take care of both their own children and their aging parents

PETS ARE FAMILY, TOO!

It will probably come as no surprise that pets are considered to be family members for millions of consumers worldwide. Dogs, cats, fish, birds, and reptiles are all popular pets for millions of consumers. Taking care of these pets can be costly, and the industry continues to grow. In the United States alone, consumers spend an estimated 62.75 billion on pet care annually, and the total is expected to increase. To put this into perspective, this is more than consumers spend on personal entertainment like watching movies, playing video games, or listening to music.

While most of the spending is attributed to food and basic medical care, one growing segment in the industry is pet services. Pet services include things like walking, boarding, and even doggie day care! Another booming segment is pet insurance. In fact, it is becoming popular for insurance policies to include coverage for pets. It seems that there is no limit to what some people will do for their pets. For most consumers, the money is well spent, considering the loyalty, comfort, and friendship that come from our furry friends.

Sources: "Pet Industry Market Size & Ownership Statistics," American Pet Products Association, http://www.americanpetproducts.org/press_industrytrends.asp (accessed April 6, 2016); Amy Silverstein, "Americans Spent Record Amount of Money Grooming Their Pets Last Year," Globalpost.com, March 3, 2012, http://www.globalpost.com/dispatches/globalpost-blogs/weird-wide-web/americans-spent-record-amount-money-grooming-their-pets (accessed April 13, 2012); "The Pet Economy: More than Movies, Music & Video Games Combined," Globalanimal.org, http://www.globalanimal.org/2010/10/20/the-pet-economy-more-than-movies-music-video-games-combined/20226/ (accessed April 12, 2012); C. Taylor, "The U.S. Pet Economy Didn't Go to the Dogs," Reuters, http://www.reuters.com/article/2013/02/08/us-economy-spending-pets-idUSBRE9170ZP20130208 (accessed February 11, 2013).

8-6c Household Purchase Roles

Five important roles in the household purchase process can be identified, and each member of a household plays at least one of these roles:

▶ *Influencer.* The person in the household who recognizes a need and provides information about a potential purchase to others

▶ *Gatekeeper.* The person who controls information flow into the household (for example, a mother who blocks unwanted email solicitations from her child's email account)

▶ *User.* The actual user of the product under consideration

▶ *Decision maker.* The person who makes the final decision regarding product purchase or nonpurchase

▶ *Purchaser.* The person who actually buys the product under consideration

sex role orientation (SRO) family's set of beliefs regarding the ways in which household decisions are reached

Each role is important in product consideration and selection. The final purchase of the product is largely influenced by beliefs regarding the role of each person in the household.

GENDER ROLES AND HOUSEHOLD DECISION MAKING

Like many of the concepts pertaining to household composition, societal views on gender roles and family decision making have evolved over time. Traditionally, men were viewed as having the primary responsibility of providing for the family, while women were expected to meet everyday family needs and take care of the home.[81] However, changes in the education of women and the acceleration in the number of double-income families have challenged these conceptualizations.

An important concept in gender roles and family decision making is **sex role orientation (SRO)**. A family's SRO influences the ways in which household decisions are reached. Families that have a traditional SRO believe that it is the responsibility of the male head of household to make large purchase decisions, while families with a "modern" SRO believe in a more democratic approach.[82] Given the evolving nature of the typical household in the United States, it is not surprising that SROs are changing. In particular, the role of women in household decision making is more prevalent than in previous years. Indeed, studies have revealed that women are playing a bigger role in decision making in all household areas. This, in part, reflects the fact that the percentage of women with higher education and income levels than their spouses has grown significantly over the last few decades.[83]

KID POWER

The role of children in household decision making is also evolving.[84] Although children were once thought to have little impact on purchasing decisions beyond what toy to buy, marketers are realizing that children are playing a large role in influencing many household purchases. One study found that 36% of parents with children between the ages of 6 and 11 reported that kids significantly influence their purchases. Even in times of economic instability, parents still try to spend on their kids, even if it means cutting back on other things.

Though it is difficult to measure kids' spending precisely, it has been estimated that kids command more than $1 trillion annually in personal spending and family influence.[85] Furthermore, the teen segment frequently sees its disposable income grow at a rate that is unlike that found in any other segment. For example,

the typical American 12-year-old has $1,500 per year to spend. However, this number leaps to $4,500 per year by the time the child reaches age 17. Much of this income is earned income, even if it is simply a weekly allowance. Older children earn much of their income from jobs outside of the house.

An important issue in the development of the child consumer is known as consumer socialization. Consumer socialization is defined as the process through which young consumers develop attitudes and learn skills that help them function in the marketplace.[86] Sometimes these skills are learned at a surprisingly young age, and children have largely begun to seek products that were once considered "too old" for their age segment. This has led to the development of a common marketing acronym, KGOY (Kids Growing Older, Younger).

Although many consider the issue of kid power and marketing to children controversial, it is clear that children do exert a significant influence on household decision making, and it is likely that this trend will continue.

consumer socialization the process through which young consumers develop attitudes and learn skills that help them function in the marketplace

STUDY TOOLS 8

LOCATED AT BACK OF THE TEXTBOOK
☐ Tear out Chapter Review Card

LOCATED AT WWW.CENGAGE.COM/LOGIN
☐ Review Key Term flashcards and create your own cards
☐ Track your knowledge and understanding of key concepts in consumer behavior
☐ Complete practice quizzes to prepare for tests
☐ Complete interactive content within CB Online
☐ Review the Chapter Highlight boxes for CB Online

9 | Consumer Culture

JGI/Jamie Grill/Getty Images

Remember to visit PAGE 201 for additional STUDY TOOLS

9-1 CULTURE AND MEANING ARE INSEPARABLE

Do love and marriage go together? One thing that might be even more certain is the fact that marriage and consumption go together. No matter where one gets married, the wedding typically involves an elaborate celebration. The site costofwedding.com tracks the average cost of weddings across the United States. In 2016, the average cost of a U.S. wedding was $26,500 according to their data.[1] The high cost of getting hitched is not confined to the United States—Chinese weddings cost an average $20,000. Both the U.S. and Chinese weddings seem like a bargain compared to the U.A.E., where an average wedding costs over $80,000. The disparity between economical and expensive weddings is tremendous. Some couples opt for "naked weddings," meaning no wedding dress, no flowers, no reception; just the *bare* essentials.

The way consumers find mates, however, is not so universal. In Western cultures, romantic marriage rules are ingrained so strongly that other concepts come across as strange, unusual, or even illegal. Consumers in other cultures often do not have much say in exactly whom they marry. Although this seems strange for most readers of this book, consumers from those cultures accept and even find comfort in the notion of an arranged marriage. Arab and Eastern consumers often end up getting married based on arrangements between families. This eliminates the need for match.com subscriptions, dating rituals, anxiety, and stress over popping the question—the couples never face this climactic moment. Polygamy is even an accepted form of marriage in some cultures, although it is illegal in many Western cultures. Culture drives differences in the customs associated with weddings, marriages, and the family life that follows.

9-1a What Is Culture?

Consumers make very simple decisions involving things like coffee drinking and very important and meaningful decisions involving things like getting married. In all cases, what a person consumes helps determine acceptance by other consumers in society. The consumption

act itself generally has no absolute meaning, only meaning relative to the environment in which the act takes place. Culture, therefore, embodies meaning.

Consumer culture represents the commonly held societal beliefs that define what is socially gratifying within a specific society. Culture shapes value by framing everyday life in terms of these commonly held beliefs. The fact that the average price for a cup of coffee in the United States has risen in the last quarter century indicates that American beliefs about the coffee-drinking experience have certainly changed and define a more valuable experience than in decades past. Nearly two in three consumers in the United States are coffee drinkers.[2] In contrast, although the average wedding still represents a large sum of money, the average spending on U.S. weddings is less now than it was in 2008. Is this due to the economy or to changing values? The answer is uncertain at this point but culture ultimately determines what consumption behaviors are acceptable.

At what age is it okay to have a cup of coffee, drink a glass of wine with the family, or go to the mall without an adult chaperone? Like other activities, the appropriateness of these activities varies. Exhibit 9.1 lists some consumption behaviors that vary in meaning, value, and acceptability from culture to culture.

9-1b Culture, Meaning, and Value

Today's marketplace is truly global. Consumers can easily interact with marketers from all parts of the world both virtually through the Internet and in person. Without culture, consumers would have little guidance as to the appropriate actions in many common consumer situations. Thus, culture performs important functions for consumers. These functions shape the value of consumer activities and include:

1. **Giving meaning to objects.** Consider how much culture defines the meaning of furniture, religious objects, and everyday items like food and drink. For instance, Dunkin' Donuts sells nearly 200 million cups of coffee annually in the United States with slogans like #KeepOn as part of its "America Runs on Dunkin" campaign. But in India, that slogan doesn't work, because breakfast on the run is not part of the Indian diet. Instead,

> **consumer culture**
> commonly held societal beliefs that define what is socially gratifying

Exhibit 9.1

Culture Shapes Value of Activities

Consumer behavior	Appropriateness in U.S. today	Alternative meaning
Texting or making Facebook posts while driving	U.S. society seems to accept the behavior, with 40 percent of teens admitting to the behavior.[1] Staying "connected" is greatly valued in today's U.S. consumer culture.	An insanely irresponsible behavior with the potential for great harm, including death, to the self and innocent others.
Kissing in public	Primarily a romantic activity although an acceptable family greeting.	In many cultures, kissing is common when greeting a friend or making a new acquaintance.
Consumers under 21 consuming beer or wine with dinner	Unacceptable or even illegal in many parts of the world, including much of the U.S.	Part of a nice family meal in many cultures including much of Western Europe. Not considered "drinking."
Supervisors and employees socializing together	Supervisors and coworkers can be friendly and socialize in public.	Employees and supervisors keep their distance away from work.
A get-together for BBQ pork ribs	A pleasant part of summertime backyard barbeques or tailgates.	Pork is an unacceptable food in many non-Christian cultures for religious reasons.

[1]https://www.fcc.gov/consumers/guides/dangers-texting-while-driving, accessed May 23, 2016.

Dunkin' Donuts encourages customers to "Get Your Mojo Back" with a visit, where customers can enjoy a beefless meal such as the Big Joy potato-and-pea-patty burger. ADD coffee is not so much the way to freshen up one's mind.[3]

2. **Giving meaning to activities.** Consider, for example, the role of things as simple as tipping, recreational activities, and even washing (hygiene). A daily shower still is not a universally accepted norm.

3. **Facilitating communication.** The shared meaning of things facilitates communication. When strangers meet, culture indicates whether a handshake, hug, or kiss is most appropriate. Things as simple as making eye contact can take on dramatically different meanings from one culture to another.

cultural norm rule that specifies the appropriate consumer behavior in a given situation within a specific culture

cultural sanction penalty associated with performing a nongratifying or culturally inconsistent behavior

9-1c Cultural Norms

Culture, meaning, and value are very closely intertwined. For this reason, culture determines things that are socially rewarding (valuable) or socially

unrewarding (not valuable). A consumer who acts inconsistently with cultural expectations risks getting the cold shoulder or worse from others. The term **cultural norm** refers to a rule that specifies the appropriate behavior in a given situation within a specific culture. Most, but not all, cultural norms are unwritten and simply understood by members of a cultural group.

In many countries, consumers do not routinely drink out of a bottle or can. It's considered impolite. Rather, particularly when one is at the table, a server always provides a glass, and the cultural expectation is a consumer should pour their drink into the glass before drinking. Koreans hold this custom strongly; many European cultures also practice this custom but perhaps not as strongly, whereas in North American cultures, drinking from a bottle is routine even in public places like bars and restaurants. Thus, in places like Korea and Europe, by pouring the drink into a glass before drinking the consumer performs a socially rewarding (valuable) act consistent with the norms of that society.

9-1d Cultural Sanctions

So, what happens to a consumer who performs an act inconsistent with cultural norms? Unfortunately, the consumer is likely to experience a cultural sanction. A **cultural sanction** refers to the penalties associated with performing a nongratifying or culturally inconsistent

CONSUMERS AND TECHNOLOGY

How Culture Gets Social

Marketing efforts rely heavily on Internet-based social media to reach consumers around the world. More than half the world's population engages in some form of social media. But, consumers around the world interact with social media in different amounts and in different ways. Consumers in the Philippines are best reached through Facebook with over 90 percent of consumers using Facebook at least monthly, the highest rate in the world. Want to reach potential customers through Twitter? That should work fine if your customers are in Indonesia with nearly 70 percent monthly penetration but not nearly so well in Germany where penetration is less than 20 percent. Mexican consumers have the highest rate of Instagram users (just under 100 percent) with France and China on the opposite side with very low penetrations. Where are U.S. consumers? They are in the middle of the pack for all the Internet usage statistics—maybe not the best global targets for social media marketing! Additionally, consumers do not use social networks the same way. Brazilian consumers, coming in about the median for all networks, use social networking to extract hedonic value through entertainment more than any other purpose.

Sources: Chaffey, D. (2016), "Global Social Media Research Summary 2016," Smart Insights, smartinisghts.com, accessed October 24, 2016. Charron, C. (2016), "Global Twitter Trends: Brazil," 360.com, accessed October 24, 2016.

behavior. Cultural sanctions often are relatively innocuous. For instance, if a man were to drink a soda from a bottle in Korea, he would be likely to get only a curious look or suffer some innocent teasing from members of the group. In other instances however, a consumer performing a culturally inconsistent act may be shunned or suffer banishment from a group.

Many societies still have strong cultural norms about marrying outside of one's social class, religion, or ethnic group. Violation of this norm can result in isolation from family or worse. Physically or socially harming a family member for fraternizing beyond one's cultural group represents a fairly strong cultural sanction.

POPULAR CULTURE

Popular culture captures cultural trends and shapes norms and sanctions within society. A few decades ago, U.S. college students routinely smoked cigarettes in college classroom buildings, filling the hallways with clouds of smoke. This is not only against university and local regulations in most places, but other students would likely find the behavior offensive today. Pop icons such as Miley Cyrus and Justin Bieber help determine acceptable style for many groups of admirers who desire to fit in with today's popular culture. For example, before her 20th birthday, Miley Cyrus generated quite a bit of

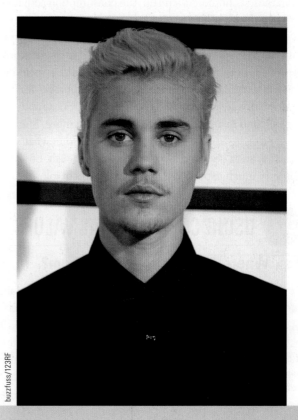

Pop star icons may establish cultural norms among pop culture members.

controversy by taking part in public displays of nudity and sensual behavior aimed at members of both sexes, as well as flaunting her use of marijuana.[4] Do such behaviors challenge cultural norms?

ROLE EXPECTATIONS

Every consumer plays various roles within society. Culture expects people to play these roles in a culturally rewarding fashion. In other words, when a consumer interacts with another person, any characteristic upon which that person can be categorized activates certain behavioral expectations. Recall that in a previous chapter we described how social schemata (stereotypes) help consumers organize knowledge about people. **Role expectations** are the specific expectations that are associated with each type of person. One's sex, one's occupation, one's social class, one's age: All are relevant bases for forming societal role expectations. Role expectations become a primary basis for cultural norms and sanctions. They define not only the way one should act to play the role but also the types of products that are appropriate for a person within a role. When a consumer travels to a foreign country, she may well find that expectations for a given role are different from those at home. As a result, the consumption activities associated with roles can also vary from culture to culture.

In most parts of the United States, for example, typical service employees in a restaurant, a department store, or even a hotel play their societal role well by speaking English only. However, in much of Scandinavia, for instance Norway, consumers expect that a service employee can respond in at least two languages, if not more. Service employees in Norway would generally be somewhat surprised even to be asked if they can speak English, because it is very much expected of them within their role.

9-2 USING CORE SOCIETAL VALUES

9-2a **Where Does Culture Come From?**

Consumer researchers commonly use culture to explain and predict consumer behavior, including Asian weddings.[5] More than 10% of all explanations of some consumer behavior include culture as a key factor.[6] Cultural beliefs define what religion is acceptable, what types of art and recreation are preferred, what manners are considered

role expectations the specific expectations that are associated with each type of person within a culture or society

ecological factors physical characteristics that describe the physical environment and habitat of a particular place

XiXinXing/Shutterstock.com

polite, the roles for different types of individuals including expectations for men and women in a society, and much more. Distinguishing the unique effects of culture over these more specific things is extremely difficult since as part of culture these things tend to function together. But as a whole there is little doubt that culture causes differences in the value consumers perceive from different products and experiences.[7]

> **There is little doubt that culture causes differences in the value consumers perceive in different products and experiences.**

How do people in one nation end up with a culture distinct from that of people in another? In other words, what causes culture? The answer to this question involves two important components.

First, ecological factors cause differences in culture because they change the relative value of objects. **Ecological factors** are the physical characteristics that describe the physical environment and habitat of a particular place. Thus, for example, consumers from groups that have traditionally lived in desert areas place a great value on water relative to consumers from areas filled with freshwater lakes. As a result, consumers from this area may have different habits when it comes to hygiene, including the frequency and duration of baths or showers. This can affect sales of beauty products, soaps, and toilet water and things like hotel room and building design.

Second, over time tradition develops among groups of peoples, and these traditions carry forward to structure society. **Tradition** in this sense refers to the customs and accepted ways of structuring society. Traditions include things like the family and political structures of a society. In the United States, Australia, Canada, and much of Europe, families traditionally consist of two generations (parents and children) living in a household, where a husband and wife share decision making. In other cultures, India for instance, more than two generations (grandparents, parents, and children) may share a household, and the key decision maker is the oldest male living in the house. Thus, consumer advertising may need to differ based on the traditional family decision-making style associated with a culture. While tradition can be thought of as influencing culture, one can safely say that in the long run culture also defines tradition.

Exhibit 9.2 illustrates how tradition and ecology come together to influence culture, with each culture being described by different amounts of core societal values (discussed later in this chapter), and these values driving differences in consumer behaviors and the value derived from them. Over time, traditions become embedded in culture and become relatively stable. However, while stable, they do slowly change, as illustrated by the changes in places where people traditionally smoke without fear of sanctions. In this sense, not only does culture influence the choices and behaviors of consumers, but in the end, subtle changes in these choices and behaviors also influence culture.

9-2b Dimensions of Cultural Values

Although conflicting views exist on what exactly are the best dimensions to describe differences in cultural values, the most widely applied dimensions are those developed by Geert Hofstede.[8] This theory of value-based differences in cultures is based on multiple dimensions, with each representing an identifiable core societal

Exhibit 9.2

Inputs and Outputs of Culture

value aspect. **Core societal values (CSVs)**, or cultural values, represent a commonly agreed-upon consensus about the most preferable ways of living within a society. Even though not all members of a culture may share precisely the same values to the same degree, a specific cultural group will tend to have common worldviews along these dimensions. Exhibit 9.2 illustrates how core societal values serve as the mechanism by which culture affects value. In some cases, the core societal value dimensions relate to or overlap with each other. Thus, some dimensions share some meaning. Also, when we discuss behavioral patterns associated with CSVs, we should realize they are generalities and thus we also can find exceptions to these patterns. Exhibit 9.3 provides a summary of each dimension.

Core societal values can be described along seven dimensions. Exhibit 9.3 lists and briefly summarizes each dimension. The sections below describe core societal values in more detail.

INDIVIDUALISM

The first CSV dimension contrasts cultures based on relative amounts of individualism and collectivism.[9] **Individualism** as a CSV means the extent to which people expect each other to take responsibility for themselves and their immediate family. Highly individualistic societies place high value on self-reliance, individual initiative, and personal

tradition customs and accepted ways of everyday behavior in a given culture

core societal values (CSVs) commonly agreed-upon consensus about the most preferable ways of living within a society, also known as cultural values

individualism extent to which people are expected to take care of themselves and their immediate families

Exhibit 9.3

Core Society Value Dimensions

Individualism	Masculinity	Power Distance	Uncertainty Avoidance	Long-Term Orientation	Indulgence
• High Score: Society expects one to take responsibility for self and family • Low Score: Life intertwined with large cohesive group	• High Score: Society values assertiveness and control • Low Score: Values caring, conciliation, and community	• High Score: Society values the division of authority and privilege • Low Score: Society blurs distinction among classes	• High Score: Society values novelty, risk-taking • Low Score: Society values clarity and familiarity and avoids risks	• High Score: Society values future rewards over short-term rewards • Low Score: Society oriented in the present	• High Score: Values happiness and extraversion • Low Score: Values restraint and reserved personality

achievement. In contrast, nations with low individualism are high in **collectivism**, which refers to the extent to which an individual's life is intertwined with a large cohesive group. Highly collectivistic societies tend to live in extended families, take their identity from the groups to which they belong, and be very loyal to these groups.

Clearly, this dimension has important implications for the way consumers make decisions and the way that consumers extract value from consumption (see the CVF in Chapter 2 for an illustration). In the United States, marketers often communicate the value of various products by illustrating the extent to which they help one achieve personal freedom. American consumers often see important purchases as an extension of themselves. Advertisements for jeans, shoes, and even laptop computers commonly use adjectives such as *rugged, tough,* and *dependable*.[10] In contrast, an advertisement for a collective culture may rely more on adjectives such as *honest* or *friendly*.

Generally, Western societies tend to be more individualistic, whereas Eastern nations tend to be more collectivistic. Collectivist societies tend to be more compliant with requests from group members. The high collective value scores associated with Chinese consumers may contribute to a relatively high incidence of smoking. In particular, Chinese workers feel strongly compelled to participate in smoke breaks with their co-workers to the extent that the behavior is ritualized.[11] In contrast, personal choice enhances one's self-concept more strongly under high individualism.[12]

MASCULINITY

The **masculinity** CSV dimension captures societal distinctions based on mannerisms typically associated with Western male traits such as valuing assertiveness and control over traditional feminine traits such as caring, conciliation, and community. **Femininity** represents the opposite end of the scale, but in this case, the term does not refer to the prominence that women have within a society. In a culture with low masculinity, men also tend to share some *feminine* traits.[13]

Advertisements for tablet computers in a highly masculine nation such as Japan may emphasize product benefits such as one's ability to get ahead. So a newer, faster computer with more features can help one assert himself in the workplace or at school. In contrast, in a more feminine country such as Brazil, an advertisement for the same tablet might emphasize the benefit of being able to stay in touch with family and friends through ready access to social networks via various apps.

POWER DISTANCE

Power distance is the extent to which people accept as fact the principle of the division of authority and privilege among different groups within society. Social class distinctions become a very real issue among consumers

collectivism extent to which an individual's life is intertwined with a large cohesive group

masculinity sex role distinction within a group that values assertiveness and control; CSV opposite of femininity

femininity sex role distinction within a group that emphasizes the prioritization of relational variables such as caring, conciliation, and community; CSV opposite of masculinity

power distance extent to which authority and privileges are divided among different groups within society and the extent to which these facts of life are accepted by the people within the society

How might differing cultural values create different meanings for this product?

© iStockphoto.com/LPETTET

in high-power-distance nations. These distinctions go beyond just social class and affect relationships between supervisory and subordinate employees and even between students and teachers.

Low-power-distance nations tend to be more egalitarian. As a result, people refer commonly to each other by first names even when a discussion involves people from different social classes and often even between employees and supervisors. In high-power-distance nations, those with less status must show deference to those with greater status; therefore, the lower-status person would not likely call a person of higher status by first name.

In many Asian nations, where power distance is relatively high compared to that in the United States, people often use the terms *senior* and *junior* to capture status distinctions. A student might be junior to a faculty supervisor or even to another student who preceded her through a program of study. When one is unclear about whether or not she is junior or senior to another, she might well ask the other consumer, "How old are you?" Age would be a tiebreaker, with older people having more status than younger people. Senior and junior status can affect simple things such as seating arrangements and whether or not one gets served first or last. Juniors may need to be careful in what they buy and do so as not to seem superior in any substantive way to a senior. A consumer violating a custom and acting more "senior" than appropriate may well face cultural sanctions for the behavior.

In high-power-distance nations, consumers consider certain consumer behaviors as appropriate only for those with sufficient class or status. For example, in high-power-distance nations people view activities like tennis as only for those with very high status. Authority appeals in marketing are more effective when power distance is high.[14]

UNCERTAINTY AVOIDANCE

Uncertainty avoidance is just what the term implies. A culture high in uncertainty avoidance is uncomfortable with things that are ambiguous or unknown. Consumers high in uncertainty avoidance prefer the known, avoid taking risks, and like life to be structured and routine. Uncertainty avoidance has important implications for consumer behavior, because marketing success and improved quality of life often depend on obtaining value from something innovative and therefore somewhat unfamiliar. The task becomes making the unfamiliar seem familiar in appealing to consumers who are high in uncertainty avoidance.

Nations that are high in uncertainty avoidance will be slower to adopt new products or react to novel price promotions. High uncertainty avoidance, such as exists in France, may make consumers more skeptical of promotions that seem too good to be true.[15] In addition, consumers in high-uncertainty-avoidance cultures are quicker to buy something because of perceived scarcity possibly because of doubt over when the product might be available again. In much the same way, the effect of star power on box office sales for motion pictures is stronger in nations with high uncertainty avoidance.[16]

> ## In high-power-distance nations, certain consumer behaviors are designated exclusively to individuals by class or status.

Superstitions and myths also play a bigger role among cultures high in uncertainty avoidance.[17] Although consumers with high uncertainty avoidance are slightly less likely to gamble than others, when they do, they may use astrological charts to help plan visits to casinos. Thus, the casinos in these cultures can somewhat predict peak periods of traffic based on these types of beliefs. Research also suggests that low uncertainty avoidance leads to a higher degree of implicit trust as the exchange partners' ethics guide marketing transactions. This means that fewer issues need to be governed by explicit rules.[18] Consumers from high-uncertainty-avoidance cultures also

uncertainty avoidance
extent to which a culture is uncomfortable with things that are ambiguous or unknown

demand greater amounts of product information and explanation. German consumers, like other consumers high in uncertainty avoidance, find more value from the detailed product presentations that others may not have the patience for.

LONG-TERM ORIENTATION

Long-term orientation reflects values consistent with Confucian philosophy and a prioritization of future rewards over short-term benefits. As such, high long-term orientation means that a consumer values thriftiness, pragmatism, and perseverance as well as the maintenance of long-term relationships.[19] Relationships need time to develop and are intended to last a lifetime. As a result, negotiations between suppliers and buyers are more likely to consider long-term effects to both parties in high-long-term-orientation cultures such as Japan.[20] At the other end of the spectrum, a short-term orientation is associated more with immediate payoffs and face saving. While some may break pragmatism out as a distinct cultural element, the close overlap with LTO suggests that the pragmatic approach is to consider pragmatism as part of LTO.

Guanxi (pronounced "gawn-zeye") is the Chinese term for a way of doing business in which parties must first invest time and resources in getting to know one another and becoming comfortable with one another before consummating any important deal. Guanxi is a common mode of operation among cultures with high long-term orientation—as with many nations in the Far East.[21] The principles of guanxi and long-term orientation present barriers for credit card companies.[22] Chinese consumers were slow to adopt Western-style credit cards. The slow diffusion of credit systems was due in part to consumers and in part to lenders who avoided the uncertainty involved in credit. Regulatory reform, however, has led to lower risk perceptions of consumer credit and thus the demand for credit has grown. That said, even with more than six times

vepar5/Shutterstock.com

the population of the United States, Chinese consumer credit is about two-thirds of total U.S. consumer credit.[23]

Renquing is another phenomenon associated with long-term orientation.[24] **Renquing** is the idea that when someone does a good deed for you, you are expected to return that good deed. The reciprocation need not be immediate, however. In fact, the expectation of reciprocation at some point in the future fosters long-term relationships, since individuals are forever trying to balance the renquing score with each other. Thus, a consumer and personal service provider may end up in a long-term relationship facilitated in part by renquing.

INDULGENCE-RESTRAINT

Indulgent cultures value immediate gratification, particularly for natural human needs associated with fun and enjoyment. Low scores on indulgence are associated with restraint. Restrained cultures tend to be reserved and regulate such desires through the means of societal norms.[25] Clearly, the **indulgence-restraint** dimension shows similarity to the distinction between hedonic and utilitarian value and motivation. Societies with high restraint scores will tend to prioritize utilitarian value in consumption, whereas societies with high indulgence will tend to prioritize hedonic value in consumption. Advertising appeals can easily be adopted for this dimension.

9-2c The CSV Scoreboard

A CSV scoreboard can be put together using historical CSV dimension scores found in many resources, including the Hofstede website (www.geert-hofstede.com). Before doing business in another culture, it's best to know how "foreign" it truly is. The CSV scores for a given

---

long-term orientation values consistent with Confucian philosophy and a pragmatic prioritization of future rewards over short-term benefits

guanxi Chinese term for a way of doing business in which parties must first invest time and resources in getting to know one another and becoming comfortable with one another before consummating any important deal

renquing the idea that favors given to another are reciprocal and must be returned

indulgence-restraint a cultural value dimension distinguishing societies based on how oriented people are toward immediate fun and enjoyment versus restraining oneself from much indulgence in such things

Exhibit 9.4

CSV Scoreboard for a Sample of Nations

	Power distance	Individualism	Masculinity	Uncertainty avoidance	Long-term orientation	Indulgence
United States	40	91	62	46	26	68
Australia	36	90	61	51	21	71
United Kingdom	35	89	66	35	25	69
Canada	39	80	52	48	36	68
Brazil	69	38	49	76	65	59
Ghana	80	15	40	65	32	72
South Africa	49	65	63	49	34	63
Russia	93	39	36	95	81	20
India	77	48	56	40	51	26
Pakistan	55	14	50	70	50	0
China*	80	20	66	30	87	24

country can be essential information for marketers wishing to appeal to consumers in another country. The more similar the CSV scores, the more likely consumers find value in the same or similar products and experiences.

BRIC

Exhibit 9.4 shows a CSV scoreboard for a few select nations. Brazil, Russia, India, and China often are considered emerging economies. The acronym **BRIC** refers to the collective economies of these nations. Each nation's large population makes it impossible to ignore as a potential consumer market. Together, the BRIC nations account for 270 million households with an income of at least $10,000 per year.[26] However, investors are looking beyond BRIC, particularly as Chinese growth slows and both India and Brazil struggle with internal problems. Indonesia and Poland represent alternatives showing signs of growth, as does Mexico, Columbia, Ghana, and Kenya. Doing business in these emerging markets is hardly the same as in the United States or the same as each other, as the CSV scores show. Thus, in this truly global marketplace, serving

consumers in emerging markets can be an important route to business success.

CSV LEADERS

Among all nations with CSV scores, Austria has the lowest power-distance scores and Malaysia has the highest. The United States has relatively low power distance, with only 15 nations reporting lower scores. For individualism, Guatemala reports the lowest score, and the United States has the highest. Sweden reports the lowest masculinity score, and Japan the highest. The United States is neither clearly masculine nor clearly feminine. Singapore reports the lowest uncertainty avoidance score and Greece the highest. The United States is relatively low on uncertainty avoidance, with only 12 nations reporting a lower score. Australia has the lowest long-term orientation scores (meaning that it is the most short-term oriented), and China has the highest. Puerto Rico gets the highest score on indulgence and Pakistan the lowest.

BRIC acronym that refers to the collective economies of Brazil, Russia, India, and China

Exhibit 9.5

CSV Difference Scores Relative to the Culture of the United States

	Power distance	Individualism	Masculinity	Uncertainty avoidance	Long-term orientation	Indulgence	Total
Australia	−4	−1	−1	5	−5	3	8.8
United Kingdom	−5	−2	4	−11	−1	1	13.0
Canada	−1	−11	−10	2	10	0	18.1
South Africa	9	−26	1	3	8	−5	29.3
India	37	−43	−6	−6	25	−42	75.4
Brazil	29	−53	−13	30	39	−9	79.5
Ghana	40	−76	−22	19	6	4	91.0
Pakistan	15	−77	−12	24	24	−68	109.9
China*	40	−71	4	−16	61	−44	112.1
Russia	53	−52	−26	49	55	−48	118.0

9-2d Cultural Distance

Consider businesses like Starbucks, Subway, IKEA, Sephora, and Zara. Each already operates many stores in many countries. Subway alone has over 33,000 stores across more than 100 countries. How should a company decide where it should expand internationally? In other words, where will it be successful?

Two approaches can be considered. First, perhaps the most intuitive response is to look to countries with which the home country shares a border. Certainly, many U.S. businesses exist in Canada and vice versa. Geographic distance forms the basis for international expansion. Countries are attractive because they are nearby and easily reached in terms of both marketing communications and physical distribution.

The second approach looks more at how similar a target nation's consumers are to the home consumers. The **cultural distance (CD)** approach represents how disparate one nation is from another in terms of their CSVs. Thus, with this approach, consumers can be compared by using

> **cultural distance (CD)**
> representation of how disparate one nation is from another in terms of their CSV

scores available in a CSV scoreboard. For example, Exhibit 9.5 shows the difference scores for all nations

How should a company decide where it should expand internationally?

Contrasting appeals from an indulgent above left, and a restrained culture above right.

in the previous exhibit. These are obtained simply by subtracting the score for each nation on each dimension from the corresponding score for U.S. consumers.

Notice the small scores on each dimension for the differences between Australia, the United Kingdom, Canada, South Africa, and the United States compared to the other nations. A simple distance formula can summarize the cultural differences between two nations. One might consider simply adding up the difference scores; however, the negative and positive scores could cancel each other out, making two quite different nations appear similar. Thus, one way to correct this problem is by using the squared differences, much as would be the case in computing statistical variation. For example, the following formula computes the total cultural distances and is illustrated by examining CD from the United States for each nation shown in Exhibit 9.5:

$$CD = \sqrt{\sum_{i=1}^{K}(TCSV_i - BCSV_i)^2}$$

where i = a specific cultural value dimension, K = the number of dimensions for which comparative data are available, CD = cultural distance, TCSV = target country value score on dimension i, and BCSV = baseline country value score on dimension i.

Thus, for example, the CD for Australia from the United States is 8.8:

$$CD = \sqrt{(36-40)^2 + (90-91)^2 + (61-62)^2 + (51-46)^2}$$

$$CD = 8.8$$

Among all comparisons, few would show as little difference as this. Exhibits 9.5 and 9.6 (one shown in a table and the other graphically) show the total CD from the United States for each of nine countries. Australia may be the most

Exhibit 9.6

Graphical Depiction of Cultural Distance

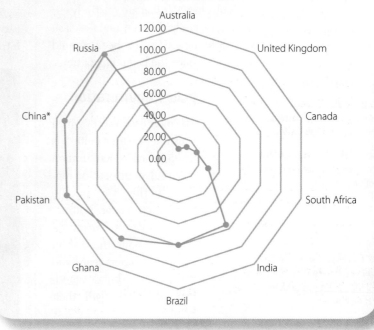

distant geographically, but it is closest culturally. Among the nations in the exhibit, the USA is most distant to China.

Countries with relatively low CD scores are more similar, and thus they tend to value the same types of consumption experiences. In fact, the term **CANZUS** is sometimes used to refer to the close similarity in values between Canada, Australia, New Zealand, and the United States.[27] Additionally, the U could also represent the United Kingdom because the nations are nearly identical from a CD perspective. Not surprisingly, common consumer products, retailers, and restaurant chains that are successful in one of these countries tend to be successful in the others as well.

International expansion decisions should consider CD as well as geography.

9-3 HOW IS CULTURE LEARNED?

Culture is a learned process. Consumers learn culture through one of the two socialization processes discussed in this section. **Socialization** involves learning through observation and the active processing of information about lived, everyday experience. The process takes place in a sequence something like this:

Social interaction
↓
Modeling
↓
Reinforcement

As consumers interact they begin to model (meaning enact) behaviors learned or seen. Reinforcement occurs through the process of rewarding reactions or sanctions. Additionally, learning results in CSVs that are relatively enduring. Societal values are not easily changed, and the clash between peoples with differing CSVs has been around since the beginning of time.

9-3a Enculturation

The most basic way by which consumers learn a culture is through an enculturation process. **Enculturation** represents the way people learn their native culture. In other words, enculturation represents the way in which consumers learn and develop shared understandings of things with their families.

Why do some consumers like wasabi or hot peppers? The answer is enculturation. Consumers are not born liking very pungent food. But early in life, children observe the diets of their parents and relatives and come to mimic those behaviors. When they do, they receive overt social rewards, thereby reinforcing their dietary choice. How about some sannakji for lunch? While some Americans still find the idea of sashimi (raw fish) extreme, sannakji is a Korean dish that goes a couple of steps further. Instead of raw salmon or tuna, sannakji is live octopus. The entire idea of habituation, discussed in an earlier chapter, provides a mechanism that helps make this type of enculturation possible. Consumers who grow up eating sannakji, Vegemite, Surströmming, tartare, or corn dogs easily see the products as food, although consumers from other cultures may disagree.

9-3b Acculturation

Acculturation is the process by which consumers come to learn a culture other than their natural, native culture—that is, the culture to which one may adapt when exposed to a new set of CSVs. Acculturation is a learning process. When a consumer becomes acculturated, chances are that old beliefs have been replaced by new beliefs. Therefore, children generally become acculturated more quickly than adults, because the old rules are not as old and are thereby less resistant to change.[28] Not all cultures appreciate cleanliness to the same degree, sometimes with dire consequences in terms of health. Unilever's Lifebuoy soap brand has made a huge difference in developing nations like India with a campaign teaching children the proper way to wash their hands with soap. The campaign aims at school-aged children and uses songs to go along with hand-washing. The result is a significant reduction in diarrhea and respiratory infections, two major causes of childhood mortality.[29] The brand has introduced young consumers to new, healthier habits with

Bloomberg/Getty Images

CANZUS acronym that refers to the close similarity in values among Canada, Australia, New Zealand, and the United States

socialization learning through observation of and the active processing of information about lived, everyday experience

enculturation way people learn their native culture

acculturation process by which consumers come to learn a culture other than their natural, native culture

slogans and promotions such as "Dr. Lifebuoy says 5 times a day!"

You may be surprised to know that the house party is a relatively novel event in Japan. Japanese typically go out to party. But Japanese consumers who have spent time in the United States and experienced the typical Western house party have become enamored with the concept. In fact, they were so enamored that a Home Party Association emerged in Japan and actually gives classes and exams designed to teach Japanese consumers what is needed to throw a genuine house party!

However, several factors can inhibit acculturation. For example, strong ethnic identification, the degree to which consumers feel a sense of belonging to the culture of their ethnic origins, can make consumers feel close-minded about adopting products from a different culture. When ethnic identification is strong, consumers in a new land may even avoid learning the language of the new land. For instance, pockets of Chinese immigrants in Canada with strong ethnic identification choose to live the majority of their lives interacting only with other Chinese immigrants, purchasing Chinese products nearly exclusively, and paying attention only to Chinese language media.[30] Although this may be in part a matter of taste and custom, diet can influence immigrants' health.[31] Chinese immigrants who retain a Chinese diet are generally healthier than are Canadian-born people of Chinese descent.

Consumer ethnocentrism is a belief among consumers that their ethnic group is superior to others and that the products that come from their native land are superior to other products. Consumers who are highly ethnocentric believe that it is only right to support workers in their native country by buying products from that country. Ethnocentrism is highly related to the concept of uncertainty avoidance. When ethnocentrism is very high, consumers who are in a foreign land may create their own communities within a larger enclave and display little interaction with the outside world. Social media usage also plays a role. Consider immigrants from Latin America who come to the United States. Those who engage only in English-language social media will acculturate more quickly than those who engage in Spanish social media.[32]

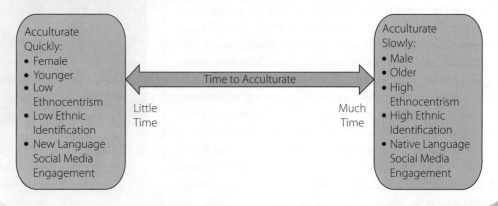

Exhibit 9.7

Characteristics of Fast and Slow Acculturation

Acculturate Quickly:
- Female
- Younger
- Low Ethnocentrism
- Low Ethnic Identification
- New Language Social Media Engagement

Little Time

Time to Acculturate

Much Time

Acculturate Slowly:
- Male
- Older
- High Ethnocentrism
- High Ethnic Identification
- Native Language Social Media Engagement

Exhibit 9.7 summarizes factors that either inhibit or encourage consumer acculturation. Simply put, male consumers who have high ethnic identification, high ethnocentrism, and are relatively old are the worst targets for adopting products of a different or new culture. Interestingly, from an international marketing perspective, CSV profiles characterized by high uncertainty avoidance and strong masculinity are likely not good targets for imported goods relative to other countries. The inhibitions that consumers have about "foreign" products distract from the value the products offer, because their very meaning is inconsistent with the consumer's current belief structure.

9-3c Quartet of Institutions

Whether consumers get culture from enculturation or acculturation, culture adoption is a learning process. Consumers learn primarily through the influence of cultural institutions. We recognize that a quartet of institutions are largely responsible for communicating CSVs through both formal and informal processes. The four institutions comprising the quartet are (see Exhibit 9.8):

1. **Family**
2. **School**
3. **Church**
4. **Media**

ethnic identification
degree to which consumers feel a sense of belonging to the culture of their ethnic origins

consumer ethnocentrism
belief among consumers that their ethnic group is superior to others and that the products that come from their native land are superior to other products

quartet of institutions
four groups responsible for communicating the CSVs through both formal and informal processes: family, school, church, and media

Sociology theory long recognizes the family, school, and church as primary acculturation and enculturation agents. Each serves as a vehicle for teaching values to children; therefore, they are agents of enculturation. The knowledge and behavior associated with each institution socialize those within the institution. In more recent times, the influence of popular media, including electronic media, also merits consideration as an influential institution. Media, thus, offers another channel through which consumers learn.

Many consumers, particularly young consumers, spend a lot of time interacting with media ranging from magazines, television, and radio to web-based social networks and sites like Instagram, Tumblr and Habbo. Here, they observe behavior (sometimes acted out in fiction), receive information about celebrities and pop culture, and exchange ideas, likes, and thoughts with both real and virtual acquaintances. From time to time, controversy will surround media outlets like these. For instance, Habbo chat often involves sexually explicit language and has even been accused of appealing to pedophiles.[33]

The relative influence pushed through the media raises concerns about public policy potentially restricting media access. Many governments actively limit the amount of "American" media allowed in the country, believing that this will protect their culture from becoming overly Americanized or Westernized. An influx of nonnative media can indeed influence the rate of acculturation.[34] Children may be particularly susceptible to media influence. More time watching videos online or in front of the television can distort perceptions of reality.[35] Teens and young adults, particularly immigrants, who are more involved with media like that offered by MTV may end up with different ideas about what makes up appropriate dating behavior based on idealized portrayals of attraction often depicted in media.[36] Therefore, many families try to actively limit their children's Internet media and television exposure.[37]

CULTURE AND POLICY-RELATED CONSUMER COMMUNICATION

Differences in CSVs may have public policy implications as well. A study of teen consumers in countries including Italy, Austria, Slovenia, Uzbekistan, Russia, and the United States found that antismoking ads were not equally effective. The results suggest that antismoking ads targeted toward countries high in individualism should emphasize the ill effects of smoking to one's self. In contrast, in countries with high collectivism, antismoking ads that emphasize the negative effects of smoking on other consumers are more effective.[38]

modeling process of imitating others' behavior; a form of observational learning

LATEST NEWS

BAW: THE CRYSTAL QUEST WEEK 2 »
Jun 10, 2016 | Builders At Work, Campaigns & Activities

As the fog lifts on a new day, you discover a new room with four mysterious portals. The second one has now opened!

GET STRANDED IN THE JUNGLE!
May 31, 2016 | Campaigns & Activities

It's here! A brand new fun time, a bunch of activities and interactive jungle fun or...

I'M A HABBO... GET ME OUT OF HERE! CHALLENGE TWO WINNERS
Jun 10, 2016 | Campaigns & Activities

Habbos, you have completely outdone yourselves! We couldn't help but...

MATURE MMO GA

SAFETY TIPS

Protect yourself with awareness. Learn how to stay safe on the internet.

PARENTS' GUIDE

Popular among teens, this social networking site involves a game where users try to end up with a better room.

Studies measuring CSV among consumers still show distinctions consistent with the profiles discussed earlier. Thus, beyond the teen years particularly, differences in tastes, political views, and preferences are expected to remain somewhat distinct from culture to culture.

MODELING

Modeling is an important way in which consumers are socialized into a specific culture either through acculturation or enculturation. A famous cliché says that imitation is the sincerest form of flattery. Well, **modeling** is precisely a process of imitating others' behavior.

Young children, for instance, observe their parents and model their behavior—at least until adolescence. As children become older, they may choose to model the behavior of older peers more than that of their parents. Adolescents' smoking behavior corresponds to that of their parents and their peers.[39] Children in their teens may be more susceptible to modeling their friends' behavior rather than that of their parents. In fact, the noun *model* captures this concept's essence. When it comes to fashion, designers hope that consumers will want to model their fashion models by selecting the clothes these models wear on the runway. Exhibit 9.8 displays ways institutions facilitate modeling.

SHAPING

Shaping is a socialization process by which consumers' behaviors slowly adapt to a culture through a series of rewards and sanctions. Think about how you might modify your behavior to win acceptance from a group. A student might decide to wear different clothes to school as a way of trying to fit in. The way that other students react to the new attire can serve to shape the student's

Exhibit 9.8

Modeling and the Quartet

Institution	Behavior	Description
School	Meals	Younger students observe senior students' behaviors and learn when it is appropriate to use the dining hall versus other options on or off campus.
Family	Timeliness	Children observe parents to see if they are on time to events.
Church	Prayer	People observe others in the church to learn the appropriate way to behave when in a church.
Media	Language	Consumers learn slang by repeating terms learned through television, movies, music, blogs, social networks, and gaming.

future behavior. Even factors such as consumer cynicism can be shared among a group and end up shaping behaviors: for instance, members of a group may take steps to avoid interacting with those institutions.[40]

The CSV profile of a culture can influence the effectiveness of cultural shaping. Consumers from highly individualistic societies may not alter their behavior so readily just to fit in.[41] In collectivistic cultures, complaining can be a sign of disrespect and may be looked at as inappropriate for minor inconveniences. American consumers who complain about their American hotel room being slightly too warm are not likely to risk sanction. However, in a more collectivistic culture, hotel staff may look down upon someone complaining about a room that is slightly warm. The extra added value that comes from group acceptance is greater among cultures where collectivism is stronger than individualism.

 9-4 FUNDAMENTAL ELEMENTS OF COMMUNICATION

9-4a Verbal Communication

Obviously, language can sometimes be a problem. If you have ever needed directions to some location in a place where you don't know the language, you can appreciate this. However, sometimes even when the correct language is used communication can still be awkward or difficult. The term *Chinglish* refers to the awkward use of English traditionally common in China. "Execution in progress" may sound alarming but it's Chinglish for "caution, work in progress."

Verbal communication refers to the transfer of information through the literal spoken or written word. Consumers will have difficulty finding value in things they cannot understand. Marketers have long wrestled with the problem of translating advertisements, research instruments, product labels, and promotional materials into foreign languages for foreign markets. Getting the meaning right is more important than ever given a truly global marketplace.

Verbal communication can even be difficult within a single language. Almost every language is spoken slightly differently from place to place—or with several unique **dialects**. English in the United States isn't exactly the same as English in England, which is not the same as English in Australia, which is not the same as English in Ireland or other places where English is spoken. In the same way, Chinese is not always Chinese and Spanish not always Spanish. Thus, translation alone is insufficient to guarantee effective communication. Exhibit 9.9 provides some examples of difficulties in communicating even simple ideas through the spoken or written word.

TRANSLATION EQUIVALENCE

Bilingual speakers often may think of more than one way to try to express the meaning of something from one language in another. In some cases, words exist in one language that have no precise equivalent in another. In other instances, even when the same word may exist, people in other cultures do not use the word the same way. Thus, interpretation errors and blunders occur unless one takes great care.

Translational equivalence exists when two phrases share the same precise meaning in two different cultures. Translation–back translation is a way to try to produce translational equivalence. With this process, one bilingual speaker takes the original phrase and translates it from the original language into the new language. Then, a second, independent bilingual speaker translates the

verbal communication transfer of information through either the literal spoken or written word

dialects variations of a common language

translational equivalence two phrases share the same precise meaning in two different cultures

TASTES *DANG-GUI* TO ME!

When did you last eat cassis berries? Sometimes known as black currant, many Americans are unfamiliar with them. Wine marketers, though, often use the term cassis to describe the flavor of wines—usually red wines. Now, imagine trying to translate traditional wine label descriptions into Chinese! The Chinese wine market is just emerging, and its growth depends on educating the market. Most Chinese consumers have never tasted blackberries, passion fruit, or many of the other flavors typically used to describe and sell wine. Complicating this is that there is little agreement among Chinese, even within the same dialect at times, about which words mean

what. No consensus seems to exist about basic terms like *savory* or even *merlot*. Even still, the same character, "mei," means both *beautiful* and *plum*. Bordeaux can taste *dang gui,* though. Verbal communication isn't as easy as it sounds!

Sources: Chow, J. (2013), "Lost in Translation: The Lingo for Tasting Wine," *Wall Street Journal*, (March 14), D4. Jasper, C. (2014), "What Do Chinese Wine Buyers Want?" *Rural* (March 14), http://www.abc.net.au/news/2014-03-14/selling-wine-in-china/5320322, accessed October 24, 2016.

phrase from the new language back into the original language. Assuming the retranslated phrase matches the first, translational equivalence exists. If not, either the phrase needs to be dropped or more work, possibly involving even other speakers fluent in both languages, is needed to determine if a common meaning can be found by changing the words in one or both languages.

METRIC EQUIVALENCE

Once a common meaning is established, things could still go wrong when consumer researchers compare consumer reactions from one country with those from another. Researchers who apply typical survey techniques such as Likert scales or semantic differentials may wish to compare scores from one culture with those from another. This is valid only if the

Exhibit 9.9

Example Problems with Verbal Communication

Communication	Situation	Intended communication	Problem
"Yo vi la Papa!"	Spanish-language slogan on t-shirts prior to Pope's visit to Mexico	"I saw the Pope!"	*La Papa* is "the potato." *El* (or al) *Papa* is the Pope. So, the t-shirts said "I saw the potato."
"Boy, am I stuffed!"	English-language restaurant slogan spoken by middle-aged man.	"Boy, am I full!" (meaning had a lot to eat)	Slogan works fine in the United States; however, in Australia, "stuffed" means pregnant. So, slogan depicts middle-aged, slightly overweight man saying "Boy, am I pregnant!"
"Strawberry Crap Dessert"	English placed on prepre-pared, refrigerated pancakes by Japanese firm intending product for Chinese market.	"Strawberry crêpe"	English can convey a quality image to products in much of Asia even if most consumers can't read the words. Here, the phonics are probably just a little off.
"Bite the waxed tadpole"	Chinese label for Coca-Cola	"Coca-Cola"	Coke tried to find the best phonetic way to produce something sounding like "Coca-Cola." In some Chinese dialects, but not all, strange interpretations like this resulted.
"miststueck!"	Clairol's name for a new hair care product introduced in Germany	Literally a Mist Stick that helped to tame unmanageable hair.	The English *Mist Stick* phonetically sounds like *Miststück*, which means something unflattering; "piece of dung" or even worse.

two culture-language combinations use numbers in a somewhat similar fashion. For example, if a Chinese consumer rated a woman who was 5 feet 5 inches tall for height, she might be rated tall. However, if a Norwegian rated the same woman, she would be rated as short.

Metric equivalence refers to using numbers to represent quantities the same way across cultures. Metric equivalence is necessary to draw basic comparisons about consumers from different countries concerning important consumer relationships. Comparing average scores for consumer attitudes from one culture to the next requires another form of equivalence known as *scalar equivalence*. The procedures for performing tests of metric equivalence are beyond the scope of this text, but students of consumer behavior and international marketing should be aware of these approaches, because comparing quantities across cultures can be tricky.[42]

GLOBISH

Through history, different languages have emerged as the international language of business communication. At one time, French was that language, but today most would consider English the language of international business. English is most common on the Internet and is the international language of marketing. But English grammar can be difficult, as illustrated by Chinglish—and some linguists believe a new form of English with simpler rules is developing. **Globish** reduces the English vocabulary to around 1,500 words and gets rid of nasty complications like contractions and silent letters. Research suggests that well-known global brands are better off sticking to real English in advertisements. However, local brands in non–English-speaking countries can improve their quality perceptions by using a little Globish.[43] Grammatically incorrect but easily recognized, Globish slogans and advertising are spreading through developing countries.

9-4b Nonverbal Communication

An American tourist who wants to know how many stops it will be until he reaches his destination approaches a conductor on a train in Germany. The train is noisy and filled with people so the conductor holds up his pointer finger in response. When the train stops, the tourist quickly exits. However, he soon realizes he is not in the right location. Why? In Germany, the hand sign for one is holding up the thumb. The pointer finger means two.

Nonverbal communication refers to information passed through some unspoken act—in other words, communication not involving the literal word. This example illustrates intentional nonverbal communication; however,

Olivier Le Moal/Shutterstock.com

much communication through this means is unintentional or automatic. Many nonverbal communication cues are culturally laden so that the meaning depends on culture.

Exhibit 9.10 depicts several aspects of nonverbal communication and the way they come together to create effective communication. High-context cultures emphasize communication through nonverbal elements. In contrast, low-context cultures, such as Denmark, emphasize the spoken word and what you say truly is what you mean. The elements of nonverbal communication are touched on briefly in the following sections.

TIME

In America, the expression "time is money" is often used. Americans typically place a high value on time and timeliness. The high value placed on timeliness may be due to the importance of individualism and achievement as core values. When an American plans a dinner meeting for 7:00 P.M., he or she expects everyone to be present at 7:00 P.M.

Consumers from some other cultures do not value timeliness in the same way. For example, in Spain, where individualism is much lower than the United States, a formal dinner scheduled for 9:00 P.M. is early by Spanish standards and will probably not begin at 9:00 P.M. The exact starting time is uncertain, but dinner will almost certainly not be served until sometime much later than 9:00 P.M.

Asian cultures also show much more patience consistent with high long-term orientation. Thus, while CANZUS and many Western European salespeople will want to close a sale on the first meeting, such an approach with Asian buyers will not come across well. Asian exchange partners need time to get to know one another and are not anxious to either close a sale or be closed until guanxi is established.

metric equivalence
statistical tests used to validate the way people use numbers to represent quantities across cultures

Globish simplified form of English that reduces the vocabulary to around 1,500 words and eliminates grammatical complications

nonverbal communication information passed through some nonverbal act

Exhibit 9.10

Nonverbal Communication Affects the Message Comprehended

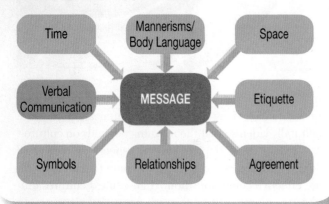

MANNERISMS/BODY LANGUAGE

Body language refers to the nonverbal communication cues signaled by somatic (uncontrollable biological) responses. Consumers may use certain mannerisms when discussing issues with other consumers or salespeople. These cues can be more telling than words. The mannerisms that reveal meaning include the following characteristics:

▶ **Facial expressions**

▶ **Posture**

▶ **Arm/leg position**

▶ **Skin conditions**

▶ **Voice tone**

Sometimes, we feel compelled to look happy just to be polite. This requires a fake smile. While most people can easily make their mouths produce a grin, smiling eyebrows, slightly dilated pupils, and a tilted head (back) also occur with true happiness. Similarly, the posture of a truly happy person generally indicates a willingness to approach the object of the emotion.

Involuntary physical mannerisms communicate in a persuasive manner. In fact, advertisements depicting celebrities displaying a genuine smile as opposed to a fake smile lead to a more effective appeal.[44] In Japan and countries with similar cultures, managing the appearance of one's emotions

body language nonverbal communication cues signaled by somatic responses

etiquette customary mannerisms consumers use in common social situations

becomes very important, because one needs to avoid doing something that may shame another. If a Japanese consumer gives a gift to another person, the reaction in written and verbal communication means a great deal to the gift giver.

SPACE

In places like the United States and Australia, there is a lot of space. Relative to many parts of the world, like Japan or Western Europe, the United States and Australia are sparsely populated. Thus, space varies in importance. The typical consumer in Seoul lives in a large high-rise building in a small flat identical to that of many neighbors living in the same building. For many Americans or Australians, the fact that so many people are packed into a tight space may make them uncomfortable. For citizens of Seoul, being very close to other people is a mere fact of life.

The value that consumers place on space affects communication styles, too. Generally, CANZUS consumers, for instance, do not like to be too close to each other. When having a conversation, they remain at "arm's length." However, Italian, Armenian, or many Arabian consumers are comfortable communicating when they are so close to each other that they are physically touching. The CANZUS consumer engaged in a conversation with an Armenian, for instance, will likely instinctively try to obtain some space in the conversation by leaning backward at the waist as if trying to escape! The differing approaches to space have implications for sales approaches, the way other consumers are depicted in advertising, and the design of retail environments.

ETIQUETTE/MANNERS

When Americans greet each other, the typical response, particularly if a man is involved, is a handshake. Different handshakes may communicate different impressions. However, Asian consumers would expect a bow as a greeting and show of respect, while many Europeans may plant a kiss or two on the cheek. Greeting a business client with a kiss on the cheek would be a definite no-no in the United States; however, in France or Italy, a couple of kisses to the cheek could be an appropriate greeting.

Different cultures have different etiquettes for handling various social situations. **Etiquette** represents the customary mannerisms consumers use in common social situations. Dining etiquette varies considerably from one culture to another. In the United States, consumers cut food with the right hand, place the knife down, then place a fork in the right hand to put food into their mouths. In Europe, however, good manners dictate that the knife stays in the right hand and the fork

Global Gaming Culture

Technology and culture do interact. Mobile technology, coupled with the increasing availability of online gaming that avoids the necessity of relatively expensive game consoles, has brought gaming to billions of consumers around the world. Language barriers are minimal as graphical communication provides a way for consumers of any language to learn how to play many games. As a result, consumers around the world are participants in online gaming. The percent of leisure time spend playing video games varies little across nations. The typical gamer in the United States spends 11 percent of his or her time playing video

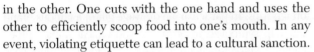

games compared to 9 percent in the U.K. and 15 percent in China. Multinational gaming communities are increasingly facilitated by web-sites that bring the multicultural consumer groups together shared more by involvement in a game than national culture.

Sources: Nielsen (2016), "Gaming Gone Global: Keeping Tabs on Worldwide Trends," A.C. Nielsen (www.nielsen.com) White Paper, May 31. www.gamewithpure.org, accessed June 19, 2016.

---

in the other. One cuts with the one hand and uses the other to efficiently scoop food into one's mouth. In any event, violating etiquette can lead to a cultural sanction.

Service providers need to be sensitive to the various differences in etiquette. For example, although no formal airline passenger etiquette exists, there is an informal code, and passengers who break these unwritten rules can actually decrease the satisfaction of other passengers. This situation is exaggerated by airlines carrying multinational groups of passengers. These passengers have different rules about space, privacy, dress, and hygiene. Passengers with body odor or who dress inappropriately (for example, men in tank tops are generally considered inappropriate for such close company in Western

Politeness is gratifying—but what is polite, like appropriate table manners, varies with culture.

cultures) can ruin the experience for other consumers. When consumers are unaware or lack concern for the proper etiquette in a given situation, the result can be awkward and diminish the value of the experience.

RELATIONSHIPS

How do consumers respond to attempts by marketers to build a personal relationship? Earlier, we discussed the Asian principle of guanxi and the different ways that a relationship may develop under this principle as opposed to conventional Western principles. However, differing CSVs have other implications for consumer-brand or consumer–service provider relationships.

For example, with high collectivism, the idea of a relationship is no longer personal. Consumers from collectivist nations define relationships in terms of the ties between a brand or service provider and a family or relevant group of consumers. Therefore, marketing appeals aimed at building personal relationships should emphasize the collective preference of this group rather than the individual.[45]

AGREEMENT

How is agreement indicated and what does it mean? An Asian consumer who responds to a sales appeal with "yes" is not indicating agreement. Instead, this "yes" is more a way of indicating that she understands what is being said. Further, many Asian cultures will avoid strong affirmative or negative responses and instead use expressions like "that is possible" or "that may be difficult" to indicate agreement or lack of agreement.

TASTES THE SAME ALL OVER

Marketers who previously tailored marketing campaigns to specific cultures are more prone than ever to try a global campaign, meaning one message for the entire world. Airbnb uses the tagline and hashtag #OneLessStranger to encourage hospitality, including renting out a spare room to strangers. Red Bull communicates with the same packaging and promotion around the world. Even Coca-Cola is launching a global campaign called "Taste the Feeling," which emphasizes the universally positive feelings that come with drinking a Coke. With this feelings-based global campaign, the same images will be seen in Japan, Mexico, and Italy. Coke, however, will not move to a universal recipe, as consumers in Israel and Mexico enjoy Coke sweetened with cane sugar instead of high fructose corn syrup, part of the standard U.S. recipe.

Sources: Businesswire (2016), "Coca-Cola Announces 'One Brand' Global Marketing Approach," http://www.businesswire.com/news/home/20160119005959/en/Coca-Cola-Announces-%E2%80%9COne-Brand%E2%80%9D-Global-Marketing-Approach, accessed June 19, 2016; Fleishman, H. (2015), "13 Businesses with Brilliant Global Marketing Strategies," http://blog.hubspot.com/blog/tabid/6307/bid/33857/10-Businesses-We-Admire-for-Brilliant-Global-Marketing.aspx, accessed October 25, 2016.

Additionally, the extent to which a contract binds varies from place to place. Traditionally, South Koreans have not been accustomed to signing contracts. The fact that someone would ask one to sign such an agreement may come across as a bit of an insult. Thus, Western firms may have to adjust their practices to indicate formal agreements when doing business in these cultures.

SYMBOLS

The chapter began by emphasizing the link between culture and meaning. Because different cultures have different value profiles, objects and activities take on different symbolic or semiotic meaning. Perhaps nowhere is this more obvious than in the arena of religious objects. A large wooden cross is a device used to execute people in some cultures, but to Christians, a cross is an important symbol signifying everlasting life.

The symbolic meaning of objects also affects gift giving from culture to culture. In some Western cultures, particularly among the French cultures of Quebec and south Louisiana, a knife is seen as an inappropriate gift because of the risk that a knife symbolizes cutting a relationship. In China, clocks and watches are inappropriate as gift items because they symbolize the finite nature of life—time is running out. Also in Japan, the term *omiyage* refers to the custom of bringing gifts to friends from foreign trips. In particular, an omiyage gift of a famous brand can help symbolize freedom for the typical female office worker.[46] Marketers need to take care not to unintentionally promote offensive items based on cultural symbolism.

9-5 EMERGING CULTURES

International marketers traditionally direct most efforts at consumers from developed nations. In the 1990s and early 2000s, marketing investment in developing nations increased dramatically. Even low-income consumers in developing nations can represent attractive markets to serve, particularly if marketers offer low-priced, basic products. Market segments in developing nations offer tremendous opportunities, but communicating and delivering value in the segments means that marketers must know and understand the nuances of culture. In recent years however, the high uncertainty associated with many emerging markets has curbed further direct foreign investment. In fact, in 2016, the United States and Canada once again represent two of three of the most attractive markets for foreign investment [course: www.atkearney.com/dbpc/foreign-direct-investment-confidence-index, accessed June 19, 2016]. China comes in at second place, with the next "emerging market" being India in 9th place.

> In China, clocks and watches are inappropriate as gift items because they symbolize the finite nature of life.

Brazil, Russia, India, and China make up the BRICs markets.

9-5a BRIC Markets

As discussed previously, the acronym BRIC stands for Brazil, Russia, India, and China. These four nations were singled out as having rapidly growing economies. In each market, large middle classes emerged as job opportunities followed the emerging consumer cultures. In 2010, South Africa was added to the list to turn BRIC into BRICS. Now that the BRICS are major players in the economy, we look to other places to find rapidly growing economies. Political changes coupled with large, growing populations mean that places like Mexico, Indonesia, Kenya, and Poland may be leaders in the next round of emerging consumer cultures.[47] Marketers look for growing populations, youthfulness, free markets, favorable cultural values, and pro-growth political climates as signs of opportunities to do business.

9-5b Chindia

The term **Chindia** refers to the combined market and business potential of China and India.

Over 190 million households call India home. In 2005, 140 million of those households were considered aspiring consumers with household incomes equal to about $2,500 per year. Today, the Indian middle class has grown to just over 100 million households. As Indian incomes rise, the market potential of India expands as well.

More and more Chindian consumers are stepping up to some luxuries that would have been out of their reach previously. Starbucks is growing in both countries, and the cosmetics market in China is about $25 billion annually. Middle-class consumers there don't seem to mind what some politicians call excessive prices for coffee and consider a visit to Starbucks a luxury more than an everyday event.

9-5c Glocalization

How should a company from another country appeal to these emerging but foreign consumer markets? Certainly, these countries offer a significantly different CSV profile than those in the United States. The term *glocalization* represents one alternative that allows flexibility in responding to the unique value profiles of consumers. **Glocalization** represents the idea that the marketing strategy may be global, but the implementation of that strategy at the marketing tactics level should be local.

Reef Brazil beachwear executes a global branding strategy that appeals to the youth market by portraying a cool, carefree image.[48] This corporate strategy may be set by executives in Brazil. However, rather than dictating how this plan would be implemented everywhere Reef is sold, Reef could allow local input into how to translate this image in a way appropriate for the local market. In Brazil, an ad depicting provocatively dressed women may help execute this message. However, in India or in much of the Middle East, this may not be an appropriate way to send the message. In contrast, global brands like Coca-Cola and Red Bull shun the glocalization approach in favor of a more global appeal as captured by Coke's "Taste the Feeling" campaign, described in the feature box above.

Chindia combined market and business potential of China and India

glocalization idea that marketing strategy may be global but the implementation of that strategy at the marketing tactics level should be local

STUDY TOOLS 9

LOCATED AT BACK OF THE TEXTBOOK

☐ Tear out Chapter Review Card

LOCATED AT WWW.CENGAGE.COM/LOGIN

☐ Review Key Term flashcards and create your own cards

☐ Track your knowledge and understanding of key concepts in consumer behavior

☐ Complete practice quizzes to prepare for tests

☐ Complete interactive content within CB Online

☐ Review the Chapter Highlight boxes for CB Online

10 | Microcultures

LEARNING OBJECTIVES

After studying this chapter, the student should be able to:

10-1 Apply the concept of microculture as it influences consumer behavior.

10-2 Know the major U.S. microcultural groups.

10-3 Realize that microculture is not a uniquely American phenomenon.

10-4 Perform a demographic analysis.

10-5 Identify major cultural and demographic trends.

Remember to visit **PAGE 221** for additional **STUDY TOOLS**

10-1 MICROCULTURE AND CONSUMER BEHAVIOR

Climate is remarkable in many ways. On a June day, Kevin drives westward through northern California, and in just a few minutes' time the temperature indicator on the car has fluctuated from 92 to 58 degrees. The sky has gone from absolutely clear to partly cloudy to a foggy mist. East of a ridge it is hot and dry, west of a ridge, cool and damp. Drive into a valley, and it is something in between. Meteorologists explain that regional climates contain many microclimates within them. Many Americans envy Californians because of the good weather associated with California. But truly, California's weather presents many different climates. The microclimates that exist throughout central and northern California are responsible for high-quality conditions for growing the grapes used to make many outstanding wines.

microculture a group of people who share similar values and tastes that are subsumed within a larger culture

In a similar way, we can think of a given culture as containing multiple smaller and more specific microcultures. A **microculture** is indeed a culture, only smaller. We define a microculture as a group of people who share similar values and tastes that are subsumed within a larger culture. The smaller group can be quite distinct from the larger group or overall culture. The term *subculture* is often used to capture much the same idea as microculture. However, the term *microculture* is used here to portray the idea that the group is smaller but in no way less significant in terms of the potential influence on consumer behavior. You may notice that the microculture concept is similar in some ways to the group influence topic. Microcultures, however, are generally based on specific variables that we detail in this chapter. How many microcultures do you belong to? Let's take a look.

10-1a Culture Is Hierarchical

Culture is a universal phenomenon. It is everywhere and ultimately explains the habits and idiosyncrasies of all groups of consumers. In fact, each consumer belongs

to many cultural groups—or more precisely, they move in and out of microcultures. For instance, a college student from Texas who is attending a state university in that state is likely part of American culture, Texas culture, an ethnically defined culture such as Hispanic culture, university culture, and possibly Greek culture, should he or she belong to a fraternity or sorority. In this way, culture is hierarchical. A consumer belongs to one large, overall culture and then to many smaller cultural groups—microcultures—existing and interlinking within the overall culture. Exhibit 10.1 illustrates a cultural hierarchy.

Exhibit 10.1

The Hierarchical Nature of Culture and Microculture

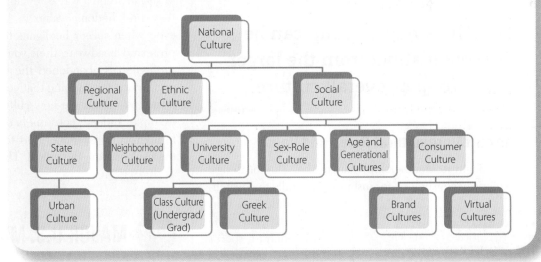

Each microculture brings with it role expectations for its members. The role provides a signal as to the behaviors that one should perform to truly belong to the group; or, in other words, what it takes to be an authentic member of the group.[1] Obviously, some of the roles are inconsistent with each group, and the consumer makes a choice to behave in ways more consistent with one group than with another. When a consumer faces a situation involving conflicting expectations based on cultural expectations, he is experiencing **role conflict**. For instance, when students attend a career fair for the first time they may experience some conflict over how to dress. Sorority sisters may see a certain outfit as business attire, but the career-oriented woman representing a company at the event may see it as too sexy and inappropriate for the office.

The fact that the college student mentioned earlier is a Texan clearly typifies culture. Texas has a unique and identifiable culture, and this point is illustrated by the fact that by now, the reader has an image of a Texan in mind. In other words, consumers have generally consistent associations with the "Texan" social schema. A college student who wears boots, jeans, and a Stetson in Massachusetts may stand out in the crowd, but this manner of dress may help a Texan fit in. This particular consumer likely also identifies with a specific age-based or generational culture, and makes consumer choices that either reinforce this social identity or send the signal that he does not wish to be part of this group. Think about how these decisions explain simple things like music preferences. Polka music may be traditional in Austria, but an Austrian university student is not likely to find being a huge polka fan very gratifying among his peers. Similarly, an authentic goth may well have to hide a liking of a country music song or two.

Texas culture is part of American culture.

> ## The smaller group can be quite distinct from the larger group or overall culture.

10-1b Microcultural Roles and Value

Microculture membership changes the value of things. American consumers, for instance, generally find watching soccer dull, and thus consider it to be a low-value activity. In contrast, soccer is the number one spectator sport all around Europe and in other parts of the world. Cultural groups even arise within sports fans, and an extreme soccer fan may even become a *soccer hooligan* who participates in extreme and sometimes violent behaviors as a way of creating a personally meaningful soccer experience. Anthropologists have studied this cultural phenomenon by immersing themselves within the hooligan group. Some hooligans are professional people who find involvement in soccer to be a way to escape other realities, and thus they find hedonic value in hooligan activities. However, when soccer hooligans took up Burberry caps as preferred headwear, then young male British business professionals abandoned the caps so as not to have a preference overlapping that could identify them as hooligans. We again see how culture is hierarchical in this example. Indeed, consumers often choose membership in microcultures in an effort to stand out or distinguish themselves from the crowd. This phenomenon is known as **divergence**.[2]

10-2 MAJOR U.S. MICROCULTURES

Marketers can divide the U.S. population into consumer groups along a number of dimensions relative to market segmentation. These groupings are particularly effective when microcultures are involved because the consumers within these groups likely have very similar preferences.

role conflict a situation involving conflicting expectations based on cultural role expectations

divergence situation in which consumers choose membership in microcultures in an effort to stand out or define themselves from the crowd

There are many types of microcultures in the United States. These include regional, sex role, age-based, generational, religious, ethnic, income/social class, and street microcultures.

10-2a Regional Microculture

We don't think about it much today, but the U.S. Declaration of Independence declares each of the original 13 colonies "free and independent states." In much of early U.S. history, the country's name was plural. "These United States are free and independent" was a commonly used phrase, as opposed to "The United States is free and independent."[3] Using the plural form more clearly reflects the fact that lifestyles and culture vary as you travel around the United States and North America. Within America, many cultural groups can be identified. In 1981, Joel Garreau published the book *The Nine Nations of North America*.[4] The book identifies nine geographical regions that supposedly share similar value profiles and thus contain consumers with similar preferences. However, they don't neatly fit with conventional regional distinctions. For example, Florida is split, with the northern part belonging to "Dixie" and the southern part belonging to "The Islands." Chicago is part of the "Breadbasket," but Indianapolis is part of "Dixie." Exhibit 10.2 illustrates this concept.

The relative usefulness of the nine-nation approach in segmentation is questionable, but it captures the fact that priorities among consumers do vary regionally.[5] Brand and food preferences, choices of favorite beverages, favorite sports, and even the names of things vary by region. For example, in the South a soda is something with ice cream in it, but in the Northeast a soda is a soft drink. Debating the best pizza—either Chicago style or New York style—is very likely to get some consumers fighting!

One area in the United States that receives significant attention is the "Borderland" region, a region that was not included in the original Nine Nations approach. The Borderland covers the southwestern U.S. states that share a border with Mexico.[6] A large Hispanic population lives in this region; consumer researchers and marketers alike pay close attention to the composition and culture of the region. It is common to experience both Mexican and American culture in the area, and many marketing communications are presented in both English and Spanish. Exhibit 10.3 presents differences and preferences among U.S. consumers by region.

10-2b Sex Roles and Microculture

Sex roles refer to the societal expectations for men and women among members of a cultural group. Sex roles are ubiquitous in society, and inconsistency with them can be a source of sanctions. The differences between societal expectations of men and women vary less in Western cultures than they do in Eastern cultures, in which sex-based divisions in roles remain more obvious.[7] Recent comparisons of brand personality tend to show greater androgyny—meaning neither clearly male nor female—among U.S. perceptions of brands relative to Korean brands.[8]

SOCIETAL ROLE EXPECTATIONS

Even in Western cultures, certain responsibilities such as child care and household cleaning are unevenly spread among cultures. In Italy, a relatively feminine culture by Western standards, women spend a great deal of time keeping their houses clean. Even an Italian woman who works outside of the home is likely to wash the floors of her home at least twice a week. Women who do not work outside the home likely wash the floors nearly every day. In addition, they tend to use stronger cleaners than their U.S. counterparts. Clearly,

sex roles societal expectations for men and women among members of a cultural group

Exhibit 10.2

North American Regions

The Empty Quarter

Quebec

Ecotopia

New England

Breadbasket

The Foundry

MexAmerica

Dixie

The Islands

Exhibit 10.3

Regional Differences and Preferences Among U.S. Consumers

Actual place	"Nine-nation region" (Garreau)	Geographical designation	Core societal value priority	Example preference
Birmingham, AL	Dixie	South	Security and self-respect	Watch Discovery Health Channel
Los Angeles, CA	MexAmerica	West	Warm relationships with others and self-fulfillment	In-home cosmetics
Boston, MA	New England	Northeast	Self-fulfillment, achievement	Viewing foreign movies
Chicago, IL	Breadbasket	Midwest	Security and warm relationships	Chicago pizza

all of this cleaning provides utilitarian value through the result of a clean house, but Italian women also take inner gratification from the activities because they help fulfill their specific societal sex role.[9] In Western culture, men have traditionally picked up the tab during a date, but as cultures become more androgynous, this tradition may be falling by the wayside.

Marketers need to be aware of the relative sex roles within societies. Men and women may share purchasing responsibilities differently from culture to culture. In the United States, the woman in the family remains the primary purchasing agent for most things. Men are generally allowed to make purchase decisions for things such as lawn care equipment and beer. Men also play a much larger role in the purchase of big-ticket items. Women tend to purchase the majority of clothing for males in U.S. households. However, in Italy, men place great pride in their business attire and are more likely to want control of these purchase decisions. Marketers therefore need to do research to help identify these roles, or else run the risk of targeting the wrong family member with marketing communications.

MALE AND FEMALE SEGMENTS

A great deal of marketing communication is directed toward either a male or female market segment. Media are often distinguished easily based on the proportion of

© Yakobchuk Vasyl/Shutterstock.com

male and female customers. ESPN channels, for example, offer an opportunity to reach out to a predominantly male market. *Cosmopolitan* and *Harper's Bazaar* magazines offer an opportunity to reach a female market. These media clearly contain appeals geared toward the respective sex.

Although role expectations associate certain types of purchases with men or women, marketers sometimes reach out to the opposite sex. Men traditionally are the household buying agent for electronics. However, Best Buy altered its marketing strategy in a special effort to appeal to female shoppers. Consumer research showed that women were not particularly enamored with the big box format, so Best Buy launched Best Buy Mobile. Best Buy Mobile units are relatively small and located in shopping centers and malls.[10] Now female consumers are exposed to mobile technologies in an environment more suited to their tastes. Marketers outside the United States are also taking this approach. Vespa, the world's top name in scooters, redesigned their basic model into the "Indian Vespa" by adding a foot-rest extension to the left side because Indian women, who wear relatively close-fitting floor-length garments, only ride in a sidesaddle style. The effort to provide cheap transportation to relatively low-income women may pay off in a big way in the long run.

CHANGING CLASS?

Middle-class growth characterizes much of the developing world, as typified by China, India, and Brazil. The United States, however, bucks this demographic trend with respect to income groups. In the United States, a shrinking middle class and a growing lower class characterizes recent times. From 2000 to 2014, the share of U.S. adults in the middle class fell nationwide, and for the first time in 40 years there were fewer people in the middle class than in either the lower or upper classes. Income inequality and the outsourcing of jobs are often given as reasons behind the decline. While some middle-class consumers have seen their income rise above the middle class designation, the average incomes of the U.S. middle and lower classes have fallen to levels below that of other countries. As an example, Canada's middle class now enjoys a higher income than America's middle class. It seems that in the United States, the rich are certainly getting richer, while the poor are not.

If household incomes continue to decrease, consumer spending may remain low overall, and premium products formerly enjoyed by middle-class consumers, such as frequently dining out, private school education, and new cars, will be in less demand. Further, over half of American consumers are on some kind of government aid, and a record 15% (over 45 million) receive food stamps. As a result, even American companies look increasingly to foreign markets for growth. Ford and GM both look to Brazil's growth in middle-class consumers as a reason to be optimistic about their near-term sales prospects.

Sources: Leonhardt, David and Kevin Quealy (2014), "The American Middle Class Is No Longer the World's Richest," *The New York Times* (online), April 22, 2014, online content retrieved at: www.nytimes.com/2014/04/23/the-american-middle-class-is-no-longer-the-worlds-richest.html?r=0, accessed June 20, 2014. Pew Research Center (2016), "America's Shrinking Middle Class: A Close Look at Changes Within Metropolitan Areas," May 11, 2016, online content retrieved at: http://www.pewsocialtrends.org/2016/05/11/americas-shrinking-middle-class-a-close-look-at-changes-within-metropolitan-areas/, accessed June 22, 2016. J. Cox, "Report: 15% of Americans on Food Stamps," http://www.nbcnews.com/business/report-15-americans-food-stamps-980690 (accessed March 19, 2013); J. Muller, "Going South," *Forbes* (October 22, 2012): 46–48.

Conversely, online fashion retailers like Gilt Groupe and Rue La La have changed their marketing approach to better appeal to men.[11] Currently, only about one in four adult men regularly purchase clothing products online. These retailers seek to entice more men to their sites by offering more sports-oriented merchandise lines, such as golf apparel. The retailers believe that appealing to men will be successful based on the relatively high amount of disposable income of many middle-aged professional men.

Marketers need to keep in mind that women and men do not make consumer decisions in the same way. Perhaps the biggest difference is in the way men and women process information. Relative to women, men tend to be more heuristic/intuitive in their processing. **Cognitive structuring** is a term that refers to the reliance on schema-based heuristics in making decisions. In contrast, women tend to process information in a more piecemeal fashion.[12] Thus, men are more likely to process information based on the way it is framed and on the categories (schema, stereotypes, scripts) it evokes, rather than on a detailed breakdown of all the information. Interestingly, this doesn't mean that men make poorer choices than women, only that they make them in a different way.

10-2c Age-Based Microculture

The term **age-based microculture** describes the concept that people of the same age end up

cognitive structuring
term that refers to the reliance on schema-based heuristics in making decisions

age-based microculture
term that describes the concept that people of the same age end up sharing many of the same values and develop similar consumer preferences

sharing many of the same values and develop similar consumer preferences. Perhaps no age-based group receives more attention than teens. Nearly 21 million Americans are between 15 and 19 years of age.[13] Teens seem to share many similar behaviors. In fact, some argue that teen behavior is not just similar within a given country, but similar across countries. Part of the similarity in behavior allows teens to fill the role expectations for a teenager in U.S. society.

WORLD TEEN CULTURE?

Consumer media involve more than just television. Radio, print publications, music, and web-based communication all can play a role in shaping culture and, therefore, the things that consumers value.[14] The Internet facilitates communication among consumers around the world, contributing to what some believe is a more universally similar **world teen culture**. Evidence of similar tastes among teenaged consumers around the world is obvious if one takes a look at teen purchase and consumption patterns. Many of these tastes are influenced by the Western media's depiction of celebrities. Thus, fashion and entertainment companies in particular may find segmenting based on age as useful as geography.

Brands listed in Exhibit 10.4 have particular appeal to teens in practically all corners of the world. Coca-Cola and McDonald's, for example, are brand names that are listed among teens' favorite brands throughout much of the world.[15] Coca-Cola takes advantage of virtual media to help stay on top. A recent Coke Super Bowl ad encouraged fans to go online to vote for their favorite way of ending the commercial. Coke fans voted on which team would win a desert race to the nearest Coca-Cola. Coke invites participation in marketing and engages young consumers worldwide in doing so.

Although teens around the world may find value in many of the same types of music and clothing, research suggests that the cultural values of their home nation remain relatively distinct from nation to nation, particularly concerning personal products.[16] American teen consumers, for instance, still rate freedom as the most important CSV. In contrast, teens from Arab countries list faith as the most important CSV.[17] These differences translate into different consumption habits. For example, even though McDonald's is popular among teens practically everywhere, preferences for fast-food brands still differ between Asians and Americans. Young consumers from different cultures around the world do appear to have similar tastes in apparel.

10-2d Generation Microculture

Age-based groups can be distinguished from generational groups. Consumers grow out of age groups. When a consumer reaches age 20, she is no longer in the teen microculture. However, she still "belongs" to a group with her peers. Notice that people who are in the same generation still belong to the same cohort. A **cohort** is a group of people who have lived the same major experiences in their lives, and the experiences end up shaping their core values. Life experiences have many different effects on a cohort. For instance, while teens tend to share some behaviors in common, such as experimenting with tobacco, their preference for music tends to be much more of a generational effect. Consumers tend to enjoy music from their own generation, and each generation seems to carry its taste for music with it to a large extent. Here, we briefly introduce some of the main generational groups in the United States. It is important to remember that not everyone always agrees on the exact dates of these groups or specific labels that are attached to them.[18]

Exhibit 10.4

Similarities and Differences Among Teen Consumers

Favorite brands	Similar activities	Less similar choices
Coca-Cola	Listening to music	Religious ideas/activities
Adidas	Using mobile phone	Cosmetic brands
Nike	Posting photos/videos on Instagram or Youtube	Political ideas
Disney	Video games	Equality of sexes
Cadbury	Smoking	

world teen culture speculation that teenagers around the world are more similar to each other than to people from other generations in the same culture

cohort a group of people who have lived the same major experiences in their lives

GREATEST GENERATION

The term "greatest generation" refers to American consumers who were young adults during World War II. These consumers were born prior to 1928. They represent approximately 11.5 million consumers living today. Their lives and values are shaped very much by World War II and their post-war experiences. These consumers tend to be more thrifty than other consumers and thus are highly price conscious. These consumers have reached their elderly years. A somber occasion was marked on June 6, 2014, which was the 70th anniversary of the D-Day invasion of then-occupied Europe by Allied troops. Several veterans returned to attend the ceremonies, and others have attended since then as well.

SILENT GENERATION

Silent generation consumers were born between 1928 and 1945. Two major events occurred during this time period. The first major event was the Great Depression, which began in 1929. The second major event was, of course, World War II. These consumers were greatly impacted by these events and, like their predecessors, are known for civic duty, conformity, and responsibility. They tend to be frugal and follow largely utilitarian motivations with their purchases. This segment is comprised of approximately 40 million consumers in the United States today.

BABY BOOMERS

The Baby Boomers were born between 1946 and 1964. Approximately 74.9 million Americans are Boomers. Boomers were born during a time in the United States that was marked by optimism and relative economic security. Many of these consumers came of age during the very turbulent 1960s, and they clearly left a mark on popular culture.

Boomers represent a major force in consumer culture, and they are a substantial force in the economy. It should not be surprising, therefore, that they receive significant marketing attention. Many Boomers have

Glynnis Jones/Shutterstock.com

saved significant sums of money for retirement and plan to enjoy good times well into their elderly years. Boomers, by and large, have a huge amount of spending power relative to other generations. They are characterized by a preference for wine and the finer things.

Although mortality will eventually lead to a decline in baby boom consumers, trends in fertility rates and migration are expected to sustain the number of older American consumers into the distant future. In fact, it has been projected that the number of U.S. consumers aged 65 or older will reach nearly 85 million by 2050.[19] The Baby Boomers enjoyed the designation as the largest cohort in the U.S. until recently, when the Millennials overtook this honor.

GENERATION X

Generation X consumers were born between 1965 and 1980. They represent 65 million consumers million consumers. Generation X consumers were long thought to be a group that was marked by alienation and cynicism. They have also been referred to as "latchkey" kids to signify the idea that many of these consumers spent a great deal of time alone due to having both parents at work. Many Generation Xers also came from divorced households, which may explain why a good number of these consumers today focus strongly on the family and traditional family values. Although marketers often viewed Generation Xers as slackers, many of these consumers have become successful business people and community leaders. Research also reveals that the majority of these consumers started saving money relatively early in life.[20]

MILLENNIALS

Millennials were born between 1981 and 1995. They represent approximately 75.4 million in the United States. This group was originally referred to as Generation Y. A lot of research attention has been focused on this group not only because of its sheer size, but also because its members are so different from other cohorts. It is important to realize that in 2016 this group was recognized as being even larger in sheer numbers than the Baby Boomers.[21]

Excited about an RV? Well, Baby Boomers with disposable income find lots of value in the RV!

These consumers tend to wholeheartedly embrace technology as no other generation before them. Many of them were cocooned by protective parents when they were young and tend to view technology as a means to build community and relationships. They also tend to keep close contact with their parents.[22] They tend to be relatively impulsive and optimistic. One of the consumer behaviors that Millennials enjoy is visiting coffee shops with in-store WiFi. In this way, they stay connected to their friends and to their interests. Younger consumers in this group tend to be so technologically savvy that they have been referred to as the first "always connected" generation, meaning that they are constantly in touch with other consumers through various technologies.[23] Of course, the older Millennials did not grow up in the same technological environment as did the younger consumers in this group. This is why only a part of this group, those in their early twenties, are referred to as "digital natives."[24] Regardless, even the older Millennials are more tech-savvy than the general population, and they do tend to be always connected.

Millennials would prefer to walk rather than drive, live in urban settings than in rural settings, and live in smaller, rather than larger, homes. The very way in which they view the concept of "freedom" is also unique. For Millennials, freedom is more closely associated with having access to the Internet and social networking sites than with the automobile. Their parents tended to view the automobile as the key to freedom. Millennials, as a group, do not.

Millennials tend to be optimistic even though older consumers in this group have been greatly impacted by economic challenges. Many of these consumers are underemployed, taking whatever job will help to pay bills, and a number of them have taken unpaid internships simply to gain experience. Economic pressures have led many of them to delay marriage and even to move in with parents for financial reasons.[25] Research also reveals that these pressures lead many Millennials to make poor choices with their finances, such as accumulating debt and saving little. Many consumers in this group see no problem with living with their parents into their late twenties.

GENERATION Z

Much attention has been given to the Millennial group, and rightfully so. However, another group of interest is "Generation Z." This group follows the Millennials and represents young consumers born between 1995 and 2010. The number of people in this group is smaller than the Millennials, with approximately 30 million consumers in the United States. Research suggests that they will be the most educated, diverse, and mobile group to date. They will also be the first truly "global" generation, due to racial and cultural diversity, increased population mobility and migration, and comfort with mobile technologies.[26] They also tend to embody the "KGOY" concept (kids growing older, younger) since information is spread so quickly through the group by social media and texting.

Given that many of these young consumers grew up with concepts like "tagging" and "liking" Facebook pages, they are also more attuned to concepts like viral marketing and self-endorsements than is any other group.[27] One of the biggest challenges for marketers and employers will be how to communicate with these consumers. Given that this generation has grown up with Internet and smartphone jargon, their use of everyday language has been affected. Popular acronyms like "LOL" and "ROTFL" have now entered into everyday conversations. This is not to suggest that these are not serious consumers. Quite the contrary. In fact, they can quickly see through marketing hype that does not come across as sincere. Consumer researchers will continue to monitor this group as they come of age.

GEN Z—THE NEXT BIG THING

Millennials, Millennials, Millennials! We hear the term so much, you'd think we were all "Millennials!" Depending on when you are reading this, most Millennials are aged somewhere between their early twenties and late thirties. In fact, many of today's traditional college students today aren't even Millennials—they are "Gen Z!"

As this chapter highlights, Gen Z consumers are different in important ways from other cohorts. As has been stated, they are clearly the most educated, diverse, mobile, and global consumers we've ever seen. But what does this mean for marketers? It's still early to tell, but one clear trend is that this group views social media as their television. In fact, they are much more focused on creating and sharing content than any other previous generation. This is not surprising when one remembers that this group grew up with the selfie and with apps like Snapchat. As a result, to say that they'll be engaged in the marketing process is an understatement. Given that they regularly create and share content, this group is a perfect target for companies seeking brand ambassadors.

As always, time will tell what the exact impact of this cohort will be on the marketing world. For now, marketers are paying close attention and trying to understand the needs and attitudes of this unique segment.

GENERATIONAL INFLUENCE AND MARKETING

Generations provide a good basis for marketing segments because a consumer's age identifies his or her generation. Not every person that is age 21 right now matches the tastes of all the other Millennial generation consumers, but the largest number of people within a generation are similar to some extent. McDonald's recent strategies illustrate the difference between appealing to an age group versus a cohort group. For decades, practically every McDonald's featured a playground built conspicuously at the front of each restaurant. Not only that, consumers also strongly associated the Happy Meal with McDonald's. Thus, in consumers' long-term memories, McDonald's was strongly defined by the play area, Happy Meals, and children. In the past few years, McDonald's has moved away from that strategy and has even removed the play areas from many of their restaurants. In some cases, they have been replaced with sections called McCafé. The Happy Meal still remains, but the shift in their marketing corresponds to the fact that they are more interested in serving the markets that grew up playing in the playgrounds and eating Happy Meals than they are in directly appealing to children themselves. In a way, McDonald's has shifted from looking at the markets based on their age to one where they are capitalizing on a cohort group. Millennial generation consumers won't be found in the play area any longer, but you can still find them at McDonald's.

Generational effects can also explain why country music has changed so dramatically over the years. Have you ever wondered why today's country music doesn't sound like your grandpa's country? The answer lies largely in the fact that many of today's biggest stars grew up listening to classic or even alternative rock music. As you may have noticed, much of country music has a rock-edge sound to it. In some cases, it's even hard to tell the difference between today's country and rock music. Many of today's country music stars were just as likely to listen to rock groups such as REM, Aerosmith, or Dave Matthews Band when they were growing up as to traditional country legends like Willie Nelson or Johnny Cash. Comparing today's country music star in his 30s with a country music star of the same age in 1950 clearly illustrates how generations change.

10-2e Religious Microculture

Recall that religion represents one of the key institutions that shape consumer culture. Not surprisingly, then, religious affiliation provides a basis for microcultures within national or regional cultures. Religion affects all manner of daily life, sometimes even among those who are not devout followers of any religion. For instance, in the United States and throughout the Western world, the weekend occurs on Saturday and Sunday. But in Arab lands and others where Islam is the predominant religion, Friday is the day of prayer, so the weekend occurs on Thursday and Friday. Exhibit 10.5 illustrates the proportion of consumers belonging to the main religions in the United States, other diverse nations, and the world at large.

Perhaps more than in other countries, U.S. Christians represent a large number of different religions. Just over half (51.3%) of Americans report belonging to a Protestant religion, with the remainder of Christians being Catholic (23.9%). One can hardly say that all Protestant denominations are the same, but generally speaking, Protestants are relatively conservative in their approach to life, and emphasize hard work and accomplishment as important goals. They also tend to be more comfortable with material acquisitions than are Catholics.[28] Some Protestant denominations are more likely than Catholics to have a moral prohibition against the consumption of beer, wine, and other forms of alcoholic beverages. In the southern United States, where large portions of the population belong to relatively conservative Protestant religions such as Southern Baptist or Pentecostal, many counties are "dry," meaning the purchase and/or possession of alcohol is prohibited by law.

Budget allocations also are associated with religion. Church organizations have not been immune from economic downturns. Many Protestant denominations have tithing requirements that strongly encourage church members to give 10% of their gross income to the church. This is a relatively high proportion compared to other religions, even while the bad economy has hit church finances very hard.[29] The resulting strain comes at a bad time for church groups as they seek to provide assistance for the unemployed. Furthermore, many church groups provide a source of low-price and free products for lower income consumers. Groups such as St. Vincent de Paul operate stores where secondhand items and retailer overstocks are made available at a fraction of normal retail price or even for free for the more needy consumers. The Jewish Federation also implements *tzedakah*, meaning giving assistance to the poor, which enables the poor to access products they may not be able to otherwise.

Consumer research examines the extent to which an overt Christian appeal influences Christians.[30] For example, an advertisement containing the ichthys symbol (Christian fish emblem) caused Evangelical Christians to rate the perceived quality of service, and their intention to use that particular service, higher than an ad that was otherwise identical. No such effect was seen among consumers of other religious affiliations. In fact, the authors of that particular research suggest that the symbol may even backfire and have negative effects on non-Evangelicals.

Religion also affects consumers' diets and the clothing they wear. During Lent each year, fast-food restaurants heavily advertise fish offerings as a way of capitalizing on the Catholic tradition of abstaining from meat during Lent, particularly on Fridays. Jewish consumers often follow a kosher diet. This places a high standard on cleanliness and purity of foods. Some

Exhibit 10.5

Religious Percentages in the World and Select Nations

Source: CIA World Factbook, https://www.cia.gov/library/publications/the-world-factbook/geos/tu.html (accessed June 27, 2016).

common Christian foods like shrimp and bacon are inconsistent with this standard. Kosher restrictions include:

▶ **Food must be prepared with a very high degree of cleanliness. Kosher packing plants are inspected by a rabbi to certify cleanliness.**

▶ **Certain meats are prohibited, such as pork and rabbit.**

▶ **Dairy products cannot be consumed simultaneously with meat.**

▶ **Fish with scales are allowed, but shellfish are not.**

In many urban areas around the United States, where relatively large Jewish populations exist, grocers dedicate entire sections of their stores to kosher goods. The Islamic religion also places dietary restrictions on its followers, and it strictly prohibits the consumption of pork. The word *halal* describes the dietary restrictions that prohibit alcohol, pork, and meats that are not slaughtered in the prescribed manner. Restaurateurs who serve these markets need to be well aware of the dietary restrictions and the sensitivity of these cultures to violations of the restrictions.

> ## Religion affects all aspects of daily life.

Additionally, various religions have rules and customs about public displays of the body. Muslim women often sport veils, or even cover their entire face. Although this practice is often stigmatized in the United States, some

Boris-B/Shutterstock.com

fashion retailers have offered fashionable veils that may even cross over into the secular market.[31] **Stigmatization** means that the consumers are marked in some way that indicates their place in society. Sometimes the mark is not particularly flattering. A fashionable veil can help overcome negative feelings about this stigmatized product. In 2010, France's legislature voted to make the public wearing of full veils (those covering the face as well as the head) illegal, arguing that the practice was demeaning to women. Other European countries are considering adopting similar legislation.[32] Friction is often inevitable as cultures interact and as consumers choose to follow their religious beliefs rather than laws that they perceive to clash with these beliefs. Consumers of all faiths often make decisions to follow their religious beliefs and customs. Without question, religion plays a major role in both culture and microculture.

10-2f Ethnic Microculture

The United States is sometimes referred to as a melting pot. The analogy tries to make the point that America is a land filled with people from a wide range of ethnic backgrounds. According to this view, these people all blend together into a single American culture. This may be an oversimplification, but the fact that the American people are very diverse is undeniable. Most Americans are aware of their heritage beyond the United States and are often proud of it. Thus, even for multigenerational Americans, consumption is affected by heritage. This can be much stronger for families with shorter roots in America, including recent immigrants. Another chapter discussed the acculturation process of consumers arriving in a new land like America. Consumption in the United States, however, remains tied to ethnicity to varying extents. We choose to use the term *culture* with these groups due to the strong ties that consumers often feel to their ethnic roots. Exhibit 10.6 breaks down the major ethnic groups in the United States.

HISPANIC CULTURE

The largest ethnic group (aside from whites) is now Hispanic. Hispanics are expected to account for nearly 20% by 2020. Nearly 11% of Americans list Spanish as their primary language. Perhaps the most important rule to remember in dealing with any large ethnic market segment is that the group is not homogeneous. Hispanic consumers vary a great deal from one

stigmatization a situation in which consumers are marked in some way that indicates their place in society

Exhibit 10.6

Ethnic/Racial Groups in the United States Based on U.S. Census Projections (2015–2020)*

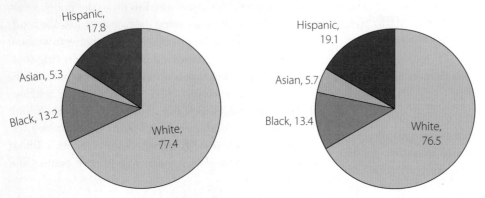

Source: U.S. Census Bureau, http://www.census.gov/population/projections/data/national/2012/summarytables.html (accessed June 17, 2014).

* The percentages do not add to 100 because the U.S. Census classifies Hispanics by racial color.

Hispanics tend to place a high value on family-oriented values and social intimacy. Thus, products that appeal to the entire family or that somehow bring the family together tend to provide high value for Hispanic consumers. The Hispanic market cannot be ignored, as it is the fastest growing market segment in the United States.

AFRICAN AMERICAN CULTURE

The African American market segment represents about 13% of the total U.S. market. Like the Hispanic culture, the African American microculture can be broken down into other more specific microcultures. Obviously, this is an important American market segment. Again, factors such as social class may have more influence in a given situation than ethnicity (such as which restaurants to patronize), but many companies, including McDonald's, have successfully capitalized on a special effort to tailor products toward the African American consumer. One of the most important trends among African American consumers is their growing affluence.

another, based on their own personal preferences, their degree of acculturation, how many generations removed they are from their ancestral country, what the ancestral country is (Mexico, the Dominican Republic, Cuba, etc.), and other demographic characteristics. Thus, we can only talk about general tendencies for this market.

The more generations removed from the ancestral country, the closer a consumer is likely to be to the mainstream culture. Hispanic consumers several generations removed from the ancestral country are likely to communicate in English, while first generation Hispanic immigrants may still communicate primarily in Spanish. However, care needs to be taken when trying to appeal to an ethnic group in their native language. Even if the children of American-born Hispanics (third generation or more) can speak Spanish, they may be somewhat insulted by being presented an ad in Spanish. Also, in all cultures, there is some risk of a backlash from other consumers who may resent an advertisement in something other than their native language. The safest approach is to use Spanish-language ads only when dealing with immigrant Hispanic populations or Spanish-language media (radio, printed media, television). The term **bicultural** is used to describe immigrants as they face decisions and form preferences based on their old or new cultures. Bicultural consumers begin to express lower ethnocentrism than their counterparts in the native country and thus are more open to products from their new country.[33]

bicultural used to describe immigrants as they face decisions and form preferences based on their old or new cultures

More than one in ten Americans list Spanish as their primary language. Carefully targeted ads attempt to reach this segment.

The number of these Americans in professional occupations has multiplied many times over in the past few decades, as has the number of African American-owned businesses. Each of these factors contributes to an even higher buying power for this important segment.

ASIAN CULTURE

The Asian segment also is growing rapidly. This segment represents between 4% and 5% of the U.S. population. Relative to other minority groups, the Asian American culture is highly educated and highly affluent.[34] Asian American consumers are very favorable toward luxury brands, tend to own their homes, and retain a preference for Asian foods. Asian Americans also are concentrated in large numbers in a few areas of the United States. For example, all the major cities of California contain high proportions of Asian Americans. The fact that they are concentrated in specific locations in the United States facilitates marketers' ability to effectively reach this market.

10-2g Income and Social Class Microculture

Two very important topics in consumer behavior are income and social class. The concepts permeate our everyday life, and it seems that consumers are always trying to better themselves by moving up the income and class ladders. To say that income and social class are variables that marketers track closely would be a huge understatement.

Income level and social class are closely related, but distinct, concepts. Income level is truly a demographic issue, based on the amount of monetary resources a person receives. We define **social class** as a culturally defined group to which a consumer belongs based on resources like prestige, income, occupation, and education. Income and occupation are two of the most recognizable determinants of social class.

Tastes and preferences are largely determined by social class, a finding that falls under the sociological concept of habitus. The term **habitus** refers to mental and cognitive structures through which individuals perceive the world based largely on their standing in a social class.[35] Although concrete generalizations regarding the influence of income and social class on purchase behavior are difficult, it can be said that social class tends to be a better predictor of purchases that involve value and lifestyles, as well as symbolic and highly visible products. Income tends to be a better predictor of purchases that require very substantial expenditures.[36]

SOCIAL CLASS IN THE UNITED STATES

Six major social classes have been identified in the United States. These include *Upper Class, Lower Upper Class, Upper Middle Class, Lower Middle Class, Upper Lower Class,* and *Lower Lower Class.*[37] Many consumers strive to move up the social ladder throughout their lifetimes, but this is not true of all consumers. Some consumers are simply content with their social standing and do not aspire to move up the social ladder. Some consumers are born into a social class (termed an *ascribed* status), whereas others work their way into a class (termed an *achieved* status).

Social class is an important concept because a class strongly influences lifestyles, opinions, attitudes, and behaviors. Sayings such as "birds of a feather flock together" and "keeping up with the Joneses" typify the social class conceptualization. That is to say, consumers in a particular class tend to behave similarly in the marketplace. Again, it should be emphasized that this does not mean that *every* consumer in a social class will exhibit the *exact* same behaviors, attitudes, and opinions. However, in general it is a good rule of thumb that they will act similarly.

Two issues regarding social class that have been discussed here illustrate the difficulties with considering class in consumer behavior. The facts that not all consumers strive to move up the social ladder, and that not every consumer in a social class will act similarly, highlight the limitations of using the concept in consumer research. Nevertheless, social class is a very important societal and cultural issue that we observe in everyday life. A simple example of the influence of social class on behavior is the finding that most marriages comprise people from similar classes. In sociology, this is referred to as **homogamy**, or *assortative mating.*[38]

SOCIAL STRATIFICATION

The concept of social stratification underscores the role of social class in society. **Social stratification** can be defined as the division of society into classes that have unequal access to scarce and valuable resources.[39] Of course, the finer things in life are generally enjoyed by the Upper Class or Lower Upper Class. Luxury items and

social class a culturally defined group to which a consumer belongs based on resources like prestige, income, occupation, and education

habitus mental and cognitive structures through which individuals perceive the world based largely on their standing in a social class

homogamy the finding that most marriages comprise people from similar classes

social stratification the division of society into classes that have unequal access to scarce and valuable resources

status symbols are enjoyed by these groups, while the bare essentials are relegated to the Lower Lower Class. Many of the Lower Lower Class even find themselves homeless.

The huge disparity between the upper and lower classes can be found in many parts of the United States. As a sad, ironic example, consider the number of homeless people that currently live in the tunnel systems under the city of Las Vegas. Under the very streets where excess is flaunted live some of the poorest and most destitute consumers in the nation.[40] The problems of poverty and homelessness are found worldwide.

SOCIAL CLASS WORLDWIDE

Social classes obviously exist throughout the world. China, with its enormous population, exhibits a range of social classes. Rapid economic development has led to recent gains in the Chinese middle class. Forecasts reveal that as many as 700 million consumers will be in the Chinese middle class by the year 2020. Middle-class consumers occupy a variety of positions in the Chinese workplace, from entrepreneurs to managers of high-tech companies.[41] Japan, on the other hand, has witnessed a gradual widening of the gap between the haves and the have-nots, along with a generally shrinking middle class. India, like China, has a large middle class, estimated at approximately 170 million. Many of these consumers are young, with nearly half of India's billion-plus population less than 25 years old. Estimates reveal that as much as 40% of the population of India will be middle class in the next two decades.[42]

10-2h Street Microculture

Microcultures can grow around any number of phenomena, not just around differences in ethnicity, income/social class, generation, region, or religion. As we have seen, sports can provide a basis for microculture. Music can as well. One way to refer to these microcultures is by using the label *street microcultures*.

The hip-hop microculture illustrates one such group. Obviously, hip-hop culture has influenced consumer tastes outside of its group (consider the pervasiveness of hip-hop apparel). "Gothic" (or "goth") microculture represents another prevalent microculture in the United States. Gothic influence can be very strong, as group members almost universally wear dark, macabre attire. The goth microculture is a great example of how strong microculture influence can be. In fact, some argue that gothic identification is even more important than

status symbols products or objects that are used to signal one's place in society

gender identification.[43] The "emo" subculture has received a lot of media attention in recent years, though its roots are thought to go back at least a few decades. Most consumers can recognize a goth or emo person easily, further evidence of how microcultures permeate our daily lives and are observed by many consumers.

Microcultures can even grow out of gaming experiences, virtual communities, and practically any other consumer activity that brings consumers with something in common together. The more easily microcultures can be reached, either physically or with various media, the better marketers can connect with them through value-added communications and products.

10-3 MICROCULTURE IS NOT UNIQUELY AMERICAN

From this discussion of microcultures, it is easy to see why this consumer behavior topic is important to researchers and managers alike. Microculture membership affects the value of things. It is important to remember that like other concepts discussed in this text, microcultures are truly global phenomena and are not confined to any one region or country.

10-3a Microcultures Around the World

We often think of foreign countries with a single stereotype. A Parisian may represent all French people to some consumers. Even a country as diverse as China might be looked at very narrowly, with unfounded stereotypes. Yet other countries also have many bases around which microcultures are formed.

Many of the examples we've discussed transcend any specific country. Germany, Spain, and South Africa, for instance, are all countries where different languages or dialects are spoken in different regions of the country. Bavarians, from the German Alps, feel quite distinct from the typical German population. Over 1,800 languages are spoken on the continent of Africa, across 53 countries. Furthermore, immigration is fast spreading through Europe, and the influx of Muslim microcultures in many European countries is adding to the diversity of these nations.

10-3b Street Microcultures Worldwide

Many street microcultures, including music, sports, and fashion, exist around the world as well. Punk, goth, and emo microcultures are all good examples. Emo, for example, represents a popular microculture in Japan. Japanese "gothic Lolita" is another popular microculture that can best be illustrated by imagining a gothic China doll. Some Japanese girls also follow the "decora" microculture, which is marked by wearing extremely bright clothing and plastic accessories. Firms need to account for the pervasiveness of microcultures when marketing products in virtually any part of the world.

Tofudevil/Shutterstock.com

 DEMOGRAPHIC ANALYSIS

Ultimately, any group or microculture has to be reached before a value proposition can be effectively delivered to them. Demographics is a term that we have used throughout this text, and it is an important concept for marketers and consumer researchers alike. Demographics refer to observable, statistical aspects of populations such as age, gender, or income.

Demographic variables are closely related to microculture. In fact, you may have noticed from previous sections that demographic variables help one to describe microcultures. As an example, we previously discussed the fact that age distinctions can be used to describe generational microcultures. Consider the fact that consumers in the Millennial microculture currently fall between the ages of 20 and 34. As such, the demographic variable "age" helps us to better understand and describe this microculture. The combination of demographic and microcultural information is therefore very valuable for today's marketers. This information becomes even more valuable when it is combined with geodemographic information, because members of many microcultures often live in close proximity to one another. Geodemographic tools such as PRIZM assist the consumer researcher with these analyses.

A **demographic analysis** develops a profile of a consumer group based on their demographics. As we have discussed, these analyses often include geodemographic approaches, because marketers find it advantageous to know where targeted consumers live. These analyses become important components of a demographic segmentation strategy. If marketers can identify where their targeted consumers live, they can implement marketing campaigns much more efficiently. Newspapers, radio, television, and even Internet communications can then be geared to specific regions.

10-4a U.S. Census Data

One very important source for performing a demographic analysis is the U.S. Census Bureau's website (www.census .gov). Exhibit 10.7 shows the interface from this website.

Exhibit 10.7

The U.S. Census Bureau's Website

A powerful source of demographic information is the U.S. Census Bureau website.

Source: U.S. Census Bureau, www.census.gov, accessed June 22, 2014.

demographic analysis
a profile of a consumer group based on their demographics

The website provides a real-time estimate of the U.S. population. The top category of options provides an entry into the search mechanisms to find details about people and households in the United States. One can find the actual counts from the most recent census, or get estimates and projections of populations up to the current date. Generally, the search engine can be used to find statistics on a region of interest. Exhibit 10.8 shows the demographic profile for the state of Missouri.

Exhibit 10.8

Demographic Profile for the State of Missouri

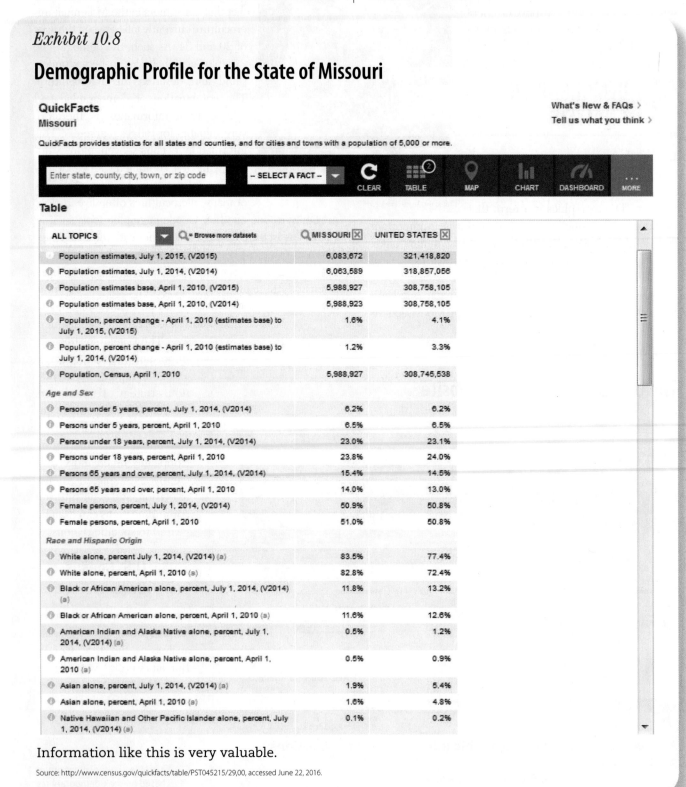

ALL TOPICS	MISSOURI	UNITED STATES
Population estimates, July 1, 2015, (V2015)	6,083,672	321,418,820
Population estimates, July 1, 2014, (V2014)	6,063,589	318,857,056
Population estimates base, April 1, 2010, (V2015)	5,988,927	308,758,105
Population estimates base, April 1, 2010, (V2014)	5,988,923	308,758,105
Population, percent change - April 1, 2010 (estimates base) to July 1, 2015, (V2015)	1.6%	4.1%
Population, percent change - April 1, 2010 (estimates base) to July 1, 2014, (V2014)	1.2%	3.3%
Population, Census, April 1, 2010	5,988,927	308,745,538
Age and Sex		
Persons under 5 years, percent, July 1, 2014, (V2014)	6.2%	6.2%
Persons under 5 years, percent, April 1, 2010	6.5%	6.5%
Persons under 18 years, percent, July 1, 2014, (V2014)	23.0%	23.1%
Persons under 18 years, percent, April 1, 2010	23.8%	24.0%
Persons 65 years and over, percent, July 1, 2014, (V2014)	15.4%	14.5%
Persons 65 years and over, percent, April 1, 2010	14.0%	13.0%
Female persons, percent, July 1, 2014, (V2014)	50.9%	50.8%
Female persons, percent, April 1, 2010	51.0%	50.8%
Race and Hispanic Origin		
White alone, percent July 1, 2014, (V2014) (a)	83.5%	77.4%
White alone, percent, April 1, 2010 (a)	82.8%	72.4%
Black or African American alone, percent, July 1, 2014, (V2014) (a)	11.8%	13.2%
Black or African American alone, percent, April 1, 2010 (a)	11.6%	12.6%
American Indian and Alaska Native alone, percent, July 1, 2014, (V2014) (a)	0.5%	1.2%
American Indian and Alaska Native alone, percent, April 1, 2010 (a)	0.5%	0.9%
Asian alone, percent, July 1, 2014, (V2014) (a)	1.9%	5.4%
Asian alone, percent, April 1, 2010 (a)	1.6%	4.8%
Native Hawaiian and Other Pacific Islander alone, percent, July 1, 2014, (V2014) (a)	0.1%	0.2%

Information like this is very valuable.

Source: http://www.census.gov/quickfacts/table/PST045215/29,00, accessed June 22, 2016.

This simple profile contains a great deal of useful information. For example, if a company were interested in marketing a product toward Asians, Missouri might not be the best target. Less than 2% of the population is Asian, which is less than half the percentage in the nation overall. In contrast, the relative proportion of white Americans versus African Americans is quite similar to that of the national profile. In other instances, one may wish to obtain these data for a smaller region. The website makes the data available at the county level, and with a bit of additional assistance, the data can be broken down by ZIP code. Also, a marketer may sometimes need a market to be of at least a certain minimum size in order to be considered a viable target. A product might be targeted toward Millennials and may require a market of at least two million consumers to be viable. The target can be compared to the demographic numbers to see if the option should be pursued.

 10-5 MAJOR CULTURAL AND DEMOGRAPHIC TRENDS

As with other consumer behavior topics, it is not enough to simply understand cultural and demographic factors as they currently exist. These factors evolve over time. For this reason, it is important to identify emerging trends that influence behavior. Cultural, microcultural, and demographic trends are especially important to monitor. In fact, it is safe to say that the use of demographic analysis today is not enough to help us understand consumer behavior. Mixing in other variables such as cultural, microcultural, lifestyle, or even life stage variables often reveals much better information about consumer behavior today. As we have stated, a 30-year-old today is much different from a 30-year-old in 1950. You are much more likely to find a 60-year-old surfer today than you would in 1950!

10-5a Trends Affecting Consumer Behavior

While there are a number of trends that could be discussed, four notable trends that are relevant to consumer researchers and managers deserve careful attention. These trends include declining birthrates, increasing consumer affluence, increasing life expectancy, and increasing cultural diversity worldwide. Each of these trends are discussed below.

DECLINING BIRTHRATES

One of the biggest trends in Western countries is the declining birthrate. In many European countries, the birthrate has dropped to 0.5 per person. That means that each couple is having at most one child. If this trend continues, these countries will experience declining populations. One particularly important trend in China, thought to be the result of the country's "one child" policy, is a relative imbalance in the number of men compared to women. Estimates reveal that by 2020, China could have as many as 30 million more men than women.[44] Exhibit 10.9 displays select birthrates. While birthrates are relatively low in many Western

Exhibit 10.9

Projected Birthrates per Couple and Life Expectancies for Countries Around the World (2016)

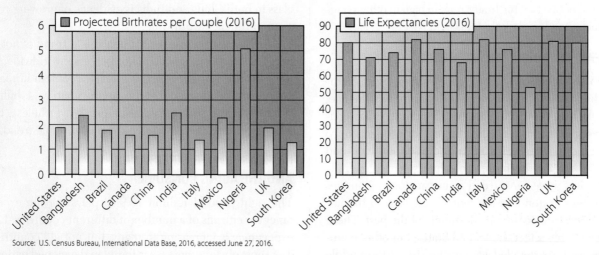

Source: U.S. Census Bureau, International Data Base, 2016, accessed June 27, 2016.

SUCCESS AT THE BOTTOM

Over 4 billion consumers worldwide live in poverty. That segment isn't expected to shrink anytime soon. However, these consumers are not to be ignored. First, they share the same basic needs as other consumers, and success can be found in the marketplace for products that provide these consumers economical ways to address basic needs for sustenance, safety, and esteem. Entrepreneurs sometimes go into these areas with the idea of providing basic goods and services to this segment, but also realize that without a way for consumers to make a living, poverty will continue.

In many instances, agricultural products still offer entrepreneurial opportunities, particularly as upper-level consumers become more attuned to natural, authentic products and avoid the synthetic. If these consumers can become part of an enterprise that nurtures the natural resources where they live into a product that offers value for other consumers, then they have a chance to earn a living and in turn become consumers for an ever-increasing array of products. For example, in many coffee-producing areas, entrepreneurs have capitalized on upper-level segments' increasing taste for gourmet coffee by teaching farmers and workers in these areas to nurture the *terroir* (the specific geographical location along with its natural and cultural resources) into a uniquely differentiated product. After all, nobody else has that terroir! Such strategic efforts provide an avenue up from the bottom of the pyramid.

© GuoZhongHua/Shutterstock.com

Sources: C. Nakata and M. Viswanathan (2012), "From Impactful Research to Sustainable Innovations for Subsistence Marketplaces," *Journal of Business Research*, 65 (12), 1655–1657. Raed Elaydi and Josetta McLaughlin, "Cultivating Terroir in Subsistence Markets: Development of Terroir Strategy through Harmony-with-Community Framework," *Journal of Business Research*, doi.org/10.1016/j.jbusres.2012.02.016.

countries, notice that birthrates remain high in other countries, including Bangladesh, India, and Nigeria.

INCREASING CONSUMER AFFLUENCE

The combination of working couples and lower birthrates has led to greater levels of consumer affluence, particularly in the United States. As a result, many consumer segments have become targets for products once considered to be luxuries, such as cruises and high-end automobiles. Furthermore, consumers have generally become less price-sensitive in many categories. Families eat out more often and are more likely to own the latest electronic devices than consumers of the past. These trends not only affect the United States, but other countries as well. As detailed earlier, the rise of the middle class in both China and India is evidence of growing consumer affluence worldwide.

To say that consumer affluence is a trend is not to imply that poverty is not a major problem worldwide. To the contrary, poverty remains a major problem in many nations, as evidenced by the approximately 4 billion "bottom of the pyramid" consumers. Nevertheless, the growth in consumer affluence is a recognizable trend.

INCREASING LIFE EXPECTANCY AND THE AGING CONSUMER

The right pane of Exhibit 10.9 displays the life expectancy for citizens of a number of different countries. Life expectancy is increasing in many, but not all, countries. The most obvious increase is found in developed nations.

If we consider life expectancy as a proxy for standard of living, we can see that as the birthrate declines, the standard of living increases. Thus, unfortunately, the countries with the highest birthrates in the world are among the poorest. In developed countries, more wealth is spread over fewer consumers.

The growth trends in population, along with birthrate and life expectancy trends, all affect consumer culture in many ways. One major issue in the United States today is the aging baby boomer population. This segment of the consumer population is expected to dramatically affect business practices for many years to come. As discussed earlier, this segment attracts much marketing attention due to its large size and overall spending power.

INCREASING CULTURAL DIVERSITY

Many societies worldwide are becoming increasingly culturally diverse. One way in which cultures become more diverse is through immigration and the growth of microcultures. There are numerous trends that could be discussed, and they range from religious to street microcultural diversity. Regarding religious microcultures, one significant trend in European countries is the growth of the Muslim faith. Islam is rapidly growing in popularity in Europe, and this religious microculture is influencing consumer behavior throughout the region. In the United States, ethnic microcultures continue to become increasingly diverse due to both legal and illegal immigration. This issue is greatly impacting the Borderland region discussed earlier in this chapter.

The United Kingdom is also experiencing a general increase in immigration, with many immigrants arriving from the European Union. As such, the United Kingdom

is realizing a growth in microcultural diversity, particularly pertaining to ethnic and religious microcultural diversity. The continued expansion of the world teen culture market is expected as many Western brands, such as Coca-Cola, McDonald's, and Starbucks, continue to succeed with foreign expansion. The influence of Western ideals and practice on the world teen culture continues. This is not to say that all young consumers will think and act completely alike. In fact, many Asian teens are carving out new and developing microcultures unlike those found in the United States. Some teens worldwide are breaking away from punk, goth, and emo microcultures to focus on more traditional clean-cut, even conservative styles.[45] As mentioned, there are many ways in which cultural diversity is increasing worldwide.

As we have seen, microcultures influence consumer behavior throughout the world, and for this reason, the study of microculture is very important for consumer researchers and marketers alike.

STUDY TOOLS 10

LOCATED AT BACK OF THE TEXTBOOK
☐ Tear out Chapter Review Card

LOCATED AT WWW.CENGAGE.COM/LOGIN
☐ Review Key Term flashcards and create your own cards
☐ Track your knowledge and understanding of key concepts in consumer behavior
☐ Complete practice quizzes to prepare for tests
☐ Complete interactive content within CB Online
☐ Review the Chapter Highlight boxes for CB Online

CASES

Rate My Professors.com: Does this Site Really Help in Choosing Classes?

Written by Robert A. Bergman, College of Business, Lewis University

When registration time comes around, convenient class times and a great schedule are just part of the picture. You also want the best professors who make the class relevant, interesting, informative, and fun. And don't forget . . . easy. As one student remarked, "keep me awake and give me an A."

Tom and Alex are a couple of marketing majors finishing their second year at State University. They're kicking back at the student union on a warm afternoon in late April, smartphones in hand. It's time to register for fall term, and they're discussing a lot more than just day and time of the available classes.

They've already met with their academic advisors and determined the classes they should take in the fall term to stay on schedule and graduate on time. They've chosen six classes to target when it's their turn for online registration. They've also determined a contingency plan in the event the courses they want are full. They've each chosen two alternative courses.

On average, each of these eight courses has a half dozen sections to choose from, and each section seems to have a different professor. It's a confusing quest for the perfect schedule.

As business students, they take a managerial approach to their decision-making process—to maximize their probability of success in taking classes. In their minds, "success" is measured in:

1. **convenient schedule**
2. **easy coursework**
3. **interesting lectures**

The schedule book allows them to evaluate each course by:

a) **day of week**

b) **time of day**

c) **professor**

While they can make educated decisions about (a) day of week, and (b) time of day, which happen to be their first evaluative criteria to consider for a *Convenient Schedule*, they are stumped to find an easy and effective way to evaluate *Easy Coursework* and *Interesting Lectures* without further data on the various professors.

Success factors		Evaluative criteria
Convenient Schedule	}	Day of week
		Time of day
Easy Coursework Interesting Lectures	}	Professor

They could create a list of all the professors teaching the classes on their list—over 40 professors. Then they could poll fellow students about their experiences with each professor, document the results, and churn the data to make the most effective decisions in choosing their class schedule for the next term.

From reading their *Principles of Marketing* textbook, Tom and Alex realize they are members of the generational microculture termed Millennials. They are technologically savvy and experts in using the Internet and social media. As they crack open a Red Bull and ponder this revelation, they think out loud: "There must be

	NAME	DEPARTMENT	TOTAL RATINGS	OVERALL QUALITY	EASINESS	HOT?	SHARE
	Bergman, Robert	Marketing	28	5.0	3.8		

Source: http://www.ratemyprofessors.com/SelectTeacher.jsp?the_dept=All&sid=515&orderb y=TLName&letter=B, accessed April 8, 2012.

Robert Bergman

no photo

Name: **Robert Bergman**
School: **Lewis University**
Location: **Romeoville, IL**
Department: **Marketing**

5.0	**5.0**	**5.0**	**3.8**	🌶
OVERALL QUALITY	HELPFULNESS	CLARITY	EASINESS	HOTNESS

ⓘ Submit a Correction

Number of ratings **28**

Source: http://www.ratemyprofessors.com/ShowRatings.jsp?tid=517521, accessed April 8, 2012.

a website where professors are rated by students." Tom pulls out his smartphone, opens a browser window, and types in "rate professors" in the search bar. In a few seconds his eyes widen to see listed a website called "Rate My Professors" at www.ratemyprofessors.com.

Their hearts start to race. Is it an adrenalin rush from finding the kind of site that would solve their dilemma, or the slurry of stimulants in the Red Bull? With a few taps of the screen, they find the "gold" they were digging for—priceless information about their university professors.

On RateMyProfessors.com, Tom and Alex find all the professors from State U listed in alphabetical order, making it easy to locate each professor they need to evaluate.

Both Tom and Alex must take consumer behavior in the fall. There are six sections, with four different professors. Registration is just a couple of days away and they need to make the right decision, factoring in the day, time, and quality of the professor.

They find the list of professors at State U rated in the following ways:

▶ **Total ratings (number of ratings students have made)**
▶ **Overall quality**
▶ **Easiness**
▶ **Hot?**

Overall quality and easiness have numerical values from 0 to 5, 5 being the highest.

The term "hot?" is noted with the graphic of a red chili pepper to designate if the professor is considered good looking.

Tom and Alex note the numerical values representing *overall quality* and *easiness* of each professor they are researching, and make their decisions based on these numbers alone.

In addition, visitors to the site can click on the name of any professor and see their ratings in more detail. The following categories and their rating are presented:

▶ **Overall quality**
▶ **Helpfulness**
▶ **Clarity**
▶ **Easiness**
▶ **Hotness**

Below these rating summaries are the individual user comments and ratings.

Tom and Alex are used to reading customer reviews of products and services on Amazon, Zappos, and Best Buy websites. They've come to rely on the feedback and opinions of people they perceive to be just like them. While they don't always read the dialogue or text of each customer review, they base a lot of their purchase decisions on the rating, or number

CASES

	User Comments and Ratings		Professor Rebuttals

DATE	CLASS	RATING	COMMENT
4/6/12	SMMS1	☺ Good Quality Easiness Helpfulness Clarity Rater Interest	The class was half really interactive lecture and half project work with Mr. Bergman working one-on-one with each project team. I learned so much about social media - and how to think outside the box to create uber strategies to get the most out of websites and social media channels. ⚑ Report this rating
4/5/12	PR2	☺ Good Quality Easiness Helpfulness Clarity Rater Interest	Great approach to topic. We took what we learned and used it for local non-profits. Bergman taught us how to use PR to advance our careers and get noticed in the world. Great professor. Great mentor. Knows his stuff and wants us to be as good. ⚑ Report this rating
2/23/12	mkt376	☺ Good Quality Easiness Helpfulness Clarity Rater Interest	Best professor ever!!!!! I took him for 3 classes and he is great. Yay Lewis! ⚑ Report this rating
12/26/11	CB2	☺ Good Quality Easiness Helpfulness Clarity Rater Interest	Awesome teacher. Relates everything to real-world situations. Lots of group work, videos, meaningful discussions and field trips. I actually enjoyed going to class. ⚑ Report this rating

Source: http://www.ratemyprofessors.com/ShowRatings.jsp?tid=517521, accessed April 8, 2012.

of stars the product or service receives in the ratings. They figure the rating tells enough of the story to make an informed decision, and "why waste time reading the entire review?"

Tom hypothesizes another thing about the ratings, and muses to Alex, "If girls are rating male professors with a chili pepper to signify they're 'hot,' then there might be more girls in the class." Alex punches him in the arm, and they continue studying the ratings.

When they finish planning their schedule, Tom and Alex look to have the perfect schedules—classes just three days a week, all taught by professors who have an overall rating of 4–5 stars and an easiness rating of 3.5 or higher. Life is good!

Tom and Alex close their schedule books, put them in their backpacks and head to the cafeteria. Their next mission is evaluating the selection of lunch entrées at the university cafeteria, affectionately known as "the slop house." They only wish there was a website called "RateMyCafeteriaFood.com."

QUESTIONS

1 What assumptions can you make about managerial decision making, as it relates to the Millennial generation, from the case?

2 Did Tom and Alex follow a logical and rational managerial decision-making process in determining their class schedules? Why or why not?

3 Identify the group influence that the information provided on RateMyProfessors.com places on Tom and Alex.

4 Describe the types of interpersonal influence that the information provided on RateMyProfessors.com places on Tom and Alex.

5 What influence do consumer ratings that fall either above or below the norm have on your managerial decision-making process? For example, when a professor (or an Amazon.com product) is rated with 3 stars, what strength do you place on the few individual reviews that rate them with 1 star or 5 stars?

CASE 3-2

Collegiate Sporting Events Attendance: Reaching Students Through Social Media

Written by Sarah Fischbach, PhD Candidate, New Mexico State University

Attendance at university sports has a unique position. Sports at the collegiate level either have a strong following where it is nearly impossible to obtain seats to the season games, or a weak following where it is a struggle to bring in fans week after week. The administration for universities with attendance challenges find themselves focusing on all target markets. Campaigns are developed to increase community involvement by bringing in local high school, even elementary school students and families. Potential attendees are offered free products such as shirts, megaphones, and meet-and-greet sessions with the players. Additionally, theme nights become popular techniques for influencing attendance for the entire population. For example, the college administration may reduce hot dog and drink prices by 25 cents for every free throw made or three-point shot hit by the home team, to the point that the hot dogs and drinks are free to the attendees.

Although promoting to the local community and their families is important, it is not really what students are looking for at a basketball game. Students are looking for a much different environment than are families with children. In a recent survey, students were asked about family and children's attendance at games.[1] Their response was somewhat of a surprise; they didn't understand why people outside the college would want to attend the games. The consensus was that college sports were meant for the students and the students' families, not the rest of the community. Encouraging local participation would only decrease their desire to attend the game.

Whatever marketing approach the university uses to increase attendance, they need to consider the impact on the students. Students seem to be forgotten in the typical sports marketing campaign. During a recent focus group of students and faculty at a university struggling with game attendance, one participant asked what kind of motivation it is for younger kids (high school and even elementary) to come to a game and see all the empty seats. If or when the students begin their tenure at the university, they will follow suit and continue to limit their attendance at games. It's not personal, it's popularity. It doesn't create much fun for potential students when current university students don't attend the games. This is why it is so important to include collegiate sports when developing the culture of the university. It's in their best interest for universities to make attending sporting events an important part of college life and not a burden on the student's time.

So why are students not attending the games? During the same qualitative research, students unanimously stated that the main reason they don't attend is because the team doesn't win.[2] It's hard to sit in the bleachers game after game watching the other team win. There are a hundred other things students could be doing rather than attending a losing basketball game. However, winning or losing doesn't matter as much if the student is having fun and hanging out with friends. Building the sports attendance culture at the university may be just what is needed to improve overall attendance. But where does administration start? The cultural selection process includes finding out how to produce a system with both formal and informal gatekeepers. Informal gatekeepers include friends, spouses, family members, and neighbors, just for a few examples. Formal gatekeepers include radio, TV, and celebrities. College administrators must take these gatekeepers' choices and opinions into consideration and continue to mold the changes students find in mass media. Building the hype among the students even if the team is failing to meet the league records will create this awareness, at least to attend. But how do universities build this hype? Where else but social media.

Social media is the component of the online world where people interact with one another, often changing roles from reader to author and seeking various benefits from social interaction.[3] Over the last two decades, research from the literacy field has been incorporated into marketing research. The researchers who pursue this avenue discuss how the characteristics of literature or drama have been important factors in consumer development of perspectives regarding ads. Academic researchers, marketing practitioners, and sports marketing professionals agree that you must use social media to gain awareness for younger generations. But merely being on the social media radar is not enough. You have to track your social return on investment. As more companies become players of social media tools,

CASES

it is important for academic researchers, practitioners, and especially sports marketers to establish relevant ground rules.

Social media can be used to tap into the social media network that students communicate through on a daily basis. Even outside of the student network, individuals of the younger generation are using social media to bring awareness to organizations and companies. Many organizations use social media to create a buzz around a new project or an event. Facebook, LinkedIn, and Twitter have become popular forms of communication for companies worldwide. Mobile communication and mobile marketing have recently become resources for companies looking for a new edge. For example, individuals may communicate through texting and other forms of social media to create a flash mob. A flash mob is when individuals get together to promote a product or organization through spontaneous, choreographed dancing. A recent episode of *Modern Family* featured a flash mob scenario. The type of organization utilizing this new wave of social media marketing is not limited to any specific category. Suave, Oscar Mayer, and Cox Wireless are just a few companies to step into this growing segment.[4]

Mobile marketing, including the use of a flash mob, is just one example of how organizations can reach out through new innovative ways to communicate with the next technology-friendly generations. Collegiate sports are no different. Connecting with students to conduct a flash mob at a basketball game or football game could increase attendance and create a buzz for students to come and watch. These new forms of communication, such as mobile marketing, can be incorporated into the university sporting culture. Feeding the "me generation" frenzy takes new forms of marketing that might not be seen as marketing techniques. This allows the student to become part of the game instead of just a bystander. During a day and age when demands on our time keep increasing, creating the desire for students to attend games can be challenging. Using social media can help.

QUESTIONS

1 What factors will likely have the greatest impact on student attendance at a basketball game for your university?

2 Describe culture. How would your university go about creating a unique culture to capture student attendance for your university?

3 What are the benefits and dangers that universities face by including social media in their marketing campaigns?

4 What types of social media campaigns could a sports marketing director implement to gain student awareness? Explain your answer.

5 Not all college sports venues are the same. For example, football is played in a stadium, and golf is an event where smaller crowds follow along with the players. What challenges and benefits does this create for a university trying to increase attendance at sporting events?

CASE 3-3

The Millennial Generation

Written by Henry Schrader, Department of Business Administration, Central State University

Julie is the owner and manager of Julie Marchese Photography (www.mar-k-zphotography.photoreflect.com). Her business has grown to more than she can handle alone and she decided to hire another photographer. Julie, being of the late baby boomer generation, wanted to hire a photographer from a younger generation to bring a new and different creative viewpoint to her customers. She hired Maggie, a twenty-something photographer who she believed would bring in fresh ideas to her company. What Julie wasn't expecting was having a hard time understanding and working with someone from the Millennial generation. Julie said, "Maggie does a good job taking pictures, but seems to have a problem staying focused on the other responsibilities of the position."

Many employers are now trying to work with and understand the generation that is called by so many names, including the Millennial Generation, Millennium Generation, Millennials, Generation Y, Generation Next, Net Generation, Always Connected Generation, Eighties Babies, or Echo Boomers. This generation is described as a group of "jugglers" who value being both footloose and connected to their peers 24/7.[1] They stay connected via technology such as Facebook, IM, and texting, and are totally comfortable in a thumb culture that communicates online and by cell phone. To an employer these could seem like distracted employees who are more interested in their best friend's dating life than serving their customers. So is this the most misunderstood generation yet or the most distracted? We really can't look at the generation born between 1981 and 1995 (give or take a few years) as baby-faced teenagers anymore. The bulk of the Millennials have struggled to find their place in the 21st century. They are the most diverse generation ever and have often grown up in nontraditional families.[2] As they age, some of the adult pressure and strain has started eating away at their celebrated optimism and good cheer as it does with every generation. Happiness is higher on their agenda than past generations, but many Millennials remain motivated by material things. They will not forgo their comfort to make a difference.[3]

The Millennial generation has been raised in a culture that places more focus on the self and less on group, society, and community.[4] The aphorisms have shifted to "believe in yourself" and "you're special." The culture emphasizes individualism, and this gets reflected in personality traits and attitudes.[5] In the same way, older generations may view Millennials' willingness to trade high pay for fewer billable hours, flexible schedules, and a better work life as a lack of commitment, discipline, and drive. Is this true? Or are they just more focused on what is really important in life? Perception seems to be a major factor in understanding the younger generations. Julie has found that Maggie's generation is looking for meaningful work and a solid learning curve. They have high expectations of their employers and don't want to do anything they feel is beneath them.

Julie has also found that Maggie works better when they work as a team versus working alone. The Millennial generation has grown up playing on teams with no winners or losers, or even all winners. They have been laden with trophies just for participating.[6] Julie may want to focus more attention on giving Maggie different forms of feedback and guidance. Millennials like to be kept in the loop and seek frequent praise and reassurance. Honesty, humor, and information are important to this generation.[7] Employers need to be aware that this generation has a tendency to move on to other employers when they feel they are not advancing or achieving in a timely manner. You can expect your Millennial employees to stay with your company three to five years on average.

Maggie has been a large help to Julie when it comes to marketing to her fellow Millennials. Where Julie's generation was easy to reach via television, Maggie's generation has grown up in the media-saturated world of their parents and responds differently to advertisements.[8] They are more likely to respond to advertisements on the Internet, at a snowboarding tournament, or on cable television. The ads may be funny or disarmingly direct. The thing to avoid is assuming that you know this generation better than they know themselves. They are more pragmatic than the Baby Boomers ever were, and they have a BS alarm that goes off quickly. They walk in and usually make up their minds very quickly about whether they want something or don't want it. They know a lot of advertising is based on lies and hype.[9]

So as soon as you have them figured out, it is likely to change tomorrow. Millennials live in a fluid world that requires an unprecedented mutability of mind and action, and flexibility of identity and disposition. Millennials expect to live their lives in constant transition, always upgrading, changing, and leapfrogging to the latest technology. Markets that are wholly dissimilar in almost every other way look strikingly alike when it comes to Millennials.[10]

Julie has seen an increase in sales and new customers, and has learned to work with her Millennial. Just as in times past, passing knowledge from one generation to the next takes place, and learning to work with the individual, not the generation, turns out to be the most important thing on the road to success. Keeping an open mind, staying flexible, and using nontraditional methods to reach today's consumers including the Millennials has become the next step on the road of marketing.

QUESTIONS

1 Can the Millennial generation be considered a microculture?

2 What type of social power, if any, does the Millennial generation hold?

3 How has social media and group influence helped to define the Millennial generation?

4 What generation has been called the boomerang kids? Why?

5 What makes the Millennial generation so different from generations before?

11 | Consumers in Situations

LEARNING OBJECTIVES

After studying this chapter, the student should be able to:

11-1 Understand how value varies with situations.

11-2 Know the different ways that time affects consumer behavior.

11-3 Analyze shopping as a consumer activity using the different categories of shopping activities.

11-4 Distinguish the concepts of unplanned, impulse, and compulsive consumer behavior.

11-5 Use the concept of atmospherics to create consumer value.

11-6 Understand what is meant by antecedent conditions.

Remember to visit **PAGE 249** for additional **STUDY TOOLS**

INTRODUCTION

This chapter focuses on a dynamic aspect of value. The focus is on ways that a particular situation alters how much value a consumer associates with and then obtains from a particular consumption act. We recognize that consumers are always free to change their minds about something, and they very frequently do!

11-1 VALUE IN SITUATIONS?

Some consumers like to travel and others find traveling a royal pain. Traveling presents consumers with a host of situations that can alter a service's value. Let's consider breakfast. How much is too much to pay for a nice breakfast with bacon, eggs, coffee, and juice? After tax and tip, this comes to $10 at Waffle House. That may not seem like too much, and many travelers visit Waffle House every day. How does $45 sound? Ordinarily, $45 would seem like a very high price to pay for breakfast. But for the millions of consumers who attend conventions and

conferences in major cities each day, a $45 breakfast, usually not cooked to order, is more the rule than the exception. The food and beverages that associations purchase for their convention delegates represent a major source of revenue for hotels. Any convention planner knows that breakfast for the delegates can easily cost $45 a person. The hotel may list the price at just over $30, but the built-in service charge will top 20%, and taxes often are 10% or more. How can breakfast be worth so much?

A partial list of considerations that might shape value for travelers and other consumers includes:

▸ Is someone else (a third-party payer) completely or partially subsidizing the consumption?

▸ Is the consumer alone or with others?

▸ What are the economic conditions like?

▸ How much time is the consumer spending in the location?

▸ If traveling abroad, what is the exchange rate?

▸ How is the consumer paying for things?

▶ **Are any items like hotel rooms prepaid?**

▶ **Can the consumer access reviews online?**

In the case of the $45 breakfast, the convention attendee is not paying for the breakfast, although he/she may pay registration to attend the convention. If the association is not supplying breakfast, the consumer may still take the breakfast buffet in the hotel restaurant, which may only run about $35. One might think about whether that can go on the expense account before heading to the restaurant. If not, there's almost certainly a coffee shop or fast-food option nearby in a major city, maybe even a Waffle House. The handy Waffle House Locator app may help save $25!

11-1a Situations and Value

This chapter focuses on precisely how the value a consumer obtains from a purchase or consumption act varies based on the context in which the act takes place. *Situational influences* is the term that captures these contextual effects, meaning effects independent of enduring consumer, brand, or product characteristics. As can be

seen in the CVF framework, situational influences directly affect both consumer decision making and the eventual value experienced. Situational influences are enduring characteristics of neither a particular consumer nor a product or brand. Indeed, situational influences are ephemeral, meaning they are temporary conditions in a very real sense. Contexts can affect communication, shopping, brand preference, purchase, actual consumption, and the evaluation of that consumption.

The movie theater experience typifies situational influences. If the movie is a matinee, the consumer expects to pay a lower price than he would pay in the evening. Even though the movie hasn't changed, the number of people available to go to the movie has changed from the evening hours. Therefore, the lower demand entices the theater to offer lower prices. Far fewer people work in the evenings, and thus more people are free to take in a movie.

How much is too much for one margarita? Consumers attending an event at the $1 billion AT&T Stadium for the Dallas Cowboys must think a margarita, or a "Cowboy" Rita, is worth at least $16. Each time a big game is played there, consumers buy thousands of "Cowboy" Ritas at $16. Outside the stadium, the consumer could mix a margarita for a couple of dollars. However, management does not allow consumers to bring those inside,

"Place" and time shape the value of margaritas and other drinks.

so the convenience factors, along with the souvenir cowboy boot cup, add to its value. Situational influences change the desirability of consuming things and therefore change the value of these things.

We can categorize situational influences into three categories:

▶ Time

▶ Place

▶ Conditions

Exhibit 11.1 illustrates each with an example. The following sections discuss each category in more detail, with an emphasis on how value changes with each.

 11-2 TIME AND CONSUMER BEHAVIOR

Is time a consumer's most valuable resource? Time is truly scarce. In some ways, time is a consumer's only real resource because when we work, we convert time into economic resources. In addition, time is necessary for consumption

temporal factors situational characteristics related to time

to occur. Time-related factors also affect a consumer's thoughts, feelings, and behavior, all of which come together to create differing perceptions of value. Time can affect consumption in any of these forms:

▶ **Time pressure**

▶ **Time of year**

▶ **Time of day**

The term **temporal factor** refers to situational characteristics related to time. Thus, each of the time forms listed here represents a different temporal factor.

11-2a Time Pressure

Bob's a busy businessperson and Christmas is coming. His inbox has been full of emails counting down the days until Christmas, or more importantly, how many days until "your purchase will arrive in time for Christmas." Now, it's December 23 and finally, he clicks through a Facebook

Exhibit 11.1

Situational Influences Can Exist in Any of These Forms

Time—As a consumer has less discretionary time, the value of many household maintenance services increases.

Conditions—A consumer's economic condition will change the value of lunch in a restaurant.

Place—An environment can make a consumer feel at ease and relaxed meaning they will linger longer in that space.

message that notes "there is still time" to buy a gift for his mom. Bob selects something by clicking through the advertisement because they can deliver the gift in time for Christmas. He isn't sure the gift is right for his mom and feels a little ashamed that he didn't search sooner.

This situation exemplifies an intense time pressure. **Time pressure** represents an urgency to act based on some real or self-imposed deadline. In the situation above, the consumer faces a firm deadline. Therefore, he rushes to make a decision without the due deliberation that would likely take place otherwise. Time has caused him to make a purchase that is likely not the best choice.

Time pressure affects consumers in several ways. First, when time is scarce, consumers process less information because time is a critical resource necessary for problem solving. Consumers who experience time pressure, for instance, are able to recall less information about product choices than are consumers in the same situation who are not under the situational influence of time pressure.[1] Second, consumers experiencing time pressure are more likely to rely on simple choice heuristics than are those in less-tense situations. Thus, rather than deciding which restaurant option is more nutritious, the consumer simply chooses the fastest option.[2] Often, this means relying on habit (habitual decision making) such as choosing a burger.[3] Third, time pressure can switch a consumer's orientation from hedonic to utilitarian. Consider a highly involved shopper. Ordinarily, the consumer would enjoy a leisurely shopping experience. However, time pressure may prevent any enjoyment, and shopping just becomes something that needs to be done. Consistent with this line of reasoning, consumers under time pressure are more likely to shop alone than with others.[4]

Consumers facing time pressure are more likely to make poor judgments about prices. In particular, they are more likely to believe that a seller-supplied reference price is indeed a fair price.[5] Time pressure shapes the value consumers perceive in products by influencing both quality and price perceptions.[6] Because consumers rely more on price–quality heuristics than they do beliefs about financial sacrifice, brands positioned as relatively high quality may benefit in situations characterized by high time pressure. Consumers may simply choose the well-known and potentially higher-priced brand because they don't have time to weigh different attributes against the price. Conversely, other consumers may simply choose the lowest-priced alternative and risk disappointment if a brand does not deliver the expected benefits.

> **Consumers facing time pressure are more likely to make poor judgments about prices.**

11-2b Spare Time

Like discretionary income, **discretionary (spare) time** represents the days, hours or minutes that are not obligated toward some compulsory and time-consuming activity. The biggest constraint on most consumers' time is their job. Consumers who work 60 hours a week or more feel a great deal of time pressure even when going through routine consumer behaviors like dropping off dry cleaning or getting a check-up. When consumers feel like they lack spare time, personalized services that make routine activities convenient, such as getting service on the car or, house cleaning, or electronic appointments with a doctor increase hedonic value as the feelings of relief bring about instant gratification. Conversely, consumers with a lot of spare time find little hedonic value in such things, and instead seek such services out only as a way of increasing utilitarian value.[7]

Service providers need to be able to detect whether consumers are time starved or have extra time. Consider how different consumers with varying amounts of spare time for lunch will react. A consumer with 30 minutes only needs a utilitarian experience. However, even that same consumer might wish to have a leisurely and relaxing lunch experience if she is dining on her day off. Consumers who are hedonically motivated will more likely trade time for money, but when consumers have utilitarian motivations they will more likely trade money for time.[8]

Many consumers face chronic time pressure because so much of their time is obligated to work and family responsibilities that they have little time for leisure. Conversely, consumers today with more spare time can offer their services for hire. With little or no training, Internet-based communications allow consumers to "share" for hire. Uber, the best known ride-sharing service, provides one such opportunity. Consumers with no training as a cab driver can find business online in the form of people who need a ride at times when the consumer need not be

time pressure urgency to act based on some real or self-imposed deadline

discretionary (spare) time the days, hours, or minutes that are not obligated toward some compulsory and time-consuming activity

at work. The consumer becomes the marketer as part of the sharing economy.

11-2c Time of Year

Seasonality refers to regularly occurring conditions that vary with the time of year. The fact is, consumers' value perceptions also vary with the time of year. Iced tea is worth more to a consumer on a hot, sunny summer afternoon than it might be on a cold, cloudy winter day.

Even though this tendency may seem as obvious as consumers purchasing more coats and sweaters during the winter, seasonality has other effects that are perhaps not so obvious.[9] Consumers tend to shop earlier in the day during winter months, and, overall, they tend to spend more during the summer months.[10] Almost all products are susceptible to some type of seasonal influence. Fashion may lead the way with traditional spring, summer, fall, and winter fashions. However, many food items vary in demand with the season. People consume champagne predominantly during the holidays. The effectiveness of social media marketing depends strongly on seasonality and timing the market push when demand for the product is highest.[11]

11-2d Cycles

The increase in coffee consumption in the United States over the last few years has come largely at the expense of carbonated soft drinks. Tea sales are also increasing in the United States, and although tea has largely been an afternoon and evening beverage in the past, Americans now are turning to tea as a beverage to wake up to. Whether it's beverage consumption, attire, or choice of entertainment, the time of day affects the value of products and activities. Some of this influence is due to scheduled events during the day such as one's working hours. But part is also biological. In fact, our bodies have a rhythm that varies with the time of day, or a **circadian cycle**. One aspect of the circadian cycle deals with our sleeping and waking times. Consumers would prefer to sleep between the hours of midnight and 6 am and from about 1 to 3 pm. Consumers who tend to shop during the "odd hours" will do so with less energy and efficiency, and deprived cognitive

seasonality regularly occurring conditions that vary with the time of year

circadian cycle rhythm (level of energy) of the human body that varies with the time of day

advertiming ad buys that include a schedule that runs the advertisement primarily at times when customers will be most receptive to the message

capacity.[12] However, they can also do so with less interference from other consumers.

Our circadian cycle is responsible for productivity in many activities. A host of products exist to try to aid consumers through the low-energy periods of the day, but perhaps the best fix is a quick nap! Products like Kombucha and 5-Hour Energy, vitamin B–based pick-me-ups, offer a value proposition built around trying to help consumers get through the sleepy times of day. These products also offer an alternative to controversial caffeine-based pick-me-ups like Monster.

Other types of physical cycles also can create situational influences on consumers. Consumer researchers examined women's purchasing patterns over the menstrual cycle. The research demonstrates that women purchase more beauty-related products during the fertile phase and more food-related products during the non-fertile phase.[13] The explanation involves instinctive mechanisms related to the need for a mate, which are heightened cyclically during this time. During the day, hunger cycles occur but do not always coincide with an opportunity to eat.[14] Research suggests that from a health perspective, consumers who eat when they are either not very hungry or very hungry experience fewer health benefits from eating compared to those who eat when moderately hungry.

The value of products like 5-Hour Energy depends on the circadian cycle.

11-2e Advertiming

Companies sometimes buy advertising with a schedule that runs the advertisement primarily at times when customers will be most receptive to the message. This practice is known as **advertiming**. Advertisers traditionally practice advertiming based on seasonal patterns and even on day-to-day changes in the weather. Advertisements for gold purchases typically go up in times when the economy is uncertain. Social networking provides a twist on advertiming. Did you ever notice an online ad that seemed uncanny in touching on some recent event in your life? Internet users often inadvertently allow their identity to be known through procedures related to "growth hacking." Companies are using Instagram posts to time online advertising specifically to these types of consumers. People love to post Instagram photos of their new pet. Almost as soon as the posts appear, those consumers may notice a large number of ads for pet-related products. Growth-hacking involves engineering mechanisms that drive up interactions between brands and consumers. Airbnb grew in large part due to growth hacking approaches that embedded it within craigslist.

In addition, **near-field communication (NFC)** technologies using RFID, GPS, or Bluetooth capabilities alert marketers when someone, or at least someone's smartphone or tablet, has entered an area. A retailer (or the retailer's computers) taking advantage of this type of technology might spot a consumer near the store, perhaps someone who has been browsing for kitchen tables online, and push out messages or coupons for kitchen tables to entice them into the store.

 ## 11-3 PLACE SHAPES SHOPPING ACTIVITIES

Many of the activities involved in the CVF and consumer behavior theory in general take place in the shopping process. What exactly is shopping? Perhaps the following questions can help put shopping in perspective:

▶ **Do consumers have to buy to shop?**

▶ **Is a store necessary for shopping?**

▶ **What motivates consumer shopping?**

Marketers naturally hope that consumers will purchase things while shopping. But not every shopping act culminates in a purchase. Sometimes a consumer shops only to find out that the desired product is out of stock. Rather than buying a less desirable product, the consumer may simply pass or put off product acquisition indefinitely.

Consumers shop using their computers, tablets, phones, vending machines, or other nonstore alternatives, like physical mail-order catalogs. Sometimes, consumers facing an important decision like a new home or an upcoming vacation are so involved in the buying process that they can't stop thinking about their choices. In this case, they may be shopping simply from the things they hold in memory.

11-3a What Is Shopping?

Shopping can be defined as the set of potentially value-producing consumer activities that directly increase the likelihood that something will be purchased. Thus, when a consumer surfs iTunes looking for a song, he is shopping. A consumer searching Pinterest at 3 am for comments about new dress shoes because she can't sleep is shopping. When a consumer visits the mall as a regular weekend activity, she is shopping. Earlier, we described marketing as a set of business activities that enhances the likelihood of purchase. In this sense, shopping represents the inverse of marketing. Both marketing and shopping make purchase more likely, but one involves activities of marketing people and the other involves activities of shoppers.

11-3b Virtual Shopping Situations

Shopping via the Internet brings 24/7 access to shopping environments. Many effects seen in real bricks-and-mortar shopping environments exist in the virtual shopping world too. For example, color and sounds can work in much the same way. Images placed in the background of a website can produce active thoughts, particularly when consumer expertise or knowledge is low. A web-based furniture retailer using pictures of clouds in the background of a web page, for instance, can produce thoughts of soft and comfortable furniture. Images play a key role in shaping the virtual shopping experience. For example, the display of clothing items on a headless mannequin may produce more positive effects online than in a physical store.[15] However, care should be taken, as aesthetics often take a backseat to the need for an easy-to-use site that facilitates easy transactions—especially for task-oriented shoppers that frequent the Internet. This is particularly the case for shoppers interacting through a smartphone or tablet computer, due to the smaller screen and limited functionality.

Typically, we think of shopping as a volitional activity, meaning the consumer is the active decision maker. Smart-agent technology raises questions about how volitional shopping might be. **Smart agent software** is capable of learning an Internet user's preferences and automatically searching out information and distributing the information to a user's computer. Numerous vendors offer smart agent software for sale or lease. Companies that purchase software hope to leverage the information that consumers leave behind into more customized and therefore more effective

near-field communication (NFC) Wi-fi–like systems communicating with specific devices within a defined space like inside or around the perimeter of a retail unit or signage

shopping set of value-producing consumer activities that directly increase the likelihood that something will be purchased

smart agent software software capable of learning an Internet user's preferences and automatically searching out information in selected websites and then distributing it

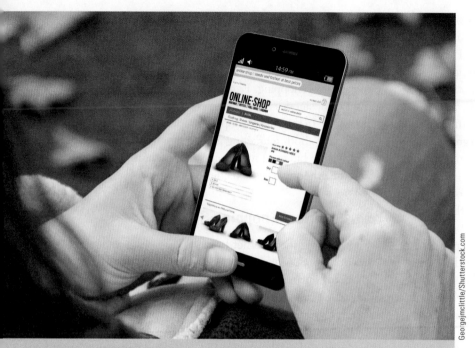

People shop online and experience the same four types of shopping activities as when shopping in a physical store.

front lawn.[16] Are consumers shopping if Amazon makes their minds up for them? As of now, society is uncertain as to when technologies allow too much to be known about or done for us. What do you think?

11-3c Shopping Activities

Shopping activities take place in specific places, over time, and under specific conditions or contexts. Shopping thus occurs in situations that consumers and marketers cannot easily control. The consumer may be either alone or in a crowded place, rushed or relaxed, in a good mood or a bad mood. In other words, shoppers are subject to many situational influences that affect decision making and value.

Four different types of shopping activities exist. At least one of these types characterizes any given shopping experience, but sometimes the shopper can combine more than one type into a single shopping trip. The four types of shopping activities are:

sales appeals. As an illustration, even a casual virtual visit to Michael Kors will set in motion push technologies that will generate Michael Kors banner ads within the browser for days after the visit.

Amazon Prime account holders leave behind browsing history, allowing Amazon to build models of what a particular consumer is going to buy. Amazon believes the models are highly accurate; so much so that they would like to ship things to consumers before they even physically make a purchase. Technology exists to have Amazon make the "purchase" on the consumer's behalf. The added convenience of the consumer not even having to make a decision might add utilitarian value. Amazon also has the capability of delivering those products with a fleet of GPS-directed drones that could take the item that was not purchased and drop it off right to your

acquisitional shopping activities oriented toward a specific, intended purchase or purchases

epistemic shopping activities oriented toward acquiring knowledge about products

experiential shopping recreationally oriented activities designed to provide interest, excitement, relaxation, fun, social interaction, or some other desired feeling

impulsive shopping spontaneous activities characterized by a diminished regard for consequences, spontaneity, and a desire for immediate self-fulfillment

1. **Acquisitional shopping.** Activities oriented toward a specific, intended purchase or purchases

2. **Epistemic shopping.** Activities oriented toward acquiring knowledge about products

3. **Experiential shopping.** Recreationally oriented activities designed to provide interest, excitement, relaxation, fun, social interaction, or some other desired feeling

4. **Impulsive shopping.** Spontaneous activities characterized by a diminished regard for consequences, heightened emotional involvement, and a desire for immediate self-fulfillment

> Both marketing and shopping make purchase more likely, but one involves activities of marketing people and the other involves activities of shoppers.

CONSUMERS AND TECHNOLOGY

Where's the Cash?

Remember when a line of cash registers stood at the front or rear of many retail stores? It used to be easy to find the cash register. More and more, however, retailers are replacing the traditional bulky units with hand-held devices or even small tablets armed with a cash register app. Retailers hope such moves will increase sales in three ways. First, the space taken up by bulky cash registers now can be used for merchandising. Second, customers end up interacting with sales associates more when they have to seek somebody out to find out how to make a purchase. Third, the interaction between customer and employee

allows the sales associate to provide key assurances and information at the critical time when a consumer is most likely to follow through with a purchase. Thus, sales can be rung up without a register to ring them.

Source: Smith. R.A. (2016), "Where Did the Register Go?" *Wall Street Journal*, March 9, D1–D3. http://marginalrevolution.com /marginalrevolution/2016/03/why-is-it -so-hard-to-find-the-cash-register.html, accessed October 21, 2016.

Ivan Smuk/Shutterstock.com

Exhibit 11.2 lists each type of shopping activity and depicts the type of shopping value generally associated with each type.

ACQUISITIONAL SHOPPING

A consumer who has to get an airline ticket to go on a business trip begins checking options at airline websites and through online travel agents. Chances are, the task is not very gratifying in and of itself. Thus, shopping like this is a chore depending on high utilitarian value to create satisfaction.

EPISTEMIC SHOPPING

An epistemic orientation motivates the shopper to increase knowledge. Epistemic activities include finding information on some imminent purchase. After the purchase situation is finished, the consumer stops looking for information. Alternatively, epistemic activities also include shopping simply to increase an ever-growing body of knowledge about some product category of interest. In this sense, epistemic activities can be associated with either situational involvement or enduring involvement, respectively. Online shopping provides a convenient forum for epistemic shopping activities that can be directly gratifying and value producing.[17] A consumer reading restaurant reviews while traveling to a city is practicing epistemic shopping. Depending on the situation, the activity could produce utilitarian value (the consumer is taking a client to dinner just after arrival) and/or hedonic value (the consumer is curious about the local restaurants).

EXPERIENTIAL SHOPPING

Experiential activities include things done just for the experience. Many consumers go shopping on the weekends just to do something. In other words, experiential shopping can be motivated by boredom or loneliness. On the other hand, consumers who are on vacation often take in the local shopping venues. In this way, they experience something new and possibly unique. **Outshopping** is a term used to refer to consumers who are shopping in a city or town they must travel to rather than in their own hometown. Outshopping is often motivated simply by the desire for the

> **outshopping** shopping in a city or town to which consumers must travel rather than in their own hometowns

Exhibit 11.2

Types of Shopping Activities

Type of Shopping Activity	Example	Utilitarian Shopping Value	Hedonic Shopping Value
Acquisitional shopping	Buying printer cartridges	☆☆☆	
Epistemic shopping	Studying vacation destinations	★★	★★
Experiential shopping	Shopping with friends		★★★
Impulsive shopping	Buying 4 pairs of shoes	☆	★★

Outshopping provides value by allowing consumers to experience new or unique things.

experience. The outshopping consumer sees this as a value opportunity and is more likely to make purchases in this less familiar and perhaps more intriguing place.

Other customers within the shopping environment help shape the experience. Consumers will seek to avoid shopping environments containing other people deemed to be difficult to identify with.[18] Other consumers sometimes distract from the experience. On the other hand, consumers who live alone go shopping to experience interacting with other people. These experiential shoppers desire more of a social experience when shopping. Experiential shoppers tend to be less averse to crowds and thus cope better with a crowded shopping environment.[19] Experiential shopping activities demonstrate that a lot of the reason for shopping lies in the experience itself.

IMPULSIVE SHOPPING

Impulsive behaviors represent a unique group of shopping activities, as we will see in detail later. However, impulsive activities also illustrate how a single shopping experience can result in more than one type of activity. A shopper visits a department store simply to acquire the baby shower gift. Unexpectedly,

she finds that the store has shoes at half off! So the consumer buys four pairs of shoes and "saves a lot of money" doing so. In this instance, the consumer may have entered the store with an acquisitional orientation but the environment triggers a reversal that leads to more impulsive activities. A body of theory known as **reversal theory** tries to explain how environmental elements can lead to near 180-degree changes in shopping orientation. In other words, reversal theory suggests consumers can switch from the pursuit of utilitarian to the pursuit of hedonic value.[20]

11-3d Shopping Value

All shopping activities are aimed at one key result—value. Consistent with the view of value from a previous chapter, **personal shopping value (PSV)** is the overall subjective worth of a shopping activity considering all associated costs and benefits. Like value overall, PSV can be usefully divided into two types. **Utilitarian shopping value** represents the worth obtained because some shopping task or job is completed successfully. **Hedonic shopping value** represents the worth of an activity because the time spent doing the activity itself is personally gratifying.[21]

VALUE AND SHOPPING ACTIVITIES

Thus, the activities shown in Exhibit 11.2 all provide value, but they provide value in different ways to different consumers. The old term *window shopping* illustrates this point. Some consumers *window-shop* to find information so that an upcoming shopping trip might be more successful. In this way, window shopping is epistemic and provides a means to the end of a more successful future shopping task. Consumers may also window-shop simply as a way of passing time in a gratifying way. Thus, window shopping can provide utilitarian and/or hedonic shopping value, respectively. A lot of *window shopping* takes place on the screen of a consumer's smartphone or tablet and serves much the same purposes as actual window shopping.[22]

Situational influences may affect the type of shopping value desired by consumers. Time pressure, for example, may lead consumers to be more concerned with simple product acquisition than they might otherwise be. On the other hand, consumers who are in a bad mood may choose to change it by going shopping. The pleasant emotions can be personally gratifying and can potentially improve a shopper's mood.

RETAIL PERSONALITY

Retailers specializing in things like a wide selection of goods, low prices, guarantees, and knowledgeable

reversal theory tries to explain how environmental elements can lead to near 180-degree changes in shopping orientation

personal shopping value (PSV) overall subjective worth of a shopping activity considering all associated costs and benefits

utilitarian shopping value worth obtained because some shopping task or job is completed successfully

hedonic shopping value worth of a shopping activity because the time spent doing the activity itself is personally gratifying

employees can provide high proportions of utilitarian shopping value. This type of positioning emphasizes the **functional quality** of a retail store by facilitating the task of shopping. In contrast, retailers specializing in a unique environment, impressive décor, friendly employees, and pleasant emotions can provide relatively high hedonic shopping value. This type of positioning emphasizes the **affective quality** of a retail store. The affective quality can be managed to create an emotionally rewarding environment capable of producing high hedonic shopping value. Together, the functional and affective qualities come together to shape retail personality. More specifically, **retail personality** is the way a retail store is defined in the mind of a shopper based on the combination of functional and affective qualities.[23]

 ## 11-4 IMPULSIVE SHOPPING AND CONSUMPTION

Impulsive shopping activities take place every day. Some retailers and service providers survive largely as a result of consumers' impulsive activities. For instance, many behaviors associated with indulgence can be driven by impulsive motivations.

So, just what is an impulsive consumption act? **Impulsive consumption** is largely characterized by three components:

1. Impulsive acts are usually spontaneous and involve at least short-term feelings of liberation.

2. Impulsive acts are usually associated with a diminished regard for any costs or consequences (negative aspects) associated with the act.

3. Impulsive acts are usually motivated by a need for immediate self-fulfillment and are thus usually highly involved emotionally and associated with hedonic shopping value.

Activities characterized by these features are likely to be impulsive. For example, a consumer might have a bad morning at work and decide to cancel a business lunch to take a break shopping for self-gifts or "happies" via the Internet. This activity is likely characterized as impulsive and can be a way to suppress negative emotions and evoke more positive feelings.[24] The behavior can be broken down to demonstrate the impulsiveness involved as follows:

1. The act involves willingly deviating from previous plans and thus shows spontaneity and no doubt feelings of liberation from the negative events of the day.

2. The act shows diminished regard for consequences either for missing the business lunch or for any expense incurred.

3. The act fulfills the need to maintain a positive outlook on the self and thus provides hedonic value.

Internet shopping, although often viewed as utilitarian in nature, can provide hedonic value in this way.[25] Additionally, consumers who feel they have restrained their spending behavior in the past may indulge in impulsive purchases as a reward for past good behavior.[26] Thus, when a down economy turns around, consumers may let loose with a lot of impulsive purchases.

11-4a Impulsive versus Unplanned Consumer Behavior

Impulsive purchasing is not synonymous with unplanned purchasing behavior. **Unplanned shopping**, buying, and consuming share some, but not all, characteristics of truly impulsive consumer behavior. Exhibit 11.3 illustrates the relationship between impulsive and unplanned consumer activity. The right side of the exhibit shows that unplanned consumer acts are characterized by:

1. **Situational memory**

2. **Utilitarian orientation**

3. **Spontaneity**

Situational memory characterizes unplanned acts because something in the environment, such as a point-of-purchase display, usually triggers the knowledge in memory that something is needed. A consumer may enter the grocery store without AA batteries on her grocery list. However, the battery display at the checkout provides a convenient reminder that her office inventory of batteries for wireless devices is depleted.

Simply put, utilitarian motivations drive many unplanned purchases. This consumer who purchases

functional quality retail positioning that emphasizes tangible things like a wide selection of goods, low prices, guarantees, and knowledgeable employees

affective quality retail positioning that emphasizes a unique environment, exciting décor, friendly employees, and, in general, the feelings experienced in a retail place

retail personality way a retail store is defined in the mind of a shopper based on the combination of functional and affective qualities

impulsive consumption consumption acts characterized by spontaneity, a diminished regard for consequences, and a need for self-fulfillment

unplanned shopping shopping activity that shares some, but not all, characteristics of truly impulsive consumer behavior; being characterized by situational memory, a utilitarian orientation, and feelings of spontaneity

Exhibit 11.3

Impulsive versus Unplanned Shopping Behavior

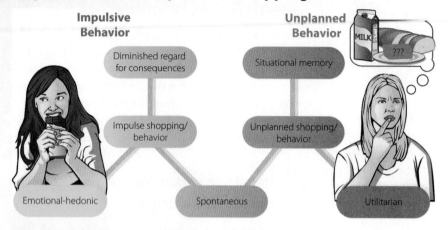

are, by definition, unplanned and therefore done without any significant deliberation or prior decision making. The grocery shopper certainly had not thought about buying AA batteries as she planned the shopping trip.

11-4b Distinguishing Impulsive and Unplanned Consumer Behavior

The line between impulsive and unplanned purchases is not always clear because some unplanned acts are impulsive and many impulsive acts are unplanned. Las Vegas tourism for years used this tagline:

What Happens in Vegas, Stays in Vegas

AA batteries is probably not very emotionally moved by the purchase. However, the purchase allows her to fulfill a need to maintain items needed to work efficiently.

Unplanned acts are spontaneous and, to some extent, they share this characteristic with impulsivity. They

INSIDE BOXES

One situation that nonstore shoppers have to deal with is their living arrangement. Nonstore shopping means having packages delivered. For most homeowners, this is not complicated unless the delivery needs a signature. For instance, wine sales made online require someone to be home for the delivery because an adult signature is needed. However, for people living in an apartment, any delivery can be a challenge. Landlords, or their management companies, are home when the renters are away, but many do not want to be responsible for signing for packages. Furthermore, many apartment complexes are gated, meaning the deliveries cannot be made at the apartment door. Consequently, the apartment office personnel are tasked with taking deliveries and finding a place to hold packages for the renters. Camden Holding Company claims that for 59,000 units it received nearly 1 million packages—it's Packagegate! Thus, some management companies no longer agree to accept and hold deliveries for tenants. What's a tenant to do? While some may curb online shopping, others take advantage of businesses like nearby convenience stores that agree to accept deliveries and hold packages in return for a modest fee. Situations and shopping create market opportunities.

Frank Gaertner/Shutterstock.com

Sources: Kusisto, L. (2015), "Web Shopping Deluge Boxes in Landlords," *Wall Street Journal,* 10/21, A1–A2. https://operationsroom.wordpress.com/2015/10/21/apartments-packages-and -e-commerce/, accessed June 22, 2016.

While some trips to Vegas may be completely spontaneous, most involve some degree of planning. But the tagline emphasizes the impulsive nature of consumption in Las Vegas. Certainly, the campaign illustrates the high hedonic value that can be obtained and encourages consumers not to worry so much about the consequences. So perhaps an impulsive consumption act, like going to Vegas, can even be planned. Simple unplanned purchases may lack the impulsive characteristics captured so well by this campaign.

Simple unplanned purchases usually lack any real emotional involvement or significant amounts of self-gratification. Additionally, unplanned purchases often involve only minimal negative consequences and thus fail to qualify as having negative consequences. A pack of gum or breath mints is not likely to cause severe financial problems for very many consumers.

11-4c Susceptibility to Situational Effects

Are all consumers susceptible to unplanned and impulsive behavior? The answer is yes, but not all consumers are equally susceptible. Individual difference characteristics can play a role. For example, **impulsivity** is a personality trait that represents how sensitive a consumer is to immediate *rewards*. A consumer shopping for a gift for a friend may see shoes on sale at half off and be compelled to purchase these and obtain the *reward*.[27]

Online retailers can facilitate the impulse buying process by making the transaction a simple one-step process.[28] If online shoppers have their credit card information stored with the retailer or have some other easy payment app in play, they are more likely to go through with an impulsive purchase, because the deliberation time is reduced by the speed of the easy transaction.

Facebook use also provides a situation ripe for impulsive buying urges. Consumers with high compulsivity are particularly prone to make purchases through Facebook, including C2C purchases through the "buy and sell" group. Complete information and numbers of likes for an item are factors that may contribute to an impulsive tendency to buy while browsing.[29]

11-4d Consumer Self-Regulation

Another key personality trait that affects a consumer's tendency to do things that are unplanned or impulsive is self-regulatory capacity. **Consumer self-regulation** in this sense refers to a tendency for consumers to inhibit outside, or situational, influences from interfering with shopping intentions. Consumers with a high capacity to self-regulate their behavior are sometimes referred to as

A great deal of the allure of Las Vegas vacations is the opportunity to participate in impulsive consumer behavior.

action-oriented, whereas consumers with a low capacity to self-regulate are referred to as **state-oriented**.[30] Action-oriented consumers are affected less by emotions generated by a retail atmosphere than are state-oriented consumers. Recall the three dimensions of atmospheric emotions discussed in an earlier chapter: pleasure, arousal, and dominance. State-oriented shoppers who are emotionally aroused are far more likely to make additional purchases beyond what was planned than are action-oriented shoppers. Likewise, state-oriented shoppers' spending behavior is strongly affected by feelings of dominance in the environment. Further, feelings of dominance among state-oriented shoppers increase hedonic shopping value and decrease utilitarian shopping value. In contrast, action-oriented shoppers' purchasing and shopping value perceptions are unaffected by dominance.

New technologies represent tempting items in a shopping environment. Self-regulation is related to a consumer's desire, and intention, to purchase such new products. A state-oriented consumer who discovers an innovative new technology is more likely to buy the new product than would be an action-oriented consumer in the same situation.[31] Retailers with a high proportion of state-oriented consumers in their target market are more likely to thrive on consumers' impulse purchases.

> **impulsivity** personality trait that represents how sensitive a consumer is to immediate rewards
>
> **consumer self-regulation** tendency for consumers to inhibit outside, or situational, influences from interfering with shopping intentions
>
> **action-oriented** consumers with a high capacity to self-regulate their behavior
>
> **state-oriented** consumers with a low capacity to self-regulate their behavior

Exhibit 11.4

Questions Distinguishing Low from High Self-Regulatory Capacity

Statement	Action-oriented consumers' typical response	State-oriented consumers' typical response
If I had to work at home…	I would get started right away.	I would often have problems getting started.
When I have important things to buy…	I make a shopping plan and stick to it.	I don't know how to get started.
When I have an important assignment to finish in an afternoon…	I can easily concentrate on the assignment.	It often happens that things will distract me.
When it is absolutely necessary to do some unpleasant task…	I finish it as soon as possible.	It takes a while before I can start on it.

Exhibit 11.4 lists some questions that help distinguish consumers based on self-regulatory capacity. The exhibit shows a statement and then demonstrates the way a consumer would respond to the situation. Consumers with a high ability to self-regulate their behavior—in other words, the action-oriented consumers—generally form rules that they stick by to limit the extent to which situational influences determine their behavior. For example, if they know they will be tempted to overspend during a shopping trip, they may decide not to take their credit cards with them while shopping. In this way, they can resist the overspending that sometimes accompanies unplanned and impulse purchases.

Considering that consumers are more or less vulnerable to certain marketing approaches to encourage impulsive buying, one might ask, are such actions ethical? Or do such actions simply encourage consumers to buy things wastefully? This certainly can be the case, but unplanned purchases are often simply things consumers would indeed intend to buy if they had remembered them before they started shopping. Impulse purchases can also be a relatively harmless way that consumers control their emotions and improve their outlook on life, providing them with value. In this way, impulse shopping can be therapeutic and emotionally uplifting. This isn't always the case, though.

Exhibit 11.5 summarizes ways retailers can encourage unplanned or impulse purchases.

Exhibit 11.5

Retail Approaches Aimed at Encouraging Impulse Purchases

Tool	Example
1. Merchandise complementary products together.	Peruse social networking entries on the Internet for consumers talking about recent purchases and generate push advertising aimed at complementary products.
2. Encourage "add-on" purchases.	Asking consumers to buy socks after they have agreed to buy shoes seems like a small request, and turning the request down risks creating negative feelings. Smart agents generate suggested add-ons of the type, "other consumers who purchased x also purchased y."
3. Create an emotionally charged atmosphere.	Creating an upbeat, exciting dining atmosphere encourages customers to linger and order something extra.
4. Make things easy to buy.	Storing credit card information using an instant pay app, which makes transactions easy and quick, reduces time for consumers to have second thoughts.
5. Provide a discount.	Offering an instant discount at checkout diminishes the perceived consequences associated with a purchase.

11-4e Impulsive versus Compulsive Behavior

Impulsive and compulsive consumer behavior share many of the same characteristics. Compulsive behavior can be emotionally involving and can certainly entail negative consequences. Compulsive consumer behavior can be distinguished from impulsive consumer behavior. The three distinguishing characteristics are:

- ▸ **Compulsive consumer behavior is harmful.**
- ▸ **Compulsive CB seems to be uncontrollable.**
- ▸ **Compulsive CB is driven by chronic depression.**

The urge to buy among compulsive buyers dominates rationale thought. Daily deal websites like wtso.com and dailysteals.com prove very tempting to compulsive buyers.[32] Compulsive consumer behavior is defined and discussed in more detail in a later chapter.

11-5 PLACES HAVE ATMOSPHERES

All consumption takes place in some physical space. Sometimes marketing managers easily forget that the physical environment can play a significant role in shaping buying behavior and the value a consumer receives from shopping or service. Perhaps nowhere is the true impact of place more obvious than in retail and service environments.

11-5a Retail and Service Atmospherics

In consumer behavior, **atmospherics** refers to the emotional nature of an environment or, more precisely, to the feelings created by the total aura of physical attributes that comprise the physical environment. A total list of things that make up the atmosphere would be difficult to compile, but they can be summarized by two dimensions.[33] Exhibit 11.6 provides a summary of the dimensions and what they can create.

The term **servicescape** refers to the physical environment in which consumer services are performed.[34] Each servicescape has its own unique environment. Others have used terms like *e-scape* to refer to a virtual

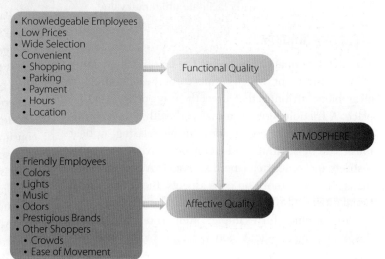

Exhibit 11.6

The Qualities of an Environment

shopping environment as portrayed by a website or *festivalscape* to refer to the array of environmental characteristics a consumer encounters when attending a festival.[35] Thus, Mardi Gras in New Orleans creates an atmosphere where consumers feel uninhibited and sometimes perform extreme behaviors, including acts of public nudity, that they probably would not even consider doing in another atmosphere. While consumers sometimes do things they may regret later, this feeling is a defining part of the Mardi Gras experience. No matter the "scape," atmosphere works through the same sequence:

FUNCTIONAL QUALITY

The functional quality of an environment describes the meaning created by the total result of attributes that facilitate and make efficient the function performed there. In a shopping environment, this includes convenience in all forms: the number and helpfulness of employees, ease of parking and movement through the environment, and the breadth and depth of merchandise, along with other characteristics that facilitate the shopping task. In a service

atmospherics emotional nature of an environment or the feelings created by the total aura of physical attributes that comprise a physical environment

servicescape physical environment in which consumer services are performed

environment, the amount and expertise of service employees, the convenience of the environment, and the capability of the support staff, among other things, all contribute to the functional quality of the service environment.[36] These core benefits greatly facilitate utilitarian value.

AFFECTIVE QUALITY

The affective quality represents the emotional meaning of an environment, which results from the sum effect of all ambient attributes that affect the way one feels in that place. A friendly nurse can make a health care environment less anxious, cool colors can be relaxing, upbeat music can be exciting, and a crowded environment that restricts movement can be distressing. Although many managers focus more on core aspects, these more relational aspects also influence value and satisfaction.

Restaurants, for example, often go out of business despite having excellent food and a good location. A primary reason for their lack of competitiveness is a lack of attention to the environment. As a result, the restaurant lacks style or creates a distressing or boring affective quality. All consumers are susceptible to the effects of affective quality, but female consumers appear much more demanding based on how they react to a place with a negative affective quality.[37]

So, does a retail environment with a distinctly high functional quality necessarily have an uninteresting or poor affective quality? Quite the contrary! If anything, the two dimensions are positively related. An environment with a favorable functional quality tends to be associated with some degree of positive affect. Thus, retailers should keep this in mind and realize that even things they build to create shopper safety can affect both the functional and affective meaning of a particular retailer.

11-5b Atmosphere Elements

The way an atmosphere makes a consumer feel is really determined by the consumer's perception of all the elements in a given environment working together. Therefore, naming all the elements that eventually affect the retail or service atmosphere is impossible. However, a more distinct atmosphere creates a feeling that can ultimately result in a core competitive advantage based on the unique feeling. Two factors help merchandisers and retail designers create just such an atmosphere:[38]

fit how appropriate the elements of a given environment are

congruity how consistent the elements of an environment are with one another

olfactory refers to humans' physical and psychological processing of smells

▶ **Fit** refers to how appropriate the elements of an environment are for a given environment.

▶ **Congruity** refers to how consistent the elements of an environment are with each other.

Panera Bread is one of the fastest growing food chains in the United States. Panera illustrates that it takes more than good food to deliver a total value experience. A big secret to their success is the relaxing atmosphere. The design concept is visually appealing, with interesting shapes and colors. This design is accented by soft jazz music and wonderful aromas of fresh baked bread. Like Starbucks, consumers feel comfortable just being in the Panera Bread atmosphere, and many will linger there even after their meal is done. Panera also presents an inviting atmosphere for families—including families with small children. The informality of the design makes everyone feel welcome.

Although a combination of elements come together to create an atmosphere, researchers often study the elements in isolation or in combination with only one or two other elements. The following sections single out a few of the more prominent environmental elements as being particularly effective in controlling an environment's atmosphere.

ODORS

Believe it or not, in Manchester, UK, the industrial revolution museum includes a tribute to sewer systems with a sewer exhibit. What should a sewer exhibit smell like? Well, the folks at the museum in Manchester have a sewer that smells like a sewer—it certainly wouldn't be authentic with the scent of roses piped in. The fact is, odors are prominent environmental elements that affect both a consumer's cognitive processing and affective reaction.

Olfactory is a term that refers to humans' physical and psychological processing of smells. When shoppers process ambient citrus odors, they tend to feel higher levels of pleasant emotions while shopping and to be more receptive to product information. Citrus odors produce positive responses in practically all consumers. Even more positive reactions can be obtained by matching odors with a target market. For example, women respond more favorably to floral scents, while men respond more favorably to food scents like pumpkin pie. No kidding! Perhaps the way to a man's heart, or wallet, really is through his stomach. Research suggests that consumers express a higher maximum acceptable price in the presence of pleasant odors.[39]

Designers need to keep in mind that a scent, like other elements, works best when it fits with the setting. In an experimental study, wine store consumers paid more attention to label information when an incongruent and slightly less pleasant odor was present and became less risk aversive and more willing to try different wines when more pleasing and consistent odors were present.[40] In a doctor's office, a strong floral scent may not produce a positive reaction because the smell does not fit the office. But one reason for Ulta's success and growth is the fact that Ulta *smells* like beauty and allows women to indulge in a wide array of beauty products and services.[41]

MUSIC

Fast music means fast dancing. Slow music means slow dancing. Even though consumers don't always dance through the aisles of stores, this image is fairly accurate in describing the way background music affects consumers. Both foreground and background music affect consumers, but they do so in different ways. **Foreground music** is music that becomes the focal point of attention and can have strong effects on a consumer's willingness to approach or avoid an environment. Consumers who dislike rap or country music will likely have a difficult time hanging around a place with loud rap or country music.

From a consumer behavior standpoint, **background music**, which is music played below the audible threshold that would make it the center of attention, is perhaps more interesting than foreground music. Service providers and retailers generally provide some type of background music for customers. Muzak was the leader in providing background music to retailers for decades. Today, Muzak and competitors like Mood Media and PlayNetwork consider themselves in the mood management business, not the background music business.[42] The extended service touches on all other sensory elements of the service environment including scent. Retailers like Urban Outfitters and The North Face use services like these to help produce the right combination of elements to produce the desired cognitive, affective, and behavioral effects among consumers.

> ▸ The speed of the background music determines the speed at which consumers shop. Slower music means slower shopping. Faster music means faster shopping.
>
> ▸ The tempo of music affects the patience of consumers. Faster music makes consumers less patient.

August_0802/Shutterstock.com

The decor and atmosphere of the luxury IAPM shopping mall in Shanghai is filled with elements that affect the retail atmosphere.

> ▸ The presence of background music enhances service quality perceptions relative to an environment with no background music.
>
> ▸ Pop music used in the background contributes to discount store perceptions.
>
> ▸ Incongruent music lowers consumers' quality perceptions.
>
> ▸ The fit of the music to other elements in the environment and to the type of service offered shapes consumer reactions.

These factors are important for retail managers interested in managing quality and value perceptions. However, background music can also affect the bottom line. In restaurants, for instance, consumers who dine with slow background music are more patient and in less of a hurry to leave. As a result, they linger longer and tend to buy more beverages than consumers dining with faster background music. Consequently, gross margins can actually be increased by slowing down the background music, particularly in light of the higher margins realized on drink sales relative to food sales.[43]

The fit of the music to the environment helps explain consumer reactions. Imagine browsing for a hotel room. What type of music might enhance the image of the hotel? Well, West African djembe (pronounced "JEM-bay") drumming is not it. An

foreground music music that becomes the focal point of attention and can have strong effects on a consumer's willingness to approach or avoid an environment

background music music played below the audible threshold that would make it the center of attention

JUST LET GO

While we may sometimes use the term web *atmospherics* to refer to the physical design of a website, a website just can't quite do all the things that a carefully created physical space can do. Indeed, a well-designed consumer environment creates a place for consumers to become mesmerized and truly escape their real-world problems. From a cost standpoint, one might wonder why malls or hotels would spend so much money building and maintaining elaborate atriums that bring the sensation of outdoors indoors. The answer is that consumers are fascinated, whether they want to be or not, with things like waterfalls and high spaces. The ambience, decorations, and other elements replenish a consumer's senses and shape value both directly and through the fact that consumers leave the environment better able to engage in their daily routine.

S-F/Shutterstock.com

Sources: Kusmowidagdo, A., A. Sachan, and P. Widnodo (2016), "Visitors' Perceptions on the Important Factors of Atrium Design in Shopping Centers: A Study of Gandaria City Mall and Ciputra World in Indonesia," *Frontiers in Architectural Research*, 5, 52–62; Krey, Nina (2016), "Enough Is Enough," Doctoral Dissertation, Louisiana Tech University; Shows, D. (2013), "Escape Experiences, Restorative Environments and Consumer Self-Regulation," Doctoral Dissertation, Louisiana Tech University.

experiment's results showed that only 5% of people exposed to a hotel site with djembe drumming in the background liked the room.[44] In contrast, 80% of browsers liked the room when jazz music played in the background. Conversely, the djembe drumming enhanced perceptions of a campground. Like other elements, music has to work together to create the right feel.

COLOR

Color is another tool that marketing managers can use to alter consumer reactions by enhancing visual appeal. Some colors are more liked than other colors, but liking isn't really the key to understanding consumer reactions to color. Blue is perhaps the most universally liked color. Blue presents few cultural taboos. Red, white, and black, however, all present cultural barriers associated with bad omens and death in some cultures. Red is a risky color in Japan, as is white in China and black in Western cultures. Color, like other environmental elements, helps frame the shopping experience. Therefore, choosing the right color depends on how consumers react in terms of both their thoughts and their feelings.

Color, for example, affects both quality and price perceptions. Consumers who perceive a product in a predominantly blue background tend to think the product is of higher quality, and they are willing to pay more for that product.[45] In contrast, warm colors like red and orange tend to promote expectations of poor quality and low price.

Exhibit 11.7 illustrates the way these effects can play out in a retail environment. Color changes behavior by

Exhibit 11.7

The Way Color Works

$100

- High quality
- Worth $100
- Believe price is fair
- Feel pleased
- More willing to buy

$100

- Low quality/discount
- Not worth $100
- Believe price is not as fair
- Feel more distressed
- Less willing to buy

framing the way consumers think about a product and also by changing the way they feel. The same product at the identical price, in this case $100, will be viewed as priced more fairly with a blue background than with an orange or red background. Consumers also express more positive feelings when presented with a blue background. Not surprisingly, consumers are also more willing to buy a product presented in a blue background than a red or orange background. Thus, the perceived value of an object can vary with color.

Red isn't always bad though. Sometimes people use the term "power tie" to refer to a red tie. The idea is that a red tie makes someone come across as more influential. Well, research suggests there may be something to this. A message given by a man dressed in a suit with a blue tie comes across as less influential than the same message given by the same man dressed in a red tie.[46]

LIGHTING

Lighting can have dramatic effects on the environment and even reverse the effect of color. Change a store's lighting to soft lights and consumers' opinions regarding the product with a warm background change considerably. For instance, soft lights and an orange background can eliminate the advantage that blue has in that the price fairness perceptions, quality perceptions, affect, and purchase intentions are now equal to or slightly better than the combination of blue and soft lights.[47] Research also suggests that warm colors accented with soft, colored lights lead consumers to a more favorable image of retailers.[48] Luxury retailers, including designers like Burberry and Victoria's Secret, pay careful attention to their lighting and colors to create the right mood and get good reactions to their merchandise.

Next time you visit a retail clothing store, pay attention to the lighting. Unless the store is a discounter, chances are you will see limited use of direct fluorescent (white) lighting. More and more, retailers are using indirect and soft lighting. Fluorescent lights not only provide bright white light that can seem unnatural, but they oscillate, meaning they turn off and on about a hundred times per second. Some people find the lighting very annoying and claim that it leads to eyestrain and headaches. If you are one of these people, it's likely because you have a threshold of perception that detects the oscillation at frequencies of 100 or more.[49] Thus, this type of lighting can be bad for customers and employees, the latter who have to spend hours per day in the environment.

Poor merchandising can increase the sense of crowding in a store environment.

MERCHANDISING

Merchandising's point is to provide the customer with the best opportunity to purchase something. This is done by the placement of goods and store fixtures, along with the use of signage. The angles or racks and the visual image of the store provide a way for consumers to view and move through a store. Signs change consumers' perceptions. For example, signs that emphasize price by using large numerals create the perception of a discount store. An up-scale store uses little signage. Increasingly, digital signage is delivered with electronic display boards. Digital signage can attract a shopper's attention and influence feelings, and digital signs that emphasize price can increase sales, particularly in large stores emphasize price.[50] In some cases, the consumer can even interact with the display board.

SOCIAL SETTINGS

An old saying about Bishop Berkeley's forest goes:

If a tree falls in the forest and nobody is there to hear it, does it make any noise?

Well, if a consumer shops on the Champs Elysées in Paris and no other shoppers are present, is there an atmosphere? People are a huge part of the environment, and if people are removed, the atmosphere changes entirely. Thus, researchers cannot ignore the social environment, meaning the other customers and employees in a service or shopping environment, when explaining how atmosphere affects CB.

Crowding refers to the density of people and objects within a given space. A space can be crowded without any people. However, *shopper density,*

crowding density of people and objects within a given space

Exhibit 11.8

The Way Crowding Affects Consumers

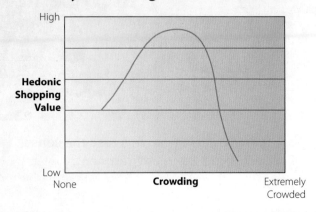

generate an effect that produces hedonic value. Further, crowding can be caused by stuff and not just customers. Even web pages that crowd too many things into a given space can create the perception of a dense and crowded environment.

Both the number and type of salespeople can also affect shoppers. For example, the presence of more salespeople in a shopping environment can actually increase shopper purchase intentions. However, the type of salespeople can also influence shoppers' purchasing and value perceptions. In particular, salespeople and service providers should have an appropriate appearance for the type of product sold. The salespeople should simply fit the part. At Disney theme parks, employees are referred to as "cast members" in part because their appearance is tightly controlled to fit the particular environment in which they work.

Salespeople and service providers are an important source of information and influence. **Source attractiveness** is defined as the degree to which a source's physical appearance matches a consumer's prototype (expectations) for beauty and elicits a favorable or desirable response. Intuitively, one would think that a more attractive person always is a good idea compared to a relatively less attractive person. This idea is known as the "beauty is good" hypothesis. One can't overlook the way a salesperson makes a consumer feel in understanding whether or not a consumer makes a purchase.[53] **Emotional ability** refers to a salesperson who is capable of conveying emotional information to shape a more valuable outcome for consumers.

However, a consumer who encounters an attractive salesperson may end up making an upward social comparison. **Social comparison** is a naturally occurring mental personal comparison of the self with a target individual. Simply, it's a self-other comparison that helps give the self-relative meaning. An upward comparison means the target is better and a downward comparison means the target is inferior. In the case of attractiveness, an upward comparison (the salesperson perceived as more attractive than the consumer) can cause negative feelings that reduce the likelihood of purchase.[54] The presence of other attractive customers may even cause another consumer to feel embarrassed if the upward comparison is strong. This effect is more likely for same-sex comparisons when the service is unrelated to beauty-related products. Think about how a very attractive appliance salesperson may come across.

Shopping buddies, meaning shopping companions, also cause consumers to react differently than when shopping alone. A shopping companion can be more fun and be a source of objective opinion. In this way, the

meaning the number of consumers in a given space, can still exert relatively strong influences on consumer behavior. Crowding actually exerts a **nonlinear effect** on consumers, meaning that a plot of the effect by the amount of crowding does not make a straight line.

Exhibit 11.8 illustrates the way crowding works, particularly with respect to shopper density. Generally, consumers are not particularly attracted to an environment with no other consumers. The lack of consumers might signal poor quality or, in other cases, an absence of other consumers is simply awkward. For example, a consumer who enters a restaurant alone, particularly with no other diners, may well feel quite uncomfortable. In contrast, a mild degree of crowding produces the most positive outcomes in terms of shopping affect, purchase behavior, consumer satisfaction, and shopping value; high degrees of crowding lower these outcomes.[51] Expectations and shopping orientation can alter the effect of crowding. If a consumer seeking utilitarian value unexpectedly finds an uncrowded service environment, he or she is likely to experience higher satisfaction.[52] In a hedonic situation, a surprisingly crowded environment can

nonlinear effect a plot of an effect that does not make a straight line

source attractiveness the degree to which a source's physical appearance matches a prototype for beauty and elicits a favorable or desirous response

emotional ability capability of a salesperson to convey emotional information to shape a more valuable outcome for consumers

social comparison a naturally occurring mental personal comparison of the self with a target individual within the environment

companion can affect hedonic and utilitarian value. The shopping buddy can help reinforce positive feelings about products and thus encourage purchase. A simple statement like "those jeans look great on you" can tilt the scale toward purchase. Consumers who shop with a companion tend to buy more than those who shop alone. Teens' behavior is particularly affected by mall shopping companions who are members of their peer group. Research shows limits to positive effects of group shopping, however. Consumers who shop with a spouse or other family member report lower hedonic value. The family members interfere or get in the way of what could otherwise be a gratifying time alone or with a friend.[55]

11-6 ANTECEDENT CONDITIONS

The term **antecedent conditions** refers to situational characteristics that a consumer brings to a particular information processing, purchase, or consumption environment. Events occurring prior to this particular point in time have created a situation. Antecedent conditions include things like economic resources, orientation, mood, and other emotional perceptions such as fear. They can shape the value in a situation by framing the events that take place. The following sections elaborate.

11-6a Economic Resources

BUYING POWER

The economic resources a consumer brings to a particular purchase setting refer to the consumer's buying power. Buying power can be in the form of cash on hand, credit, money available by draft (check), systems like PayPal, iTunes, or debit card. Among all methods of payment, cash payments have a way of emphasizing the sacrifice required for purchase. Overall, the method of payment represents a situational influence on consumers in several ways.

However, other issues arise. What if consumers are near their credit limits? This can also change their shopping behavior. Companies may put together special financing packages to deal with consumers whose credit is good enough to receive a major credit card, even though they maintain high debt levels. Many consumers live paycheck to paycheck. Buying increases on and just after payday because consumers perceive themselves as better off financially; they believe their buying power is higher. Check advance services, sometimes called payday loans, take advantage of payday timing by offering to prepay consumers in return for a portion of the total paycheck. Thus, these consumer services offer utilitarian value to consumers by providing a way for them to receive their pay before the company they work for actually issues a check.

THIRD PARTY PAYMENTS

Sometimes, consumers need not spend their own money to make purchases. Instead, some third party provides the financial backing for the purchase. Sometimes, the third party is another consumer, like a parent or guardian, or an institution, like an insurance company or charity. The consumer's employer or even the government sometimes pays for expenses or other items, particularly if the employee is traveling. When consumers are in essence spending somebody else's money, they tend to be less price sensitive. The payments for consumer purchases of opioid drugs have shifted substantially from consumers to government and insurance providers. At the same time, the number of deaths from opioid overdose has quadrupled.[56] Workers at a campus McDonald's at a large southeastern university swindled customers for years by adding extra money, sometimes twice as much, to patrons' orders when students paid with their student debit card, typically funded by parents or as a result of scholarship money. The workers had figured out how to cash in and pocket the extra charges. The scam went on for so long that it got handed down from one generation of workers to the next. If the students had been using their own cash to buy their burgers, would it have gone unnoticed for so long?

CONSUMER BUDGETING

Once upon a time, young consumers found it difficult to get credit because a track record of payments was necessary to establish credit. For the past 20 years or so, high interest rates have compensated for high-risk consumers, and young consumers, even those still in college, now find it easy to get a credit card.

Instant credit enables consumers to avoid delaying gratification. "Why wait when you can buy it today?" However, when consumers find themselves having difficulty making payments, their spending habits must change or they run the risk of losing their credit and worse. Even the manner with which one uses a credit card can influence spending. The easier it is to use the card, the more consumers spend. Consumers who store their card numbers online or use smartphone apps to make payments are more willing to spend than are consumers who have to

antecedent conditions situational characteristics that a consumer brings to information processing

> **Consumers who store their card numbers online or use smartphone apps are more willing to spend than are consumers who have to take their cards out to pay.**

take their cards out and swipe them in card readers.[57] Consumers concerned about spending habits may find this fact useful as a tip to saving money.

Most consumers do not prepare a formal budget and instead rely on mental budgeting. **Mental budgeting** is simply a memory accounting for recent spending.[58] One result is that a consumer who has recently splurged on spending in one category will tend to make up for the exuberance through under-consumption in another category. In other words, they buy less than they typically would because of the antecedent condition of having recently overspent.

GIFT (PREPAID) CARDS

> *Would you prefer receiving a gift valued at $45 or a $25 gift card?*

In what seems to defy economic theory, most consumers prefer the gift card despite the lower economic value. Gift cards provide value in other ways, including the feelings that come from a branded experience. For the past decade, surveys suggest gift cards are the most frequently requested gift item in the United States, which explains in part why over two billion of them are sold annually. Their popularity is also growing in other parts of the world.[59]

Gift cards come in different types. Open-loop gift cards can be redeemed at any number of merchants accepting the form of payment. Closed-loop gift cards can be redeemed only at a single merchant. Starbucks is among the largest purveyors of gift cards. The e-gift card is increasingly common, too, although the physical card conveys greater value than an actual gift due to the symbolic benefits of passing an item from the giver to the receiver, and the fact that the card can be wrapped or

mental budgeting memory accounting for recent spending

otherwise embellished. The symbolic and emotional benefits of a gift card add to its hedonic value, but the card also provides utilitarian value to the giver because it is often an easy gift solution!

Merchants get value from gift cards as well. The average gift card carries a value of about $50. Thus, let's say a consumer picks up a $50 Outback Steakhouse gift card at CVS. CVS is happy, because they keep a small percentage of that sale ($2 to $3). Black National, the company that sets up the gift card kiosks at CVS and many other places, also is happy because they keep a similar percentage of the $50. Outback now has just over $40 in revenue from the sale, but not to worry: they are happy too because the typical consumer who redeems the card will spend well over $50 on their visit. In department stores, $50 gift cards often turn into sales of $200 or more. Thus, the gift card creates a unique purchase situation for the consumer.

Not all cards get redeemed. Estimates of nonredemption rates for traditional gift cards vary from 5 to 10 percent (over $100 billion every year). Consumers sometimes forget them, don't find the opportunity to use them, or just don't want to deal with the hassle of redemption. E-gift cards are far less likely to be redeemed than physical gift cards. Thus, one might think merchants would be happy about getting revenue but never providing the service. However, this is a complicated issue. From a legal perspective, firms cannot carry liability indefinitely. Although some firms write off the liability as unearned income, every state in the U.S. determines laws for unclaimed property (known as *escheat* laws), a category that unused gift cards can fall into. For example, some states declare that the monetary value of the unclaimed card has to be returned to the "last address holder" after five years. Good luck finding those addresses! And if you can't identify the holder, the state may be able to claim the money. The legalities of this issue are complicated and continue to evolve.

11-6b Orientation

Gift shopping can change a consumer's orientation. When gift shopping, things that might otherwise be pleasant distract the consumer. This effect is even true on the Internet, as an aesthetically pleasing website can actually cause lower satisfaction among consumers who are highly task-oriented.[60] Employees who sense the orientation and can adjust their approach will create higher value for the consumer. Gift shopping can dramatically shift a shopper's orientation and change the shopping experience altogether.

11-6c Mood

Mood was defined earlier as a transient affective state. While shopping and consuming can alter a consumer's mood, consumers bring their current moods to the particular consumption situation. Consumers in particularly bad moods may have a tendency to binge-consume. For example, a consumer in a foul mood may down an entire pint of Bi-Rite Creamery ice cream. If the mood is particularly disagreeable, perhaps a quart is more likely to do the trick. The foul mood enhances the value of the ice cream temporarily because it provides the normal hedonic value from the good taste, but it is also therapeutic and, at least temporarily, helps restores a more favorable affective state.

Mood affects shopping behavior. Consumers in good moods find more hedonic shopping value, but they can be more prone to buy as well. Technicians are developing mood detection devices using webcams and other devices that can detect what kind of mood an Internet user is in at any moment.[61] Such technologies may enable coupling of electronic sales appeals through social networks based on the mood of a consumer. Clearly, such technologies will generate some controversy.

11-6d Security and Fearfulness

Consumers today live with ever-present reminders of vandalism, crime, and even terrorism. Large parking lots such as commonly found at Walmart stores or conventional shopping centers attract criminals who prey on seemingly defenseless consumers. Stories of abductions, muggings, assaults, carjackings, and other heinous criminal acts taking place understandably create fear among some shoppers, particularly those who view themselves as vulnerable.[62] Shopping malls, markets, airports, cafés, and other places where consumers frequently gather are all too often the site of terrorist attacks. In fact, some

Exhibit 11.9

Enhancing Value by Making Consumers Feel Safer

▶ Increase number and visibility of security personnel

▶ Increase number and prominence of security cameras in parking lots

▶ Have brightly lit parking lots

▶ Add carry-out service for consumers—particularly for those shopping alone

▶ Maintain an uncrowded, open entrance

▶ Clearly mark all exits

▶ Prevent loitering

▶ Discourage gangs from visiting the center

consumers give fear of terrorism as one reason why they prefer to do their holiday shopping online rather than in crowded shopping venues. In December 2015, the grand department stores of Paris helped create a sense of security by closely monitoring every person who entered the store using metal detectors and even light pat-downs.

Fearfulness can affect consumers in multiple ways. A consumer who goes shopping in a fearful mood will not go about her shopping in the same way. A fearful consumer will tend to buy less and enjoy the experience less. Alternatively, a consumer may cope with the fear of shopping by turning to nonstore outlets such as the Internet as a seemingly safer way of doing business. But even here, consumers sometimes fear providing private information often needed to complete a transaction. Thus, retailers who pay attention to making their parking and shopping environments more secure can help eliminate the feelings of fear some shoppers may have otherwise. Exhibit 11.9 lists some ways fearfulness may be reduced among consumers.

STUDY TOOLS 11

LOCATED AT BACK OF THE TEXTBOOK
☐ Tear out Chapter Review Card

LOCATED AT WWW.CENGAGE.COM/LOGIN
☐ Review Key Term flashcards and create your own cards
☐ Track your knowledge and understanding of key concepts in consumer behavior
☐ Complete practice quizzes to prepare for tests
☐ Complete interactive content within CB Online
☐ Review the Chapter Highlight boxes for CB Online

12 | Decision Making I: Need Recognition and Search

LEARNING OBJECTIVES

After studying this chapter, the student should be able to:

12-1 Understand the activities involved in the consumer decision-making process.

12-2 Describe the three major decision-making research perspectives.

12-3 Explain the three major types of decision-making approaches.

12-4 Understand the importance of the consideration set in the decision-making process.

12-5 Understand the factors that influence the type and amount of search performed by consumers.

Noel Hendrickson/Getty Images

Remember to visit **PAGE 265** for additional **STUDY TOOLS**

12-1 CONSUMER DECISION MAKING

Consumers are continually making decisions that are meant to solve problems. Consumers encounter problem situations every day, and choices have to be made. Most of the time there are so many of these situations that it's hard to recall them all. We run low on gas, pay bills, search for a new apartments, take cars to repair shops, and think about new cell-phone contracts. In each of these situations, needs are recognized and choices are made. When needs occur, decision making must take place. Where should I buy milk? Should I change cell-phone carriers? Should I check craigslist for a used mountain bike? EBay?

Some situations require big decisions. For example, finding a new apartment is usually tough. In other situations, the decisions are small. For example, when you blow a lightbulb, you might simply grab any brand you see.

You may recall the basic CB consumption process that was presented in our opening chapter. This process is shown again in Exhibit 12.1. The process revolves around value-seeking activities that consumers perform as they go about satisfying needs. The consumer first realizes she has a particular need. For example, maybe she needs a new dress for a special dinner. She then moves through a series of steps that will help her find a desirable way to fill the need. Exchange then takes place, and she ultimately derives value from the process. As with other consumer behavior concepts, value is at the heart of decision making.

The decision-making process has been added to the exhibit. As you can see, decision-making processes generally include five activities: (1) need recognition, (2) search for information, (3) evaluation of alternatives, (4) choice, and (5) postchoice evaluation. In the current chapter, we focus on the first two stages of the process: need recognition and information search. The following chapter discusses evaluation of alternatives and choice.

To better visualize this process, consider Exhibit 12.2. Here, Aaron is faced with a need for a new business suit as he begins interviewing for jobs. To learn about his options, he begins to pay attention to ads for men's apparel and may begin doing a search on the Internet. He asks friends and refers to his social network for

their input while using search apps on his phone. After considering all of the information that he has gathered, he evaluates the alternatives that are realistically available. From there, he makes a choice and an exchange occurs. He then considers all the costs and benefits of his purchase and the overall value that he has received.

Note that the activities found in the decision-making process are not referred to as steps. The reason is that consumers do not always proceed through the activities in sequential fashion, nor do they always complete the process. Because consumers face numerous decision-making situations daily, they often decide to simply defer a decision until a later time. Consumers can also uncover additional problems or unmet needs as they search for information—moving them from information search to need recognition.

12-1a Decision Making and Choice

Decision-making processes lead to consumer choice. The term *choice* is important. *Choice* does not necessarily mean identifying what brand of product to buy. In fact, one of the very first choices that consumers need to make when facing a decision is whether any purchase will be made at all.[1] Consumers commonly either delay the purchase of a product or forgo the purchase altogether. As discussed elsewhere, consumers may also

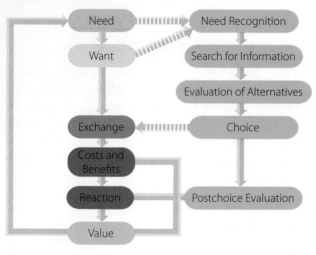

Exhibit 12.1

Basic Consumption Process and Decision Making

- Need ⇢ Need Recognition
- Want → Search for Information
- Evaluation of Alternatives
- Exchange ⇠ Choice
- Costs and Benefits
- Reaction → Postchoice Evaluation
- Value

Exhibit 12.2

Consumer Decision-Making Process

Process	Example
Need Recognition	James realizes he needs a new business suit.
Search for Information	He pays attention to ads for apparel, considers input from his social network, searches the Internet, scans QR codes, and uses visual search apps to learn about options.
Evaluation of Alternatives	James compares three different brands of suits on attributes that he considers to be relevant.
Choice	He selects a Stafford suit because he thinks it best fits his needs and budget.
Postchoice Evaluation	Looking back at his choice, James considers the value of the Stafford suit and thinks that he made a good overall decision.

decide to take part in the sharing economy by sharing a product or renting it from someone else.

Decision-making processes don't always involve a tangible product. And consumers make choices about behaviors not relating directly to a purchase. For example, a consumer may be trying to decide if she should volunteer at a community theater. Here, the decision involves whether time should be exchanged in return for greater involvement with the theater. Thus, consumer decision making does not always focus on the purchase of a tangible product, but always involves choices linked to value.

DECISION MAKING AND VALUE

Both utilitarian value and hedonic value are associated with consumer decision making. As we have discussed previously, the car-buying experience involves both value types. First, a car is in itself a means to an end. That is, owning cars enables consumers to transport themselves from place to place. As such, an automobile delivers utilitarian value. Second, much of the car-buying experience is based on hedonic value. The image associated with a particular model of car and the feelings that go with sporty handling or comfort are hedonic benefits. Many other consumption activities also provide both hedonic value and utilitarian value. For example, a $5,000 Gibson Les Paul guitar may provide the same utilitarian value as a $300 Squire Stratocaster guitar. However, guitarists

will recognize that the hedonic value of each would differ based on the feelings involved with consumption. A Les Paul is a classic guitar!

Value perceptions influence decision making activities. For example, consumers generally continue searching for information about products only as long as the perceived benefits that come from searching exceed the perceived costs associated with the process. In today's smartphone world, it is easier than ever to obtain information very quickly and easily, thereby making it beneficial for consumers to extend the search process. Smartphone apps, including visual search and augmented reality-based applications have made search much easier.

DECISION MAKING AND MOTIVATION

You may recall that motivations are the inner reasons or driving forces behind human actions as consumers are driven to address needs. It isn't surprising, therefore, that decision making and motivation are closely related concepts.[2] For example, a student may notice that the ink in his printer is low and perceive a need to fix the problem (a utilitarian motivation). Or the same student may be bored on a Saturday afternoon and decide to go longboarding (a hedonic motivation). The relationship between decision making and motivation is well-known, and almost all consumer decisions revolve around goal pursuit.[3]

Apps can make decision making fun!

DECISION MAKING AND EMOTION

Consumer decision making is also closely related to emotion. Quite frankly, some decisions can be very emotional and exhausting. Because the decision-making process can be draining, consumers frequently have feelings of frustration, irritation, or even anger as they attempt to satisfy needs. This is especially true when consumers must make difficult decisions, cannot find acceptable solutions to problems, or must make trade-offs by giving up one alternative for another.[4] As a college student, you may soon face the difficult task of deciding which job offer to take. Perhaps there will be a job offer many miles away, or one that is closer to your family. Decisions like these can be quite emotional.

Marketers also realize that sometimes the decision-making process can actually be enjoyable, especially if consumers use search apps that they actually enjoy. App developers work to ensure that consumers enjoy using their products as much as possible.

 12-2 DECISION-MAKING PERSPECTIVES

Consumer researchers view the decision-making process from three perspectives: the rational decision-making perspective, the experiential decision-making perspective, and the behavioral influence decision-making perspective.[5] These perspectives are similar to the attitude hierarchies that we discussed in the attitude chapter.

It is important to remember two important aspects of these perspectives. First, each perspective serves as a theoretical framework from which decision making can be viewed. That is, the perspectives pertain to how consumer researchers view the decision-making process, and they are not consumer decision-making approaches. Second, most consumer decisions can be analyzed from a combination of these perspectives. The perspectives are presented in Exhibit 12.3.

> Value perceptions influence decision-making activities.

Exhibit 12.3

Perspectives on Consumer Decision Making

Perspective	Description	Example
Rational Perspective	Consumers are rational and they carefully arrive at decisions.	Jamal carefully considers the various features of apartment complexes.
Experiential Perspective	Decision making is often influenced by the feelings associated with consumption.	Riley goes longboarding just for the fun of it.
Behavioral Influence Perspective	Decisions are responses to environmental influences.	A product display leads Karissa to buy a snack.

12-2a Rational Decision-Making Perspective

In the early days of consumer research, researchers focused on what is referred to as the rational decision-making perspective. This perspective is considered by many to be the traditional approach to studying decision making. The rational decision-making perspective assumes that consumers diligently gather information about purchases, carefully compare various brands of products on salient attributes, and make informed decisions regarding what brand to buy. This approach centers on the assumption that human beings are rational creatures who carefully consider their decisions and that they can identify the expected value associated with a purchase. The act of selecting a cell-phone plan often follows a rational process. Consumers compare service, features, and prices carefully when making these purchases. The rational perspective fits well within the concept of utilitarian value.

A problem with this perspective is that we cannot assume that consumers are always rational, nor do they always follow a well-planned decision-making process. In fact, consumers often make purchases and satisfy needs with very little cognitive effort or rationality. We simply don't want to think extensively about every single product choice that we make. Nor could we!

The assumption that consumers are rational is debatable. Of course, what is rational to some may be irrational to others. Paying over $1,000 to enjoy a wine-tasting event may seem irrational to many consumers, but some people do it regularly. Although researchers focused on the rational perspective for several years, the experiential and behavioral influence perspectives have recently gained significant attention.

12-2b Experiential Decision-Making Perspective

The experiential decision-making perspective assumes that consumers often make purchases and reach decisions based on the affect, or feeling, attached to the product or behavior under consideration. Recall from the discussion in our attitude chapter that consumers sometimes follow an "affect-behavior-cognition" hierarchy. That is, behaviors are based largely on the sheer enjoyment involved with consumption rather than on extensive cognitive effort.

Experiential decision processes often focus on hedonic value. For example, a consumer may decide to spend time at a day spa as the result of an experiential decision-making process. Here, decisions are based on feeling—not on a drawn-out decision-making process. Value comes from the experience, not necessarily from an end result. Variety-seeking behavior often results from feelings of boredom or a perceived need for change. Consumers will sometimes switch brands or look for new products simply because they want something different. Snack and fast food marketers often capitalize on variety-seeking behavior by introducing new flavors of products and short-term deals to generate excitement.

12-2c Behavioral Influence Decision-Making Perspective

The behavioral influence decision-making perspective assumes that many decisions are learned responses to environmental influences. For example, soft music and dim lighting can have a strong influence on consumer behavior in a restaurant. These influences generally lead consumers to slow down, stay in the restaurant for a longer time, and buy more drinks and dessert. This perspective follows the behavioral learning concept that was discussed in a previous chapter.

The behavioral influence perspective also helps to explain how consumers react to store layout, store design, and POP (point-of-purchase) displays. Traffic flow in a grocery store greatly influences shopping behavior, and POP displays are especially effective. In fact, consumers often buy products that are placed on display simply because they are on display. Retailers use the "brand-lift index" to measure the incremental sales that occur when a product is on display. Lift indices can be impressive. In fact, one study indicated that POP displays in convenience stores can increase product sales by nearly 10%. This is a sizable amount. Considering that incremental sales opportunities for POP materials in grocery stores can be in the billions of dollars, retailers should pay close attention to the behavioral influence perspective.[6]

rational decision-making perspective assumes consumers diligently gather information about purchases, carefully compare various brands of products on salient attributes, and make informed decisions regarding what brand to buy

experiential decision-making perspective assumes consumers often make purchases and reach decisions based on the affect, or feeling, attached to the product or behavior under consideration

variety-seeking behavior seeking new brands or products as a response to boredom or to satisfy a perceived need for change

behavioral influence decision-making perspective assumes many consumer decisions are actually learned responses to environmental influences

Store layout greatly impacts decision making. IKEA stores famously move people through the store in arrowed paths to encourage impulse buying.

12-3 DECISION-MAKING APPROACHES

Consumers reach decisions in a number of different ways. The decision-making approach that is used depends heavily on the amount of involvement a consumer has with a product category or purchase and the amount of perceived risk involved with the decision. Note that involvement can be associated with the product, the purchase situation, or both. In general, as involvement and

risk increase, consumers are motivated to move more carefully through the decision-making process.

You may remember from an earlier chapter that consumer involvement represents the degree of personal relevance that a consumer finds in pursuing value from a given act. **Perceived risk** refers to the perception of the negative consequences that are likely to result from a course of action and the uncertainty of which course of action is best to take. Consumers face several types of risk, including:[7]

▸ **Financial risk.** Risk associated with the cost of the product

▸ **Social risk.** Risk associated with how other consumers will view the purchase

▸ **Performance risk.** Risk associated with the likelihood of a product performing as expected

▸ **Physical risk.** Risk associated with the safety of the product and the likelihood that physical harm will result from its consumption

▸ **Time risk.** Risk associated with the time required to search for the product and the time necessary for the product to be serviced or maintained

Risk varies across consumers and situations. Signing a year-long apartment lease is a financially risky process for most consumers. For the very wealthy, this may not be the case at all. Some risks are hidden or not completely understood. For example, evidence shows that wearing earphones when playing music loudly on a phone can damage hearing, though few consumers think of this.

Decision-making approaches can be classified into three categories: extended decision making, limited decision making, and habitual (or "routine") decision making. Remember, these are approaches that consumers use, and they differ from the researcher perspectives discussed previously. Exhibit 12.4 presents these categories in the form of a continuum based on involvement and risk.

perceived risk perception of the negative consequences that are likely to result from a course of action and the uncertainty of which course of action is best to take

Exhibit 12.4

Decision-Making Approaches

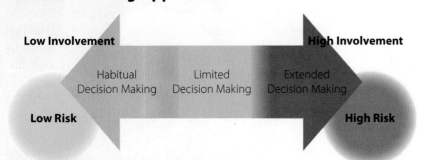

Low Involvement — High Involvement

Habitual Decision Making — Limited Decision Making — Extended Decision Making

Low Risk — High Risk

12-3a Extended Decision Making

When consumers engage in **extended decision making**, they tend to search diligently for information that will help them reach a satisfactory decision. This information can come from both internal sources (for example, previous experiences) and external sources (for example, websites such as craigslist). Consumers carefully assimilate the information they have gathered and evaluate each alternative based on its potential to satisfy their need. This process is generally rather lengthy. Extended decision making occurs when involvement is high and when there is a significant amount of purchase risk involved with the decision. Expensive products such as houses, automobiles, and televisions are usually purchased only after an extended decision-making process has occurred.

12-3b Limited Decision Making

With **limited decision making**, consumers search very little for information and often reach decisions based on prior beliefs about products and their attributes. There is little comparison between brands. Given the time constraints that consumers often feel, this type of decision making occurs with great frequency.

Limited decision making usually occurs when there are relatively low amounts of purchase risk and product involvement. For example, a consumer may need to buy a new roll of adhesive tape, and there may be very few attributes that are considered in the process. Perhaps the consumer will want to find a tape that is designed to be invisible. Any brand that offers this feature would likely be selected.

12-3c Habitual Decision Making

With **habitual decision making** (sometimes referred to as "routine" decision making), consumers generally do not seek information at all when a problem is recognized. Choice is often based on habit. Here, consumers generally have a specific brand in mind that will solve the problem, and they believe that the consumption of the product will deliver value. For example, most consumers have a favorite type of drink that they habitually buy when they are thirsty.

Two topics are of special importance concerning habitual decision making: *brand loyalty* and *brand inertia*. **Brand loyalty** may be defined as a deeply held commitment to rebuy a product or service regardless of situational influences that could lead to switching behavior.[8] For consumers to truly be brand loyal, they must have a bond with the product and believe that the consumption activity delivers value. Companies often attempt to reward loyalty with rewards programs as found in frequent flier miles, hotel reward points, and credit card cash-back deals. However, in order for these tactics to be successful, consumers must ultimately value both the product and the incentives offered.[9] These programs must also have clear rules and rewards.[10] This leads to a key difference between loyalty and what is referred to as brand inertia. **Brand inertia** is present when a consumer simply buys a product repeatedly without any real attachment. Loyalty includes an attitudinal component that reflects a true affection for the product.[11] Strictly speaking, a consumer is not considered loyal if she simply buys the same product habitually.

Brand loyalty affects consumption value in a number of ways. First, loyalty enables consumers to reduce searching time drastically by insisting on the brand to which they are loyal. This leads to a benefit of convenience. Second, loyalty creates value for a consumer through the benefits associated with brand

extended decision making consumers move diligently through various problem-solving activities in search of the best information that will help them reach a decision

limited decision making consumers search very little for information and often reach decisions based largely on prior beliefs about products and their attributes

habitual decision making consumers generally do not seek information at all when a problem is recognized and select a product based on habit

brand loyalty deeply held commitment to rebuy a product or service regardless of situational influences that could lead to switching behavior

brand inertia occurs when a consumer simply buys a product repeatedly without any real attachment

Reward cards can be a successful method of rewarding loyalty if consumers value both the product and the incentives offered.

Guy Bouchet/Getty Images

GIVE ME SHELTER

Many problems that consumers face are routine. We run out of milk or gasoline. But sometimes, our problems can be unexpected and very serious. Researchers refer to unforeseen needs as "unanticipated needs."

The last few years have brought about a number of severe weather incidents around the world, and tornado outbreaks in the United States have been particularly deadly. The storm shelter industry has been greatly impacted. Shelters of all types, including both underground and above-ground models, are in high demand across the United States and particularly in the tornado alley states of the Midwest. Demand has also grown in the Southeastern United States, where tornadoes have been striking more frequently.

Sometimes the perception of a need is greater than the real need. Nevertheless, the demand for shelters is likely to grow as consumers witness the horrors that tornadoes bring. The need for safety and security is a critical part of Maslow's Hierarchy of Needs, and the storm shelter industry works hard to meet this need. Taking shelter from the storm is definitely serious business.

Sources: Anonymous (2015), "Federal Funding for Storm Shelter Rebates Running Low," *Newschannel10*.com, online content retrieved at: http://www .newschannel10.com/story/28835775 /federal-funding-for-storm-shelter -rebates-running-low, accessed April 25, 2016; Sheila Stogsdill, "High Demand for Storm Shelters Means the Wait Is Long," *Tulsa World*, October 28, 2011, http://www.tulsaworld.com/news /article.aspx?subjectid=11&articleid=20110528_19_A10_CUTLIN111108 (accessed April 25, 2012); Brian Richardson, "Storm Shelters in High Demand Following Joplin Tornado," *Ozarksfirst*, June 6, 2011, http://ozarksfirst.com/fulltext?nxd_id=467967 (accessed April 25, 2012); Meghan McCormick,

image. Ford trucks are well-known for their ruggedness and durability. Ford owners benefit from this image. Finally, loyalty enables consumers to enjoy the benefits that come from long-term relationships with companies. For example, a consumer might enjoy special incentives that are offered to long-time Ford purchasers.

Brand loyalty also has an impact on the value of the brand to the firm. As branding expert David Aaker asserts, consumer brand loyalty influences the value of a product to a firm because (a) it costs much less to retain current customers than to attract new ones, and (b) highly loyal customers generate predictable revenue streams.[12] As can be seen, brand loyalty has benefits for both the consumer and the marketer. Brand loyalty is discussed in more detail in a subsequent chapter.

FINAL THOUGHT ON DECISION-MAKING APPROACHES

Consumers go through decision-making processes, but these processes do not guarantee maximum value. Consumers often make mistakes or settle for alternatives that they are unsure of. In reality, many purchases are made with little prepurchase decision effort.[13] Most purchases made daily are low-involvement purchases that do not entail significant risk. Also, consumers are not always motivated to make the "best" decision. In many situations, consumers engage in what is called **satisficing**, the practice of using decision-making shortcuts to arrive at satisfactory, rather than optimal, decisions.[14] Other consumers, like "maximizers," work to find the best solution. Research also indicates that consumer decision making may be influenced by heredity.[15] Some consumers may be predisposed genetically to arrive at some decisions. One recent study found that some decisions, including compromises, can be influenced by heredity.

12-4 NEED RECOGNITION, INTERNAL SEARCH, AND THE CONSIDERATION SET

As we have discussed, the recognition of a need leads the consumer to begin searching for information. Several important issues are relevant here.

> **satisficing** practice of using decision-making shortcuts to arrive at satisfactory, rather than optimal, decisions

12-4a Need Recognition

The decision-making process begins with the recognition of a need. Simply put, a need is recognized when a consumer perceives a difference between an actual state and a desired state. A consumer's **actual state** is his perceived current state, while the **desired state** is the perceived state for which the consumer strives. A consumer recognizes a need when there is a gap between these two. Note that either the actual state or the desired state can change, leading to a perceptual imbalance between the two. When the actual state begins to drop, for example when a consumer runs out of deodorant, a need is recognized. Obviously, needs like this are recognized many times each day. Importantly, however, marketers also focus on what they term *opportunity recognition*. Here, a consumer's actual state doesn't change, but her desired state changes in some significant way.

To illustrate how a desired state can be changed, consider how happy consumers once were with their cell phones—that is, before the iPhone was released. After the iPhone was introduced, the desired state for many consumers changed dramatically. Phones became much more than just phones. Apple then introduced the iPad, and now tablets are overtaking laptops in popularity.

Desired states can be affected by many factors, including reference group information, consumer novelty seeking, and cognitive thought processes.[16] As we discussed in the group influence chapter, reference groups are important sources of information for consumers, and the information that is gathered from others directly affects what consumers think they should do and what types of products they think they should buy. Desired states are also influenced by novelty. Many times consumers desire to try a new product simply because of boredom or because of a motivation to seek variety. Finally, consumers have the ability to plan their actions by anticipating future needs. For example, college graduates realize after graduation that they face the need for all types of insurance they may not have considered before, including life, health, and homeowner's insurance.

Not all needs are satisfied quickly, nor does the recognition of a need always trigger the other activities found in the decision-making process. Value is again important here. If the end goal is not highly valued, consumers may simply put off a decision. For example, a consumer may realize that the leather cushion on her couch is ripped, but this does not necessarily mean

Wants and needs are often confused.

that she will begin to search for information on where to buy a new couch. She may simply realize that there is a problem that eventually needs to be fixed. In fact, she may have to be reminded of this need several times before she does anything about it. Or, she may simply decide to do nothing about it at all. From this example, we are again reminded of why we don't refer to the activities found in decision making as steps. That is, the sequential ordering of the activities is not concrete.

We should once again clarify the distinction between a want and a need. Both of these terms have been discussed in a previous chapter. As you may remember, a want is the way in which a consumer goes about addressing a need. It's quite common for marketers to be criticized for attempting to turn wants into needs. For example, a consumer may want to fulfill a need for a watch by purchasing a Michael Kors, even though a much less expensive watch would suffice.

12-4b Search Behavior

When consumers perceive a difference between an actual state (an empty gas tank) and a desired state (a full tank), the decision-making process is triggered.[17]

actual state consumer's perceived current state

desired state perceived state for which a consumer strives

Radius Images/Getty Images

CONSUMERS AND TECHNOLOGY

A Big Decision

One of the biggest decisions that consumers make in their lifetimes is the purchase of a new home. In years past, the process usually revolved around meeting with a realtor, scanning the local newspapers, and logging countless miles driving around select neighborhood and locations. All of these efforts represent an external search.

In today's app world, however, things have changed dramatically. Currently, consumers have many different apps at their fingertips that can make the home searching process much easier. Popular apps such as Realtor, Zillow, Trulia, and Homes aid consumers in all aspects of the home search. All a consumer needs to do is enter selected search criteria into the apps and many options pop up automatically. Popular search criteria include square footage, number of bedrooms, number of bathrooms, garage size, lot size, swimming pool, and school district. Using these criteria, the apps are able to quickly produce a listing

Richard Levine/Alamy Stock Photo

of available properties that match the needs of the consumer.

Like other aspects of consumer behavior that have been impacted by technology, the house searching process is now easier than ever before. Thanks to apps such as these, the big decision has been made just a little bit easier.

Consumer search behavior refers to the behaviors that consumers engage in as they seek information that can be used to satisfy needs. Consumers seek all types of information about potential solutions to needs, including: (1) the number of alternatives available, (2) the price of various alternatives, (3) the relevant attributes that should be considered and their importance, and (4) the performance of each alternative on the attributes.[18] Consumer search behaviors can be categorized in a number of ways, including ongoing search, prepurchase search, internal search, and external search. Some consumer researchers have suggested using the term "discovery" in place of "search" because of all the new technologies that are available to consumers. That is, consumers continually discover new information whether or not they are searching.

ONGOING AND PREPURCHASE SEARCH

A consumer performs an **ongoing search** when she seeks information simply because she is interested in a particular topic (such as a product or an organization). Here, the search effort is not necessarily focused on an upcoming purchase or decision; rather, the effort is focused on simply staying up to date on a topic of interest.

Consumers who perform ongoing searches are usually highly involved with the product category and seek information simply for enjoyment. They also tend to spend more in the relevant product category than do consumers who do not regularly search for information.[19]

Prepurchase search activities are focused on locating information that will enable the consumer to reach a decision for a specific problem. These searches are purchase-specific. Prepurchase search can also be exhibited in browsing behavior. When consumers browse, they are simply gathering information that can be used in decisions that involve a longer time frame. Note that browsing and ongoing searches are similar. The difference between ongoing searches and browsing behavior is that an ongoing search is performed when consumers have an enduring interest or involvement with the product, not simply

consumer search behavior behaviors that consumers engage in as they seek information that can be used to satisfy needs

ongoing search search effort that is not necessarily focused on an upcoming purchase or decision but rather on staying up to date on the topic

prepurchase search search effort aimed at finding information to solve an immediate problem when information is being gathered for a specific purchase.

The concept of information search has changed dramatically in recent years due to the mass adoption of the Internet as well as the proliferation of mobile information technologies like cell phones and personal data assistants. In today's environment, finding information generally isn't a problem. The problem is that there is simply too much information out there. Information overload is an important research topic.[20] **Information overload** refers to the situation in which consumers are presented with so much information that they cannot assimilate it all. The search engine Bing humorously devised an advertising campaign aimed at highlighting the downside of what they term "search overload." The campaign targeted Google as presenting too much information in an unfiltered way.

One way that consumers can try to minimize information overload in the online environment is by joining a specific group for a product or brand on a site like Facebook. By focusing specifically on a group or fan page, consumers are able to look for relevant information in one place and can gain a sense of which other posters they can and cannot trust for information. Information search on social network sites can be either ongoing or prepurchase.

12-4c The Consideration Set

Internal search includes the retrieval of knowledge about products, services, and experiences that is stored in memory. This type of knowledge is related directly to consumers' experiences with products and services. When confronted with a need, consumers begin to scan their memories for available solutions to the problem that can aid in decision making. As such, consumers most often perform internal searches before any other type of search begins.

Marketers find it valuable to understand the **consideration set** of their customers in order to learn about the total number of brands, or alternatives, that are considered in consumer decision making.[21] The conceptualization of a consideration set is presented in Exhibit 12.5.

The total collection of all possible solutions to a recognized need (for example, the total number of brands of deodorant available on the market) is referred to as the **universal set** of alternatives. Although the universal set may be quite large, consumers generally do not realize how many solutions are potentially available when a need arises. In fact, decision making is limited by what is referred to as the awareness set. The **awareness set** includes, quite simply, the set of brands

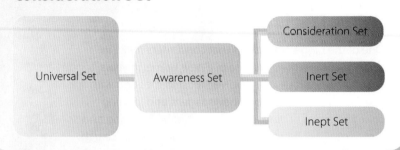

Exhibit 12.5
Consideration Set

- Universal Set
- Awareness Set
  - Consideration Set
  - Inert Set
  - Inept Set

Consumers are able to learn about new developments with products by following them online.

Source: www.facebook.com

or alternatives of which a consumer is aware. Alternatives that have been previously selected are included in this set, and the size of the awareness set increases as external search proceeds.[22]

Within the awareness set, three categories of alternatives are found. The first is the consideration set (or the "evoked set"). The consideration set includes the brands or alternatives that are considered acceptable for further consideration in decision making. There are also alternatives in the awareness set that are deemed to be unacceptable for further consideration. These alternatives comprise the inept set. The inert set includes those alternatives to which consumers are indifferent, or for which strong feelings are not held.

Exhibit 12.5 demonstrates how the size of both the awareness set and the consideration set is smaller than the universal set—a situation typical for most decisions. Research confirms that consumers generally consider only a small fraction of the actual number of problem solutions that are available.[23] Note that although the consideration set is held internally in a consumer's memory, alternatives that are found in external search can be added to the set as the decision-making process continues. As such, the consideration set plays an important role in advertising effectiveness.[24]

 12-5 EXTERNAL SEARCH

Frequently, consumers don't have enough information stored in memory that will enable them to reach a decision. For this reason, external search efforts are often necessary. External search includes the gathering of information from sources external to the consumer, including friends, family, salespeople, advertising, independent research reports (such as *Consumer Reports*), the Internet, and search apps. In selecting the best information source, consumers consider factors such as:

▸ **The ease of obtaining information from the source**

▸ **The objectivity of the source**

▸ **The trustworthiness of the source**

▸ **The speed with which the information can be obtained**

In general, consumers find that information from family and friends is dependable but that information from commercial sources (like advertising or salespeople) is less credible for input into decision making.[25] Personal factors like self-esteem play a role, however. Research indicates that consumers with low self-esteem tend to favor impersonal sources of information such as media advertising and the Internet.[26]

12-5a The Role of Price and Quality in the Search Process

The term *evaluative criteria* is used to refer to the product attributes that consumers consider when reviewing possible solutions to a problem. Many things can become evaluative criteria. However, two evaluative criteria are used across almost all consumer decisions: price and quality. Consumers turn to price and quality very quickly as they consider most products.

Price represents an important type of information that consumers generally seek. But what is a price? A price is really a piece of information. More specifically, price is information signaling how much potential value may be derived from consuming something. In this sense, price is like the physical concept of potential energy.

Generally, we think of a high price as being a bad thing. In other words, a higher price means greater sacrifice to obtain some product. This view of price is referred to as the negative role of price. From this view, needless to say, a lower price is more desirable. Some consumers are very sensitive to the negative role of price. They tend to be very bargain conscious and do things like collect and redeem coupons.

However, a positive role for price also exists[27]. In this sense, price signals how desirable a product is and how much prestige may be associated with owning the product. Some consumers are more sensitive to the positive role of price and tend to desire things with high prices as a way of signaling prestige and desirability to others.[28] You may remember from an earlier discussion that a backward sloping demand curve is not necessarily rare.

Consider a consumer shopping for a new outfit to wear during an evening on the town. She may find a cute outfit at Target, but this outfit may not offer enough value given that it will be worn in a socially sensitive situation. Therefore, she may opt for a higher-priced outfit that may be somewhat similar. The higher price will signal more prestige. Thus, she may feel more comfortable shopping at Chico's or some other more prestigious fashion retailer.

Consumers also commonly search for information about a product's quality. Consumers nearly

inept set alternatives in the awareness set that are deemed to be unacceptable for further consideration

inert set alternatives in the awareness set about which consumers are indifferent or do not hold strong feelings

external search gathering of information from sources external to the consumer such as friends, family, salespeople, advertising, independent research reports, and the Internet

price information that signals the amount of potential value contained in a product

> **Consumers almost always use price and quality when making decisions.**

always consider quality an important evaluative criterion. Although quality can mean many things to many people, from a consumer perspective, **quality** represents the perceived overall goodness or badness of some product. In other words, consumers generally use the word *quality* as a synonym for relative goodness. A high-quality hotel room is a good hotel room; a low-quality hotel room is a bad one.

Quality perceptions take place both before and after purchase. However, consumers do not always seek high quality, because many times consumers do not need the "best" product available. Although Holiday Inn Express may not offer as high quality an experience as does a Hyatt Regency hotel, it does adequately address the need for a place to sleep on a cross-country drive.

Consumers almost always use price and quality when making decisions. Indeed, price and quality perceptions are related, as consumers generally assume that higher prices mean higher quality. This relationship is altered, however, by other variables. For example, when consumers view a purchase as coming in the distant future they tend to view price as a stronger indicator of quality (the positive role of price). When the purchase is imminent, however, they tend to view price as more of a monetary sacrifice (the negative role of price).[29]

A relatively new tactic regarding pricing and quality is the "pay what you want" (PWYW) phenomenon. To say that this is completely new is a bit misleading, because some marketers have done this for years. However, the tactic is gaining in popularity. Products and services ranging from music downloads to sporting events to restaurants now include PWYW options. Research in the area is still developing, but early indications reveal that consumers are happy to pay what they choose to pay and that the option can lead to profitability, especially if consumers understand a company's cost structure.[30]

12-5b External Search and Emerging Technologies

quality perceived overall goodness or badness of some product

As discussed previously, in today's fast-paced, information-rich environment, a tremendous amount of information

is at our fingertips. There's no denying that the advent of the Internet and emerging technologies quickly affected search behavior.[31] Due to the popularity of search engines, social networking sites, and smartphone apps, consumers can find solutions to all sorts of problems at their fingertips.

Since the Internet is now firmly entrenched in consumers' lives, it is easy to overlook just how much it originally changed consumer search and decision making. Most traditional college students grew up in a world that always included widespread Internet and app access, but that wasn't always the case. What was once a novel computer tool has now become the first place that many consumers go to find information. The Internet has dramatically affected search behavior. First, it lowers the costs associated with search and can make the process more productive.[32] Second, the search process itself has become more enjoyable by delivering hedonic value to the consumer.[33] Third, consumers now have the ability to control information flow much more efficiently than if they are viewing product information from a television commercial. The ability to control information flow increases informational value and increases the consumers' ability to remember information that is gathered.[34]

While many consumers now check smartphone apps first, websites are still popular. Craigslist, in particular, remains extremely popular. Consumers search craigslist every day for solutions to problems they face. While the site is useful in many different contexts, evidence suggests that it is especially useful for helping consumers locate apartments and rental properties. Decreases in vacancies can be directly attributed to the site.[35] Online shopping sites such as Overstock.com and auction sites such as eBay and Ubid are popular as well.

Website construction is very important in impacting online search success. One study found that consumers spend more time searching in three-dimensional interactive web environments than in two-dimensional web spaces. However, the study also revealed that the number of brands examined was actually higher for two-dimensional web pages than for three-dimensional sites.[36] Consumers can become so immersed in virtual worlds that they neglect to consider brand information.

12-5c Consumer Search and Smartphone Applications

Smartphone capabilities have greatly impacted search. Recall that one criterion that consumers consider when searching for information is the ease of obtaining information from the source. Smartphone apps have made it easier for consumers to search for information from practically any location, and they have played a major role in the advent of mobile commerce. Although new technologies are introduced daily, the following four advancements apply well to smartphone apps and mobile commerce. These technologies have also contributed to the growing use of the phrase *consumer discovery*, which describes how consumers are constantly discovering new information about products, services, experiences, and locations.[37]

QR Codes. QR codes (*quick response codes*) dramatically changed information availability. With a QR code reader, consumers gain access to all types of product-related information. Early on, marketers viewed QR codes as an essential part of marketing strategy whereby *promotional conversion rates* (that is, the rate at which a promotion is transitioned into a sale) could be improved. To some extent, marketers still reap the rewards of QR codes. However, the codes have gradually decreased in popularity due to other types of visual recognition technologies.

Mobile Visual Search. Mobile visual search (MVS) technologies allow consumers to simply take a photo of an object or scan it into their screen and quickly receive information about it. Apps such as Google Goggles, CamFind, and Veracity enable consumers to perform searches without having to enter text into a search engine. Not only does this make it easier for consumers to gain information, it also makes the process faster.

Augmented Reality. A number of apps are currently available that bring the physical and virtual worlds together in new and exciting ways. Augmented reality apps do simply that—they *augment* reality with computer simulated information. Apps such as *Blippar*, *Wikitude*, and *Layar Reality* create entirely new interactive experiences for the consumer. Other apps, such as *Snapshot Showroom*, allow consumers to visualize how products purchased will look in their homes.

GPS-Based Technologies. Other search technologies combine elements of GPS capabilities with consumer needs. Currently, most smartphones such as the iPhone include features that show popular retailers nearby. There are also popular apps such as Around Me, Around Town, and Find NearMe that allow consumers to find information about nearby points of interest like restaurants, gas stations, parks, and hospitals. These apps allow consumers to quickly address specific needs that they have while they are traveling.

It is easy to see how technologies such as these have affected consumer search processes. In fact, it can be argued that neither *search* nor *discovery* accurately

DWD-Media/Alamy Stock Photo

Augmented reality technologies have greatly affected CB.

describes what these technologies enable the consumer to do. The search and discovery processes really become "branded consumer experiences." The experience enables the consumer to learn about the product, interact with it, and begin to forge relationships with it.

12-5d Amount of Search

The amount of search that a consumer performs related to decision making can be measured in a number of ways, including the number of stores visited, the number of websites and apps visited, the number of personal sources (friends, family, salespeople) used, the number of alternatives considered, and the number of advertisements studied.

Many factors influence the information search effort, including previous experience with a product, involvement, perceived risk, value of search effort, time availability, attitudes toward shopping, personal factors, and situational influencers.[38]

Product Experience. Prior experience with a product has been shown to influence how much a consumer searches. A number of researchers have examined this issue, sometimes with conflicting results. As a general statement, evidence shows that moderately experienced

Exhibit 12.6

Experience and External Search

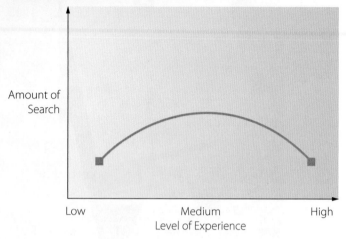

Amount of Search

Low   Medium   High

Level of Experience

Value of Search Effort. Value can be obtained from the search process itself. When the benefits received from searching exceed the associated costs, consumers derive value. When searching costs are greater than the benefits of the search process, consumers no longer value the activity and search stops.[43] Costs associated with search can be either monetary (for example, the cost of driving around town looking for a new bedroom dresser) or nonmonetary (for example, psychological or physical exhaustion or stress). Even online searching brings about certain mental costs.[44] As we have discussed, mobile technologies have increased the ease of search activities.

Time Availability. All other things being equal, more time to spend on search usually results in increased search activity.[45] Because time is valued so highly by most consumers, search will decrease when time constraints are present.

consumers search for purchase-related information more than do either experienced or inexperienced consumers. This finding is shown in Exhibit 12.6.[39]

One explanation for the finding that moderately experienced consumers search more than other consumers is that individuals with little experience are unable to make fine distinctions between product differences and will likely see product alternatives as being similar. As such, they find little value in extensive information search. Highly experienced consumers can make fine distinctions between products and may know so much about products that they do not need to search at all. Moderately experienced consumers, on the other hand, perceive some differences among brands and are more likely to value information about these distinctions.[40]

Involvement. As noted earlier, purchase involvement is positively associated with search activities, especially for ongoing searches. Because involvement represents a level of arousal and interest in a product, search tends to increase when a consumer possesses a high level of purchase involvement.[41]

Perceived Risk. As perceived risk increases, search effort increases.[42] As discussed earlier in the chapter, a number of risks can be associated with the consumption act, including financial, social, performance, physical, and time risks. Consumers are usually motivated to reduce these risks as much as possible and will therefore expend considerable time and effort in searching for information.

Attitude toward Shopping. Consumers who value shopping and who possess positive attitudes toward shopping generally spend more time searching for product information.[46]

One controversial method for introducing new products to consumers requires marketers to pay retailers what are known as *slotting allowances* or *slotting fees*. Slotting allowances are sums of money paid by a vendor to a retailer for specific locations or shelf placement in a store. These fees are often required for new products and can play a big role in the success of these products.

Personal Factors. Search tends to increase as a consumer's level of education and income increase. Search also tends to decrease as consumers become older.[47]

Situational Influencers. Situational factors also influence the amount of search that takes place. Perceived urgency, financial pressure, and mood can all impact search behavior. The purchase occasion can also affect the search. Consumers sometimes have such an urgent need for a product that they will select the first option they come across. When a product is being purchased as a gift, the amount of search will depend on the relationship between the giver and the receiver and on the amount of time before the occasion.

EXTERNAL SEARCH OFTEN MINIMIZED

While many factors influence the amount of search that takes place, consumers tend to search surprisingly little

THAT'S CONVENIENT!

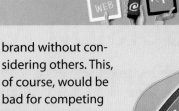

onvenience. We all want it. Along with price and quality, convenience often ranks highly on what consumers seek. Now, the shopping process is easier than ever thanks to Amazon's "Dash Button." This button is making waves in the retail world and changing the way that consumers find solutions to their problems.

The Dash Button, which is a small device that is attached to various consumer goods, allows consumers to simply push a button when they run low on products and automatically place orders for replacements. The technology is available through Amazon, which has been working for years to simplify consumer shopping and decision making. From predictive analytics, including anticipatory shipping, to drone-based product delivery to the Dash Button, Amazon has successfully leveraged technology to present the consumer with convenient home shopping. Obviously, the button encourages consumers to continue to buy the same

brand without considering others. This, of course, would be bad for competing brands. However, the convenience advantage is clear for Amazon customers.

Time will tell

Amazon/Splash News/Newscom

just how successful the Dash Button will become. For now, however, the consumer decision-making process has become just that much easier.

Sources: Mark Wilson, "Life with The Dash Button: Good Design for Amazon, Bad Design for Everyone Else," *Fastcodesign.com*, September 19, 2015, online content retrieved at http://www.fastcodesign.com/3050044/life-with-the-dash-button-good-design-for-amazon-bad-design-for-everyone-else, accessed April 26, 2015; Josh Lowensohn, "Amazon Has Invented Tiny Plastic Buttons That Allow for Instant Product Ordering," *theverge.com*, March 31, 2015, online content retrieved at http://www.theverge.com/2015/3/31/8316775/amazon-dash-buttons-turn-homes-into-shopping-carts; Ian Crouch, "The Horror of Amazon's New Dash Button," *NewYorker.com*, April 2, 2015, online content retrieved at http://www.newyorker.com/culture/culture-desk/the-horror-of-amazons-new-dash-button.

for most products.[48] This is true for both high- and low-involvement products. Consumers may already have a stored rule in memory for low-involvement products and may engage in extensive ongoing search activities and have acceptable alternative solutions in mind for high-involvement categories.[49]

12-5e Search Regret

As we have discussed, emotions and decision making are closely related topics. The search process can lead directly to emotional responses for consumers as well. The term search regret refers to the negative emotions that come from failed search processes. Many times, consumers are simply not able to find an acceptable solution to their problems. As a result, the decision-making process stops. In these situations, consumers may feel as if the entire search process was a waste of time, and they will start to feel search regret. Regret is related to the amount of search effort, the emotions felt during the process, and the use of unfamiliar search techniques.[50] Regret is more likely to be experienced when consumers exert much energy, experience more emotion, and utilize unfamiliar techniques during the search process.

Many issues relate to the topics of need recognition and search. Our next chapter discusses evaluation of alternatives and choice.

search regret negative emotions that come from failed search processes

Decision Making II: Alternative Evaluation and Choice

LEARNING OBJECTIVES

After studying this chapter, the student should be able to:

13-1 Understand the difference between evaluative criteria and determinant criteria.

13-2 Comprehend how value affects the evaluation of alternatives.

13-3 Explain the importance of product categorization in the evaluation of alternatives process.

13-4 Distinguish between compensatory and noncompensatory rules that guide consumer choice.

Remember to visit PAGE 280 for additional STUDY TOOLS

INTRODUCTION

Selecting a new apartment is obviously a big decision. But what about selecting a beverage? For decades, colas were the beverage of choice for millions of young consumers. But now, it seems that something is changing. Cola sales have gradually slipped in recent years. This was once unheard of. Everyone drank cola! For the health conscious consumer, however, colas have clearly dropped in popularity. What is it that consumers are looking for and why?

As you will remember from the first decision-making chapter, the decision-making process includes need recognition, search for information, alternative evaluation, choice, and postchoice evaluation. The decision-making model is shown once again in Exhibit 13.1.

In this chapter, we focus on evaluation of alternatives and choice.

13-1 EVALUATION OF ALTERNATIVES: CRITERIA

An important part of decision making is evaluating alternative solutions to problems. As we have discussed throughout this text, consumers are bombarded daily by a dizzying array of product varieties, brands, and experiences from which to choose. For example, consumers can select from dozens of varieties of athletic shoes and deodorants. Quite often the deodorant section in a store takes up 10 feet or more of aisle space! Marketers sometimes refer to this situation as "hyperchoice" because so many alternatives are available. Trying to make sense out of all the alternatives can be very difficult. Fortunately, consumer researchers have learned much about how consumers evaluate alternatives. In some situations, consumers simply look for one or two attributes to consider. This is relevant in the choice of beverage. Many young consumers today seek healthy alternatives when they consider which type of beverage to buy.

Exhibit 13.1

Consumer Decision-Making Process

Process

Need Recognition

↓

Search for Information

↓

Evaluation of Alternatives

↓

Choice

↓

Postchoice Evaluation

They often seek low sugar content and few additives. This has brought about an increased demand for waters, teas, and juices in recent years. In other cases, consumers consider products across several different attributes. To begin a discussion of the criteria that consumers seek, it is important to understand the different criterion classifications.

13-1a Evaluative Criteria

After a need is recognized and a search process has taken place, consumers begin to examine the criteria that will be used for making a choice. **Evaluative criteria** are the attributes, features, or potential benefits that consumers consider when reviewing possible solutions to a problem. A **feature** is a performance characteristic of an object. Remember from our attitude chapter that features are often referred to as attributes. A **benefit** is a perceived favorable

evaluative criteria attributes that consumers consider when reviewing alternative solutions to a problem

feature performance characteristic of an object

benefit perceived favorable results derived from a particular feature

Exhibit 13.2

Product, Feature, Benefit

Product	Feature	Benefit
Smartphone	Screen size	Easy viewing
Garage door opener	Programmable code	Security
Tablet case	Detachable front	Ease of use

result that is derived from the presence of a particular feature.[1] Screen size on phone is a feature. The benefit is ease of viewing. These concepts are illustrated in Exhibit 13.2.

Benefits play an important role in the value equation. Consumers don't really buy a garage door because of programmable codes. They are seeking security! If there was some other way to deliver this benefit without the feature, consumers would be quick to buy this other solution. You may remember that benefits represent "what you get" in the value equation.

$$\boxed{\text{Value}} = \boxed{\begin{array}{c}\text{What you get}\\(\textit{Benefits})\end{array}} - \boxed{\begin{array}{c}\text{What you give}\\(\textit{Costs})\end{array}}$$

13-1b Determinant Criteria

Not all evaluative criteria are equally important. Determinant criteria (sometimes called determinant attributes) are the evaluative criteria that are related to the actual choice that is made.[2]

Consumers don't always reveal, or may not even know, the criteria that truly are determinant. This is true even when several attributes are considered to be important. For example, airline safety is definitely an important feature of an airline, and consumers would quickly voice this opinion. But because consumers do not perceive a difference in safety among major airlines, safety does not actually determine the airline that is eventually selected. For this reason, statistical tools are often needed to establish determinance.

Which criteria are determinant can depend largely on the situation in which a product is consumed. For example, a consumer might consider gas mileage as a determinant criterion when buying a car for himself. However, the safety of a car would likely be a determinant factor if he were buying a car for his daughter. Marketers therefore position products on the determinant criteria that apply to a specific situation.

determinant criteria criteria that are most carefully considered and directly related to the actual choice that is made

13-2 VALUE AND ALTERNATIVE EVALUATION

To understand how alternatives are evaluated and how final choices are made, we must again highlight the key role that value plays in decision making. The value that consumers believe they will receive from a product has a direct impact on their evaluation of that product. In fact, the word *evaluate* literally means to set a value or worth to an object. Remember that benefits are at the heart of the value equation, and value is a function of both benefits and costs.

13-2a Hedonic and Utilitarian Value

It should be clear that consumers seek both hedonic and utilitarian value. The criteria that consumers use when evaluating a product can also often be classified as either hedonic or utilitarian.[3] Hedonic criteria include emotional, symbolic, and subjective attributes or benefits that are associated with an alternative. For example, the prestige that one associates with owning a BMW is a hedonic criterion. These criteria are largely experiential. Utilitarian criteria pertain to functional or economic aspects associated with an alternative. For example, safety of a BMW is a utilitarian criterion.

Marketers often promote both the utilitarian and hedonic potential of a product. For example, the advertisements presented in Exhibit 13.3 promote utilitarian and hedonic automobile attributes. Consumers often use

Denys Prykhodov/Shutterstock.com

Screen size is an important feature on a phone.

Exhibit 13.3

Utilitarian and Hedonic Criteria in Advertising

Ads promote utilitarian and hedonic value.

Utilitarian Ad—Nissan   Hedonic Ad—Alfa Romeo

both categories of criteria when evaluating alternatives and making a final choice.

RATIONALITY, EFFORT, AND VARIETY

As discussed previously, consumers are not always rational when they are evaluating and choosing from possible solutions to a problem. What's more, consumers often have limited ability to process all the information that's available in the environment. The term **bounded rationality** describes the idea that perfectly rational decisions are not always feasible due to constraints found in information processing.

Even when consumers have the ability to consider all possible solutions to a problem, they do not always do so. Quite simply, sometimes the task just isn't worth it. In fact, consumers often minimize the effort that they put into alternative evaluation and choice. As we discussed in our need recognition and information search chapter, consumers often settle for a solution that is simply good enough to solve a problem. Realistically, there are just too many choices out there. In fact, even though variety is a good thing, studies indicate that too much variety actually contributes to feelings of discontent and unhappiness![4] The attractiveness of alternatives also impacts satisfaction. More attractive alternatives reduce satisfaction with a selected product, while more unattractive ones increase this satisfaction.[5]

13-2b Affect-Based and Attribute-Based Evaluations

We can distinguish between two major types of evaluation processes: affect-based and attribute-based. With **affect-based evaluation**, consumers evaluate products based on the overall feeling that is evoked by the alternative.[6] A consumer remark like "I'm not even sure why I bought this sweater; I just liked it" reflects an affect-based process. Emotions play a big role in affect-based evaluation, as do mood states.[7]

In general, positive mood states lead to positive evaluations, while negative mood states lead to negative evaluations. Mood is also influential when limited information is found about an alternative.[8]

For example, when you are in a good mood, you may evaluate a product positively even if there is not a lot of information given about the product. Happiness affects product choices in many ways. And being "happy" can mean different things at different times. For example, some people may need to feel nice and calm to be happy. In this case, they might seek out a relaxing trip to a day spa. Others may seek excitement as a means to finding happiness. In this case, they might decide to go to an amusement park. In either case, the decision is influenced by the overall feeling that is sought.[9]

As discussed elsewhere, consumers often seek variety in order to combat the feeling of boredom. Fast food marketers are constantly adding variety to their menus. For example, restaurants like Subway and Taco Bell have moved into the breakfast market. These moves not only fulfill consumers' needs, but they also help build excitement toward the brand. The fast food industry knows that consumer excitement plays a key role in success. The selection of a restaurant is often based on hedonic criteria, and variety plays a role in the decision.[10]

> **bounded rationality**
> idea that consumers attempt to act rationally within their information-processing constraints
>
> **affect-based evaluation**
> evaluative process wherein consumers evaluate products based on the overall feeling that is evoked by the alternative

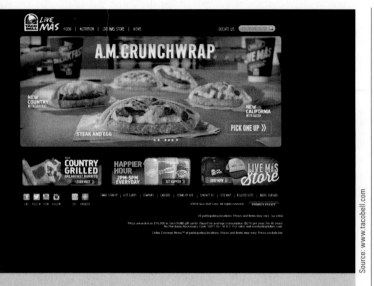

Taco Bell's move into breakfast encourages consumer excitement.

Product categories are mental representations of stored knowledge about groups of products. When considering a new product, consumers rely on the knowledge that they have regarding the relevant product category. Knowledge about the existing category is then transferred to the novel item. For example, when consumers view a tablet for the first time, they start to compare it with existing tablets. Even if a product is very different from products that are currently available, consumers still draw on existing category knowledge to guide their expectations and attitudes toward the new product.[11] Consumers now use their existing knowledge about phones and tablets to guide their comprehension of the products.

13-3a Category Levels

Consumers possess different levels of product categories. The number of levels and details within each level is influenced by familiarity and expertise with products.[12] For example, consumers know the differences between snacks, breakfast, and dinner. Further distinctions can be made within any of these categories. Within the snack category, distinctions can be made between salty snacks, sweet snacks, fruits, and vegetables. Even finer distinctions can be made at yet a third level. Salty snacks may be broken down into crackers, chips, snack mix, and so on. Therefore, distinctions at basic levels are generally made across product categories (for example, snacks, breakfast foods, dinner foods). Distinctions at subsequent levels increase in specificity, ultimately to the brand and attribute level.[13] Expertise and familiarity play important roles in this process.

SUPERORDINATE AND SUBORDINATE CATEGORIES

The different levels of product categories are referred to as being either superordinate or subordinate.[14] *Superordinate categories* are abstract in nature and represent the highest level of categorization. An example of a superordinate category would be "beverages." *Subordinate categories* are more detailed. Here, the consumer examines the knowledge that she has stored about various options. For example, a consumer would proceed through the beverage superordinate category to the subordinate categories of "colas," "sports drinks," and "juices." As a hypothetical example, assume that Alyssa visited the websites for sports drinks

> ## Consumers often seek variety in order to combat feelings of boredom.

With **attribute-based evaluation**, alternatives are evaluated across a set of attributes that are considered relevant to the purchase situation. As we have noted, the rational decision-making process assumes that consumers carefully integrate information about product attributes and make careful comparisons between products. For example, a consumer may want to find a television that has at least a 50-inch screen, has the best picture clarity, a good warranty and surround sound. All of these features would be considered in the selection process.

13-3 PRODUCT CATEGORIZATION AND CRITERIA SELECTION

One of the first things that a consumer does when she receives information from the environment is attempt to make sense of the information by placing it in the context of a familiar category. Existing schemata, as discussed in our comprehension chapter, allows consumers to provide meaning to objects. Within these schemata, both product categories and brand categories are found.

attribute-based evaluation evaluative process wherein alternatives are evaluated across a set of attributes that are considered relevant to the purchase situation

product categories mental representations of stored knowledge about groups of products

Recommend an App

One of the most useful advances in technology in terms of consumer behavior is the advent of recommendation algorithms. Consumers are familiar with these: Netflix presents movies and sitcoms based on viewing habits, Amazon features products such as "you might like," and YouTube presents us with recommended videos based on the types of videos we often watch.

Now, new recommendation services are popping up that help consumers find new apps for their phones. Searching the vast array of apps on the iTunes App Store or Google Play can be a daunting task. But, thanks to apps such as AppZapp, AppWatch, and BAM, finding a new app can be easier than ever. These apps use information such as app habits and preferences and other recommendation technologies to help you find new apps that you might like. Here, both the information search and alternative evaluation stages of decision making are greatly simplified. The apps give you plenty of alternatives and the alternatives have been pre-screened based on your own habits.

Gonzalo Aragon/Shutterstock.com

There's no doubt that thousands of apps are developed every year. Thanks to discovery and recommendation technologies, the app decision making process has become easier than ever.

and found the information listed in Exhibit 13.4.

We should note that evaluations are generally more relevant and meaningful at subordinate levels.[15] For example, assume that Alyssa notices specific differences in the brands at the subordinate level. Hypothetically, she may notice that G-02 has fewer calories than the other products. Or she may notice that All-Sport has less sodium than the competitors. Or she may notice that Powerade ION4 has less potassium than the others. This information would then guide her final decision for which sports drink to buy.

Recall from the memory chapter that exemplars are first

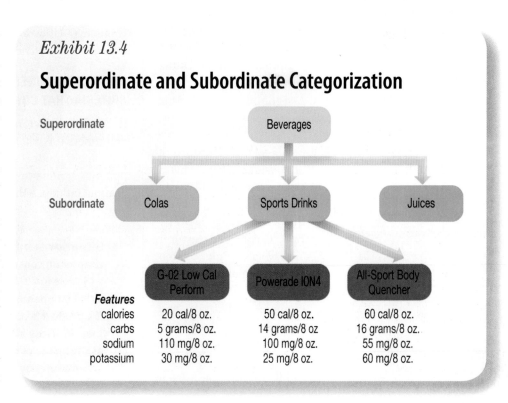

Exhibit 13.4

Superordinate and Subordinate Categorization

Features	G-02 Low Cal Perform	Powerade ION4	All-Sport Body Quencher
calories	20 cal/8 oz.	50 cal/8 oz.	60 cal/8 oz.
carbs	5 grams/8 oz.	14 grams/8 oz	16 grams/8 oz.
sodium	110 mg/8 oz.	100 mg/8 oz.	55 mg/8 oz.
potassium	30 mg/8 oz.	25 mg/8 oz.	60 mg/8 oz.

thought of within any category. An exemplar for sports drinks may be G. New alternatives will be compared to exemplars first and then to other brands that are found in the brand category. For example, when Alyssa sees an advertisement for a new brand of sports drink, she will quickly move through the beverage and sports drinks categories and arrive at G and use G as the first benchmark. Other brand comparisons will then occur.

© Jessmine/Shutterstock.com

PERCEPTUAL AND UNDERLYING ATTRIBUTES

When evaluating products, consumers also distinguish between perceptual and underlying attributes. **Perceptual attributes** are visually apparent and easily recognizable. Size, shape, color, and price are perceptual attributes. These attributes are sometimes referred to as search qualities, because they can easily be evaluated prior to actual purchase.

Underlying attributes are not readily apparent and can only be learned through experience with the product. These attributes are sometimes referred to as experience qualities, because they are often perceived only during consumption. An example of an underlying attribute is product quality. The distinction between the two types of attributes is important, because consumers most often infer the existence of underlying attributes through perceptual attributes. As we discussed in the previous chapter, the price of a product often tells the consumer something about its quality. In this way, price is used as a signal of quality. A **signal** is a characteristic that allows a consumer to diagnose something distinctive about an alternative.

An example of a signal is the color and texture of fruits and vegetables. A lot of consumers know that a green banana will taste bitter. And they know that a soft orange is overly ripe. Colors and textures are signals. Colors often signal something about nutritional content. For example, red fruits and vegetables are thought to reduce the risk of some cancers. Blue fruits, such as blue berries, have been shown to reduce the risk of stroke and heart disease. In this case, the perceptual attribute of color signals something about the underlying attribute of health benefit and nutrition.

Consumers tend to use information about color, feel, brand name, price, and retailer reputation as signals about quality in the following situations:

> ▶ **When the consumer is trying to reduce risk**
> ▶ **When purchase involvement is low**
> ▶ **When the consumer lacks product expertise**[16]

Interestingly, young and inexperienced consumers rely more heavily on perceptual attributes than do older consumers.[17]

13-3b Criteria Selection

There are a number of issues that relate to the selection of criteria that consumers use when evaluating products. What determines the type of evaluative criteria that consumers use? Are consumers accurate in their assessment of evaluative criteria? How many criteria are necessary to evaluate alternatives effectively? What if information is missing? How do marketers determine which criteria consumers use? These issues are discussed below.

WHAT DETERMINES THE TYPE OF EVALUATIVE CRITERIA THAT CONSUMERS USE?

A number of factors influence the type of criteria that consumers use when evaluating alternatives. Situational influences, product knowledge, social influences, expert opinions, online sources, and marketing communications all influence the type of criteria that are used.

> 1. **Situational Influences.** As discussed in the chapter on consumers in situations, situations play a big role in CB. The type of criteria that are considered depends heavily on situational influences. If a product is being purchased as a gift, the buyer may pay close attention to hedonic attributes such as the image of the product and its reputation. When a girl buys a dress for a high school prom

---

perceptual attributes attributes that are visually apparent and easily recognizable

underlying attributes attributes that are not readily apparent and can be learned only through experience or contact with the product

signal attribute that consumers use to infer something about another attribute

or college formal, attributes like quality and look are important and are weighted heavily in the evaluation process. When purchasing a dress for other occasions, the consumer would likely rely more heavily on other criteria such as price and, perhaps, comfort or convenience.

2. **Product Knowledge.** As a consumer's level of knowledge increases, he is able to focus on criteria that are most important in making a selection and to discount irrelevant information.[18] A college basketball player would be able to quickly discern what information about athletic shoes is important.

3. **Expert Opinions.** Because brand experts have well-developed knowledge banks for products and services, they can be used to help others determine what types of information to pay attention to when evaluating products. For example, a lapidary would be able to guide consumers in the types of evaluative criteria to consider when buying a diamond ring. Market mavens are also trusted sources who can guide consumers in focusing on various product attributes.

4. **Social Influences.** Friends, family members, and reference groups also have an impact on the type of criteria that are used for decision making. This is especially true for socially visible products like automobiles or clothing.[19] Friends and families are considered to be trustworthy sources of information, and guidance that they give as to what type of attributes to consider is usually closely followed.

5. **Online Sources.** Numerous websites can assist consumers with information on product attributes and brand differences. ConsumerReports.com explains what types of criteria to consider when buying products. Popular retail sites like Staples.com also explain what attributes consumers should consider.

6. **Marketing Communications.** Marketers assist consumers in deciding what features to consider when buying a particular product. They generally promote the attributes that their products excel on and attempt to convince consumers that these are the most important. For example, Hallmark Cards tells consumers to choose their cards when they "care enough to send the very best."

ARE CONSUMERS ACCURATE IN THEIR ASSESSMENT OF EVALUATIVE CRITERIA?

The accuracy of a consumer's evaluation depends heavily on the quality of judgments that they make. **Judgments** are mental assessments of the presence of attributes and the benefits associated with those attributes. Consumer judgments are affected by the amount of knowledge or experience a consumer has with a particular object. During the evaluation process, consumers make judgments about the following:

▸ **Presence of features.** Does this car stereo store music?

▸ **Feature levels.** How many songs does it store?

▸ **Benefits associated with features.** I won't have to carry my mp3 player or CDs with me.

▸ **Value associated with the benefit.** Both utilitarian and hedonic value are derived.

▸ **How objects differ from each other.** The other stereos don't offer this attribute.

There are several issues that affect consumer judgments. We review a few of these issues here.

1. **Just Noticeable Difference.** The ability of consumers to make accurate judgments when evaluating alternatives is influenced by their ability to perceive differences in levels of stimuli between two options. As was discussed in our perception chapter, the just noticeable difference (JND) represents how much stronger one stimulus must be compared to another if someone is to notice that the two are not the same. For example, when judging picture quality on an HDTV, a consumer may not be able to discern the difference between refresh rates of 120 Hz and 240 Hz. In fact, most consumers can't see the difference. If consumers cannot tell the difference, then their judgments about the products may not be accurate.

   Sometimes, the same manufacturer offers different brands or models that are very similar to each other. The term *branded variants* is used to describe the practice of offering essentially identical products with different model numbers or names.[20] Even if differences are perceived, the differences might not be very meaningful.

   The impact of the JND on consumer judgments also applies to how consumers react to counterfeit products. Some counterfeits are so much like the original that consumers simply can't perceive the difference. This is, of course, a bad situation for marketers of the original.

judgments mental assessments of the presence of attributes and the benefits associated with those attributes.

WHY ARE WE FLIPPING OUT?

So, your phone has the latest and the greatest: the most up-to-date operating system, processor, camera, and voice recognition technology. But are you happy? Well, many in the industry are beginning to ask this question.

Just what are consumers looking for? Is technology feeding technology? Do consumers really need their smartphones to start their coffee pots, find their cars, or take time-lapse video? Or do they simply want a phone that won't crack easily and that has a good battery?

It seems that consumers are beginning to see through the gimmicks and the "clutter" of features they'll rarely use. Many consumers are second-guessing the marketing and asking themselves what is really important in a phone. And it appears that it's really pretty simple stuff—a phone that won't break, a phone that has good security, and a battery that won't run out. In fact, the years 2016 and 2017 saw a real rebound of the old-school flip phone. After all, flip phones can't be hacked, they have good battery life, they don't break easily, and their small screens are a default privacy filter. You might think about this in your next purchase. But if you do need your phone to tell you where you left your car, you can have that, too.

Sources: Lucy Bayly (2016), "iPhone Sales Are Down: Are We Flipping for 'Dumb' Phones Instead?", NBCNews.com, May 8, 2016, online content retrieved at: http://www.nbcnews.com/tech/tech-news/smartphone-sales-are-down-are-we-flipping-dumb-phones-instead-n564911, accessed May 11, 2016; Versace, Christopher (2014), "What Do Consumers Want in a New Smartphone?," Forbes.com, August 21, 2014, online content retrieved at: http://www.forbes.com/sites/chrisversace/2013/08/21/what-do-consumers-want-in-a-new-smartphone/, accessed June 6, 2014; Hide, Nick (2014), "Kazam's James Atkins: Consumers Don't Want Smartphone Gimmicks," Cnet.com, February 26, 2014, online content retrieved at: http://www.cnet.com/news/kazams-james-atkins-consumers-dont-want-smartphone-gimmicks/, accessed June 6, 2014.

2. **Attribute Correlation.** Consumers often make judgments about features based on their perceived relationship with other features. For example, earlier we stated that price is often used as a signal for quality. Here, consumers rely on **attribute correlation** to describe the perceived relationship between attributes of products.[21] Recall from the discussion of consumer search that price and quality are often assumed to be positively correlated. That is, when a product has a high price, consumers often assume it will be high quality.

Attributes can also be negatively correlated. For example, if a consumer's wait time at a bank is long, he might think that the bank offers poor service. Here, the consumer assumes that as wait time goes up, service quality goes down (hence, a negative correlation). This can be a faulty assumption, because a long wait time may simply mean that consumers get individualized attention and really good service. Some things are worth waiting for. In fact, perceived quality, purchase intentions, and customer satisfaction can even be improved by making consumers wait![22]

attribute correlation
perceived relationship between product features

Personality traits also affect consumer judgments.

3. **Quality Perceptions.** Marketers have long realized that consumer perception is critical to marketing success. As we have discussed, perceptions are not always in line with reality. One issue that pertains to consumer judgments is the difference between objective quality and perceived quality. *Objective quality* refers to the actual quality of a product that can be assessed through industry specification or expert rating. For example, a cell phone provider may advertise that its service has been proven to have the fewest dropped calls in the industry. *Perceived quality* is based on consumer perceptions. Even if the cell phone has objectively been shown to have the best coverage in the industry, consumers may still perceive poor quality if the coverage in their immediate area is not good.

Companies spend a great deal of time and money on improving the objective quality of their products. These efforts are limited, however, by consumer perceptions of quality. In fact, a recent study revealed that improvements in objective quality may take as many as six years to be fully recognized by consumers![23] You may remember from our discussion in the comprehension chapter that consumers act on declarative knowledge even if the knowledge is incorrect. The Ford Motor Company has been successful with its "Swap Your Ride" promotion, which allows consumers to directly experience the quality of its products, influencing their perceptions.[24]

4. **Brand Name Associations.** Brand names also have an impact on consumer judgments. Much like price, brand names can be used as signals of quality. In fact, studies have found that brand names are even stronger signals of quality than is price.[25] For example, Energizer batteries are assumed to last a long time, and Gillette razors are believed to be the best a man can get.

Unusual product names also influence consumer judgments. Marketers therefore pay close attention to the names they place on their products. This is true across consumer product industries. Chewing gum brands are known for being very descriptive and sometimes humorous. Names like "Double Bubble," "CinnaBurst," and "Extra" tell consumers what to expect from the products. Research indicates that unexpected and novel names can lead to increased product preference and choice.[26]

5. **Consumer Personality.** Personality traits also affect consumer judgments. Highly impulsive consumers

digitalreflections/Shutterstock.com

often make poor judgments, while consumers with a high need for cognition can overthink their decisions and sometimes regret the judgments that they've made. High self-monitors can also ruminate on their judgments by focusing too intensely on the consequences associated with various attributes.

HOW MANY CRITERIA ARE NECESSARY TO EVALUATE ALTERNATIVES EFFECTIVELY?

As we have discussed, too many alternatives can be draining for consumers. However, research suggests that consumers can handle a surprisingly high number of comparisons before overload sets in. One study revealed that consumers can evaluate as many as 10 product alternatives and 15 attributes before overload occurs.[27] Even though consumers can handle this much information, they rarely like to do so. And they generally do not consider this many alternatives. In fact, consumers are often able to make good choices when considering only a single attribute.[28]

WHAT IF INFORMATION IS MISSING?

Consumers may have a good understanding of the types of attributes that they would like to use for alternative evaluation, but sometimes attribute information is not available. This actually happens quite frequently in the marketplace. For example, consider the information given in Exhibit 13.5. Here, information is given for two televisions that a consumer collects from print advertisements. Assume that both televisions cost roughly the same amount, for example $1,000. As you can see, the information for television A lacks the details for picture quality, while the information given for television B lacks the details regarding the product's warranty. Consumer satisfaction ratings are available for both products.

To help solve this dilemma, consumers tend to weigh the criteria that are common to both alternatives quite heavily in the evaluation. They also tend to discount information that is missing for the option that performs better on the common criteria. For example, satisfaction ratings are given for both TV sets in this exhibit. Consumers would likely discount the missing warranty information for television B because this alternative performs better on the common criteria of consumer satisfaction ratings.[29]

Exhibit 13.5

Missing Information

Features	Television A	Television B
Consumer satisfaction ratings	Good	Excellent
Warranty	2 years parts and labor	Not given
Picture quality	Not given	Good

Source: Kivetz, R., and I. Simonson (2000), "The Effects of Incomplete Information on Consumer Choice," *Journal of Marketing Research*, 37 (4), 427–448.

Interestingly, consumers jump to all kinds of conclusions when faced with missing information. Recent research in services marketing reveals that consumers display the tendency to jump to negative conclusions about service providers who promote themselves positively on one feature but omit information on another feature. This is called an "innuendo effect." For example, a doctor who promotes himself as highly competent but doesn't include information about his personality may be perceived by consumers as being relatively uncaring.[30]

> Consumers jump to all kinds of conclusions when faced with missing information.

HOW DO MARKETERS DETERMINE WHICH CRITERIA CONSUMERS USE?

Marketers can use several techniques to determine the criteria that consumers use when judging products. They can directly ask consumers through surveys. They can also gather information from warranty registrations that ask consumers to indicate the specific criteria that were used in arriving at a purchase decision.

Marketers also use techniques such as perceptual mapping and conjoint analysis to assess choice criteria. Perceptual mapping was discussed in a previous chapter. Conjoint analysis is used to understand the attributes that guide preferences by having consumers compare products across levels of evaluative criteria and the expected utility associated with the alternatives.[31]

13-4 CONSUMER CHOICE: DECISION RULES

Once consumers have evaluated alternative solutions to a problem, they begin to make a choice. *Choice* does not mean that a particular alternative will be chosen, as consumers may simply choose to delay a choice until a future date or to forgo a selection indefinitely.

There are two major types of rules that consumers use when selecting products: compensatory rules and noncompensatory rules. Compensatory rules allow consumers to select products that may perform poorly on one attribute by compensating for the poor performance by good performance on another attribute. A consumer using a compensatory rule might say something like "It's OK that this car isn't very stylish; it gets good gas mileage. I'll buy it."

Noncompensatory models do not allow for this process to take place. Rather, when noncompensatory rules are used, strict guidelines are set prior to selection, and any option that does not meet the specifications is eliminated from consideration. For example, a consumer might say, "I'll only choose a car that gets good gas mileage. I am not budging on that."

13-4a Compensatory Models

The attitude-toward-the-object model (Fishbein model) that was presented in our attitude chapter represents a compensatory approach. The formula $A_o = \Sigma(b_i)(e_i)$ allows for poor scores on one attribute to be compensated for by good scores on another. Our example from that chapter is again shown in Exhibit 13.6. This example revealed that Crown View was the apartment complex to which Jamal held the most positive attitude, even though it scored highest on the attribute that Jamal rated very poorly: high rent/fees. The high ratings on other attributes compensated for his belief that the complex has high fees.

conjoint analysis technique used to develop an understanding of the attributes that guide consumer preferences by having consumers compare product preferences across varying levels of evaluative criteria and expected utility

compensatory rule decision rule that allows consumers to select products that may perform poorly on one criterion by compensating for the poor performance by good performance on another

noncompensatory rule decision rule in which strict guidelines are set prior to selection and any option that does not meet the guidelines is eliminated from consideration

IS IT A BOY OR A GIRL?

Consumer researchers study all kinds of issues relating to decision making. Sometimes the issues studied are surprising. One area of study is learning the factors that influence consumers' decisions to follow doctors' orders. Another area is understanding why consumers don't follow safety warnings about not texting and driving. Recent findings regarding storm precautions are particularly surprising.

It was found that female-named hurricanes are often more deadly than are male-named storms. The reason? People tend to think that female-named storms will be less aggressive, and therefore they don't take precautions as seriously. The issue comes down to the gender stereotypes that consumers hold. Women are often thought to be more compassionate and more caring than are men. As such, people tend to think that female storms will be relatively easygoing. The problem is that data reveals that female-named storms like Katrina and Sandy are among the worst in history. As such, the entire naming scheme for hurricanes might need to be reconsidered.

The moral of the story is simple: When it comes to hurricanes, don't ask if it's a boy or a girl. Follow safety precautions and make good decisions!

Harvepino/Shutterstock.com

Sources: Jung, K., Shavitt, S., Viswanathan, M., and Hilbe, J. (2014). "Female Hurricanes Are Deadlier than Male Hurricanes," Proceedings of the National Academy of Sciences, doi: 10.1073/pnas. 1402786111; Samenow, Jason (2014), Female-Named Hurricanes Kill More Than Male Hurricanes Because People Don't Respect Them, Study Finds," The Washington Post (online), June 2, 2014, online content retrieved at: http://www.washingtonpost.com /blogs/capital-weather-gang/wp/2014/06/02/female-named-hurricanes-kill-more-than -male-because-people-dont-respect-them-study-finds/, accessed June 6, 2014; Cary, John (2014), "Hurricanes with Women's Names Significantly More Deadly, Study Finds," Chicago Tribune (online), online content retrieved at: http://articles.chicagotribune.com/2014-06-02 /news/chi-hurricanes-names-study-20140602_1_storm-surge-national-hurricane-center -names, accessed June 6, 2014.

Exhibit 13.6

Attitude-Toward-the-Object Model Applied to Apartment Complexes

Attribute	e	City pointe b	City pointe (b)(e)	Crown view b	Crown view (b)(e)	Kings landing b	Kings landing (b)(e)
Location	3	7	21	9	27	6	18
High rent/fees	−2	8	−16	9	−18	7	−14
Security	3	7	21	8	24	6	18
Fitness center	1	5	5	7	7	10	10
Pet friendliness	−3	5	−15	2	−6	9	−27
A_0			16		34		5

Note: e = evaluative ratings. These ratings are generally scaled from −3 to +3, with −3 being very negative and +3 being very positive. b = strength of belief that the object possesses the attribute in question. Beliefs are generally scaled from 1 to 10, with 1 meaning "highly unlikely" and 10 meaning "highly likely." (b)(e) is the product term that is derived by multiplying the evaluative ratings (e) by belief strength (b). A_0 is the overall attitude toward the object. This is determined by adding the (b)(e) product terms for each object.

Exhibit 13.7

Noncompensatory Decision Approaches

Attribute	Importance	Chevy Spark belief ratings	Ford Fiesta belief ratings	Honda Fit belief ratings	Hyundai Accent belief ratings
Gas mileage	10	5	7	9	8
Low price	9	8	6	7	10
Styling	8	9	8	4	4
Warranty	5	4	8	9	8
Service	6	5	6	7	3
Handling	7	6	5	3	3

Note: Belief ratings are performance judgments scaled from 1 = very poor to 10 = very good. Importance ratings are scaled so that 10 = most important, 9 = next most important, and so on.

Source: P. Wright, "Consumer Choice Strategies: Simplifying vs. Optimizing," *Journal of Marketing Research*, 12, no. 1 (1975): 60–67.

13-4b Noncompensatory Models

Consumer researchers have identified four major categories of noncompensatory decision rules.[32] They include the conjunctive rule, the disjunctive rule, the lexicographic rule, and the elimination-by-aspects (EBA) rule.

conjunctive rule noncompensatory decision rule where the option selected must surpass a minimum cutoff across all relevant attributes

disjunctive rule noncompensatory decision rule where the option selected surpasses a relatively high cutoff point on any attribute

lexicographic rule noncompensatory decision rule where the option selected is thought to perform best on the most important attribute

elimination-by-aspects rule (EBA) noncompensatory decision rule where the consumer begins evaluating options by first looking at the most important attribute and eliminating any option that does not meet a minimum cutoff point for that attribute, and where subsequent evaluations proceed in order of importance until only one option remains

1. Following the conjunctive rule, the consumer sets a minimum mental cutoff point for various features and rejects any product that fails to meet or exceed this cutoff point across all features.

2. Following the disjunctive rule, the consumer sets a minimum mental cutoff for various features. This is similar to the conjunctive rule. However, with the disjunctive rule, the cutoff point is usually high. The product that meets or exceeds this cutoff on any feature is selected.

3. Following the lexicographic rule, consumers select the product that they believe performs best on the most important feature.

4. Following the elimination-by-aspects rule (EBA), consumers set minimum cutoff points for the attributes. Beginning with the most important feature, they then eliminate options that don't meet or surpass the cutoff point on this important feature. The consumer then moves on to the next most important feature and repeats the process, doing this until only one option remains and a choice is made.

To illustrate these rules, consider the information that is presented in Exhibit 13.7. Here, the consumer is evaluating different makes and models of cars. She is considering the Chevy Spark, Ford Fiesta, Honda Fit, and Hyundai Accent. Assume these are her belief ratings for each car.

The process involved with each decision rule would be as follows:

1. **Conjunctive Rule.** Assume that all features must meet or surpass a mental cutoff of 5 in order for the car to be selected. Looking across the various features for the cars, we see that only the Ford Fiesta has performance ratings at or above 5 on all features. Using this rule, the Ford Fiesta would therefore be selected. Its performance ratings are, respectively, 7, 6, 8, 8, 6, 5. Notice that at least one of the performance ratings for the attributes of the other cars falls below the cutoff of 5.

2. **Disjunctive Rule.** Assume that the consumer wants a car that excels at any of the features. Here, she would set a high cutoff of, say, 10. The only car that offers a performance rating of 10 on any attribute is the Hyundai Accent. The "low price" criterion is particularly strong for this car, and the consumer rates this feature as a 10. Using the disjunctive rule, the Hyundai Accent would be selected. She is considering performance ratings, not the importance of the attributes.

3. **Lexicographic Rule.** Here, the product that is thought to perform best on the most important attribute is selected. In this example, the consumer would select the Honda Fit because it scores highest (9) on the most important attribute, gas mileage.

4. **EBA Rule.** Assuming a minimum cutoff point of 5 once again, the consumer begins with the most important attribute, gas mileage. Any product that does not meet or surpass the cutoff of 5 on this attribute would be eliminated. All options meet or surpass 5 on the gas mileage attribute, and no products are eliminated. Next, the consumer looks at the next most important attribute, low price. Again, all options meet the 5 criterion, and no options are eliminated.

   On the next most important attribute, styling, two options are eliminated because they don't reach the 5 cutoff—the Honda Fit and the Hyundai Accent. The consumer continues on with the next most important attribute, handling. Both the Spark and the Fiesta surpass the 5 cutoff on this attribute. The same is true for the next most important attribute, service. Finally, on the final attribute, warranty, the Spark is eliminated from consideration because it does not reach the cutoff, and the Ford Fiesta is ultimately selected. Notice that the conjunctive and EBA rules can result in the same decision. This will occur if the same cutoff points are used for both rules.

13-4c Use of Decision Rules

Noncompensatory rules are often used in low-involvement situations, because these rules allow consumers to simplify their thought processes. However, these rules

Choosing a car is a highly involved decision and probably uses both compensatory and noncompensatory rules.

are also used in high-involvement purchase situations. The decision of what car to buy is certainly a high-involvement decision for most people.

Consumers can combine decision rules in order to arrive at a final solution. For example, a consumer might begin with a conjunctive rule to narrow down the choices and then use a compensatory approach to finalize the decision.

You may be wondering what type of rule consumers use most often. Studies have revealed that the lexicographic rule is very common. This is because consumers usually know what features are most important, and they simply select the product that offers the best performance on that feature.

You may also wonder how often consumers use these rules. Actually, the rules are used quite frequently. We should emphasize, however, that the processes are indeed mental. That is, the comparisons are almost always made mentally, without the strict use of a mathematical formula. Nevertheless, by considering issues such as cutoff points, researchers are able to gain a better understanding of the processes behind consumer choice.

13-4d Retail Outlet Selection

Up to this point, we have emphasized the processes that consumers use when selecting from alternative solutions to a problem. Consumers must also choose where they will buy the product. Sometimes, consumers will decide *where* they will buy before they determine *what* they will buy. One consumer says to another, "I'm going to the store; what do we need?" The other replies, "Where are you going?" Here, the decision of what product to buy hinges on where you are shopping. In fact, one trend that researchers have noticed is that consumers have gradually become less brand-loyal and more store-loyal. This means that consumers tend to have favorite stores that they visit regularly and first consider the products that are carried by those stores. Of course, retail marketers encourage this behavior by offering club memberships and reward points. Marketing managers realize that much of the power in the marketing channel has moved from manufacturer to retailer.

Several factors influence the choice of retail outlet, including objective and subjective criteria such as product variety, store image, location, service, and product quality.[33] Location is particularly important, as is store image. Consumers still prefer to shop in shopping malls, although many cities have successfully implemented "shop downtown" or "Main Street" campaigns.

ONLINE RETAIL SELECTION

The Internet has also become the channel of choice for many consumers. And consumers continue to shop online by using mobile devices like smartphones and tablets. Estimates are that online sales in the United States alone will top $500 billion by 2020.[34]

Consumers clearly enjoy the convenience and selection that come from online shopping. In the United States, this is most evident during "Black Friday" and "Cyber Monday" each year. In 2015, bricks-and-mortar sales during these events were down, while online sales grew to approximately $11 billion.[35]

Of course, Amazon is the online retailing giant, but new competitors such as Jet.com have emerged. Convenience plays a big role in online retail selection, but other factors such as the availability of variety and product information, customer service, security, and navigational ease also play important roles. Amazon obviously excels at each of these criteria.

Many large retailers have both a physical presence (a bricks-and-mortar store) and an online presence.

Maglara/Shutterstock.com

Best Buy is a good example of a store that has successful physical and online presence. What is even more interesting is a gradual move from "click to brick." That is, online retailers are beginning to build physical stores. For example, Amazon opened a new bricks-and- mortar bookstore in Seattle in late 2015. The company has used its knowledge to move into the physical retail business, and has continued this push into 2017, with moves into the convenience grocery store market.[36]

As you can tell, evaluating alternatives and making final purchase decisions are part of an involved process. Our next chapter will consider the processes that occur after a choice has been made.

STUDY TOOLS 13

LOCATED AT BACK OF THE TEXTBOOK

☐ Tear out Chapter Review Card

LOCATED AT WWW.CENGAGE.COM/LOGIN

☐ Review Key Term flashcards and create your own cards

☐ Track your knowledge and understanding of key concepts in consumer behavior

☐ Complete practice quizzes to prepare for tests

☐ Complete interactive content within CB Online

☐ Review the Chapter Highlight boxes for CB Online

CASE 4-1

Smartphones, Tablets, Laptops, and PCs: What's the World Coming To?

Written by Eric G. Harris, Pittsburg State University

2011 was a very significant year in the computer world. It was during 2011 that smartphones officially outsold personal computers (PCs) for the first time ever. For a society that is always "on the go," the PC and laptop can stay at home. Smartphones and tablets are changing both the consumer and business worlds, and they are greatly impacting the global economy.

The numbers are truly astonishing. In the fourth quarter alone, 158 million smartphones were shipped, as compared to a total of 120 million PCs, tablets, netbooks, and laptops combined![1] The total shipments of smartphones totaled 488 million in 2011, which was an increase of over 60% from 2010.[2] These numbers indicate that smartphones are currently the hot consumer electronic product. Even though smartphones are hot, tablets are gaining ground very quickly. Their sales grew 274% in 2011 (63 million total units shipped for the year).[3] To put these growth rates into perspective, desktops and laptops grew only 2% and 7%, respectively, while netbook sales declined 25%. The proliferation of mobile devices, including laptops, is a clear indication that we truly live in a mobile society and that mobile technology is the wave of the future.

So what is driving the demand for these devices? As smartphones and tablets have quickly gained consumer acceptance, the products are approaching the point where they've gained mass-market appeal, analysts say. They are no longer considered a niche market for business people or the affluent. Consumers from all demographic groups seek mobile access to the Internet. And the popularity of social media and smartphone apps continues to grow in popularity for most all consumer groups at the same time that consumers realize that they don't have to be home to enjoy their availability. What this means is that consumers are no longer content with just surfing the Web; they now consider mobile

technologies as essential parts of their social lives. It seems that maintaining a presence in cyberspace all but requires mobile technologies today. More consumers access social media sites by mobile technologies than through desktop computers.

Which consumer need do mobile devices fill? Smartphones and tablets deliver both utilitarian and hedonic value. For many business people, smartphones and tablets have become an essential part of everyday work life. Many business travelers prefer the smaller size of smartphones and tablets to the larger, more bulky, laptops.[4] Business travelers can perform many work-related duties on smartphones, from checking email to checking warehouse inventories. And many nonusers report the intention to adopt them if manufacturers can improve applications, power, and projection availabilities. Cloud technologies also make it more reasonable for the business traveler to access vital company information from the cloud. These are very rational reasons to use smartphones or tablets.

The average consumer also tends to prefer the smartphone and tablet to laptops when they are traveling. And, of course, they're fun to use! Most consumers are familiar with all of the apps that are available. Consumers also enjoy having a music player, camera, Internet connectivity, and games at their fingertips. For many consumers, social media connectivity also provides hedonic value. Many consumers simply enjoy the ability to keep up on sites such as Facebook, Twitter, and Instagram through their smartphones or tablets while they are on the go.

What attributes and benefits do consumers seek with mobile devices? Attributes such as screen size, battery life, and storage capability are important. For some consumers, computing power is a consideration. App availability is also very important for most consumers. Of course, the reputation of the manufacturer and the warranty are important as well. The physical design of the products is also important, as are their accessories such as carrying cases and external keyboards.

So what has happened with the laptop? Laptop sales, as previously mentioned, have grown but they haven't kept up with smartphone or tablet sales growth. That doesn't mean that there aren't hardcore laptop fans out there. In fact, many consumers insist on the laptop.

CASES

Laptop fans tend to lament the small size of the smart-phone and the lack of computing power of the tablet.[5] In response, smartphone marketers have developed a number of projection techniques for screens and keyboards, along with motion technologies such as Microsoft Kinect technologies for smartphones. Tablet manufacturers are researching ways to make their products more powerful. Will tablets overtake the laptop in the business world? At a growth rate of over 200% in the last year, this appears likely. Most consumers prefer to type on a regular keyboard versus a tablet keyboard (even when external keyboards are available for many tablets).[6] But tablets tend to be more portable than laptops. Also, tablets are less intrusive in business meetings because they fit nicely on a desk without having to extend a viewing screen abruptly. They also tend to have much better battery life as compared to the battery life of the average laptop. Of course, it takes more power to handle the computing strength of the laptop.

For many consumers, the debate is not really about tablets versus laptops, but rather about tablets versus smartphones. It may be that smartphone sales will eventually fall victim to tablets and that it won't be laptops or even PCs that disappear. Some analysts already predict this, suggesting that the most dramatic decrease in sales will soon be found with smartphones. Given that most consumers use smartphones for data capabilities, they really don't have many advantages over tablets other than simply having the telephone feature.[7] The key question appears to be what the optimal size should be. But are tablets better than smartphones simply because of their size? One interesting thing to note is that smartphones are getting bigger while tablets are getting smaller. However, this doesn't address the issue of telephone capability. What if you could speak through a tablet like you can through a smartphone? Many tablets already include technologies such as FaceTime and Skype. As such, telephone capabilities might not be that big of an issue.

In 2011, it looked possible that smartphones would begin to decline in 2012 or shortly thereafter. If laptops or PCs do not disappear, then the growth in tablets will most likely come at the expense of smartphones. Will smartphones, which have enjoyed record sales, soon be in decline? Initial estimates in 2016 suggests this just may be the case.

QUESTIONS

1 What type of decision-making approach do most consumers use when deciding between smartphones, tablets, laptops, or desktop computers?

2 What factors influence the amount of search that most consumers will exert when buying a smartphone or a tablet?

3 How does superordinate and subordinate categorization apply to this case from a consumer's perspective?

4 What factors do consumers consider when making judgments about smartphones?

5 What type of decision rule would a consumer most likely use when selecting between smartphone brands? How could they use such a rule?

CASE 4-2

New Balance, Out of Step?

Written by Kristen Regine, Johnson & Wales University

New Balance (NB) is a privately held corporation based out of Brighton, MA, selling men's and women's athletic shoes and apparel for running, hiking, tennis, cross-training, golf, and fitness. The company operates in 120 countries worldwide. There are 157 licensed New Balance stores in North America; 140 are independently owned and operated.[1] This number does not include its three corporate stores located in Dedham, MA. The experience stores are in the Flatiron district in New York and the Pentagon in Washington, DC. The company expects to open another twelve stores over the next year.[2]

Some of their top competitors include Nike, K-Swiss, Saucony, Adidas, and Fila USA. The NB claim is substance over style; unlike their competitors, they do not promote their products with celebrity endorsements. They have developed an "endorsed by no one" philosophy. When compared to their competitors, this might be viewed as a weakness, since brands such as Nike, Adidas, and Reebok have become well-established based on the premise of using celebrities as endorsers to build brand awareness.

Their focus in the marketplace is on technology and innovation, with a wide product portfolio. In 2011, the company's products NBX and WW86 were named as "Best Fitness Buys" by *Health* magazine, and the MR/WR890 and MR/WR1080 shoes were selected as the "Best Neutral Shoe" by *Women's Running* and *Running Network* magazines. In such a competitive market, New Balance expects 15% growth this year, and for the first time since 2004 expects double-digit growth globally.[3]

NEW BALANCE BRAND GOALS[4]

▶ Solidify top placement within the athletic shoe market and among the key target market/core consumers with research, development, and strategic tactics that showcase NB as an innovator/cutting-edge brand in the athletic shoe category.

▶ Reinforce the brand anthem of "Make Excellent Happen" by raising awareness to the fact that NB is invested in the consumer's performance as an athlete, comfort as an athlete, and investment in fashion as a man or woman. The idea is to market to all the needs and wants of the consumer athlete: fashion/form/function/fun.

▶ Demonstrate a dedication to "American-made"/"made in the USA" products. (This is a critical attribute that NB is proud of and promotes with enthusiasm.)

▶ Expand upon the brand legacy of being a runners' shoe company and grow into a holistic brand that is a leader in the athletic show category and serves not just the runner, but the athlete.

▶ Promote a fashion-forward, functional perception among consumers that builds upon the trusted New Balance product legacy.

Judy Piktelis, the general market manager from New Balance, explained that their new experience store opened in the Flatiron district due to its historic roots in New York City, to unprecedented numbers. The 4000-square-foot Flatiron store opened in August 2011. Consumers are able to see their shoes completed in an hour. "I think customers expect a lot more in their shopping experience," said Tracy Knauer, New Balance's head of marketing for retail. There's a running track, a shoemaker from Maine in a glass booth assembling shoes, and an over-the-top shopping experience. In New

York, a creative tactic was utilized to drive traffic into the store: customization of the 875 shoe.[5] Shoppers were even able to purchase shoes from the glass booth with an "assembled in New York" tote bag. The shoe was a sellout. This is not the first experience store for New Balance. The others are located in Beijing, Hong Kong, and Australia.[6]

However, in New Balance's backyard and home market the company-owned store in Dedham, MA, a suburb located south of Boston,[7] is showing a slowdown in sales. Dedham's demographics are mainly families (56%). Eighty percent of families own their own homes, the median age is 39 years, and the largest age group is 35–44 years old with an average household income of $80,000 per year, which is substantially higher than the national average of $51,914.[8] Legacy Place was a prime target to develop a new retail center in 2009. The open-air shopping center covers 675,000 square feet, featuring over 60 retail shops, restaurants, and entertainment such as a movie theater and bowling alley.[9]

However, the NB store in Legacy Place is problematic. There is a lot of competition: City Sports, Urban Outfitters, and Lululemon Athletica. One destination in particular was always jam-packed; King's Bowling Alley.[10]

The Dedham New Balance store decided to start with a grassroots marketing program, since discounting was a tactic employed only twice a year for friends and family days. Their grassroots campaign included partnering with Kings Bowling Alley. Kings offers its patrons a trivia night, karaoke nights, all-you-can-bowl nights for $10, live music, bowling leagues, and industry nights.[11] New Balance posted information in the restrooms and offered employees of Kings a discount. Additionally, the marketing program included the formation of a walking club for the outdoor shopping plaza, which was sponsored by Whole Foods.

The one tactic that did require a small budget was to partner with the local Massachusetts Red Cross mobile unit; blood donors received a gift from New Balance.[12] Recently, the company struck a deal with the Boston Red Sox to become the official apparel and footwear sponsor of the team.[13] Could the Legacy Place store feature a Boston sports connection to get foot traffic moving their way? Will their grassroots marketing program develop a loyal customer base? What type of experience can Legacy Place create for its customers?

CASES

1 Explain the consumer decision-making process when purchasing a new pair of sneakers.

2 What is the consumer's motivation for wanting to have the customized pair of 875 New Balance shoes? Explain.

3 Should New Balance consider a specialty sneaker for the Boston market? If so, what do you envision?

4 What is the effect of the New Balance brand on the consumers' judgment to buy or not to buy?

5 Discuss the atmospherics of the two shopping areas, Legacy Place in Dedham, MA, and the Flatiron district in New York City.

6 Visit three stores selling running shoes. Describe how the atmospherics differ across the stores. Why do these differences exist?

CASE 4-3

Consumer Confidence: Preparation Pays Off

Written by Mohan Menon, University of South Alabama

It's time to make a decision on a new car. Maya has been preparing for the moment when she will finally buy her own new car for the first time in her life, but she has waited to break the news to her family until closer to graduation. She now feels that she has done her homework and is ready to discuss her choices with her family before making the purchase.

It all started about a year ago, when she was in the last year of medical school. Maya had been thinking about her residency in a city hospital, one that is well-known for her specialty, neuroradiology. Along with moving away from home and fitting into the hospital culture, Maya would have to buy a car. Until now, she has been driving an older model Prius that was given to her by her dad, who bought it new. She likes the car, but wants to upgrade to a new car when she starts her residency. She has never had a new car and believes that the changes that will take place in her life over the next year will warrant one.

She feels confident in her ability to select a suitable new car. Having grown up in a family that subscribed

to *Consumer Reports* ever since she can remember, she seems well-informed about many products, including automobiles. Her parents have always been careful shoppers. They taught her and her older brother how to save money, spend less, and not to give in to impulses. Moreover, her dad and brother are knowledgeable about cars. Her brother, who has just started his private practice, will be of tremendous help in the process. With his extensive toy car collection from childhood, he has been a car enthusiast and is highly knowledgeable about automobiles.

However, her plan has been to go through the car-buying process with as minimal outside help as possible. Maya has done some serious research on cars she is considering. She has a set of basic criteria, such as miles per gallon (MPG) of 40 or more, interior (leather only), body style (4-door), no built-in GPS-Nav system, iPhone/iPad and Bluetooth connectivity, ample trunk space, low maintenance, minimum 4-star safety rating, ABS system, electronic displays on the dashboard, smooth handling and ride, manual transmission, and so on. Because she is likely to move to a northern city, having heated seats are preferable but not a must. She has also heard of other features such as independent suspension and all-wheel-drive options, but is not quite sure how they would benefit her. At the same time, there are options and features that Maya does not care for: acceleration/performance, V-6 engine, off-road ability, extended warranty, towing capacity, sun or moon roof, and so on. The realizes that she will never find her ideal car and that she will have to compromise on a few items.

Even though price is not likely to be a major factor in her decision, she had an upper limit of $35,000 for her car. Maya is not very familiar with financing options available to her, and leaving the nest for the very first time, she is aware that she will have to buy her own car insurance. Despite her accident-free record, she was concerned about her premiums. Because financing and insurance are the two areas that Maya is most unfamiliar with, she knows she will need to rely on her family to explain them to her.

Maya is anxious about starting out on her own in a new city, yet with regard to buying her own car for the very first time, she feels confident. She has had the luxury of time, since she has delayed buying the car until after her graduation but before leaving for the residency. She has gathered most of her information from magazines and various websites. She has watched very little TV and thus paid scant attention to the car ads. She is more interested in non-biased sources of car information. Even though she has steered family conversations to include cars, she has not informed them of her intent to buy a new car before her residency begins. She has also brought up the topic subtly with her friends, who have given her a variety of opinions on various makes and models. Her plan has been to first gather information from trustworthy sources, mull over it, and possibly narrow down her options before seeking some assistance from her family.

She has positive impressions of the Prius she has been driving, and she knows she wants an environmentally friendly vehicle. Given the number of cars that fit the description, she knows she has a long road ahead. But her informal discussions with family and friends have helped.

Maya considers herself to be a very logical person and thus is more interested in the functional aspects of the car. The look and feel of the car are important to her, but they are secondary in nature. Her color choices are basic: silver or black. Yet one aspect of research she has avoided up to this point is visiting local dealerships. Having gone car shopping with her family in the past, she is realistic about her own experience. For instance, she is not comfortable negotiating prices or making instant decisions about certain aspects of the purchase. She plans to take her dad or brother along when visiting dealerships.

Now that she has had a chance to review the information she has gathered, she feels confident about four

specific models: Toyota Prius V, Hyundai Sonata Hybrid, Ford Fiesta Hybrid, and Volkswagen TDI Diesel. Brands she has rejected for one reason or the other include Chevy Volt, Nissan Leaf, Toyota Camry Hybrid, and Honda Civic Hybrid. Having been involved in her family's car buying decisions in the past, she knows that she has to also order *Consumer Reports'* new car pricing reports before visiting car dealerships. Also, given how selective her dad and brother can be about cars, she wants to narrow down her choices before seeking specific brand advice from them. She is sure that they will approve of her initial choices.

It's now a few days after the graduation ceremony. Maya and her family are preparing for her move to New York-Presbyterian Hospital for her residency. It's finally time to make a decision and buy that new car.

QUESTIONS

1 Based on the various perspectives of consumer decision making, what type of a shopper is Maya and why?

2 Apply the consumer decision-making process stages to Maya's actions as a consumer, or describe Maya's actions within the framework of the consumer decision-making process.

3 Is Maya utilizing the affect-based or attribute-based evaluation process? Justify your answer.

4 Based on the information provided in the case, what are the determinants of the evaluative criteria that the customer is using? Explain each in detail.

5 In your opinion, which decision rule (compensatory or noncompensatory) is Maya utilizing in her car-buying process?

PART 5

14 | Consumption to Satisfaction

LEARNING OBJECTIVES

After studying this chapter, the student should be able to:

14-1 Know the connections among consumption, value, and satisfaction.

14-2 Discuss the relative importance of satisfaction and value in marketing and consumer behavior.

14-3 Understand how emotions other than satisfaction can affect post-consumption behavior.

14-4 Use expectancy disconfirmation, equity, and attribution theory approaches to explain consumers' post-consumption reactions.

14-5 Avoid problems associated with typical satisfaction measures.

14-6 Describe ways that consumers dispose of products.

michaeljung./Shutterstock.com

Remember to visit PAGE 303 for additional STUDY TOOLS

INTRODUCTION

For several reasons, one might think that CB ends after a consumer buys something. However, as the CVF illustrates, a host of other things go on after exchange and consumption. This chapter focuses on what happens after purchase and consumption. This is a critical stage for marketers, because among those things is the decision whether or not to do business again with the marketers who helped create the value.

 ## 14-1 CONSUMPTION, VALUE, AND SATISFACTION

Consumption is at the heart of all consumer behavior. Obviously, a consumer *consumes*. In fact, one might say that all human activity focuses on some form of consumption. Even when we work, we consume time so that we can earn money to consume other things. In the consumption process, consumers use the product, service, or experience that they selected through the consumer decision-making process. Ultimately, consumers use or experience products and receive value in return.

14-1a Consumption Leads to Value

The important role of consumption becomes apparent when one considers that without consumption, there is no value. Consumers derive value from consumption, and marketers derive value from continued exchange.[1] Earlier, we defined consumption as the process that converts time, goods, ideas, or services into value for consumers. Consumption experiences possess a potential to produce utilitarian and/or hedonic value. In this way, consumption experiences are like physical objects that contain potential energy. If one places a rock into a sling shot and pulls back the band, the rock contains unrealized energy. As long as the band is held tight, nothing happens; release the band, and the rock now has energy as it flies through

Exhibit 14.1

Basic Consumption Process

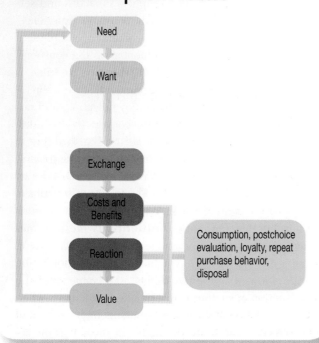

the air. **Potential value** represents the benefits not yet realized from service because consumption has yet to take place. A bottle of Dasani water only has the potential to quench thirst until it is consumed. Value thus comes from use or experience, which unleashes the value potential. Sometimes, various factors interfere with the full realization of potential value. The basic consumption process that is at the heart of the CVF is shown again in Exhibit 14.1.

14-1b Consumption and Product Classification

Many issues go along with the consumption of goods, services, and experiences. Important differences exist for the consumption of durable and nondurable goods. **Durable goods** are typically relatively expensive goods consumed over a long time period. Dishwashers, furniture, automobiles, and many electronics like personal computers represent durable goods. Durable

> **potential value** benefits not yet realized from a service because they have yet to be consumed
>
> **durable goods** goods that are typically expensive and usually consumed over a long period of time

Coke Life appeals to not just diet-conscious but health-conscious consumers.

much smaller than today—holding a mere 6½ ounces. Pepsi's selling point was a 10-ounce bottle at the same price. Over time, the average bottle size grew to the point where consumers often consume 20-ounce or even 1-liter bottles a number of times per day. The soft drink industry has slowly facilitated an increase in the average soft drink serving size. Within the last few years though, carbonated soft drink sales have shown slowed consumption as consumers turn to noncarbonated alternatives, energy drinks, and alternatives perceived as more healthy, including water. In response, Coca-Cola rolled out a new product, Coke Life. Coke Life, in its smart green can, contains about half the sugar of a typical Coke and shuns sweeteners typically used in diet soft drinks. The hope is to get health-conscious consumers to rediscover "good old" Coke.

Services and experiences are usually classified as nondurable by default. However, some services are more clearly consumed over extended periods. For example, we consume insurance daily even though consumers may pay premiums only periodically. Experiences are complete when consumption stops. However, marketers of these products encourage repeat consumption of their products by offering season tickets, club memberships, and special invitations to events. By encouraging increased consumption, these marketers are able to foster customer relationships.

14-1c Situations and Consumer Reactions

As discussed previously, consumption situations and settings have a significant impact on the consumer experience. The temporal factors, antecedent conditions, and physical environment are particularly influential on the consumption experience. How, what, and when we consume is largely dependent upon the environment that we are in.

For example, football fans enjoy tailgating, and numerous products are essential to convert the occasion into value. Beer, burgers, and brats are standard fare at typical midwestern tailgates. In Louisiana, jambalaya, gumbo, gator tail, and perhaps even a Cajun band may accompany the beer. The products become artifacts in part of a tailgating ritual. Without them, the experience is less than authentic. **Authenticity** means something (goods, services, people, experiences, etc.) is real, genuine, unique, and has a history or tradition.[2] The consumption of authentic things adds value over the consumption of synthetic experiences, particularly when the consumption environment contains high degrees of symbolism or consumers are highly involved in some activity. The very same products, such as fried gator tail,

goods that do not perform well cause consumers major problems. **Nondurable goods** are typically inexpensive and consumed quickly. Soft drinks, pencils, and Kleenex are nondurable goods. Nondurable goods that do not perform well do not present major problems for consumers.

For nondurable goods especially, marketers try to increase consumption frequency as much as possible. **Consumption frequency** refers to the number of times a product or service is consumed in a given time period. Credit card companies have made it easier and easier for consumers to use their cards on routine shopping trips. Consumers today, though, routinely use cards for all types of purchases. The card number can even be stored for ready use online via PayPal, iTunes, or Google Checkout.

Marketers also attempt to increase the amount of product consumed per occasion. For example, soft drink marketers gradually increased the average size of soft drinks over time. Many students may be surprised to find out that the traditional Coke bottle was

nondurable goods goods that are typically inexpensive and usually consumed quickly

consumption frequency number of times a product or service is consumed in a given period of time

authenticity the degree to which an object, person, or experience seems real, genuine, unique, and part of history or tradition

YOU DON'T ALWAYS GET WHAT YOU PAY FOR

The most basic element of authenticity is that a product really is what it is labeled to be. Thinking about a Rolex one day? For every real Rolex watch there are multiple counterfeits, and some of them make their way into legitimate jewelry stores. Fake branded products are a problem in all types of industries. In the wine business, among the most stolen products in a winery are labels. Sometimes, relatively inexpensive pinot noir is relabeled as Romanée St. Vivant or Richebourg—some of the most expensive wines in the world. The fakes have been sold at auction as authentic or offered for sale to restaurants. On a larger scale, Italian police uncovered bottles of Moet & Chandon Champagne, with a retail value of about $50 a bottle, which were actually cheap sparkling wine from the Prosecco region. One of the clues is that the fake bottles did not contain individual identification numbers, a measure taken by many wine producers to make fakes easier to detect. The counterfeiters were sending the fake products to market areas in northern Europe where they believed consumers would not detect the difference. Make sure you get what you pay for!

ERIC FEFERBERG/Getty Images

Source: Frank, M. (2016), "Italian Police Uncover Counterfeit Champagne Scheme," Wine Spectator, (2/2), http://www.winespectator.com/webfeature/show/id/52684, accessed June 27, 2016.

offer less value when they are not contributing to an authentic consumer experience.

The environment plays a large role in influencing consumption and consumer satisfaction. Although a hot dog might not be considered gourmet dining, when it's a Chicago hot dog, it's more than just a hot dog! The ingredients that make a Chicago hot dog are the bun, a Vienna wiener, mustard, onion, pickle, tomato, peppers, and celery salt. And of course it really should come from a street-side cart to be completely authentic.

Authenticity is not always easy to detect. Etsy.com, a huge online retailer of low-priced jewelry, contains many pages from merchants openly selling fake designer jewelry. The Internet—and the streets of major cities around the world—are also replete with merchants openly offering fake Rolexes. Of course, these fake products benefit from the real brands that they mimic. But luxury brands need to take steps to protect their image from counterfeits, particularly those that are sold as authentic.

14-1d Consumption, Meaning, and Transference

Consumers' lives are very much intertwined with consumption. Value depends on a process called **meaning transference**. From a utilitarian standpoint, the meaning of consumption is straightforward. A consumer downloads an app to do online banking. That's easy. What is not as straightforward is the hedonic component of consumption.

Meaning transference begins with culture. Value is affected largely by the meaning of goods, services, and experiences. Marketers work to transfer important cultural ideals or values into products via advertising and the word of mouth that occurs between consumers. For instance, consider what happens when a brand becomes closely associated with a celebrity endorser and that endorser ends up committing a crime or publicly performing some embarrassing behavior. One of the dangers of celebrity endorsement is that the meaning of celebrity behavior is transferred to the brand.[3] Consider also how meaning might transfer from a branded product to the celebrity. For example, Taylor Swift is an endorser for Diet Coke. What meaning transference might occur as a result?

14-1e Consumption Outcomes and Emotion

Consumers choose products, services, and experiences that they believe will deliver value by addressing their wants and needs.

> **meaning transference**
> process through which cultural meaning is transferred to a product and onto the consumer

Exhibit 14.2

Emotion Affects Consumption and Consumption Outcomes

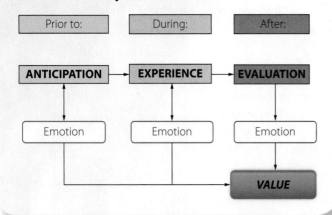

experience will be like based on cognitions that give the concept meaning (i.e., schema), the meaning is either realized or not during a visit to a French restaurant, and the evaluation of that experience in turn creates emotion and adjustments to meaning. The shopping experience provides value directly when consumers search through alternatives that are personally interesting.[6] Search isn't a task so much as an experience when the consumer enjoys the time spent with the activity. The concept of value extracted from experience matches with hedonic value more than utilitarian.

> **The concept of value extracted from experience matches with hedonic value more than utilitarian.**

They anticipate good outcomes from their choices or else they would have made a different choice. Emotions influence CB before, during, and after consumption. Emotions play a role prior to exchange as expectations manifest emotions like anxiety, apprehension, or fear. Imagine the emotions accompanying a student just prior to going off to university for the first time. Emotions taking place during a consumption experience affect value directly. Finally, emotions naturally result from consumer appraisals of consumption outcomes. Thus, emotions are involved in all phases of consumption and they influence value both directly and indirectly, as illustrated in Exhibit 14.2.

In this portion of the CVF, and in this chapter, we stress how consumer emotions influence consumption outcomes. Consumption, value, and satisfaction are tied closely together. Not surprisingly, consumers tend to be more satisfied with exchanges they find valuable, as value is at the heart of marketing transactions. Value perceptions, therefore, directly influence consumer satisfaction.[4] However, the link between value and satisfaction is nowhere near perfect, as will be seen later.

14-1f Value in Experience

Often, marketing experts acknowledge that products alone cannot produce value. Rather, the value comes from use of the service provided by the product, thus the idea of value in use.[5] This concept fits particularly well with utilitarian value.

Use is not always straightforward. Consumers, for example, anticipate what an authentic French restaurant

14-2 VALUE AND SATISFACTION

Many companies try hard to satisfy customers. However, is satisfaction *the* key outcome variable for marketers and consumers? Consider Exhibit 14.3. This chart plots scores for major retailers from the ACSI, which is the American Consumer Satisfaction Index.[7] This index provides satisfaction scores for many major companies across many industries and even some governmental organizations.

Notice that Wegmanns (a supermarket chain with stores along the U.S. mideastern Atlantic coast) has the highest customer satisfaction rating in the latest period, with Trader Joe's, Publix, and Nordstrom also scoring relatively high. JCPenney, Dillard's, Target, Kroger, and Whole Foods all have higher satisfaction ratings than Walmart. Walmart scores have generally declined in recent years. What does this mean? How many retailers in recent history enjoyed more success than Walmart? Yet, Walmart is hardly the satisfaction leader. In fact, Walmart's satisfaction ratings are the lowest of all retailers listed, according to the ACSI. What can explain this? The answer lies in value. Even if Walmart does not provide high customer satisfaction, it does provide value leadership, particularly the perception that high utilitarian value results from shopping there. Thus, the track record says Walmart should continue to prioritize value over satisfaction.

Exhibit 14.3

U.S. Retail Consumer Satisfaction Scores

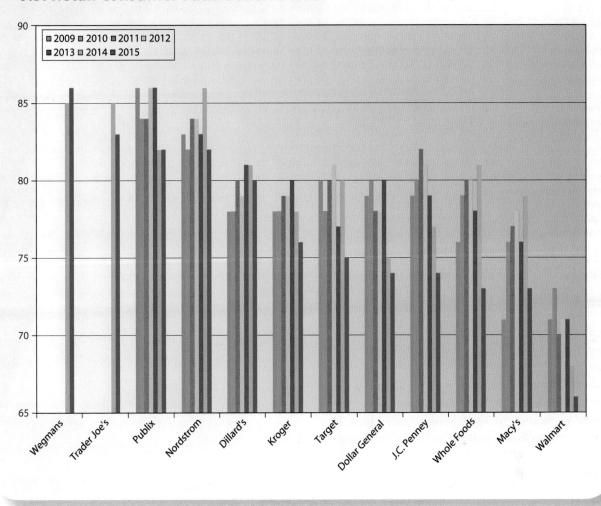

Indications are that Walmart executives have learned what drives customers to Walmart. Walmart more recently is de-emphasizing growth in supercenters (hypermart-style stores) and concentrating growth in neighborhood markets. These markets are intended to be smaller, more conveniently located near population centers, and more shopper-friendly. While these steps may help create a more rewarding shopping environment, the mass merchandising mindset emphasizing large assortments and low prices, and getting as much merchandise onto the sales floor as possible, may detract from a pleasant shopping experience. Managers acknowledge that initiatives that increase customer satisfaction do not always improve **top-line performance**, a business term referring to sales growth. Top-line referring to sales being reported at the top of earnings statements.

The importance of value in the consumption experience cannot be overstated. In fact, the reason a firm exists at all is to create value.[8] Value and satisfaction relate to one another to some degree, but value is the heart of CB and is what consumers seek from consumption experiences.[9] If marketers ever face the decision of providing value or satisfaction, value should be prioritized because, as illustrated by the ACSI, firms can do well even when they do not enjoy the highest industry satisfaction scores, but the firm that does not provide value in some form

top-line performance
a business term referring to sales growth (sales being at the top of an earnings statement)

Limited-Service Restaurants

	Base-line	95	96	97	98	99	00	01	02	03	04	05	06	07	08	09	10	11	12	13	14	15	16	Previous Year % Change	First Year % Change
Chick-fil-A	NM	NM	NM	NM	NM	NM	NM	NM	NM	NM	NM**	NM	NM	NM	NM	NM	NM	NM	NM	NM	NM	86	87	1.2	1.2
Papa John's	NM	NM	NM	NM	NM	76	77	78	76	76	NM**	78	79	77	76	75	80	79	83	82	82	78	82	5.1	7.9
All Others	73	74	75	73	74	74	72	73	74	75	NM**	78	80	79	80	83	76	81	82	82	84	81	81	0.0	11.0
Little Caesars	72	69	69	73	71	NM	69	70	74	75	NM**	74	77	75	75	75	78	80	82	82	80	74	81	9.5	12.5
Panera Bread	NM	NM	NM	NM	NM	NM	NM	NM	NM	NM	NM**	NM	NM	NM	NM	NM	NM	NM	NM	NM	NM	80	81	1.3	1.3
Dunkin' Donuts	NM	NM	NM	NM	NM	NM	NM	NM	NM	NM	NM**	NM	NM	NM	NM	NM	NM	NM	79	80	75	78	80	2.6	1.3
Subway	NM	NM	NM	NM	NM	NM	NM	NM	NM	NM	NM**	NM	NM	NM	NM	NM	NM	NM	82	83	78	77	80	3.9	−2.4
Arby's	NM	NM	NM	NM	NM	NM	NM	NM	NM	NM	NM**	NM	NM	NM	NM	NM	NM	NM	NM	NM	NM	74	80	8.1	8.1
Limited-Service Restaurants	69	70	66	68	69	69	70	71	71	74	NM**	76	77	77	78	78	75	79	80	80	80	77	79	2.6	14.5
Chipotle Mexican Grill	NM	NM	NM	NM	NM	NM	NM	NM	NM	NM	NM**	NM	NM	NM	NM	NM	NM	NM	NM	NM	NM	83	78	−6.0	−6.0
KFC (Yum! Brands)	67	68	69	67	64	64	65	63	69	71	NM**	69	70	71	70	69	75	75	75	81	74	73	78	6.8	16.4
Domino's	67	70	68	68	70	67	69	73	75	75	NM**	71	75	75	75	77	77	77	77	81	80	75	78	4.0	16.4
Pizza Hut (Yum! Brands)	69	66	63	71	71	68	70	71	70	75	NM**	71	76	72	76	74	78	81	78	80	82	78	77	−1.3	11.6
Wendy's	72	73	71	69	73	71	70	72	74	74	NM**	75	76	78	73	76	77	77	78	79	78	73	76	4.1	5.6
Burger King	66	65	67	68	64	66	67	65	68	68	NM**	71	70	69	71	69	74	75	75	76	76	72	76	5.6	15.2
Taco Bell (Yum! Brands)	66	66	66	67	64	64	63	66	67	68	NM**	72	70	69	70	73	74	76	77	74	72	72	75	4.2	13.6
Starbucks	NM	NM	NM	NM	NM	NM	NM	NM	NM	NM	NM**	NM	77	78	77	76	78	80	76	80	76	74	75	1.4	−2.6
Jack in the Box	NM	NM	NM	NM	NM	NM	NM	NM	NM	NM	NM**	NM	NM	NM	NM	NM	NM	NM	NM	NM	NM	72	74	2.8	2.8
McDonald's	63	63	60	60	61	61	59	62	61	64	NM**	62	63	64	69	70	67	72	73	73	71	67	69	3.0	9.5

The ACSI for fast-food restaurants. How do success and satisfaction relate?

can't succeed for long.[10] Walmart annual sales growth for 2016 is around −0.5%, whereas Trader Joe's, now one of America's favorite shopping experiences, has experienced double-digit growth for much of the 2000s. Walmart's attempts to counter competition[11] through smaller stores rather than supercenters, enhanced online shopping, and the introduction of standalone stores that sell wine, beer, and spirits[12] show that Walmart is trying to increase value through a more personalized service touch.

14-2a What Is Consumer Satisfaction?

Customer satisfaction receives a lot of attention from consumer researchers and marketing managers. However, different people may define satisfaction differently and this causes confusion over the exact meaning. As a result, satisfaction is at times confused with numerous closely related concepts like quality, loyalty, and cognitive dissonance. However, satisfaction is distinct from these concepts.

consumer satisfaction
mild, positive emotion resulting from a favorable appraisal of a consumption outcome

Consumer satisfaction is a mild, positive emotional state resulting from a favorable appraisal of a consumption outcome. Several points distinguish consumer satisfaction from other important consumer behavior concepts:

1. Consumer satisfaction is a *post-consumption* phenomenon because it is a reaction to an outcome.

2. Like other emotions, satisfaction results from a cognitive appraisal. Some refer to this appraisal as the satisfaction judgment; however, the appraisal and the emotional reaction are distinct events.

3. Satisfaction as an emotion is relatively mild and does not create strong behavioral motivations.

Other key consumer variables like expectations, quality, or attitude are generally more relevant in explaining pre-consumption or even pre-purchase phenomena.[13] Nevertheless, managers consider consumer satisfaction important because they believe consumers' word of mouth, repeat purchases, and ultimately, consumer loyalty correlate with reported customer satisfaction. These relationships are discussed in detail in the next chapter. As we

YOU DID IT? NO, I DID IT!

As alluded to earlier, CB recognizes that consumer experiences are co-created. That is, the consumer and the service provider play a role in shaping the value extracted. The understanding of co-creation, though, complicates our understanding of consumer satisfaction. Consider a consumer who spends at least 15 minutes a day taking care of their teeth by flossing, brushing multiple times, cleaning the tongue, etc. Similarly, think of a vacationer who researches a destination and carefully plans activities. What happens when things turn out great? Paradoxically, although consumers realize greater value (in these cases, healthier teeth or a great holiday), they may actually report lower satisfaction with the service provider than a consumer who put less effort into the experience! One explanation is that the consumer naturally takes credit for the good outcome.

Sources: Grissemann, U.S., and N.E. Stockburger-Sauer (2012), "Customer Co-Creation of Travel Services: The Role of Company Support and Customer Satisfaction with the Co-Creation Performance," *Tourism Management*, 33, 1483–1492; Navarro, S., C. Linares, and D. Garzon (2016), "Exploring the Relationship between Co-Creation and Satisfaction Using QCA," *Journal of Business Research*, 69, 1336–1339.

dachazworks/Shutterstock.com

will see, many managers tend to overstate the positive benefits of customer satisfaction relative to other outcomes.[14]

14-2b What Is Consumer Dissatisfaction?

Recall from the material on consumer information processing (CIP) that consumers react quite differently when responding to losses than when responding to gains. Additionally, some debate exists over whether or not low satisfaction necessarily means a consumer has high dissatisfaction. For reasons like these, consumer behavior theory distinguishes consumer dissatisfaction from consumer satisfaction. Therefore, **consumer dissatisfaction** can be defined as a mild, negative affective reaction resulting from an unfavorable appraisal of a consumption outcome.[15] Even though conceptually dissatisfaction is an opposite concept to satisfaction, the fact that consumers react differently to negative contexts means that dissatisfaction will explain behaviors that satisfaction cannot.

Phoenixns/Shutterstock.com

14-3 OTHER POST-CONSUMPTION REACTIONS

Although people often use *satisfaction* as a colloquialism for everything that happens after a consumer buys something, many other things, including other emotions, may also occur post consumption. Among the other important post-consumption reactions that can be overlooked are specific emotions, including delight, disgust, surprise, exhilaration, and even anger. These particular emotions are often much more strongly linked to behavior, because although they are also emotional reactions to appraisals, they are often much stronger.

An angry consumer exhibits much more noticeable and persistent behavior than does a consumer with low satisfaction. The

> **consumer dissatisfaction**
> mild, negative affective reaction resulting from an unfavorable appraisal of a consumption outcome

angry consumer likely complains and sometimes shouts and, in extreme cases, begins boycott initiatives against a company that is the target of anger. A consumer with low satisfaction would not likely exhibit any visible signs of irritation. The particular emotion experienced by consumers will do much to determine the behavioral reaction, as we will see in the next chapter, when we discuss complaining in more detail. Any model of what happens after purchase would be remiss not to include possibilities beyond satisfaction.

14-4 THEORIES OF POST-CONSUMPTION REACTIONS

Imagine a consumer placing an online order for some perishable food items—say peaches. What does the consumer expect the peaches to be like when they arrive? When will they arrive? How long will they last? Will they taste better than store-bought peaches? The answer to each of these questions involves an expectation before the peaches arrive. Afterwards, the actual outcomes are compared to these expectations. If the event turns out to be less than satisfying, perhaps the expectations were too high or the performance of the company was too poor.

14-4a Expectancy/ Disconfirmation

The most commonly accepted theory of consumer satisfaction is the **expectancy/disconfirmation theory**. The basic disconfirmation model proposes that consumers enter into a consumption experience with predetermined cognitive expectations of consumption. These expectations provide a benchmark against which actual performance perceptions are judged.

Disconfirmation becomes central in explaining consumer satisfaction. When performance perceptions are more positive than what was expected, **positive disconfirmation** occurs. Positive disconfirmation leads to consumer satisfaction. When performance perceptions do not meet expectations, meaning performance is less than expected, **negative disconfirmation** occurs. Negative disconfirmation leads to dissatisfaction. Finally, if performance perceptions exactly match what was expected, confirmation (sometimes referred to as *neutral disconfirmation*) is said to occur.

The expectancy/disconfirmation approach is shown in Exhibit 14.4. Taken together, disconfirmation represents the cognitive appraisal that produces post-consumption emotions like consumer satisfaction. Using different terminology, disconfirmation is the satisfaction judgment. The blue boxes represent cognitive postconsumption reactions, whereas the green box represents an affective or emotional post-consumption reaction. Various factors moderate the strength of relationships constituting the disconfirmation process.[16] The sections that follow explain these relationships briefly.

EXPECTATIONS

Expectations are pre-consumption beliefs concerning what will occur during an exchange and/or consumption of a product. Consumer expectations have two components: (1) the probability that something will occur and (2) an evaluation of that potential occurrence.[17] Exhibit 14.4 reveals that expectations also can have a direct impact on satisfaction (by the dotted line), independent of their role in the disconfirmation process.[18] This can occur when the consumer has very little involvement. In these cases, little effort is put into either expectation or performance appraisal, and satisfaction formation is largely shaped by consumer expectations alone. In other words,

---

Exhibit 14.4

Basic Disconfirmation Process

Expectations

Performance Perceptions

Disconfirmation

Satisfaction

Performance > Expectations = +Disconfirmation ➡ Satisfaction
Expectations < Performance = −Disconfirmation ➡ Dissatisfaction

---

expectancy/ disconfirmation theory satisfaction formation theory that proposes that consumers use expectations as a benchmark against which performance perceptions are judged

positive disconfirmation according to the expectancy/ disconfirmation approach, a perceived state wherein performance perceptions exceed expectations

negative disconfirmation according to the expectancy/ disconfirmation approach, a perceived state wherein performance perceptions fall short of expectations

expectations pre-consumption beliefs of what will occur during an exchange and consumption of a product

with low involvement, high expectations will be associated directly with increased satisfaction, and low expectations will be associated directly with increased dissatisfaction. Using terminology from earlier in the book, involvement serves to moderate the disconfirmation process.

Very high involvement creates a similar moderating effect. When consumers are very involved with a situation and filled with anticipation, their ability to judge performance objectively can be impaired. Balance theory kicks in and consumers may adjust their reactions automatically as a way of protecting themselves from the realization that they may have made a poor choice. Consumers who are highly involved in a brand find it difficult to see flaws. Among technology brands, Apple likely has the largest following of loyal customers. The flaws like uneven surfaces on the iPhone, an iTunes system that has grown overly complex, lack of a touch screen on MacBooks, etc. do not affect highly involved consumers because the products are so greatly anticipated that mental adjustments are made to overcome problems, and satisfaction corresponds more to expectations.[19] Thus, under conditions of very low or very high involvement, expectations can influence satisfaction directly.

Expectations are the cognitive component of anticipation. Anticipation, though, also involves emotions. Hope, for example, is a fundamental emotion evoked by positive, anticipatory appraisals that signal uncertainty about a positive outcome. The consumer anticipates an outcome that could bring about a better situation in some way, and he feels the emotion of hope in return. In this way, hope contrasts with fear, the anticipation of a negative outcome. Consumers who experience anticipatory hope show a greater tendency toward being satisfied relative to consumers who frame expectations based on what ought to happen. Consumers often anticipate deals, especially during events like Black Friday. Daily deal websites like 1sale.com offer daily discounts beginning at midnight that last for 24 hours or until products are sold out. Deal-prone consumers hope to find good deals—and that hope can lead to satisfaction.

TYPES OF EXPECTATIONS

Consumers bring different types of expectations into a consumption situation.

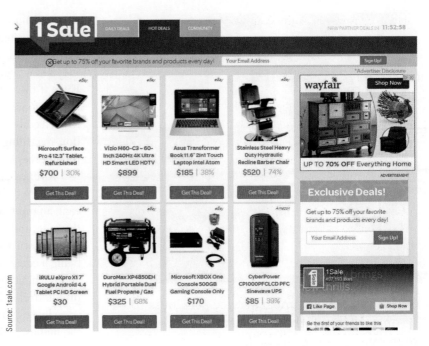

Source: 1sale.com

Predictive Expectations. Expectations that form about what a consumer thinks will actually occur during an experience.

Normative Expectations. Expectations of what a consumer thinks should happen given past experiences with a product or service.

Ideal Expectations. Expectations about what a consumer really wants to happen during an experience if everything were ideal. In terms of regulatory focus theory, these could be referred to as promotion-based expectations (the expectation being that the experience will improve their overall status and not just maintain the current state).

Equitable Expectations. Expectations that a consumer forms regarding what she thinks should or ought to happen given the level of work that she has put into the experience. From a regulatory focus viewpoint, these can be called prevention-based expectations.

SOURCE OF EXPECTATIONS

How do consumers form expectations? In other words, what are the sources of information that allow consumers to form expectations? In reality, consumers form expectations based on a number of different sources.[20] Word-of-mouth communication from other consumers is an important source of information. When a close friend tells you that a new television show is good, you'll probably hope

> **hope** a fundamental emotion evoked by positive, anticipatory appraisals that signal uncertainty about a potentially positive outcome

Consumers expect most service providers to be empathetic. If those expectations are not met, quality is diminished.

that this is the case if you plan on watching it. A consumer's experience also influences expectations. If you've gone to a dentist who was caring and respectful of your feelings on the first visit, then you would expect the same kind of treatment during the next visit. Explicit promises such as advertisements and promotions create consumer expectations as well. If a company promises that it will deliver a package within two days, a two-day delivery is what you probably expect. Personal factors also influence expectations. Some people simply expect more out of products and services than do others. Perhaps you know people who expect to never have to wait for a haircut or flights to arrive on time in any weather conditions. Here, personal factors influence the expectations that they have about the service.

PERFORMANCE PERCEPTIONS

Recall that perception plays a very important role in CB. "Perception *is* reality." Marketers are well aware of this. Perception directly influences how a consumer interacts with the world.

confirmatory bias
tendency for expectations to guide performance perceptions

self-perception theory theory that states that consumers are motivated to act in accordance with their attitudes and behaviors

Perception is also very important for the consumption and post-consumption processes. As is the case with expectations, performance perceptions can also directly influence consumer satisfaction formation independent of the

disconfirmation process (dotted line in Exhibit 14.4). This is particularly the case when expectations are low. For example, if consumers buy a brand of product that they know will be bad, expectations are likely to be low. Even if these low expectations are met by performance perceptions, consumers may not feel very satisfied. Also, when a consumer has no previous experience or expectation regarding a product (for example, a new product), then perception directly influences satisfaction.[21]

Airlines have to walk a fine line in setting expectations. Scheduled flight times now incorporate a significant amount of time to account for taxiing, holding at the gate and delays in boarding, so that the amount of time shown to get from one place to another ends up being a conservative estimate. Airlines have to be careful about what they promise. JetBlue and Southwest Airlines promise reliable no-frills service at good prices. The ability to live up to expectations helps them maintain some of the highest satisfaction scores in the industry.

CONFIDENCE IN EXPECTATIONS AND THE CONFIRMATORY BIAS

Not only do expectations play a key role in satisfaction formation, they also can affect how consumers see things. That is, expectations can affect performance perceptions.[22] Imagine a student who goes into a class thinking, "This class is going to be really bad!" An expectation like this tends to alter her perception of the class experience. If the student thinks it's going to be bad, she may very well look for evidence to support this expectation. The term to explain this phenomenon is **confirmatory bias**.

Research shows the confirmatory bias to be particularly present when consumers receive recommendations from the marketer, and return policies are lenient. A consumer who has doubts about switching to a different phone is more likely to confirm those doubts and interpret the phone's performance as bad when purchased from a retailer with lenient return policies. In contrast, when a retailer makes no recommendation and has restrictive policies, consumers rely more on actual performance perceptions.[23] The confirmatory bias works in conjunction with self-perception theory. **Self-perception theory** states that consumers are motivated to act in accordance with their attitudes and behaviors. Here, consumers are motivated to perceive their environment through the lens of their expectations. The confirmatory influence of expectations on perceptions is especially strong when consumers are quite confident in what to expect.

Once consumers view themselves as loyal to a particular cause or choice, their judgment may become clouded by confirmatory bias. Consider the case of organic foods.

A consumer who considers himself loyal to organic foods and is willing to pay more for them is likely to expect organic foods to be better in multiple ways than non-organic foods. Consumers tend to believe organic foods are healthier to eat and better for the environment, in part justifying their higher cost, which is particularly burdensome for those with low incomes.[24] However, the science on the healthiness and environmental impact of organic foods is very much in doubt. Loyal consumers expect organics to have benefits, and their perceptions may be adjusted by a combination of their perception of themselves as healthy and environmentally concerned and the confirmation bias.

EXPECTATIONS AND SERVICE QUALITY

Service quality can be thought of as the overall goodness or badness of a service provided. Service quality sometimes is seen as determined by the difference between consumer expectations of different service aspects and the actual service that is delivered. When a gap exists, for example, when a dental hygienist is not as empathetic as a consumer expected, then quality perceptions are diminished. In fact, the **SERVQUAL** scale, a commonly applied approach for measuring service quality, takes this approach. From this perspective, service quality is really a disconfirmation approach.[25] Perhaps it goes without saying, but service quality then becomes a key driver of consumer satisfaction or dissatisfaction. Social media provides marketers with tremendous opportunities to connect with customers. However, consumers are often disappointed with attempts to deliver quality service through social media.[26]

DESIRES AND SATISFACTION

Although expectations play a major role in satisfaction formation, consumer desires are also very important. A **desire** is the level of a particular benefit that will lead to a valued end state. Studies have shown that desires directly impact satisfaction, beyond the influence of disconfirmation alone.[27] The anticipation of receiving a gift can provide value directly at times, and if desires go unfulfilled,[28] can lower satisfaction thereafter.

14-4b Equity Theory and Consumer Satisfaction

Perceptions of fairness can also have an impact on consumer satisfaction. **Equity theory** proposes that consumers cognitively compare their own level of inputs and outcomes to those of another party in an exchange.[29] Equitable exchanges occur when these ratios are equal. In equation form:

$$outcomes_A/inputs_A \approx outcomes_B/inputs_B$$

A computer salesperson should put time into understanding a consumer's desire and the way he or she will use the computer.

The equation states that as long as comparisons of outcomes to inputs for consumer A are approximately the same as the same ratio for another party (for example, a company or another consumer), then satisfaction will be positively affected. So an inequitable exchange can occur when a consumer believes that he or she has been taken advantage of by a company or another customer has been treated more favorably.

When a consumer sets out to buy a computer, she will put quite a bit of effort into finding just the right one. She will take time to visit a store such as Best Buy, talk with friends about what brand to buy, visit websites such as Apple.com, and try to figure out the best way to finance the computer. She considers all these inputs before conducting the transaction. What will the consumer get when she buys the computer? Of course, she will get a computer, but she will also get a warranty, service contract, and maybe even in-home installation. These things represent her outcomes. The term **distributive fairness** refers to the way a consumer judges the outcomes of an exchange. When a consumer

service quality overall goodness or badness of a service experience, which is often measured by SERVQUAL

SERVQUAL way of measuring service quality that captures consumers' disconfirmation of service expectations

desire level of a particular benefit that will lead to a valued end state

equity theory theory that proposes that people compare their own level of inputs and outcomes to those of another party in an exchange

distributive fairness refers to the way a consumer judges the outcomes of an exchange

asks, "Did I get what I paid for?" she is asking a question of distributive fairness.

The computer salesperson should put time into understanding the consumer's desires and the way she will use the computer and then try to match these with a good arrangement of product features. Perhaps the salesperson will show effort by listening and physically searching store inventory for the most appropriate product. These are inputs for the salesperson. Salesperson outcomes include a salary and any commission tied directly to the sale. When consumers put a lot into an important purchase, they don't like to be shortchanged by an apathetic employee. That wouldn't be fair, and the output-to-input ratios would reflect this. Fairness perceptions affect satisfaction in addition to any influence of disconfirmation. In fact, consumers sometimes feel over-rewarded in a service recovery effort. For instance, a passenger whose bags were delayed for an hour was offered $200 from an airline for the inconvenience. This act may come across as more than adequate for what was a relatively small transgression. However, consumers with this impression tend to pay the business back with very high satisfaction.[30] In particular, equity theory plays a role in explaining how consumers react to complaints. The term **interactional fairness** captures how fairly a consumer believes he is treated when dealing with service personnel in resolving some issue.[31]

INEQUITABLE TREATMENT

Perhaps more often, equity perceptions involve inequitable treatment of customers. A single customer enters a restaurant for lunch and puts in an order. A few minutes later, a couple enters and sits beside the first customer at the next table. They place their order. After ten minutes, the couple receives their food and the original customer is still waiting. To the original customer, this may seem unfair and be a source of dissatisfaction. Thus, service providers need to be keenly aware of how customers are treated in public to maintain perceptions that all customers are treated in much the same way—or at least treated in a fair way.

INEQUITABLE CONSUMERS

Some consumers will try to take advantage of situations. Even though treatment is inequitable, if the inequity is in the consumers' favor, these particular

interactional fairness captures how fairly a consumer believes he or she was treated when dealing with service personnel in resolving some issue

attribution theory theory that proposes that consumers look for the cause of particular consumption experiences when arriving at satisfaction judgments

customers may be very satisfied. For example, some consumers may take a minor mishap and complain so fiercely that managers feel compelled to offer something overly generous as a way of calming the consumer down. Other consumers may realize that a cashier has made a significant error and given them significantly too much change and not correct the mistake. These consumers may be satisfied because the equity balance favors them. However, their actions can disadvantage other consumers.

14-4c Attribution Theory and Consumer Satisfaction

Another satisfaction theory focuses on consumer attributions. **Attribution theory** focuses on explaining why a certain event has occurred. When consumers select and consume products, they are motivated to make attributions as to why good or bad things happen. Humans are innately curious. There are three key elements to the attribution theory approach: *locus, control,* and *stability*.[32]

1. **Locus.** Judgments of who is responsible for an event. Consumers can assign the locus to themselves or to an external entity like a service provider. A self-ascribed event occurs when a consumer blames himself for a bad event. For example, a consumer might say to himself, "I have not followed the fitness program; no wonder I haven't lost any weight." Self-ascribed causes are referred to as internal attributions. If an event is attributed to a product or company, an external attribution is made. For example, a consumer might say, "I exercised just like my personal trainer said and I've still gained weight. She is clueless!" This type of attribution of blame toward a marketing entity increases consumer dissatisfaction.

2. **Control.** The extent to which an outcome was controllable or not. Here, consumers ask themselves, "Should this company have been able to control this event?" Two consumers are stranded in the Frankfurt airport in Germany overnight because their destination airport, Dallas/Fort Worth, is iced over. One consumer is irate (beyond dissatisfaction) with the airline because he believes the airline should have equipment

to clear the ice off the runway—even in the southern part of the country. Another consumer who is booked on the same flight is not happy about the situation but does not blame the airline because she understands that weather events are uncontrollable. Therefore, the situation does not significantly affect her satisfaction process.

3. **Stability.** The likelihood that an event will occur again in the future. Here, consumers ask themselves, "If I buy this product again, is another bad outcome likely to happen?" Let's briefly return to the Frankfurt airport example. If a customer recently found himself stranded because of weather problems in Dallas due to something other than an ice storm, he naturally comes to believe that this is a stable situation, and his satisfaction with the airline is reduced. On the other hand, if the other consumer never found herself stranded due to problems at the Dallas airport, her satisfaction with the airline is not likely to be affected by the current situation. She, unlike the previous consumer, does not have a track record showing a stable problem.

14-4d Cognitive Dissonance

Consumers also can experience what is known as cognitive dissonance following a purchase or a big decision. As was discussed with the balance theory approach, consumers prefer consistency among their beliefs. When faced with the knowledge that a bad decision may have been made, consumers experience dissonance (literally meaning "lack of agreement") between the thought that they are good decision makers and that they made a bad decision. **Cognitive dissonance** refers to thoughts that are inconsistent with one's preconceived notions. In this case, dissonance takes the form of lingering doubts about a decision that has already been made.[33] Dissonance is sometimes known as buyer's regret. Itsjustlunch.com succeeds in part by lessening the consequences of a first date. By using the site, a couple meeting for the first time, with limited information about each other, can establish more realistic opinions of each other without commitment.

Cognitive dissonance does not occur for all decisions. For high-ticket items like automobiles or homes, though, dissonance is a real possibility if not a probability. Dissonance has also been responsible for more than a

few cold feet in the days before a wedding. These are situations that naturally lend themselves to the experience of dissonance. A consumer is more likely to experience true dissonance following a purchase when the following conditions exist:

1. The consumer is aware that there are many attractive alternatives that may offer comparable value relative to the product/brand purchased.
2. The decision is difficult to reverse.
3. The decision is important and involves risk.
4. The consumer has low self-confidence.

The dissonance among consumers' beliefs following a consumption experience can be very discomforting and be a source of negative post-consumption emotions.

marino bocelli/Shutterstock.com

Consumers may therefore be motivated to lessen this discomfort. Furthermore, effective marketing can target consumers after purchase to take steps to reinforce their customers' decisions to select a brand. Many universities automatically send graduates university-sponsored magazines in order to maintain relationships and to reinforce the idea that choosing the school was indeed a good idea.

To lessen feelings of discomfort following purchase, consumers may engage in any, or all, of the activities listed in Exhibit 14.5.

COGNITIVE DISSONANCE AND SATISFACTION

Satisfaction and cognitive dissonance are closely related topics. The major difference between the two concepts is that satisfaction is generally felt *after* a consumption experience, but dissonance may be experienced even *before* consumption begins. For example, immediately after a decision has been made, a consumer might think, "I should have bought the other one." The uncertainty of events that might occur provides the basis for dissonance.[34]

> **cognitive dissonance**
> an uncomfortable feeling that occurs when a consumer has lingering doubts about a decision that has occurred

Exhibit 14.5

Dissonance Reduction Strategies

Complain about the experience

Return the product if possible

Seek positive information about the alternative selected

Seek negative information about alternatives not selected

Minimize the perceived consequences of the decision

14-5 CONSUMER SATISFACTION/ DISSATISFACTION MEASUREMENT ISSUES

Marketers assess customer satisfaction perhaps more than any other psychological concept. Three common measurement approaches include direct measures, difference scores, and disconfirmation.

▶ **Direct, Global Measure.** Simply asks consumers to assess their satisfaction on a scale such as:

How do you rate your overall satisfaction with your stove?

completely dissatisfied	dissatisfied	satisfied	completely satisfied
☐	☐	☐	☐

▶ **Attribute-Specific.** Assesses a consumer's satisfaction with various components, or attributes, of a product, service, or experience, such as:

How satisfied are you with the following attribute of your stove?

Heat of Burners

completely dissatisfied				completely satisfied
1	2	3	4	5

▶ **Disconfirmation.** Compares the difference between expectations and performance perceptions. This measure can be taken in a direct, subjective fashion, such as:[35]

Compared to my expectations, this stove performs . . .

much worse than I expected				much better than I expected
1	2	3	4	5

14-5a Improving Satisfaction Measures

Satisfaction is one of the most commonly measured concepts in consumer behavior but also one of the most difficult to measure accurately. For example, the typical four-choice satisfaction approach, as shown in the direct global measure example, actually proves quite problematic in practice. The problems can be severe and limit the ability to use satisfaction ratings to explain or predict other outcomes, including whether or not the consumer will return.

Consider that marketers measure satisfaction among existing customers most frequently. These customers have already decided to patronize a business. So a pop-up window on Amazon.com may ask a consumer to rate satisfaction with a simple measure of this type. This consumer should already be favorable because she has decided to purposefully visit Amazon.com and shop using this site. Thus, she already feels favorable toward Amazon.com. Therefore, we would expect even without knowing what happened during the visit that the customer would report some degree of satisfaction. In fact, typical consumer responses to this type of measure show that the vast majority of consumers, 80% or more, choose "satisfied" or "completely satisfied." Statistically speaking, these data are **left skewed**, in this instance meaning that the bulk of consumers have indicated that they are satisfied or completely satisfied with the product or service.

Does this reflect reality, or is the scale simply inadequate in truly differentiating consumers experiencing different levels of satisfaction? The truth is that both possibilities are likely true to some extent. From a measurement perspective, giving consumers more choices to respond to may increase the amount of variance displayed in the satisfaction measure and thereby increase its usefulness in trying to use satisfaction to predict and explain other behaviors. An alternative would be to have consumers score their satisfaction on a 0 (no satisfaction) to 100 (complete satisfaction) point scale. The results will still typically show an average satisfaction score above 50 points; however, the statistical properties are much improved, making for a more useful measure. Even better, a researcher might have respondents rate their satisfaction with multiple scale items.

Exhibit 14.6 displays an improved way of measuring consumer satisfaction using multiple scale items.[36] The scale mitigates problems with skewness and bias by providing scales with more response points and by using different response formats for each response item. The scale also focuses only on satisfaction. Although a marketer may choose to measure only satisfaction, this scale suggests that dissatisfaction should be measured with its own scale. A dissatisfaction scale can be formed by substituting the word *dissatisfaction* for satisfaction in each of the four items. Even if a total of eight items are used (four satisfaction and four dissatisfaction items),

Exhibit 14.6

A Multi-Item Satisfaction Scale

Please rate your satisfaction with your experience in the Delta Airlines Sky Club using the following items. It will take you no longer than 1 minute to complete this survey.

Place an X in the box that best describes the way you feel about your stay in the Delta Airlines Sky Club.

Indicate the percent to which you feel satisfied with your stay in the Delta Airlines Sky Club using a 100 point scale where 0 = no satisfaction at all and 100 = total satisfaction.

_____ %

Indicate the extent to which you experienced the feeling of satisfaction with your visit to the Delta Airlines Sky Club. Place an X in the box that matches the way you feel.

To what extent do you agree with the following statement:
I feel completely satisfied with my experience with the Delta Airlines Sky Club.

Source: Adapted from Barry J. Babin and Mitch Griffin, "The Nature of Satisfaction: An Updated Examination and Analysis," *Journal of Business Research* 41 (1998): 127–136.

a consumer can typically respond to these items in less than one minute. The question of whether or not dissatisfaction is more than just low satisfaction can be sorted out statistically. That topic is left for another course.

14-6 DISPOSING OF REFUSE

14-6a Disposal Decisions

A final step in consumption is disposal of any consumer refuse. **Consumer refuse** is any packaging that is no longer necessary for consumption to take place or, in some cases, the actual

left skewed distribution of responses consistent with most respondents choosing responses so the distribution is clustered toward the positive end of the scale

consumer refuse any packaging that is no longer necessary for consumption to take place or, in some cases, the actual good that is no longer providing value to the consumer

CONSUMERS AND TECHNOLOGY

Paper or e-Plastic?

There are countless thousands of studies trying to assess the environmental impact of consumer goods. Despite all of this effort, questions about the what is best for the environment are difficult. We used to think plastic was better than paper. Now, paper is considered better than plastic. We've all seen the common phrases at the bottom of many emails to encourage recipients to limit printing. The majority of paper used in the United States is recycled. Currently, e-waste is becoming more and more of a concern given the proliferation of battery-run devices. Batteries involve toxic chemicals and processes in both their manufacturing and disposal. Did you know that good practice means not disposing of batteries with household refuse? Thus, weighing the plastic devices run by batteries, not to

Piotr Zajic/Shutterstock.com

mention batteries that help power Tesla and other e-cars, against pages of paper, in terms of impact may not be as simple as it first seems.

Sources: www.cleanup.org.au/PDF/aubatteries_final.pdf, accessed July 4, 2016; https://www.theguardian.com/vital-signs/2015/jun/10/tesla-batteries-environment-lithium-elon-musk-powerwall, accessed July 4, 2016.

---

good that is no longer providing value to the consumer. A growing source of refuse falls under the category of **e-waste**, consisting of discarded electronics such as cell phones, old computers, and tablets and their components. Many of these are powered by batteries, with chemicals like cadmium and lithium, which, although small, leave a toxic footprint. Consumers express little awareness of the potential harmfulness of e-waste. Many consumers have old computers that they no longer use but have not yet disposed of because of other concerns including security issues. At first, this may seem like a straightforward process: Consumers simply throw away their trash. However, a number of disposal alternatives are available. These include trashing, recycling, converting to another use, trading, donating, or reselling.[37]

▶ **Trashing.** One alternative that a consumer has is to simply throw away waste material including unused products, packaging, and by-products. Of course, there are environmental concerns with this alternative. For instance, fast-food consumers sometimes dispose of their product packaging and remnants by littering. Fast-food wrappers are one of the largest sources of litter in developed nations.[38]

> **e-waste** the mass of discarded electronics such as cell phones, old computers, and tablets

▶ **Recycling.** Another alternative for consumers is to recycle used

products or packaging. Recycling cuts down on garbage while providing raw materials for other new products. Consumers can then buy new products made of recycled materials.

▶ **Converting.** Consumers can convert products or product packaging into new products in a number of creative ways. For example, consumers often use old t-shirts and socks as car-wash rags.

© Mr.Reborn55/Shutterstock.com

▶ **Trading.** Another alternative for consumers is to trade in old products for new products. The automotive industry has encouraged this practice for years. Consumers can often get thousands of dollars off of a new automobile purchase by trading in an old model. Even a car that doesn't run has some value in the form of spare parts.

▶ **Donating.** Consumers also have the ability to donate used products to various causes. Eyeglasses, clothing, and (surprisingly) automobiles are often donated in order to help other consumers who may not be able to afford new products.

▶ **Reselling.** One of the most popular methods for permanently disposing of used products is to simply sell them. Garage sales and swap meets are popular means of disposing of products in this way. Of course, online methods such as eBay and craigslist are also quite popular with consumers.

14-6b Disposal, Emotions, and Product Symbolism

Consumers often develop emotional bonds with their possessions. As discussed in an earlier chapter, possessions can help express a consumer's self-concept. The decision to part with belongings can therefore be very emotional, especially for older consumers who place much symbolic value on many products.[39] Strong feelings of attachment may be placed on many goods, especially those goods that are considered to be family heirlooms. Selling, giving away, or donating goods can lead some consumers to feel as if they have lost a part of themselves. In other situations, consumers can be quite ready to dispose of products that bring back bad memories, or that lead consumers to have uneasy feelings about themselves or their past.[40]

The willingness to let go of possessions varies from consumer to consumer. **Packrats** possess a lifestyle trait leading to a strong tendency toward retaining consumption-related possessions.[41] Packrats also are likely to visit garage sales, swap meets, and flea markets to purchase products that serve no immediate need.[42] Even though the term *packrat* is often used loosely, packrat behavior can be associated with various psychological conditions including obsessive-compulsive disorder. In contrast, most consumers hang onto a relatively manageable number of cherished mementos from the past that bring a great deal of value through nostalgia or personal memories. Things like family photos and love letters are understandably difficult to simply throw away.

One method of disposal is to sell an item. Ebay makes selling unwanted items easy. Also, recent television shows like Cajun Pawn Stars have glamorized pawnshops. A pawnshop provides evidence that there is something to the old cliché that one person's garbage is another's treasure. Even emotional value has a price.

> **packrats** consumers possessing high levels of a lifestyle trait leading to a strong tendency toward retaining consumption-related possessions

STUDY TOOLS 14

LOCATED AT BACK OF THE TEXTBOOK
☐ Tear out Chapter Review Card

LOCATED AT WWW.CENGAGE.COM/LOGIN
☐ Review Key Term flashcards and create your own cards
☐ Track your knowledge and understanding of key concepts in consumer behavior
☐ Complete practice quizzes to prepare for tests
☐ Complete interactive content within CB Online
☐ Review the Chapter Highlight boxes for CB Online

15 | Beyond Consumer Relationships

LEARNING OBJECTIVES

After studying this chapter, the student should be able to:

15-1 List and define the behavioral outcomes of consumption.

15-2 Know why and how consumers complain and spread word-of-mouth and know how word-of-mouth helps and hurts marketers.

15-3 Use the concept of switching costs to understand why consumers do or do not continue to do business with a company.

15-4 Describe each component of true consumer loyalty.

15-5 Link the concept of consumer co-creation of value to consumption outcomes.

Remember to visit **PAGE 323** for additional **STUDY TOOLS**

INTRODUCTION

For companies and consumers alike, transactions hopefully represent only a single touch-point among many that represent a long-term relationship. This chapter focuses on how single interactions between consumers and companies have potential to develop into long-term relationships. More importantly, both consumers and marketers benefit from relationships that are not just long lasting, but also mutually beneficial.

15-1 OUTCOMES OF CONSUMPTION

The story of CB does not end with the transaction. In fact, a transaction can be a starting place. To help bring customers back, many companies offer satisfaction guarantees:

100% Satisfaction or Your Money Back!

Are all companies really interested in complete satisfaction? If consumers could not return to do business

again, the pursuit of satisfaction would represent a purely altruistic exercise. Many firms might lose interest in serving customers if the only opportunity to do business with them is in the first transaction. The majority of businesses depend on consumers' repeat purchase behavior. One of the most important things that happens after the first transaction is another transaction. Therefore, businesses should be very interested in what happens after consumption—the outcomes of consumption—and the climax of CB.

This chapter focuses squarely on what happens after purchase and even after consumption. Exhibit 15.1 illustrates post-consumption CB by expanding the disconfirmation framework traditionally used to represent consumer satisfaction. The green colored boxes represent cognitive reactions consumers experience, including those that make up the actual disconfirmation process. Disconfirmation results from a cognitive comparison of what a consumer thought would happen (expectations) with the consumer's actual performance perception. A consumer's attributions represent cognitions about why the performance turned out as it did, and equity perceptions are cognitive reactions related to fairness or justice.

CUSTOMER LOYALTY

BUILD CUSTOMER TRUST

Procedural justice, in particular, refers to the extent that consumers believe the processes involved in processing a transaction, performing a service, or handling a complaint are fair. At times, a consumer may think the process to get a refund was too difficult but may think the refund itself was fair. In such a case, procedural justice contributes to inequity, but distributive fairness contributes to equity, since the consumer believes the refund was just.

Post-consumption cognitions lead to an affective reaction most conventionally represented by consumer satisfaction or dissatisfaction (CS/D). This particular model recognizes that the evaluation process could lead to any number of varying affective outcomes, many of

Exhibit 15.1

What Happens After Consumption

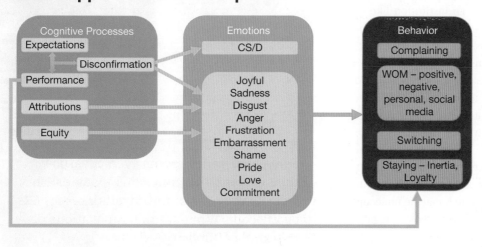

procedural justice
an equity-based cognition representing the extent that consumers believe the processes involved in processing a transaction, performing a service, or handling any complaint are fair

which have stronger behavioral reactions than CS/D. The blue sections in Exhibit 15.1 show the affective variables.

Finally, the exhibit shows behavioral outcomes of the post-consumption process in magenta boxes. Indeed, this is why marketers are interested in pursuing satisfaction. The behaviors that complete this process do much to determine the success or failure of competitive enterprises. Never has this been truer than in today's relationship marketing era. While negative behaviors like complaining perhaps receive more attention as reactions to consumption, positive outcomes, including positive word-of-mouth behavior and ultimately the development of a strong relationship, are essential elements to success.

We begin this chapter by looking at some common behaviors that follow consumption. Exhibit 15.1 lists the behaviors; although three of them seem negative, if companies possess the expertise to respond to the behaviors appropriately the result can be a positive value experience for company and customer alike. The term **critical incident** refers to exchanges between consumers and businesses that the consumer views as unusually negative.[1] Customers who believe a firm has adequately responded to some negative critical incident are likely to become more loyal, and loyalty is the positive outcome relationship-oriented firms seek.

15-2 COMPLAINING AND SPREADING WOM

15-2a Complaining Behavior

Complaining behavior occurs when a consumer actively seeks out someone to share an opinion with regarding a negative consumption event. The person may be a service provider, a supervisor, someone designated by a company to take complaints, or an institution like the Better Business Bureau (BBB) or Federal Trade Commission (FTC). Typically, a consumer who complains is seeking some type of action to address what he/she sees as a service failure resulting in a value deficit.

Consider a consumer faced with a wait. Making a consumer wait 30 minutes for lunch may be unacceptable and evoke negative disconfirmation, a negative affective consequence,

critical incident exchange between consumers and businesses that the consumer views as unusually negative with implications for the relationship

complaining behavior action that occurs when a consumer actively seeks out someone (supervisor, service provider, etc.) with whom to share an opinion regarding a negative consumption event

and encourage the consumer to complain. However, a consumer waiting 30 minutes to see a doctor may not experience the same reaction because the expectation is that one will wait for 30 minutes or more. Even if one waits longer than expected to see a doctor, the consumer still may not complain for other reasons. Marketers' online platforms have to adjust for media devices or risk aggravating potential customers. A wait of even a few seconds for a page to load can be a source of complaints. Thus, investments in technology make sense—to the extent that such things as Internet speed can be controlled. High-speed Internet providers like Cox suffer from low customer satisfaction scores and complaints whenever customers perceive the technology is slow.

COMPLAINERS

As you probably know from your own behavior, not all dissatisfied customers complain. In fact, far less than half of customers experiencing some dissatisfaction complain to management. Marketers have to assume that for every customer who complains about a problem, there are ten more who experienced one but didn't complain. To someone outside a marketing-related field, it may seem strange to think of the lack of complaints as a potential problem. Complaints, however, are a prime source of information that can be used to make improvements to goods and services.

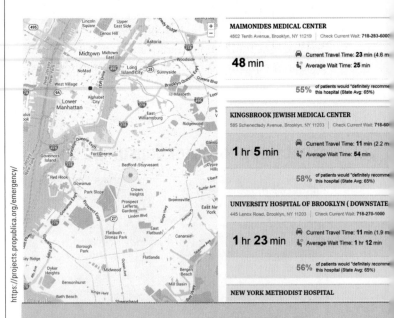

Some emergency rooms even advertise their current wait times on billboards. This website provides current wait times for ERs by ZIP code. What are the implications of this kind of publicity?

What makes a *complainer* different? Consumers who complain experience different emotions than do those who do not complain. In contrast to consumers who are merely dissatisfied, angry consumers are very likely to complain and, at times, the anger becomes very strong and reaches the stage of rage.[2] These consumers complain and more. In addition, consumers high in price sensitivity are more likely to complain than consumers with some indifference about the price paid for a service.[3] In turn, price-sensitive consumers become less loyal following the complaint than do those with less price sensitivity. Also, culture influences complaining. Consumers from collectivist cultures are less likely to complain than those from individualist cultures, unless the consumer feels embarrassed by the incident.[4] Demographically, male consumers aged 30–39 are the most likely to complain.[5]

> When a customer complains, the marketer has a chance to rectify the negative situation. . . . An angry customer is a valuable asset.

Compared to the angry customer, a disgusted or hopeless consumer is not likely to complain.[6] Consumers' behavioral reactions can be understood by considering whether the emotions they experience evoke approach or avoidance reactions. Negative approach emotions like anger are most likely to precede complaining behavior. Complaining is a relatively mild way of coping with anger.

The consumer who reacts with disgust is unlikely to complain. Disgust evokes an avoidance response, and as a result, a disgusted consumer avoids a potential confrontation and simply goes away. When the disgusted consumer simply goes away, the information about what caused the problem in the first place also goes away. Complainers, although sometimes unpleasant to deal with, are valuable sources of feedback about potential problems in service quality, product performance, or system malfunction. Unfortunately, the disgusted consumer copes by going away.

When a consumer complains, the marketer has a chance to rectify the negative situation. A consumer who sulks away takes valuable information with her. A truly consumer-oriented company should encourage customers to complain when things go wrong. If "100% satisfaction" is not just a slogan, the company must encourage its customers to act like whistle-blowers when something goes wrong. In this sense, an angry customer is a valuable asset for a business!

THE RESULTS OF COMPLAINING

Exhibit 15.2 provides a summary of what happens when consumers do or do not complain. The fact of the matter is that for consumers as well as marketers, complaining pays off. When consumers complain, more often than not some corrective action is taken that culminates with the consumer feeling satisfied when he reevaluates the situation. A consumer who complains about a noisy hotel room gets moved to another room, perhaps a suite! In such a case, the customer is likely to believe that he was treated fairly after complaining, and these thoughts evoke a more positive outcome. This positive outcome can represent a win-win situation.

Exhibit 15.2

Complainers versus Non-Complainers

Complainers:
- Tell others when company performs poorly
- Potentially valuable source of information
- More likely to become satisfied with company intervention
- More likely to return following exchange

Non-complainers:
- May tell others (friends/family) when company performs poorly
- Post negative messages on social network sites
- Not as valuable to firm because they don't complain
- Unlikely to return
- Firm must take preemptive action to create satisfaction

© Elena Elisseeva/Shutterstock.com

© Selecstock/Shutterstock.com

Some industries attract a lot of complaining customers. Home improvement services, used auto sales (both B2C and C2C), credit/loan/debt services, and utilities attract complaints more than other industries. The BBB reports that over three out of four consumer complaints across all industries are resolved satisfactorily. Perhaps high switching costs are associated with more complaints? Loan and debt services also report relatively low satisfaction with the complaints compared to more service-oriented industries like hospitality. Here are some tips for handling consumer complaints:[7]

1. **Thank the customer for providing the information.**
2. **Listen carefully to understand the facts.**
3. **Apologize sincerely.**
4. **Show empathy for the customer.**
5. **Explain the corrective action that will take place.**
6. **Empower people to take corrective action quickly.**
7. **Communicate clearly and professionally.**

Today it's easier than ever for consumers to complain publicly. Both the BBB (bbb.org) and FCC (fcc .gov/complaints) offer formal opportunities to complain. These organizations help facilitate responses from companies but they also make the complaints public.

▶ **Complaints.com (www.complaints.com)**
▶ **Federal Communications Commission (www.fcc.gov/complaints)**
▶ **Better Business Bureau (www.bbb.org)**

RESPONSES PAY OFF

A host of evidence suggests that it's better for companies to respond aggressively to complaining. Companies sometimes do more than just offer a refund when a service has gone bad. Sometimes, the something more comes in the form of a coupon or voucher that amounts to a prepayment for future purchases. One study of this type of behavior suggested that it more than pays for itself in terms of customer retention if the store provides the compensation quickly.[8] However, for firms that act slowly, taking a week or more to respond, complaining consumers reduce their spending by a total of over $1 million per year.

THE RESULT OF NOT COMPLAINING

So, what happens when a consumer does not complain? Let's return to the noisy hotel room. Our customer may simply put up with the inconvenience and end up leaving miserable after a poor night's sleep. Is this the end of the story? Not really! The consumer may well remember this incident and be less likely to do business with this hotel again. He may also complain to others about the episode. Interestingly, though, when marketers can take action to address a negative situation before a consumer complains, a very positive outcome can result. So, imagine that a bell clerk reports the noise in one of the halls of the hotel to management. Management then takes action by calling the adjacent guests to suggest that they move to better rooms. These customers are likely to be very appreciative and become more likely to maintain a relationship with the firm.[9]

REVENGE

On occasion, consumers' verbal complaints to the marketing company do not eliminate the negative emotions they are experiencing. In these instances, consumers may retaliate in the form of revenge-oriented behaviors. These could be as simple as trying to prevent others from using the business by spreading the word about how bad the business is, but the behaviors can become more aggressive. **Rancorous revenge** is when a consumer yells insults and makes a public scene in an effort to harm the business.[10] A vengeful consumer may make derogatory posts on social networks as a way of taking out frustrations. In extreme cases the furious consumer can become violent or try to vandalize the business. **Retaliatory revenge** is a term that captures these extreme types of behavior. Revenge often occurs out of feelings of inequity; in particular, violations of procedural or interactional justice can lead to revenge.[11] After two transgressions from the same business, a consumer becomes particularly vengeful unless the company can demonstrate that their intentions were to serve the customers' best interests all along.[12]

When it comes to rancorous or retaliatory revenge, the customer is definitely not always right. From time to time news stories report extreme consumer behaviors. A New York Malibu Diner customer became irate after a manager confronted her about her loud and profane cell phone conversation.[13] She continued the conversation

rancorous revenge
is when a consumer yells insults and makes a public scene in an effort to harm the business in response to an unsatisfactory experience

retaliatory revenge
consumer becomes violent with employees and/or tries to vandalize a business in response to an unsatisfactory experience

Reading is Believing?

Today it's easy for consumers to turn complaining into publicity by posting reviews online at amazon.com, yelp.com, tripadvisor.com or any one of hundreds of websites and social networking sites. More than half of consumers agree that they pay at least some attention to online reviews. The reality, however, is that a significant portion of online reviews are fake. Sometimes fake reviews are just attempts to be funny (you can find lots of examples online). Exaggerated negative reviews can be a form of revenge. But, based on a recent Amazon lawsuit, positive reviews also stand a good chance of being fake. Technology allows crowdsourced workers to write and post fake reviews in return for small payments. Websites like fiverr.com and (ironically) Amazon's Mechanical Turk facilitate these transactions, and a business can quickly accumulate "reviews." Consequently, consumers need to be wary and stay attuned to clues that may indicate fake reviews, such as overzealousness in praise and multiple postings of very similar reviews.

Sources: http://money.cnn.com/2015/10/18/technology/amazon-lawsuit-fake-reviews/index.html, accessed July 7, 2016; http://www.foxnews.com/tech/2015/10/31/4-ways-to-spot-fake-online-review.html, accessed July 9, 2016.

for nearly half an hour before being asked to leave. She became irate at that point and began hurling ketchup bottles across the restaurant.

15-2b Word-of-Mouth/Publicity

Just because a consumer doesn't complain to the offending company doesn't mean she just keeps the episode inside. **Negative word-of-mouth** (negative WOM) takes place when consumers pass on negative information about a company from one to another. Realize that one does not have to be a complainer to spread negative WOM. Some estimates suggest that consumers who fail to achieve a valuable consumption experience are likely to tell their story to an average of 16 others, not including social media.[14] Recall that as a source of information, WOM is powerful because of relatively high source credibility. The fact that most consumers who participate in WOM speak to multiple consumers makes the matter all the more important.

WOM is not always negative. In fact, **positive WOM** occurs when consumers spread information from one to another about positive consumption experiences with companies. Overall, consumers are about half as likely to spread positive as negative WOM. However, in the entertainment industry, consumers appear more likely to spread the word about shows they find valuable rather than those they do not.[15] Another study shows that when a shopper has a reversal in orientation from a browser to a buyer within a retail store, she becomes highly likely to tell others about the great experience.[16] Further, consumers who have bad experiences with companies become agents of positive WOM if they believe the transgression was handled with high procedural justice.[17]

Whether positive or negative, WOM exerts very strong influences on other consumers. Recipients of WOM become particularly receptive when they see the giver as

negative word-of-mouth (negative WOM); action that takes place when consumers pass on negative information about a company from one to another

positive WOM action that occurs when consumers spread information from one to another about positive consumption experiences with companies

trustworthy and experienced within the consumption domain.[18] Most consumers say they pay attention to online reviews. Given the sheer volume of such WOM, marketers have to pay close attention. Indeed, the reviews can function like complaints in pointing out potential service problems. However, the credibility is still suspect given that recipients of this WOM cannot usually judge the trustworthiness of the information. The fact that firms take legal action to try to stop organized efforts at fake reviews indicates that reviews influence sales.

What happens to WOM when a consumer is shopping online versus shopping in a physical store? For example, if an online shopper encounters information they deem deceptive, their satisfaction with the product will be reduced but the likelihood of WOM is unaffected. In contrast, when a shopper encounters deception in a store, this can lower their satisfaction with the retailer and reduce the likelihood of positive WOM.[19] Thus, retailers need to make sure their in-store staff are knowledgeable and portray accurate information.

NEGATIVE PUBLIC PUBLICITY

When negative WOM spreads on a relatively large scale, it can result in **negative public publicity**. Negative public publicity could even involve widespread media coverage. The outcome of such events questions the old cliché that bad publicity is better than no publicity at all. Lululemon, which markets yoga pants that retail for over $100, has faced significant amounts of negative publicity, beginning with changes in production that lowered quality and left the yoga pants transparent! Formerly loyal consumers sometimes become the biggest sources of negative WOM. For lululemon, at least one post about an unwanted "thigh-gap" design led to a viral video exposing what the customer perceived as a drop in quality and generating empathy for the consumer.[20]

More and more consumers are turning to social media as a way of spreading negative publicity. YouTube contains many videos with various consumer rants about different companies. Spirit Airlines seems to have their share of videos about unresponsive employees and long wait times. SiriusXM customers also demonstrate considerable creativity expressing problems with service quality. These sites can turn a complaint into negative publicity—particularly when the complaint goes viral!

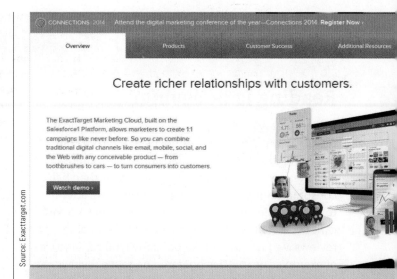

Radian 6 monitors what is being said about companies online.

Companies can use software such as Salesforce.com's Radian6 to monitor posts on social media that use the brand's name.[21] Products like Radian help make the massive amounts of data available about big brand names in social media scalable (meaning "manageable"). The technology helps not only in lead generation but in brand management. Gatorade automates some responses to social media as a way of protecting the brand from negative publicity. In the social media world, the key is to respond quickly before negative news goes viral.

Negative publicity can do considerable harm to a brand. In 2016, IKEA faced potentially damaging negative publicity when a problem surfaced with one of its bestselling furniture products, a stand-up dresser. The deaths of several children were attributed to their using the open drawers as a ladder to climb toward the top. The dresser was found to be prone to tipping and toppling onto a child. IKEA issued a recall of nearly 30 million dressers and offered owners the option of having an employee come to their home to anchor the dresser to the wall. IKEA, already suffering from controversy about tainted cakes in China and Swedish meatballs with traces of horsemeat, needed to take swift and drastic action to protect the brand. One response was the tip-over campaign for furniture safety.[22]

How should a firm handle negative public publicity? Here are some alternative courses of action:

1. **Do nothing; the news will eventually go away.**

2. **Deny responsibility for any negative event.**

negative public publicity
action that occurs when negative WOM spreads on a relatively large scale, possibly even involving media coverage

Secure it!
Creating safer homes together

We all want our homes to be a safe place. When we work together, we can reduce the risk of accidents.

We all want our homes to be a safe place. But in our homes, accidents can put children at risk. By working together, we can help prevent these accidents and make the home a safer place.

The best way to help prevent furniture tip over accidents is to secure furniture to the wall. IKEA urges customers to inspect their IKEA chests of drawers and dressers to ensure that they are securely anchored to the wall using the restraints provided in the packaging.

Should you need a replacement restraint kit to secure the IKEA furniture in your home, you can call us on 0203 6450010 (UK) to order one free of charge. Alternatively, click here, to fill out an online form to place your order.

We all want our home to be a safe place.

Source: ikea.com

IKEA's website and Facebook profile featured pages and videos like this one in response to problems with product safety.

Source: http://www.ikea.com/gb/en/tip_over_campaign/index.html.

3. **Take responsibility for any negative events and be visible in the public eye.**

4. **Release information allowing the public to draw its own conclusion.**

What is the best approach?

DOING NOTHING

Doing nothing is neither the best nor the worst option. Taking action seems to be a responsible thing to do, but the action might backfire and bring more attention to the issue. Sometimes, an issue may be so politically sensitive that any response has the chance of being misinterpreted. Other times, a claim is just ridiculous, and responding may only give it some credibility that it does not deserve. KFC stood accused of using genetically modified non-chickens to produce the meat sold in its restaurants. Word spread over a few years that the reason KFC changed its name from Kentucky Fried Chicken was because the government ruled that the meat was not really chicken. In reality KFC changed their name to deemphasize "fried chicken" as its only product. Had KFC issued a vigorous response to this rumor, they would only have provided awareness that could further fuel the belief.

DENYING RESPONSIBILITY

Denials can also be tricky given the potential to bring attention to something that may not even be true. Denials should be made only when the evidence unambiguously supports the actual truth. In 2014, Facebook was accused of conducting experiments that involved manipulating information presented in consumer newsfeeds.[23] The experiments involved emotional contagion. If they could make the news seem more negative or positive than it otherwise might come across, could Facebook determine reactions to advertised brands, including the tendency to "like" a brand? Initially, Facebook denied any wrongdoing in conducting the experiments. A great deal of negative publicity followed these denials, particularly because Facebook had no institutional body to review the ethics of such experimentation.

TAKING RESPONSIBILITY

One might easily see that attribution theory plays a role in dealing with negative publicity. If consumers blame the company for the event surrounding the negative publicity, then the potential repercussions appear serious. However, public action to deal with any consequences of a negative event can mollify any negative effects.

One of the most famous negative publicity cases of all time involves Tylenol pain medicine. In the fall of 1982, over half a dozen consumer deaths in the Chicago area were attributed to cyanide traces in Tylenol capsules. Tylenol executives considered their options, including plausible deniability, and decided to take action by immediately having all Tylenol removed from shelves all around the country immediately. In addition, they agreed to take steps to investigate how this happened and to ensure that it could not happen again. The dramatic action helped convince consumers that Tylenol truly cared about the welfare of customers and wanted to make sure this never happened again. Even though they were quite certain they had no culpability in what appears to be senseless murder, they acted in a way that led to a huge short-term loss. However, this action saved Tylenol's reputation. In fact, many younger consumers may wonder how

The media are a vehicle both for spreading negative publicity and for managing the implications of negative publicity.

of canning plants that exist and how they are spread around the country. This action worked to prevent any negative fallout for Pepsi. The media coverage allowed consumers to draw their own conclusions. Obviously, if a needle would get into some Pepsi cans, the chances that this would happen at multiple canning plants all around the country seemed unlikely. Thus, how could this be happening all over? Also, watching the canning operations made clear the fact that nobody could possibly slip a needle into a can at the speeds the assembly line operates. This entire incident was over in just a couple of weeks. All of the alleged needle victims confessed to making up the stories with the hope of getting some part of any settlement that Pepsi might be forced to pay. Thus, this appears to be a textbook way to deal with negative publicity for an implausible event.

we came to have tamperproof packaging for over-the-counter medications and now practically all food products. While today government mandates require such packaging in many instances, the beginning of tamperproof packaging goes back to Tylenol's response to this potentially damaging negative publicity associated with the murders.

RELEASING INFORMATION

Sometimes, a company may be able to release some counter-PR to media that allows consumers to make up their own minds about the potential source of any negative PR. If this is done properly, the company does not publicly deny any allegation about the event and instead insists that actions are being taken to get to the bottom of the event.

In the mid-1990s, a consumer made the news by claiming that he was simply drinking a Pepsi when a hypodermic needle began to flow out of the can and stuck his lip. Within two days of this story going public, dozens of consumers from all around the country made the same claim. Pepsi, rather than denying any responsibility, opened the doors of canning operations around North America. Film crews were allowed to come in and videotape cans streaming down an assembly line at high speed. Pepsi released information about the number

PARTICIPATING IN NEGATIVE WOM

One of the factors that helps determine negative word-of-mouth returns to the issue of equity. Consumers who believe they have not been treated with fairness or justice become particularly likely to tell others and, in some cases, report the incident to the media.[24]

Consumers can be angry when they believe they have been wronged in this way, and these actions are a small way of trying to get revenge. Consumers who spread negative WOM without complaining to the company itself are particularly likely to never do business with that company again.[25] This tendency provides all the more reason for companies to make consumers feel comfortable about complaining and creating the impression of genuine concern for the consumer's situation.

IMPLICATIONS OF NEGATIVE WOM

One reason consumers share negative WOM is as a way of preventing other consumers from falling victim to a company. Thus, negative WOM can hurt sales. However, this is not the only potential effect. Negative WOM also can damage the image of the firm. When a consumer hears the negative WOM from a credible source, that information gets stored and associated with the schema for that brand. Thus, not only is the consumer's attitude toward the brand lowered, but the consumer will also find the firm's advertising harder to believe.[26]

In extreme cases, the negative WOM attached to one company can have effects that spill over to an entire industry. For instance, news attributing accidents at one amusement park to a lack of maintenance will certainly damage the image of that particular amusement park. However, a consumer hearing this news may end up not feeling very comfortable about any similar amusement park. Thus, firms must be wary of negative WOM not just for their own brand, but for the industry as well.[27]

Negative WOM does not affect all consumers and all brands in the same way. Consumers who have very strong, positive feelings about a brand may have a difficult time accepting negative WOM. One reason is due to balance theory, as consumers try to maintain their existing belief systems. If the relationship with the brand is strong, accepting negative information also diminishes the consumer's self-concept. Online reviews do not affect all brands in the same way. In fact, consumer opinions will be more shaped by reviews for technologically oriented products and for relatively unfamiliar brands compared to established brands.[28] Therefore, tech brands and new brands need to be particularly wary of "the word of mouse."

THIRD-PARTY ENDORSEMENTS

Consumers often see publicity as more credible than advertising because the source is someone other than the firm. A **third-party endorsement** represents one form of publicity in which an ostensibly objective outsider (neither the customer nor the business) provides publicly available purchase recommendations. These come in two forms.

The first type makes recommendations based on cumulative consumer ratings. TripAdvisor is one site that collects consumers' post-consumption evaluations of restaurants, airlines, and hotels, and provides an overall recommendation based on the average ratings. Consumers tend to trust each other, so these ratings can be influential. However, are all the ratings supplied by actual customers? Recall that earlier in the chapter the topic of fake reviews was discussed. Once a review is spreading false information, it becomes unethical.

The second type involves recommendations from subject experts. Numerous media organizations endorse higher education institutes and programs. Each has its own system for determining the best schools in

> **Consumers tend to trust each other more than they do advertisements. Thus, online reviews and ratings are influential.**

each category. Universities put considerable effort into finding a place near the top of at least one of these lists. The Academy of Motion Pictures Oscar Award may be the best-known third-party product endorsement. Movies that were merely nominated for an Oscar see spikes in sales at the box office and online. Several "authorities" score wines; retailers routinely use these scores as point-of-purchase promotional materials as these endorsements are very influential in a category where most buyers have difficulty discriminating among alternatives. The following are examples of such rating authorities:

1. *Financial Times*: ranks business schools and graduate business programs
2. *U.S. News and World Report*: ranks universities and programs, ranks hospitals
3. *Consumer Reports*: rates the latest consumer products from soap to automobiles
4. *Wine Spectator* and *Wine Advocate*: rate wines based on blind taste tests by editors on a scale of 50 to 100
5. J.D. Power: rates autos and many other industries
6. CNET: rates many consumer products, with an emphasis on electronics (reviews.cnet.com)

15-3 SWITCHING BEHAVIOR

Exhibit 15.1 suggests that a consumer evaluates a consumption experience, reacts emotionally, and then, perhaps, practices switching behavior. **Switching**, in a consumer behavior context, refers to the times when a consumer chooses a competing choice, rather than the previously purchased choice, on the next purchase occasion. If a consumer visited Waffle House for breakfast last Tuesday, and chooses Panera Bread the next

third-party endorsement one form of publicity in which an ostensibly objective outsider (neither the customer nor the business) provides publicly available purchase recommendations or evaluations

switching times when a consumer chooses a competing choice, rather than the previously purchased choice, on the next purchase occasion

time she goes out for breakfast, the consumer has practiced switching behavior. This could be due to any number of reasons, but perhaps the last experience at Waffle House was less than satisfying.

All things considered, consumers prefer the status quo. Change brings about, well . . . change, and this can mean costs that diminish the value of an experience. If the consumer has been a regular Waffle House customer, she now has to learn the new assortment of items available at Panera Bread, may lose any accumulated benefits from being a loyal Waffle House customer, and cannot get all of those free coffee refills at Waffle House.

Thus, the consumer will incur some **switching costs**, or the costs associated with changing from one choice (brand/retailer/service provider) to another. Switching costs are one reason why a consumer may be dissatisfied with a service provider but will continue to do business with them. Switching costs can be divided into three categories:[29]

1. **Procedural**

2. **Financial**

3. **Relational**

Rawpixel.com/Shutterstock.com

switching costs costs associated with changing from one choice (brand/retailer/service provider) to another

procedural switching costs lost time and extended effort spent in learning ways of using some product offering

financial switching costs total economic resources that must be spent or invested as a consumer learns how to obtain value from a new product choice

relational switching cost emotional and psychological consequences of changing from one brand/retailer/service provider to another

15-3a Procedural Switching Costs

Procedural switching costs involve lost time and effort. Although Apple computers have a stellar reputation for being easy to use, many computer users stick with PC models. Why? Even if an Apple MacBook is easy to use, a consumer familiar with a PC-based Windows operating platform would have to forgo this knowledge to learn how to use a MacBook. Thus, the effort that went into learning the PC system is lost and replaced by effort that would be needed to learn how to use an Apple. Thus, when consumers master a technologically complex product, they become very resistant to switching. When Windows introduced Windows 8, with near instant start-up times, they made sure the old Windows desktop view was easily accessible to reduce the costs of adopting a new version of the familiar product.

15-3b Financial Switching Costs

Financial switching costs consist of the total economic resources that must be spent or invested as a consumer learns how to obtain value from a new product choice. A new car purchase may involve an increase in insurance, for instance. Switching cell phones without switching service also could involve a financial switching cost, given that the phone cost is generally bundled with a service plan.[30]

15-3c Relational Switching Costs

The **relational switching cost** refers to the emotional and psychological consequences of changing from one brand/retailer/service provider to another. Imagine a consumer who has used the same hairstylist for five years. When she goes to college, however, she finds another hair salon that is more convenient. She is greeted by a stylist named Karla just after entering

Exhibit 15.3

Factors Contributing to Switching Costs

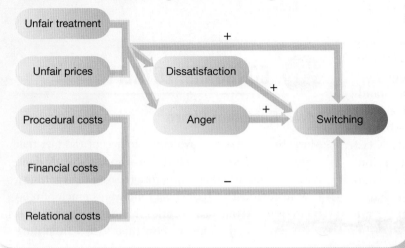

make a point of advertising policies that they maintain prices during weather crises like hurricanes.

Furthermore, even though all types of functional costs can prevent switching, evidence suggests that relational barriers may be the most resistant to influence. Retailers who build up procedural switching costs, particularly through the use of loyalty cards and other similar programs, may gain temporary repeat purchase behavior, but they fail to establish the connection with the customer that wins them true loyalty.[32] Additionally, the inability of web-based retailers to create anything other than procedural loyalty may be responsible for low levels of loyalty observed for many pure-play (Internet-only) retailers.[33]

the salon. Although Karla seems nice, the consumer is very uneasy during the entire salon visit. In fact, she even feels a bit guilty for letting Karla do her hair. This uneasiness is an example of a typical relational switching cost.

15-3d Understanding Switching Costs

Exhibit 15.3 demonstrates conventional consumer behavior theory that explains switching costs. Consumers become dissatisfied for any number of reasons, and these reasons and dissatisfaction together determine how likely a consumer is to return on the next purchase occasion.[31] Equity judgments, in particular perceptions of unfair treatment, are particularly prone to lead consumers to switch. Perceptions of unfair prices may make consumers temporarily angry, but they also create lasting memories. When coastal building centers raise plywood prices immediately before a hurricane's landfall, they may enjoy a short-term profit, but consumers will probably remember this and switch to a different retailer the next time they need a building center. Retailers like Home Depot

15-3e Satisfaction and Switching

The intermingling of consumer satisfaction/dissatisfaction and switching costs has received considerable attention. In fact, in addition to the measurement difficulties associated with CS/D, switching costs are another important reason why CS/D results often fail to predict future purchasing behavior. Exhibit 15.4 summarizes how vulnerable a company is to consumer defections based on the interaction between switching costs, competitive intensity, and consumer satisfaction.

As can be seen in Exhibit 15.4, dissatisfaction does not always mean that the consumer is going to switch. Before reaching a conclusion on vulnerability to losing a customer, one also has to take into account at least two

Exhibit 15.4

Vulnerability to Defections Based on CS/D

Customers are relatively:	High competitive intensity		Low competitive intensity	
	Switching costs		Switching costs	
	Low	High	Low	High
Satisfied	Vulnerable	Low vulnerability	Low vulnerability	No vulnerability
Dissatisfied	High vulnerabilty	Vulnerable	Vulnerable	Low vulnerability

other factors. For instance, the amount of competition and the competitive intensity also play a role in determining who switches. **Competitive intensity** refers to the number of firms competing for business within a specific category. A student today has many choices on where and how to pursue a college degree. Thus, higher education institutions feel a great deal more competitive pressure than they did a few decades ago.

This exhibit drives home the fact that customer satisfaction is not a panacea for marketers. In fact, brands with low customer satisfaction can have high market share. The low satisfaction/high market share situation is typical among mass marketers.[34] McDonald's is last in restaurant satisfaction among national chains but not last in profitability.[35] In addition, given that companies must invest considerable resources to enhance satisfaction, not all high satisfaction conditions are highly profitable. By limiting spending on satisfaction, a firm can sometimes find profitability. The areas shaded in green suggest conditions that tend to be profitable.

When competitive intensity is high and switching costs are low, a company is vulnerable to consumers who will switch providers even when satisfied. The consumer has many companies vying for the business, and changing presents little barrier. Consumers looking for take-out food have many choices. Even if a consumer is satisfied with Chili's take-out, he may try Boston Market next time if a traffic situation makes Boston Market's location slightly more convenient.

In contrast, Exhibit 15.4 suggests that even when consumers are dissatisfied, they may not switch. Consider the case when competitive intensity is low, meaning there are few alternatives for the consumer and switching costs are high. In this case, even dissatisfied consumers may return repeatedly. In many small- to medium-size markets in the United States, Walmart Supercenters dominate the mass merchandising landscape. Many conventional grocery stores were unable to compete in these markets; as a result, Walmart Supercenter became practically the only choice for buying groceries on any large scale. Thus, although consumers may experience

Sergiy1975/Shutterstock.com

competitive intensity number of firms competing for business within a specific category

customer share portion of resources allocated to one brand from among the set of competing brands

share of wallet customer share

dissatisfaction, the fact that there are few places to turn to and the costs of switching might involve a long drive to the next larger city in the area makes Walmart only slightly vulnerable to defections due to low consumer satisfaction.

15-4 CONSUMER LOYALTY

15-4a Customer Share

Marketing managers have come to accept the fact that getting business from a customer who has already done business with the company before is easier than getting a new customer. This basic belief motivates much of relationship marketing. The rubrics that determine marketing success then switch from pure sales and profit margin toward indicators that take into account marketing efficiencies. One important concept is **customer share**, which is the portion of resources allocated by a consumer to one brand from among the set of competing brands. Here, *brand* is used loosely to capture any type of consumer alternative including a retailer, service provider, or actual product brand. Some managers use the term **share of wallet** to refer to customer share.

Exhibit 15.5 illustrates customer share. The exhibit shows the choices made by two consumers who each make daily coffee shop visits. On July 1, Bill goes to Starbucks (SB) and spends $5 and Erin does the same thing. On July 2, Bill returns to Starbucks and spends $10. Erin however, goes to CC's (CC) and spends $15. In ten days, Bill chose Starbucks (SB) eight out of ten times and spent $60 out of the $80 total at Starbucks. Erin chose Starbucks only three times out ten visits and spent $20 out of the $70 total at Starbucks. Thus, Starbucks gets considerably greater customer share from Bill than from Erin. The tenet of relationship marketing is that a company's marketing is much more efficient when most of the business comes from repeat customers. In this sense, Bill is a more valuable consumer to Starbucks than Erin is. Starbucks gets a greater share of Bill's coffee business than they do Erin's.

Customer share represents a behavioral component that is indicative of customer loyalty. Behaviorally, Bill is more loyal than Erin. When customers don't

Exhibit 15.5

Customer Share Information for Two Coffee Shop Customers

	Date of visit										Total spent
	7-1	7-2	7-3	7-4	7-5	7-6	7-7	7-8	7-9	7-10	
Bill's Choice	SB	SB	CC	SB	SB	CC	SB	SB	SB	SB	
$$ Spent	5	10	10	5	15	10	5	5	10	5	$80
Erin's Choice	SB	CC	M	M	SB	M	CC	SB	CC	M	
$$ Spent	5	15	5	5	5	5	10	10	5	5	$70

SB = Starbucks   CC = CC's   M = McDonald's

switch, they repeat their purchase behavior over again. At times, they repeat the behavior over and over and over again. We examine the question of whether or not a consumer is truly loyal by examining why a consumer is repeating behavior. This brings us to the concept of consumer inertia.

CONSUMER INERTIA

In physics, inertia refers to the fact that a mass that is in motion (or at rest) will stay in motion (at rest) unless the mass is acted upon by a greater force. The concept of consumer inertia presents an analogy.

Do apps like this one build loyalty or only inertia?

Consumer inertia means that consumers will tend to continue a pattern of behavior until some stronger force motivates them to change. In fact, resistance to change is one of the biggest reasons why new products fail in the marketplace.[36] Change often means consumers must give up something. For example, many grocers try to take advantage of technology to increase the utilitarian value of getting groceries. The latest approach involves a regular grocery purchase where the customer simply drives up, pays using a credit card, and drives away in a matter of minutes. This seems like a great value-added service. However, it comes at the price of the value that a customer gets by actually entering in the store and getting to see, touch, and smell the products beforehand. Once consumers adopt the "more convenient" option, they build up an inertia that may take a large perceived gain to overcome.

LOYALTY PROGRAMS

Many marketers have experimented with loyalty cards or programs as a way of increasing customer share. Apps sometimes function as an actual card these days. Loyalty cards also allow marketers to learn more about customer groups' demographics and shopping patterns. A **loyalty card/program** is a device that encourages repeated purchasing and keeps track of the amount of purchasing a consumer has had with a given marketer (as well as a list of actual items purchased by

consumer inertia
situation in which a consumer tends to continue a pattern of behavior until some stronger force motivates him or her to change

loyalty card/program
device that encourages repeated purchasing and keeps track of the amount of purchasing a consumer has had with a given marketer once some level is reached

the consumer); more spending generally brings more rewards in one form or another. Loyalty programs differ somewhat depending on the firms offering them. Today, European firms typically offer the standard reward in terms of a future purchase incentive, but in the United States, loyalty programs more often work by offering on-the-spot discounts on selected items. One result is a two-tiered pricing system where there is one price for customers who comply with the card program, and a higher price for those who do not use the card on those selected items. Other programs, like Amazon Prime, allow a consumer to buy into a program to receive rewards like free shipping and faster delivery.

However, the results are mixed with respect to loyalty programs' effectiveness. In fact, they can sometimes backfire by appealing too strongly to consumers who are bargain shoppers. Consumers with a strong economic orientation display lower customer share with all competitors, instead choosing to shop in the place with the current best offer.[37]

While these programs are referred to as "loyalty" programs, the question occurs as to exactly what constitutes loyalty. Customer share reflects a behavioral component of loyalty by reflecting repeated behavior.

customer commitment
sense of attachment, dedication, and identification

Starbucks is noted for having one of the most successful loyalty programs. It periodically rewards consumers with free drinks and other extras based on points earned through purchasing behavior. As recorded in Exhibit 15.5, Bill repeats similar behavior over again and appears to be loyal to Starbucks, but is he really? This question is the focus of the next section.

15-4b Customer Commitment

Bill does appear at least partially loyal to Starbucks. However, repeated behavior alone cannot answer the loyalty question. True consumer loyalty consists of both a pattern of repeated behavior as evidenced by high customer share and a strong feeling of attachment, dedication, and sense of identification with a brand. **Customer commitment** captures this sense of attachment, dedication, and identification. Exhibit 15.6 depicts the components of loyalty. Customer share is behavioral, and commitment is an affective component of loyalty.

Highly committed customers are true assets to a company. They are willing to sacrifice to continue doing business with the brand and serve as a source of promotion by spreading positive WOM. If we look at a consumer with a pattern of consistent behavior like Bill in Exhibit 15.5, the question becomes whether

Exhibit 15.6

True Loyalty Requires Customer Commitment

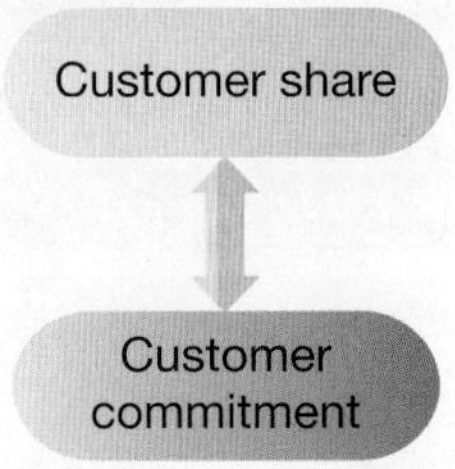

```
Customer share
      ↕
Customer
commitment
```

the behavior is simply inertia or motivated by true commitment. Perhaps this particular customer just happens to live next door to a Starbucks and thus getting coffee there is merely the easiest thing to do. If a CC's Coffee Shop were to take over the current Starbucks location, the customer would then buy his coffee there. However, if Bill were truly committed, he would seek out another Starbucks location even if the one next to his place were to close or get leased to a different coffee competitor. This distinguishes inertia from a truly loyal customer. Even if Starbucks is not convenient or the least expensive alternative, the truly loyal consumer will still seek out Starbucks. Indeed, the Starbucks loyalty card is successful not just for the points, but because the visit to Starbucks often brings hedonic value.

The CLV (Customer Lifetime Value equation from Chapter 2) concept demonstrates why high customer commitment is so beneficial to a company. The certainty of a lengthy stream of revenues is much less for a customer acting only on inertia. In addition, the customer acting on inertia alone is likely not contributing on the equity side of the equation as is the truly committed customer. A firm that concentrates on repeated behavior alone, perhaps by always being convenient, can do well but remains more vulnerable to competitors. The reason for the vulnerability is that competitors easily duplicate tangible assets like convenience; but the intangible assets, like the feel associated with a choice or place, or the feelings consumers have for Louis Vuitton or drinking a Coke, are very hard to duplicate.

Which brands have the most "loyalty"? At the top of the chart are brands like Apple, which has a high

switching cost plus an image of technological superiority going for it; AT&T, also a master of switching costs; BMW; and Walt Disney and Harley Davidson, both of which generate higher affective commitment. Brands with high loyalty are brands with high value. Casper Mattresses, while not a household name yet, is winning a loyal customer base for its high-end mattresses by having a mascot called Casper the Mattress communicate through its own Twitter site.

15-4c Preferred Customer Perks

Loyalty programs reward good customers with perks. From a behavioral learning perspective, these can be regarded as rewards that condition behavior so that consumers repeat good behavior (like buying drinks at Starbucks). The Starbucks Gold Card is often looked at as a successful program; the better customers get rewarded perks in the form of free drinks, free additions to drinks, and free refills on some items. Airlines use terms like gold, platinum, and diamond to refer to good, better, and best customers, respectively. Good customers get perks like upgrades to first class, access to comfortable airport lounges where passengers can wait in style, and preferential positions on waitlists for flights. A diamond passenger doesn't need to worry so much about a connection after a flight delay. If one spot is open on a plane heading home, they will likely zoom ahead of other passengers waiting to *earn* that spot.

Although perks often are very expensive for companies to provide, they make sense because the so-called good customers are disproportionately profitable for the companies. How do the consumers who get the perks feel? Well, generally, recipients feel grateful and look for ways to reciprocate such as with increased positive WOM.[38] Companies also need to be somewhat discrete in providing perks so as not to create embarrassment among recipients or anger among those who do not receive perks. But star customers provide disproportionate shares of profits to firms in competitive industries, so firms are justified in investing in ways to keep them from looking for opportunities to do business elsewhere.[39]

15-4d Antiloyalty

Loyalty is almost always discussed from a positive perspective. However, at times consumers act in an antiloyal way. **Antiloyal consumers** are those who

antiloyal consumers
consumers who will do everything possible to avoid doing business with a particular marketer

will do everything possible to avoid doing business with a particular marketer. These consumers generally dislike this particular company severely and the negative emotions that go along with the aversion determine the subsequent reactions. Antiloyalty is often motivated by a bad experience between a consumer and the marketer that the marketer could not redress.

Attributes marketers build into a product to create procedural switching costs are one source of frustration. These procedural costs sometimes build into so much frustration that consumers will just avoid anything to do with that brand, sometimes even forgoing the entire product category. Some consumers become so frustrated with cable TV services that they just give up their TV.

Antiloyal customers often are former customers who switched and treat the former marketing firm as a jilted partner. They obviously have no net positive lifetime value for the target firm. Moreover, these antiloyal consumers, who are former customers, become perhaps the most frequent source for negative word-of-mouth.[40] Thus, antiloyal consumers can be a major force to reckon with. Customers on board one of several Carnival Cruise Liners that lost power and got stuck adrift for a few days were disenchanted with the company's response and are likely to be antiloyal to Carnival.[41]

15-4e Value and Switching

Exhibit 15.7 reproduces the center portion of the Consumer Value Framework (CVF). The exhibit clearly shows that value plays a role in the post-consumption process. During an exchange, the consumer goes through the consumption process, and the result produces some amount and type of value. The value, in turn, shapes what happens next. Thus, the CVF makes up for a shortcoming of the disconfirmation theory approach (as displayed in Exhibit 15.1) by explicitly accounting for value.

For a host of reasons, consumers may end up maintaining a relationship even if they experience dissatisfaction. However, consumers do not maintain relationships in which they find no value. Even if consumers do not enjoy shopping at

> The Consumer Value Framework (CVF) makes up for a shortcoming of disconfirmation theory by explicitly accounting for value.

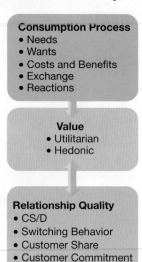

Exhibit 15.7
Value and Relationship Outcomes

Consumption Process
- Needs
- Wants
- Costs and Benefits
- Exchange
- Reactions

Value
- Utilitarian
- Hedonic

Relationship Quality
- CS/D
- Switching Behavior
- Customer Share
- Customer Commitment

Walmart, they tend to repeat the behavior because of high utilitarian value. Also, even though a consumer may be able to bank at a more convenient location, he might continue doing business with his original bank because he enjoys the personal relationships he has developed with bank personnel. Thus, both utilitarian and hedonic value can be key to preventing consumers from switching to a competitor and creating true loyalty among consumers.

Is one type of value more important in preventing switching behavior? The answer to this question depends on the nature of the goods or services being consumed. For functional types of services, such as banking, utilitarian value is more strongly related to customer share (and therefore preventing switching) than is hedonic value.[42] However, for more experiential types of services, such as fashion shopping, hedonic value is more strongly related to customer share.[43]

Value also is linked to the affective side of loyalty: customer commitment. Again, both value dimensions relate positively to commitment. Hedonic value, however,

Exhibit 15.8
Value Types and Loyalty

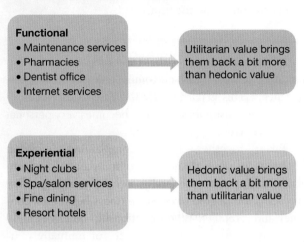

Functional
- Maintenance services
- Pharmacies
- Dentist office
- Internet services

→ Utilitarian value brings them back a bit more than hedonic value

Experiential
- Night clubs
- Spa/salon services
- Fine dining
- Resort hotels

→ Hedonic value brings them back a bit more than utilitarian value

plays a larger role in creating commitment. The receipt of hedonic value pays off as time goes by, because consumers' memories of hedonic value remain relatively strong.[44] In particular, customers who have switched service providers are more likely to become loyal customers when they experience increased hedonic value compared to the previous service provider. Exhibit 15.8 suggests ways that value plays a role in shaping loyalty and preventing switching behavior for different types of businesses.

15-5 LINK THE CONCEPT OF CONSUMER CO-CREATION OF VALUE TO CONSUMPTION OUTCOMES

In an earlier chapter, we introduced the concept of value co-creation. Co-creation recognizes that the value received from consumption depends not only on the product or service providers, but also on the customer him- or herself! When a consumption experience turns out really well, for example a vacation experience to the Top of the Rock in Missouri or the Palms Hotel and Spa at Miami Beach, the customer plays a role in creating the experience and may end up taking credit for that good outcome. At the very least, the customer has done enough research to find the place. That may

LOYALTY'S IN THE BOTTLE

CB theory recognizes that consumers play a role in creating value from relationships with marketers. Sometimes the consumer plays a small role and sometimes they play a large role. Most consumers probably wouldn't go to an expensive restaurant and begin to tell the chef how to cook the food. But marketers see opportunity in giving the customer a role in producing the outcome in all sorts of industries. No region is more synonymous with world-class wine than the Bordeaux region of France. Winemakers in Bordeaux are among the world's best. That said, consumers who are willing to pay $12,500 to $25,000 a barrel can have a Bordeaux blended to their own specification. Viniv, operated by Château Lynch-Bages, allows customers to create their own custom blends by specifying vineyard and varietal blends. Perhaps Viniv is onto a formula for high customer loyalty, since customers like to take credit for success!

Sources: Stanley, A. (2016), "A Wine of One's Own? They'll Drink to That," *The New York Times*, (July 2), http://nyti.ms/29nZ4Rz, accessed July 2, 2016; Cossío-Silva, F. J., Revilla-Camacho, M. Á., Vega-Vázquez, M., & Palacios-Florencio, B. (2016), "Value Co-creation and Customer Loyalty," *Journal of Business Research*, 69, 1621–1625.

mean hours on the Internet comparing vacation destinations, reading reviews at sites like tripadvisor.com, or searching out vacation-related hashtags on Instagram, Pinterest, or Twitter for good leads. After choosing a site, that consumer may spend more hours planning every detail of the vacation. Another consumer may just phone a human travel agent and say "Book us for five days at Disney World!"

Recall that attribution theory plays a role in what happens after purchase and consumption. When a consumer is highly engaged, and has put a lot of effort into producing and creating the consumption experience, he or she may be very much inclined to take credit when things go well. When things don't go so well at first, though, the confirmatory bias may kick in and the consumer may deny that things are going poorly. But when things go well, the consumer is likely to become more convinced that their brand choice was correct, become even more engaged with the brand, and be very willing to tell others about the experience by spreading positive word-of-mouth (WOM). Thus, customer engagement in co-creation of both utilitarian and hedonic value creates a *stickiness* that encourages them to tell others about their experience and exhibit loyalty-related behaviors.[45] In other words, consumers will stick with the choice regardless of whether the experience is virtual (e.g., through online social networking) or actual (as with vacation resorts).

Not all consumers want to put a lot of effort into shaping the consumption experience. Consider a busy consumer who needs to get a wedding gift for a cousin. Perhaps the easiest choice is to select something "acceptable" from a gift registry. In this case, even if the consumer spends a little more than they planned, they will be more satisfied because of the minimal effort needed to get this job done. Utilitarian value is clearly the focus.[46] One of the tricks for marketers is to be able to tell the difference between the two types of consumers—the one who is highly engaged in co-creation and the one who is unengaged and very willing to be efficiently served—and adjust their behaviors accordingly.

15-5a Relationships and the Marketing Firm

Marketers have come to realize that the exchange between a business and a consumer constitutes a relationship. Two factors help make this clear:

relationship quality
degree of connectedness between a consumer and a retailer

1. **Customers have a lifetime value to the firm.**

2. **True loyalty involves both a continuing series of interactions and feelings of attachment between the customer and the firm.**

In return, many firms that truly adopt a relationship marketing approach with customers enjoy improved performance.[47] This is particularly the case as the relationship between customer and seller becomes very personal and involves trust.

Taken together, CS/D, complaining behavior, switching, customer share, and commitment all indicate relationship quality. Generally, relationship quality represents the degree of connectedness between a consumer and a retailer. When relationship quality is high, the prospects for a continued series of mutually valuable exchanges exist. Relationship quality represents the health of the relationship so that, in all likelihood, healthy relationships continue. When consumers are truly loyal, and this loyalty is returned by the marketer, relationship quality is high.

15-5b Value and Relationship Quality

A healthy relationship between a consumer and a marketer enhances value both for the consumer and the marketer.[48] For the consumer, decision making becomes simpler, enhancing utilitarian value, and relational exchanges often involve pleasant relational and experiential elements, enhancing hedonic value. For the marketer, the regular consumer does not have to be resold and thus much of the selling effort required to convert a new customer is not necessary.

In fact, when relationship quality is very strong, the marketer and the customer act as partners. When something bad happens to the marketer, the customer is affected. When something bad happens to the customer, the marketer is affected. Customers and sellers often act very closely as partners in business-to-business contexts. However, relationship quality can be very important in business-to-consumer contexts, too. When a parent sends a child off to college, chances are that a strong relationship exists or will soon exist between the family and the college. The family will don school colors on game day and become a prime target for fundraising campaigns. The strong relationship quality means that the family and the university share many common goals.

Exhibit 15.9

The Characteristics of Relationship Quality

▶ **Competence.** Consumer views company and service providers as knowledgeable and capable.

▶ **Communication.** Consumer and firm understand each other and "speak the same language."

▶ **Trust.** Buyer and seller can depend on each other.

▶ **Equity.** Both buyer and seller see equity in exchange and are able to equitably resolve conflicts.

▶ **Personalization.** Buyer treats the customer as an individual with unique desires and requirements.

▶ **Gratifying.** The relationship provides for gratifying (value-added) experiences.

▶ **Customer oriented.** Strong relationships are more likely to develop when a firm practices a marketing orientation, and this filters down to service providers and salespeople.

Exhibit 15.9 displays some of the characteristics of a marketing relationship that is very healthy. Consider this example. A consumer uses the same travel agent for practically all travel. When the consumer calls the agent, the agent does not have to ask the customer for preferences or personal information, not even a credit card number, because she has all the information about the customer. She knows the customer is a Delta SkyMiles member so she books on Delta whenever possible. She knows the customer doesn't like close connections (under an hour), so she tries to always allow at least an hour and a half between connecting flights. Whenever the customer flies, the agent monitors the flight status. If there is a delay, she phones the customer to exchange information and rebooks any connecting flights, hotel reservations, or car rentals if the delay disrupts the original plans. In this case, we can see that many of the characteristics displayed in Exhibit 15.9 are illustrated. This agent is customer oriented, has a personal relationship with the customer, communicates well, and is competent; the relationship is characterized by trust. Chances are that this customer will be loyal for quite some time.

STUDY TOOLS 15

LOCATED AT BACK OF THE TEXTBOOK

☐ Tear out Chapter Review Card

LOCATED AT WWW.CENGAGE.COM/LOGIN

☐ Review Key Term flashcards and create your own cards

☐ Track your knowledge and understanding of key concepts in consumer behavior

☐ Complete practice quizzes to prepare for tests

☐ Complete interactive content within CB Online

☐ Review the Chapter Highlight boxes for CB Online

16 | Consumer and Marketing Misbehavior

LEARNING OBJECTIVES

After studying this chapter, the student should be able to:

16-1 Understand the consumer misbehavior phenomenon and how it affects the exchange process.

16-2 Distinguish between consumer misbehavior and consumer problem behavior.

16-3 Discuss marketing ethics and how marketing ethics guide the development of marketing programs.

16-4 Comprehend the role of corporate social responsibility in the field of marketing.

16-5 Understand the various forms of regulation that affect marketing practice.

16-6 Comprehend the major areas of criticism to which marketers are subjected.

Remember to visit **PAGE 345** for additional **STUDY TOOLS**

INTRODUCTION

Most of the time when students think about the field of consumer behavior, they think about behaviors that are generally considered "acceptable" or "normal" by societal standards. They tend to think about things like buying products, watching advertisements, developing budgets, and deciding on solutions to problems. A number of important topics, however, fall outside of what would be considered acceptable. In this chapter, we focus on what is referred to as consumer and marketer misbehavior. The term *misbehavior* is used cautiously because opinions regarding what is acceptable or normal depend on our ethical beliefs, ideologies, and even culture. For consumers, examples include shoplifting, downloading music illegally, drinking and driving, engaging in fraud, and bullying one another on the internet. Marketers sometimes engage in unethical activities as well. They mislead consumers through deceptive advertising, state that regular prices are "sale" prices, and artificially limit the availability of products in order to increase prices. Some marketers will do anything to profit at the cost of consumer satisfaction and value. As we discuss, a fair marketplace depends on ethical behavior by *both* consumers and marketers. When the marketplace is disrupted by misbehavior, both consumers and marketers eventually lose.

16-1 CONSUMER MISBEHAVIOR AND EXCHANGE

Consumer misbehavior may be viewed as a subset of the *human deviance* topic. This topic has a long history of research in the fields of sociology and social psychology. We consider misbehavior a subset in part because the term covers only negative or destructive deviance and does not consider positive deviance. Sometimes consumers can deviate from norms with the intention of doing good.

Consumer misbehavior can be defined in numerous ways. We define it as behaviors that are in some way unethical and that potentially harm the self or others.[1] Misbehavior violates norms and also disrupts the flow of consumption activities. For example, a consumer cursing at employees in a grocery store because she thinks her wait is too long makes other consumers feel uncomfortable. Her actions disrupt others' shopping and may affect their entire afternoon. Chances are the employees who endure the outburst will perform poorly, at least for a while. This single consumer's actions potentially affect all the other customers in the store.

Consumer misbehavior is sometimes called the "dark side" of CB, and words such as *aberrant*, *illicit*, *dysfunctional*, and *deviant* have been used to describe it. Some behaviors are clearly illegal, while others are simply immoral. There's a difference. For example, shoplifting is illegal and almost always considered immoral. Illicitly downloading music, however, is illegal but not always considered immoral. Many students think that if "everyone's doing it," then there's not a problem. Not returning excess change that is mistakenly given at a store is immoral but not illegal.[2] A consumer might purchase a product one day, use it, and then return it for a refund. This may be immoral but not illegal. This practice is called *retail borrowing* and it costs the retail sector billions of dollars annually.

In order for exchanges to occur in an orderly fashion, the expectations of the consumer, the marketer, and even other consumers must coincide with one another.[3] When we see consumers becoming abusive, cutting in line at a movie theatre, or making other people uncomfortable, the exchange process is disrupted. Consumers who make fraudulent insurance claims increase insurance costs. Consumers who engage in retail borrowing increase product costs. Belligerent sports fans turn otherwise joyous occasions into annoying events for everybody. All sorts of misbehaviors affect exchange.

16-1a The Focus of Misbehavior: Value

As we have discussed throughout this text, a central component for understanding consumer behavior is value. It shouldn't

> **consumer misbehavior** behaviors that are in some way unethical and that potentially harm the self or others

Consumers who misbehave harm themselves and others.

decision making and consumer misbehavior is shown in Exhibit 16.1.

MORAL BELIEFS

Moral beliefs, or beliefs about the perceived ethicality or morality of behaviors, play a very important role in misbehavior.

Notice that a consumer's moral beliefs are made up of three components: moral equity, contractualism, and relativism.[6]

▸ **Moral equity** represents beliefs regarding an act's fairness or justness. Do I consider this action to be fair? Is it fair for me to illegally download a video?

▸ **Contractualism** refers to beliefs about the violation of written (or unwritten) laws. Does this action break a law? Does it break an unwritten promise of how I should act? Is pirating videos illegal?

▸ **Relativism** represents beliefs about the social acceptability of an act. Is this action culturally acceptable? Is pirating acceptable in this culture?

ETHICAL EVALUATIONS

Consumers bring their moral beliefs into all decision-making settings. Once a consumer enters into a situation that calls for an ethical decision (*Should I download this movie?*), she considers the various alternative courses of action. Here, two sets of ethical evaluations occur: deontological evaluations and teleological evaluations.[7]

Deontological evaluations focus on specific *actions*. Is this action "right"? As such, deontology focuses on *how* people accomplish their goals. The deontological perspective is, in large part, attributed to the work of Immanuel Kant. Kant's *categorical imperative* suggests that one should act in a way that would be considered a universal law for all people facing the same situation.

Teleological evaluations focus on the *consequences* of the behaviors and the individual's assessment of those consequences. How much "good" will

be surprising then that the focal motivation for consumer misbehavior is value.[4] However, *how* consumers obtain value is the key issue. Rowdy sports fans think that the best way to obtain value is to be obnoxious. Identity thieves believe that the best way to obtain value is to steal from others. In each instance, consumers seek to maximize the benefits they receive from an action while minimizing, or eliminating, their own costs. Ultimately, others' costs increase. Consumer misbehavior is, quite simply, selfish!

16-1b Consumer Misbehavior and Ethics

Moral beliefs and evaluations influence decisions pertaining to marketplace behaviors.[5] The effect of moral beliefs on ethical

moral beliefs beliefs about the perceived ethicality or morality of behaviors

moral equity beliefs regarding an act's fairness or justness

contractualism beliefs about the violation of written (or unwritten) laws

relativism beliefs about the social acceptability of an act in a culture

deontological evaluations evaluations regarding the inherent rightness or wrongness of specific actions

teleological evaluations consumers' assessment of the goodness or badness of the consequences of actions

> Moral beliefs and evaluations influence decisions pertaining to marketplace behaviors.

Exhibit 16.1

Moral Beliefs, Ethical Evaluations, and Behavior

Moral Beliefs
- Moral equity
- Contractualism
- Relativism

→

Ethical Evaluations
- Deontology
- Teleology

→

Consumer Behavior/ Misbehavior

result from this decision? With teleological evaluations, consumers consider the perceived consequences of the actions for various stakeholders, the probability that the consequence will occur, the desirability of the consequences for the stakeholders, and the importance of the stakeholder groups to the consumer.[8] Notice from Exhibit 16.1 that moral beliefs influence ethical evaluations, which in turn influence the decision to engage in misbehavior.

16-1c Motivations of Misbehavior

Moral beliefs and behavioral evaluations indeed play important roles in consumer misbehavior. However, the question remains: why do consumers misbehave? Researchers Ronald Fullerton and Girish Punj offer the following motivations of consumer misbehavior:[9]

- **Unfulfilled Aspirations.** Many consumers have unfulfilled aspirations that influence their misbehavior. An important concept here is *anomie*. Anomie has been conceptualized as both a response to rapid cultural change and an explanation for deviance. To understand anomie as an explanation for deviance, consider the goals that are generally accepted in a culture. The U.S. culture places a great deal of emphasis on attaining material possessions and "getting ahead." However, not all members of the society have the necessary resources to be able to get ahead and enjoy the things that society deems important. As a result, some consumers turn to deviant actions in order to acquire these things. It's when societal goals are out of reach given the accepted means of achieving them that deviance occurs.[10]

- **Thrill Seeking.** The thrill of the action may lead consumers to misbehave. Some consumers get a thrill from defacing the property of companies.

- **Lack of Moral Constraints.** Some consumers simply don't have a set of moral beliefs that are in agreement with society's expectations and see no problem with their behavior. For example, some

consumers who sell illegal drugs don't see a problem with the behavior.

- **Differential Association.** Differential association explains why groups of people replace one set of acceptable norms with another set that others view as unacceptable. By acting in opposition to acceptable standards, group members forge their own identities and strengthen group cohesion.[11] For example, prospective gang members may assault innocent bystanders as a way of gaining acceptance into their group.

- **Pathological Socialization.** Consumers may view misbehavior as a way of getting revenge against companies. Stealing from large corporations may seem less severe than stealing from a family-owned retailer, and consumers may believe that big companies somehow deserve what they get. Numerous groups have targeted Walmart over the last few years simply because they believe that the company "deserves it."

- **Provocative Situational Factors.** Factors like crowding, wait times, excessive heat, and noise can contribute to consumer misbehavior. A well-mannered, quiet person may become combative if his order is wrong at a busy restaurant.

- **Opportunism.** Misbehavior can also be the outcome of a deliberate decision-making process that weighs the risks and rewards of the behavior. For example, consumers may believe that the rewards associated with stealing outweigh the risks of getting caught.

16-2 DISTINGUISH CONSUMER MISBEHAVIOR FROM PROBLEM BEHAVIOR

Consumer misbehavior can be distinguished from what we refer to as consumer "problem behavior." The misbehavior term is used to describe behavior deliberately harmful to the self or another party during an exchange. **Consumer problem behavior** refers to behaviors that are seemingly outside of a

> **consumer problem behavior** consumer behavior that is deemed to be unacceptable but that is seemingly beyond the control of the consumer

Exhibit 16.2

Consumer Misbehavior and Problem Behavior

Consumer misbehavior	Consumer problem behavior
▸ Shoplifting	▸ Compulsive buying
▸ Computer-mediated behaviors: illicit sharing of software and music, computer attacks, cyberbullying	▸ Compulsive shopping
▸ Fraud	▸ Eating disorders
▸ Abusive consumer behavior	▸ Binge drinking
▸ Illegitimate complaining	▸ Problem gambling
▸ Product misuse: aggressive driving, drunk driving, cell phone use while driving, sexting	▸ Drug abuse

consumer's control. For example, some people compulsively shop. Some people are addicted to drugs or alcohol. In cases like these, consumers may express a desire to stop the behaviors but simply find quitting too difficult.

Although the line between consumer misbehavior and problem behaviors can be blurred, we distinguish between the two areas by considering the issue of self-control. Exhibit 16.2 presents examples of consumer misbehaviors and problem behaviors, but again the line is blurry. Drug addiction is listed as a problem behavior, but when someone drives under the influence of drugs, the individual risks injuring or killing someone else. Shoplifting could also be considered either a problem behavior or misbehavior, as the behavior can sometimes be clinically diagnosed as *kleptomania*.

16-2a Consumer Misbehavior

Many of the behaviors that are listed in Exhibit 16.2 are discussed frequently in the popular press. For example, you may have heard stories in the news media about the devastating effects of binge drinking or problem gambling. Although there are many different types of consumer misbehavior, we limit our discussion to behaviors that have gathered significant attention.

SHOPLIFTING

Did you know that consumers steal more than $35 million of products every day? That's over $13 billion per year! Shoplifting has become one of the most common

U.S. crimes, averaging over 500,000 cases per day! Many shoplifters are repeat offenders, shoplifting on average 1.6 times per week. Sadly, even kids shoplift. Statistics reveal that approximately 25 percent of shoplifters are children. And many adults say they started in their teens.[12] Employees also steal products: a 2015 study revealed that half of total shoplifting is done by store employees.[13]

Consumers' motivations for shoplifting are similar to motivations for other forms of misbehavior. Specifically, consumers shoplift because the temptation can be very strong, they believe that retailers can afford the monetary loss, they believe they probably won't get caught, they seek acceptance into a group, and the act can be exciting.[14]

As we have mentioned, shoplifting can sometimes be diagnosed as kleptomania. Kleptomania is generally triggered by a strong compulsion and the inability of the consumer to fight the urge.

Emotions and Shoplifting. Emotions play a large role in shoplifting. Fear of being caught plays a role in predicting shoplifting intentions, especially among young consumers. Interestingly, the shoplifting intentions of adolescents appear to be more heavily influenced by emotions than by moral beliefs. The opposite occurs in older consumers. Research also shows that consumers who shoplift are sometimes motivated by repressed feelings of stress and anger.[15]

Age and Shoplifting. Shoplifting behavior appears to peak during the adolescent years. This may be because adolescents are yet to fully mature and often find themselves in the stressful transition from childhood to adulthood. Adolescents also tend to consider shoplifting as being more ethical than do adult shoppers.[16]

COMPUTER-MEDIATED BEHAVIORS: ILLEGAL SHARING OF SOFTWARE AND MUSIC

Due to improvements in technology, consumers often have the ability to illicitly download electronic material from a number of sources. Major problems here include the pirating of computer software, video games, and music.

Some consumers cannot resist the temptation to shoplift.

The software industry continues to lose billions of dollars annually due to piracy, and the amount is increasing. A recent study from the Business Software Alliance estimates that nearly $70 billion is lost globally each year due to unlicensed and improper software usage.[17] What's more, over half of computer users worldwide admit to pirating software.

The music industry has also been hit hard by these actions. The U.S. Digital Millennium Copyright Act deems the sharing of copyrighted music as illegal. Although there are numerous legal download services available, such as iTunes, consumers continue to share music in illegal ways. Interestingly, research reveals that how consumers view illegal downloading depends on the motivation for the behavior. That is, if the motivation is primarily based on utilitarian value (that is, for personal gain), then the act is viewed as less morally ethical and socially acceptable than if the behavior occurs based on hedonic value (that is, for "fun").[18]

COMPUTER-MEDIATED BEHAVIORS: ATTACKS

Computers present other opportunities for misbehavior. Did you know that consumers in the United States send more spam than do consumers in any other nation? Spam, which clogs up computers and slows internet connectivity, results in billions of dollars of lost business productivity annually.[19] Computer viruses are another major problem. In fact, it has been estimated that viruses cost U.S. businesses over $55 billion annually.[20] U.S. households suffer losses of nearly $5 billion annually due to viruses. By far the most common form of computer-aided attacks is the spreading of malicious URL links.[21]

Another form of computer misbehavior is *cyberbullying*. Cyberbullying, the attack of innocent people on the internet, is especially a problem for young consumers. Current research indicates that girls tend to be targeted by, and instigate, cyberattacks more often than boys.[22] However, cyberbullying is a serious issue for both genders. Statistics from a recent study reveal that as many as 32% of online teens have been victims of some type of cyberbullying.[23] However, the true percentage may be much higher, as another recent study reported that fully 87% of teens surveyed witnessed cyberbullying.[24] The disparity in the statistics suggests that some teens may be bullied but may not want to admit to it. Fortunately, a more recent study from 2016 revealed that over 90% of parents surveyed regularly speak to their children about inappropriate internet behavior like cyberbullying. Teens can experience lower self-esteem, depression, anxiety, and suicidal thoughts when victimized by cyberbullying.[25]

CONSUMER FRAUD

There are many types of consumer fraud. For instance, consumers fraudulently obtain credit cards, open bank accounts, and turn in insurance claims. Although it is difficult to estimate exactly how much consumer fraud ends up costing consumers, the Coalition Against Insurance Fraud estimates that insurance fraud alone costs Americans at least $80 billion per year.[26]

Identity theft is another major public concern. Statistics reveal that as many as 15 million Americans are victimized by identity theft each year.[27] The Identity Theft and Assumption Deterrence Act of 1998 and the Identity Theft Penalty Enhancement Act of 2004 were passed in order to curb the crime, but the increased reliance on computers for transactions has contributed to its spread. It is no wonder that information privacy and security concerns are hot topics for consumers.

ABUSIVE CONSUMER BEHAVIOR

As we have discussed, abusive consumers can be a real problem. Consumers who are aggressive or rude to employees and other consumers are considered to be abusive.[28] One early study in the area of problem customers suggested that four categories of customers can be identified: verbally or physically abusive customers, uncooperative customers, drunken customers, and customers who break company policy.[29] Needless to say, employees don't like to deal with customers who act this way, and abusive behaviors can have negative effects on other consumers as well.[30]

One area of abusive behavior that has gained attention is dysfunctional fan behavior. *Dysfunctional fan behavior* is abnormal functioning relating to sporting event consumption. Several college towns have seen riots that have occurred after big losses (or wins) of the home team. Unfortunately, riots can get out of hand quickly. While there are many explanations for such behavior, some think that dysfunctional fan behavior is simply a result of an increasingly violent society.[31]

Another controversial issue today is culture jamming. *Culture jamming* refers to attempts to disrupt marketing campaigns by altering the messages in some meaningful way. For example, billboards are often altered in a way that delivers messages that conflict with those originally intended. Also, websites that attempt to disrupt marketing efforts are often created. Sites like Amexsux.com have popped up in the online world. Of course, calling culture jamming an abusive behavior depends on your own perspective. Proponents believe that their behaviors are a matter of free speech and good for society.

ILLEGITIMATE COMPLAINING

Consumers also complain about products and services even when there really isn't a problem. To date, the research on illegitimate complaining remains relatively scarce. However, one study did find that illegitimate complaining is motivated by a desire for monetary gain, a desire to evade personal responsibility for product misuse, a desire to enhance the consumer's ego and look good to others, or a desire to harm a service provider or company.[32]

PRODUCT MISUSE

Consumers also may use products in ways that were clearly not intended. In some cases, consumers simply misuse products by accident. In others, they knowingly misuse them. For example, some consumers will sniff glue or household

BLACK (AND BLUE) FRIDAY

Idaho Statesman/Getty Images

"Black Friday" has become a ritual for millions of consumers. For some, it's a fun-filled family tradition. For others, the entire weekend is seen as nothing more than madness. And as retailers continue to move Black Friday back to Thanksgiving Day, the madness only intensifies. Each year there are numerous reports of injuries and assaults that occur during the rush. Sadly, some consumers add to the problem by just going to watch the event, or to cause trouble.

Nationwide, local police forces are put on alert each year on Black Friday, and hospitals know that they will be busier than usual as well. One especially violent act occurred during Black Friday 2013, when thieves dragged a police officer with their car as they tried to escape after shoplifting at an Illinois Kohl's department store. The violence continued to escalate in 2015 and 2016, when a number of videos from around the U.S. went viral.

Although Black Friday is an opportunity for retailers to operate in the "black" by realizing a profit, it seems that some consumers will stop at nothing to get what they want. For some, Black Friday might as well be called "Black and Blue Friday."

Sources: David Boroff and Nicole Hensley, "Black Friday Brawls Break Out Across the Country, Including Several Ugly Incidents at Walmart and Food Court Melee – VIDEO," *New York Daily News*, November 27, 2015, http://www.nydailynews.com/news/national/kentucky-mall-brawl-kicks-black-friday -violence-article-1.2448085, accessed May 23, 2016; Sege, Adam and Juan Perez Jr. (2013), "Charges Filed After Shoplifting Suspect Shot by Police," Chicago Tribune (online edition), November 29, 2013, online content retrieved at: http://www.chicagotribune.com/news/local/suburbs/joliet_romeoville /chi-black-friday-kohls-shooting-20131128,0,1973578.story, accessed June 30, 2014. Philip Caulfield, "As Anxious Black Friday Shoppers Swarm Sale Stores to Nab Post-Thanksgiving Deals, Fights and Hot Tempers Mar Holiday Shopping and Lead to Injuries, Arrests Across the Country," NYDailyNews.com, November 23, 2012, http://www.nydailynews.com/news/national/tensions-black-friday-u-s -article-1.1206877 (accessed March 7, 2013).

cleaners to get high. Marketers therefore work hard to ensure that consumers understand the ways in which products should be used. However, even when warnings and instructions are provided, consumers still misuse products. Injuries that result can be very costly. In fact, statistics from the Consumer Product Safety Commission reveal that deaths and injuries resulting from product consumption cost the United States over $800 billion annually.[33]

Why do consumers use products in unsafe ways? A number of explanations have been offered. Consumers may simply not pay attention to what they are doing, may feel as though they generally get away with risky behaviors, may have a tendency to be error prone, or may focus more on the thrill of misuse rather than the actual risk of the behavior.[34] Although product misuse may apply to any number of products, many issues revolve around automobiles, cell phones, and prescription medication.

Aggressive Driving. Aggressive driving may range from mild displays of anger to seriously violent acts while driving. Although aggressive driving is often thought of as an act by a solitary consumer, aggressive driving problems often involve multiple drivers, as victims retaliate with their own aggression.[35] Younger, less-educated males have been shown to be more likely to engage in aggressive driving behavior.[36] Situational factors, such as intense traffic congestion and driver stress, as well as personality traits play a part. Traits like instability and competitiveness have been found among aggressive drivers.[37]

Drinking and Driving. Statistics reveal that as many as 13,000 people die from alcohol-related traffic accidents in the United States each year and that nearly three out of every ten Americans will be involved in an alcohol-related crash at some point in their lives. Although drunk driving incidents have decreased in recent years, on average, approximately 30 Americans die from these accidents each day.[38] Sadly, one out of every six fatalities among children aged 14 and younger is due to an alcohol-related accident.[39] Statistics also reveal that men are responsible for four in five episodes of drinking and driving and that young men aged 21–34 are responsible for 32% of all instances of drinking and driving. This is a telling statistic, given that this group only makes up 11% of the total U.S. population.[40] While the cost in terms of human life is high, there is a high monetary cost of drinking and driving. Estimates reveal that drinking and driving costs over $52 billion annually, based on the most recent data.[41]

Texting while driving is extremely dangerous

Furthermore, one study estimates that nearly 25% of all drivers aged 15–20 who are killed in fatal accidents have blood alcohol levels above 0.08.[42] Of course, this group is under the legal drinking age. Drunk driving and binge drinking are often related. In fact, one study indicated that over 80% of respondents who reported alcohol-impaired driving also reported engaging in binge drinking behaviors.[43]

Cell Phone Use and Driving. There were more than 7 billion cellular subscriptions worldwide as of 2015 and there are currently over 355 million wireless subscriptions in the United States alone.[44] The effective U.S. penetration rate is now over 100% (many consumers have more than one subscription) and more than 90% of American adults have cell phones.[45] With such widespread adoption, one area of concern involves the use of cell phones while driving. While not everyone will agree that simply using a cell phone while driving is a consumer misbehavior, texting and driving is certainly a dangerous issue. And, this behavior is against the law in many states. Texting while driving is currently the single largest form of distracted driving. While the phrase may sound funny, "DWI—Driving While Intexticated" is anything but.

Studies reveal that consumers who use cell phones while driving are four times as likely to get into serious accidents, and the problem is particularly serious for teens particularly when it comes to texting. One recent study found that only 43% of teens surveyed, aged 16–17, had *never* texted while driving, which of course suggests that 57% have![46] A 2012 study also revealed that teen girls are twice as likely as teen boys to use cell phones while driving.[47] While the problem appears to be serious among younger drivers, the behavior actually cuts across age groups, and texting is not the only problem. One study revealed that 43% of drivers 18–29 surfed the internet while driving.[48]

As of late 2016, eighteen U.S. states prohibit all drivers from using handheld cell phones while driving, and while no state completely bans cell phone use, 38 states ban all use by novice drivers. Regarding texting, as of late 2016, Montana and Arizona were the only states that did not have at least some ban on texting while driving.[49]

SEXTING

One growing form of misbehavior is "sexting." Sexting is taking nude photos of oneself and sending them to another person via cell phone. It seems to occur most frequently among teen-aged consumers, and the app Snapchat has been criticized by some as making sexting easy and secure.

Multiple media reports indicate that many teens feel like sexting isn't harmful. Parents and school administrators don't feel the same way. Parents are concerned that the images can be passed from person to person, and even onto the internet. Sexting also raises moral, ethical, and legal issues.[50] The behavior can result in severe psychological and social problems. The effects of sexting range from minor psychological distress to intense emotional trauma.[51] As of mid-2016, 20 states had reportedly enacted legislation aimed at banning the practice.[52]

16-2b Consumer Problem Behavior

Consumer problem behaviors include other acts that do not necessarily break any specific laws or societal norms. For example, consumers shop too much, rack up large amounts of debt, and sometimes harm their own bodies in desperate attempts to look thin. Psychological problems can cause or influence these behaviors.

COMPULSIVE CONSUMPTION

Compulsive consumption refers to repetitive, excessive, and purposeful consumer behaviors that are performed as a response to tension, anxiety, or obtrusive thoughts.[53] The term *compulsive consumption* is often used broadly and consists of a number of specific behaviors related to the purchase and use of consumer products and services.[54] Compulsive consumption should not be confused with *addictive consumption*. **Addictive consumption** refers to a physiological dependency on the consumption of a product. The word *dependency* is important, and in the strictest sense, addictions are characterized by the physical inability to discontinue a behavior, or a physical reliance. A person who is addicted to a product physically needs it. Compulsive consumption often takes two forms: *compulsive buying* and *compulsive shopping*.

Compulsive Buying. **Compulsive buying** may be defined as chronic, repetitive *purchasing* behaviors that are a response to negative events or feelings.[55] The behavior has harmful effects, such as the accumulation of debt, domestic problems, and feelings of frustration. Influencers of the behavior include feelings of low self-esteem, obsessive-compulsive tendencies, fantasy-seeking motivations, and materialism,[56] as well as a focus on the short term.[57] Research reveals that a need for prestige also motivates the behavior, particularly among college students.[58] Among adolescents, the behavior can be a response to family problems.[59] The same negative feelings that influence compulsive buying can also result from the behavior itself. So a consumer who buys compulsively as a reaction to negative feelings often experiences even more negative feelings after going on buying binges.[60] In short, it can be a vicious cycle.

Compulsive Shopping. **Compulsive shopping** refers to repetitive *shopping* behaviors. The word *oniomania* is sometimes used to describe this behavior. Compulsive shoppers often feel preoccupied with shopping, exhibit uncontrollable shopping tendencies, and experience guilt from their behaviors.[61] The key difference between compulsive shopping and buying is the buying process

compulsive consumption repetitive, excessive, and purposeful consumer behaviors that are performed as a response to tension, anxiety, or obtrusive thoughts

addictive consumption physiological dependency on the consumption of a consumer product

compulsive buying chronic, repetitive purchasing that is a response to negative events or feelings

compulsive shopping repetitive *shopping* behaviors

Vladimir Sazonov/Shutterstock.com

Exhibit 16.3

Binge Eating Disorder

Binge eating disorder consists of:

▶ Frequent eating episodes that include large quantities of food in short time periods

▶ A felt loss of control over eating behavior

▶ Feelings of shame, guilt, and/or disgust about the amount of food consumed

▶ The consumption of food when one is not hungry

▶ The consumption of food in secret

Source: Based on National Eating Disorders Association, www.nationaleatingdisorders.com.

itself. Compulsive shoppers tend to focus on the mental highs associated with "the hunt,"[62] whereas compulsive buyers feel the need to buy. Although early research on this issue revealed that compulsive shopping was predominately a problem for women, more recent evidence suggests that both women and men engage in compulsive shopping. One study confirmed that equal proportions of men and women are compulsive shoppers (6% of women, 5.5% of men).[63]

EATING DISORDERS

Binge eating refers to the consumption of large amounts of food while feeling a general loss of control over intake. Binge eating may result in medical complications, including high cholesterol, high blood pressure, and heart disease. Exhibit 16.3 presents a description of the binge eating disorder. The disorder is thought to affect as many as 3.5% of all women and 2% of all men at some point in their lives.[64]

Binge eating has been shown to be associated with compulsive buying and impulsivity, and it is often related to obesity. Consumers who binge-eat and who are also obese are likely to have other psychiatric disorders that require treatment.[65] Unfortunately, many consumers who binge-eat fail to seek treatment. Binge eating is also often associated with *bulimia*, a disorder that includes binge eating episodes followed by self-induced vomiting. *Anorexia*, or the starving of one's body in the pursuit of thinness, is another consumer eating disorder. Eating problems are often associated with other consumer issues. For example, it has been shown that simply paying for food with a credit card leads to unhealthy food choices.[66]

BINGE DRINKING

Binge drinking is defined as the consumption of five or more drinks in a single drinking session for men and four or more drinks for women,[67] and the behavior is particularly prevalent among full-time college students. A report from 2012 revealed that binge drinking rates among full-time college students are over 39%, compared to 35% for students who are not enrolled full time.[68] Binge drinking occurs globally. In fact, one study revealed that students in the United Kingdom binge-drink for the sole purpose of getting drunk and feel that getting drunk is a key part of college life.[69]

Binge drinking has been linked to suicide attempts, unsafe sexual practices, legal problems, academic disruptions, and even death.[70] Sadly, over 1,800 college students between the ages of 18 and 24 die each year from alcohol-related unintentional injuries.[71] College students who have higher self-actualization values generally have lower attitudes toward binge drinking, whereas students who value social affiliation tend to have more positive attitudes toward the behavior.[72] Studies also reveal that students who drink excessively often brag about it on apps like Facebook, Instagram, or Snapchat.[73]

Binge drinking behavior actually cuts across demographic groups. One alarming trend is the occurrence of binge drinking among underage consumers, with one study indicating that nearly half of the alcohol consumed on four-year college campuses is consumed by underage consumers.[74] Other statistics reveal that one in five teenagers binge-drink.[75]

PROBLEM GAMBLING

Problem gambling is another serious issue. This behavior may be described as an obsession with gambling and the loss of control over gambling behavior and its consequences.[76] Consumers who are problem gamblers frequently gamble longer than planned, borrow money to finance their gambling,

binge eating consumption of large amounts of food while feeling a general loss of control over food intake

binge drinking consumption of five or more drinks in a single drinking session for men and four or more drinks for women

problem gambling obsession over the thought of gambling and the loss of control over gambling behavior and its consequences and feel major depression due to their gambling behaviors. Although casino and online gambling receive much research attention, lottery ticket and scratch ticket purchases can also be considered problem gambling behaviors.[77]

Estimates reveal that as many as two million consumers meet the criteria of pathological gambling and another four to six million could be considered problem gamblers.[78] Problem gamblers exhibit at least some of the criteria for pathological gambling. Although problem gambling is often thought of as being primarily an issue for middle-aged consumers, approximately 8% of college students gamble problematically.[79] What's more, one study revealed that nearly 70% of seniors older than 65 had gambled at least once in the previous year and nearly 11% were considered at risk for problem gambling.[80] Research indicates that problem gambling is often associated with compulsive buying and drug abuse.[81]

DRUG ABUSE

Both illegal and prescription drugs are problem areas for some consumers. The problem is especially alarming among teens. One study by the Partnership for a Drug-Free America revealed that nearly one in five teenagers report using prescription drugs to get high, and nearly one in ten report abusing cough medicine.[82] The study did reveal, however, that the percentage of high school seniors who abuse prescription drugs has declined slightly over the most current ten-year period, down from 17.1% in 2005 to 12.9% in 2015.

The abuse of drugs, which cuts across demographic groups, has been a problem for years.

Recreational use of marijuana was legalized in the states of Washington and Colorado during 2012, and later in Oregon, Alaska, and Washington, D.C. in 2014. Even more states legalized marijuana in 2016. Nevertheless, the majority of U.S. states still have laws against the drug, and there has been a general decline in use among young consumers over the last few decades. Data from 2015 reveal that 6% of high school seniors surveyed reported smoking marijuana daily, while approximately 37% reported having smoked it within the last twelve months.[83]

Of course, it's not only teens who smoke marijuana. Estimates reveal that over 17 million consumers use the drug regularly.[84] A relatively new trend is also the use of "synthetic" marijuana, which many consumers view as being safer than the actual drug. This drug, however, has come under tighter Drug Enforcement Agency control, which has led to a gradual decrease in its use. Other drugs, such as cocaine and methamphetamine, are also often abused at alarmingly high rates.

We've discussed only a handful of behaviors that may be considered consumer problem areas here and we again emphasize that these issues are largely impacted by individual beliefs and ethical perspectives. Space prohibits a complete discussion of several other consumer problem areas.

16-3 MARKETING ETHICS AND MISBEHAVIOR

karamysh/Shutterstock.com

As we have stated, a fair marketplace depends on each party in an exchange acting fairly and with due respect for each other. Whenever anyone acts unethically, inefficiencies result and chances are that somebody will suffer. Marketers, like consumers, can act unethically. Media reports all too often describe company actions that are at best questionable, at times immoral, and at worst illegal. Unscrupulous actions of companies directly impact the marketplace because they upset the value equation associated with a given exchange. When a company misrepresents a product, consumers are led to expect more than is actually delivered.

Not everyone will agree on what behaviors should be considered marketing "misbehaviors." The topic again centers on ethics. The term ethics refers to standards or moral codes of conduct to which a person, group, or organization adheres. Marketing ethics consist of societal and professional standards of right and fair practices that are expected of marketing managers as they develop and implement marketing strategies.[85] More simply, ethics determines how much tolerance one has for actions that take advantage of others.

Many organizations have explicitly stated rules or codes of conduct for their employees. Exhibit 16.4 presents the Code of Ethics for the American Marketing Association.

Like consumer misbehavior, marketer misbehavior can be viewed as a subset of *deviance*. For marketers

ethics standards or moral codes of conduct to which a person, group, or organization adheres

marketing ethics societal and professional standards of right and fair practices that are expected of marketing managers as they develop and implement marketing strategies

Exhibit 16.4

American Marketing Association Code of Ethics

Preamble The American Marketing Association commits itself to promoting the highest standard of professional ethical norms and values for its members. Norms are established standards of conduct that are expected and maintained by society and/or professional organizations. Values represent the collective conception of what people find desirable, important and morally proper. Values serve as the criteria for evaluating the actions of others. Marketing practitioners must recognize that they not only serve their enterprises but also act as stewards of society in creating, facilitating and executing the efficient and effective transactions that are part of the greater economy. In this role, marketers should embrace the highest ethical norms of practicing professionals and the ethical values implied by their responsibility toward stakeholders (e.g., customers, employees, investors, channel members, regulators and the host community).

General Norms:

1. Marketers must do no harm. This means doing work for which they are appropriately trained or experienced so that they can actively add value to their organizations and customers. It also means adhering to all applicable laws and regulations and embodying high ethical standards in the choices they make.

2. Marketers must foster trust in the marketing system. This means that products are appropriate for their intended and promoted uses. It requires that marketing communications about goods and services are not intentionally deceptive or misleading. It suggests building relationships that provide for the equitable adjustment and/or redress of customer grievances. It implies striving for good faith and fair dealing so as to contribute toward the efficacy of the exchange process.

3. Marketers must embrace, communicate and practice the fundamental ethical values that will improve consumer confidence in the integrity of the marketing exchange system. These basic values are intentionally aspirational and include honesty, responsibility, fairness, respect, openness and citizenship.

Ethical Values

Honesty—to be truthful and forthright in our dealings with customers and stakeholders. We will tell the truth in all situations and at all times. We will offer products of value that do what we claim in our communications. We will stand behind our products if they fail to deliver their claimed benefits. We will honor our explicit and implicit commitments and promises.

Responsibility—to accept the consequences of our marketing decisions and strategies. We will make strenuous efforts to serve the needs of our customers. We will avoid using coercion with all stakeholders. We will acknowledge the social obligations to stakeholders that come with increased marketing and economic power. We will recognize our special commitments to economically vulnerable segments of the market such as children, the elderly and others who may be substantially disadvantaged.

Fairness—to try to balance justly the needs of the buyer with the interests of the seller. We will represent our products in a clear way in selling, advertising and other forms of communication; this includes the avoidance of false, misleading and deceptive promotion. We will reject manipulations and sales tactics that harm customer trust. We will not engage in price fixing, predatory pricing, price gouging or "bait-and-switch" tactics. We will not knowingly participate in material conflicts of interest.

Respect—to acknowledge the basic human dignity of all stakeholders. We will value individual differences even as we avoid stereotyping customers or depicting demographic groups (e.g., gender, race, sexual orientation) in a negative or dehumanizing way in our promotions. We will listen to the needs of our customers and make all reasonable efforts to monitor and improve their satisfaction on an ongoing basis. We will make a special effort to understand suppliers, intermediaries and distributors from other cultures. We will appropriately acknowledge the contributions of others, such as consultants, employees and coworkers, to our marketing endeavors.

Openness—to create transparency in our marketing operations. We will strive to communicate clearly with all our constituencies. We will accept constructive criticism from our customers and other stakeholders. We will explain significant product or service risks, component substitutions or other foreseeable eventualities that could affect customers or their perception of the purchase decision. We will fully disclose list prices and terms of financing as well as available price deals and adjustments.

Citizenship—to fulfill the economic, legal, philanthropic and societal responsibilities that serve stakeholders in a strategic manner. We will strive to protect the natural environment in the execution of marketing campaigns. We will give back to the community through volunteerism and charitable donations. We will work to contribute to the overall betterment of marketing and its reputation. We will encourage supply chain members to ensure that trade is fair for all participants, including producers in developing countries.

Implementation Finally, we recognize that every industry sector and marketing subdiscipline (e.g., marketing research, e-commerce, direct selling, direct marketing, advertising) has its own specific ethical issues that require policies and commentary. An array of such codes can be accessed through links on the AMA website. We encourage all such groups to develop and/or refine their industry and discipline-specific codes of ethics to supplement these general norms and values.

CSR Apps

Given the increased public scrutiny of corporate social responsibility and sustainability, it was only a matter of time before app developers began to offer apps that enable consumers to have valuable marketplace information at their fingertips. Now company efforts to "do well by doing good" are more visible than ever before.

Currently there are a number of apps that help consumers make informed choices about the products they buy and the companies that supply them. Corporate social responsibility (CSR) apps allow consumers to receive information about and recommendations for companies and products that match their beliefs about important issues. Apps such as Ethical Barcode, Seafood Watch, and OpenLabel help consumers to make informed decisions. Consumers know that purchasing a product from a company signals support of the company and its practices, and thanks to these apps it's often as easy as scanning a barcode on a product to receive relevant information.

Consumers are now more empowered than ever to ensure that they are making the most informed decisions possible. Of course, not all consumers care about these issues. But for the millions of consumers who do care, these apps are likely to continue to grow in popularity.

garagestock/Shutterstock.com

Sources: Timothy Pratt, "New OpenLabel App Offers Product Information for Eco-Minded Consumers," *Theguardian.com*, February 10, 2015, http://www.theguardian.com/sustainable-business/2015/feb/10/openlabel-app-consumer-information-google-facebook, accessed May 23, 2016; Brandon Baker, "Ethical Barcode App Uses 20 Nonprofits to Ensure Sustainable Grocery Shopping," *Ecowatch.com*, June 9, 2014, http://ecowatch.com/2014/06/09/ethical-barcode-app-sustainable-shopping/, accessed May 23, 2016; Lindsey Hoshaw, "Top 3 Sustainable Seafood Apps," *Fortune.com*, October 11, 2011, http://www.forbes.com/sites/lindseyhoshaw/2011/10/25/top-3-sustainable-seafood-apps/#7050722721fa5, accessed May 23, 2016.

to misbehave, they must be aware that an action will be considered unethical and act with deviance to cover intent. Sometimes, marketers don't intend to misbehave, but mistakes are made in marketing execution. As in a court of law, proving intent is rarely an easy thing to do.

16-3a Consumerism

The **marketing concept** proposes that all the functions of the organization should work together in satisfying its customers' wants and needs. This is important for any business. When businesses begin taking advantage of consumers, consumers lose, businesses lose, and society as a whole eventually loses. In fact, it can be said that the ethical treatment of consumers is a cornerstone of a fair marketplace.[86]

Much of the pressure that has been placed on marketers comes directly from consumer groups. **Consumerism** is used to describe the activities of various groups to protect basic consumer rights. Many years ago, the voice of the consumer simply didn't garner much attention at all. In the early days of mass production, much of the focus was on production efficiencies rather than on the consumer. This changed gradually throughout the 20th century as the marketplace became more competitive. The voice of the consumer grew steadily. The **Consumer Bill of Rights**, which today stands as a foundation of the consumerism movement, was introduced in 1962, and includes:

1. The right to safety
2. The right to be informed
3. The right to redress and to be heard
4. The right to choice

16-3b The Marketing Concept and the Consumer

The marketing concept developed greatly in the 1960s. It was early in this time period that Theodore Levitt published the article "Marketing Myopia." Among other

marketing concept states a firm should focus on consumer needs as a means of achieving long-term success

consumerism activities of various groups to voice concern for, and to protect, basic consumer rights

Consumer Bill of Rights introduced by President John F. Kennedy in 1962, list of rights that include the right to safety, the right to be informed, the right to redress and to be heard, and the right to choice

things, Levitt's work brought about a new perspective that argued that businesses should define themselves in terms of the consumer needs that they satisfy rather than in terms of the products they make. He argued that a firm's long-term health depends on its ability to exist as a consumer-satisfying entity rather than a goods-producing entity. As we have discussed in this text, companies should focus on the *total value concept* and remember that products provide value in multiple ways.

While many companies today adhere to the marketing concept, numerous questions arise regarding actual marketing practice. For example, companies often come under criticism for marketing products that some consider harmful. In particular, the fast-food, cereal, tobacco, and alcohol industries are often under fire from various groups. Even though freedom of choice is a central tenet of the U.S. economic system, these products are among the many that society often considers harmful.

THE MARKETING MIX AND THE CONSUMER

Marketers should use the tools found in the marketing mix carefully as they target consumers. When consumers question the way in which they are treated, they are likely to spread negative information through word of mouth and seek some form of remedy.

One of the most visible elements of the marketing mix is pricing. When consumers believe that a firm's prices are unfair, they are likely to leave the firm and spread negative information about it.[87] Consumers also complain that marketing efforts lead to higher overall prices. Marketers counter by explaining that marketing expenditures allow for increased economies of scale that contribute to lower overall production costs. Pricing issues are certainly

debatable. Exhibit 16.5 presents the four Ps of marketing, as well as their ethical and unethical uses.

The product portion of the marketing mix also commonly comes under fire. Consumers question the extent to which products are actually harmful to them or society in the long run. Many products can lead to short-term satisfaction, but they can also lead to long-term consumer and/or societal problems. Consider the following categories of products, as originally discussed by Philip Kotler:[88]

> - **Deficient products** are products that have little to no potential to create value of any type (for example, faulty appliances).
>
> - **Salutary products** are products that are good for both consumers and society in the long run (for example, air bags). These products offer high utilitarian value, but do not provide hedonic value.
>
> - **Pleasing products** are products that provide hedonic value to consumers but may be harmful in the long run (for example, energy drinks).

© iStockphoto.com/Skip O'Donnell

> - **Desirable products** are products that deliver high utilitarian and hedonic value and that benefit both consumers and society in the long run (for example, pleasant-tasting weight-loss products).

Exhibit 16.5

The Marketing Mix and Business Ethics

Tool	Common use	Unethical use
Product	The development of a good, service, or experience that will satisfy consumers' needs.	Failure to disclose that product won't function properly without necessary component parts.
Place	The distribution of a marketing offer through various channels of delivery.	Limiting product availability in certain markets as a means of raising prices.
Price	The marketer's statement of value received from an offering, which may be monetary or nonmonetary.	Stating that a regular price is really a "sales" price. This practice is prohibited by law.
Promotion	Communicating an offering's value through techniques such as advertising, sales promotion, and word of mouth.	Promoting one item as being on sale and then informing the customer that the product is out of stock and that a more expensive item should be bought. This practice, known as "bait and switch," is illegal.

Marketers clearly want to avoid offering *deficient* products. The difficult issue comes with the marketing of *pleasing* products. Many consumers know that the products they enjoy are harmful, but they buy them anyway. Needless to say, the tobacco industry has been under criticism for years for marketing products that many think are unsafe. Individual responsibility and freedom are important factors in consumer decisions to use these products. Most of the time, these companies deliver both customer satisfaction and value.

The promotion and place elements of the marketing mix can also be questioned. Consumers often question distribution tactics used by marketers. For example, they complain about tickets to major events being made available in only a few select channels. In 2009, Bruce Springsteen fans were enraged when trying to buy tickets to his concerts through Ticketmaster. After logging onto the website, they were redirected to the Ticketmaster-owned site TicketsNow.com. Ticket prices were much higher than face value on TicketsNow. Springsteen condemned the practice and Ticketmaster later apologized.[89] A settlement was reached with the FTC in 2010. Ticketmaster was to repay fans the difference between a ticket's face value and the amount paid to a broker through TicketsNow. Brokers on TicketsNow must now disclose when they are listing tickets that they do not actually have.[90] Unfortunately, ticket scandals are all too common. The 2012 Olympic Games were marred with a ticket scandal, and in 2016 a ticket scandal was uncovered that included employees of the world-famous Madison Square Garden in New York City.[91]

CONSUMER VULNERABILITY AND PRODUCT HARMFULNESS

Two important issues to consider when discussing marketing ethics are product harmfulness and consumer vulnerability.[92] A classification of product harmfulness versus consumer vulnerability applied to marketing decision making is presented in Exhibit 16.6. Public criticism of marketing strategies tends to be most intense when a marketer targets vulnerable consumer groups with harmful products. A major debate raged during the 2016 U.S. presidential election regarding gun control: many consumers view guns as inherently harmful, while others believe that it is people, not guns, that are harmful.

Of course, what constitutes a "harmful" product is a question of interpretation, as is the definition of a "vulnerable" consumer. What is a harmful product? What is a vulnerable consumer? Obesity continues to be a major issue in the United States. Public pressure has led fast-food marketers to rethink their menus. Some people

Exhibit 16.6

Product Harmfulness and Consumer Vulnerability

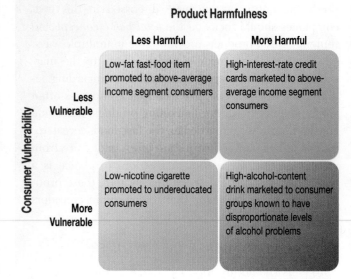

Source: Adapted from N. C. Smith, and E. Cooper-Martin (1997), "Ethics and Target Marketing: The Role of Product Harm and Consumer Vulnerability," *Journal of Marketing* 61 (3), 1–20.

believe the problems originate with the marketer, while others point to the consumer.

EMPLOYEE BEHAVIOR

Individual employees play an important part in the execution of marketing programs. Although consumers hope that a firm's employees are acting in good faith, this is not always the case. A used car salesperson who sets the odometer back on automobiles should know that the act is unethical and illegal. Some situations, however, are not as straightforward. Consider a salesperson facing the temptation to use bribery as a means of obtaining a sale. In some cultures, this practice is commonplace and acceptable; however, the practice is prohibited in the United States. But what if the

> **Many consumers know that the products they enjoy are harmful, but they buy them anyway.**

salesperson is dealing with a customer who is living in the United States but is from a country where bribes are commonplace?

Individual behavior is guided largely by morals. **Morals** are personal standards and beliefs that are used to guide individual action. Certainly, individuals must answer to their own belief systems.

16-4 CORPORATE SOCIAL RESPONSIBILITY

Corporate social responsibility (CSR) may be defined as an organization's activities and status related to its societal obligations.[93] Due to increased pressure from consumer groups, companies are finding that they must be socially responsible. In fact, a popular catchphrase for socially responsible businesses is "doing well by doing good."

There are many ways in which companies can be responsible. Activities such as making donations to causes, supporting minority programs, ensuring responsible manufacturing processes and environmental protectionism, acting quickly when product defects are detected, focusing on employee safety, and encouraging employees to volunteer for local causes are some of the many ways in which companies can exhibit their social responsibility.[94] Basically, the actions described fall into one of three categories:

▶ *Ethical duties* **include acting within expected ethical boundaries.**

▶ *Altruistic duties* **include giving back to communities through philanthropic activities.**

▶ *Strategic initiatives* **include strategically engaging in socially responsible activities in order to increase the value of the firm.**[95]

Socially responsible marketing is associated with favorable consumer evaluations, increased customer satisfaction, and the likelihood of increased sales. This is particularly the case when an individual consumer identifies with the company and the causes to which it contributes. Managers should ensure that their social responsibility efforts guide their marketing programs, as research indicates that brand promotion influences how consumers respond to CSR initiatives.[96]

16-4a The Societal Marketing Concept

Part of being socially responsible is adopting the **societal marketing concept**. This concept considers the needs of society along with the wants and needs of individual consumers.[97] All firms have many stakeholders, and the effects of marketing actions on all these stakeholder groups should be considered. Some argue that if a product promotion achieves profitability at the expense of the general good, then the effort should not be undertaken. All of the stakeholders of a firm should be considered when marketing programs are initiated. Exhibit 16.7 presents prescriptions for improved marketing ethics.

morals personal standards and beliefs used to guide individual action

corporate social responsibility (CSR) organization's activities and status related to its societal obligations

societal marketing concept marketing concept that states that marketers should consider not only the wants and needs of consumers but also the needs of society

Exhibit 16.7

Prescriptions for Improved Marketing Ethics

▶ Marketers must put people first and consider the effects of their actions on all stakeholders.

▶ Actions must be based on standards that go beyond laws and regulations.

▶ Marketers must be held responsible for the means they use to achieve their desired ends. Focusing on profit motivations is not enough.

▶ Marketing organizations should focus on training employees in ethical decision making.

▶ Marketing organizations should embrace and disseminate a core set of ethical principles.

▶ Decision makers must adopt a stakeholder orientation that leads to an appreciation of how marketing decisions affect all relevant parties.

▶ Marketing organizations should specify ethical decision-making protocols.

Source: G. R. Laczniak and P. E. Murphy, "Normative Perspectives for Ethical and Socially Responsible Marketing," Journal of Macromarketing 26, no. 2 (2006): 154–177.

16-5 REGULATION OF MARKETING ACTIVITIES

Many federal, state, and local laws were established in order to protect consumers from marketer misbehavior. Federal regulatory bodies such as the Federal Trade Commission (FTC) and the Food and Drug Administration monitor exchanges that take place between consumers and marketers. Other groups, such as the Better Business Bureau and the American Association of Advertising Agencies (AAAA), also play important roles in monitoring marketing activities. Although these groups attempt to bring fairness to the marketplace, it is ultimately up to managers to ensure that the actions of their firms fall within generally accepted business guidelines.

16-5a Marketing and the Law

Exhibit 16.8 presents legislation that has been enacted in an effort to regulate commerce, promote free trade, and ensure consumer safety. Many of these acts are

Exhibit 16.8

Major Acts Affecting Commerce and Consumer Safety

Sherman Antitrust Act (1890)	Prohibits restraint of free trade
Federal Food and Drug Act (1906)	Prohibits misleading practices associated with food and drug marketing
Clayton Act (1914)	Restricts price discrimination, exclusive dealing, and tying contracts
Wheeler–Lea Act (1938)	Provides FTC with jurisdiction over misleading or false advertising
Fair Packaging and Labeling Act (1966)	Marketers must present proper packaging and content information about products
Child Protection Act (1966)	Prohibits the marketing of dangerous toys
Truth in Lending Act (1968)	Lenders required to disclose complete costs associated with loans
Children's Online Privacy Protection Act (1998)	Establishes rules governing online marketing practices aimed at children
Credit Card Accountability, Responsibility, and Disclosure Act (2009)	Amends Truth in Lending Act to establish fair and transparent practices relating to consumer credit
Helping Families Save Their Homes Act (2009)	Prevents mortgage foreclosures and enhances mortgage availability
Family Smoking Prevention and Tobacco Control Act of 2009	Protects public health by giving the Food and Drug Administration certain authority to regulate the tobacco industry
Wall Street Reform and Consumer Protection Act (2010)	Regulation of financial market practices and consumer protection from various financial and credit practices
Food Safety Modernization Act of 2010	Aims at ensuring the safety of U.S. food supply
Patient Protection and Affordable Care Act of 2010	Aims at decreasing the number of Americans without health insurance
Health Care and Education Reconciliation Act of 2010	Aims at providing college graduates relief from student loan debt
Child Protection Act of 2012	Protects young victims of child pornography, sexual abuse, and human trafficking
Drug Quality and Security Act of 2013	Grants the FDA additional authority to regulate and monitor the manufacturing of compound drugs.
Cybersecurity Enhancement Act of 2014	Provides for ongoing public–private partnerships to improve cybersecurity and to strengthen cybersecurity research
Ensuring Patient Access and Effective Drug Enforcement Act of 2016	Clarifies standards to ensure that prescription drugs are available to legitimate patients and not diverted to illicit use

aimed at maintaining or improving the general welfare of consumers in a free marketplace. They also protect the value that consumers receive from exchanges by prohibiting acts such as deceptive advertising and the selling of defective or unreasonably dangerous products. Sometimes, however, legislation can have adverse effects. For example, evidence suggests that the imposition of rent controls (restricting rent prices below market equilibrium price) actually increases homelessness in urban areas.[98]

16-6 PUBLIC CRITICISM OF MARKETING

Unethical marketers intend to do harm in some way, act negligently, and/or manipulate consumers. As we have stated, however, marketers can simply make innocent mistakes. For example, a company may not discover a product defect until it has been released for public consumption. It would then issue a product recall. At issue is the *intent* and *knowledge* of the firm. Consumer perception is also important, as bad events can mean disaster for the firm in terms of lost business, customer boycotts, and bad publicity. We could discuss any number of different issues regarding public criticism of marketing; however, we focus on only a handful of issues here.

16-6a Deceptive Advertising

Deceptive advertising (sometimes called false or misleading advertising) is an important issue for marketers. Deceptive advertising is covered under the Wheeler–Lea Act (1938). This act amended the Federal Trade Commission Act to include false advertising issues. The FTC protects consumers from acts of fraud, deception, and unfair business practices, and the Wheeler–Lea amendment plays an important role in regulating advertising. The FTC has the power to issue cease-and-desist orders and to issue fines against firms that are found guilty of deceptive advertising.

According to the FTC, **deceptive advertising** is advertising that (a) contains or omits information that is important in influencing a consumer's buying behavior and (b) is likely to mislead consumers who are acting reasonably.[99] The extent to which advertisers *intentionally* misrepresent their products is crucial. Although the FTC defines what deceptive advertising is, actual deception can be difficult to prove.

An important distinction in practice is the difference between deceptive advertising and *puffery*. The term **puffery** describes making exaggerated claims about a

product's superiority. Puffery differs from deceptive advertising in that there is no overt attempt to deceive a targeted consumer. Consumers often complain that advertisers create unrealistic expectations in their advertisements. For example, marketers of weight-loss products often promote lofty expectations. Advertisers include disclaimers such as "results vary" or "results are not typical" in their advertisements, but consumers rarely notice them. Quite often disclaimers are given very quickly; research indicates that consumers are less likely to purchase products when disclaimers are presented very quickly, especially for unknown or untrusted brands.[100]

In general, objective claims must be substantiated. In fact, the American Advertising Federation (AAF) promotes the idea that advertising claims must be, among other things, truthful and substantiated.[101] The line between puffery and deception can be blurry.

Although regulatory mechanisms are in place to protect consumers from deceptive advertising, most businesses prefer forms of self-regulation over governmental regulation. For this reason, self-regulatory bodies such as the National Advertising Review Council (NARC) work to ensure that advertisements are truthful. The NARC provides guidelines and sets standards for truth and accuracy for national advertisers.[102] National organizations such as the AAAA and the AAF also monitor the advertising practices of their members.

16-6b Marketing to Children

Children typify a vulnerable group because they often lack the knowledge of how to behave as responsible consumers. Two important issues arise with marketing to children. First, there is the question of whether children can understand that some marketing messages do not offer literal interpretations of the real world. For example, many toys are shown in unrealistic settings. Second, the quantity of marketing messages to which children are exposed can be called into question. It has been estimated that the average American child sees more than 40,000 television commercials per year—or an average of over 100 commercials per day.[103] The Children's Television Act was put into effect to limit the amount of advertising to which children are exposed, with a limit of 10.5 minutes of commercials per hour on weekends and 12 minutes on weekdays. Even with these limitations,

deceptive advertising message that omits information that is important in influencing a consumer's buying behavior and is likely to mislead consumers acting reasonably

puffery practice of making exaggerated claims about a product and its superiority

Advertisers must take into account that children have limited knowledge and comprehension when it comes to issues in marketing

approximately $17 billion is spent each year by advertisers targeting the children's market.[104]

The Children's Advertising Review Unit (CARU) of the Better Business Bureau is a self-regulatory body that examines marketing activities aimed at children. Among other things, the CARU guidelines state that advertisers should take into account the limited knowledge and comprehension that children have regarding marketing issues. Furthermore, the CARU maintains that advertisers should pay close attention to the educational role that advertising plays in a child's development and that advertising should stress positive behaviors.[105]

Internet marketing is another issue. The Children's Online Privacy Protection Act focuses on the online collection of personal information from children who are 13 years or younger. It specifies what marketers must include in privacy policies, when and how to seek consent from parents, and the responsibilities that marketers have to protect children's privacy and safety online.[106] Yet another issue is how violent advertisements affect children. Research indicates that children who are exposed to these ads may have violent thoughts.[107]

16-6c Pollution

planned obsolescence
act of planning the premature discontinuance of product models that perform adequately

Marketing a product can lead to pollution. Of course, consumption also leads to pollution,[108] and both marketers and consumers play roles in environmental stewardship.

Environmental protection continues to grow in importance, and popular movies and events highlight consumer pressure on businesses and government to increase their role. The Live Earth organization focuses on solving environmental problems, and the group has held several successful events that have highlighted these concerns.[109] For example, the group sponsored a "24 Hours of Reality" webcast that highlighted climate issues during the 2015 UN COP21 climate talks. These events are examples of millions of consumers coming together to support a cause. Although experts disagree on the effects of pollution, the issue remains important.

16-6d Planned Obsolescence

Marketers are also criticized for intentionally phasing out products before their usefulness wears out. For example, video game manufacturers are criticized for releasing new and seemingly "improved" gaming consoles even when older models haven't been on the market very long. The practice of managing and intentionally setting discontinue dates for products is known as **planned obsolescence**. Critics charge that it is both wasteful and greedy for marketers to engage in planned obsolescence. Marketers counter by arguing that by continually offering improved products, consumers are able to enjoy improved standards of living and innovation.

16-6e Price Gouging

One area of consumer interest is price gouging. Price gouging is the act of charging a higher than reasonable price for a good, following some kind of natural disaster or event. Price gouging is most often aimed at commodity goods like gasoline. However, it also occurs for other kinds of products and services. Following natural disasters, it is common for state officials to warn potential violators to not engage in price gouging. Most laws prohibit sellers from increasing prices from anywhere between 10–25% or more over a thirty-day period after a disaster. Several businesses were found guilty of price gouging after Hurricane Sandy in the northeastern United States. Later, following the devastating tornadoes of 2013 in Oklahoma, one retailer was allegedly selling bottle water for $40 per case.[110] More recently, complaints of price gouging occurred after the historic floods in Texas during the spring of 2016.[111] While some argue that the laws amount to price controls, there is no doubt that gouging ultimately harms consumers.[112]

16-6f Manipulative Sales Tactics

High-pressure and manipulative sales pitches are often the cause of consumer dissatisfaction. For example, a realtor might tell a client that several other people have looked at a particular house when they actually haven't. Or a salesperson might tell a customer that a product is in short supply when it really isn't.

Salespeople who adhere to a **sales orientation** are often guilty of these types of high-pressure tactics. To have a sales orientation means that the salesperson is more focused on the immediate sale and short-term results than on long-term customer satisfaction and relationship de-

Lisa Young/123RF

velopment. A more appropriate way to approach a sale is to adhere to what is referred to as a customer orientation. When using a **customer orientation**, the salesperson focuses on customer needs. Several studies have shown that having a customer orientation leads to favorable results for salespeople.

Ingratiation tactics are sometimes used by salespeople in order to get a sale. These techniques are often viewed as being manipulative.[113] Techniques such as the foot-in-the-door technique, the door-in-the-face technique, the even-a-penny-will-help technique, and the "I'm working for you!" technique can be called into question. These methods are considered unethical to the extent they are used for manipulation.

▶ A salesperson using the **foot-in-the-door technique** focuses on simply getting a "foot in the door." When consumers realize that they have opened themselves up to a sales pitch, they are more likely to listen to the pitch and they are also more likely to buy a product. The salesperson first makes a small request such as "May I have a few minutes of your time?" and follows with larger request such as "May I show you how this works?" and finally by the largest request of "May I have your order?" The foot-in-the-door technique is based on *self-perception theory,* which proposes that consumers use perceptions of their own actions when forming attitudes. The consumer realizes that he has "let the salesperson in" and has given in to a small request; therefore, he must be the type of person who would give in to larger requests and ultimately buy the product. Of course, salespeople could argue that this is simply good salesmanship.

▶ With the **door-in-the-face technique**, a salesperson begins by making a really large request such as "Can I get you to buy this car today?" Realizing that very few, if any, customers would say "Yes!" the salesperson prepares for the dreaded "No!" Showing that her feelings are hurt, she guilt-trips the customer with a statement like "Well, can I show you its features?" Many consumers would feel bad about responding negatively to the first request and would allow the salesperson to explain the car's features. This tactic relies on the *reciprocity norm,* which states that individuals are motivated to give back to those who have given them something. By feeling that he just rejected a salesperson, the customer feels that he at least owes the salesperson the courtesy of listening.

▶ Using the **even-a-penny-will-help technique**, cause-related marketers suggest to potential donors that even the smallest donation will go a long way toward reaching the desired goal, such as ending child abuse, feeding the hungry, or sheltering the homeless.[114] The idea is to make the donor feel ashamed to give such a small amount. Instead of giving the penny, they may give a dollar. This technique is considered unethical to the extent that it relies on feelings of guilt.

sales orientation practice of using sales techniques that are aimed at satisfying the salesperson's own needs and motives for short-term sales success

customer orientation practice of using sales techniques that focus on customer needs

foot-in-the-door technique ingratiation technique used in personal selling in which a salesperson begins with a small request and slowly leads up to one major request

door-in-the-face technique ingratiation technique used in personal selling in which a salesperson begins with a major request and then follows with a series of smaller requests

even-a-penny-will-help technique ingratiation technique in which a marketing message is sent that suggests that even the smallest donation, such as a penny or a dollar, will help a cause

▶ Using the **"I'm working for you!" technique**, salespeople attempt to lead customers into believing that they are working as hard as possible to give them the best deal when in reality they are following a script or routine. A salesperson walks away from his office during a negotiation to "go check with the manager" when he is really going to get coffee. The salesperson returns and says something like "I'm really working for you and here's a good deal!" This technique relies on *equity theory*. Here, the consumer would think that the salesperson is working hard, thereby raising the denominator in the equity theory comparison equation and leading to higher levels of satisfaction, and potentially purchase likelihood. Of course, salespeople often do consult with managers and work as hard as possible to give their customers the best deal.

16-6g Stealth Marketing

One area of marketing that is currently receiving increased attention is the use of stealth marketing. This type of marketing was discussed in another chapter. Is it ethical for businesses to market products to consumers when the consumers do not realize that they are being targeted by marketing messages? As you may remember from our earlier discussion, with *stealth marketing*, consumers are completely unaware that they are being marketed to (hence, the term stealth). Again, WOMMA (Word of Mouth Marketing Association) is opposed to such tactics and considers their use to be unethical.[115]

16-6h Products Liability

Big business is often criticized for marketing unsafe products. The Consumer Product Safety Commission is the main body that monitors product safety, and the right to be safe is a basic consumer right listed in the Consumer Bill of Rights. Deaths, injuries, and/or property damage from consumer products in the United States cost the nation more than $800 billion annually.[116] Another organization with which consumers are familiar is the Insurance Institute for Highway Safety. This organization focuses on deaths, injuries, and property damage from automobile accidents on the nation's highways.

Product safety is governed in different ways around the world. American consumers are largely protected by regulations resulting from tort law. When a consumer is harmed by a product, he has the right to sue the party believed to be responsible. The issue of **products liability**, which is the extent to which businesses are held responsible for product-related injuries, is determined through this process. At one extreme, the consumer could live by the "buyer beware" principle and face responsibility for all injuries. At the other, firms could be responsible for any consumer injury. In the latter case, the marketplace would be so restricted that few firms could afford to operate.

The primary legal doctrine governing products liability in the United States today is strict liability. With **strict liability**, consumers can win a legal action against a firm if it can be demonstrated in court that an injury occurred and that the product associated with the injury was faulty in some way. This doctrine has become more prominent recently than the former guiding doctrine of negligence. With **negligence**, an injured consumer would have to show that the firm could foresee a potential injury that might occur and then decided not to act on that knowledge. The doctrine of strict liability means that firms face increased exposure to costs associated with product injury lawsuits.

A famous consumer incident involved McDonald's and a customer in the United States who spilled coffee onto her legs, burning herself. She obtained counsel and sued McDonald's. Under the negligence doctrine, the plaintiff would have to prove that McDonald's knew such an injury could occur and did nothing to prevent such a mishap, but under strict liability, the consumer needed to demonstrate that an injury occurred and that the product was faulty. In this case, an action under strict liability was pursued on the basis that the consumer was burned and the coffee, being hot, was faulty. The woman ended up winning the lawsuit. A similar action led to Wendy's discontinuing the sale of hot chocolate, because if "being hot" made the chocolate faulty, it was pointless to offer the product for sale. Warning labels are now commonplace.

Mariyana M/Shutterstock.com

"I'm working for you!" technique technique used by salespeople to create the perception that they are working as hard as possible to close a sale when they really are not doing so

products liability extent to which businesses are held responsible for product-related injuries

strict liability legal action against a firm whereby a consumer demonstrates in court that an injury occurred and that the product associated with the injury was faulty in some way

negligence situation whereby an injured consumer attempts to show that a firm could foresee a potential injury might occur and then decided not to act on that knowledge

The costs of products liability are high in many industries. Physicians in the United States face huge costs due to the expensive liability insurance they must carry. Some claim that one of the biggest cost elements to an automobile is the amount of liability exposure, and companies have little choice but to pass these costs on to consumers. So, when a consumer purchases a ladder, a big part of the price covers liability exposure. A potentially bigger cost comes from stifled innovation, as firms fear introducing products that are novel because they could be considered faulty. Companies like Cessna, Piper, and Beechcraft produce piston engine aircraft using the same basic technology that existed in 1950. More innovative aircraft are produced in the "kit plane" industry where consumers have the responsibility of manufacturing the airplane themselves, limiting company liability.

Generally, firms face higher liability costs in the United States than in most other countries. One reason is because liability lawsuits that actually reach a courtroom often involve jury trials. In Europe, most liability actions would be overseen by a magistrate rather than a jury. Juries tend to be more sympathetic and are much more likely to award substantial punitive damages as well as compensatory damages. **Punitive damages** are intended to punish a company for injuries; **compensatory damages** are intended to cover costs incurred by a consumer due to an injury.

The issue of products liability is a good way to illustrate the importance of public policy to consumer behavior. The issue can be complicated and emotional. But while tilting the balance of bearing the burden of product injuries toward firms may, at times, seem reasonable, such tilting actually restricts the market by driving businesses out of certain industries and restricting the choices of consumers. If pharmaceutical firms face costs that are too high and regulations that are too stringent, they may simply stop producing potentially life-saving medications because of product risk. The key to effective public policy is finding the proper balance: offering consumers protection but still providing a high degree of freedom in the marketplace. This, of course, is no easy task.

punitive damages damages that are sought to punish a company for behavior associated with an injury

compensatory damages damages that are intended to cover costs incurred by a consumer due to an injury

CASES

Culture Creates Customer Dissatisfaction?

Written by Mohan Menon, University of South Alabama

It was close to lunch time in Singapore when a long-time customer, Mr. Joe Teng, walked into the offices of Global Voyages and began to raise his voice in anger. He was not in a joyful mood. When employees at the travel agency offered to help, he brushed them aside. He wanted to see the owner to demand his three airline tickets for a flight that night. Mr. Teng had planned to travel to Australia with his family to plan the wedding of his daughter in Sydney. His daughter, who completed her graduate program in environmental sciences at Macquarie University, is working in Sydney. She invited her parents to visit and help her with planning her wedding, which would take place in a couple of months.

As Mr. Teng rushed past the row of employee desks, heading toward the back of the office, the owner, Mr. Tarun Yadav, walked out of his office to meet him. "I've been getting my tickets from you for the past four years, and now you make me lose face with my future son-in-law. If I can't leave tonight I will have to postpone the wedding." Mr. Yadav kept his cool in front of his employees and tried in vain to calm the customer down. Mr. Teng was in no mood to reason. He wanted his three tickets, and nothing else mattered.

The genesis of this service encounter began a few years ago when one of Mr. Teng's business acquaintances, who was himself a customer of Global Voyages, referred Mr. Teng to the travel agency. Global Voyages is a full-service travel agency that primarily serves the corporate market in Singapore and countries in the Asia-Pacific region, including China and India. But through referrals Global Voyages has developed a significant proportion of business in the retail sector over the years with little or no promotion.

Global Voyages' owner, Mr. Yadav, worked for Thomas Cook, a global full-service travel agency, before establishing his own business. He was with them for about ten years in their Kuala Lumpur, Malaysia, office. He was involved with both corporate and retail clients during that time. At Thomas Cook, Mr. Yadav experienced the peril of retail travel business in the Asian markets and has been deliberate in his attempt to target the corporate marketplace with Global Voyages. As with other businesses in the high-context Asian region, retail referrals are sustained if not sought after. Small- and medium-scale businesses welcome referrals, which provide higher marginal revenues with little effort.

Yet many small business owners, like Mr. Yadav, deal with referrals such as Mr. Teng's with trepidation. The reason is cultural, in that consumers develop the bonds of trust with business owners and thus expect to be served without regard for their own "deficient" payment habits. The situation with Mr. Teng's dealings with Global Voyages is illustrative of this phenomenon. Consumers expect prompt and high-quality personal service but seem reluctant to make timely payments. For various reasons, consumers expect unsecured credit for services. Seldom do they skip town without paying, but delayed payments affect a business's cash flow situation.

At the same time, in such high-context cultural societies, repeated pleas or threats for payment are frowned upon and most business owners, such as Mr. Yadav, feel uncomfortable doing so anyway. In the past, he's tried having his employees do this "dirty" job with mixed success. Longtime customers sometimes feel slighted by the approach. Travel business is personal in the region; therefore, a high level of satisfaction among customers is a prerequisite for building loyalty. Meeting or exceeding customer expectations is the name of the game.

The travel industry has been battered in recent years on several fronts. The economic downturn across the world, including in southeast Asia, a rise in aviation fuel prices, and competition among the major carriers and the low-cost airlines have had a profound negative effect on the travel business. Add to this the pricing pressure from airline websites, third-party consolidator sites, and meta-search sites such as Kayak.com, and it is easy to understand the scope of the problems that contribute to full-service travel agencies being squeezed.

Since travel site switching costs are negligible, younger customers tend to price-shop online and thus are harder for full-service agents to attract. Older travelers, on the other hand, are generally in need of additional help with their travel arrangements and tend to value relationships they've cultivated through the years.

They are not very price sensitive and thus patronizing businesses such as Global Voyages provides higher levels of service and satisfaction.

But given his earlier experiences with Thomas Cook, Mr. Yadav also feels that some consumers take advantage of this cultural peculiarity in Asia. Both his corporate accounts and retail clients are generally satisfied with his company, and 80% of them are repeat buyers. His own surveys and audits of travel-related blogs and forums confirm his belief that the company is doing well in the satisfaction ratings. He is fond of adding personal touches to his client interactions. For instance, he and his employees call clients once they reach their destinations to make sure they had pleasant trips and reassure them of help if they need it. At the same time, he uses these personal calls to subtly upsell local attractions or other arrangements they might need. Older clients appreciate this level of attention and often refer their friends and family to the business.

But he has had enough with a few consumers such as Mr. Teng. He feels that their service expectations of Global Voyages are high, yet their reimbursements for services rendered are protracted beyond reason. Customers' vision of what they want from businesses is sometimes colored by their unrealistic expectation of the level of service they feel they deserve within a cultural context. Mr. Teng is not likely to delay payments to service providers in Australia, a country he visits often. Other customers also tend to exhibit such behaviors to varying degrees, and Global Voyages has had to resort to intense coaxing to get paid. Legal maneuvers are rarely utilized, since they might backfire in the high-context culture of Singapore. This time, he wants to take a stand, yet not in a manner his customers or employees might find hostile. He needs to set the right tone and be the role model that his employees have come to expect. Mr. Yadav also wants his employees to take a stand in similar situations in the future.

QUESTIONS

1 What type of expectation does Mr. Joe Teng have about his ticketing situation?

2 Which of the theories of postconsumption reactions might explain Mr. Teng's experience? Why?

3 If the customer is likely to mention his dissatisfaction or negative experience with Global Voyages to his friends and acquaintances, what can Mr. Yadav's business do to combat it?

4 In your opinion, is this a case of customer misbehavior or not? Please justify your answer.

5 Which of the characteristics of relationship quality does Global Voyages exhibit in the case?

6 What would you do if you were the owner of Global Voyages; in other words, how would you deal with the situation?

CASE 5-2

Susan G. Komen for the Cure: Can This Relationship Be Saved?

Written by Mary Anne Doty, Texas A&M University–Commerce

On January 31, 2012, news reports circulated that Susan G. Komen for the Cure had decided to stop funding clinical breast exams through a grant to Planned Parenthood. Initially, Komen cited the congressional investigation of Rep. Cliff Stearns, a conservative legislator who has pushed for abortion restrictions, as the reason for the change in policy barring grants to groups under government investigation. This decision had been made quietly in late November 2011, with notification to Planned Parenthood in mid-December. As the story broke, Komen found itself in the middle of a controversy. Overnight the organization faced severe criticism (and some praise) as the story mushroomed through television and newspapers, as well as Facebook, Twitter, and other social media.[1]

Susan G. Komen for the Cure has become the largest source of nonprofit funds dedicated to the fight against breast cancer in the world, investing more than $1.9 billion since 1982. In April 2012 their website listed 124 corporate sponsors from varying organizations, including product brands (American Airlines, Ford Motor Company, Mohawk Flooring, and Yoplait Yogurt), retailers (Belk, Lowe's, Old Navy, Walgreens), and sports organizations (Dallas Cowboys,

CASES

Major League Baseball, Ladies PGA).[2] In thirty years the brand had reached iconic proportions, beloved by people on all parts of the political spectrum. Charity Navigator, a website that rates nonprofit organizations on the percentage of funds used for the organization's mission and on transparency, gave Komen a rating of 4/4 stars, with a score of 62/70.[3] Supporters have a very personal link with the organization because volunteers have given (or walked) in honor of loved ones affected by breast cancer.

As word trickled out about the Komen decision, supporters and critics began sharing opinions through social networking sites. Former Komen supporters responded with anger and disappointment, many expressing feelings of betrayal. While the Komen grants totaled only $680,000 in 2011, an outpouring of donations to Planned Parenthood raised $3 million in three days, including over 10,000 new donors. As the lines were drawn for supporters of both organizations, most chose Planned Parenthood.[4]

The negative publicity also drew attention to many of Komen's practices that had not faced public scrutiny.[5] Among the complaints were: (1) the relatively small percentage of Komen funds that go to medical research for a cure (less than 19%); (2) high salaries of the founder and board members (founder Nancy Brinker is reportedly paid over $400,000 annually); (3) large legal expenses incurred from suing other charities defending the words "for the Cure" in their trademark; and (4) making women's health a political issue.

Susan G. Komen for the Cure did not respond to the social media uproar initially, which angered many of their former supporters.[6] Komen received a strong defense from people who disapproved of Planned Parenthood. Many of these were people who previously did not support Komen's activities because of their grants to Planned Parenthood. In spite of the approval, it was not clear that this segment would replace the funding and other support at risk by the decision.

Corporate sponsors, who generally fear controversial issues, complained that Komen had not informed them of the policy change in advance.[7] While none of the sponsors publicly abandoned Susan G. Komen for the Cure in the short term, they made it clear that better communication was expected if the relationship was to thrive. After four days of intense negative publicity, Komen announced they were reversing their decision and would consider reinstating the Planned Parenthood grants.[8] Komen founder Nancy Brinker apologized and announced that in the future groups will only be disqualified from receiving grants when they are under investigations that are "criminal and conclusive in nature and not political."

This response was probably a case of "too little, too late" that angered those on both sides of the debate. Planned Parenthood supporters claimed the wording was full of loopholes and not a strong repudiation of the initial decision. Planned Parenthood opponents were angry that the decision was reversed and vowed not to support Komen in the future. The slow response managed to alienate a majority of the public.[9]

When the decision to defund Planned Parenthood's grant became public on February 1, 2012, a number of Komen executives and employees resigned in protest, including a medical advisory board member, a health official, and the directors of several large Komen chapters. After the reversal on February 3, public outcry did not fade away. Karen Handel, senior vice president for public affairs, received most of the blame for the initial decision and for politicizing Komen policies by focusing on abortion politics rather than detecting and treating breast cancer. Handel, a former political candidate who had campaigned on an anti–Planned Parenthood platform, resigned on February 7.[10]

By February 23, news stories reported Komen hired a consulting firm to assess damage to their brand among supporters.[11] The 20-minute survey tested the wording of various apologies and then measured the credibility of the Komen foundation and its leaders, along with the credibility of other public figures. Komen's problems continued into March when two top executives resigned, the executive VP and chief marketing officer, as well as the CEO of Komen's New York City affiliate. As the organization struggled to repair its relationship with supporters, some Komen affiliates reported revenues were substantially lower than in previous campaigns, and participation in the Race for the Cure was also down.

It may take years to determine if Komen can repair its relationships and be restored as a premiere charity brand. The damage of these events affects employees in the form of poor morale, former supporters who are angered by Komen's initial decision and are not mollified by the reversal of that decision, corporate sponsors who are leery of future controversy, a public that views Susan G. Komen for the Cure as a tarnished organization, and disappointed anti-abortion groups who remain opposed to Komen. Moving forward, it may be time to reexamine their mission. When the organization was founded in 1982, breast cancer was often a death sentence for women (and a few men) because the prognosis was poor when cancer was detected in later stages. Komen raised awareness of breast cancer and spent millions of dollars on public education and breast cancer screening. By any measure, those efforts were a resounding success. It may be time for Komen to focus their strategy on research and treatment (as implied by the trademark name, "…for the Cure") and save their education campaigns for less informed segments.

QUESTIONS

1 How did social media impact the complaining behaviors of donors and participants for Susan G. Komen for the Cure activities? What types of complaining behaviors were most apparent?

2 What was the response by Susan G. Komen for the Cure to negative public publicity after their decision to stop funding mammograms in partnership with Planned Parenthood? Would you have responded differently had you been in charge?

3 Officials at Susan G. Komen for the Cure seemed unprepared for the intensity of response that they encountered. How would an understanding of the difference between customer loyalty and customer inertia have prepared the Komen officials for the reactions they experienced?

4 Does the Komen organization demonstrate characteristics of relationship loyalty with their donors? Why or why not?

5 Many Komen supporters switched their donations to Planned Parenthood after the negative public publicity. Use the concept of share of wallet to explain why this might have happened.

CASES

CASE 5-3

Sports Fans Behaving Badly

Written by Dr. Venessa Funches, Auburn University–Montgomery

It is becoming more and more commonplace to turn on the television, pick up a newspaper, or browse the Web and find out about another sports fan behaving badly. You can attend a sporting event from professional to little leagues, and you are likely to encounter fans misbehaving. The misbehavior of fans has become legendary. The offenses run the gamut from simple mischief all the way to criminal behavior.

In fact, researchers have identified a subset of fans they term *dysfunctional fans*. "These fans tend to be overly aggressive with opposing teams, fans, and officials oftentimes yelling obscenities or throwing things. These fans are typically disruptive, confrontational, complain a great deal, and abuse alcohol while attending sporting events."[1] In addition, these fans tend to be highly identified with a particular team.[2]

Team identification is defined as the degree to which the fan feels a psychological connection to the team.[3] Fans exhibit high levels of team identification in numerous ways: following the players' careers, being students of team history, attending or watching games, closely watching news coverage, wearing team apparel, just to name a few. There are additional benefits associated with high levels of team identification: an improved state of well-being, a greater sense of community, and strong social connections.[4] In addition, high team identification is also positively correlated to game attendance and merchandise purchasing. Fans who identify highly with their teams consume sports-related products, services, and media such as television, talk radio, and websites at greater levels than their low-identifying counterparts. These high consumption levels are good for business. Unfortunately, there is also a dark side. Some researchers believe that excessive team identification is a determinant factor in fan misbehavior.

Dysfunctional fans are characterized as aggressive males who lack self-control and have positive attitudes toward violent actions.[5] Anecdotal evidence supports the research in this area.

CASES

Examples of legendary fan misbehavior include the 2004 NBA brawl between the Pacers and Pistons. A fight broke out between players. After it was brought under control, Ron Artest lay on the scoring table. Suddenly an upset fan threw a drink at him. Artest responded by entering the crowd and throwing punches. The resulting altercation was enormous and included both fans and players. In the end, nine people were injured. Several players were fined and/or suspended from the game as a result of their participation in the fight.[6]

More recently, Harvey Updyke, a 62-year-old avid Alabama fan and retired Texas highway patrolman, called into a popular sports talk show to announce his misbehavior. Updyke told the radio host that he became upset after a disappointing loss to archrival Auburn and decided to retaliate. He allegedly poisoned the famous Toomer's oak trees located on the Auburn campus with a lethal herbicide. The Toomer oak trees represent a coveted symbol for Auburn Tiger fans. The fans traditionally roll these trees with toilet paper after every victory. Updyke is facing criminal charges.[7]

In the latest instance, several Crimson Tide fans poked, prodded, and taunted an incapacitated LSU fan at a burger joint following the BCS championship game. Eventually one of the fans sexually assaulted the unconscious man in the restaurant. Although many people witnessed the incident, no one intervened. The incident was recorded and posted on the Web, where it eventually came to the attention of local authorities in New Orleans.[8]

In the heat of the moment sports fans either fail to consider the consequences or believe their inappropriate exploits will remain an unspoken part of the game day experience, repeated only as part of sports folklore. However, this is not the case. Just as in the aforementioned examples, all of these occurrences were heavily scrutinized and reported by the media and gained national attention. Additionally, all of these occurrences were punished and criminally prosecuted. But this inappropriate behavior is not limited to professional sports.

At the conclusion of a teenage baseball tournament, a player from the losing team left the field, making loud and disrespectful comments about the opposing team. A supporter of the winning team consequently punched the player in the head and a fight broke out. By the end of the fight, a spectator had bitten off a man's earlobe and knocked a baby from its mother's arms.[9]

In 2009, sheriff's deputies had to be called out to a little league championship. Apparently, words were exchanged after the game. Then the mother of one player threw a punch at a father of a player from the opposing team. Deputies moved in and quickly gained control of the scene. Both parents were taken into custody.[10]

While this type of fan misbehavior may not be new, it certainly appears to be more frequent and widespread in today's society. Unfortunately, this type of behavior is detrimental to numerous stakeholders, including employees and other consumers. The misbehavior is especially concerning for management of sports organizations because it is their job to deliver positive consumer experiences. Sports fans are expecting to experience an exciting game filled with suspense, drama, and emotional swings. Fan misbehavior like shouting obscenities at officials, throwing items on the field of play, drunken displays, and confrontations can disrupt not only the game but also the positive experience of other fans. Sports fans have many choices when it comes to where to spend their entertainment dollars. Event managers are afraid some fans may decide that sporting events are either unsafe or inappropriate family outings.

As a result, reducing incidents of fan misbehavior is an important concern for managers of sports organizations. Obviously, no one has found the answer yet, but several strategies are presently being used: increasing the number of security personnel present at games, proactively seeking out misbehaving fans through fan tips and increased security surveillance and removing them, and limiting the sale of alcohol. Is this enough? What can be done about fan misbehavior outside of the stadiums? Are the teams responsible in any way? Could teams like Alabama play a role in reducing this type of behavior? If so, what could they do?

CASES

QUESTIONS

1 Have you ever witnessed fan misbehavior? Describe the experience and how it impacted the value you received from the experience.

2 Is fan misbehavior unethical? Explain your answer.

3 What are the motivations of fan misbehavior?

4 What measures can be taken to prevent or reduce incidents of fan misbehavior?

5 Is fan misbehavior appropriately described as abusive consumer behavior?

ENDNOTES

1

1. http://www.alexa.com/siteinfo/pinterest.com rates Pinterest the 12th most visited web site, accessed February 4, 2016.

2. http://data.bls.gov/timeseries/LNS11300000, accessed February 4, 2016.

3. http://blog.fieldagent.net/the-staying-power-of -smartwatches-and-what-it-means-for-apple-watch-, accessed Feb. 4, 2016.

4. http://theadvocate.com/news/14727494-123 /lsu-engineering-students-envision-hyperloop -pods-carrying-riders-from-baton-rouge-to-new -orleans-in-, accessed February 6, 2016.

5. F. Alan (2016), "Fitbit Blaze Smartwatch Has Comparibility Issues with Windows Phone Devices," phonearena.com (January 10), accessed February 2016).

6. See C. Glenn Walters and Gordon W. Paul, *Consumer Behavior: An Integrated Approach*, 3rd ed. (Homewood, IL: Irwin, 1970); John L. Howard and Jagdish Sheth, *The Theory of Buyer Behavior* (New York: Wiley, 1969).

7. Deborah J. MacInnis and Valerie S. Folkes, "The Disciplinary Status of Consumer Behavior: A Sociology of Science Perspective on Key Controversies," *Journal of Consumer Research*, 36 (April 2010): 899–914.

8. MacInnis and Folkes, "Disciplinary Status."

9. J. Tucker and J. Ryan, *Economics with Emphasis on the Free Enterprise System* (Mason, OH: Cengage Learning, 2013).

10. "The Big Mac Index," *The Economist* (January 24, 2014), available at http://www.economist.com /content/big-mac-index, accessed February 16, 2014.

11. http://www.infomine.com/investment/metal-prices /crude-oil/5-year/, accessed February 6, 2016.

12. B. McFerran, D. W. Dahl, G. J. Fitzsimons, and A. C. Morales, "I'll Have What She's Having: Effects of Social Influence and Body Type on the Food Choices of Others," *Journal of Consumer Research*, 40 (June 2013): 61–75.

13. P. Chandon and B. Wansink, "The Biasing Health Halos of Fast-Food Restaurant Health Claims: Lower Calorie Estimates and Higher Side-Dish Consumption Intentions," *Journal of Consumer Research*, 34 (October 2007): 301–314.

14. Leona E. Tyler, "More Stately Mansions— Psychology Extends Its Boundaries," *Annual Review of Psychology*, 32 (1981): 1–20.

15. Carolyn Yoon, Gilles Laurent, Helen H. Fung, Richard Gonzales, Angela H. Gutchess, Trey Hedden, Raphaelle Lambert-Pandraud, et al., "Cognition, Persuasion and Decision Making in Older Consumers," *Marketing Letters* 16, no. 3 (2005): 429–441.

16. David J. Moore, "Is Anticipation Delicious? Visceral Factors as Mediators of the Effect of Olfactory Cues on Purchase Intentions," *Journal of Business Research*, 67, no. 9 (September 2014), http:// dx.doi.org/10.1016/j.jbusres.2013.10.005.

17. W. Pride and O. C. Ferrell, *Foundations of Marketing* (Mason, OH: Cengage Learning, 2015).

18. Robert A. Mittelstaedt, "Economics, Psychology, and the Literature of the Subdiscipline of Consumer Behavior," *Journal of the Academy of Marketing Science* 18, no. 4 (1990): 303–311. Interested readers can see MacInnis and Folkes (2010) for more on this debate.

19. T. Gilovich, A. Kumar, and L. Jampol (2015), "A Wonderful Life: Experiential Consumption and the Pursuit of Happiness," *Journal of Consumer Psychology*, 25, 152–165.

20. Klein, J.G., T.M. Lowery, and C.C. Otnes (2015), "Identity-Based Motivations and Anticipated Reckoning: Contributions to Gift-Giving Theory from an Identity-Stripping Context," *Journal of Consumer Psychology*, 25, 431–448.

21. http://denver.cbslocal.com/2015/02/11 /dmv-waits-longer-than-ever-despite-assurances/, accessed February 7, 2016.

22. Thibodeaux, E. (2015), "After the VA Scandal, Veterans Were Told Their Wait for Care would get Shorter. But, It's Actually Getting Worse," *Washington Post* (September 18), 9. E. Wax-Thibodeaux (2015), "Report on VA health care says long waits are far from over." *The Washington Post*, 9. Newspaper Source, EBSCOhost (accessed February 7, 2016).

23. M. Schwanke, "Searching for a Better DMV: Is a Private Model the Answer?" KWCH, http://www .kwch.com/news/local-news/searching-for-a-better -dmv-is-a-private-model-the-answer/22822936, accessed February 16, 2014.

24. http://www.theguardian.com/technology/2015 /dec/16/eu-agrees-draft-text-pan-european-data -privacy-rules, accessed February 7, 2016.

25. J. C. Narver and S. F. Slater, "The Effect of a Market Orientation on Business Profitability," *Journal of Marketing*, 54 (October 1990): 20–35.

26. K. Reed, J.R. Goolsby, and M.K. Johnston (2016), "Listening In and Out: Listening to Customers and Employees to Strengthen an Integrated Market-Oriented System," *Journal of Business Research*, in press, http://dx.doi .org/10.1016.01.002).

27. T. Hult, J. A. Mena, O. C. Ferrell, and L. Ferrell, "Stakeholder Marketing: A Definition and Conceptual Framework," *AMS Review* 1, no. 1 (2011): 44–65.

28. I. Skogland and J. A. Siguaw, "Are Your Satisfied Customers Loyal?" *Cornell Hotel and Restaurant Administration Quarterly*, 45 (2004): 221–234. P. D. Berger, N. Eechambadi, G. Morris, D. R. Lehmann, R. Rizley, and R. Venkatesan, "From Customer Lifetime Value to Shareholder Value: Theory, Empirical Evidence and Issues for Future Research," *Journal of Services Research*, 9 (2006): 156–167.

29. Y. L. Zhao and C. A. Di Benedetto, "Designing Service Quality to Survive: Empirical Evidence from Chinese New Ventures," *Journal of Business Research*, 66 (2013): 1098–1107. S. A. Neslin, D. Grewal, R. Leghorn, V. Shankar, M. L. Teerling, J. S. Thomas, and P. C. Verhoef, "Challenges and Opportunities in Multichannel Customer Management," *Journal of Services Research*, 9 (2006): 95–112.

30. S. D. Hunt, "Developing Successful Theories in Marketing: Insights from Resource-Advantage Theory," *AMS Review* 1, no. 2 (2011): 72–84.

31. B. Carson (2015), "In Memoriam: 7 Once-Hot Startups that Shut Their Doors in 2015; D. Goldman (2015), "10 Big Dot-Com Flops," http://money .cnn.com/gallery/technology/2015/03/02/dot-com -flops/index.html, accessed February 4, 2016.

32. http://www.pewinternet.org/data-trend/mobile /device-ownership/, accessed February 7, 2016; T. Welch (2014), "More Have Access to Cell Phones than Toilets," US News, http://www.usnews.com /news/blogs/data-mine/2014/11/18/on-un-world -toilet-day-more-have-access-to-cell-phones-than -toilets, accessed February 7, 2016.

33. T. Chen, "American Household Credit Card Debt Statistics: 2014," NerdWallet, http://www .nerdwallet.com/blog/credit-card-data/average -credit-card-debt-household/, based on Federal Reserve statistics, accessed February 17, 2014.

34. US Debt Clock, http://www.usdebtclock.org/, accessed February 16, 2014.

35. W. G. Zikmund and B. J. Babin, *Essentials of Marketing Research* (Mason, OH: Cengage Learning, 2013).

36. R. A. Tiwsakul and C. Hackley, "Postmodern Paradoxes in Thai-Asian Consumer Identity," *Journal of Business Research*, 65 (April 2012): 490–496.

37. M. Tadajewski, "Remembering Motivation Research: Toward an Alternative Genealogy of Interpretive Consumer Research," *Marketing Theory*, 6 (2006): 429–466.

38. Miguel Del Fresno, *Netnografía: Investigación, Análisis e Intervención Social Online* (Barcelona, Spain: Editorial UOC, 2011).

39. Kashmir Hill, "How Target Figured Out a Teen Girl Was Pregnant Before Her Father Did," *Forbes* (February 16, 2012), http://www.forbes.com, accessed February 19, 2012.

40. P. Sarantopoulos, A. Theotokis, K. Pramatan, and G. Doukidis (2016), "Shopping Missions: An Analytical Method for the Identification of Shopper Need States," *Journal of Business Research*, 69, 1043–1052].

41. E.M. Gonzalez, E. Esteva, A. Roggeveen, and D. Grewal (2016), "Amount Off versus Percentage Off—When Does It Matter?" *Journal of Business Research*, 69, 1023–1027.

42. "Company Profile," Starbucks, http://www .starbucks.com/about-us, accessed February 16, 2014.

43. Sears Archives, http://www.searsarchives.com /catalogs/history.htm, accessed July 19, 2012.

44. Based on final quarter 2015 data, https://www.census .gov/retail/index.html, accessed February 8, 2016.

45. C. Malamut (2016), "Statistics the Prove Email Marketing Is Not Dead," (February 6), http://blog .capterra.com/statistics-email-marketing-not-dead/, accessed February 8, 2016.

46. C. Birkner (2016), "Scoping It Out," Marketing News (January), 10–11.

47. R. Karlgaard, "Big Data's Promise: Messy, Like Us," *Forbes*, 191, no. 11 (2013), 36.

48. Brad Plumer, "The U.S. Labor Force Is Still Shrinking. Here's Why," Wonk blog, November 18, 2013, http://www.washingtonpost.com/blogs /wonkblog/wp/2013/11/08/the-u-s-labor-force-is -still-shrinking-rapidly-heres-why/, accessed February 16, 2014.

2

1. G. Seidman (2014), "Can You Really Trust The People You Meet Online?" *Psychology Today*, https://www.psychologytoday.com/blog/close-encounters/201407/can-you-really-trust-the-people-you-meet-online, accessed February 8, 2016. "The 10 Most Common Lies in Online Dating," http://www.womansday.com/relationships/dating-marriage/advice/a6759/online-dating-profile-lies/, accessed February 9, 2016.

2. Yany Grégoire, T. M. Tripp, and R. Legoux, "When Customer Love Turns into Lasting Hate: The Effects of Relationship Strength and Time on Customer Revenge and Avoidance," *Journal of Marketing*, 73 (November 2009): 18–32.

3. Yany Grégoire and Robert Fisher, "The Effects of Relationship Quality on Customer Retaliation," *Marketing Letters*, 17, no. 1 (2006): 31–46.

4. Frank Kressmann, M. Joseph Sirgy, Andreas Herrmann, Frank Huber, Stephanie Huber, and Dong-Jin Lee, "Direct and Indirect Effects of Self-Image Congruence on Brand Loyalty," *Journal of Business Research*, 59 (September 2006): 955–964.

5. K. Kim, J. Park and J. Kim (2014), "Consumer Brand Relationship Quality: When and How It Helps Brand Extensions," *Journal of Business Research*, 67, 591–597.

6. Schroeder, B. (2015). Leaders: Build customer truth into your company DNA. *Leader to Leader*, 2015(78), 19–24.

7. E. O'Toole, "The Numerous Legal Traps of the Zero Moment of Truth," *Marketing* (August 12, 2012): 19.

8. H. Kim, "Situational Materialism: How Entering Lotteries May Undermine Self-Control," *Journal of Consumer Research*, 40 (December 2013): 759–772.

9. B. J. Babin, W. R. Darden, and M. Griffin, "Work and/or Fun: Measuring Hedonic and Utilitarian Shopping Value," *Journal of Consumer Research*, 20 (March 1994): 644–656.

10. Movie facts found at Box Office Mojo, www.boxofficemojo.com, accessed February 23, 2014.

11. T. Levitt, "Marketing Myopia," *Harvard Business Review*, 38 (July–August 1960): 57–66.

12. K. Badenhausen, "Shoe Salesman," *Forbes* (June 10, 2013): 1. C. Salter, "Putting a Weird Foot Forward," *Fast Company*, 172 (February 2013): 36–38. "Marketing A-List," *Advertising Age*, 42 (November 26, 2012): 1. T. Wasserman, "Puma Celebrates Darts and Other Hip Pastimes," *Adweek* (August 22, 2010): 26. V. Reklatis, "Analysts See Market-Share Gains for Nike," *Investors' Business Daily* (November 16, 2010): B03.

13. S. L. Vargo and R. F. Lusch, "Service-Dominant Logic: Continuing the Evolution," *Journal of the Academy of Marketing Science*, 36 (March 2008): 1–10.

14. P. R. Dickson and J. L. Ginter, "Market Segmentation, Product Differentiation and Marketing Strategy," *Journal of Marketing*, 51 (1987): 1–10.

15. More precisely, in economics *price elasticity* represents the proportionate change in demand associated with a proportionate change in price. The slope parameter represents the parameter of the line showing how demand responds to price. Thus, the slope of the line is constant over the range, while the elasticity changes at any point on the line. In addition, to get the actual total quantity demanded, the total size of the population would have to be included in the equation. For simplicity of illustration, they are omitted here.

16. See W. C. Kim and R. Mauborgne, "Blue Ocean Strategy," *Harvard Business Review* (October 2004): 2–10. From a creative thinking view, blue ocean strategies are built around the key words of Reduce, Eliminate, Raise, and Create. Blue ocean strategists often refer to perceptual maps as a strategy canvas.

17. For similar perceptual map illustrations: R. T. Kuo, K. Aksana, and B. Subrota, "Application of Particle Swarm Optimization and Perceptual Map to Tourist Market Segmentation," *Expert Systems with Applications*, 39 (August 2012): 5726–8735. L. Xiang, F. Meng, M. Uysal, and B. Milhalik, "Understanding China's Long-Haul Outbound Travel Market: An Overlapped Segmentation Approach," *Journal of Business Research*, 66, no. 6 (June 2013): 786–793.

18. L. M. Sciulli and C. Bebko, "Positioning Strategies for Social Cause Organizations: A Multivariate Analysis of Dimensions and Ideals," *Journal of Nonprofit and Public Sector Marketing*, 23, no. 2 (2012): 99–133.

19. G. Sunil, D. Hanssens, B. Hardie, W. Kahn, V. Kumar, L. Nathaniel, and N. R. Sriram, "Modeling Customer Lifetime Value," *Journal of Service Research*, 9 (November 2006): 139–155.

20. V. Kumar, D. Shah, and R. Venkatesan, "Managing Retailer Profitability—One Customer at a Time!" *Journal of Retailing*, 82 (2006): 277–294.

21. Kumar et al., "Managing Retailer Profitability."

Case 1–1

1. IDEO, http://www.ideo.com, accessed April 11, 2012.

2. Cliff Kuang, "IDEO and Steelcase Unveil a School Desk for the Future of Teaching," *Fast Company*, June 16, 2010, http://www.fastcompany.com/1660576/ideo-and-steelcase-unveil-schooldesk-for-the-future-of-teaching, accessed August 1, 2012.

3. Vivek Kemp, "Pediatric Adventures," GE Healthymagination, http://www.healthymagination.com/stories/pediatric-adventures/, accessed August 1, 1012.

Case 1–2

1. T. Shimp and S. Subash, "Consumer Ethnocentrism: Construction and Validation of the CETSCALE," *Journal of Marketing Research*, 24, no. 3 (1987): 280–289.

2. "Made in America," *World News with Diane Sawyer*, ABC, 2012, http://abcnews.go.com/WN/fullpage/tour-made-america-house-13001236, accessed October 1, 2012.

3. T. A. Shimp, S. Samiee, and S. Sharma, "The Country-of-Origin Effect and Brand Origin Knowledge: How Little Consumers Know and How Important Knowledge Is," in *European Advances in Consumer Research*, ed. A. Groeppel-Klien and R. E. Frank, 325–326 (Provo, UT: Association for Consumer Research, 2001).

Case 1–3

1. Kashmir Hill, "How Target Figured Out a Teen Girl Was Pregnant before Her Father Did," *Forbes*, February 16, 2012, www.forbes.com, accessed August 1, 2012.

2. Charles Duhigg, "How Companies Learn Your Secrets," *The New York Times*, February 16, 2012, www.nytimes.com/2012/02/19/magazine/shopping-habits.html, accessed August 1, 2012.

3. Eric Savitz, "IBM Buying DemandTec for $13.20/Share in $440M Deal," *Forbes.com*, December 8, 2011, 21.

4. "The Collaborative Analytics Cloud," *DemandTec, an IBM Company*, 2012, http://www.demandtec.com/mydemandtec/home.

5. Ladka Bauerova, Chris Burritt, and Joao Oliveira, "A Three-Way Food Fight in Brazil," *Businessweek*, no. 4172 (April 5, 2010): 70.

6. Ibid.

7. Michael Garry, "GPA Deploys Price Optimization," *SN: Supermarket News* 59, no. 39 (2011): 11.

8. Ibid.

9. Ibid.

10. "SKU (inventory)," Britannica Online Encyclopedia, n.d., http://www.britannica.com/EBchecked/topic/1242199/SKU, accessed August 1, 2012.

11. Garry, "GPA Deploys Price Optimization."

12. Ibid.

13. Ibid.

Case 1–4

1. Laura Petrecca, "Sears, Kmart Parent Company Details 80 Store Closings," *USA Today*, December 29, 2011, http://www.usatoday.com/money/industries/retail/story/2011-12-29/sears-releases-sears-kmart-closings-list/52272742/1, accessed August 2, 2012.

3

1. K. Richards, (2015), "Here's What the Most Popular Brands' Logos Have in Common," *AdWeek*, (7/17), 1.

2. A. Sundar and J.J. Kellaris (2015), "How Logo Colors Influence Shoppers' Judgments of Retailer Ethicality: The Mediating Role of Perceived Eco-Friendliness," *Journal of Business Ethics*, 1–17.

3. P. Raghubir and A. Krishna, "Vital Dimensions in Volume Perception: Can the Eye Fool the Stomach?" *Journal of Marketing Research*, 36 (1999): 313–326.

4. Y. Tu, Z. Yang, and C. Ma (2015), "Touching Tastes: The Haptic Perception Transfer of Liquid Food Packaging Materials," *Food Quality and Preference*, 39 (January), 124–130.

5. Dengfeng Yan, Jaideep Sengupta, and Robert S. Wyer Jr., "Package Size and Perceived Quality: The Intervening Role of Unit Price Perceptions," *Journal of Consumer Psychology*, 24, no. 1 (January 2014), doi: 10.1016/j.jcps.2013.08.001.

6. A. Krishna, "An Integrative Review of Sensory Marketing: Engaging the Senses to Affect Perception, Judgment and Behavior," *Journal of Consumer Psychology*, 22 (2012): 332–351; Krishna, A., L. Cian and T. Sokolova (2016), "The Power of Sensory Marketing in Advertising," *Current Opinion in Psychology*, 10, 142–147.

7. T. Powers, D. Advincula, M. S. Austin, S. Graiko, and J. Snyder, "Digital and Social Media in the Purchase Process," *Journal of Advertising Research*, 52 (December 2012): 479–489.

8. G. Antonides, P. C. Verhoef, and M. van Aalst, "Consumer Perception and Evaluation of Waiting Time: A Field Experiment," *Journal of Consumer Psychology*, 12, no. 3 (2002): 193–202. V. M. Patrick (2016). "Everyday consumer aesthetics," *Current Opinion in Psychology*, 10, 60–64.

9. P. Aggarwal and Z. Min (2015). "Seeing the Big Picture: The Effect of Height on the Level of Construal," *Journal of Marketing Research (JMR)*, 52(1), 120–133.

10. See the archive at www.damnyouautocorrect.com for more examples like these. The intended meanings are crushed Oreos (for a recipe), get Hunan (a restaurant dish's name) beef, dear husband.

11. J. J. Argo, M. Popa, and M. C. Smith, "The Sound of Brands," *Journal of Marketing*, 74 (July 2010): 97–109.

12. Joan Meyers-Levy and Alice M. Tybout, "Schema Congruity as a Basis for Product Evaluation," *Journal of Consumer Research*, 16, no. 1 (1989): 39–54.

13. Espinosa, J.A. and D.J. Ortinau (2016), "Debunking Legendary Beliefs about Student Samples in Marketing Research," *Journal of Business Research*, doi:10.10-16/jbusres.2015.12.003

14. Zheng, X. Z. Schwarts. J.H. Gerdes, M Uysal (2015), "What Can Big Data and Text Analytics Tell Us about Hotel Guest Experience and Satisfaction?" *International Journal of Hospitality Management*, 44, 120–130.

15. P. Aggarwal and A. L. McGill, "Is That Car Smiling at Me? Schema Congruity as a Basis for Evaluating Anthropomorphized Products," *Journal of Consumer Research*, 14 (December 2007): 468–479.

16. A. Waytz, J. Heafner, and N. Epley, "The Mind in the Machine: Anthropomorphism Increases Trust in Autonomous Vehicle," *Journal of Experimental Social Psychology*, 52 (2014): 113–117.

17. P. M. Merkile, "Subliminal Perception," *Encyclopedia of Psychology* 7 (2000): 497–499.

18. M. Gable, H. Wilkens, L. Harris, and R. Feinbert, "An Evaluation of Subliminally Embedded Sexual Stimuli in Graphics," *Journal of Advertising*, 16 (1987): 26–31.

19. S. J. Broyles, "Misplaced Paranoia over Subliminal Advertising: What's the Big Uproar?" *Journal of Consumer Marketing*, 23 (2006): 312–313.

20. T. Verwijerman, J. C. Karremans, W. Stroebe, and D. H. T. Wigboldus, "The Workings and Limits of Subliminal Advertising: The Role of Habits," *Journal of Consumer Psychology*, 21 (April 2011), 206–213.

21. S. J. Broyles, "Subliminal Advertising and the Perceptual Popularity of Playing to People's Paranoia," *Journal of Consumer Affairs*, 40 (2006): 392–406.

22. G. Lantos, "Ice Cube Sex: The Truth about Subliminal Advertising; Book Review," *Journal of Consumer Marketing*, 13 (1996): 62–64.

23. W. B. Key, *Subliminal Seduction: Ad Media's Manipulation of a Not So Innocent America* (New York: Signet, 1974). V. Packard, *The Hidden Persuaders* (New York: D. McKay Co., 1957).

24. W. A. Cook, "Looking Behind Ice Cubes," *Journal of Advertising Research*, 33 (March/April 1993): 7–8.

25. "Subliminal Seduction and Other Urban Myths," *Advertising Age*, 71 (September 18, 2000): 104–105.

26. J. Vroomen and M. Keetels, "The Spatial Constraint in Intersensory Pairing: No Role in Temporal Ventriloquism," *Journal of Experimental Psychology*, 32 (2006): 1063–1071.

27. Richard L. Miller, "Dr. Weber and the Consumer," *Journal of Marketing*, 26 (1962): 57–67.

28. K. D. Hoffman, L. W. Turley, and S. W. Kelley, "Pricing Retail Services," *Journal of Business Research*, 55 (December 2002): 1015–1023.

29. K. Kalyanam and T. S. Shively, "Estimating Irregular Pricing Effects: A Stochastic Spline Regression Approach," *Journal of Marketing Research*, 35 (1998): 16–29.

30. D. Biswas, L. I. Labrecque, D. R. Lehmann, and E. Markos, "Making Choices While Smelling, Tasting and Listening: The Role of Sensory Dissimilarity When Sequentially Sampling Products," *Journal of Marketing*, 78 (January 2014): 112–126; Aktar, T., J. Chen, R. Ettelaiaie (2015), "Evaluation of the Sensory Correlation between Touch Sensitivity and the Capacity to Discriminate Viscosity," *Journal of Sensory Studies*, 30, 98–107.

31. D. McShefferty, W. Whitmer, and M. A. Akeroyd, (2016), "The Just-Meaningful Difference in Speech-to-Noise Ratio," *Trends in Hearing*, 20, 2331216515626570.

32. D. Chaffey (2015), "Display Advertising Click-through Rates," Smart Insights, http://www.smartinsights.com/internet-advertising/internet-advertising-analytics/display-advertising-clickthrough-rates/, accessed February 25, 2016. J. Lee, J. H. Ahn, and B. Park (2015). "The effect of repetition in Internet banner ads and the moderating role of animation," *Computers in Human Behavior*, 46, 202–209.

33. Chris Janiszewski, "Preattentive Mere Exposure Effects," *Journal of Consumer Research*, 20, no. 3 (1993): 376–392.

34. Nunes, J.C., A. Ordanini, and F. Valsesia (2015), "The Power of Repetition: Repetitive Lyrics in a Song Increase Processing Fluency and Drive Market Success," *Journal of Consumer Psychology*, 25, 187–199.]

35. C. V. Dimofte and R. F. Yalch, "The Mere Association Effect and Brand Attitudes," *Journal of Consumer Psychology* 21 (2011): 24–37.

36. M. Yang, D. Roskos-Ewoldson, L. Dinu, and L. M. Arpan, "The Effectiveness of 'In-Game' Advertising," *Journal of Advertising*, 35 (Winter 2006): 143–152.

37. http://brandchannel.com/2015/02/20/announcing-the-2015-brandcameo-product-placement-awards/, accessed March 11, 2016

38. B. David and D. W. Wooten, "From Labeling Possessions to Possessing Labels: Ridicule and Socialization among Adolescents," *Journal of Consumer Research*, 33 (2006): 188–198.

39. B. F. Skinner, "The Origins of Cognitive Thought," *American Psychologist*, 44, no. 1 (1989): 13–18.

40. Ibid.

41. John C. Malone, Jr., and Natalie M. Cruchon, "Radical Behaviorism and the Rest of the Psychology: A Review/Precis of Skinner's *About Behaviorism*," *Behavior and Philosophy* 29 (2001): 31–57.

42. Saul McLeod, "Behaviorism: Learning Theory," 2007, http://www.simplypsychology.org/behaviorism.html, accessed June 29, 2012.

43. Cindy Chan, LeafVan Boven, Eduardo B. Andrade, and Dan Ariely, "Moral Violations Reduce Oral Consumption," *Journal of Consumer Psychology*, 24, no. 3 (July 2014): 381–386. DOI: http://dx.doi.org/10.1016/j.jcps.2013.12.003

4

1. Metro, November 12, 2013, http://metro.co.uk/2013/11/12/domestic-incident-turns-out-to-be-couple-struggling-with-ikea-furniture-4184295/, accessed March 25, 2014.

2. E. Lepkowska-White and A. Parsons, "Comprehension of Warnings and Resulting Attitudes," *Journal of Consumer Affairs*, 35 (2001): 278–194. A. D. Cox, D. Cox, and S. Powell Mantel, "Consumer Response to Drug Risk Information: The Role of Positive Affect," *Journal of Marketing*, 74 (July 2010): 31–44.

3. M. O'Hegarty, L. L. Pederson, K. J. Asman, A. M. Malarcher, and J. Kruger, "Reactions of Adult Smokers and Former Smokers to Current US Warning Labels," *American Journal of Health Behavior*, 37 (Sept./Oct. 2013): 654–659. J. J. Argo and K. J. Main, "Meta-Analysis of the Effectiveness of Warning Labels," *Journal of Public Policy & Marketing*, 23 (Fall 2004): 193–208.

4. T. F. Thrasher, M. C. Rousu, D. Hammond, A. Navarro, and J. Corrigan, "Estimating the Impact of Pictorial Health Warnings and 'Plain' Cigarette Packaging: Evidence from Experimental Auctions among Adult Smokers in the U.S.," *Health Policy*, 102 (September 2011): 41–48.

5. Adam E. Green, Darren Mays, Emily B. Falk, Donna Vallone, Natalie Gallagher, Amanda Richardson, Kenneth P. Tercyak, David B. Abrams, Raymond S. Niaura (2016), "Young Adult Smokers' Neural Responses to Graphic Cigarette Warning Labels," *Addictive Behavior Reports*, 3, 28–32.

6. A. Borges and B. Babin, "Revisiting Low Price Guarantees: Does Consumer versus Retailer Governance Matter?" *Marketing Letters*, 23, no. 3 (2012): 777–791. Monika Kukar-Kinney and Dhruv Grewal, "Comparison of Consumer Reactions to Price-Matching Guarantees in Internet and Bricks-and-Mortar Retail Environments," *Journal of the Academy of Marketing Science*, 35, no. 2 (Summer 2007): 197–207.

7. L. Bix, S. Wontae, and R. P. Sundar, "The Effect of Colour Contrast on Consumers' Attentive Behaviours and Perception of Fresh Produce," *Packaging Technology & Science*, 26 (March 2013): 96–104.

8. C. Areni and C. Sutton-Brady, "The Universal Color Grid: Color Research Unbiased by Verbal Labels and Prototypical Hues," *Journal of Marketing Development and Competitiveness*, 5 (2011): 98–102. D. Tsiantar, J. Brau, E. Florian, B. Dumaine, and M. Kimes, "25 Green Myths Debunked," *Fortune*, 161 (April 12, 2010): 101–112.

9. B. Grohmann, J. L. Giese, and I. D. Parkman, "Using Type Font Characteristics to Communicate Brand Personality of New Brands," *Journal of Brand Management*, 20 (2013): 389–403.

10. J. R. Doyle and P. A. Bottemly, "Dressed for the Occasion: Font-Product Congruity in the Perception of Logotype," *Journal of Consumer Psychology*, 16, no. 2 (2006): 112–123.

11. H. Noel and B. Vallen, "The Spacing Effect in Marketing: A Review of Extant Findings and Directions for Future Research," *Psychology & Marketing*, 26 (November 2009): 951–969.

12. K. Svobodova, P. Sklenicka, K. Molnarova, and J. Vojar, "Does the Composition of Landscape Photographs Affect Visual Preferences? The Rule of the Golden Section and the Position of the Horizon," *Journal of Environmental Psychology*, 38 (2014): 143–152.

13. Kurtzman, E. and J. Greene (2016), "Effective Presentation of Health Care Performance Information for Consumer Decision Making: A Systematic Review," *Patient Education and Counselling*, 99, 36–43.

14. Yoon, D. and Y. Kim (2015), "The Roles of a Spokesperson and Brand-Message Congruity in Advertising Effectiveness of Coffeehouse Brands," *Journal of Quality Assurance in Hospitality & Tourism*, 16, 347–368.

15. R. R. Burke and T. K. Srull, "Competitive Interference and Consumer Memory for Advertisements," *Journal of Consumer Research*, 15 (June 1988): 55–68.

16. A. Kronrod and S. Danziger, "Wii Will Rock You!! The Use and Effect of Figurative Language in Consumer Reviews of Hedonic and Utilitarian Consumption," *Journal of Consumer Research*, 40 (December 2013): 726–739.

17. R. R. Dholokia and B. Sternthal, "Highly Credible Sources: Persuasive Facilitator or Persuasive Liabilities?" *Journal of Consumer Research*, 3 (1997): 223–232.

18. V. A. Taylor and A. B. Bower, "Improving Product Instruction Compliance: If You Tell Me Why, I Might Comply," *Psychology & Marketing*, 21 (2004): 229–245.

19. "Avoid Black Cats? Walk Around Ladders? Are Americans Superstitious?" Harris Polls, February 27, 2014, http://www.harrisinteractive.com/NewsRoom/HarrisPolls/tabid/447/mid/1508

/articleId/1388/ctl/ReadCustom%20Default/Default.aspx, accessed March 2, 2014.

20. Richard L. Celsi and Jerry C. Olson, "The Role of Involvement in Attention and Comprehension Processes," *Journal of Consumer Research*, 15, no. 2 (1988): 210–224.

21. S. Menon and D. Soman, "Managing the Power of Curiosity for Effective Web Advertising Strategies," *Journal of Advertising*, 31 (2004): 1–14.

22. S. Lee, K. Kim and S. Sundar (2015), "Customization in Location-Based Advertising: Effects of Tailoring Source, Locational Congruity, and Product Involvement on Ad Attitudes," *Computers in Human Behavior*, 51.A., 336–343.

23. J. P. Redden, "Reducing Satiation: The Role of Categorization Level," *Journal of Consumer Research*, 34 (February 2008): 624–634. C. L. Nordhielm, "The Influence of Levels of Processing on Advertising Repetition Levels," *Journal of Consumer Research*, 29 (December 2002): 371–82.

24. M. Griffin, B. J. Babin, and D. Modianos, "Shopping Values of Russian Consumers: The Impact of Habituation in a Developing Economy," *Journal of Retailing*, 76 (2000): 33–52.

25. Ralph I. Allison and Kenneth P. Uhl, "Influence of Beer Brand Identification on Taste Perception," *Journal of Marketing Research*, 1 (August 1964): 36–39.

26. C. Kaufman-Scarborough, "Seeing Through the Eyes of the Color-Deficient Shopper: Consumer Issues for Public Policy," *Journal of Consumer Policy*, 23 (2000): 461–492.

27. K. Vance and S. Virtue, "Metaphoric Advertisement Comprehension: The Role of Cerebral Hemispheres," *Journal of Consumer Behaviour*, 10 (2011): 41–50.

28. A. D. Cox, D. Cox, and G. Zimet, "Understanding Consumer Responses to Product Risk Information," *Journal of Marketing*, 70 (January 2006): 79–91.

29. A. Tversky and D. Kahneman, "The Framing of Decisions and the Psychology of Choice," *Science*, 211 (1981): 453–458. J. Cesario, K. S. Corker, and S. Jelinek, "A Self-Regulatory Framework for Message Framing," *Journal of Experimental Social Psychology*, 49 (2013): 218–249.

30. S. Rick, "Losses, Gains, and Brains: Neuroeconomics Can Help to Answer Open Questions about Loss Aversion," *Journal of Consumer Psychology*, 21 (2011): 453–463.

31. R. Saini, R. S. Rao, and A. Monga, "Is That Deal Worth My Time? The Interactive Effect of Relative and Referent Thinking on Willingness to Seek a Bargain," *Journal of Marketing*, 74 (January 2010): 34–48.

32. H. Deval, S. P. Mantel, F. R. Kardes, and S.S. Posavac, "How Naïve Theories Drive Opposing Inferences from the Same Information," *Journal of Consumer Research*, 39 (April 2013): 1185–1200.

33. Mangen, A., B. R. Walgermo, K. Bronnick (2013), "Reading Linear Texts on Paper versus Computer Screen: Effects on Reading Comprehension," *International Journal of Educational Research*, 58, 61–68

34. Coulter, K.S. (2016), "How Hand Proximity Impacts Consumer Response to a Persuasive Communication," *Psychology & Marketing*, 33, 135–149.

35. Macdonnell, R. and K. White (2015), "How Construals of Money Versus Time Impact Consumer Charitable Giving," *Journal of Consumer Research*, ucv042.

36. Charles Spence, "Managing Sensory Expectations Concerning Products and Brands: Capitalizing on the Potential of Sound and Shape Symbolism," *Journal of Consumer Psychology*, 22, no. 1 (2012): 37–54.

37. Sandra Littel and Ulrich R. Orth, "Effects of Package Visuals and Haptics on Brand Evaluations," *European Journal of Marketing*, 47, no. 1/2 (2013): 198–217.

38. Keith S. Coulter, Pilsik Choi, and Kent B. Monroe, "Comma N'cents in Pricing: The Effects of Auditory Representation Encoding on Price Magnitude Perception," *Journal of Consumer Psychology*, 22 (2012): 395–407. D. Luna and H. M. Kim, "How Much Was Your Shopping Basket? Working Memory Processes in Total Basket Price Estimation," *Journal of Consumer Psychology*, 19 (2009): 346–355.

39. Baker, M.A., J.T. Shin and Y.W. Kim (2016), "An Exploration and Investigation of Edible Insect Consumption: The Impacts of Image and Description on Risk Perceptions and Purchase Intent," *Psychology & Marketing*, 33, 94–112.

40. D. Luna, M. Carnevale, and D. Lerman, "Does Brand Spelling Influence Memory? The Case of Auditorily Presented Brand Names," *Journal of Consumer Psychology*, 23 (2013): 36–48.

41. J. C. K. Chan, K. B. McDermott, J. M. Watson, and D. A. Gallo, "The Importance of Material-Processing Interactions in Inducing False Memories," *Memory & Cognition*, 33 (2005): 389–395.

42. A. Debenedetti and P. Gomez, "Mental Rumination: How Unwanted and Recurrent Thoughts Can Perturbate the Purchasing Behavior," *Advances in Consumer Research*, 37 (2010): 1–6.

43. A. Kähr, B. Nyffenegger, H. Krohmer, and W. D. Hoyer (2017), "When Consumers Harm Your Brand—The Phenomenon of Consumer Brand Sabotage," *Journal of Marketing*, In-Press.

44. J. J. Sierra and S. McQuitty, "Attitudes and Emotions as Determinants of Nostalgic Purchases: An Application of Social Identity Theory," *Journal of Marketing Theory and Practice*, 15 (2007): 99–112.

45. Celsi and Olson, "The Role of Involvement."

46. J. Saegert, "A Demonstration of Levels of Processing Theory in Memory for Advertisements," *Advances in Consumer Research*, 6 (1979): 82–84.

47. R. Winkler, "Google Deal with Luxottica Will Bring Glass to Ray-Ban, Oakley," *The Wall Street Journal*, March 24, 2014, D1.

48. B. M. Fennis, L. Janssen, K. D. Vohs, "Acts of Benevolence: A Limited-Resource Account of Compliance with Charitable Requests," *Journal of Consumer Research*, 35 (April 2009): 906–924.

49. R. S. Moore, "The Sociological Impact of Attitudes toward Smoking: Secondary Effects of the Demarketing of Smoking," *Journal of Social Psychology*, 145 (2005): 703–718.

50. B. McFerran, D. W. Dahl, G. J. Fitzsimons, and A. C. Morales, "Might an Overweight Waitress Make You Eat More? How the Body Type of Others Is Sufficient to Alter Our Food Consumption," *Journal of Consumer Psychology*, 20 (2010): 146–151.

51. Kim Peterson, "Wealthy Prius Drivers Can Be Huge Jerks," MSN Money, August 13, 2013, http://money.msn.com/now/wealthy-prius-drivers-can-be-huge-jerks, accessed August 13, 2013.

52. Moore,"The Sociological Impact of Attitudes toward Smoking."

5

1. K. Rosman and E. Dwoskin, "Marketers Want to Know What You Feel, Not Just What You Say," *The Wall Street Journal*, March 24, 2014, R3.

2. R.Govind, N. Garg, and W. Sun, "Geographically Varying Effects of Weather on Tobacco Consumption: Implications for Health Marketing Initiatives," *Health Marketing Quarterly*, 31, no. 1 (2014): 46–64; S. Stockli, A.E. Stampfli, C. Messuer, and T.A. Brunner (2016), "An Unhealthy Poster: When Environmental Cues Affect Consumers' Food Choices at Vending Machines," *Appetite*, 96, 368–374.

3. S. Motyka, et al., "Regulatory Fit: A Meta-Analytic Synthesis," *Journal of Consumer Psychology* (July 2014), http://dx.doi.org/10.1016/j.jcps.2013.11.004. S. Chatterjee, R. Roy, and A. V. Malshe, "The Role of Regulatory Fit in the Attraction Effect," *Journal of Consumer Psychology*, 21 (2011): 473–481. M. Touré-Tillery and A. Fishbach, "The Course of Motivation," *Journal of Consumer Psychology*, 21 (2011): 414–423.

4. M. Kukar-Kinney and A.C. Scheinbaum (2016), "Compulsive Buying in Online Daily Deal Settings: An Investigation of Motivations and Contextual Elements," *Journal of Business Research*, 69, 691–699.

5. G. Laurent and J. N. Kapferer, "Measuring Consumer Involvement Profiles," *Journal of Marketing Research*, 22 (February 1985): 41–53.

6. D. J. Howard and R. A. Kerin, "Broadening the Scope of Reference Price Advertising Research: A Field Study of Shopping Involvement," *Journal of Marketing*, 70 (October 2006): 185–204.

7. H. Kim, K. Park, and N. Schwarz, "Will This Trip Be Exciting? The Role of Incidental Emotions in Product Evaluations," *Journal of Consumer Research*, 36 (April 2010): 983–991.

8. R. K. Madupalli and A. Poddar, "Problematic Customers and Customer Service Employee Retaliation," *Journal of Services Marketing*, 28, no. 3 (2014): 244–255.

9. E. Fonberg, "Amygdala: Emotions, Motivation, and Depressive States," in *Emotion: Theory, Research, and Experience*, ed. R. Plutchik et al. (New York: Kluwer Press, 1986), 302.

10. B. J. Babin, W. R. Darden, and L. A. Babin, "Negative Emotions in Marketing Research: Affect or Artifact?" *Journal of Business Research*, 42 (1998): 271–285. J. A. Russell and J. Snodgrass, "Emotion and the Environment," in *Environment and Psychology*, ed. D. Stokols and I. Altman (New York: John Wiley and Sons, 1987), 245–280.

11. A. De Nisco and G. Warnaby, "Urban Design and Tenant Variety Influences on Consumers' Emotions and Approach Behavior," *Journal of Business Research*, 67 (2014): 211–217.

12. J. Calanchini, W. G. Moons, and D. M. Mackie (2016). "Angry expressions induce extensive processing of persuasive appeals," *Journal of Experimental Social Psychology*, 64, 88–98.

13. L. Watson and M. Spencer, "Causes and Consequences of Emotions on Consumer Behaviour: A Review and Integrative Cognitive Appraisal Theory," *European Journal of Marketing*, 41 (2007): 487–511.

14. J. G. Moulard, M. Kroff, and J. A. G. Folse, "Unraveling Consumer Suspense: The Role of Fear, Hope and Probability Fluctuations," *Journal of Business Research*, 65 (March 2012): 340–346. L. Brennan and W. Binney, "Fear, Guilt and Shame Appeals in Social Marketing," *Journal of Business Research*, 62 (2010): 140–146.

15. H. Zourrig, J. C. Chebat, and R. Toffoli, "Consumer Revenge Behavior: A Cross-Cultural Perspective," *Journal of Business Research*, 62 (2009): 995–1001.

16. B. J. Babin and W. R. Darden, "Good and Bad Shopping Vibes: Spending and Patronage Satisfaction," *Journal of Business Research*, 35 (1996): 201–206.

17. N. M. Pucinelli, "Putting Your Best Foot Forward: The Impact of Customer Mood on Salesperson Evaluation," *Journal of Consumer Psychology*, 16 (2006): 156–162.

18. S. J. Stanton, C. Reeck, S. A. Huettel, and K. S. LaBar, "Effects of Induced Moods on Economic Choices," *Judgment and Decision Making*, 9, no. 2 (2014): 167–175.

19. Y. Jiang, A. Choi, and R. Adaval, "The Unique Consequences of Feeling Lucky: Implications for Consumer Behavior," *Journal of Consumer Psychology*, 19 (2009): 171–184.

20. A. S. Koch and J. P. Forgas, "Feeling Good and Feeling Truth: The Interactive Effects of Mood and Processing Fluency on Truth Judgments," *Journal of Experimental Social Psychology*, 48 (2012): 481–485.

21. J. Hong and H.H. Chang (2016), "'I' Follow My Heart and 'We' Rely on Reasons: The Impact of Self-Construal on Reliance on Feelings versus Reasons in Decision Making," *Journal of Consumer Research*, 41, 1392–1411.

22. D. Keltner, A. Kogan, P. K. Piff, and S. R. Saturn, "The Sociocultural Appraisals, Values, and Emotions (SAVE) Framework of Prosociality: Core Processes from Gene to Meme," *Annual Review of Psychology*, 65 (2014): 425–460.

23. P. Raghubir, "An Information Processing View of the Subjective Value of Money and Prices," *Journal of Business Research*, 59 (2006): 1053–1062.

24. See P. Karolein and S. Dewitte, "How to Capture the Heart? Twenty Years of Emotion Measurement in Advertisement," *Journal of Advertising*, 46 (2006): 18–37.

25. T. Bakalash and H. Riemer, "Exploring Ad-Elicited Emotional Arousal and Memory for the Ad Using fMRI," *Journal of Advertising*, 42, no. 4 (2013): 275–291.

26. C. Rasch, J.L. Louviere, and T. Teichert (2015), "Using Facial EMG & Eye-Tracking to Study Integral Affect in Discrete Choice Experiments," *Journal of Choice Modeling*, 14 (March), 32–47.

27. J. A. Russell and G. Pratt, "Affect Space Is Bipolar," *Journal of Personality and Social Psychology*, 37 (1979): 1161–1178. Babin, Darden, and Babin, "Negative Emotions in Marketing Research."

28. See E. Mazaheri, M. O. Richard, M. Laroche, and L. C. Ueltschy (2014). "The influence of culture, emotions, intangibility, and atmospheric cues on online behavior," *Journal of Business Research*, 67(3), 253–259, for a review.

29. V. A. Vieira, "Stimuli–Organism-Response Framework: A Meta-Analytic Review in the Store Environment," *Journal of Business Research*, 66 (2013): 1420–1426.

30. K. P. Newman, and M. Brucks (2016), "When Are Natural and Urban Environments Restorative? The Impact of Environmental Compatibility on Self-Control Restoration," *Journal of Consumer Psychology*, doi:10.1016/j.jcps.2016.02005.

31. N. McDougal, *The Impact of Neuroticism on Online Gaming Emotions and Value*. PhD Diss., Louisiana Tech University, 2013.

32. D. L. Hoffman and T. P. Novak, "Flow Online: Lessons Learned and Future Prospects," *Journal of Interactive Marketing*, 23 (2009): 23–24.

33. K.-K. Mak, C.-M. Lai, C.-H. Ko, C. Chou, D.-I. Kim, H. Watanabe, and R. C. M. Ho, "Psychometric Properties of the Revised Chen Internet Addiction Scale (CIAS-R) in Chinese Adolescents," *Journal of Abnormal Child Psychology* (March 2014): 19. A. Patterson, "Social Networkers of the World Unite and Take Over: A Meta-Introspective

Perspective on the Facebook Brand," *Journal of Business Research*, 65 (2012): 527–534. Harry Wallop, "12 Signs That You're Addicted to Social Media," *The Telegraph*, September 12, 2013, http://www.telegraph.co.uk/technology/social-media /10304570/12-signs-that-youre-addicted-to-social -media.html, accessed April 10, 2014.

34. Donnavieve N. Smith and K. Sivakumar, "Flow and Internet Shopping Behavior," *Journal of Business Research*, 57, no. 10 (2004): 1199–1208.

35. L. Dailey, "Navigational Web Atmospherics: Explaining the Influence of Restrictive Navigation Cues," *Journal of Business Research*, 57 (2004): 795–803.

36. J. M. Gottman and R. W. Leveson, "Emotional Suppression: Physiology, Self-Report, and Expressive Behavior," *Journal of Personality and Social Psychology*, 64 (April 1992): 970–986.

37. J. J. Gross and O. P. John, "Revealing Feelings: Facets of Emotional Expressivity in Self-Reports, Peer Ratings, and Behavior," *Journal of Personality and Social Psychology*, 72 (February 1997): 435–448.

38. B. J. Babin, M. Griffin, A. Borges, and J. S. Boles, "Negative Emotions, Value and Relationships: Differences between Women and Men," *Journal of Retailing and Consumer Services*, 20 (September 2013): 471–478.

39. H. A. Taute, B. A. Huhmann, and R. Thakur, "Emotional Information Management: Concept Development and Measurement in Public Service Announcements," *Psychology & Marketing*, 27 (May 2010): 417–444.

40. B. Kidwell, J. Hassford, and D.M. Hardesty (2015), "Emotional Ability Training and Mindful Eating," *Journal of Marketing Research*, 52, 105–19.

41. B. Kidwell, D. M. Hardesty, B. R. Murtha, and S. Sheng, "Emotional Intelligence in Marketing Exchanges," *Journal of Marketing*, 75, no. 1 (2011): 78–95. C. C. Chen and F. Jaramillo, "The Double-Edged Effects of Emotional Intelligence on the Adaptive Selling–Salesperson-Owned Loyalty Relationship," *Journal of Personal Selling & Sales Management*, 34, no. 1 (2014): 33–50.

42. S. Weems, "It's Funny How Humor Actually Works," *The Wall Street Journal*, March 22, 2014, C3.

43. P. Ferrè, "Effects of Level of Processing on Memory for Affectively Valenced Words," *Cognition and Emotion*, 17 (2003): 859.

44. Thomas R. Baird, R. G. Wahlers, and C. K. Cooper, "Non Recognition of Print Advertising: Emotion Arousal and Gender Effects," *Journal of Marketing Communications*, 13 (2007): 39–57.

45. K. White and C. McFarland, "When Are Moods Likely to Influence Consumers' Product Preferences? The Role of Mood Focus and Perceived Relevance of Moods," *Journal of Consumer Psychology*, 19 (2009): 526–536; A. Merchant, J. B. Ford, and G. Rose, "How Personal Nostalgia Influences Giving to Charity," *Journal of Business Research*, 64 (June 2011): 610–616.

46. J. P. Forgas and J. Ciarrochi, "On Being Happy and Possessive: The Interactive Effects of Mood and Personality on Consumer Judgments," *Psychology & Marketing*, 18 (2001): 239–260.

47. H. H. Chang and M. T. Pham, "Affect as a Decision-Making System of the Present," *Journal of Consumer Research*, 40, no. 1 (2013): 42–63.

48. K. Pounders, B.J. Babin, and A. Close, "All the Same to Me: Outcomes of Aesthetic Labor Performed by Frontline Service Providers," *Journal of the Academy of Marketing Science*, DOI: 10.1007 /s11747-014-0407-4; K.R. Pounders, B.J. Babin, and A.G. Close (2015), "All the Same to Me: Outcomes of Aesthetic Labor Performed by Frontline Service

Providers," *Journal of the Academy of Marketing Science*, 43, 670–693.

49. K. H. Chu, M. A. Baker, and S. K. Murrmann, "When We Are Onstage, We Smile: The Effects of Emotional Labor on Employee Work Outcomes," *International Journal of Hospitality Management*, 31 (2012): 906–915.

50. S. Fournier and C. Alvarez. "Relating Badly to Brands," *Journal of Consumer Psychology*, 23, no. 2 (2013): 253–264.

51. Hasford et al. (2015); Gabriel, A.S., J.D. Acosta, A.A. Grandey (2015), "The Value of a Smile: Does Emotional Performance Matter More in Familiar or Unfamiliar Exchanges?" *Journal of Business and Psychology*, 30, 37–50.

52. I. A. Castro, A. C. Morales, and S. M. Nowlis, "The Influence of Disorganized Shelf Displays and Limited Product Quantity on Consumer Purchase," *Journal of Marketing*, 77, no. 4 (2013): 118–133.

53. J. L. Argo, D. W. Dahl, and A. C. Morales, "Positive Consumer Contagion: Responses to Attractive Others in a Retail Context," *Journal of Marketing Research*, 45 (December 2008): 690–701.

1. For a discussion of individual difference variables in consumer research and marketing practice, see John C. Mowen, *The 3M Model of Motivation and Personality: Theory and Empirical Applications to Consumer Behavior* (Boston: Kluwer Academic Publishers, 2000).

2. This definition is based on a number of different sources in personality psychology literature, including G. W. Allport, *Pattern and Growth in Personality* (New York: Holt, Rinehart, and Winston, 1961); L. A. Pervin and O. P. John, *Personality Theory and Research* (New York: John Wiley & Sons, 1977); Nathan Brody and Howard Ehrlichman, *Personality Psychology: The Science of Individuality* (Upper Saddle River, NJ: Prentice Hall, 1998); and Mowen, *The 3M Model of Motivation and Personality*.

3. Alois Angleitner, "Personality Psychology: Trends and Developments," *European Journal of Personality*, 5 (1991): 185–197.

4. A discussion of the debate regarding personality and behavioral consistency across situations may be found in W. Mischel and P. K. Peake, "Some Facets of Consistency: Replies to Epstein, Funder, and Bem," *Psychological Review*, 89 (1983): 394–402; S. Epstein, "The Stability of Confusion: A Reply to Mischel and Peake," *Psychological Review*, 90 (1983): 179–194; David Buss, "Personality as Traits," *American Psychologist*, 44 (1989): 1378–1388.

5. For a discussion of psychoanalytical theory and applications to marketing, see Harold H. Kassarjian, "Personality and Consumer Behavior: A Review," *Journal of Marketing Research*, 8 (November 1971): 409–18. Also see Harold H. Kassarjian and Mary Jane Sheffet, "Personality and Consumer Behavior: An Update," in *Perspectives in Consumer Behavior*, 4th ed., ed. Harold H. Kassarjian and Thomas S. Robertson (Upper Saddle River, NJ: Prentice Hall, 1991), 81–303. For a general description of the psychoanalytical approach in psychology, see Brody and Ehrlichman, *Personality Psychology*.

6. Interesting examples of the early use of these motivational techniques can be found in Philip Gustafson, "You Can Gauge Customers' Wants," *Nation's Business*, 49 (April 1958): 76–84.

7. Kassarjian, "Personality and Consumer Behavior: A Review."

8. Brody and Ehrlichman, *Personality Psychology*.

9. P.A. Rosen, B.D. McLarty, C. Esken, S. Solomon, and E. Taylor (2014), "The Use of Twitter Profiles to Assess Personality and Hireability," *Academy of Management Annual Meeting Proceedings*, (1), 17496.

10. Stephen J. Gould, "The Emergence of Consumer Introspection Theory (CIT): Introduction to a JBR Special Issue," *Journal of Business Research*, 65 (2012): 453–460. Barbara Olsen, "Reflexive Introspection on Sharing Gifts and Shaping Stories," *Journal of Business Research* 65 (2012): 467–474.

11. A. Keinan and R. Kivetz, "Productivity Orientation and the Consumption of Collectible Experiences," *Journal of Consumer Research*, 37, no. 6 (2011): 935–950.

12. Buss, "Personality as Traits."

13. G. W. Allport and H. S. Odbert, "Trait Names," *Psychological Monographs*, 47, no. 211 (1936): 1–37.

14. Donald R. Lichtenstein, Richard G. Netemeyer, and Scot Burton, "Distinguishing Coupon Proneness from Value Consciousness: An Acquisition-Transaction Utility Theory Perspective," *Journal of Marketing*, 54, no. 3 (1990): 54–67.

15. Russell W. Belk, "Materialism: Trait Aspects of Living in the Material World," *Journal of Consumer Research*, 12, no. 3 (December 1985): 265–280.

16. Marsha L. Richins, "Special Possessions and the Expression of Material Values," *Journal of Consumer Research*, 21, no. 3 (December 1994): 522–533. Belk, "Materialism."

17. Aric Rindfleisch, James E. Burroughs, and Nancy Wong, "The Safety of Objects: Materialism, Existential Insecurity, and Brand Connection," *Journal of Consumer Research*, 36 (June 2009): 1–16.

18. Sigal Segev, Aviv Shoham, and Yossi Gavish, "A Closer Look into the Materialism Construct: The Antecedents and Consequences of Materialism and It's Three Facets," *Journal of Consumer Marketing*, 32 no. 2 (2015): 85–98.

19. Kelly Tian and Russell W. Belk, "Extended Self and Possessions in the Workplace," *Journal of Consumer Research*, 32, no. 2 (September 2005): 297–310.

20. Melanie Wallendorf and Eric J. Arnould, "My Favorite Things: A Cross-Cultural Inquiry into Object Attachment, Possessiveness, and Social Linkage," *Journal of Consumer Research*, 14, no. 4 (March 1988): 531–547.

21. Belk, "Materialism."

22. Mary Loftus, "Till Debt Do Us Part," *Psychology Today*, 37, no. 6 (November/December 2004): 42–50.

23. John L. Lastovicka, Lance A. Bettencourt, Renee Shaw Hughner, and Ronald J. Kuntze, "Lifestyle of the Tight and Frugal: Theory and Measurement," *Journal of Consumer Research*, 26, no. 1 (June 1999): 85–98.

24. This definition is based on the works of David F. Midgley and Grahame R. Dowling, "Innovativeness: The Concept and Its Measurement," *Journal of Consumer Research* (1978): 229–242; Everett M. Rogers and Floyd F. Shoemaker, *Communication of Innovations* (New York: The Free Press, 1971); Jonathan B. Hartman, Kenneth C. Gerht, and Kittichai Watchravesringkan, "Re-Examination of the Concept of Innovativeness in the Context of the Adolescent Segment: Development of a Measurement Scale," *Journal of Targeting, Measurement and Analysis for Marketing*, 12 (2004): 353–366; Stacy L. Wood and Joffre Swait, "Psychological Indicators of Innovation Adoption: Cross-Classification Based on Need for Cognition and Need for Change," *Journal of Consumer Psychology*, 12 (2002): 1–13;

Ronald E. Goldsmith and Charles E. Hofacker, "Measuring Consumer Innovativeness," *Journal of the Academy of Marketing Science*, 19 (1991): 209–221; Meera A. Venkatraman, "The Impact of Innovativeness and Innovation Type on Product Adoption," *Journal of Retailing*, 67 (1991): 51–67.

25. Nasir Salari and Eric Shiu, "Establishing a Culturally Transferrable Consumer Innovativeness Scale for Radical and Really New Innovations in New Markets," *Journal of Marketing Analytics*, 3, no.2, (2015): 47–68.

26. Tanawat Hirunyawipada and Audhesh K. Paswan, "Consumer Innovativeness and Perceived Risk: Implications for High Technology Product Adoption," *Journal of Consumer Marketing*, 23/24 (2006): 182–198. Elizabeth C. Hirschman, "Innovativeness, Novelty Seeking, and Consumer Creativity," *Journal of Consumer Research*, 7 (1980): 283–295. Kenneth C. Manning, William O. Bearden, and Thomas J. Madden, "Consumer Innovativeness and the Adoption Process," *Journal of Consumer Psychology*, 4 (1995): 329–345. A. V. Citrin, D. E. Sprott, S. N. Silverman, and D. E. Stem, "Adoption of Internet Shopping: The Role of Consumer Innovativeness," *Industrial Management & Data Systems*, 100 (2000): 294–300.

27. John Cacioppo and Richard Petty, "The Need for Cognition," *Journal of Personality and Social Psychology*, 42 (January 1982): 116–131.

28. Curt Haugtvedt, Richard Petty, John Cacioppo, and Thresea Steidley, "Personality and Ad Effectiveness: Exploring the Utility of Need for Cognition," *Advances in Consumer Research*, Vol. 15, ed. Michael Houston (Provo UT: Association for Consumer Research, 1988): 209–212.

29. Angeline Close, Russell Lacey, and T. Bettina Cornwell (2015), "Visual Processing and Need for Cognition Can Enhance Event-Sponsorship Outcomes: How Sporting Event Sponsorships Benefit from the Way Attendees Process Them," *Journal of Advertising Research*, 55, no. 2, (2015): 206–215.

30. These assertions based on Yong Zhang, "Responses to Humorous Advertising: The Moderating Effect of Need for Cognition," *Journal of Advertising*, 25, no. 1 (1996): 15–31; Sanjay Putrevu, "Consumer Responses toward Sexual and Nonsexual Appeals: The Influence of Involvement, Need for Cognition, and Gender," *Journal of Advertising*, 37, no. 2 (2008): 57–70.

31. John C. Mowen, "Exploring the Trait of Competitiveness and Its Consumer Behavior Consequences," *Journal of Consumer Psychology*, 14 (2004): 52–63.

32. Robert B. Cialdini, Richard J. Borden, Avril Thorne, Marcus R. Walker, Stephen Freeman, and Lloyd R. Sloan, "Basking in Reflected Glory: Three (Football) Field Studies," *Journal of Personality and Social Psychology*, 34, no. 3 (1976): 366–375.

33. Anat Keinan and Ran Kivetz, "Productivity Orientation and the Consumption of Collectable Experiences," *Journal of Consumer Research*, 37, no. 6 (April 2011): 935–950.

34. Ibid.

35. Researchers who have contributed to the development of the Five-Factor Model and associated consumer research include: P. T. Costa and R. R. McCrae, *The NEO Personality Inventory Manual* (Odessa, FL: Psychological Assessment Resources, 1985); L. R. Goldberg, "The Development of Matters for the Big-Five Factor Structure," *Psychological Assessment*, 4 (1992): 26–42; J. Wiggins, *The Five-Factor Model of Personality* (New York: Guilford Press, 1996); Eric G. Harris and John C. Mowen, "The Influence of Cardinal, Central-, and Surface-Level Personality Traits on Consumers' Bargaining and Complaining Behaviors,"

Psychology & Marketing, 18, no. 11 (November 2001): 1150–1185; Eric G. Harris and David E. Fleming, "Assessing the Human Element in Service Personality Formation: Personality Congruency and the Five Factor Model," *Journal of Services Marketing*, 19, no. 4 (2005): 187–198; John C. Mowen and Nancy Spears, "Understanding Compulsive Buying among College Students," *Journal of Consumer Psychology*, 8, no. 4 (1999): 407–430; Seth Finn, "Origins of Media Exposure: Linking Personality Traits to TV, Radio, Print, and Film Use," *Communication Research*, 24, no. 5 (October 1997): 507–530; Elena Fraj and Eva Martinez, "Influence of Personality on Ecological Consumer Behaviour," *Journal of Consumer Behaviour*, 5 (2006): 167–181.

36. Notable works in this area include H. J. Eysenck, *Dimensions of Personality* (London: Routledge & Kegan Paul, 1947); Allport, *Pattern and Growth in Personality*; S. V. Paunonen, "Hierarchical Organization of Personality and Prediction of Behavior," *Journal of Personality and Social Psychology*, 74 (1998): 538–556; Mowen, *The 3M Model of Motivation and Personality*.

37. This section is based on a number of sources that have discussed problems with the trait approach in CB, including Kassarjian, "Personality and Consumer Behavior: A Review"; Kassarjian and Sheffet "Personality and Consumer Behavior: An Update"; John L. Lastovicka and Eric A. Joachimsthaler, "Improving the Detection of Personality-Behavior Relationships," *Journal of Consumer Research*, 14, no. 4 (March 1988): 583–587; Mowen, *The 3M Model of Motivation and Personality*.

38. Hans Baumgartner, "Toward a Personology of the Consumer," *Journal of Consumer Research*, 29, no. 2 (September 2002): 286–292; also Dan P. McAdams, "Personality, Modernity, and the Storied Self: A Contemporary Framework for Studying Persons," *Psychological Inquiry*, 7, no. 4 (1996): 295–321.

39. Jennifer Aaker, "Dimensions of Brand Personality," *Journal of Marketing Research*, 34, no. 3 (August 1997): 347–356.

40. K. P. Gwinner and J. Eaton, "Building Brand Image through Event Sponsorship: The Role of Image Transfer," *Journal of Advertising*, 38 (1999): 47–57.

41. Vanitha Swaminathan, Karen M. Stilley, and Rohini Ahluwalia, "When Brand Personality Matters: The Moderating Role of Attachment Styles," *Journal of Consumer Research*, 35 (April 2009): 985–1002.

42. R. Tsiotsou, "Developing a Scale for Measuring the Personality of Sports Teams," *Journal of Services Marketing*, 26, no. 4/5 (2012): 238–252.

43. David A. Aaker, *Building Strong Brands* (New York: Free Press, 1996); also Bill Snyder, "Highly Trusted Brands Run More Risk of Offending Customers," March 1, 2003, http://www.gsb .standford.edu/news/research/mktg_goodbrands .shtml, accessed May 24, 2010.

44. L. Malar, B. Nyffeneggar, H. Krohmer, and W. Hoyer, "Implementing an Intended Brand Personality: A Dyadic Perspective," *Journal of the Academy of Marketing Science*, 40, no. 5 (2012): 728–744.

45. Traci H. Freling, Jody L. Crosno, and David H. Henard, "Brand Personality Appeal: Conceptualization and Empirical Validation," *Journal of the Academy of Marketing Science*, 39 (2011): 392–406.

46. Susan Fournier, "Consumers and Their Brands: Developing Relationship Theory in Consumer Research," *Journal of Consumer Research* (March 1998): 343–373. Jennifer Aaker, Susan Fournier, and S. Adam Brasel, "When Good Brands Do Bad," *Journal of Consumer Research* (June 2004): 1–16.

47. S. J. Long-Tolbert and B. S. Gammoh, "In Good and Bad Times: The Interpersonal Nature of Brand Love in Service Relationships," *Journal of Services Marketing*, 26, no. 6/7 (2012): 391–402.

48. Harris and Fleming, "Assessing the Human Element in Service Personality Formation."

49. Aaker, Fournier, and Brasel, "When Good Brands Do Bad."

50. W. Lazer, "Lifestyle Concepts and Marketing," in *Towards Scientific Marketing*, ed. S. Greyer (Chicago: American Marketing Association, 1963).

51. Rob Lawson and Sarah Todd, "Consumer Lifestyles: A Social Stratification Perspective," *Marketing Theory*, 2 (2002): 295–307.

52. Ana M. Gonzalez and Laurentino Bello, "The Construct 'Lifestyle' in Market Segmentation: The Behaviour of Tourist Consumers," *European Journal of Marketing*, 36 (2002): 51–85.

53. These assertions come from the works of Karen Benezra, "The Fragging of the American Mind," *Brandweek*, June 1998, S12–S19; Trent Johnson and Johan Bruwer, "An Empirical Confirmation of Wine-Related Lifestyle Segments in the Australian Wine Market," *International Journal of Wine Marketing*, 15 (2003): 5–33; A. Taylor, "Porsche Slices Up Its Buyers," *Fortune*, January 16, 1995, 24; Natural Marketing Institute website, www.nmisolutions.com/lohasd_segment.html, accessed May 24, 2010.

54. This section is based on information obtained on the SBI International website, http://www.strategicbusinessinsights.com/vals/presurvey.shtml, accessed May 25, 2010.

55. This information is based on materials found at http://enus.nielsen.com/tab/product_families/nielsen_claritas/prizm, accessed May 25, 2010.

56. Trendwatching.com (2014), "Post-Demographic Consumerism," Trend Briefing, online content accessed at: http://trendwatching.com/trends/post-demographic-consumerism/, accessed February 19, 2016.

57. Cecilia L. Ridgeway and Henry A. Walker, "Status Structures," in *Sociological Perspectives on Social Psychology*, ed. Karen S. Cook, Gary A. Fine, and James S. House (Boston: Allyn and Bacon, 1995), 281–310.

58. George H. Mead, *Mind, Self, and Society* (Chicago: University of Chicago Press, 1934); David Glen Mick, "Consumer Research and Semiotics: Exploring the Morphology of Signs, Symbols, and Significance," *Journal of Consumer Research*, 13, no. 2 (September 1986): 196–213. Morris B. Holbrook, "The Millennial Consumer in the Texts of Our Times: Exhibitionism," *Journal of Macromarketing*, 21 (2001): 81–95. Himadri Roy Chaudhuri and Sitanath Majumdar, "Of Diamonds and Desires: Understanding Conspicuous Consumption from a Contemporary Marketing Perspective," *Academy of Marketing Science Review*, (2006): 1.

59. See also Hope Jensen Schau and Mary Gilly, "We Are What We Post? Self-Presentation in Personal Web Space," *Journal of Consumer Research*, 30, no. 3 (December 2003): 385–404; Kaye D. Trammell and Ana Keshelashvili, "Examining the New Influencers: A Self-Presentation Study of A-List Blogs," *Journalism and Mass Communication Quarterly*, 82, no. 4 (Winter 2005): 968–983.

60. Jennifer Aaker, "The Malleable Self: The Role of Self-Expression in Persuasion," *Journal of Marketing Research*, 36, no. 1 (February 1999): 45–57.

61. These concepts are based on M. Joseph Sirgy, "Self-Concept in Consumer Behavior: A Critical Review," *Journal of Consumer Research*, 9, no. 3 (December 1982): 287–300; Russell Belk, "Possessions and the Extended Self," *Journal of Consumer Research*, 15, no. 2 (September 1988): 139–168.

62. Aaron C. Ahuvia, "Beyond the Extended Self: Loved Objects and Consumers' Identity Narratives," *Journal of Consumer Research*, 32, no. 1 (June 2005): 171–184. Jennifer Escalas and James R. Bettman, "Self-Construal, Reference Groups, and Brand Meaning," *Journal of Consumer Research*, 32, no. 3 (December 2005): 378–389.

63. Lon Nguyen Chaplin and Debrah Roedder John, "The Development of Self-Brand Connections in Children and Adolescents," *Journal of Consumer Research*, 32, no. 1 (June 2005): 119–130.

64. Debra Trampe, Diederik A. Stapel, and Frans W. Siero, "The Self-Activation Effect in Advertisements: Ads Can Affect Whether and How Consumers Think About the Self," *Journal of Consumer Research*, 37, no. 6 (2011): 1030–1045.

65. Dirk Smeesters and Naomi Mandel, "Positive and Negative Media Image Effects on the Self," *Journal of Consumer Research*, 32, no. 4 (March 2006): 576–582. Marsha Richins, "Social Comparison and the Idealized Images of Advertising," *Journal of Consumer Research*, 18, no. 1 (June 1991): 71–83. Sarah Grogan, *Understanding Body Dissatisfaction in Men, Women, and Children* (London: Routledge, 1999).

66. Darren W. Dahl, Jennifer J. Argo, and Andrea C. Morales, "Social Information in the Retail Environment: The Importance of Consumption Alignment, Referent Identity, and Self-Esteem," *Journal of Consumer Research*, 38 (February 2011): 860–871.

67. Cheryl Lu-Lien Tan, "Fashion Group Sets Guides to Rein in Ultra-Thin Models," *The Wall Street Journal*, January 8, 2007, B4.

68. Brandon Keim, "Media Messes with Mens' Minds Too," *Psychology Today*, 39, no. 5 (September/October 2006): 26.

69. Michael Hafner, "How Dissimilar Others May Still Resemble the Self: Assimilation and Contrast after Social Comparison," *Journal of Consumer Psychology*, 14 (2004): 187–196.

70. The American Society of Plastic Surgeons (2016), "2015 Plastic Surgery Statistics Report," http://www.plasticsurgery.org/news/plastic-surgery-statistics, accessed October 11, 2016

71. Eric Bui, Rachel Rodgers, Lionel Cailhol, Phillippe Birmes, Henri Chabrol, and Laurent Schmitt, "Body Piercing and Psychopathology: A Review of the Literature," *Psychotherapy and Psychosomatics*, 79 (2010): 125–129.

72. Joan Jacobs Brumberg, "Are We Facing an Epidemic of Self-Injury?" *Chronicle of Higher Education*, 53 (2006): B6–B8.

73. R. Braithwaite, A. Robillard, T. Woodring, T. Stephens, and K. J. Arriola, "Tattooing and Body Piercing among Adolescent Detainees: Relationship to Alcohol and Other Drug Use," *Journal of Substance Abuse*, 13 (2001): 5–16. J. Grief and W. Hewitt, "The Living Canvas: Health Issues in Tattooing, Body Piercing, and Branding," *Advances for Nurse Practitioners*, 12 (1998): 26–31. Jonathan W. Roberti and Eric A. Storch, "Psychosocial Adjustment of College Students with Tattoos and Piercings," *Journal of College Counseling*, 8, no. 1 (Spring 2005): 14–19.

74. Jeff W. Totten, Thomas J. Lipscomb, and Michael A. Jones, "Attitudes toward and Stereotypes of Persons with Body Art: Implications for Marketing Management," *Academy of Marketing Studies Journal*, 13, no. 2 (2009): 77–96.

75. M. Joseph Sirgy, Dhruv Grewal, Tamara Mangleburg, and Jae-ok Park, "Assessing the Predictive Validity of Two Methods of Measuring Self-Image Congruence," *Journal of the Academy of Marketing Science*, 25, no. 3 (Summer 1997): 229–241.

76. M. Joseph Sirgy and A. Coskun Samli, "A Path Analytic Model of Store Loyalty Involving Self-Concept, Store Image, Geographic Loyalty, and Socioeconomic Status," *Journal of the Academy of Marketing Science*, 13, no. 3 (Summer 1985): 265–291.

77. S. Hosany and D. Martin, "Self-Image Congruence in Consumer Behavior," *Journal of Business Research*, 65, no. 5 (2012): 685–691.

78. Aaker, "The Malleable Self."

79. Alexander Chernev, Ryan Hamilton, and David Gal, "Competing for Consumer Identity: Limits to Self-Expression and the Perils of Lifestyle Branding," *Journal of Marketing*, 75 (May 2011): 66–82; also Urska Tuskej, Ursa Golob, and Klement Podnar, "The Role of Consumer-Brand Identification in Building Brand Relationships," *Journal of Business Research*, 66, no. 1 (January 2013): 53–59.

80. Melea Press and Eric J. Arnould, "How Does Organizational Identification Form? A Consumer Behavior Perspective," *Journal of Consumer Research*, 38 (December 2011): 650–666. Grahame R. Dowling and Tayo Otubanjo, "Corporate and Organizational Identity: Two Sides of the Same Coin," *AMS Review*, 1, no. 3/4 (2011): 171–182.

81. P. W. Fombelle, C. B. Jarvis, J. Ward, and L. Ostrom, "Leveraging Customers' Multiple Identities: Identity Synergy as a Driver of Organizational Identification," *Journal of the Academy of Marketing Science*, 40, no. 4 (2012): 587–604.

7

1. Erin Bury, "Why the New Generation Is Turning Away from Facebook," *The Huffington Post*, January 7, 2015; online content retrieved at http://www.huffingtonpost.ca/erin-bury/facebook-new-generation_b_6431322.html.

2. This definition is based on a summary of several works in the social psychology and consumer behavior literature, including Alice Eagly and Shelly Chaiken, *The Psychology of Attitudes* (New York: Harcourt Brace, 1993); John Cacioppo, Stephen Harkins, and Richard Petty, "The Nature of Attitudes and Cognitive Responses and Their Relations to Behavior," in *Cognitive Responses in Persuasion*, ed. Richard Petty, Thomas Ostrom, and Timothy C. Brock (Hillsdale, NJ: Lawrence Erlbaum, 1981); L. L. Thurstone, "The Measurement of Social Attitudes," in *Readings in Attitude Theory and Measurement*, ed. M. Fishbein (New York: Wiley, 1931).

3. The information in this section is based on Daniel Katz, "The Functional Approach to the Study of Attitudes," *Public Opinion Quarterly*, 24, no. 2 (1960): 163–204.

4. Heather Gibson, Cynthia Willming, and Andrew Holdnak, "We're Gators . . . Not Just Gator Fans: Serious Leisure and University of Florida Football," *Journal of Leisure Research*, 34, no. 4 (2003): 397–425.

5. Michael Ray, "Marketing Communications and the Hierarchy-of-Effects," in *New Models for Mass Communications*, ed. P. Clarke, 147–76 (Beverly Hills, CA: Sage, 1973).

6. Herbert Krugman, "The Impact of Television Advertising: Learning without Involvement," *Public Opinion Quarterly*, 29 (Fall, 1965): 349–356.

7. A recent example of the experiential nature of consumption may be found in Russell Belk, Guliz Ger, and Soren Askegaard, "The Fire of Desire: A Multisited Inquiry into Consumer Passion," *Journal of Consumer Research*, 30, no. 3 (2003): 326–351.

8. Martin Fishbein and Icek Ajzen, *Belief, Attitude, Intention, and Behavior: An Introduction to Theory and Research* (Reading, MA: Addison-Wesley, 1975).

9. A number of researchers have addressed this issue, including Linda F. Alwitt and Ida E. Berger, "Understanding the Link Between Environmental Attitudes and Consumer Product Usage: Measuring the Moderating Role of Attitude Strength," in *Advances in Consumer Research*, vol. 20, ed. Leigh McAlister and Michael Rothschild, 189–194 (Provo, UT: Association for Consumer Research, 1992); Allan Wicker, "Attitudes Versus Actions: The Relationship of Verbal and Overt Behavioral Responses to Attitude Objects," *Journal of Social Issues,* 25 (Autumn 1969): 41–78.

10. Icek Ajzen and Martin Fishbein, "Attitude-Behavior Relations: A Theoretical Analysis and Review of Empirical Research," *Psychological Bulletin,* 84, no. 5 (September 1977): 888–918.

11. Michael J. Ryan and E. H. Bonfield, "Fishbein's Intentions Model: A Test of External and Pragmatic Validity," *Journal of Marketing,* 44, no. 2 (1980): 82–95.

12. More on this model may be found in Art Sahni Notani, "Moderators of Perceived Behavioral Control's Predictiveness in the Theory of Reasoned Action," *Journal of Consumer Psychology,* 7, no. 3 (1998): 247–271. Also, an interesting presentation of the planned behavior model applied to food choice may be found in Mark T. Conner, "Understanding Determinants of Food Choice: Contributions from Attitude Research," *British Food Journal,* 95, no. 9 (1993): 27–32.

13. Andrew A. Mitchell and Jerry Olson, "Are Product Attribute Beliefs the Only Mediator of Advertising Effects on Brand Attitude?" *Journal of Marketing Research,* 18 (1981): 318–332.

14. Several studies have approached this issue, including Scott MacKenzie and Richard Lutz, "An Empirical Examination of the Structural Antecedents of Attitude towards the Ad in an Advertising Pretesting Context," *Journal of Marketing,* 53 (April 1989): 48–65; Scot Burton and Donald Lichtenstein, "The Effect of Ad Claims and Ad Context on Attitude towards the Advertisement," *Journal of Advertising,* 17, no. 1 (1988): 3–11.

15. Tom J. Brown and Peter A. Dacin, "The Company and the Product: Corporate Associations and Consumer Product Responses," *Journal of Marketing,* 61 (January 1997): 68–84.

16. Sankar Sen and C. B. Bhattacharya, "Does Doing Good Always Lead to Doing Better? Consumer Reactions to Corporate Social Responsibility," *Journal of Marketing Research,* 38 (May 2001): 225–243.

17. Bydamon Poeter, "Study: U.K. Teens Fleeing 'Dead and Buried' Facebook," *Pcmag.com,* December 27, 2013, http://www.pcmag.com/article2/0,2817,2428773,00.asp, accessed April 4, 2014.

18. Edward Group, "The Benefits of Apple Cider Vinegar," Global Healing Center, August 4, 2008, http://www.globalhealingcenter.com/natural-health/the-benefits-of-apple-cider-vinegar/, accessed April 18, 2012.

19. Richard E. Petty, John T. Cacioppo, and David Schuman, "Central and Peripheral Routes to Advertising Effectiveness: The Moderating Role of Involvement," *Journal of Consumer Research,* 10, no. 2 (1983): 135–146.

20. Richard L. Celsi and Jerry C. Olson, "The Role of Involvement in Attention and Comprehension Processes," *Journal of Consumer Research,* 15, no. 2 (September 1988): 210–224. Deborah J. MacInnis and C. Whan Park, "The Differential Role of Characteristics of Music on High- and Low-Involvement Consumers' Processing of Ads," *Journal of Consumer Research,* 18, no. 2 (September 1991): 161–173.

21. Fritz Heider, *The Psychology of Interpersonal Relations* (New York: John Wiley, 1958).

22. Steve DiMeglio, "Tiger Woods Gets New Endorsement with Nutrition Company," *USA Today,* November 21, 2011, http://content.usatoday.com/communities/gameon/post/2011/11/tiger-woods-new-endorsement-fuse-science-/1, accessed April 18, 2012.

23. A number of studies have addressed these issues, including Cristel Russell and Barbara B. Stern, "Consumers, Characters, and Products: A Balance Model of Sitcom Product Placement Effects," *Journal of Advertising,* 35, no. 1 (2006): 7–21; Arch Woodside, "Advancing Means-End Chains by Incorporating Heider's Balance Theory and Fournier's Consumer-Brand Relationship Typology," *Psychology & Marketing,* 21, no. 4 (2004): 279–94; Jennifer Edson Escalas and James R. Bettman, "Self-Construal, Reference Groups, and Brand Meaning," *Journal of Consumer Research,* 32, no. 3 (2005): 378–389; Janet S. Fink, Heidi Parker, Brett Martin, and Julie Higgins, "Off-Field Behavior of Athletes and Team Identification: Using Social Identity and Balance Theory to Explain Fan Reactions," *Journal of Sport Management,* 23, no. 2 (2009): 142–157.

24. Muzafer Sherif and Carl Hovland, *Social Judgment: Assimilation and Contrast Effects in Communication and Attitude Change* (New Haven, CT: Yale University Press, 1961).

25. D. Allan, "Radio Advertising: Blip Commercials," *Journal of Business Research,* 65, no. 6 (2013): 880–881.

26. Donna L. Hoffman and Thomas P. Novak, "Marketing in Hypermedia Computer-Mediated Environments: Conceptual Foundations," *Journal of Marketing,* 60, no. 3 (1996): 50–68.

27. This estimate based on data from "ICT Facts & Figures," International Telecommunications Union (ITU), Geneva (2015), www.itu.int/en/ITU-D/Statistics/Documents/facts/ICTFactsFigures2015.pdf, accessed February 29, 2016.

28. Hoffman and Novak, "Marketing in Hypermedia Computer-Mediated Environments."

29. A. O'Cass and J. Carlson, "An Empirical Assessment of Consumers' Evaluations of Web Site Service Quality: Conceptualizing and Testing a Formative Model," *Journal of Services Marketing* 26, no. 6 (2012): 419–434.

30. Sid C. Dudley, "Consumer Attitudes toward Nudity in Advertising," *Journal of Marketing Theory and Practice,* 7, no. 4 (1999): 89–96.

31. Enny Das, Maryna Galekh, and Charlotte Vonkeman, "Is Sexy Better than Funny? Disentangling the Persuasive Effects of Pleasure and Arousal Across Sex and Humour Appeals," *International Journal of Advertising,* 34, no. 3 (2015), 406–420.

32. Michael S. LaTour, "Female Nudity in Print Advertising: An Analysis of Gender Differences in Arousal and Ad Response," *Psychology & Marketing,* 7, no. 1 (1990): 65–81.

33. Penny M. Simpson, Steve Horton, and Gene Brown, "Male Nudity in Advertisements: A Modified Replication and Extension of Gender and Product Effects," *Journal of the Academy of Marketing Science,* 24, no. 3 (1996): 257–262.

34. Ming-Hui Huang, "Romantic Love and Sex: Their Relationship and Impacts on Ad Attitudes," *Psychology & Marketing,* 21, no. 1 (2004): 53–73.

35. E.J. Schultz, "Bud Light Goes Back to Humor for Super Bowl," *Advertising Age,* 87, no. 2, (2016): 3.

36. Martin Eisend, "A Meta-Analysis of Humor in Advertising," *Journal of the Academy of Marketing Science,* 37 (Summer 2009): 191–203.

37. H. S. Krishnan and D. Chakravarti, "A Process Analysis of the Effects of Humorous Advertising Executions on Brand Claims Memory," *Journal of Consumer Psychology,* 13, no. 3 (2003): 230–245.

38. Uta Schwarz, Stefan Hoffman, and Katharina Hutter, "Do Men and Women Laugh About Different Types of Humor? A Comparison of Satire, Sentimental Comedy, and Comic Wit in Print Ads," *Journal of Current Issues and Research in Advertising,* 36, no. 1, (2015): 70–87.

39. Yong Zhang, "The Effect of Humor in Advertising: An Individual-Difference Perspective," *Psychology & Marketing,* 13, no. 6 (1996): 531–545.

40. Thomas W. Cline, Moses B. Altsech, and James J. Kellaris, "When Does Humor Enhance or Inhibit Ad Responses?" *Journal of Advertising,* 32, no. 3 (2003): 31–46.

41. Amitava Chattopadhyay, "Humor in Advertising: The Moderating Role of Prior Brand Evaluations," *Journal of Marketing Research,* 29 (November 1990): 466–476.

42. Stephen M. Smith, "Does Humor in Advertising Enhance Systematic Processing?" in *Advances in Consumer Research*, vol. 20, ed. L. McAlister and M. Rothschild, 155–158 (Provo, UT: Association of Consumer Research, 1993).

43. Michael S. LaTour and Herbert J. Rotfeld, "There Are Threats and (Maybe) Fear-Caused Arousal: Theory and Confusions of Appeals to Fear and Fear Arousal Itself," *Journal of Advertising,* 3 (Fall 1997): 45–59.

44. Punam Anand Keller and Lauren Goldberg Block, "Increasing the Persuasiveness of Fear Appeals: The Effect of Arousal and Elaboration," *Journal of Consumer Research,* 22, no. 4 (1996): 448–459.

45. Ron Lennon, Randall Renfro, and Bay O'Leary, "Social Marketing and Distracted Driving Behaviors among Young Adults: The Effectiveness of Fear Appeals," *Academy of Marketing Studies Journal,* 14, no. 2 (2010): 95–113.

46. John C. Mowen, Eric G. Harris, and Sterling A. Bone, "Personality Traits and Fear Response to Print Advertisements: Theory and an Empirical Study," *Psychology & Marketing,* 21, no. 11 (2004): 927–943.

47. Robert F. Potter, Michael S. LaTour, Kathryn A. Braun-LaTour, and Tom Reichert, "The Impact of Program Context on Motivational System Activation and Subsequent Effects on Processing a Fear Appeal," *Journal of Advertising,* 35, no. 3 (2006): 67–80.

48. John F. Tanner, James B. Hunt, and David R. Eppright, "The Protection Motivation Model: A Normative Model of Fear Appeals," *Journal of Marketing,* 55, no. 3 (1991): 36–45.

49. Charles R. Duke, Gregory M. Pickett, Les Carlson, and Stephen J. Grove, "A Method for Evaluating the Ethics of Fear Appeals," *Journal of Public Policy & Marketing,* 1 (Spring 1993): 120–130.

50. E. Deanne Brocato, Douglas A. Gentile, Russell N. Laczniak, Julia A. Maier, and Mindy Ji-Song, "Television Commercial Violence: Potential Effects on Children," *Journal of Advertising,* 39, no. 4 (2010): 95–107.

51. Michael L. Capella, Ronald Paul Hill, Justine M. Rapp, and Jeremy Kees, "The Impact of Violence Against Women in Advertisements," *Journal of Advertising,* 39, no. 4 (2010): 37–51.

52. Benjamin J. Blackford, James Gentry, Robert L. Harrison, and Les Carlson, "The Prevalence and Influence of the Combination of Humor and

Violence in Super Bowl Commercials," *Journal of Advertising*, 49, no. 4 (2011): 123–133.

53. Charles S. Gulas, Kunal Swani, and Marc G. Weinberger, "Comedic Violence in Advertising: A Test of Gender Commonality," *Proceedings of the American Academy of Advertising*, (2015), online content.

54. Alan G. Sawyer and Daniel J. Howard, "Effects of Omitting Conclusions in Advertisements to Involved and Uninvolved Audiences," *Journal of Marketing Research*, 28 (November 1991): 467–474.

55. William L. Wilkie and Paul W. Ferris, "Comparison Advertising: Problems and Potential," *Journal of Marketing*, 39 (October 1973): 7–15.

56. Paul W. Miniard, Michael J. Barone, Randall L. Rose, and Kenneth C. Manning, "A Further Assessment of Indirect Advertising Claims of Superiority over All Competitors," *Journal of Advertising*, 35, no. 4 (2006): 53–64.

57. Dennis D. Stewart, Cheryl B. Stewart, Clare Tyson, Vinci Gail, and Tom Fioti, "Serial Position Effects and the Picture-Superiority Effect in the Group Recall of Unshared Information," *Group Dynamics: Theory, Research, and Practice*, 8, no. 3 (2004): 166–181.

58. Curtis P. Haugtvedt and Duance T. Wegener, "Message Order Effects in Persuasion: An Attitude Strength Perspective," *Journal of Consumer Research*, 21 (June 1994): 205–218.

59. H. Rao Unnava, Robert E. Burnkrant, and Sunil Erevelles, "Effects of Presentation Order and Communication Modality on Recall and Attitude," *Journal of Consumer Research*, 21 (December 1994): 481–490.

60. Cong Li, "Primacy Effect or Recency Effect? A Long-Term Memory Test of Super Bowl Commercials," *Journal of Consumer Behaviour*, 9 (October 2009): 32–44.

61. Alison Jing Xu and Robert S. Wyer, Jr., "The Role of Bolstering and Counterarguing Mind-Sets in Persuasion," *Journal of Consumer Research*, 38 (February), 920–932.

62. S. P. Jain and S. S. Posavac, "Prepurchase Attribute Verifiability, Source Credibility, and Persuasion," *Journal of Consumer Psychology*, 11, no. 3 (2001): 169–180.

63. Pamela M. Homer and Lynn R. Kahle, "Source Expertise, Time of Source Identification, and Involvement in Persuasion," *Journal of Advertising*, 19, no. 1 (1990): 30–39.

64. Xiaoli Nan, "The Influence of Source Credibility on Attitude Certainty: Exploring the Moderating Effects of Timing of Source Identification and Individual Need for Cognition," *Psychology & Marketing*, 26, no. 4 (2009): 321–332.

65. Elizabeth Wilson and Daniel L. Sherrell, "Source Effects in Communication and Persuasion Research: A Meta-Analysis of Effect Size," *Journal of the Academy of Marketing Science*, 21, no. 2 (1993): 101–112.

66. Josh Wiener and John C. Mowen, "The Impact of Product Recalls on Consumer Perceptions," *The Journal of the Society of Consumer Affairs Professionals in Business* (Spring 1985): 18–21.

67. Barbara A. Lafferty, Ronald E. Goldsmith, and Stephen J. Newell, "The Dual Credibility Model: The Influence of Corporate and Endorser Credibility on Attitudes and Purchase Intention," *Journal of Marketing Theory & Practice*, 10, no. 3 (2002): 1–12.

68. Brian D. Till and Michael Busler, "The Match-Up Hypothesis: Physical Attractiveness, Expertise, and the Role of Fit on Brand Attitude, Purchase Intent, and Brand Beliefs," *Journal of Advertising*, 3 (Fall 2000): 1–13. Shelly Chaiken, "Communicator Physical Attractiveness and Persuasion," *Journal*

of *Personality and Social Psychology*, 37 (August 1979): 1387–1397.

69. Michael Baker and Gilbert Churchill, "The Impact of Physically Attractive Models on Advertising Effectiveness," *Journal of Marketing Research*, 14 (November 1977): 538–555.

70. Yoon-Soon Kang and Paul M. Herr, "Beauty and the Beholder: Toward an Integrative Model of Communication Source Effects," *Journal of Consumer Research*, 33, no. 1 (2006): 123–130; also Debra Trampe, Diederik A. Stapel, Frans W. Siero, and Henriette Mulder, "Beauty as a Tool: The Effect of Model Attractiveness, Product Relevance and Elaboration Likelihood on Advertising Effectiveness," *Psychology & Marketing*, 27 (December 2010): 1101–1121.

71. Marketing Evaluations, Inc., http://www.qscores.com, accessed May 28, 2010.

72. Marc-Andre Reinhard and Matthias Messner, "The Effects of Source Likeability and Need for Cognition on Advertising Effectiveness under Explicit Persuasion," *Journal of Consumer Behaviour*, 8, no. 4 (2009): 179–191.

73. James Lynch and Drue Schuler, "The Matchup Effect of Spokesperson and Product Congruency: A Schema Theory Interpretation," *Psychology & Marketing*, 11 (September–October 1994): 417–445; Michael A. Kamins, "An Investigation into the 'Match-Up' Hypothesis in Celebrity Advertising: When Beauty May Be Only Skin Deep," *Journal of Advertising*, 19, no. 1 (1990): 4–13.

Case 2–1

1. "Indoor Rock Climbing," Find Sports Now, http://www.findsportsnow.com/learn/indoor-rock-climbing.

2. Jessika Toothman, "What Is the History of Rock Climbing?" How Stuff Works, http://adventure.howstuffworks.com/outdoor-activities/climbing/history-of-rock-climbing1.htm.

3. "Climbing Gyms," Centrahealth, http://www.centrahealth.com/health-library/c/609-climbing-gyms.

Case 2–2

1. David Katzmaier and Matthew Moskovciak, "The Basics of TV Power," *CNET*, April 21, 2010, http://reviews.cnet.com/green-tech/tv-power-efficiency/.

2. Gary Merson, "HDTV Viewing Distance Chart," HD Guru, 2006, http://hdguru.com/wp-content/uploads/2006/11/hdtv_distance_chart.pdf.

Case 2–3

1. A. Troianovski, S. E. Ante, and J. E. Vascellaro, "Mom, Please Feed My Apps!" *The Wall Street Journal*, June 11, 2012, C1.

2. Steven Russolillo, "Zynga Shares Plunge Below $5; Circuit Breaker Triggered," *The Wall Street Journal*, June 12, 2012, C1.

3. Daisuke Wakabayashi and Spencer E. Ante, "Mobile Game Fight Goes Global," *The Wall Street Journal*, June 14, 2012, B1.

4. Troianovski, Ante, and Vascellaro, "Mom, Please Feed My Apps!"

5. Wakabayashi and Ante, "Mobile Game Fight Goes Global."

8

1. C. Whan Park and V. Parker Lessig, "Students and Housewives: Differences in Susceptibility to Reference Group Influence," *Journal of Consumer Research*, 4 (September 1977): 102–110.

2. H. Andrew Michener and Michelle P. Wasserman, "Group Decision Making," in *Sociological Perspectives on Social Psychology*, ed. Karen S.

Cook, Gary Alan Fine, and James S. House (Boston: Allyn and Bacon, 1995), 336–361.

3. Paul Webley and Ellen K. Nyhus, "Parents' Influence on Children's Future Orientation and Saving," *Journal of Economic Psychology*, 27, no. 1 (2006): 140–149.

4. Albert M. Muniz, Jr., and Thomas C. O'Guinn, "Brand Community," *Journal of Consumer Research*, 27, no. 4 (2001): 412–432.

5. Z. Zhou, Q. Zhang, S. Chenting, and N. Zhou, "How Do Brand Communities Generate Brand Relationships? Intermediate Mechanisms," *Journal of Business Research*, 65 (2012): 890–895.

6. James H. Alexander, John W. Schouten, and Harold F. Koening, "Building Brand Community," *Journal of Marketing*, 66, no. 1 (2002): 38–54.

7. Dana-Nicoleta Lascu and George Zinkhan, "Consumer Conformity: Review and Applications for Marketing Theory and Practice," *Journal of Marketing Theory and Practice*, 7, no. 3 (1999): 1–12.

8. Jill Ross and Ross Harradine, "I'm Not Wearing That! Branding and Young Children," *Journal of Fashion Marketing and Management*, 8, no. 1 (2004): 11–26.

9. Juan Ramos, "Tobacco Company Undermines Global Treaty on Facebook," Suite101 website, May 28, 2010, http://www.suite101.com/article/tobacco-company-undermines-global-treaty-on-facebook-a242242, accessed June 17, 2010.

10. Karen H. Smith and Mary Ann Stutts, "The Influence of Individual Factors on the Effectiveness of Message Content in Antismoking Advertisements Aimed at Adolescents," *Journal of Consumer Affairs*, 40, no. 2 (2006): 261–293. Merri Rosenberg, "Anti-Smoking Ads Aimed at Peers," *New York Times*, February 17, 2002, http://query.nytimes.com/gst/fullpage.html?sec=health&res=9D06E5D8163FF934A25751C0A9649C8B63.

11. Nancy Albers-Miller, "Consumer Misbehavior: Why People Buy Illicit Goods," *The Journal of Consumer Marketing*, 16, no. 3 (1999): 273–287.

12. Kenneth J. Gergen and Mary Gergen, *Social Psychology* (New York: Harcourt Brace Jovanovich, 1981).

13. J. R. P. French and B. Raven, "The Bases of Social Power," in *Studies in Social Power*, ed. D. Cartwright (Ann Arbor, MI: Institute for Social Research, 1959).

14. William O. Bearden and Michael J. Etzel, "Reference Group Influence on Product and Brand Purchase Decisions," *Journal of Consumer Research*, 9, no. 2 (1982): 183–194.

15. Bearden and Etzel, "Reference Group Influence."

16. Park and Lessig, "Students and Housewives."

17. ibid

18. Aaron Smith, "Neighbors Online," Pew Research Center, June 9, 2010, http://pewresearch.org/pubs/1620/neighbors-online-using-digital-tools-to-communicate-monitor-community-developments, accessed July 17, 2012.

19. Sarah Perez, "Social Networking Now More Popular on Mobile than Desktop," ReadWriteWeb, February 18, 2010, www.readwriteweb.com/archives/social_networking_now_more_popular_on_mobile_than_desktop.php, accessed July 17, 2012.

20. Statistics from Facebook.com website, http://newsroom.fb.com/company-info/, accessed April 13, 2016.

21. Statistics obtained from http://newsroom.fb.com/company-info, accessed April 21, 2014.

22. ibid

23. Lang, Nico, "Why Teens Are Leaving Facebook: It's 'Meaningless'," *The Washington Post* (online edition), February 21, 2105, https://www.washingtonpost

.com/news/the-intersect/wp/2015/02/21/why-teens-are-leaving-facebook-its-meaningless/, accessed April 13, 2016.

24. Statistics obtained from about.twitter.com /company, accessed April 21, 2014.

25. "Facebook to Acquire Instagram," Facebook, April 9, 2012, http://newsroom.fb.com/News /Facebook-to-Acquire-Instagram-141.aspx, accessed September 12, 2012.

26. Covert, Adrian, "Facebook Buys Whatsapp for $19 Billion," *Money.cnn.com*, February 19, 2014, http://money.cnn.com/2014/02/19/technology /social/facebook-whatsapp/, accessed April 25, 2014.

27. Stylehive.com blog, http://blog.stylehive.com /index.php/about/, accessed July 17, 2012; also Foursquare, www.foursquare.com, accessed June 10, 2010.

28. Jessica Guynn, "Pinterest Pierces the Ranks of the Social-Networking Elite," *Los Angeles Times*, April 13, 2012, http://articles.latimes.com/2012 /apr/12/business/la-fi-pinterest-20120413, accessed April 12, 2012.

29. William O. Bearden, Richard G. Netemeyer, and Jesse E. Teel, "Measurement of Consumer Susceptibility to Interpersonal Influence," *Journal of Consumer Research*, 15, no. 4 (1989): 473–481.

30. Rajeev Batra, Pamela M. Homer, and Lynn R. Kahle, "Values, Susceptibility to Normative Influence, and Attribute Importance Weights: A Nomological Perspective," *Journal of Consumer Research*, 11, no. 2 (2001): 115–128.

31. David B. Wooten and Americus Reed II, "Playing It Safe: Susceptibility to Normative Influence and Protective Self- Presentation," *Journal of Consumer Research*, 31, no. 3 (2004): 551–556.

32. David B. Wooten and Randall L. Rose, "Attention to Social Comparison Information: An Individual Difference Variable Affecting Consumer Conformity," *Journal of Consumer Research*, 16, no. 4 (1990): 461–471.

33. Ronald A. Clark and Ronald E. Goldsmith, "Global Innovativeness and Consumer Susceptibility to Interpersonal Influence," *Journal of Marketing Theory and Practice*, 14, no. 4 (2006): 275–285.

34. Cheng Lu Wang and Allan K. K. Chan, "A Content Analysis of Connectedness vs. Separateness Themes Used in U.S. and P.R.C. Print Advertisements," *International Marketing Review*, 18, no. 2 (2001): 145–157. Cheng Lu Wang and John C. Mowen, "The Separateness-Connectedness Self-Schema: Scale Development and Application to Message Construction," *Psychology & Marketing*, 14 (March 1997): 185–207.

35. Wang and Mowen, "The Separateness-Connectedness Self-Schema."

36. Jiang Lan, Joandrea Hoegg, Darren W. Dahl, and Amitava Chattopadyhay, "The Persuasive Role of Incidental Similarity on Attitudes and Purchase Intentions in a Sales Context," *Journal of Consumer Research*, 36, no. 5 (2010): 778–791.

37. Wang and Chan, "A Content Analysis of Connectedness vs. Separateness Themes."

38. Jennifer J. Argo, Darren W. Dahl, and Rajesh V. Manchanda, "The Influence of a Mere Social Presence in a Retail Context," *Journal of Consumer Research*, 32, no. 2 (2005): 207–212.

39. Darren W. Dahl, Rajesh V. Manchanda, and Jennifer J. Argo, "Embarrassment in Consumer Purchase: The Roles of Social Presence and Purchase Familiarity," *Journal of Consumer Research*, 28, no. 3 (2001): 473–481.

40. He Yi, Qimei Chen, and Dana L. Alden, "Consumption in the Public Eye: The Influence of

Social Presence on Service Experience," *Journal of Business Research*, 65 (2012): 302–310.

41. "WOM 101: Organic vs. Amplified Word of Mouth," Word of Mouth Marketing Association (WOMMA), http://www.womma.org/wom101/04/, accessed July 18, 2012.

42. Tom J. Brown, Thomas E. Berry, Peter A. Dacin, and Richard F. Gunst, "Spreading the Word: Investigating Antecedents of Consumers' Positive Word-of-Mouth Intentions and Behaviors in a Retailing Context," *Journal of the Academy of Marketing Science*, 33, no. 2 (2005): 123–138.

43. Cindy M. Y. Chung, "The Consumer as Advocate: Self-Relevance, Culture, and Word-of-Mouth," *Marketing Letters*, 17, no. 4 (2006): 269–284; Florian von Wangenheim, "Postswitching Negative Word-of-Mouth," *Journal of Service Research*, 8, no. 1 (2005): 67–78.

44. Paula Bone, "Word-of-Mouth Effects on Short-Term and Long-Term Product Judgments," *Journal of Business Research*, 32, no. 3 (1995): 213–223.

45. Barry J. Babin, Yong-Ki Lee, Eun-Ju Kim, and Mitch Griffin, "Modeling Consumer Satisfaction and Word-of-Mouth: Restaurant Patronage in Korea," *Journal of Services Marketing*, 19, no. 3 (2005): 133–139.

46. "Health," Pew Internet & American Life Project, http://www.pewinternet.org/topics/Health.aspx, accessed June 11, 2010.

47. "Teens and Mobile Phones," Pew Research Center, http://www.pewinternet.org/Reports/2010 /Teens-and-Mobile-Phones.aspx?r=1, accessed June 12, 2010.

48. See www.bzzagent.com, yelp.com/faq, and www.digg.com.

49. "How Ford Got Social Marketing Right," *Bloomberg Businessweek*, January 8, 2010, http:// www.businessweek.com/managing/content/jan2010 /ca2010018_445530.htm, accessed June 12, 2010.

50. Andrew M. Kaikati and Jack G. Kaikati, "Stealth Marketing: How to Reach Consumers Surreptitiously," *California Management Review*, 46, no. 4 (2004): 6–22.

51. "Days of Our Lives Botches Product Placements," Fox News, November 16, 2010, http://www .foxnews.com/entertainment/2010/11/16/days-lives -product-placements-cheerios-chex/, accessed April 14, 2012.

52. Federico de Gregorio and Yongjun Sung, "Understanding Attitudes Toward and Behaviors in Response to Product Placement: A Consumer Socialization Framework," *Journal of Advertising*, 39, no. 1 (2010): 83–96.

53. "Ford Gets Women Involved in 'What Women Want' for Instant Buzz," Market Autopsy Blog, http://www.marketing-autopsyblog.com/customer -facing/ford-bloggers-involved-women-instant -buzz/, accessed April 14, 2012.

54. Michael Solomon, "The Missing Link: Surrogate Consumers in the Marketing Chain," *Journal of Marketing*, 50 (October 1986): 208–218.

55. Everett M. Rogers, *Diffusion of Innovations*, 4th ed. (New York: The Free Press, 1995).

56. Ayalla Ruvio, Yossi Gavish, and Aviv Shoham, "Consumer's Doppelganger: A Role Model Perspective on Intentional Consumer Mimicry," *Journal of Consumer Behaviour*, 12, no. 1 (2013): 60–69.

57. AARP Public Policy Institute, "Multigenerational Households Are Increased," Fact Sheet 221, April 2011, assets.aarp.org/rgcenter/ppi/econ-sec /fs221-housing.pdf, accessed September 12, 2012.

58. U.S. Census Bureau, http://factfinder2.census .gov/faces/tableservices/jsf/pages/productview

.xhtml?pid=ACS_12_1YR_DP02&prodType=table, accessed April 28, 2014.

59. Olivia Winslow, "Census: Nonfamily Households Surge," *News Day*, April 25, 2012, www .newsday.com/news/nation/census-nonfamily -households-surge-1.3682787, accessed February 11, 2013.

60. Claire Cain Miller, "The Divorce Surge Is Over, But the Myth Lives On," *The New York Times*, December 2, 2014.

61. DivorceRate, http://www.divorcerate.org/, accessed April 12, 2012.

62. Steve Matthews, "Worsening U.S. Divorce Rate Points to Improving Economy, *Bloomberg.com*, February 18, 2014, http://www.bloomberg.com /news/2014-02-18/worsening-u-s-divorce-rate -points-to-improving-economy.html, accessed April 28, 2014.

63. Nanette Fondas, "Millennials: Too Realistic to Have Children?" *Huffingtonpost.com*, November 17, 2013, http://www.huffingtonpost.com/nanette -fondas/are-millennials-too-realistic-to-have -children_b_4221885.html, accessed April 28, 2014.

64. Statistics obtained from statisticbrain.com/ marriage-statistics, based on CDC data, accessed April 28, 2014.

65. D'Vera Cohn, "Marriage Rate Declines and Marriage Age Rises," Pew Research Center, December 14, 2011, http://www.pewsocial-trends .org/2011/12/14/marriage-rate-declines-and -marriage-age-rises/, accessed April 12, 2012.

66. "51% of American Women Living Without a Spouse," Women Lifestyle website, April 8, 2012, http://womenlifestyle.com/entry/51-american -women-living-spouse/, accessed April 12, 2012.

67. census.gov, http://factfinder.census.gov/faces /tableservices/jsf/pages/productview.xhtml?pid =ACS_14_5YR_DP02&src=pt, accessed April 7, 2016.

68. "The New Demography of American Motherhood," Pew Research Center, http://pewsocialtrends .org/pubs/754/new-demography-of-american -motherhood, accessed June 11, 2010.

69. Joseph Lawler, "Women Are Having Fewer Kids and Demographers Don't Know Why," *The Washington Examiner*, June 7, 2014, www .washingtonexaminer.com/women-are-having-fewer -kids-and-demographers-dont-know-why/article /2549445; Emma Gray, "A Record Percentage of Women Don't Have Kids, and Here's Why That Makes Sense," *The Huffington Post*, April 9, 2015, http://www.huffingtonpost.com/2015/04/09/childless -more-women-are-not-having-kids-says-census _n_7032258.html.

70. Wendy Koch, "Number of Single Men Adopting Foster Kids Doubles; Historic Shift from When Kids Went Only to Married Couples," *USA Today*, June 15, 2007, 5A.

71. Robert E. Wilkes, "Household Life-Cycle Stages, Transitions, and Product Expenditures," *Journal of Consumer Research*, 22, no. 1 (1995): 27–41.

72. Jessica Dickler, "Boomerang Kids: 85% of College Grads Moving Home," CNN Money, October 14, 2010, http://money.cnn.com/2010/10/14/pf /boomerang_kids_move_home/index.htm, accessed April 25, 2011.

73. Kim Parker, "The Boomerang Generation," Pew Social and Demographic Trends, Pew Research Center, March 15, 2012, http://pewsocialtrends. org/2012/03/15/the-boomerang-generation/, accessed April 12, 2012.

74. Ibid.

75. Richard Fry, Kim Parker, and Molly Rohal, "More Millennials Living with Family Despite

Improved Job Market," Pew Research Center, July 29, 2015, http://www.pewsocialtrends.org/2015/07/29/more-millennials-living-with-family-despite-improved-job-market/, accessed April 13, 2016.

76. John Chatzky, "Your Adult Kids Are Back. Now What?" *Money*, 36, no. 1 (2007): 32–35.

77. Richard Fry, Kim Parker, and Molly Rohal, "More Millennials Living with Family Despite Improved Job Market," *Pew Research Center*, July 29, 2015, http://www.pewsocialtrends.org/2015/07/29/more-millennials-living-with-family-despite-improved-job-market/, accessed April 13, 2016.

78. Kim Parker and Eileen Patten, "The Sandwich Generation," Pew Research Center, January 30, 2013, http://www.pewsocialtrends.org/2013/01/30/the-sandwich-generation/, accessed April 13, 2016.

79. Ari Houser and Mary Jo Gibson, "Valuing the Invaluable: The Economic Value of Family Caregiving, 2008 Update," AARP Public Policy Institute, November 2008, http://assets.aarp.org/rgcenter/il/i13_caregiving.pdf, accessed April 3, 2009.

80. Houser and Gibson, "Valuing the Invaluable."

81. James W. Gentry, Suraj Commuri, and Sunkyu Jun, "Review of Literature on Gender in the Family," *Academy of Marketing Science Review*, 1 (2003): 1–18.

82. Christina K. C. Lee and Sharon E. Beatty, "Family Structure and Influence in Family Decision Making," *Journal of Consumer Marketing*, 19, no. 1 (2002): 24–41.

83. Michael A. Belch and Laura A. Willis, "Family Decisions at the Turn of the Century: Has the Changing Structure of Households Impacted the Family Decision-Making Process?" *Journal of Consumer Behaviour*, 2, no. 2 (2002): 111–125.

84. Richard Fry and D'Vera Cohn, "New Economics of Marriage: The Rise of Wives," Pew Research Center, January 19, 2010, http://pewresearch.org/pubs/1466/economics-marriage-rise-of-wives?src=prc-latest&proj=peoplepress, accessed June 11, 2010.

85. Statistics in this section are based on the following: "Kid Power," *Chain Store Age*, 83, no. 3 (2007): 20; "Spending on Kids Seems Recession-Resistant," MSNBC, http://www.msnbc.msn.com/id/27312338/ns/business-eye_on_the_economy/, accessed April 25, 2011; Michelle Koetters, "Tweeners' Money Talks," *Knight Ridder Tribune Business News*, May 14, 2007, 1; Steve Maich, "The Little Kings and Queens of the Mall," *Maclean's*, 119, no. 25 (2006): 37.

86. This definition is based on Scott Ward, "Consumer Socialization," in *Perspectives in Consumer Behavior*, ed. Harold H. Kassarjian and Thomas S. Robertson (Glenview, IL: Scott, Foresman, 1980), 380.

9

1. costofwedding.com, accessed May 12, 2016.

2. Ajita Shashidhar, "Dunkin' Donuts India Has Lots on Its Plate," *Business Today*, January 29, 2014, http://businesstoday.intoday.in/story/dunkin%25E2%2580%2599-donuts-india-has-lots-on-its-plate/1/202820.html, accessed September 18, 2014; S. Malhotra, "The Creative Marketer," *Business Today*, March 16, 2014, 64–65.

3. Maria Tadeo, "Miley Cyrus Strips Naked, Smokes Weed . . ." *The Independent*, February 3, 2014, http://www.independent.co.uk/news/people/news/miley-cyrus-strips-naked-talks-to-ronan-farrow-i-like-that-im-associated-with-sexuality-9104790.html, accessed October 14, 2014. "Miley Cyrus Appears in Creepy New Video that Features Nudity, Drugs, Profanity and a Stolen

Brain," Foxnews.com, July 9, 2014, http://www.foxnews.com/entertainment/2014/07/09/miley-cyrus-appears-in-creepy-new-video-that-features-nudity-drugs-profanity/, accessed October 14, 2014.

4. Thuc-Doan T. Nguyen and Russell W. Belk, "Harmonization Processes and Relational Meanings in Constructing Asian Weddings," *Journal of Consumer Research*, 40, no. 3 (2013): 518–538.

5. T. Lenartowicz and K. Roth, "A Framework for Culture Assessment," *Journal of International Business Studies*, 30 (1999): 781–798; T. Lenartowicz and K. Roth, "Culture Assessment Revisited: The Selection of Key Informants in IB Cross-Cultural Studies," Annual Meeting of the Academy of International Business, Sydney, Australia, November 16–19, 2001.

6. J. W. Overby, R. B. Woodruff, and S. F. Gardial, "The Influence of Culture on Consumers' Desired Value Perceptions: A Research Agenda," *Marketing Theory*, 5 (June 2005): 139–163.

7. Geert Hofstede, The Hofstede Centre, http://geert-hofstede.com/, accessed April 25, 2014.

8. For a concise review of Hofstede's original value dimensions, see A. M. Soares, M. Farhangmehr, and A. Shoham, "Hofstede's Dimensions of Culture in International Marketing Studies," *Journal of Business Research*, 60 (2007): 277–284.

9. E. C. Hirschman, "Men, Dogs, Guns and Cars," *Journal of Advertising*, 32 (Spring 2003): 9–22.

10. H. G. Cheng, O. McBride, and M.R. Phillips (2015), "Relationship between Knowledge about the Harms of Smoking and Smoking Status in the 2010 Global Adult Tobacco China Survey," *Tobacco Control*, 24(1), 54–61.

11. G. Zhao, W. Li, L. Teng, and T. Lu, "Moderating Role of Consumer Self-Concept on the Effectiveness of Two Nostalgia Appeals," *Journal of Promotion Management*, 20, no. 1 (2014): 1–19.

12. Geert Hofstede, The Hofstede Centre, http://geert-hofstede.com/, accessed April 25, 2014.

13. J. M. Jung and J. J. Kellaris, "Responsiveness to Authority Appeals among Young French and American Consumers," *Journal of Business Research*, 59 (June 2006): 735–744.

14. B. J. Babin, A. Borges, and K. James (2016), "The Role of Retail Price Image in a Multi-Country Context: France and the USA," *Journal of Business Research*, 69, 1074–1081.

15. M. B. Akdeniz and M. B. Talay, "Cultural Variations in the Use of Marketing Signals: A Multilevel Analysis of the Motion Picture Industry," *Journal of the Academy of Marketing Science*, 41, no. 5, 601–624.

16. D. Martin, "Uncovering Unconscious Memories and Myths for Understanding International Tourism Behavior," *Journal of Business Research*, 63 (2010): 372–383. J. C. Mowen, X. Fang, and K. Scott, "A Hierarchical Model Approach for Identifying the Trait Antecedents of General Gambling Propensity and of Four Gambling-Related Genres," *Journal of Business Research*, 62 (2009): 1262–1268.

17. J. K. M. Marta, A. Singhapakdi, D. Lee, M. J. Sirgy, K. Koonmee, and B. Virakul, "Perceptions about Ethics Institutionalization and Quality of Work Life: Thai versus American Marketing Managers," *Journal of Business Research*, 66 (March), 381–389.

18. Geert Hofstede, The Hofstede Centre, http://geert-hofstede.com/, accessed April 25, 2014.

19. K. Keysuk and C. Oh, "On Distributor Commitment in Marketing Channels for Industrial Products: Contrast Between the United States

and Japan," *Journal of International Marketing*, 10 (2002): 72–107. S. Ryu, S. Kabadavi, and C. Chung, "The Relationship Between Unilateral and Bilateral Control Mechanisms: The Contextual Effect of Long-Term Orientation," *Journal of Business Research*, 60 (July 2007): 681–689.

20. C. L. Wang, "Guanxi vs. Relationship Marketing: Exploring Underlying Differences," *Industrial Marketing Management*, 36 (2007): 81–86. Z. Shou, J. Chen, W. Zhu, and L. Yang, "Firm Capability and Performance in China: The Moderating Role of Guanxi and its Institutional Forces in Domestic and Foreign Contexts," *Journal of Business Research*, 67 (February 2014): 77–82.

21. S. Worthington, "Entering the Market for Financial Services in Transitional Economies," *International Journal of Bank Marketing*, 23 (2005): 381–396; W. Gong, R. L. Stump, and L. M. Maddox, "Factors Influencing Consumers' Online Shopping in China," *Journal of Asia Business Studies*, 7, no. 3 (2014): 214–230.

22. China Economic Review (2015), "China's Consumers Emrace Credit Cards as Regulator Rebuff New Industry Entrants," China Economic review, Chinaeconomicreview.com, accessed June 13, 2016.

23. S. Manjeshwar, B. Sternquist, and L. K. Good, "Decision Making of Retail Buyers: Perspectives from China and India," *Qualitative Market Research: An International Journal*, 16, no. 1 (2013): 38–52.

24. Geert Hofstede, The Hofstede Centre, http://geert-hofstede.com/, accessed April 25, 2014.

25. Ibid.

26. S. Boumphrey and E. Bevis, "Reaching the Emerging Middle Classes Beyond BRIC" (Euromonitor International: London, UK, 2014).

27. S. Gardiner, C. King, and D. Grace, "Travel Decision Making: An Empirical Examination of Generational Values, Attitudes, and Intentions," *Journal of Travel Research*, 52, no. 3 (2013): 310–324.

28. M. Laroche, Z. Yang, C. Kim, and M. O. Richard, "How Culture Matters in Children's Purchase Influence: A Multi-Level Investigation," *Journal of the Academy of Marketing Science*, 35 (Winter 2007): 113–126.

29. https://www.unilever.com/brands/our-brands/lifebuoy.html, accessed June 14, 2016. The brand has introduced young consumers to new, healthier habits with slogans and promotions such as "Dr. Lifebuoy says 5 times a day!"

30. K. Chankon, M. Laroche, and M. Tomiuk, "The Chinese in Canada: A Study of Ethnic Change with Emphasis on Gender Roles," *Journal of Social Psychology*, 144 (February 2004): 5–27.

31. D. Sanou, E. O'Reilly, I. Ngnie-Teta, M. Batal, N. Mondain, C. Andrew, et al., "Acculturation and Nutritional Health of Immigrants in Canada: A Scoping Review," *Journal of Immigrant and Minority Health*, 16, no. 1 (2014): 24–34.

32. Li, C. and S. T. Wan-Hsiu (2015), "Social Media Usage and Acculturation: A Test with Hispanics in the U.S.," Computers in Human Behavior, 45, 204–212.

33. http://www.bbc.com/news/technology-18424400, accessed June 16, 2016.

34. M. Laroche, K. Chankon, M. Tomiuk, and D. Belisle, "Similarities in Italian and Greek Multidimensional Ethnic Identity: Some Implications for Food Consumption," *Canadian Journal of Administrative Science*, 22 (2005): 143–167.

35. K. Bissell, "Understanding the Role of Cognition and Media in Body Image Disturbance and Weight Bias in Children, Adolescents, and Adults," *The International Encyclopedia of Media Studies* (West Sussex, UK: Wiley-Blackwell, 2013).

36. H. L. Adams and L. R. Williams, "Advice from Teens about Dating: Implications for Healthy Relationships," *Children and Youth Services Review,* 33 (2011): 254–264.

37. R. A. Tiwsakul and Ch. Hackley, "Postmodern Paradoxes in Thai-Asian Consumer Identity," *Journal of Business Research,* 65 (2012): 490–496.

38. A. Bakir, G. M. Rose, and A. Shoham, "Consumption Communication and Parental Control of Children's Viewing: A Multi-Rater Approach," *Journal of Marketing Theory and Practice,* 13 (Spring 2005): 47–58. L. Carlson and S. Grossbart, "Parental Style and Consumer Socialization in Children," *Journal of Consumer Research,* 15 (June 1988): 77–94.

39. C. Miller, F. Bram, J. Reardon, and I. Vida, "Teenagers' Response to Self- and Other-Directed Anti-Smoking Messages," *International Journal of Market Research,* 49 (2006): 515–533.

40. Z. Yang and R. Netemeyer (2015), "Differential Effects of Parenting Strategies on Child Smoking Trajectories: A Longitudinal Assessment over Twelve Years," *Journal of Business Research,* 68, 1273–1282.

41. Doréen Pick and Martin Eisend, "Buyers' Perceived Switching Costs and Switching: A Meta-Analytic Assessment of Their Antecedents," *Journal of the Academy of Marketing Science* (January 2014): 1–19.

42. See M. Griffin, B. J. Babin, and D. Modianos, "Shopping Values of Russian Consumers: The Impact of Habituation in a Developing Economy," *Journal of Retailing,* 76 (2000): 33–52.

43. N. Spielmann and M. Delvert, "Adapted or Standardized Copy: Is Non-cultural English the Answer?" *Journal of Business Research,* 67 (2014): 434–440.

44. J. Illcic, A. Kulcynski, and S. Baxter (2016), "How a Smile Can Make a Difference: Enhancing the Persuasive Appeal of Celebrity Endorsers," *Journal of Advertising Research,* JAR-2016.

45. T. Kramer, S. Spolter-Weisfeld, and M. Thakker, "The Effect of Cultural Orientation on Consumer Responses to Personalization," *Marketing Science,* 26 (March/April 2007): 246–258.

46. G. C. Pigliasco, "Lost in Translation: From Omiyage to Souvenir: Beyond Aesthetics of the Japanese Ladies' Gaze in Hawaii," *Journal of Material Culture,* 10 (July 2005): 177–196.

47. I. Bremmer (2015), "The New World of Business," *Fortune,* http://fortune.com/2015/01/22/the-new-world-of-business/, accessed June 20, 2016. Marketers look for growing populations, youthfulness, free markets, favorable cultural values, and pro-growth political climates as signs of opportunities to do business.

48. Y. Strizhakova, R. A. Coulter, and L. Price, "Branded Products as a Passport to Global Citizenship: Perspectives from Developed and Developing Countries," *Journal of International Marketing,* 16, no. 4 (2008): 57–85.

10

1. M. B. Beverland, F. Farrelly, and P. G. Quester, "Authentic Subcultural Membership: Antecedents and Consequences of Authenticating Acts and Authoritative Performances," *Psychology & Marketing,* 27 (July 2010): 608–716.

2. J. Berger and C. Heath, "Who Drives Divergence? Identity Signaling, Outgroup Similarity, and the Abandonment of Cultural Tastes," *Journal of Personality and Social Psychology,* 95 (2008): 593–607.

3. Benjamin Zimmer, "Life in These, Uh, This United States," Language Log, November 24, 2005, http://itre.cis.upenn.edu/~myl/languagelog/archives/002663.html, accessed October 26, 2016.

4. Joel Garreau, *The Nine Nations of North America* (New York: Avon, 1981).

5. L. R. Kahle, "The Nine Nations of North America and the Value Basis of Geographic Segmentation," *Journal of Marketing,* 50 (April 1986): 37–47.

6. Blayne Cutler, "Welcome to the Borderlands," *American Demographics* (February 1991): 44–49, 57.

7. S. Guimond, S. Brunot, A. Chatard, D. M. Garcia, D. Martinot, N. R. Branscombe, M. Desert, et al., "Culture, Gender, and the Self: Variations and Impact of Social Comparison Processes," *Journal of Personality and Social Psychology,* 92 (June 2007): 1118–1134.

8. Y. Sung and S. F. Tinkham, "Brand Personality Structures in the United States and Korea: Common and Culture-Specific Factors," *Journal of Consumer Psychology,* 15, no. 4 (2005), 334–350.

9. D. Ball, "Women in Italy Like to Clean but Shun the Quick and Easy," *The Wall Street Journal,* April 25, 2006, A1.

10. M. Bustillo and M. E. Lloyd, "Best Buy Seeks Female Shoppers," *The Wall Street Journal,* June 16, 2010, B5.

11. R. A. Smith, "Wanted: Guy Shoppes for Fashion Sites," *The Wall Street Journal,* July 22, 2010, B1.

12. B. T. Yoram and M. Jarymowicz, "The Effect of Gender on Cognitive Structuring: Who Are More Biased, Men or Women?" *Psychology,* 1 (2010): 80–87.

13. Statistics in this chapter are taken from the U.S. Census Bureau (www.census.gov) or the CIA Factbook (www.cia.com).

14. J. E. Lueg and R. Z. Finney, "Interpersonal Communication in the Consumer Socialization Process: Scale Development and Validation," *Journal of Marketing Theory and Practice,* 15 (Winter 2007): 25–39.

15. http://www.prweb.com/releases/TRUGlobalTeenStudy/GlobalTeenBrands/prweb2193514.htm, accessed October 26, 2016.

16. "Global Teen Culture—Does It Exist?" *Brand Strategy,* 167 (January 2003): 37–38.

17. R. S. Parker, A. D. Schaefer, and C. M. Hermans, "An Investigation into Teens' Attitudes Towards Fast-Food Brands in General: A Cross-Culture Analysis," *Journal of Foodservice Business Research,* 9, no. 4 (2006): 25–40.

18. Demographic categories in this section are based on Paul Taylor and Scott Keeter, eds., "Millennials: A Portrait of Generation Next," Pew Research Center online report, 2011, http://pewresearch.org/millennials, accessed April 28, 2011.

19. "Fueled by Aging Baby Boomers, Nation's Older Population to Nearly Double, Census Bureau Reports," www.census.gov, May 6, 2014, http://www.census.gov/newsroom/releases/archives/aging_population/cb14-84.html, accessed June 20, 2014.

20. Catherine Siskos, "Generation X Socks It Away," *Kiplinger's Personal Finance Magazine,* 52, no. 5 (1998): 20.

21. This information based on Nancy Gibbs, "Generation Next," *Time,* March 11, 2010, http://www.time.com/time/magazine/article/0,9171,1971433-2,00.html, accessed August 10, 2010.

22. Richard Fry, "Millennials Overtake Baby Boomers as America's Largest Generation," Pew Research Center, April 25, 2016, www.pewresearch.org/fact-tank/2016/04/25/millennials-overtake-baby-boomers/, accessed June 27, 2016.

23. Paul Taylor and Scott Keeter, eds., "Millennials: A Portrait of Generation Next," Pew Research Center, February 2010, http://pewsocialtrends.org/assets/pdf/millennials-confident-connected-open-to-change.pdf, accessed October 26, 2016.

24. B. Steinberg, "Study: Young Consumers Switch Media 27 Times in an Hour," *Advertising Age,* April 9, 2012, http://adage.com/article/news/study-young-consumers-switch-media-27-times-hour/234008/, accessed October 26, 2016.

25. "Young, Underemployed and Optimistic," Pew Research Center, February 9, 2012, http://www.pewsocialtrends.org/files/2012/02/young-underemployed-and-optimistic.pdf, accessed October 26, 2016. Hadley Malcolm, "Millennials Use Alternative Financial Services," *USA Today,* May 17, 2012, B1.

26. The Center for Generational Diversity Studies, www.generationaldiversity.com/index.php?/fap.html, accessed June 14, 2012.

27. Angela Cross-Bystrom, "What You Need to Know about Generation Z," IMediaConnection, www.imediaconnection.com/content/27425.asp, accessed October 26, 2016.

28. P. Boski, "Humanism-Materialism: Centuries-Long Polish Cultural Origins and 20 Years of Research," in *Indigenous and Cultural Psychology: Understanding People in Context,* ed. U. Kim, K. S. Yang, and K.-K. Hwang (New York: Springer, 2006), 373–402.

29. T. Benning, "Slump Strains Church Finances as Need Grows," *The Wall Street Journal,* August 11, 2009, A13.

30. Valerie A. Taylor, Diane Halstead, and Paula J. Haynes, "Consumer Responses to Christian Religious Symbols in Advertising," *Journal of Advertising,* 39, no. 2 (2010): 79–92.

31. O. Sandikci and G. Ger, "Veiling in Style: How Does a Stigmatized Practice Become Fashionable?" *Journal of Consumer Research,* 37 (June 2010): 15–36.

32. "French MPs Vote to Ban Islamic Full Veil in Public," BBC News, July 13, 2010, http://www.bbc.co.uk/news/10611398, accessed August 9, 2010.

33. M. A. Zolfagharian and Q. Sun, "Country of Origin, Ethnocentrism and Bicultural Consumers: The Case of Mexican Americans," *The Journal of Consumer Marketing,* 27 (2010): 345.

34. "Marketing to Asian Americans," *AdWeek Media,* May 26, 2008, http://www.adweekmedia.com/aw/content_display/custom-reports/mtaa/e3i70fa56666e6c5bccfb3fe3b2dc4c015b, accessed August 8, 2010.

35. This definition based on George Ritzer, *Sociological Theory,* 4th ed. (New York: McGraw-Hill, 1996).

36. Charles M. Schaninger, "Social Class Versus Income Revisited: An Empirical Investigation," *Journal of Marketing Research* (May 1981): 192–208.

37. Lloyd W. Warner and Paul S. Hunt, eds., *The Social Life of a Modern Community* (New Haven, CT: Yale University Press, 1941).

38. C. R. Schwartz and R. D. Mare, "Trends in Educational Assortative Marriage from 1940 to 2003," *Demography,* 42, no. 4 (2005): 621–646.

39. E. C. Snyder, "Attitudes: A Study of Homogamy and Marital Selectivity," *Journal of Marriage and Family,* 26, no. 3 (1964): 332–336.

40. This definition based on Jack Eller, *Cultural Anthropology: Global Forces, Local Lives* (New York: Routledge, 2009), and Jonathan H. Turner, *Sociology: Studying the Human System* (Santa Monica, CA: Goodyear Publishing, 1981).

41. Lisa Ling and Katie Hinman, "Under Las Vegas: Tunnels Stretch for Miles," ABC News, September 23, 2009, http://abcnews.go.com/Nightline/las-vegas-strip-home-homeless/story?id=8652139,

accessed August 11, 2010; also Ashley Powers, "A Life Saved from the Shadows," *Los Angeles Times,* December 22, 2009, http://articles.latimes.com/2009/dec/22/nation/la-na-tunnel22-2009dec22, accessed August 11, 2010.

42. An Hodgson, "China's Middle Class Reaches 80 Million," Euromonitor International, July 25, 2007, http://www.euromonitor.com/Chinas_middle _class_reaches_80_million, accessed August 11, 2010.

43. This section based on Vincent Fernando, "Faber: India's Middle Class Will Soon Be Larger than America's," *Business Insider,* February 15, 2010, http://www.businessinsider.com/faber-dont -ignore-india-2010-2, accessed August 11, 2010; also Eric Beinhocker, Diana Ferrell, and Adil Zainulbhai, "Tracking the Growth of India's Middle Class," *McKinsey Quarterly,* August 2007, http://www.mckinseyquarterly.com/Tracking_the_growth _of_Indias_middle _class_2032, accessed August 11, 2010.

44. C. Goulding and M. Saren, "Performing Identity: An Analysis of Gender Expressions at the Whitby Goth Festival," *Consumption Markets & Culture,* 12 (March 2009): 27–46.

45. Bob Martin, "Wife Shortage Looms in China," *Culture Briefings,* Geotravel Research Center, http://www.culturebriefings.com/articles/chwifesh .html, accessed August 12, 2016; also "Study: China Faces 24M Bride Shortage by 2020," CNN, January 11, 2010, http://www.cnn.com/2010 /WORLD/asiapcf/01/11/china.bride.shortage /index.html, accessed August 12, 2016.

46. "Asian Youth Trends," *American Demographics,* 26, no. 8 (2004): 14.

Case 3–2

1. Focus groups conducted at New Mexico State University, 2011.

2. Focus groups conducted at New Mexico State University, 2011.

3. Laura Deaton Morarity, "Whisper to a Scream," *Marketing Health Services* (Summer 2009): 9–13.

4. http://www.flashmobamerica.com/, accessed April 1, 2012.

Case 3–3

1. Michael R. Solomon, *Consumer Behavior,* 9th ed. (Upper Saddle River, NJ: Prentice Hall, 2011).

2. Ellen Neuborne and Kathleen Kerwin, "Generation Y," *BusinessWeek* Online, February 15, 1999, accessed March 23, 2012.

3. J. Walker Smith, "10 Truths about Millennials," Warc, July 8, 2011, http://popsurvey.blogspot .com/2011/07/10-truths-about-millennials.html, accessed October 26, 2016.

4. Joanna Chau, "Millennials Are More 'Generation Me' Than 'Generation We,'" *The Chronicle of Higher Education,* March 15, 2012, http://chronicle .com/article/Millennials-Are-More/131175/, accessed April 13, 2012.

5. Barry Babin and Eric Harris, *Consumer Behavior,* 4th ed. (Mason, Ohio: South-Western/Cengage Learning, 2012).

6. Sally Kane, "Common Characteristics of Generation Y Professionals" https://www.thebalance.com /common-characteristics-of-generation-y-professionals -2164683, accessed October 26, 2016.

7. Babin and Harris, *CB4.*

8. Chau, "Millennials Are More 'Generation Me' Than 'Generation We.'"

9. Babin and Harris, *CB4.*

10. Smith, "10 Truths about Millennials."

11

1. R. Dhar and S. M. Nowlis, "The Effect of Time Pressure on Consumer Choice Deferral," *Journal of Consumer Research,* 25 (March 1999): 369–384.

2. M. G. Bublitz, L. A. Peracchio, and L. G. Block, "Why Did I Eat That? Perspectives on Food Decision Making and Dietary Restraint," *Journal of Consumer Psychology,* 20 (July 2010): 239–258.

3. C. M. Henderson, J. T. Beck, and R.W. Palmatier, "Review of the Theoretical Underpinnings of Loyalty Programs," *Journal of Consumer Psychology,* 21 (2011): 256–276.

4. Junsang Lim and Sharon E. Beatty, "Factors Affecting Couples' Decisions to Jointly Shop," *Journal of Business Research,* 64, no. 7 (2011): 774–781.

5. B. C. Krishnan, S. Dutta, and S. Jha, "Effectiveness of Exaggerated Advertised Reference Prices: The Role of Decision Time Pressure." *Journal of Retailing,* 89, no. 1 (2013): 105–113.

6. R. Suri and K. B. Monroe, "The Effects of Time Constraints on Consumers' Judgments of Prices and Products," *Journal of Consumer Research,* 30 (June 2003): 92–104.

7. Alison Elizabeth Lloyd, Ricky Y. K. Chan, Leslie S. C. Yip, Andrew Chan, "Time Buying and Time Saving: Effects on Service Convenience and the Shopping Experience at the Mall," *Journal of Services Marketing,* 28 (2014): 36–49.

8. S. Chatterjee, D. Rai, and T. B. Heath (2016). "Tradeoff between Time and Money: The Asymmetric Consideration of Opportunity Costs," *Journal of Business Research,* 69, 2560–2566.

9. J. Wagner and M. Mokhtari, "The Moderating Effect on Household Apparel Expenditure," *Journal of Consumer Affairs,* 34, no. 2 (2000): 22–78.

10. S. Roslow, T. Li, and J. A. F. Nicholls, "Impact of Situational Variables and Demographic Attributes in Two Seasons on Purchase Behavior," *European Journal of Marketing,* 34, no. 9 (2000): 1167–1180.

11. V. Kumar, J.B. Choi, and M. Greene (2016), "Synergistic Effects of Social Media and Traditional Marketing on Brand Sales: Capturing the Time-Varying Effect," *Journal of the Academy of Marketing Science,* DOI 10.1007/s11747-016-0484-7.

12. C. Yoon, C. Cole, and M. P. Lee, "Consumer Decision Making and Aging: Current Knowledge and Future Decisions," *Journal of Consumer Psychology,* 19 (2009): 2–16. Bublitz et al., "Why Did I Eat That?"

13. G. Saad and E. Stenstrom, "Calories, Beauty and Ovulation: The Effects of the Menstrual Cycle on Food and Appearance-Related Consumption," *Journal of Consumer Psychology* 22 (2012): 102–113.

14. D. Gal (2016), "Let Hunger Be Your Guide? Being Hungry Before a Meal Is Associated with Healthier Levels of Post-Meal Blood Glucose," *Journal of the Association for Consumer Research,* 1, 1.

15. A. Lindström, H. Berg, J. Nordfält, A.L. Roggeveen, and D. Grewal (2016), "Does the Presence of a Mannequin Head Change Shopping Behavior?" *Journal of Business Research,* 69, 517–524.

16. G. Bensinger, "Amazon Wants to Ship Your Package Before You Buy It," *The Wall Street Journal,* January 21, 2014, B1. "Amazon Files Patent for 'Anticipatory' Shipping," CBS News, cbsnews.com/news/amazon-files-patent-for-anticipatory-shipping/, accessed January 21, 2014. F. Manjoo, "Why Bezos's Drone Is More Than a Joke," *The Wall Street Journal,* December 5, 2013, B1–B7.

17. D. M. Koo and Y. Y. Choi, "Knowledge Search and People with High Epistemic Curiosity," *Competence in Human Behavior,* 26 (2010): 12–22.

18. E. D. Brocato, C. M. Voorhees, and J. Baker, "Understanding the Influence of Cues from Other Customers in the Service Experience: A Scale Development and Validation," *Journal of Retailing,* 88 (2012): 384–398.

19. T. J. L. Van Rompay, J. Krooshoop, J. W. M. Verhoeven, and A. T. H. Pruyn, "With or Without You: Interactive Effects of Retail Density and Need for Affilliation on Shopping Pleasure and Spending," *Journal of Business Research,* 65 (2012): 1126–1131.

20. J. M. Jung, H. Ch. Hui, K. S. Min, and D. Martin, "Does Telic/Paratelic User Mode Matter on the Effectiveness of Interactive Internet Advertising? A Reversal Theory Perspective," *Journal of Business Research,* 67 (2014): 1303–1309. In Apter's Reversal Theory terminology, the shift is from a telic orientation, meaning oriented toward task completion, to a paratelic orientation, meaning oriented toward submissiveness to the experience, or vice versa.

21. B. J. Babin, W. R. Darden, and M. Griffin, "Work and/or Fun: Measuring Hedonic and Utilitarian Shopping Value," *Journal of Consumer Research,* 20, no. 4 (1994), 644–656.

22. A. G. Close and M. Kukar-Kineey, "Beyond Buying: Motivations Behind Consumers' Online Shopping Cart Use," *Journal of Business Research,* 63 (September 2010), 986–992.

23. W. R. Darden and B. J. Babin, "Exploring the Concept of Affective Quality: Expanding the Concept of Retail Personality," *Journal of Business Research,* 29 (February 1994): 101–109.

24. S. Ramanathan and P. Williams, "Immediate and Delayed Emotional Consequences of Indulgence: The Moderating Influence of Personality Type on Mixed Emotions," *Journal of Consumer Research,* 34 (2007): 212–223.

25. T. L. Childers, C. L. Carr, J. Peck, and S. Carson, "Hedonic and Utilitarian Motivations for Online Shopping Behavior," *Journal of Retailing,* 77 (2001): 511–535.

26. A. Mukhopadhyay and G. V. Johar, "Indulgence as Self-Reward for Prior Shopping-Restraint: A Justification Based Mechanism," *Journal of Consumer Psychology,* 19 (July 2009): 334–345.

27. I. H. A. Franken and P. Muris, "Gray's Impulsivity Dimension: A Distinction Between Reward Sensitivity and Rash Impulsiveness," *Personality & Individual Differences,* 40 (July 2006): 1337–1347; Ramanathan and Williams, "Immediate and Delayed Emotional Consequences of Indulgence."

28. X. Zhang, V. R. Prybutok, and D. Strutton, "Modeling Influences on Impulse Purchasing Behaviors During Online Marketing Transactions," *Journal of Marketing Theory and Practice,* 15 (Winter 2007): 79–89.

29. J. V. Chen, B. Su, and A.E. Wedjaja (2016), "Facebook C2C Social Commerce: A Study of Online Impulse Buying," *Decision Support Systems,* 83, 57–69.

30. B. J. Babin and W. R. Darden, "Consumer Self-Regulation in a Retail Environment," *Journal of Retailing,* 71 (Spring 1995): 47–70.

31. M. Herzenstein, S. S. Posavac, and J. J. Brakus, "Adoption of New and Really New Products: The Effects of Self-Regulation Systems and Risk Salience," *Journal of Marketing Research,* 44 (May 2007): 251–260.

32. M. Kuka-Kinney, A.C. Scheinbaum, and T. Schaefers (2016)," Compulsive Buying in

Online Daily Deal Settings: An Investigation of Motivations and Contextual Elements," *Journal of Business Research*, 69, 691–699.

33. Darden and Babin, "Exploring the Concept of Affective Quality"; J. A. Russell and G. Pratt, "A Description of the Affective Quality Attributable to Environments," *Journal of Personality and Social Psychology*, 38 (1980): 311–22.

34. M. J. Bitner, "Servicescapes: The Impact of the Physical Environment on Customers and Employees," *Journal of Marketing*, 56 (April 1992): 57–71.

35. S. K. Koernig, "E-Scapes: The Electronic Physical Environment and Service Tangibility," *Psychology & Marketing*, 20 (2003): 151–167. Yong-Ki Lee, Choong-Ki Lee, Seung-Kon Lee, and Barry J. Babin, "Festivalscapes and Patrons' Emotions, Satisfaction, and Loyalty," *Journal of Business Research*, 61, no. 1 (2008): 56–64.

36. M. K. Brady, C. M. Voorhees, J. J. Cronin, and B. L. Boudreau, "The Good Guys Don't Always Win: The Effect of Valence on Service Perceptions and Consequences," *Journal of Services Marketing*, 20 (2006): 83–91.

37. G. Williams, "It's a Style Thing," *Entrepreneur*, 32 (March 2004): 34. Dawn Iacobucci and Amy Ostrom, "Gender Differences in the Impact of Core and Relational Aspects of Services on the Evaluation of Service Encounters," *Journal of Consumer Psychology*, 2, no. 3 (1993): 257–286. C. Spence, N. M. Puccinelli, D. Grewal, and A. L. Roggeveen, "Store Atmospherics: A Multisensory Perspective," *Psychology & Marketing*, 31 (2014): 472–488.

38. Barry J. Babin, Jean-Charles Chebat, and Richard Michon, "Perceived Appropriateness and Its Effect on Quality, Affect and Behavior," *Journal of Retailing and Consumer Services*, 11 (September 2004): 287–298; R. Michon, J. C. Chebat, and L.W. Turley, "Mall Atmospherics: The Interaction Effects of the Mall Environment on Shopping Behavior," *Journal of Business Research*, 58 (May 2005): 576–583.

39. See Spence et al., "Store Atmospherics: A Multisensory Perspective" (2014) for a brief review.

40. O. R. Orth and A. Bourrain, "Ambient Scent and Consumer Exploratory Behavior: A Causal Analysis," *Journal of Wine Research*, 16 (2005): 137–150.

41. Holmes, E. (2016), "Beauty Retail's Sweet Spot," *Wall Street Journal*, June 22, D1–D3.

42. See muzak.com for more. Accessed June 22, 2016.

43. L. W. Turley and J. C. Chebat, "Linking Retail Strategy, Atmospheric Design and Shopping Behavior," *Journal of Marketing Management*, 18 (2002): 125–144. R. E. Milliman, "The Influence of Background Music on the Behavior of Restaurant Patrons," *Journal of Consumer Research*, 13 (September 1986): 286–89. Spence et al., "Store Atmospherics: A Multisensory Perspective."

44. A. Lukits, "Music Genres May Influence What We Buy Online," *The Wall Street Journal*, February 4, 2014, D2.

45. A. E. Crowley, "The Two-Dimensional Impact of Color on Shopping," *Marketing Letters*, 4 (1993): 59–69. J. Bellizi and R. E. Hite, "Environmental Color, Consumer Feelings and Purchase Likelihood," *Psychology & Marketing*, 59 (Spring 1992): 347–363. B. J. Babin, D. M. Hardesty, and T. A. Suter, "Color and Shopping Intentions: The Intervening Effect of Price Fairness and Affect," *Journal of Business Research*, 56 (2003): 541–551.

46. N. Y. Ashir and N. O. Rule, "Shopping Under the Influence: Nonverbal Appearance-Based Communicator Cues Affect Consumer Judgments," *Psychology & Marketing*, 31 (2014): 539–548.

47. Babin, Hardesty, and Suter, "Color and Shopping Intentions."

48. W. Tantanatewin and V. Inkarojnit (2016), "Effects of Color and Lighting on Retail Impression and Identity," *Journal of Environmental Psychology*, 46, 197–205.

49. I. Knez, "Affective and Cognitive Reactions to Subliminal Flicker from Fluorescent Lighting," *Consciousness and Cognition*, 26 (2014): 97–104.

50. C. Dennis, A. Newman, R. Michon, J. J. Brakus, and L. T. Wright, "The Mediating Effects of Perception and Emotion: Digital Signage in Mall Atmospherics," *Journal of Consumer and Retail Services*, 17 (2010): 205–215; A.L. Roggeveen, J. Nordfait, and D. Grewal (20016), "Do Digital Displays Enhance Sales? Role of Retail Format and Message Content," *Journal of Retailing*, 92, 122–131.

51. P. Cotlet, M. C. Lichtlé, and V. Plichon, "The Role of Value in a Services: A Study in a Retail Environment," *Journal of Consumer Marketing*, 23 (2006): 219–227; S. A. Eroglu, K. Machleit, and T. F. Barr, "Perceived Retail Crowding and Shopper Satisfaction: The Role of Shopping Values," *Journal of Business Research*, 58 (August 2005): 1146–1153.

52. F. Pons, M. Giroux, M. Mourali, and M. Zins (2016), "The Relationship between Density Perceptions and Satisfaction in the Retail Setting: Mediation and Moderation Effects," *Journal of Business Research*, 69, 1000–1007.

53. B. Kidwell and J. Hasford, "Emotional Ability and Nonverbal Communication," *Psychology & Marketing*, 31 (2014): 526–538.

54. B. Price and D. Murray, "Match-Up Revisited: The Effect of Staff Attractiveness on Purchase Intentions in Younger Adult Females: Social Comparative and Produce Relevance Effects," *Journal of International Business and Economics*, 9 (2010): 55–76. S. K. Koering and A. L. Page, "What If Your Dentist Looked Like Tom Cruise? Applying the Match-up Hypothesis to a Service Encounter," *Psychology & Marketing*, 19 (January 2002): 91–110. D. Grace, "An Examination of Consumer Embarrassment and Repatronage Intentions in the Context of Emotional Service Encounters," *Journal of Retailing and Consumer Services*, 16 (January 2009): 1–9.

55. A. Borges, J. C. Chebat, and B. J. Babin, "Does a Companion Always Enhance the Shopping Experience?" *Journal of Retailing and Consumer Services*, 17 (July 2010): 294–299. Lim Beatty, "Factors Affecting Couples' Decisions to Jointly Shop."

56. C. Zhou, C.S. Florence, and D. Dowell (2016), "Payments for Opioids Shifted Substantially to Public and Private Insurers while Consumer Spending Declined," *Health Affairs*, 35, 824–831.

57. B. O'Connell, "MasterCard: 'Contactless' Consumers Spend More Cash," Main Street, http://www.mainstreet.com/article/moneyinvesting/credit/debt/mastercard-contactless-consumers-spend-more-cash, accessed June 2, 2012.

58. C. Heath and J. B. Soll, "Mental Budgeting and Consumer Decisions," *Journal of Consumer Research*, 23 (June 1996): 40–52.

59. D. Horne and N. Bendle (2016). "Gift Cards: A Review and Research Agenda," *The International Review of Retail, Distribution and Consumer Research*, 26, 154–170; Apparel.edgl.com/news/Unused-Gift-Cards—A-Ticking-Time-Bomb-100239, accessed June 25, 2016; http://money.cnn.com/2015/08/10/investing/gift-cards-soar-in-popularity/, accessed June 25, 2016.

60. Y. J. Wang, M. D. Hernandez, and M. S. Minor, "Web Aesthetics Effects on Perceived Online Service Quality and Satisfaction in an E-Tail Environment: The Moderating Role of Purchase Task," *Journal of Business Research*, 53 (2010): 935–942.

61. R. Crouser, L. Harrison, D. Afergan, and E.M. Peck," (2016), "Beyond Detection: Investigating in Practical and Theoretical Applications of Emotion Visualization," Proceedings of EMOVis2016, March 10, 2016, No. 103.

62. Luiza Oleszczuk, "Worst Black Friday Casualties: Is Walmart the Most Dangerous Place to Shop?" November 26, 2011, http://www.christianpost.com/news/worst-black-friday-casualties-is-walmart-the-most-dangerous-place-to-shop-video-63055/, accessed June 3, 2012.

12

1. Alison Jing Xu and Robert W. Wyer, Jr., "The Effect of Mind-Sets on Consumer Decision Strategies," *Journal of Consumer Research*, 34, no. 4 (2007): 556–566.

2. Richard P. Bagozzi and Utpal Dholakia, "Goal Setting and Goal Striving in Consumer Behavior," special issue, *Journal of Marketing*, 63 (1999): 19–32.

3. Robert Lawson, "Consumer Decision Making within a Goal-Driven Framework," *Psychology & Marketing*, 14, no. 5 (1997): 427–449.

4. Mary Frances Luce, James R. Bettman, and John W. Payne, "Trade-Off Difficulty: Determinants and Consequences for Consumer Decisions," *Monographs of the Journal of Consumer Research Series*, 1 (Spring 2001). Kalyani Menon and Laurette Dube, "Ensuring Satisfaction by Engineering Salesperson Response to Customer Emotions," *Journal of Retailing*, 76, no. 3 (2000): 285–307.

5. John C. Mowen, "Beyond Consumer Decision Making," *Journal of Consumer Marketing*, 5, no. 1 (1988): 15–25.

6. "POP Sharpens Its Focus," *Brandweek*, 44, no. 24 (2003): 31–36.

7. V. Kanti Prasad, "Socioeconomic Product Risk and Patronage Preferences of Retail Shoppers," *Journal of Marketing*, 39 (July 1975): 42–47. Grahame R. Dowling and Richard Staelin, "A Model of Perceived Risk and Intended Risk-Handling Activity," *Journal of Consumer Research*, 21, no. 1 (1994): 119–134.

8. This definition is based on Richard Oliver, *Satisfaction: A Behavioral Perspective on the Consumer* (New York: McGraw-Hill, 1997).

9. Louise O'Brien and Charles Jones, "Do Rewards Really Create Loyalty?" *Harvard Business Review*, 73 (May/June 1995): 75–82.

10. Leon Steinhoff and Robert W. Palmatier, "Understanding Loyalty Program Effectiveness: Managing Target and Bystander Effects," *Journal of the Academy of Marketing Science*, 44 (2016): 88–107.

11. Kevin Lane Keller, *Strategic Brand Management: Building, Measuring, and Managing Brand Equity* (Upper Saddle River, NJ: Prentice Hall, 1998).

12. David A. Aaker, *Building Strong Brands* (New York: The Free Press, 1997), 21.

13. Richard W. Olshavsky and Donald H. Granbois, "Consumer Decision Making—Fact or Fiction?" *Journal of Consumer Research*, 6, no. 2 (1979): 93–100.

14. Don Moyer, "Satisficing," *Harvard Business Review*, 85, no. 4 (2007): 144. Barry Schwartz, Andrew Ward, John Monterosso, Sonja Lyubomirsky,

Katherine White, and Darrin R. Lehman, "Maximizing versus Satisficing: Happiness Is a Matter of Choice," *Journal of Personality and Social Psychology*, 83, no. 5 (2002): 1178–1197.

15. Itamar Simonson and Aner Sela, "On the Heritability of Consumer Decision Making: An Exploratory Approach for Studying Genetic Effects on Judgment and Choice," *Journal of Consumer Research*, 37, no. 6 (2011): 951–966.

16. Gordon C. Bruner III and Richard J. Pomazal, "Problem Recognition: The Crucial First Stage of the Consumer Decision Process," *Journal of Consumer Marketing*, 5, no. 1 (1988): 51–63.

17. M. Joseph Sirgy, *Social Cognition and Consumer Behavior* (New York: Praeger, 1983).

18. Sharon Beatty and Scott M. Smith (1987), "External Search Effort: An Investigation across Several Product Categories," *Journal of Consumer Research*, 14 (1): 83–95.

19. Peter H. Bloch, Daniel L. Sherrell, and Nancy M. Ridgway, "Consumer Search: An Extended Framework," *Journal of Consumer Research*, 13, no. 1 (1986): 119–126.

20. Benjamin Scheibehenne, Rainer Greifeneder, and Peter M. Todd, "Can There Ever Be Too Many Options? A Meta-Analytic Review of Choice," *Journal of Consumer Research*, 37, no. 3 (2011): 409–425. Nicholas H. Lurie, "Decision Making in Information-Rich Environments: The Role of Information Structure," *Journal of Consumer Research*, 30, no. 4 (2004): 473–487.

21. Girish Punj and Richard Brookes, "Decision Constraints and Consideration Set Formation in Consumer Durables," *Psychology & Marketing*, 18, no. 8 (2004): 843–864. Allan D. Shocker, Moshe Ben-Akiva, Bruno Boccara, and Prakash Nedungadi, "Consideration Set Influences on Consumer Decision Making and Choice: Issues, Models, and Suggestions," *Marketing Letters*, 2, no. 3 (1991): 181–197.

22. Bas Donkers, "Modeling Consideration Sets across Time: The Relevance of Past Consideration," in *American Marketing Association Conference Proceedings*, vol. 13 (Chicago: American Marketing Association, 2002), 322.

23. John R. Hauser and Birger Wernerfelt, "An Evaluation Cost Model of Consideration Sets," *Journal of Consumer Research*, 16, no. 4 (1990): 393–408.

24. Nobuhiko Terui, Masataka Ban, and Greg M. Allenby, "The Effect of Media Advertising on Brand Consideration and Choice," *Marketing Science*, 30 (2011): 74–91.

25. Cheryl Burke Jarvis, "An Exploratory Investigation of Consumers' Evaluations of External Information Sources in Prepurchase Search," in *Advances in Consumer Research*, vol. 25, ed. Joseph W. Alba and J. Wesley Hutchinson (Provo, UT: Association for Consumer Research, 1998).

26. Melissa Bishop and Nelson Barber, "A Market Segmentation Approach to Esteem and Efficacy in Information Search," *Journal of Consumer Marketing*, 29, no. 1 (2012): 13–21.

27. Koen Pauwels and Richard D'Aveni, "The Formation, Evolution and Replacement of Price-Quality Relationships," *Journal of the Academy of Marketing Science*, 44 (2016): 46–65.

28. D. R. Lichtenstein, N. M. Ridgway, and R. P. Netemeyer, "Price Perceptions and Consumer Shopping Behavior," *Journal of Marketing Research*, 30 (1993): 234–245.

29. Torsten Bornemann and Christian Homberg, "Psychological Distance and the Dual Role of Price," *Journal of Consumer Research*, 38 (October 2011): 490–504.

30. Lara Marie Schons, Mario Rese, Jan Wieseke, Wiebke Rasmussen, Daniel Weber, and Wolf-Christian Strotmann, "There Is Nothing Permanent Except Change—Analyzing Individual Price Dynamics in 'Pay-What-You-Want' Situations," *Marketing Letters*, 25 (2014): 25–36.

31. Barbara Bickart and Robert M. Schindler, "Internet Forums as Influential Sources of Consumer Information," *Journal of Interactive Marketing*, 15, no. 3 (2001): 31–40.

32. Brian T. Ratchford, Myung-Soo Lee, and Debabrata Talukdar, "The Impact of the Internet on Information Search for Automobiles," *Journal of Marketing Research*, 40, no. 2 (2003): 193–209.

33. Moutusy Maity, Maxwell K. Hsu, and Lou E. Pelton, "Consumers' Online Information Search: Gen Yers Finding Needles in the Internet Haystack," *Journal of Marketing Channels*, 19, no. 1 (2012): 49–76. Charla Mathwick and Edward Rigdon, "Play, Flow, and the Online Search Experience," *Journal of Consumer Research*, 31, no. 2 (2004): 324–332.

34. Dan Ariely, "Controlling the Information Flow: Effects on Consumers' Decision Making and Preferences," *Journal of Consumer Research*, 27, no. 2 (2000): 233–248.

35. Kory Kroft and Devin G. Pope, "Does Online Search Crowd Out Traditional Search and Improve Matching Efficiency? Evidence from Craigslist," *Journal of Labor Economics*, 32, no. 2 (2014): 259–303.

36. David Mazursky and Gideon Vinitzky, "Modifying Consumer Search Processes in Enhanced On-Line Interfaces," *Journal of Business Research*, 58, no. 10 (2005): 1299–1309.

37. Information in this section based in part on "February/March 2012 Trend Briefing: Point-Know-Buy: Why Infolusty, Spontaneity-Loving Consumers Will Embrace Instant Visual Information Gratification," Trendwatching, 2012, http://trend-watching.com/trends/pointknowbuy/, accessed October 1, 2012.

38. Beatty and Smith, "External Search Effort."

39. Narasimhan Srinivasan and Brian T. Ratchford, "An Empirical Test of a Model of External Search for Automobiles," *Journal of Consumer Research*, 18 (1991): 233–242. Eric J. Johnson and Edward J. Russo, "Product Familiarity and Learning New Information," *Journal of Consumer Research*, 11 (1984): 542–550. William L. Moore and Donald R. Lehmann, "Individual Differences in Search Behavior for a Nondurable," *Journal of Consumer Research*, 7 (1980): 296–307.

40. Sridhar Moorthy, Brian T. Ratchford, and Debabrata Talukdar, "Consumer Information Search Revisited: Theory and Empirical Analysis," *Journal of Consumer Research*, 23, no. 4 (1997): 263–277; also see Joseph W. Alba and J. Wesley Hutchinson, "Dimensions of Consumer Expertise," *Journal of Consumer Research*, 13, no. 4 (1987): 411–454.

41. Beatty and Smith, "External Search Effort."

42. G. R. Dowling and R. Staelin, "A Model of Perceived Risk and Intended Risk-Handling Activity," *Journal of Consumer Research*, 21, no. 1 (1994): 119–134. Konrad Dedler, I. Gottschalk, and K. G. Grunert, "Perceived Risk as a Hint for Better Information and Better Products," in *Advances in Consumer Research*, vol. 8, ed. Kent Monroe (Ann Arbor, MI: Association for Consumer Research, 1981), 391–397.

43. Nitin Mehta, Surendra Rajiv, and Kannan Srinivasan, "Price Uncertainty and Consumer Search: A Structural Model of Consideration Set Formation," *Marketing Science*, 22, no. 1 (2003): 58–84.

44. Charles F. Hofacker and Jamie Murphy, "Consumer Web Page Search, Clicking Behavior, and Reaction Time," *Direct Marketing: An International Journal*, 3, no. 2 (2009): 88–96.

45. Beatty and Smith, "External Search Effort."

46. Ibid.

47. Noel Capon and Mariane Burke, "Individual, Product Class, and Task-Related Factors in Consumer Information Processing," *Journal of Consumer Research*, 7, no. 3 (1980): 314–326. Joseph Newman and Richard Staelin, "Prepurchase Information Seeking for New Cars and Major Household Appliances," *Journal of Marketing Research*, 7 (August 1972): 249–257.

48. Cathy J. Cobb and Wayne D. Hoyer, "Direct Observation of Search Behavior in the Purchase of Two Nondurable Products," *Psychology & Marketing*, 2, no. 3 (1988): 161–179. Newman and Staelin, "Prepurchase Information Seeking."

49. Girish Punj, "Presearch Decision Making in Consumer Durable Purchases," *Journal of Consumer Marketing*, 4, no. 1 (1987): 71–83.

50. Kristy E. Reynolds, Judith Anne Garretson Folse, and Michael A. Jones, "Search Regret: Antecedents and Consequences," *Journal of Retailing*, 82, no. 4 (2006): 339–348.

13

1. Charles M. Futrell, *ABCs of Relationship Selling*, 7th ed. (Boston: McGraw-Hill, 2003).

2. James H. Myers and Mark Alpert, "Determinant Buying Attitudes: Meaning and Measurement," *Journal of Marketing* (October 1968): 13–20.

3. Terrell G. Williams, "Social Class Influences on Purchase Evaluation Criteria," *Journal of Consumer Marketing*, 19, no. 2/3 (2002): 249–276. Ravi Dhar and Klaus Wertenbroch, "Consumer Choice between Hedonic and Utilitarian Goods," *Journal of Marketing Research*, 37 (February 2000): 60–71. Elizabeth C. Hirschman and S. Krishnan, "Subjective and Objective Criteria in Consumer Choice: An Examination of Retail Store Choice," *Journal of Consumer Affairs*, 15, no. 1 (1981): 115–127.

4. Barry Schwartz, "The Tyranny of Choice," *Scientific American*, 290, no. 4 (2001): 70–75.

5. Eugene Y. Chan, "Attractiveness of Options Moderates the Effect of Choice Overload," *International Journal of Research in Marketing*, 32, no. 4 (2015): 425–427.

6. Michel T. Pham, Joel B. Cohen, John W. Pracejus, and G. David Hughes, "Affect Monitoring and the Primacy of Feelings in Judgment," *Journal of Consumer Research*, 28, no. 2 (2001): 167–188.

7. Gerald J. Gorn, Marvin E. Goldberg, and Kunal Basu, "Mood, Awareness, and Product Evaluation," *Journal of Consumer Psychology*, 2, no. 3 (1993): 237–256.

8. Georgios A. Bakamitsos, "A Cue Alone or a Probe to Think? The Dual Role of Affect in Product Evaluations," *Journal of Consumer Research*, 33 (December 2006): 403–412.

9. Cassie Mogliner, Jennifer Aaker, and Sepandar D. Kamvar, "How Happiness Affects Choice," *Journal of Consumer Research*, 39 (August 2012): 429–443.

10. Jooyeon Ha and SooCheong Jang, "Determinants of Diners' Variety Seeking Intentions," *Journal of Services Marketing*, 27, no. 2 (2013): 155–165.

11. C. Page Moreau, Arthur B. Markman, and Donald R. Lehmann, "What Is It? Categorization Flexibility and Consumers' Responses to Really

New Products," *Journal of Consumer Research*, 27, no. 4 (2001): 489–498.

12. This discussion is based on Joseph W. Alba and J. Wesley Hutchinson, "Dimensions of Consumer Expertise," *Journal of Consumer Research*, 13, no. 4 (1987): 411–454.

13. Michael D. Johnson and Claes Fornell, "The Nature and Methodological Implications of the Cognitive Representation of Products," *Journal of Consumer Research*, 14, no. 2 (1987): 214–228.

14. Madhubalan Viswanathan and Terry L. Childers, "Understanding How Product Attributes Influence Product Categorization: Development and Validation of Fuzzy Set-Based Measures of Gradedness in Product Categories," *Journal of Marketing Research*, 36, no. 1 (1999): 75–94.

15. Mita Sujan and Christine Dekleva, "Product Categorization and Inference Making: Some Implications for Comparative Advertising," *Journal of Consumer Research*, 14, no. 3 (1987): 372–378.

16. Niraj Dawar and Philip Parker, "Marketing Universals: Consumers' Use of Brand Name, Price, Physical Appearance, and Retailer Reputation as Signals of Product Quality," *Journal of Marketing*, 58, no. 2 (1994): 81–95.

17. Deborah Roedder John and Mita Sujan, "Age Differences in Product Categorization," *Journal of Consumer Research*, 16, no. 4 (1990): 452–460.

18. Alba and Hutchinson, "Dimensions of Consumer Expertise."

19. Williams, "Social Class Influences on Purchase Evaluation Criteria."

20. Mark Bergen, Shantanu Dutta, and Steven M. Shugan, "Branded Variants: A Retail Perspective," *Journal of Marketing Research*, 33, no. 1 (1996): 9–19.

21. Barbara Fasolo, Gary H. McClelland, and Peter M. Todd, "Escaping the Tyranny of Choice: When Fewer Attributes Make Choice Easier," *Marketing Theory*, 7, no. 1 (2007): 13–26.

22. Michael D. Giebelhausen and Stacey G. Robinson, "Worth Waiting For: Increasing Satisfaction by Making Consumers Wait," *Journal of the Academy of Marketing Science*, 39 (2011): 889–905.

23. Debanjan Mitra and Peter N. Golder, "How Does Objective Quality Affect Perceived Quality?" *Marketing Science*, 25, no. 3 (2006): 230–247.

24. Ford Motor Company, "Ford's Swap Your Ride Campaign Proves a Real Eye-Opener for Consumers," April 5, 2011, https://media.ford.com/content/fordmedia/fna/us/en/news/2011/04/05/ford_s-_swap-your-ride-ad-campaign-proves-a-real-eye-opener-for-.html, accessed September 24, 2014.

25. Dawar and Parker, "Marketing Universals."

26. Elizabeth G. Miller and Barbara E. Kahn, "Shades of Meaning: The Effect of Color and Flavor Names on Consumer Choice," *Journal of Consumer Research*, 32, no. 1 (2006): 86–92.

27. J. Jacoby, D. E. Speller, and C. A. Kohn, "Brand Choice Behavior as a Function of Information Load: Replication and Extension," *Journal of Consumer Research*, 1 (1974): 33–41. Naresh K. Malhotra, "Information Load and Consumer Decision Making," *Journal of Consumer Research*, 8 (1982): 419–430.

28. Fasolo et al., "Escaping the Tyranny of Choice."

29. Ran Kivetz and Itamar Simonson, "The Effects of Incomplete Information on Consumer Choice,"

Journal of Marketing Research, 37, no. 4 (2000): 427–448.

30. Lauren Brewer, "May I help you? How stereotypes and innuendoes influence service encounters," PhD diss., Department of Marketing & Analysis, Louisiana Tech University, 2014.

31. Joseph F. Hair, Jr., Rolph Anderson, Ronald L. Tatham, and William C. Black, *Multivariate Data Analysis*, 5th ed. (Upper Saddle River, NJ: Prentice Hall, 1998).

32. Peter Wright, "Consumer Choice Strategies: Simplifying vs. Optimizing," *Journal of Marketing Research*, 12 (February 1975): 60–67.

33. Hirschman and Krishnan, "Subjective and Objective Criteria in Consumer Choice." Julie Baker, A. Parasuraman, Dhruv Grewal, and Glenn B. Voss, "The Influence of Multiple Store Environmental Cues on Perceived Merchandise Value and Purchase Intentions," *Journal of Retailing*, 66, no. 2 (2002): 120–142.

34. Matt Lindner, "Online Sales Will Reach $523 Billion by 2020 in the U.S.," *Internet Retailer* (online), online content retrieved at https://www.internetretailer.com/2016/01/29/online-sales-will-reach-523-billion-2020-us, accessed May 11, 2016.

35. Alex Fitzpatrick, "See Proof Everybody Is Doing Their Black Friday Shopping Online Now," *Time*, December 1, 2015, online content retrieved at http://time.com/4130835/online-shopping-black-friday-cyber-monday/, accessed May 11, 2016.

36. Greg Bensinger and Laura Stevens, "Amazon to Expand Grocery Business with New Convenience Stores," *The Wall Street Journal* (online), October 12, 2016.

Case 4–1

1. Jeff Bertolucci, "Smartphone Sales Boom—Who Needs a Laptop?" *PCWorld*, February 4, 2012, http://www.pcworld.com/article/249313/smartphone_sales_boom_who_needs_a_laptop.html, accessed June 5, 2012.

2. Erik Kain, "Smartphone Shipments Top PCs for First Time Ever," *Forbes*, February 4, 2012, http://www.forbes.com/sites/erikkain/2012/02/04/smartphone-shipments-top-pcs-for-the-first-time-ever/, accessed June 5, 2012.

3. Knowlton Thomas, "Smartphones Outsell PCs for First Time Ever, Tablets Lead Growth by a Long Shot," Techvibes.com, February 3, 2012, http://www.techvibes.com/blog/smartphones-outsell-pcs-for-the-first-time-ever-tablets-lead-growth-by-a-long-shot-report-2012-02-03, accessed September 25, 2014.

4. Mark Kyrnin, "Tablet PCs vs. Laptops," About.com, 2012, http://compreviews.about.com/od/buyers/a/Tablets-vs-Laptops.htm, accessed June 5, 2012.

5. Ibid.

6. Nick Wingfield, "Time to Leave the Laptop Behind," *The Wall Street Journal*, February 23, 2009, http://online.wsj.com/article/SB122477763884262815.html, accessed June 5, 2012.

7. Eric Chan, "Size Matters: Tablets vs. Smartphones," *Businessweek*, March 16, 2011, http://www.businessweek.com/technology/content/mar2011/tc20110316_121017.htm, accessed June 5, 2012.

Case 4–2

1. Datamonitor, 2012. New Balance Athletic Shoe Company.

2. Tiffany Yannetta, "The Flatiron New Balance Concept Store Is No Joke," August 12, 2011, http://ny.racked.com/archives/2011/08/12/the_flatiron_new_balance_concept_store_is_no_joke.php, accessed March 28, 2012.

3. "New Balance Sees 15 Percent Growth This Year." SGB, September 2011. Available at http://www.alacrastore.com/storecontent/Business-and-Industry/275234714.

4. Natalie Bergeron, New Balance interview via email, March 17, 2012.

5. Mary Johnson, "New Balance Opens Its First North American 'Experience' Store in the Flatiron," August 12, 2011, http://www.dnainfo.com/20110812/murray-hill-gramercy/new-balance-opens-its-first-north-american-experience-store-flatiron (accessed March 28, 2012).

6. Judy Piktelis, New Balance interview, March 18, 2012.

7. Dedham Quick facts, 2012, http://quickfacts.census.gov/qfd/states/25/2516530.html.

8. Dedham Demographics, http://dedham.areaconnect.com/statistics.htm.

9. Legacy Place, http://www.legacyplace.com/.

10. Piktelis.

11. Kings Events (2012). http://www.kingsdedham.com/kings/events.php.

12. Piktelis.

13. "New Balance, Red Sox Strike Sponsorship Deal," *Team Business*, 3 no. 2 (April 4, 2011): 12.

14

1. Robert B. Woodruff, "Customer Value: The Next Source for Competitive Advantage," *Journal of the Academy of Marketing Science*, 25, no. 2 (1997): 139–153.

2. M. B. Beverland and F. Farrelly, "The Quest for Authenticity in Consumption: Consumers' Purposive Choice of Authentic Cues to Shape Experienced Outcomes," *Journal of Consumer Research*, 36 (February 2010): 838–856.

3. V. L. Thomas and K. Fowler (2016) "Examining the Impact of Brand Transgressions on Consumers' Perceptions of Celebrity Endorsers," *Journal of Advertising*, 1–14.

4. Paul G. Patterson and Richard G. Spreng, "Modeling the Relationship Between Perceived Value, Satisfaction, and Repurchase Intentions in a Business-to-Business, Services Context: An Empirical Investigation," *International Journal of Industry Management*, 8, no. 5 (1997): 414–434.

5. R. F. Lusch and S. L. Vargo, *Service-Dominant Logic: Premises, Perspectives, Possibilities* (Cambridge University Press, UK, 2014).

6. D. Maity and T. J. Arnold, "Search: An Expense of an Experience? Exploring the Influence of Search on Product Return Intentions," *Psychology & Marketing*, 30 (July 2013): 576–587.

7. The American Consumer Satisfaction Index, www.theacsi.org, accessed June 27, 2016.

8. Stanley Slater, "Developing a Customer Value-Based Theory of the Firm," *Journal of the Academy of Marketing Science*, 25, no. 2 (1997): 162–167.

9. Morris B. Holbrook, "Emotion in the Consumption Experience: Toward a Model of the Human Consumer," in *The Role of Affect in Consumer Behavior: Emerging Theories and Applications*, ed. Robert A. Peterson et al. (Lexington, MA: Heath, 1986), 17–52.

10. Barry J. Babin and Kevin William James, "A Brief Retrospective and Introspective on Value," *European Business Review*, 22 (2010): 471–478.

11. http://www.coriolisresearch.com/pdfs/coriolis _understanding_trader_joes_final.pdf, accessed June 27, 2016; http://money.cnn.com/2016/03/31/pf /trader-joes-whole-foods-prices/index.html, accessed June 27, 2016.

12. S. Banjo, "Wal-Mart Looks to Grow by Getting Smaller," *The Wall Street Journal*, July 8, 2014, A1, A12.

13. This definition is based in part on Robert A. Westbrook and Richard L. Oliver, "The Dimensionality of Consumption Emotion Patterns and Consumer Satisfaction," *Journal of Consumer Research*, 18, no. 1 (1991): 84–91.

14. T. Keningham, S. Gupta, L. Aksoy, and A. Buoye, "The High Price of Customer Satisfaction," *Sloan Management Review* (Spring 2014): 37–46.

15. Barry J. Babin and Mitch Griffin, "The Nature of Satisfaction: An Updated Examination and Analysis," *Journal of Business Research*, 41 (1998): 127–136.

16. M. Eisenbeiss, M. Cornelißen, K. Backhaus, and W. D. Hoyer, "Nonlinear and Asymmetric Returns on Customer Satisfaction: Do They Vary Across Situations and Consumers?" *Journal of the Academy of Marketing Science*, 42, no. 3 (2014): 242–263.

17. Richard L. Oliver, "Measurement and Evaluation of Satisfaction Processes in Retail Settings," *Journal of Retailing*, 57 (Fall 1983): 25–48.

18. Gilbert A. Churchill, Jr., and Carol Surprenant, "An Investigation into the Determinants of Consumer Satisfaction," *Journal of Marketing Research*, 19, no. 4 (1982): 491–504.

19. Villapez, L. (2016), "Apple Inc. Design Fails: 7 Design Flaws That Remind Us Steve Jos Is Gone," *International Business Times*, http://www .ibtimes.com/apple-inc-product-fails-7-design -flaws-remind-us-steve-jobs-gone-2292569

20. Valarie A. Zeithaml, Leonard L. Berry, and A. Parasuraman, "The Nature and Determinants of Customer Expectations of Service," *Journal of the Academy of Marketing Science*, 21, no. 1 (1993): 1–12.

21. David K. Tse and Peter C. Wilton, "Models of Consumer Satisfaction Formation: An Extension," *Journal of Marketing Research*, 24, no. 2 (1988): 204–212.

22. Stephen J. Hoch and John Deighton, "Managing What Consumers Learn from Experience," *Journal of Marketing*, 53, no. 2 (1989): 1–20.

23. Y. Kim and B. Wansink, "How Retailers' Recommendations and Return Policies Alter Product Evaluations," *Journal of Retailing*, 88, no. 4 (2012): 528–541.

24. J.G. Olson, B. McFerran, A.C. Morales, and D. Dahl (2016), "Wealth and Welfare: Divergent Moral Reactions to Ethical Consumer Choices," *Journal of Consumer Research*, 42, 869–896. http:// www.webmd.com/food-recipes/organic-food -better, accessed July 4, 2016; S.B. Lange (2016), "No Scientific Proof Organic Food Is Healthier than Non-Organic," *ScienceNordic*, (January 26, 2016), http://sciencenordic.com/no-scientific-proof -organic-food-healthier-non-organic-food, accessed July 4, 2016.

25. For a discussion of this topic, see F. A. Carrilat, J. Fernando, and J. P. Mulki, "The Validity of the SERVQUAL and SERVPREF Scales," *International Journal of Service Industry Management*, 18 (May 2007): 472–490. Also see C. Bebko, L. M. Sciulli, and R. K. Garg, "Consumers' Level of Expectations for Services and the Role of Implicit Service Promises," *Services Marketing Quarterly*, 28 (2006): 1–23.

26. R. Lasonsky (2016), "Social Media Customer Service Isn't All It's Cracked Up to Be," *Nextiva*, (June 14, 2016), nextiva.com/voip/tuesday-tip -social-media-customer-service-isnt-all-its-cracked -up-to-be, accessed July 4, 2016.

27. Richard A. Spreng, Scott B. MacKenzie, and Richard W. Olshavsky, "A Reexamination of the Determinants of Consumer Satisfaction," *Journal of Marketing*, 00, no. 3 (1990): 15–32.

28. B. Olsen, "Reflexive Introspection on Sharing Gifts and Shaping Stories," *Journal of Business Research*, 65 (April 2012): 467–474.

29. J. Stacey Adams, "Inequity in Social Exchange," in *Advances in Experimental Social Psychology*, vol. 2, ed. Richard Berkowitz (New York: Academic Press, 1965), 267–299.

30. D. C. Barnes, M. B. Beauchamp, and C. Webster, "To Delight, or Not to Delight? This Is the Question Service Firms Must Address," *Journal of Marketing, Theory and Practice*, 18 (Summer 2010): 275–283.

31. P. Aggarwal and R. P. Larrick, "When Consumers Care About Being Treated Fairly: The Interaction of Relationship Norms and Fairness Norms," *Journal of Consumer Psychology*, 22 (2012): 114–127.

32. Bernard Wiener, "Attributional Thoughts about Consumer Behavior," *Journal of Consumer Research*, 27, no. 3 (2000): 382–387.

33. L. Festinger, *A Theory of Cognitive Dissonance* (Stanford, CA: Stanford University Press, 1957).

34. Jillian C. Sweeney, Douglas Hausknecht, and Geoffrey N. Soutar, "Cognitive Dissonance after Purchase: A Multidimensional Scale," *Psychology & Marketing*, 17, no. 5 (2000): 369–387.

35. J. Paul Peter, Gilbert A. Churchill, Jr., and Tom J. Brown, "Caution in the Use of Difference Scores in Consumer Research," *Journal of Consumer Research*, 19, no. 4 (1993): 655–662.

36. Babin and Griffin, "The Nature of Satisfaction."

37. Jacob Jacoby, Carol K. Berning, and Thomas F. Dietvorst, "What About Disposition?" *Journal of Marketing*, 41, no. 2 (1977): 22–28.

38. S. Roper and C. Parker, "Doing Well by Doing Good: A Quantitative Investigation of the Litter Effect," *Journal of Business Research*, 66 (2013): 2262–2268.

39. Linda L. Price, Eric J. Arnould, and Carolyn Folkman Curasi, "Older Consumers' Disposition of Special Possessions," *Journal of Consumer Research*, 27, no. 2 (2000): 179–182.

40. John L. Lastovicka and Karen V. Fernandez, "Three Paths to Disposition: The Movement of Meaningful Possessions to Strangers," *Journal of Consumer Research*, 31, no. 4 (2005): 813–823.

41. K. L. Haws, R. W. Naylor, R. A. Coulter, and W. O. Bearden, "Keeping It All without Being Buried Alive: Understanding Product Retention Tendency," *Journal of Consumer Psychology*, 22 (2012): 224–236.

42. Robin A. Coulter and Mark Ligas, "To Retain or to Relinquish: Exploring the Disposition Practices of Packrats and Purgers," *Advances in Consumer Research*, 30 (2003): 38–43.

15

1. J. Van Doorn and P. C. Verhoef, "Critical Incidents and the Impact of Satisfaction on Customer Share," *Journal of Marketing*, 72 (July 2008): 123–142.

2. M. Kalamas, M. Laroche, and L. Makdessian, "Reaching the Boiling Point: Consumers' Negative Affective Reactions to Firm-Attributed Service Failures," *Journal of Business Research*, 61 (2008): 813–824.

3. P. Williams, M. Sajid Khan, N. Ul Ashil, and E. Naumann, "Customer Attitudes of Stayers and Defectors in B2B Services: Are They Really Different?" *Industrial Marketing Management*, 40 (July 2011): 805–815.

4. L. C. Wan, "Culture's Impact on Consumer Complaining Responses to Embarrassing Service Failure," *Journal of Business Research*, 66 (2014): 298–305.

5. Survey: Twice as many people tell others about bad service than good. http://www.retailcustomerexperience .com/articles/survey-twice-as-many-people-tell-others -about-bad-service-than-good/, accessed July 9, 2016.

6. C. M. Voorhees, M. K. Brady, and D. M. Horowitz, "A Voice from the Silent Masses: An Exploratory and Comparative Analysis of Non-Complaining," *Journal of the Academy of Marketing Science*, 34 (September 2006): 513–527.

7. https://www.bbb.org/north-east-florida/for -businesses/how-to-handle-a-customer-complaint/, accessed July 9, 2016.

8. K. Goudarzi, A. Borges, and J. C. Chebat, "Should Retailers Pay to Bring Customers Back? The Impact of Quick Response and Coupons on Purchase Outcomes," *Journal of Business Research*, 66 (2013): 665–669.

9. L. S. Alvarez, R. V. Casielles, and A. M. D. Martin, "Analysis of the Role of Complaint Management in the Context of Relationship Marketing," *Journal of Marketing Management*, 27 (February 2011): 143–164.

10. J. R. McColl-Kennedy, P. G. Patterson, A. K. Smith, and M. K. Brady, "Customer Rage Episodes: Emotions, Expressions and Behaviors," *Journal of Retailing*, 85 (2009): 222–237.

11. H. Zourrig, J.C. Chebat, and R. Tofoli, "Consumer Revenge Behavior: A Cross-Cultural Perspective," *Journal of Business Research*, 62 (2009): 995–1001. Kalamas et al., "Reaching the Boiling Point."

12. J. Joireman, Y. Gregoire, B. Devezer, and T. M. Tripp, "When Do Customers Offer Firms a 'Second Chance' Following a Double Deviation? The Impact of Inferred Firm Motives on Customer Revenge and Reconciliation," *Journal of Retailing*, 89 (September 2013): 315–337.

13. H. Holland, "Woman Hurls Ketchup Bottles After Being Shushed for Talking on Cell," DNAinfo, April 9, 2014, http://www.dnainfo.com/new-york /20140409/flatiron/woman-hurls-ketchup-bottles -after-being-shushed-for-talking-on-cellphone, accessed July 20, 2014.

14. Ibid.

15. J. Romaniuk, "Word of Mouth and the Viewing of Television Programs," *Journal of Advertising Research*, 47 (December 2007), 462–470.

16. K. E. Reynolds, M. A. Jones, C. F. Musgrove, and S. T. Gillison, "An Investigation of Retail Outcomes Comparing Two Types of Browsers," *Journal of Business Research*, 65 (2012): 1090–1095.

17. J. Gebauer, J. Fuller, and R. Pezzei, "The Dark and the Bright Side of Co-Creation: Triggers of Member Behavior in Online Innovation Communities," *Journal of Business Research*, 66 (2013): 1516–1527.

18. W. C. Martin and J. E. Lueg, "Modeling Word-of-Mouth Usage," *Journal of Business Research*, 66 (2013): 801–808.

19. I.P. Riquelme, S. Romn, and D. Iacobucci (2016), "Consumers' Perceptions of Online and Offline Retailer Deception: A Moderated Mediation Analysis," *Journal of Interactive Marketing*, 35, 16–26.

20. yogabycandace.com/blog/2016/3/14/confessions-of-ayoga-teacher-lululemon, accessed October 28, 2016.

21. L. Klie, "Hearing 140 Million Voices," *Customer Relationship Management* (June 2012): 21–26.

22. S. Chaba (2016), "Ikea Recalls 29 Million Dressers After Death of Third Child," ibtimes, http://www.ibtimes.com/ikea-recall-29-million-dressers-after-death-third-child-two-years-2387515, accessed October 28, 2016.

23. Kim Komando, "Facebook Ran a Secret Psychology Experiment on 700,000 Users," June 30, 2014, http://www.komando.com/happening-now/260080/facebook-ran-a-secret-psychology-experiment-on-700000-users/all; Samuel Gibbs, *The Guardian*, July 4, 2014, http://www.theguardian.com/technology/2014/jul/04/facebook-denies-emotion-contagion-study-government-military-ties, accessed July 21, 2014.

24. J. G. Blodgett, D. H. Granbois, and R. G. Walters, "The Effects of Perceived Justice on Complainants' Negative Word-of-Mouth Behavior and Repatronage Intentions," *Journal of Retailing*, 69 (Winter 1993): 399–428.

25. P. M. Nyer and M. Gopinath, "Effects of Complaining versus Negative WOM on Subsequent Changes in Satisfaction: The Role of Public Commitment," *Psychology & Marketing*, 22 (December 2005): 937–953.

26. F. Lange and M. Dahlen, "Too Much Bad PR Can Make Ads Ineffective," *Journal of Advertising Research*, 46 (December 2006): 528–542. J. Aaker, S. Fournier, and B. S. Adam, "When Good Brands Go Bad," *Journal of Consumer Research*, 31 (June 2004): 1–16.

27. Lange and Dahlen, "Too Much Bad PR Can Make Ads Ineffective."

28. Z. Feng and X. Zhang, "Impact of Online Consumer Reviews on Sales: The Moderating Role of Product and Consumer Characteristics," *Journal of Marketing*, 74 (March 2010): 133–148.

29. T. A. Burnham, J. K. Frels, and V. Mahajan, "Consumer Switching Costs: A Typology, Antecedents and Consequences," *Journal of the Academy of Marketing Science* 31 (Spring 2003): 109–126.

30. M. L. Andrews, R. L. Benedicktus, and M. K. Brady, "The Effect of Incentives on Customer Evaluations of Service Bundles," *Journal of Business Research*, 63 (2010): 71–76.

31. C. Antón, C. Camarero, and M. Carrero, "The Mediating Effect of Satisfaction on Consumers' Switching Intention," *Psychology & Marketing*, 24 (June 2007): 511–538.

32. M. A. Jones, K. E. Reynolds, D. L. Mothersbaugh, and S. E. Beatty, "The Positive and Negative Effects of Switching Costs on Relational Outcomes," *Journal of Services Research*, 9 (May 2007): 335–355.

33. G. Balabanis, N. Reynolds, and A. Simintiras, "Base of E-Store Loyalty: Perceived Switching Barriers and Satisfaction," *Journal of Business Research*, 59 (February 2006): 214–224.

34. T. Keiningham, S. Gupta, L. Aksoy, and A. Buoye, "The High Price of Customer Satisfaction," *Sloan Management Review*, 55 (Spring 2014): 37–46.

35. B. Horovitz, "McDonald's: Last in Satisfaction—Again," *The Wall Street Journal*, June 20, 2014, B6.

36. J. T. Gourville, "Eager Sellers and Stony Buyers: Understanding the Psychology of New-Product Adoption," *Harvard Business Review*, 84 (June 2006): 99–106.

37. A. W. Magi, "Share of Wallet in Retailing: The Effects of Consumer Satisfaction, Loyalty Cards and Shopper Characteristics," *Journal of Retailing*, 79 (Summer 2003): 97–106.

38. L. Xia and M. Kukar-Kinney, "For our valued customers only: Examining consumer responses to preferential treatment practices," *Journal of Business Research*, 67, no. 11, 2014, doi: 10.1016/j.jbusres.2014.02.002.

39. Keiningham et al., "The High Price of Customer Satisfaction."

40. F. V. Wangenheim, "Postswitching Negative Word of Mouth," *Journal of Services Research*, 8 (2005): 67–78.

41. "Carnival Dream Turns Nightmare: Power Outages, Overflowing Toilets Reported," Fox News, March 14, 2013, http://www.foxnews.com/us/2013/03/14/power-outages-overflowing-toilets-reportedly-plague-another-carnival-cruise/, accessed July 23, 2014.

42. H. C. Chiu, Y. C. Hsieh, Y. C. Li, and L. Monle, "Relationship Marketing and Consumer Switching Behavior," *Journal of Business Research*, 58 (December 2005): 1681–1689.

43. B. J. Babin and J. P. Attaway, "Atmospheric Affect as a Tool for Creating Value and Gaining Share of Customer," *Journal of Business Research*, 49 (August 2000): 91–99.

44. E. C. Chang, Y. Lv, T. J. Chou, Q. He, and Z. Song, "Now or Later: Delay's Effects on Post-Consumption Emotions and Consumer Loyalty," *Journal of Business Research*, 67, no. 7 (2014), 1368–1375.

45. M. Zhang, L. Guo, M. Hu, and W. Liu (2016), "Influence of Customer Engagement with Company Social Networks on Stickiness: Mediating Effect of Customer Value Creation," *International Journal of Information Management*, dx.doi.org/10.1016/j.ijinfomgt.2016.04.010.

46. W. Zhuang (2010). *Balancing customer and marketing inputs to maximize the value experience.* Louisiana Tech University.

47. R. W. Palmatier, R. P. Dant, D. Grewal, and K. R. Evans, "Factors Influencing the Effectiveness of Relationship Marketing: A Meta-Analysis," *Journal of Marketing*, 70 (October 2006): 136–153.

48. R. W. Palmatier, L. K. Scheer, M. B. Houston, K. R. Evans, and S. Gopalakrishna, "Use of Relationship Marketing Programs in Building Customer-Salesperson and Customer-Firm Relationships: Differential Influences on Financial Outcomes," *International Journal of Research in Marketing*, 24 (2007): 210–223.

16

1. R. A. Fullerton and G. Punj, "Repercussions of Promoting an Ideology of Consumption: Consumer Misbehavior," *Journal of Business Research*, 57 (2004): 1239–1249.

2. Aubry R. Fowler III, Barry J. Babin, and Amy K. Este, "Burning for Fun or Money: Illicit Consumer Behavior in a Contemporary Context," paper presented at the Academy of Marketing Science Annual Conference, May 27, 2005, Tampa, FL.

3. Fullerton and Punj, "Repercussions of Promoting an Ideology of Consumption."

4. Fowler et al., "Burning for Fun or Money."

5. Scott J. Vitell, "Consumer Ethics Research: Review, Synthesis and Suggestions for the Future," *Journal of Business Ethics*, 43, no. 1/2 (March 2003): 33–47.

6. Barry J. Babin and Laurie A. Babin, "Effects of Moral Cognitions and Consumer Emotions on Shoplifting Intentions," *Psychology & Marketing*, 13 (December 1996): 785–802.

7. Vitell, "Consumer Ethics Research."

8. Shelby Hunt and Scott Vitell, "A General Theory of Marketing Ethics," *Journal of Macromarketing*, 6, no. 1 (Spring 1986): 5–16.

9. This section is based on Fullerton and Punj, "Repercussions of Promoting an Ideology of Consumption."

10. Robert Merton, *Social Theory and Social Structure* (New York: Free Press, 1968).

11. V. Lee Hamilton and David Rauma, "Social Psychology of Deviance and Law," in *Sociological Perspectives on Social Psychology*, ed. Karen S. Cook, Gary A. Fine, and James S. House (Boston: Allyn and Bacon, 1995), 524–547.

12. Clint Rainey and Allegra Hobbs, "Been Caught Stealing," *New York Magazine*, December 8, 2013, nymag.com/news/intelligencer/topic/shoplifting-2013-12/, accessed May 19, 2016.

13. National Retail Federation, "The 2015 National Retail Security Survey," June 2015, https://nrf.com/resources/retail-library/national-retail-security-survey-2015, accessed May 19, 2016.

14. Dena Cox, Anthony D. Cox, and George P. Moschis, "When Consumer Behavior Goes Bad: An Investigation of Adolescent Shoplifting," *Journal of Consumer Research*, 17, no. 2 (September 1990): 149–159.

15. Babin and Babin, "Effects of Moral Cognitions." Cynthia Webster, "Exploring the Psychodynamics of Consumer Shoplifting Behavior," *American Marketing Association Conference Proceedings*, 11 (2000): 360–365.

16. Barry J. Babin and Mitch Griffin, "A Closer Look at the Influence of Age on Consumer Ethics," *Advances in Consumer Research*, 22 (1995): 668–673.

17. "The Compliance Gap: BSA Global Software Survey 2014," Business Software Alliance, 2014, http://globalstudy.bsa.org/2013/downloads/studies/2013GlobalSurvey_inbrief_en.pdf, accessed May 20, 2016.

18. Fowler et al., "Burning for Fun or Money."

19. Corilyn Shropshire, "Spam Floods Inboxes," *Knight Ridder Tribune Business News*, January 23, 2007, 1. "U.S. Branded 'Biggest Spam and Virus Host,'" *Precision Marketing*, January 26, 2007, 9.

20. Mark Smail, "Are We Risking Our Digital Lives?" Technewsworld.com, January 20, 2010, http://www.technewsworld.com/story/69145.html, accessed June 30, 2010.

21. "Online Computer Virus Statistics," Statisticbrain.com, June 27, 2014, http://www.statisticbrain.com/online-computer-virus-statistics/, accessed June 27, 2014.

22. Beth Herskovits, "APA Shows Public How Psychology Fits into Their Lives," *PR Week*, January 2, 2006, 19.

23. Amanda Lenhart, "Cyberbullying: What the Research Is Telling Us . . . ," Pew Internet & American Life Project, http://www.pewinternet.org/Presentations/2010/May/Cyberbullying-2010.aspx, accessed May 27, 2011.

24. Online content retrieved at McAfee.com, "Cyberbullying Triples According to New McAfee 2014 Teens and the Screen Study," June 3, 2014,

http://www.mcafee.com/us/about/news/2014 /q2/20140603-01.aspx, accessed June 27, 2014.

25. Monica Anderson, "Parents, Teens and Digital Monitoring," Pew Research Center, January 7, 2016, http://www.pewinternet.org/2016/01/07 /parents-teens-and-digital-monitoring/, accessed May 18, 2016.

26. Coalition Against Insurance Fraud, http://www .insurancefraud.org, accessed May 18, 2016.

27. Indentitytheft.info, http://www.identitytheft .info/victims.aspx, accessed May 18, 2016..

28. Kathryne Dupre, Tim Jones, and Shirley Taylor, "Dealing with the Difficult: Understanding Difficult Behaviors in a Service Encounter," *American Marketing Association Proceedings,* 2001, 173–80.

29. Mary J. Bitner, Bernard H. Booms, and Lois Mohr, "Critical Service Encounters: The Employee's Viewpoint," *Journal of Marketing,* 58, no. 4 (1994): 95–106.

30. Lloyd Harris and Kate L. Reynolds, "The Consequences of Dysfunctional Customer Behavior," *Journal of Service Research,* 6, no. 2 (November 2003): 144–161.

31. Scott Thorne, "An Exploratory Investigation of the Characteristics of Consumer Fanaticism," *Qualitative Market Research,* 9, no. 1 (2006), 51–72. Robert W. Pimentel and Kristy E. Reynolds, "A Model for Consumer Devotion: Affective Commitment with Proactive Sustaining Behaviors," *Academy of Marketing Science Review,* 8, no. 7 (2004): 1–45. Kirk L. Wakefield and Daniel L. Wann, "An Examination of Dysfunctional Sports Fans: Method of Classification and Relationships with Problem Behaviors," *Journal of Leisure Research,* 38 (2006): 168–186. Kenneth A. Hunt, Terry Bristol, and R. Edward Bashaw, "A Conceptual Approach to Classifying Sports Fans," *Journal of Services Marketing,* 13 (1999): 439–449. Bill Saporito, "Why Fans and Players Are Playing So Rough," *Time,* December 6, 2004, 30–35.

32. Kate L. Reynolds and Lloyd C. Harris, "When Service Failure Is Not Service Failure: An Exploration of the Forms and Motives of 'Illegitimate' Customer Complaining," *Journal of Services Marketing,* 19 (2005): 321–335.

33. Consumer Products Safety Commission, http:// www.cpsc.gov, accessed March 17, 2008.

34. Jeffrey Stoltman and Fred Morgan, "Psychological Dimensions of Unsafe Product Usage," in *Marketing Theory and Applications,* 4th ed., ed. Rajan Varadarajan and Bernard Jaworski (Chicago: American Marketing Association, 1993).

35. "Road Rage Leads to More Road Rage," National Safety Commission, December 6, 2006, http://www.nationalsafetycommission.com, accessed March 17, 2008.

36. Jim Crimmins and Chris Callahan, "Reducing Road Rage: The Role of Target Insight in Advertising for Social Change," *Journal of Advertising Research* (December 2003): 381–390.

37. Sterling A. Bone and John C. Mowen, "Identifying the Traits of Aggressive and Distracted Drivers: A Hierarchical Trait Model Approach," *Journal of Consumer Behaviour,* 5, no. 5, (2006): 454–465; also D. A. Hennessy and D. L. Wiesenthal, "The Relationship Between Traffic Congestion, Driver Stress, and Direct Versus Indirect Coping Behaviors," *Ergonomics,* 40 (1997): 348–361.

38. Centers for Disease Control and Prevention, http://www.cdc.gov/motorvehiclesafety/impaired _driving/impaired-drv_factsheet.html, accessed May 18, 2016.; Lifetips.com, "Useful Drunk Driving Facts", http://dui.lifetips.com//cat/61352/drunk -driving-facts-stats/index.html, accessed May 18, 2016.

39. "Impaired Driving: Get the Facts," Centers for Disease Control and Prevention, http://www .cdc.gov/MotorVehicleSafety/Impaired_Driving /impaired-drv_factsheet.html, accessed June 17, 2009.

40. "Drinking and Driving: A Threat to Everyone," Centers for Disease Control and Prevention, October 4, 2011, http://www.cdc.gov/vitalsigns /drinkinganddriving/?s_cid=vitalsigns-092 -bb#LatestFindings, accessed May 8, 2012.

41. National Traffic Safety Administration, "The Economic and Societal Impact of Motor Vehicle Crashes 2010 (Revised)," May 2015.

42. "Underage Drinking," Under *Your* Influence website (National Highway Traffic Safety Administration), http://underyourinfluence.org/underage -drinking, accessed March 4, 2013.

43. Kyran P. Quinlan, Robert D. Brewer, Paul Siegel, David A. Sleet, Ali H. Mokdad, Ruth A. Shults, and Nicole Flowers, "Alcohol Impaired Driving among U.S. Adults 1993–2003," *American Journal of Preventive Medicine* (May 2005): 346–350.

44. International Telecommunication Union, May 2016, http://www.itu.int/en/ITU-D/Statistics /Pages/stat/default.aspx, accessed May 18, 2016.

45. "Mobile Technology Fact Sheet," Pew Research Center, January 2014, http://www.pewinternet.org /fact-sheets/mobile-technology-fact-sheet/, accessed June 27, 2014.

46. "Cell Phones and Driving," Insurance Information Institute, http://www.iii.org/issues _updates/cellphones-and-driving.html, accessed May 8, 2012.

47. Carol Ronis, "Teen Driver Safety," AAA Foundation, 2012, http://www.aaafoundation.org/pdf /DistractedDrivingAmongNewlyLicensedTeen- DriversPR.pdf, accessed May 8, 2012.

48. "Cell Phones and Driving," Insurance Information Institute.

49. Governors Highway Safety Association, "Distracted Driving Laws, " May 2016, http://www .ghsa.org/html/stateinfo/laws/cellphone_laws.html, accessed November 9, 2016.

50. D. Searcy, "Currents: A Lawyer, Some Teens and a Fight over Sexting," *The Wall Street Journal,* April 21, 2009, A17. A. Kingston, "The Sexting Scare," *Maclean's,* March 16, 2009, 52. W. Koch, "Teens Caught 'Sexting' Face Porn Charges," *USA Today,* March 11, 2009, http://www.usatoday.com /tech/wireless/2009-03-11-sexting_N.htm, accessed June 18, 2009.

51. Renee St. Pierre, "Sexting Behaviours among Teens: Dating and Romance in the Digital Age?" *International Centre for Youth Gambling Problems and High-Risk Behaviors,* 11, no. 3 (2011), available at www.youthgambling.com, accessed May 9, 2012.

52. Sameer Hinduja and Justin W. Patchin, "State Sexting Laws," *Cyberbullying Research Center,* July 2015, www.cyberbullying.us, accessed November 9, 2016.

53. This definition is based on Thomas C. O'Guinn and Ronald J. Faber, "Compulsive Buying: A Phenomenological Exploration," *Journal of Consumer Research,* 16, no. 2 (1989): 147–157.

54. Rajan Nataraajan and Brent G. Goff, "Manifestations of Compulsiveness in the Consumer-Marketplace Domain," *Psychology & Marketing,* 9 (1992): 31–44.

55. This definition is based on Ronald Faber and Thomas O'Guinn, "A Clinical Screener for Compulsive Buying," *Journal of Consumer Research,* 19, no. 3 (1992): 459–469.

56. Elizabeth C. Hirschman, "The Consciousness of Addiction: Toward a General Theory of Compulsive Consumption," *Journal of Consumer Research* (September 1992): 155–179. O'Guinn and Faber, "Compulsive Buying." Helga Dittmar, "A New Look at Compulsive Buying: Self-Discrepancies and Materialistic Values as Predictors of Compulsive Buying Tendencies," *Journal of Social and Clinical Psychology* (September 2005): 832–859.

57. Jeff Joireman, Jeremy Kees, and David Sprott, "Concern with Immediate Consequences Magnifies the Impact of Compulsive Buying Tendencies on College Students' Credit Card Debt," *Journal of Consumer Affairs,* 44, no. 1 (2010): 155–178.

58. Kay M. Palan, Paula C. Morrow, Allan Trapp II, and Virginia Blackburn, "Compulsive Buying Behavior in College Students: The Mediating Role of Credit Card Abuse," *Journal of Marketing Theory and Practice,* 19, no. 1 (2011): 81–96.

59. James A. Roberts, Chris Manolis, and John F. Tanner, Jr., "Adolescent Autonomy and the Impact of Family Structure on Materialism and Compulsive Buying," *Journal of Marketing Theory and Practice,* 14, no. 4 (2006): 301–314.

60. James A. Roberts, "Compulsive Buying among College Students: An Investigation of Its Antecedents, Consequences, and Implications for Public Policy," *Journal of Consumer Affairs,* 32, no. 2 (1998): 295–319. O'Guinn and Faber, "Compulsive Buying."

61. D. W. Black, "Assessment of Compulsive Buying," in *I Shop, Therefore I Am: Compulsive Buying and the Search for Self,* ed. A. L. Benson (Northvale, NJ: Jason Aronson, 2000), 191–216.

62. Jessica Parker-Pope, "This Is Your Brand at the Mall: Why Shopping Makes You Feel So Good," *The Wall Street Journal,* December 6, 2005, D1.

63. Lorrin M. Koran, Ronald J. Faber, Elias Aboujauode, Michael D. Large, and Richard T. Serpe, "Estimated Prevalence of Compulsive Buying Behavior in the United States," *The American Journal of Psychiatry* (October 2006): 1806–1812.

64. Binge-eating.com, http://www.binge-eating .com/, accessed May 9, 2012.

65. Susan Yanovski and Billinda K. Dubbert, "Association of Binge Eating Disorder and Psychiatric Comorbidity in Obese Subjects," *The American Journal of Psychiatry* (October 1993): 1472–1479.

66. Manoj Thomas, Kalpesh Kaushik Desai, and Satheeshkumar Seenivasan, "How Credit Card Payments Increase Unhealthy Food Purchases: Visceral Regulation of Vices," *Journal of Consumer Research,* 38 (June 2011): 126–139.

67. National Institute for Alcohol Abuse and Alcoholism, http://www.niaaa.nih.gov, accessed November 9, 2016.

68. Substance Abuse and Mental Health Services Administration, http://www.samhsa.gov/data /NSDUH/2k11Results/NSDUHresults2011 .htm#3.1.6, accessed March 7, 2013.

69. Maira G. Piacentini and Emma N. Banister, "Getting Hammered? . . . Students Coping with Alcohol," *Journal of Consumer Behaviour,* 5, no. 2 (2006): 145–156.

70. H. Wechsler, J. E. Lee, M. Kuo, M. Seibring, T. F. Nelson, and H. P. Lee, "Trends in College Binge Drinking During a Period of Increased Prevention Efforts: Findings from Four Harvard School of Public Health Study Surveys," *Journal of American College Health,* 50 (2002): 203–217. C. A. Presley, M. A. Leichliter, and P. W. Meilman, *Alcohol and Drugs on American College Campuses: A Report to College Presidents: Third in a Series* (Carbondale, IL: Core Institute, Southern Illinois University, 1998).

71. "A Snapshot of Annual High-Risk College Drinking Consequences," College Drinking—Changing the Culture, July 1, 2010, www.collegedrinkingprevention.gov/StatsSummaries/snapshot.aspx, accessed June 1, 2011.

72. Soyeon Shim and Jennifer Maggs, "A Cognitive and Behavioral Hierarchical Decision-Making Model of College Students' Alcohol Consumption," *Psychology & Marketing*, 22, no. 8 (2005): 649–668.

73. Megan A. Moreno, Dimitri A. Christakis, Katie G. Egan, Libby N. Brockman, and Tara Becker, "Associations Between Displayed Alcohol References on Facebook and Problem Drinking among College Students," *Archives of Pediatric Adolescent Medicine*, 166, no. 2 (2012): 157–163.

74. National Institute on Alcohol Abuse and Alcoholism (2002). *A Call to Action: Changing the Culture of Drinking at U.S. Colleges,* National Institutes of Health, US Department of Health and Human Services.

75. Richard J. Bonnie and Mary Ellen O'Connell, eds., *Reducing Underage Drinking: A Collective Responsibility* (Washington, DC: Institute of Medicine, The National Academies Press, 2003).

76. This definition is based on Richard G. Netemeyer, Scot Burton, Leslie K. Cole, Donald A. Williamson, Nancy Zucker, Lisa Bertman, and Gretchen Diefenbach, "Characteristics and Beliefs Associated with Probable Pathological Gambling: A Pilot Study with Implications for the National Gambling Impact and Policy Commission," *Journal of Public Policy & Marketing*, 17, no. 2 (1998): 147–160.

77. George Balabanis, "The Relationship Between Lottery-Ticket and Scratch-Card Buying Behaviour, Personality and Other Compulsive Behaviors," *Journal of Consumer Behaviour*, 2, no. 1 (2002): 7–22.

78. Statistics based on information found at National Council on Problem Gambling, http://www.ncpgambling.org/i4a/pages/Index.cfm?pageID=3315#widespread, accessed November 9, 2016.

79. J. L. McComb and W. E. Hanson, "Problem Gambling on College Campuses," *NASPA Journal,* 46, no. 1 (2009): 1–29.

80. Suzi Levens, Anne-Marie Dyer, Cynthia Zubritsky, Kathryn Knott, and David W. Oslin, "Gambling Among Older, Primary Care Patients," *American Journal of Geriatric Psychiatry,* 13 (2005): 69–76. Peggy Sue Loroz, "Golden-Age Gambling: Psychological Benefits and Self-Concept Dynamics in Aging Consumers' Consumption Experiences," *Psychology & Marketing,* 25, no. 1 (2004): 323–350.

81. Hyokjin Kwak, George M. Zinkhan, and Elizabeth P. Lester Roushanzamir, "Compulsive Comorbidity and Its Psychological Antecedents: A Cross-Cultural Comparison Between the U.S. and South Korea," *The Journal of Consumer Marketing,* 21 (2004): 418–434. Netemeyer et al., "Characteristics and Beliefs Associated with Probable Pathological Gambling."

82. Monitoring the Future, "2015 Overview: Key Findings on Adolescent Drug Abuse," *The National Institute on Drug Abuse* at The National Institutes of Health, 2015.

83. Ibid.

84. "Results from the 2010 National Survey on Drug Use and Health: Summary of National Findings," NSDUH Series H-41, HHS Publication No. (SMA) 11-4658 (Rockville, MD: Substance Abuse and Mental Health Services Administration, 2011), http://oas.samhsa.gov/SDUH/2k10NSDUH/2k10Results.pdf, accessed May 11, 2012.

85. This definition is based on Gene R. Laczniak and Patrick E. Murphy, "Normative Perspectives for Ethical and Socially Responsible Marketing," *Journal of Macromarketing,* 26, no. 2 (2006): 154–177.

86. Rhoda H. Karpatkin, "Toward a Fair and Just Marketplace for All Consumers: The Responsibilities of Marketing Professionals," *Journal of Public Policy & Marketing,* 18, no. 1 (1999): 118–122.

87. Lan Xia, Kent B. Monroe, and Jennifer L. Cox, "The Price Is Unfair! A Conceptual Framework of Price Fairness Perceptions," *Journal of Marketing,* 68 (October 2004): 1–15. Margaret C. Campbell, "Perceptions of Price Fairness: Antecedents and Consequences," *Journal of Marketing Research,* 36 (May 1999): 187–199.

88. Philip Kotler, "What Consumerism Means for Marketers," *Harvard Business Review,* 50 (May–June 1972): 48–57.

89. Larry McShan, "Bruce Springsteen Slams Ticketmaster over Working on a Dream Ticket Sales," *New York Daily News*, February 4, 2009, http://www.nydailynews.com/gossip/2009/02/04/2009-02-04_bruce_springsteen_slams_ticketmaster_ove.html, accessed June 19, 2009.

90. Ben Sisario, "Ticketmaster Reaches Settlement on Complaints of Deceptive Sales," *The New York Times,* February 19, 2010, http://www.nytimes.com/2010/02/19/arts/music/19ticket.html, accessed May 14, 2012.

91. Josh Kosman, "MSG Execs Fired After Being Caught in Ticket Scalping Scandal," *New York Post,* January 22, 2016, http://nypost.com/2016/01/22/msg-execs-fired-after-being-caught-in-ticket-scalping-scandal/, accessed May 20, 2016.

92. N. Craig Smith and Elizabeth Cooper-Martin, "Ethics and Target Marketing: The Role of Product Harm and Consumer Vulnerability," *Journal of Marketing,* 61, no. 3 (1997): 1–20.

93. This definition is based on Tom J. Brown and Peter A. Dacin, "The Company and the Product: Corporate Associations and Consumer Product Responses," *Journal of Marketing,* 61, no. 1 (1997): 68–84.

94. Sankar Sen and C. B. Bhattacharya, "Does Doing Good Always Lead to Doing Better? Consumer Reactions to Corporate Social Responsibility," *Journal of Marketing Research,* 38, no. 2 (2001): 225–243.

95. Geoffrey P. Lantos, "The Boundaries of Strategic Corporate Social Responsibility," *Journal of Consumer Marketing,* 18, no. 7 (2001): 595–630. These assertions are based on several works including Xueming Luo and C. B. Bhattacharya, "Corporate Social Responsibility, Customer Satisfaction, and Market Value," *Journal of Marketing,* 70, no. 4 (2006): 1–18; Donald R. Lichenstein, Minette E. Drumwright, and Bridgette M. Braig, "The Effect of Corporate Social Responsibility on Customer Donations to Corporate-Supported Nonprofits," *Journal of Marketing,* 68, no. 4 (2004): 16–32; Sen and Bhattacharya, "Does Doing Good Always Lead to Doing Better?"; Brown and Dacin, "The Company and the Product."

96. Carlos J. Torelli, Alokparna Basu Monga, and Andrew M. Kaikati, "Doing Poorly by Doing Good: Corporate Social Responsibility and Brand Concepts," *Journal of Consumer Research,* 38 (February 2011): 948–963.

97. Kotler, "What Consumerism Means for Marketers."

98. Paul W. Grimes and George A. Chressanthis, "Assessing the Effect of Rent Control on Homelessness," *Journal of Urban Economics*, 41, no. 1 (1997): 23–37.

99. Federal Trade Commission, www.ftc.gov/bcp/conline/pubs/buspubs/ad-faqs.shtm, accessed March 17, 2008.

100. Kenneth C. Herbst, Eli J. Finkel, David Allan, and Grainne M. Fitzsimons, "On the Dangers of Pulling a Fast One: Advertisement Disclaimer Speed, Brand Trust, and Purchase Intention," *Journal of Consumer Research,* 38 (February 2011): 909–918.

101. American Advertising Federation, www.aaf.org, accessed May 14, 2012.

102. National Advertising Review Council, www.narcpartners.org/, accessed March 17, 2008.

103. "Television Advertising Leads to Unhealthy Habits in Children, Says APA Task Force," American Psychological Association, February 23, 2004, http://www.apa.org/releases/childrenads.html, accessed August 2007.

104. Anup Shah, "Children as Consumers," Global Issues, November 21, 2010, http://www.globalissues.org/article/237/children-as-consumers#Advertisingtochildrenisbigbusiness, accessed May 14, 2012.

105. Children's Advertising Review Unit, Better Business Bureau, http://www.caru.org/guidelines/index.aspx, accessed July 2, 2010.

106. Federal Trade Commission website, http://www.ftc.gov/ogc/coppa1.htm, accessed October 29, 2012.

107. E. Deanne Brocato, Douglas A. Gentile, Russell N. Laczniak, Julia A. Maier, and Mindy Ji-Song, "Television Commercial Violence: Potential Effects on Children," *Journal of Advertising,* 39, no. 4 (2011): 95–107.

108. Marie-Louis Fry and Michael Jay Polonsky, "Examining the Unintended Consequences of Marketing," *Journal of Business Research,* 57 (2004): 1303–1306.

109. Live Earth, http://liveearth.org/en/liveearth, accessed June 1, 2011.

110. Cindy Galli, "$40 For a Case of Bottled Water? 'Preying' on Oklahoma Tornado Victims," *ABCNews.com,* May 22, 2013, http://abcnews.go.com/Blotter/40-case-bottled-water-preying-oklahoma-tornado-victims/story?id=19233126, accessed June 30, 2014.

111. ABC 13 Eyewitness News, "Reports: Out of State Businesses Price Gouging Flood Victims," May 5, 2016, online content retrieved at http://abc13.com/business/reports-businesses-are-price-gouging-houston-flood-victims/1323890/, accessed May 20, 2016.

112. M. J. Ellington, "Price Gouging Law Takes Effect with State of Disaster Declaration," TimesDaily.com, April 29, 2011, http://www.timesdaily.com/article/20110429/news/110429779?Title=Price-gouging-law-takes-effect-with-state-disaster-declaration, accessed June 1, 2011. Brent Martin, "Attorney General Worries about Price-Gouging in Wake of Joplin Tornado," Missouri.net, May 23, 2011, http://www.missourinet.com/2011/05/23/attorney-general-worries-about-price-gouging-in-wake-of-joplin-tornado-audio/, accessed June 1, 2011. "Kentucky Gas Stations Fined for Price Gouging after Katrina," Wlky.com, August 1, 2006, http://www.wlky.com/r/9608663/detail.html, accessed June 1, 2011.

113. Alice M. Tybout, Brian Sternthal, and Bobby J. Calder, "Information Availability as a Determinant of Multiple-Request Effectiveness," *Journal of Marketing Research,* 20 (August 1988): 280–290. John C. Mowen and Robert Cialdini, "On Implementing the Door-in-the-Face Compliance Strategy in a Marketing Context," *Journal of Marketing Research,* 17 (May 1980): 253–258. Jonathan L. Freedman and Scott C. Fraher,

"Compliance without Pressure: The Foot-in-the-Door Technique," *Journal of Personality and Social Psychology*, 4 (August 1966): 195–202.

114. Robert Cialdini and David Schroeder, "Increasing Compliance by Legitimizing Paltry Contributions: When Even a Penny Helps," *Journal of Personality and Social Psychology*, 34 (October 1976): 599–604.

115. "Unethical Word-of-Mouth Marketing Strategies," WOMMA, http://www.womma.org/wom101/06/, accessed March 17, 2008.

116. Consumer Product Safety Commission, http://www.cpsc.gov/about/about.html, accessed March 17, 2008.

Case 5–2

1. Associated Press, "Bloom Is Off the Pink for Some," *Dallas Morning News*, February 5, 2012, 7A.

2. "About Us," Susan G. Komen for the Cure, http://www.komen.org/AboutUs/AboutUs.html, accessed March 18, 2012.

3. Charity Navigator—America's Largest Charity Evaluator, http://www.charitynavigator.org/.

4. Alice Park, "Public Backlash Spurs Komen to Renew Ties with Planned Parenthood," *Time*, February 3, 2012, http://healthland.time.com/2012/02/03/planned-parenthood-credits-social-media-for-publicizing-its-position-against-komen-foundation/, accessed August 3, 2012.

5. Sharon Begley and Janet Roberts, "Insight: Komen Charity under Microscope for Funding, Science," Reuters.com, February 8, 2012, http://www.reuters.com/article/2012/02/08/us-usa-healthcare-komen-research-idUSTRE8171KW20120208.

6. Marc Ramizer, "Swift Outcry on Social Media Played Key Role," *Dallas Morning News*, February 4, 2012, 1A.

7. Karen Robinson-Jacobs and Melissa Repko, "Komen's Sponsors Rattled," *Dallas Morning News*, February 5, 2012, 1D.

8. Laura Bassett, "Susan G. Komen Executives Resign amid Reports of Internal Troubles," *Huffington Post*, March 20, 2012, http://www.huffingtonpost.com/2012/03/20/susan-g-komen-executives-resign_n_1368213.html, accessed August 3, 2012. Laura Bassett and Lisa Belkin, "Susan G. Komen Officials Resign as Backlash Gains Steam," *Huffington Post*, February 2, 2012, http://www.huffingtonpost.com/2012/02/02/susan-g-komen_n_1250651.html, accessed August 3, 2012.

9. Ramizer, "Swift Outcry on Social Media Played Key Role."

10. Jennifer Preston, "After Outcry, a Senior Official Resigns at Komen," *The New York Times*, February 7, 2012, http://www.nytimes.com/2012/02/08/us/after-outcry-a-top-official-resigns-at-komen-cancer-charity.html?_r=1.

11. Laura Bassett, "Susan G. Komen Hires Consulting Firm to Assess Damage to Reputation," *Huffington Post*, February 23, 2012, http://www.huffingtonpost.com/2012/02/23/susan-g-komen-planned-parenthood_n_1297483.html.

Case 5–3

1. Jesse J. Courtney and Daniel L. Wann, "The Relationship between Sport Fan Dysfunction and Bullying Behaviors," *North American Journal of Psychology*, 12, no. 1 (2010): 191–198.

2. J. Smith and D. L. Wann, "Relationship of Dysfunctional Sport Fandom with Dislike for Rivals in a Sample of College Students," *Perceptual and Motor Skills*, 102 (2006): 719–720.

3. G. T. Trail, J. S. Fink, and D. F. Anderson, "Sport Spectator Consumption Behavior," *Sport Marketing Quarterly*, 12, no. 1 (2003): 8–17.

4. Kirk L. Wakefield and Daniel L. Wann, "An Examination of Dysfunctional Sport Fans: Method of Classification and Relationships with Problem Behaviors," *Journal of Leisure Research*, 38, no. 2 (2006): 168–186.

5. Smith and Wann, "Relationship of Dysfunctional Sport Fandom with Dislike for Rivals."

6. Duane Burleson, "NBA Suspends Artest for Rest of Season," http://nbcsports.msnbc.com/id/6549074/, accessed April 10, 2012.

7. Ben Austen, "Aubs Eat Boogers," *GQ*, September 2011, http://www.gq.com/sports/profiles/201109/college-football-alabama-auburn-rivalry, accessed April 10, 2012.

8. Brendan McCarthy, "Fan Misbehavior: Revelry Gone Awry in the Sports World," *The Times-Picayune*, http://www.nola.com/crime/index.ssf/2012/01/fan_misbehavior_revelry_gone_a.html, accessed April 10, 2012.

9. Francie Grace, "Parents Brawl at Little League Game," CBS News, October 31, 2002, http://www.cbsnews.com/news/parents-brawl-at-little-league-game/, accessed October 1, 2014.

10. "Fight at Little League Game Brings Deputies to Stonehouse Park," RanchoMurieta.com, July 8, 2009, http://www.ranchomurieta.com/node/10962, accessed April 10, 2012.

GLOSSARY

A

ABC approach to attitudes approach that suggests that attitudes encompass one's affect, behavior, and cognitions (or beliefs) toward an object

absolute threshold minimum strength of a stimulus that can be perceived

accommodation state that results when a stimulus shares some but not all of the characteristics that would lead it to fit neatly in an existing category, and consumers must process exceptions to rules about the category

acculturation process by which consumers come to learn a culture other than their natural, native culture

acquisitional shopping activities oriented toward a specific, intended purchase or purchases

action-oriented consumers with a high capacity to self-regulate their behavior

actual state consumer's perceived current state

adaptation level level of a stimulus to which a consumer has become accustomed

addictive consumption physiological dependency on the consumption of a consumer product

advertiming ad buys that include a schedule that runs the advertisement primarily at times when customers will be most receptive to the message

aesthetic labor effort put forth by employees in carefully managing their appearance as a requisite for performing their job well

affect feelings associated with objects or activities

affect-based evaluation evaluative process wherein consumers evaluate products based on the overall feeling that is evoked by the alternative

affective quality retail positioning that emphasizes a unique environment, exciting décor, friendly employees, and, in general, the feelings experienced in a retail place

age-based microculture term that describes the concept that people of the same age end up sharing many of the same values and develop similar consumer preferences

agency appraisal reviewing responsibility for events; can evoke consequential emotions like gratefulness, frustration, guilt, or sadness

aggregation approach approach to studying personality in which behavior is assessed at a number of points in time

AIO statements activity, interest, and opinion statements that are used in lifestyle studies

antecedent conditions situational characteristics that a consumer brings to information processing

anthropology field of study involving interpretation of relationships between consumers and the things they purchase, the products they own, and the activities in which they participate

anthropomorphism giving humanlike characteristics to inanimate objects

anticipation appraisal appraisal focusing on the future that can elicit anticipatory emotions like hopefulness or anxiety

antiloyal consumers consumers who will do everything possible to avoid doing business with a particular marketer

apps mobile application software that runs on devices like smartphones, tablets, and other computer-based tools

aspirational group group in which a consumer desires to become a member

assimilation state that results when a stimulus has characteristics such that consumers readily recognize it as belonging to some specific category

associative network network of mental pathways linking all knowledge within memory; sometimes referred to as a semantic network

atmospherics emotional nature of an environment or the feelings created by the total aura of physical attributes that comprise a physical environment

attention purposeful allocation of information-processing capacity toward developing an understanding of some stimulus

attention to social comparison information (ATSCI) individual difference variable that assesses the extent to which consumers are concerned about how other people react to their behavior

attitude-behavior consistency extent to which a strong relationship exists between attitudes and actual behavior

attitude-toward-the-object (ATO) model attitude model that considers three key elements, including beliefs consumers have about salient attributes, the strength of the belief that an object possesses the attribute, and evaluation of the particular attribute

attitude tracking effort of a marketer or researcher to track changes in consumer attitudes over time

attitudes relatively enduring overall evaluations of objects, products, services, issues, or people

attribute a part, or tangible feature, of a product that potentially delivers a benefit of consumption

attribute-based evaluation evaluative process wherein alternatives are evaluated across a set of attributes that are considered relevant to the purchase situation

attribute correlation perceived relationship between product features

attribution theory theory that proposes that consumers look for the cause of particular consumption experiences when arriving at satisfaction judgments

augmented product actual physical product purchased plus any services such as installation and warranties necessary to use the product and obtain its benefits

authenticity the degree to which an object, person, or experience seems real, genuine, unique, and part of history or tradition

authority the ability of a person or group to enforce the obedience of others

autobiographical memories cognitive representation of meaningful events in one's life

autonomic measures means of recording responses based on either automatic visceral reactions or neurological brain activity

awareness set set of alternatives of which a consumer is aware

B

background music music played below the audible threshold that would make it the center of attention

balance theory theory that states that consumers are motivated to maintain perceived consistency in the relations found in a system

behavioral influence decision-making perspective assumes many consumer decisions are actually learned responses to environmental influences

behavioral intentions model model developed to improve on the ATO model, focusing on behavioral intentions, subjective norms, and attitude toward a particular behavior

behaviorist approach to learning theory of learning that focuses on changes in behavior due to association, without great concern for the cognitive mechanics of the learning process

benefit perceived favorable result derived from a particular feature

benefits positive results of consumption experiences

bicultural used to describe immigrants as they face decisions and form preferences based on their old or new cultures

big data term used to represent the massive amounts of data available to companies, which can potentially be used to predict customer behaviors

binge drinking consumption of five or more drinks in a single drinking session for men and four or more drinks for women

binge eating consumption of large amounts of food while feeling a general loss of control over food intake

bipolar situation wherein if one feels joy he or she cannot also experience sadness

blue ocean strategy positioning a firm far away from competitors' positions so that it creates an industry of its own and, at least for a time, isolates itself from competitors

body esteem positivity with which people hold their body image

body language nonverbal communication cues signaled by somatic responses

boomerang kids young adults between the ages of 18 and 34 who move back home with their parents after they graduate from college

bounded rationality idea that consumers attempt to act rationally within their information processing constraints

brain dominance refers to the phenomenona of hemispheric lateralization. Some people tend to be either right-brain or left-brain dominant

brand community group of consumers who develop relationships based on shared interests or product usage

brand inertia what occurs when a consumer simply buys a product repeatedly without any real attachment

brand loyalty deeply held commitment to rebuy a product or service regardless of situational influences that could lead to switching behavior

brand personality collection of human characteristics that can be associated with a brand

brand personality appeal a product's ability to appeal to consumers based on the human characteristics associated with it

BRIC acronym that refers to the collective economies of Brazil, Russia, India, and China

buzz marketing marketing efforts that focus on generating excitement among consumers and that are spread from consumer to consumer

C

CANZUS acronym that refers to the close similarity in values among Canada, Australia, New Zealand, and the United States

central cues information presented in a message about the product itself, its attributes, or the consequences of its use

central route to persuasion path to persuasion found in ELM where the consumer has high involvement, motivation, and/or ability to process a message

Chindia combined market and business potential of China and India

chunk single memory unit

chunking process of grouping stimuli by meaning so that multiple stimuli can become one memory unit

circadian cycle rhythm (level of energy) of the human body that varies with the time of day

classical conditioning change in behavior that occurs simply through associating some stimulus with another stimulus that naturally causes some reaction; a type of unintentional learning

cognition thinking or mental processes that go on as we process and store things that can become knowledge

cognitive appraisal theory school of thought proposing that specific types of appraisal thoughts can be linked to specific types of emotions

cognitive dissonance an uncomfortable feeling that occurs when a consumer has lingering doubts about a decision that has occurred

cognitive interference notion that everything else that the consumer is exposed to while trying to remember something is also vying for processing capacity and thus interfering with memory and comprehension

cognitive organization process by which the human brain assembles sensory evidence into something recognizable

cognitive psychology study of the intricacies of mental reactions involved in information processing

cognitive structuring term that refers to the reliance on schema-based heuristics in making decisions

cohort a group of people who have lived the same major experiences in their lives

collaborative consumption participation in the sharing economy that is consumer to consumer rather than business to consumer.

collectivism extent to which an individual's life is intertwined with a large cohesive group

compensatory damages damages that are intended to cover costs incurred by a consumer due to an injury

compensatory model attitudinal model wherein low ratings for one attribute are compensated for by higher ratings on another

compensatory rule decision rule that allows consumers to select products that may perform poorly on one criterion by compensating for the poor performance by good performance on another

competitive intensity number of firms competing for business within a specific category

competitiveness enduring tendency to strive to be better than others

complaining behavior action that occurs when a consumer actively seeks out someone (supervisor, service provider, etc.) with whom to share an opinion regarding a negative consumption event

comprehension the way people cognitively assign meaning to (i.e., understand) things they encounter

compulsive buying chronic, repetitive purchasing that is a response to negative events or feelings

compulsive consumption repetitive, excessive, and purposeful consumer behaviors that are performed as a response to tension, anxiety, or obtrusive thoughts

compulsive shopping repetitive shopping behaviors that are a response to negative events or feelings

conditioned response response that results from exposure to a conditioned stimulus that was originally associated with the unconditioned stimulus

conditioned stimulus object or event that does not cause the desired response naturally but that can be conditioned to do so by pairing with an unconditioned stimulus

confirmatory bias tendency for expectations to guide performance perceptions

conformity result of group influence in which an individual yields to the attitudes and behaviors of others

congruity how consistent the elements of an environment are with one another

conjoint analysis technique used to develop an understanding of the attributes that guide consumer preferences by having consumers compare product preferences across varying levels of evaluative criteria and expected utility

conjunctive rule noncompensatory decision rule where the option selected must surpass a minimum cutoff across all relevant attributes

connected self-schema self-conceptualization of the extent to which a consumer perceives himself or herself as being an integral part of a group

consideration set alternatives that are considered acceptable for further consideration in decision making

consistency principle principle that states that human beings prefer consistency among their beliefs, attitudes, and behaviors

construal level whether or not we are thinking about something using a concrete or an abstract mindset

consumer affect feelings a consumer has about a particular product or activity

consumer behavior set of value-seeking activities that take place as people go about addressing their real needs

consumer behavior as a field of study study of consumers as they go about the consumption process; the science of studying how consumers seek value in an effort to address real needs

Consumer Bill of Rights introduced by President John F. Kennedy in 1962, list of rights that include the right to safety, the right to be informed, the right to redress and to be heard, and the right to choice

consumer culture commonly held societal beliefs that define what is socially gratifying

consumer (customer) orientation way of doing business in which the actions and decision making of the institution prioritize consumer value and satisfaction above all other concerns

consumer dissatisfaction mild, negative affective reaction resulting from an unfavorable appraisal of a consumption outcome

consumer ethnocentrism belief among consumers that their ethnic group is superior to others and that the products that come from their native land are superior to other products

consumer inertia situation in which a consumer tends to continue a pattern of behavior until some stronger force motivates him or her to change

consumer involvement degree of personal relevance a consumer finds in pursuing value from a particular category of consumption

consumer misbehavior behaviors that are in some way unethical and that potentially harm the self or others

consumer problem behavior consumer behavior that is deemed to be unacceptable but that is seemingly beyond the control of the consumer

consumer refuse any packaging that is no longer necessary for consumption to take place or, in some cases, the actual good that is no longer providing value to the consumer

consumer satisfaction mild, positive emotion resulting from a favorable appraisal of a consumption outcome

consumer search behavior behaviors that consumers engage in as they seek information that can be used to satisfy needs

consumer self-construal represents whether a consumer is thinking about the self as an independent person or construing the self as an interdependent person within a network of others

consumer self-regulation tendency for consumers to inhibit outside, or situational, influences from interfering with shopping intentions

consumer socialization the process through which young consumers develop attitudes and learn skills that help them function in the marketplace

Consumer Value Framework (CVF) consumer behavior theory that illustrates factors that shape consumption-related behaviors and ultimately determine the value associated with consumption

consumerism activities of various groups to voice concern for, and to protect, basic consumer rights

consumption process by which consumers use and transform goods, services, or ideas into value

consumption frequency number of times a product or service is consumed in a given period of time

contractualism beliefs about the violation of written (or unwritten) laws

contrast state that results when a stimulus does not share enough in common with existing categories to allow categorization

core societal values (CSV) commonly agreed-upon consensus about the most preferable ways of living within a society, also known as cultural values

corporate social responsibility (CSR) organization's activities and status related to its societal obligations

corporate strategy way a firm is defined and its general goals

costs negative results of consumption experiences

counterarguments thoughts that contradict a message

credibility extent to which a source is considered to be both an expert in a given area and trustworthy

critical incident exchange between consumers and business that the consumer views as unusually negative with implications for the relationship

crowding density of people and objects within a given space

cultural distance (CD) representation of how disparate one nation is from another in terms of their CSV

cultural norm rule that specifies the appropriate consumer behavior in a given situation within a specific culture

cultural sanction penalty associated with performing a nongratifying or culturally inconsistent behavior

customer commitment sense of attachment, dedication, and identification

Customer Lifetime Value (CLV) approximate worth of a customer to a company in economic terms; overall profitability of an individual consumer

customer orientation practice of using sales techniques that focus on customer needs

Customer Relationship Management (CRM) systematic information management system that collects, maintains, and reports detailed information about customers to enable a more customer-oriented managerial approach

customer share portion of resources allocated to one brand from among the set of competing brands

D

deceptive advertising message that omits information that is important in influencing a consumer's buying behavior and is likely to mislead consumers acting reasonably

declarative knowledge cognitive components that represent facts

demographic analysis a profile of a consumer group based on their demographics

demographics observable, statistical aspects of populations such as age, gender, or income

deontological evaluations evaluations regarding the inherent rightness or wrongness of specific actions

desired state perceived state for which a consumer strives

desire level of a particular benefit that will lead to a valued end state

determinant criteria criteria that are most carefully considered and directly related to the actual choice that is made

dialects variations of a common language

differentiated marketers firms that serve multiple market segments, each with a unique product offering

diffusion process way in which new products are adopted and spread throughout a marketplace

discretionary (spare) time the days, hours, or minutes that are not obligated toward some compulsory and time-consuming activity

discriminative stimuli stimuli that occur solely in the presence of a reinforcer

disjunctive rule noncompensatory decision rule where the option selected surpasses a relatively high cutoff point on any attribute

dissociative group group to which a consumer does not want to belong

distributive fairness refers to the way a consumer judges the outcomes of an exchange

divergence situation in which consumers choose membership in microcultures in an effort to stand out or define themselves from the crowd

door-in-the-face technique ingratiation technique used in personal selling in which a salesperson begins with a major request and then follows with a series of smaller requests

dostats Russian word that can be roughly translated as "acquiring things with great difficulty"

dual coding coding that occurs when two different sensory traces are available to remember something

durable goods goods that are typically expensive and usually consumed over a long period of time

E

e-waste discarded electronics such as cell phones, old computers, tablets, etc. and their components

echoic storage storage of auditory information in sensory memory

ecological factors physical characteristics that describe the physical environment and habitat of a particular place

economics study of production and consumption

ego component in psychoanalytic theory that attempts to balance the struggle between the superego and the id

ego-defensive function of attitudes function of attitudes whereby attitudes work as defense mechanisms for consumers

elaboration extent to which a consumer continues processing a message even after an initial understanding is achieved

elaboration likelihood model attitudinal change model that shows attitudes are changed based on differing levels of consumer involvement through either central or peripheral processing

elasticity reflects how sensitive a consumer is to changes in some product characteristic

elimination-by-aspects rule (EBA) noncompensatory decision rule where the consumer begins evaluating options by first looking at the most important attribute and eliminating any option that does not meet a minimum cutoff point for that attribute, and where subsequent evaluations proceed in order of importance until only one option remains

emotion a specific psychobiological reaction to a human appraisal

emotional ability capability of a salesperson to convey emotional information to shape a more valuable outcome for consumers

emotional contagion extent to which an emotional display by one person influences the emotional state of a bystander

emotional effect on memory relatively superior recall for information presented with mild affective content compared to similar information presented in an affectively neutral way

emotional expressiveness extent to which a consumer shows outward behavioral signs and otherwise reacts obviously to emotional experiences

emotional intelligence awareness of the emotions experienced in a given situation and the ability to control reactions to these emotions

emotional involvement type of deep personal interest that evokes strongly felt feelings simply from the thoughts or behavior associated with some object or activity

emotional labor effort put forth by service workers who have to overtly manage their own emotional displays as part of the requirements of the job

encoding process by which information is transferred from workbench memory to long-term memory for permanent storage

enculturation way people learn their native culture

enduring involvement ongoing interest in some product or opportunity

episodic memory memory for past events in one's life

epistemic shopping activities oriented toward acquiring knowledge about products

equity appraisal considering how fair some event is; can evoke emotions like warmth or anger

equity theory theory that proposes that people compare their own level of inputs and outcomes to those of another party in an exchange

ethics standards or moral codes of conduct to which a person, group, or organization adheres

ethnic identification degree to which consumers feel a sense of belonging to the culture of their ethnic origins

ethnography qualitative approach to studying consumers that relies on interpretation of artifacts to draw conclusions about consumption

etiquette customary mannerisms consumers use in common social situations

evaluative criteria attributes that consumers consider when reviewing alternative solutions to a problem

even-a-penny-will-help technique ingratiation technique in which a marketing message is sent that suggests that even the smallest donation, such as a penny or a dollar, will help a cause

exchange acting out of the decision to give something up in return for something perceived to be of greater value

exemplar concept within a schema that is the single best representative of some category; schema for something that really exists

expectancy/disconfirmation theory satisfaction formation theory that proposes that consumers use expectations as a benchmark against which performance perceptions are judged

expectations preconsumption beliefs of what will occur during an exchange and consumption of a product

experiential decision-making perspective assumes consumers often make purchases and reach decisions based on the affect, or feeling, attached to the product or behavior under consideration

experiential shopping recreationally oriented activities designed to provide interest, excitement, relaxation, fun, social interaction, or some other desired feeling

expertise amount of knowledge that a source is perceived to have about a subject

explicit memory memory that develops when a person is exposed to, attends, and tries to remember information

exposure process of bringing some stimulus within proximity of a consumer so that the consumer can sense it with one of the five human senses

extended decision making consumers move diligently through various problem-solving activities in search of the best information that will help them reach a decision

extended family three or more generations of family members

external influences social and cultural aspects of life as a consumer

external search gathering of information from sources external to the consumer such as friends, family, salespeople, advertising, independent research reports, and the Internet

extinction process through which behaviors cease due to lack of reinforcement

eye-tracking technology combines hardware and software that can measure precisely where a consumer's gaze is directed and also assess pupil dilation.

F

family household at least two people who are related by blood or marriage who occupy a housing unit

feature performance characteristic of an object

femininity sex role distinction within a group that emphasizes the prioritization of relational variables such as caring, conciliation, and community; CSV opposite of masculinity

figurative language use of expressions that send a non-literal meaning

figure object that is intended to capture a person's attention; the focal part of any message

figure-ground distinction notion that each message can be separated into the focal point (figure) and the background (ground)

financial switching costs total economic resources that must be spent or invested as a consumer learns how to obtain value from a new product choice

fit how appropriate the elements of a given environment are

five-factor model multiple-trait perspective that proposes that the human personality consists of five traits: agreeableness, extroversion, openness to experience (or creativity), conscientiousness, and neuroticism (or stability)

flow extremely high emotional involvement in which a consumer is engrossed in an activity

foot-in-the-door technique ingratiation technique used in personal selling in which a salesperson begins with a small request and slowly leads up to one major request

foreground music music that becomes the focal point of attention and can have strong effects on a consumer's willingness to approach or avoid an environment

formal group group in which a consumer formally becomes a member

framing a phenomenon in which the meaning of something is influenced (perceived differently) by the information environment

functional quality retail positioning that emphasizes tangible things like a wide selection of goods, low prices, guarantees, and knowledgeable employees

functional theory of attitudes theory of attitudes that suggests that attitudes perform four basic functions

G

geodemographic techniques techniques that combine data on consumer expenditures and socioeconomic variables with geographic information in order to identify commonalities in consumption patterns of households in various regions

Globish a simplified form of English that reduces the vocabulary to around 1,500 words and eliminates grammatical complications

glocalization idea that marketing strategy may be global but the implementation of that strategy at the marketing tactics level should be local

golden section the preferred ratio of objects, equal to 1.62 to 1.00

ground background in a message

grounded cognition theory that suggests that bodily sensations influence thoughts and meaning independent of effortful thinking

group influence ways in which group members influence attitudes, behaviors, and opinions of others within the group

guanxi (pronounced "gawn-zeye") Chinese term for a way of doing business in which parties must first invest time and resources in getting to know one another and becoming comfortable with one another before consummating any important deal

guerrilla marketing marketing of a product using unconventional means

H

habitual decision making consumers generally do not seek information at all when a problem is recognized and select a product based on habit

habituation process by which continuous exposure to a stimulus affects the comprehension of, and response to, the stimulus

habitus mental and cognitive structures through which individuals perceive the world based largely on their standing in a social class

haptic perception interpretations created by the way some object feels

hedonic motivation drive to experience something emotionally gratifying

hedonic shopping value worth of a shopping activity because the time spent doing the activity itself is personally gratifying

hedonic value value derived from the immediate gratification that comes from some activity

hierarchical approaches to personality approaches to personality inquiry that assume that personality traits exist at varying levels of abstraction

hierarchy of effects attitude approach that suggests that affect, behavior, and cognitions form in a sequential order

homeostasis state of equilibrium wherein the body naturally reacts in a way so as to maintain a constant, normal bloodstream

homogamy the finding that most marriages comprise people from similar classes

hope a fundamental emotion evoked by positive, anticipatory appraisals that signal uncertainty about a potentially positive outcome

household decision making process by which decisions are made in household units

household life cycle (HLC) segmentation technique that acknowledges that changes in family composition and income alter household demand for products and services

I

iconic storage storage of visual information in sensory memory and the idea that things are stored with a one-to-one representation with reality

id the personality component in psychoanalytic theory that focuses on pleasure-seeking motives and immediate gratification

ideal point combination of product characteristics that provide the most value to an individual consumer or market segment

idiographic perspective approach to personality that focuses on understanding the complexity of each individual consumer

implicit memory memory for things that a person did not try to remember

impulsive consumption consumption acts characterized by spontaneity, a diminished regard for consequences, and a need for self-fulfillment

impulsive shopping spontaneous activities characterized by a diminished regard for consequences, spontaneity, and a desire for immediate self-fulfillment

impulsivity personality trait that represents how sensitive a consumer is to immediate rewards

"I'm working for you!" technique technique used by salespeople to create the perception that they are working as hard as possible to close a sale when they really are not doing so

individual difference variables descriptions of how individual consumers differ according to specific trait patterns of behavior

individual differences characteristic traits of individuals, including demographics, personality, and lifestyle

individualism extent to which people are expected to take care of themselves and their immediate families

indulgence-restraint a cultural value dimension distinguishing societies based on how oriented people are toward immediate fun and enjoyment versus restraining oneself from much indulgence in such things

inept set alternatives in the awareness set that are deemed to be unacceptable for further consideration

inert set alternatives in the awareness set about which consumers are indifferent or do not hold strong feelings

informal group group that has no membership or application requirements and that may have no code of conduct

information intensity amount of information available for a consumer to process within a given environment

information overload situation in which consumers are presented with so much information that they cannot assimilate the variety of information presented

information processing (or cognitive) perspective learning perspective that focuses on the cognitive processes associated with comprehension and how these precipitate behavioral changes

informational influence ways in which a consumer uses the behaviors and attitudes of reference groups as information for making his or her own decisions

ingroup a group that a person identifies with as a member

innovativeness degree to which an individual is open to new ideas and tends to be relatively early in adopting new products, services, or experiences

instrumental conditioning type of learning in which a behavioral response can be conditioned through reinforcement—either punishment or rewards associated with undesirable or desirable behavior

intentional learning process by which consumers set out to specifically learn information devoted to a certain subject

interactional fairness captures how fairly a consumer believes he or she was treated when dealing with service personnel in resolving some issue

internal influences things that go on inside of the mind and heart of the consumer or that are truly a part of the consumer psychologically

internal search retrieval of knowledge stored in memory about products, services, and experiences

interpretive research approach that seeks to explain the inner meanings and motivations associated with specific consumption experiences

involuntary attention attention that is beyond the conscious control of a consumer

involvement the personal relevance toward, or interest in, a particular product

J

JMD just meaningful difference; smallest amount of change in a stimulus that would influence consumer consumption and choice

JND just noticeable difference; condition in which one stimulus is sufficiently stronger than another so that someone can actually notice that the two are not the same

judgments mental assessments of the presence of attributes and the consequences associated with those attributes

K

knowledge function of attitudes function of attitudes whereby attitudes allow consumers to simplify decision-making processes

L

learning change in behavior resulting from some interaction between a person and a stimulus

left skewed distribution of responses consistent with most respondents choosing responses so the distribution is clustered toward the positive end of the scale

lexicographic rule noncompensatory decision rule where the option selected is thought to perform best on the most important attribute

lifestyles distinctive modes of living, including how people spend their time and money

limited decision making consumers search very little for information and often reach decisions based largely on prior beliefs about products and their attributes

long-term memory repository for all information that a person has encountered

long-term orientation values consistent with Confucian philosophy and a prioritization of future rewards over short-term benefits

loyalty card/program device that keeps track of the amount of purchasing a consumer has had with a given marketer once some level is reached

M

market maven consumer who spreads information about all types of products and services that are available in the marketplace

market orientation organizational culture that embodies the importance of creating value for customers among all employees

market segmentation separation of a market into groups based on the different demand curves associated with each group

marketing multitude of value-producing seller activities that facilitate exchanges between buyers and sellers, including production, pricing, promotion, distribution, and retailing

marketing concept states a firm should focus on consumer needs as a means of achieving long-term success

marketing ethics societal and professional standards of right and fair practices that are expected of marketing managers as they develop and implement marketing strategies

marketing mix combination of product, pricing, promotion, and distribution strategies used to implement a marketing strategy

marketing myopia a common condition in which a shortsighted company views itself in a product business rather than in a value- or benefits-producing business

marketing strategy way a company goes about creating value for customers

marketing tactics ways marketing management is implemented; involves price, promotion, product, and distribution decisions

masculinity sex role distinction within a group that values assertiveness and control; CSV opposite of femininity

Maslow's hierarchy of needs a theory of human motivation that describes consumers as addressing a finite set of prioritized needs

matchup hypothesis hypothesis that states that a source feature is most effective when it is matched with relevant products

materialism extent to which material goods have importance in a consumer's life

meaning transference process through which cultural meaning is transferred to a product and onto the consumer

meaningful encoding coding that occurs when information from long-term memory is placed on the workbench and attached to the information on the workbench in a way that the information can be recalled and used later

memory psychological process by which knowledge is recorded

memory trace mental path by which some thought becomes active

mental budgeting memory accounting for recent spending

mere association effect the transfer of meaning between objects that are similar only by accidental association

mere exposure effect effect that leads consumers to prefer a stimulus to which they've previously been exposed

message congruity extent to which a message is internally consistent and fits surrounding information

message effects how the appeal of a message and its construction affect persuasiveness

metaphor in a consumer context, an ad claim that is not literally true but figuratively communicates a message

metric equivalence statistical tests used to validate the way people use numbers to represent quantities across cultures

microculture a group of people who share similar values and tastes that are subsumed within a larger culture

modeling process of imitating others' behavior; a form of observational learning

moderating variable variable that changes the nature of the relationship between two other variables

mood transient and general affective state

mood-congruent judgments evaluations in which the value of a target is influenced in a consistent way by one's mood

mood-congruent recall consumers will remember information better when the mood they are currently in matches the mood they were in when originally exposed to the information

moral beliefs beliefs about the perceived ethicality or morality of behaviors

moral equity beliefs regarding an act's fairness or justness

morals personal standards and beliefs used to guide individual action

motivational research era era in consumer research that focused heavily on psychoanalytic approaches

motivations inner reasons or driving forces behind human actions that drive consumers to address real needs

multiattribute attitude model a model that combines a number of pieces of information about belief and evaluations of attributes of an object

multiple store theory of memory theory that explains memory as utilizing three different storage areas within the human brain: sensory, workbench, and long-term

multiple-trait approach approach in trait research wherein the focus remains on combinations of traits

N

near-field communication (NFC) wi-fi–like systems communicating with specific devices within a defined space like inside or around the perimeter of a retail unit or signage

need for cognition refers to the degree to which consumers enjoy engaging in effortful cognitive information processing

negative disconfirmation according to the expectancy/disconfirmation approach, a perceived state wherein performance perceptions fall short of expectations

negative public publicity action that occurs when negative WOM spreads on a relatively large scale, possibly even involving media coverage

negative reinforcement removal of harmful stimuli as a way of encouraging behavior

negative word-of-mouth (negative WOM); action that takes place when consumers pass on negative information about a company from one to another

negligence situation whereby an injured consumer attempts to show that a firm could foresee a potential injury might occur and then decided not to act on that knowledge

netnography a branch of ethnography that studies the behavior of online cultures and communities

neuroscience the study of the central nervous system including brain mechanisms associated with emotion

niche marketing plan wherein a firm specializes in serving one market segment with particularly unique demand characteristics

nodes concepts found in an associative network

nomothetic perspective variable-centered approach to personality that focuses on particular traits that exist across a number of people

noncompensatory rule decision rule in which strict guidelines are set prior to selection and any option that does not meet the guidelines is eliminated from consideration

nondurable goods goods that are typically inexpensive and usually consumed quickly

nonlinear effect a plot of an effect that does not make a straight line

nonverbal communication information passed through some nonverbal act

nostalgia a yearning to relive the past that can produce lingering emotions

nuclear family a mother, a father, and a set of siblings

O

olfactory refers to humans' physical and psychological processing of smells

one-to-one marketing plan wherein a different product is offered for each individual customer so that each customer is treated as a segment of one

ongoing search search effort that is not necessarily focused on an upcoming purchase or decision but rather on staying up to date on the topic

opinion leader consumer who has a great deal of influence on the behavior of others relating to product adoption and purchase

orientation reflex natural reflex that occurs as a response to something threatening

outcomes appraisal considering how something turned out relative to one's goals; can evoke emotions like joyfulness, satisfaction, sadness, or pride

outgroup a group with which a person does not identify

outshopping shopping in a city or town to which consumers must travel rather than in their own hometowns

P

PAD pleasure–arousal–dominance; a self-report measure that asks respondents to rate feelings using semantic differential items

packrats consumers possessing high levels of a lifestyle trait leading to a strong tendency toward retaining consumption-related possessions

paths representations of the association between nodes in an associative network

peer pressure extent to which group members feel pressure to behave in accordance with group expectations

perceived risk perception of the negative consequences that are likely to result from a course of action and the uncertainty of which course of action is best to take

perception consumer's awareness and interpretation of reality

perceptual attributes attributes that are visually apparent and easily recognizable

perceptual map tool used to depict graphically the positioning of competing products

peripheral cues nonproduct-related information presented in a message

peripheral route to persuasion path to persuasion found in ELM where the consumer has low involvement, motivation, and/or ability to process a message

personal elaboration process by which people imagine themselves somehow associating with a stimulus that is being processed

personal shopping value (PSV) overall subjective worth of a shopping activity considering all associated costs and benefits

personality totality of thoughts, emotions, intentions, tendencies, and behaviors that a person exhibits consistently as he or she adapts to the environment

persuasion attempt to change attitudes

phenomenology qualitative approach to studying consumers that relies on interpretation of the lived experience associated with some aspect of consumption

physical characteristics tangible elements or the parts of a message that can be sensed

planned obsolescence act of planning the premature discontinuance of product models that perform adequately

pleasure principle principle found in psychoanalytic theory that describes the factor that motivates pleasure-seeking behavior within the id

PMG price matching guarantee

positive disconfirmation according to the expectancy/disconfirmation approach, a perceived state wherein performance perceptions exceed expectations

positive reinforcers reinforcers that take the form of a reward

positive WOM action that occurs when consumers spread information from one to another about positive consumption experiences with companies

potential value benefits not yet realized from a service because they have yet to be consumed

power distance extent to which authority and privileges are divided among different groups within society and the extent to which these facts of life are accepted by the people within the society

pragmatic-normative the idea that not everything can be explained

preattentive effects learning that occurs without attention

predictive analytics the application of statistical tools in an effort to discover patterns in data that allow prediction of consumer behavior

prepurchase search search effort aimed at finding information to solve an immediate problem

price information that signals the amount of potential value contained in a product

primacy effect occurs when the information placed early in a message has the most impact

primary group group that includes members who have frequent, direct contact with one another

priming cognitive process in which context or environment activates concepts and frames thoughts and therefore affects both value and meaning

PRIZM popular geodemographic technique that stands for Potential Ratings Index by ZIP Market

problem gambling obsession over the thought of gambling and the loss of control over gambling behavior and its consequences

procedural justice an equity-based cognition representing the extent that consumers believe the processes involved in processing a transaction, performing a service, or handling any complaint are fair

procedural switching costs lost time and extended effort spent in learning ways of using some product offering

product potentially valuable bundle of benefits

product categories mental representations of stored knowledge about groups of products

product contamination refers to the diminished positive feelings someone has about a product because another consumer has handled the product

product differentiation marketplace condition in which consumers do not view all competing products as identical to one another

product enthusiasts consumers with very high involvement in some product category

product involvement the personal relevance of a particular product category

product placements products that have been placed conspicuously in movies, television shows, music, or video games

product positioning way a product is perceived by a consumer

production orientation approach where innovation is geared primarily toward making the production process as efficient and economic as possible

productivity orientation represents the tendency for consumers to focus on being productive, making progress, and accomplishing more in less time

products liability extent to which businesses are held responsible for product-related injuries

prospect theory theory that suggests that a decision, or argument, can be framed in different ways and that the framing affects risk assessments consumers make

prototype schema that is the best representative of some category but that is not represented by an existing entity; conglomeration of the most associated characteristics of a category

psychoanalytic approach to personality approach to personality research, advocated by Sigmund Freud, that suggests personality results from a struggle between inner motives and societal pressures to follow rules and expectations

psychobiological a response involving both psychological and physical human responses

psychographics quantitative investigation of consumer lifestyles

psychology study of human reactions to their environment

puffery practice of making exaggerated claims about a product and its superiority

punishers stimuli that decrease the likelihood that a behavior will persist

punitive damages damages that are sought to punish a company for behavior associated with an injury

Q

qualitative research tools means for gathering data in a relatively unstructured way, including case analysis, clinical interviews, and focus group interviews

quality perceived overall goodness or badness of some product

quantitative research approach that addresses questions about consumer behavior using numerical measurement and analysis tools

quartet of institutions four groups responsible for communicating the CSVs through both formal and informal processes from one generation to another: family, school, church, and media

R

rancorous revenge is when a consumer yells insults and makes a public scene in an effort to harm the business in response to an unsatisfactory experience

rational decision-making perspective assumes consumers diligently gather information about purchases, carefully compare various brands of products on salient attributes, and make informed decisions regarding what brand to buy

reality principle the principle in psychoanalytic theory under which the ego attempts to satisfy the id within societal constraints

recency effect occurs when the information placed late in a message has the most impact

reference group individuals who have significant relevance for a consumer and who have an impact on the consumer's evaluations, aspirations, and behavior

regulatory focus theory puts forward the notion that consumers orient their behavior either through a prevention or promotion focus

relational switching cost emotional and psychological consequences of changing from one brand/retailer/service provider to another

relationship marketing activities based on the belief that the firm's performance is enhanced through repeat business

relationship quality degree of connectedness between a consumer and a retailer

relativism beliefs about the social acceptability of an act in a culture

renquing the idea that favors given to another are reciprocal and must be returned

repetition simple mechanism in which a thought is kept alive in short-term memory by mentally repeating the thought

researcher dependent subjective data that requires a researcher to interpret the meaning

resource-advantage theory theory that explains why companies succeed or fail; the firm goes about obtaining resources from consumers in return for the value the resources create

response generation reconstruction of memory traces into a formed recollection of information

retail personality way a retail store is defined in the mind of a shopper based on the combination of functional and affective qualities

retaliatory revenge consumer becomes violent with employees and/or tries to vandalize a business in response to an unsatisfactory experience

retrieval process by which information is transferred back into workbench memory for additional processing when needed

reversal theory tries to explain how environmental elements can lead to near 180-degree changes in shopping orientation

role conflict a situation involving conflicting expectations based on cultural role expectations

role expectations the specific expectations that are associated with each type of person within a culture or society

rumination unintentional but recurrent memories of long-ago events that are spontaneously (not evoked by the environment) triggered

S

sales orientation practice of using sales techniques that are aimed at satisfying the salesperson's own needs and motives for short-term sales success

sandwich generation consumers who must take care of both their own children and their aging parents

satisficing practice of using decision-making shortcuts to arrive at satisfactory, rather than optimal, decisions

schema a portion of an associative network that represents a specific entity and thereby provides it with meaning

schema-based affect emotions that become stored as part of the meaning for a category (a schema)

script schema representing an event

search regret negative emotions that come from failed search processes

seasonality regularly occurring conditions that vary with the time of year

secondary group group to which a consumer belongs, with less frequent contact and weaker influence than that found in a primary group

selective attention process of paying attention to only certain stimuli

selective distortion process by which consumers interpret information in ways that are biased by their previously held beliefs

selective exposure process of screening out certain stimuli and purposely exposing oneself to other stimuli

self-concept totality of thoughts and feelings that an individual has about himself or herself

self-congruency theory theory that proposes that much of consumer behavior can be explained by the congruence of a consumer's self-concept with the image of typical users of a focal product

self-conscious emotions specific emotions that result from some evaluation or reflection of one's own behavior, including pride, shame, guilt, and embarrassment

self-esteem positivity of the self-concept that one holds

self-improvement motivation motivation aimed at changing the current state to a level that is more ideal, not at simply maintaining the current state

self-monitoring tendency for consumers to observe and control behavior in ways that agree with social cues and influence

self-perception theory theory that states that consumers are motivated to act in accordance with their attitudes and behaviors

semantic coding type of coding wherein stimuli are converted to meaning that can be expressed verbally

semiotics study of symbols and their meanings

sensation consumer's immediate response to a stimulus

sensory marketing actively seeking to engage customers' senses as the primary aspect of the value proposition

sensory memory area in memory where a consumer stores things exposed to one of the five senses

sentiment analysis sometimes called conversation analysis; automatic procedures that search social networking sites like Twitter for phrases/sentences that are coded for emotional meaning

separated self-schema self-conceptualization of the extent to which a consumer perceives himself or herself as distinct and separate from others

serial position effect occurs when the placement of information in a message impacts recall of the information

service an organization's efforts applied toward value creation

service quality overall goodness or badness of a service experience, which is often measured by SERVQUAL

servicescape physical environment in which consumer services are performed

SERVQUAL way of measuring service quality that captures consumers' disconfirmation of service expectations

sex role orientation (SRO) family's set of beliefs regarding the ways in which household decisions are reached

sex roles societal expectations for men and women among members of a cultural group

shaping process through which a desired behavior is altered over time, in small increments

share of wallet customer share

sharing economy the market activity involving temporary usage for hire as a replacement for traditional ownership.

shopping set of value-producing consumer activities that directly increase the likelihood that something will be purchased

shopping involvement personal relevance of shopping activities

signal attribute that consumers use to infer something about another attribute

signal theory explains ways in which communications convey meaning beyond the explicit or obvious interpretation

single-trait approach approach in trait research wherein the focus is on one particular trait

situational influences things unique to a time or place that can affect consumer decision making and the value received from consumption

situational involvement temporary interest in some imminent purchase situation

social buying consumer buying behavior that takes place on social networking sites

smart agent software software capable of learning an Internet user's preferences and automatically searching out information in selected websites and then distributing it

social class a culturally defined group to which a consumer belongs based on resources like prestige, income, occupation, and education

social comparison a naturally occurring mental personal comparison of the self with a target individual within the environment

social couponing type of buying where consumers receive a coupon, or deal, by joining a special social networking website

social environment elements that specifically deal with the way other people influence consumer decision making and value

social gaming online or app-based game played on a social media platform

social identity the idea that one's individual identity is defined in part by the social groups to which one belongs

social judgment theory theory that proposes that consumers compare incoming information to their existing attitudes about a particular object or issue and that attitude change depends upon how consistent the information is with the initial attitude

social media media through which communication occurs

social media marketing the practice of using social media to generate consumer interest in a product, service, or idea

social networking website website that facilitates online social networking

social networks consumers connecting with one another based on common interests, associations, or goals

social power ability of an individual or a group to alter the actions of others

social psychology study that focuses on the thoughts, feelings, and behaviors that people have as they interact with other people

social schema cognitive representation that gives a specific type of person meaning

social stereotype another word for social schema

social stratification the division of society into classes that have unequal access to scarce and valuable resources

socialization learning through observation of and the active processing of information about lived, everyday experience

societal marketing concept marketing concept that states that marketers should consider not only the wants and needs of consumers but also the needs of society

sociology the study of groups of people within a society, with relevance for consumer behavior because a great deal of consumption takes place within group settings or is affected by group behavior

source attractiveness the degree to which a source's physical appearance matches a prototype for beauty and elicits a favorable or desirous response

source effects characteristics of a source that influence the persuasiveness of a message

spreading activation way cognitive activation spreads from one concept (or node) to another

stakeholder marketing an orientation in which firms recognize that more than just the buyer and seller are involved in the marketing process, and a host of primary and secondary entities affect and are affected by the value creation process

state-oriented consumers with a low capacity to self-regulate their behavior

status symbols products or objects that are used to signal one's place in society

stealth marketing guerrilla marketing tactic in which consumers do not realize that they are being targeted for a marketing message

stigmatization a situation in which consumers are marked in some way that indicates their place in society

strategy a planned way of doing something to accomplish some goal

strict liability legal action against a firm whereby a consumer demonstrates in court that an injury occurred and that the product associated with the injury was faulty in some way

subliminal persuasion behavior change induced by subliminal processing

subliminal processing way that the human brain deals with very low-strength stimuli, so low that the person has no conscious awareness

superego component in psychoanalytic theory that works against the id by motivating behavior that matches the expectations and norms of society

support arguments thoughts that further support a message

surrogate consumer consumer who is hired by another to provide input into a purchase decision

susceptibility to interpersonal influence individual difference variable that assesses a consumer's need to enhance the image others hold of him or her by acquiring and using products, conforming to the expectations of others, and learning about products by observing others

switching times when a consumer chooses a competing choice, rather than the previously purchased choice, on the next purchase occasion

switching costs costs associated with changing from one choice (brand/retailer/service provider) to another

symbolic interactionism perspective that proposes that consumers live in a symbolic environment and interpret the myriad of symbols around them, and that members of a society agree on the meanings of symbols

T

tag small piece of coded information that helps with the retrieval of knowledge

target market identified segment or segments of a market that a company serves

teleological evaluations consumers' assessment of the goodness or badness of the consequences of actions

temporal factors situational characteristics related to time

theory of planned action attitudinal measurement approach that expands upon the behavioral intentions model by including a perceived control component

third-party endorsement one form of publicity in which an ostensibly objective outsider (neither the customer nor the business) provides publicly available purchase recommendations or evaluations

time pressure urgency to act based on some real or self-imposed deadline

top-line performance a business term referring to sales growth (sales being at the top of an earnings statement)

total value concept business practice wherein companies operate with the understanding that products provide value in multiple ways

touchpoints direct contacts between the firm and a customer

tradition customs and accepted ways of everyday behavior in a given culture

trait distinguishable characteristic that describes one's tendency to act in a relatively consistent manner

trait approach to personality approaches in personality research that focus on specific consumer traits as motivators of various consumer behaviors

translational equivalence two phrases share the same precise meaning in two different cultures

trustworthiness how honest and unbiased the source is perceived to be

U

uncertainty avoidance extent to which a culture is uncomfortable with things that are ambiguous or unknown

unconditioned response response that occurs naturally as a result of exposure to an unconditioned stimulus

unconditioned stimulus stimulus with which a behavioral response is already associated

underlying attributes attributes that are not readily apparent and can be learned only through experience or contact with the product

undifferentiated marketing plan wherein the same basic product is offered to all customers

unintentional learning learning that occurs when behavior is modified through a consumer-stimulus interaction without any effortful allocation of cognitive processing capacity toward that stimulus

universal set total collection of all possible solutions to a consumer problem

unplanned shopping shopping activity that shares some, but not all, characteristics of truly impulsive consumer behavior; being characterized by situational memory, a utilitarian orientation, and feelings of spontaneity

utilitarian function of attitudes function of attitudes in which consumers use attitudes as ways to maximize rewards and minimize punishment

utilitarian influence ways in which a consumer conforms to group expectations in order to receive a reward or avoid punishment

utilitarian motivation drive to acquire products that can be used to accomplish something

utilitarian shopping value worth obtained because some shopping task or job is completed successfully

utilitarian value gratification derived because something helps a consumer solve a problem or accomplish some task

V

VALS popular psychographic method in consumer research that divides consumers into groups based on resources and consumer behavior motivations

value a personal assessment of the net worth obtained from an activity

value co-creation the realization that a consumer is necessary and must play a part in order to produce value

value consciousness the extent to which consumers tend to maximize what they receive from a transaction as compared to what they give

value-expressive function of attitudes function of attitudes whereby attitudes allow consumers to express their core values, self-concept, and beliefs to others

value-expressive influence ways in which a consumer internalizes a group's values or the extent to which consumers join groups in order to express their own closely held values and beliefs

variety-seeking behavior seeking new brands or products as a response to boredom or to satisfy a perceived need for change

verbal communication transfer of information through either the literal spoken or written word

viral marketing marketing method that uses online technologies to facilitate WOM by having consumers spread messages through their online conversations

visceral responses certain feeling states that are tied to physical reactions/behavior in a very direct way

W

want a specific desire representing a way a consumer may go about addressing a recognized need

Weber's Law law that states that a consumer's ability to detect differences between two levels of a stimulus decreases as the intensity of the initial stimulus increases

word-of-mouth (WOM) information about products, services, and experiences that is transmitted from consumer to consumer

workbench memory storage area in the memory system where information is stored while it is being processed and encoded for later recall

world teen culture speculation that teenagers around the world are more similar to each other than to people from other generations in the same culture

SUBJECT INDEX

A

ABC approach to attitudes, 132
Absolute threshold, 59
Abusive consumer behavior, 329–330
Accommodation, 58
Acculturation, 192, 193
Acquisitional shopping, 234, 235
Action-oriented, 239
Actual state, 258
Adaptation level, 78
Addictive consumption, 332
Adopters, 174
Adultolescence, 176
Advertiming, 232
Aesthetic labor, 109
Affect, 27
Affect-based evaluation, 269
Affective quality, 242
Affective quality, 237
African-American culture, 214–215
Age
    as demographic variable, 125
    and shoplifting, 328
Age-based microculture, 207–208
Agency appraisal, 99
Aggregation approach, 113
Aggressive driving, 331
Agreement, indications of, 199
AIO statements, 124
American Consumer Satisfaction Index (ACSI), 290
Antecedent conditions, 247
Anthropology, 9
Anthropomorphism, 58
Anticipation appraisal, 98
Antiloyal consumers, 319
Antiloyalty, 319
Apps, 169
Asian culture, 215
Aspirational group, 160
Assimilation, 57
Associative network, 87
Atmosphere elements, 242
Atmospherics, 241
Attention, 55
Attention to social comparison information (ATSCI), 168
Attitude—behavior consistency, 138
Attitudes
    ABC approach to, 132
    alternative approaches to, 139
    behavior in relation to, 138–139
    change theories and persuasion, 140–146
    components of, 132
    consumer models, 135–140

defined, **131**
ego-defensive function of, 133
functions of, 132–133
hierarchy of effects, 133–135
knowledge function of, 133
toward advertisement, 139
toward shopping, 264
utilitarian function of, 132
value-expressive function of, 133
Attitude-toward-the-object (ATO) model, 135–136, 140, 276
Attitude tracking, 139–**140**
Attractiveness, of source, 151
Attribute, 12
Attribute-based evaluation, 270
Attribute correlation, 274
Attribution theory, 298, 311
Augmented product, 35
Augmented reality, 263
Authenticity, 288
Authority, 161
Autobiographical memories, 107
Autonomic measures, emotion, 101
Awareness set, 260

B

Baby Boomers, 209
Background music, 243
Backward sloping demand, 37
Balance theory, 144
Behavioral conditioning, 69
Behavioral influence decision-making perspective, 254
Behavioral influence hierarchy, 134, 142
Behavioral intentions model, 138
Behaviorist approach to learning, 66
Beliefs, 140
Benefits, 5, 257
Bicultural, 214
Big data, 21
Binge drinking, 333
Binge eating, 333
Bipolar, 102
Birthrates, 219
Blended families, 175
Blue ocean strategy, 39
Body esteem, 127
Body language, 198
Body piercings, 128
Boomerang kids, 176
Bounded rationality, 269
Brain dominance, 79
Brand community, 160
Brand inertia, 256
Brand loyalty, 256

Brand personality
    appeal, 122
    defined, **121**
    formation, 121–122
Brand personality appeal, 122
Brands and brand names
    associations with, 275
    country of origin, 43
    discriminative stimuli, 64
    packaging, 75
    product placements, 60–61
    reactions to new, 90
    selective distortion, 55
BRIC, 189, 200
Buying power, 247
Buzz marketing, 171

C

CANZUS, 192
Caregivers, 177
Cell phone use and driving, 331
Central cues, 143
Central route to persuasion, 142
Chindia, 201
Chinglish, 195
Choice, 251
Chunk, 85
Chunking, 84, 85
Circadian cycle, 232
Classical conditioning, 67
Clayton Act, 10
Coercive power, 163
Cognition
    defined, **27**
    need for, 118
Cognitive appraisal theory, 98
Cognitive dissonance, 299, 300
Cognitive interference, 84
Cognitive organization, 57
Cognitive psychology, 8
Cognitive structuring, 207
Cohort, 208
Collaborative consumption, 23
Collectivism, 186
Color, 73, 244
Communication
    changes in, 21
    culture and, 194
    interactive, 147
    nonverbal, 197
    verbal, 195–197
Compensatory damages, 345
Compensatory model, 138
Compensatory rules, 276
Competition and consumer orientation, 9–11
Competitive intensity, 316
Competitiveness, 118–119

Competitive pressure, 10
Complainers, 306, 307
Complaining behavior, 306
Comprehension, 55
    defined, **70**
    environmental characteristics, 80–81
    factors affecting consumer, 72
    message characteristics, 72–76
    message receiver characteristics, 76–79
    signal theory, 72
    timing on, 81
Compulsive buying, 332
Compulsive consumption, 332
Compulsive shopping, 332
Computer-mediated behaviors, 329
Conditioned response, 67
Conditioned stimulus, 67
Confirmatory bias, 296
Conformity, 161
Congruity, 242
Conjoint analysis, 276
Conjunctive rule, 278, 279
Connected self-schema, 169
Consideration set, 260
Consistency principle, 144
Construal level theory, 81
Consumer affect, 10
Consumer affluence, 220
Consumer behavior (CB). *See also* **Consumer misbehavior**
    competition and consumer orientation, 9–11
    competitive pressure, 10
    consumption, 6
    defined, **3**
    demographic changes, 22
    economics, 6–7
    economy, changing and sharing, 22–23
    effects of, 2–4
    as field of study, **6**–9
    firm orientations and consumers, 10–11
    as human behavior, 4
    internationalization, 20
    interpretive research, **17**–18
    and marketing, 8
    and marketing strategy, 12–15
    and personal growth, 17
    and personality, 112–116
    process of, 4–6
    psychology, **8**
    quantitative consumer research, 18–20
    relationship marketing, 11
    self-concept in, 126
    self-congruency and, 128–129
    and society, 15–16
    technological changes, 20–22
    traits in, 116–123
    word-of-mouth (WOM) and, 170

Consumer behavior as a field of study, 6
Consumer Bill of Rights, 336
Consumer budgeting, 247
Consumer dissatisfaction, 293, 300–301. *See also* **Consumer satisfaction**
Consumer doppelganger effect, 174
Consumer ethnocentrism, 193
Consumer identity, 129
Consumer inertia, 317
Consumer information processing (CIP), 293, 296
Consumer involvement, 95–96
Consumerism, 336
Consumer misbehavior
    abusive, 329–330
    binge drinking, 333
    compulsive consumption, 332
    computer-mediated behaviors, 329
    defined, **325**
    drug abuse, 334
    eating disorders, 333
    and ethics, 326–327
    and exchange, 324–327
    focus of, 325–327
    fraud, 329
    illegal sharing of software and music, 328–329
    illegitimate complaining, 330
    marketing ethics and, 334–339
    motivations of, 327
    problem behavior *vs.,* 327–334
    problem gambling, 333–334
    product misuse, 330–332
    sexting, 332
    shoplifting, 328
Consumer (customer) orientation, 10
Consumer perception, 53–54
Consumer problem behavior, 327
Consumer refuse, 301
Consumer relationships
    complaining behavior, 306–309
    loyalty, 316–321
    outcomes of consumption, 304–306
    switching behavior, 313–316
    word-of-mouth/publicity, 309–313
Consumers
    attention creation, 65
    external influences, 28
    firm orientations and, 10–11
    global trends, 23
    inequitable, 298
    internal influences, 27
    personality of, 27–28
    and phones, 16
    psychology of, 27
    treatment of, 9–11
Consumer satisfaction, 286–303
    and attribution theory, 298
    cognitive dissonance, 299
    and consumer reactions, 288–289
    defined, 292
    disposing of refuse, 301–303
    emotion, 289–290

equity theory and, 297
meaning transference, 289
measurement issues, 300–301
post-consumption reactions, 293–294, 294–300
product classification, 287–288
role of consumption and value, 286–287
value and, 290
Consumer search behavior, 259
Consumer self-construal, 100
Consumer self-regulation, 239
Consumer socialization, 179
Consumer Value Framework (CVF)
    components, 25–30
    defined, **25**
    and switching, 320
Consumer vulnerability and product harmfulness, 338
Consumption
    cocreation of, 321–323
    defined, **6**
    impulsive shopping and, 237
    process of, 26
    and product classification, 287
Consumption frequency, 288
Contractualism, 326
Contrast, 58
Control, 298
Conversion, of product, 302
Core societal values (CSV)
    defined, **185**
    leaders, 189
    scoreboard, 188–189, 190
Corporate associations, 139
Corporate social responsibility (CSR), 339
Corporate strategy, 33
Cosmetic surgery, 127–128
Costs, 5
Counterarguments, 76
Couponing, 168
Credibility, 76, 150
Criteria selection, 272–273
Critical incident, 306
Crowding, 245, 246
Cultural distance (CD), 190, 191
Cultural norm, 182
Cultural sanction, 182–183
Culture, 180–201
    body language, 198
    communication, 195–200
    defined, **181**
    diversity, 221
    emerging, 200–201
    etiquette/manners, 198–199
    Globish, 197
    inputs, 185
    learning of, 192–195
    meaning of, 181–182
    nonverbal communication, 197
    norms, 182
    outputs, 185
    and policy-related communication, 194
    popular, 183
    relationships, 199
    role expectations, 184
    sanction, 182–183
    sources of, 184–185
    space, 198

symbols, 200
time, 197
values, 185–186
verbal communication, 195–197
Customer commitment, 318–319
Customer Lifetime Value (CLV), 42–43
Customer orientation, 343
Customer Relationship Management (CRM), 26
Customer share, 315–316
CVF. *See* **Consumer Value Framework (CVF)**

D

Deceptive advertising, 341
Decision making
    approaches to, 255–257
    and choice, 251–253
    consideration set, 260–261
    consumption process and, 250–251
    and emotion, 253
    evaluation of alternatives, 266–268
    external search, 261–265
    household decision making, 174
    and motivation, 252
    need recognition, 258
    ongoing and prepurchase search, 259–260
    perspectives on, 253–255
    product categorization, 270–276
    rules, 276–280
    search behavior, 258–259
    and value, 252
Decision rules, 276–280
Declarative knowledge, 87
Deficient products, 337
Demographic analysis, 217, 218
Demographics, 125, 126
Demographics
    consumer behavior and, 22
Deontological evaluations, 326
Desirable products, 337
Desire, 297
Desired state, 258
Determinant criteria, 268
Dialects, 195
Differential association, 327
Differentiated marketers, 14
Diffusion process, 174
Disconfirmation, 300
Disconfirmation theory, 294
Discretionary (spare) time, 231
Discriminative stimuli, 68
Disjunctive rule, 278, 279
Disposal of refuse, 301–303
Dissociative group, 161
Distributive fairness, 297
Divergence, 204
Diversity, cultural, 221
Divorce, 175
Donation of products, 302
Door-in-the-face technique, 343
Drinking and driving, 331
Drug abuse, 334
Dual coding, 83

Dual coding, 84
Durable goods, 287

E

Eating disorders, 333
Echoic storage, 82
Ecological factors, 184
Economic resources, 247
Economics, 6
Ego, 114
Ego-defensive function of attitudes, 133
Elaboration, 87
Elaboration likelihood model (ELM), 142
Elasticity, 37
Elimination-by-aspects rule (EBA), 278, 279
Emotion
    affect, 100
    cognitive appraisal theory, 98–99
    contagion, 110–111
    and decision making, 252
    defined, **98**
    individual differences, 103–107
    measuring, 100–104
    mood, 99
    mood-congruent recall, 106–107
    and product disposal, 303
    schema-based, 108–110
    self-conscious, 110
    semantic wiring, 107
    and shoplifting, 328
Emotional ability, 246
Emotional contagion, 110
Emotional effect on memory, 107
Emotional expressiveness, 105
Emotional intelligence, 106
Emotional involvement, 97
Emotional labor, 110
Employee behavior, 338
Encoding, 83
Enculturation, 192
Enduring involvement, 97
Episodic memory, 90
Epistemic shopping, 234, 235
Epistemic shopping, 234
Equitable expectations, 295
Equity appraisal, 99
Equity theory, 297
Ethics, 334
Ethnic identification, 193
Ethnicity, 126
Ethnography, 18
Etiquette, 198
Evaluative criteria, 261
Evaluative criteria, 267
Even-a-penny-will-help technique, 343
E-waste, 302
Exchange, 5
Exemplar, 89
Expectancy/disconfirmation approach, 294
Expectations, 79
    confidence in, 296
    defined, **294**
    and service quality, 297

source of, 295–296
types of, 295
Experiential decision-making perspective, 254
Experiential hierarchy, 133, 134
Experiential shopping, 234, 235
Expertise, 76, 150
Expert power, 162, 163
Explicit memory, 62
Exposure, 54
Extended decision making, 256
Extended family, 175
External influences, 28–30
External search
  amount of, 263–264
  defined, **261**
  and emerging technologies, 262
  minimized, 264–265
  role of price in, 261
  search regret, 265
  and smartphone applications, 262–263
Extinction, 69
Eye-tracking technology, 101

F

Fair Packaging and Labeling Act, 340
Familiarity, 63, 77
Family household, 174
Fear appeals, 148
Feature, 267
Femininity, 186
Figurative language, 75
Figure, 75
Figure-ground distinction, 75
Financial risk, 255
Financial switching costs, 314
Firm orientations and consumers, 10–11
Fishbein model. *See* **Attitude-toward-the-object (ATO) model**
Fit, 242
Five factor model (FFM), 119, 120
Flow, 105
Font, 73
Foot-in-the-door technique, 343
Foreground music, 243
Formal group, 160
Framing, 80
France, 213
Fraud, 329
Freemiums, 156
Functional quality, 237, 241
Functional theory of attitudes, 132

G

Gender
  femininity, 186
  and household decision making, 178–179
  masculinity, 186
Generation X consumers, 209
Generation Z consumers, 210
Geodemographic techniques, 125
Germany, 197

Gift (prepaid) cards, 248
Gift shopping, 249
Globish, 197
Glocalization, 201
Golden section, 74
Gothic Lolita microculture, 216
Goth microculture, 216
GPS-based technologies, 263
Greatest generation, 209
Ground, 75
Grounded cognition, 56
Group influence, 159
Guanxi, 188
Guerrilla marketing, 171

H

Habitual decision making, 256
Habituation, 77
Habitus, 215
Haptic perception, 82
Hedonic motivation, 95, 96
Hedonic shopping value, 236
Hedonic value, 258
Hedonic value, 31
Hierarchical approach to personality, 120
Hierarchy of effects, 133
High-involvement hierarchy, 134
Hispanic culture, 213–214
Homeostasis, 93
Homogamy, 215
Hope, 295
Household decision making
  boomerang kids, 176
  defined, **174**
  family structure, 174–176
  gender and, 178–179
  household life cycle, 176
  kid power, 179
  purchase roles, 178
Household life cycle (HLC), 176, 177
Humor appeals, 148

I

Iconic storage, 82
Id, 114
Ideal expectations, 295
Ideal point, 39
Idiographic perspective, 115
Illegal sharing of software and music, 328–329
Illegitimate complaining, 330
Implicit memory, 62
Impulsive consumption, 237
Impulsive shopping, 234, 236
Impulsive *vs.* compulsive consumer behavior, 241
Impulsivity, 239
"I'm working for you!" technique, 344
Income, 126
Individual differences
  defined, **27**
  in susceptibility to group influence, 168
Individualism, 185
Indulgence-restraint, 188
Inept set, 261
Inert set, 261

Informal group, 160
Informational influence, 163–164
Information intensity, 80
Information overload, 260
Information processing (or cognitive) perspective., 67
Ingratiation tactics, 343
Ingroup, 159
Innovation, 13
Innovativeness, 117
Innovators, 174
Instrumental conditioning, 67–68
Intensity, 73
Intentional learning, 66
Interactional fairness, 298
Interactive communications, 147
Internal influences, 27–28
Internal search, 260
Internationalization, 20
Internet of things, 22
Interpretive research, 17
Involuntary attention, 65
Involvement, 65, 77
  consumer, 95
  purchase, 264
  types of, 96

J

JMD (just meaningful difference), **62**
JND (just noticeable difference), **60**–62
Judgments, 273

K

Kid power, 179
Knowledge
  declarative, **87**
  prior, 76
Knowledge function of attitudes, 133

L

Language, type of, 75
Latitudes of acceptance, 145
Latitudes of rejection, 145
Laughter, 106
Law, marketing and, 340–341
Learning. *See also* **Perception**
  defined, **52**
  implicit and explicit memory, 62–65
  intentional, 66–67
  message characteristics on, 73
  unintentional, 67–69
Left skewed data, 301
Legitimate power, 162, 163
Lexicographic rule, 278, 279
Life expectancy for citizens, 220–221
Lifestyles, 123
Lighting, 245
Likeable sources, 151
Limited decision making, 256
Locus, 298
Long-term memory, 86
Long-term orientation (LTO), 188

Low-involvement hierarchy, 134
Low-involvement processing, 144
Low-power-distance nations, 187
Loyalty, consumer
  consumer inertia, 317
  customer share, 315–317
  loyalty card/program, 317
Loyalty card/program, 317

M

Manipulative sales tactics, 343–344
Mannerisms, 198
Marketing
  activity regulation, 340–341
  to children, 341–342
  defined, **8**
  firm, relationships and, 322
Marketing concept, 336
Marketing ethics, 334
Marketing mix, 36
Marketing myopia, 33
Marketing strategy
  consumer behavior, 12–15
  consumer behavior theory in, 40
  and consumer value, 33–38
  defined, **33**
Marketing tactics, 34
Market maven, 173
Market orientation, 11
Markets
  with perceptual maps, 39–40
  product differentiation, 38
  segmentation, 36–38
Market segmentation, 36
Masculinity, 186
Maslow's hierarchy of needs, 94
Matchup hypothesis, 151
Materialism, 117
Meaningful encoding, 84
Meaningfulness, of sources, 151
Meaning transference, 289
Memory
  defined, 81
  episodic, 90
  long-term, 86
  multiple store theory of, 81–83
  sensory, 82
  workbench, 83, 85
Memory trace, 86
Mental budgeting, 248
Mental tagging, 86
Merchandising, 245
Mere association effect, 64
Mere exposure effect, 62
Message appeal, 147–150
Message congruity, 74
Message effects, 146
Message media, 81
Messages
  appeals of, 147–150
  construction, 149–150
  environmental characteristics, 80–81
  receiver characteristics, 76–77
  and source effects, **146,** 150–151
  sources, 75–76
Metaphor, 79
Metric equivalence, 196–197

Microcultures
age-based, 207–208
and consumer behavior, 202
cultural hierarchy, 202–204
defined, **202**
demographic analysis, 217–219
ethnic, 213
female segments, 206
generational, 208–211
income and social class, 215
international, 216
male segments, 206
regional, 205
religious, 212
role conflict, 204
sex roles, 205
societal role expectations, 205
street, 216
trends affecting consumer behavior, 219–221
U. S., 204–216
values, 204
Middle class, 216
Millennials, 209
Mobile visual search (MVS), 263
Modeling, 194, 195
Moderating variable, 96
Mood, 99, 249
Mood-congruent judgments, 100
Mood-congruent recall, 107, **108**
Moral beliefs, 326
Moral constraints, lack of, 327
Moral equity, 326
Morals, 339
Motivation
and decision making, 252
Motivational research era, 114
Motivations
classifications, 95
defined, **92**
general hierarchy of, 94–97
hedonic, 95, 96
human behavior and, 92–94
utilitarian, 95, 96
Multiattribute attitude model, 135
Multi-item satisfaction scale, 301
Multiple store theory of memory, 81–83
Multiple-trait approach, 116
Music, 243

N

Near-field communication (NFC), 233
Need for cognition, 118
Need recognition, 258
Negative disconfirmation, 294
Negative emotions, 106
Negative peer pressure, 161
Negative public publicity, 310
Negative word-of-mouth, 309, 312
Negligence, 344
Netnography, 18
Neuroscience, 8
Niche marketing, 15

Nodes, 88
Nomothetic perspective, 115
Noncompensatory rules, 276
Non-complainers, 307
Nondurable goods, 288
Nonfamily, 175
Nonlinear effect, 246
Nonverbal communication, 197, 198
Normative expectations, 295
Nostalgia, 87
Nuclear family, 175
Numbers, 73

O

Odors, 242–243
Olfactory, 242
One-to-one marketing, 14
Ongoing search, 259
Online retail selection, 280
Online social network sites. *See* **Social networking websites**
Opinion leader, 173
Opportunism, 330
Organizational identification, 129
Organizing perceptions, 56–58
Orientation, 248
Orientation reflex, 65
Outcomes appraisal, 99
Outgroup, 159
Outshopping, 235

P

Packrats, 303
PAD (pleasure–arousal–dominance), 102
PANAS (positive-affect-negative-affect scale), 103
Pathological socialization, 327
Paths, 88
Pay what you want (PWYW) phenomenon, 262
Peer pressure, 161
Perceived risk, 264
Perceived risk, 255
Perception
consumer, 53–54
defined, **53**
process of, 55–60
and reality, 53–54
selective, 58–59
Perceptual attributes, 272
Perceptual maps, 39
Performance perceptions, 296
Peripheral cues, 144
Peripheral route to persuasion, 143
Personal elaboration, 87
Personal growth, 17
Personality
and brand relationships, 122
and consumer behavior, 112–116
hierarchical approach to, 120
psychoanalytic approach to, 114–115
trait approach to, 115–116
traits, 275
Personal relationship, 199

Personal shopping value (PSV), 236
Personology, 121
Persuasion, 140
Phenomenology, 18
Physical characteristics, 73
Physical limitations, 79
Physical risk, 255
Planned obsolescence, 342
Pleasing products, 337
Pleasure principle, 114
PMG (price-matching guarantee), 72
Pollution, 342
Positive disconfirmation, 294
Positive reinforcers, 68
Positive word-of-mouth, 309
Post-consumption cognitions, 305
Potential value, 287
Power distance, 186
Preattentive effects, 62
Predictive analytics, 21
Predictive expectations, 295
Preferred customer perks, 319
Prepurchase search, 259
Price, 261
Price gouging, 342
Price-matching guarantee (PMG), 72
Primacy effect, 149
Primary group, 160
Priming, 80
Prior knowledge, 76
PRIZM, 125
Problem gambling, 333
Procedural justice, 305
Procedural switching costs, 314
Product
defined, **13**
experience, 263
harmfulness and consumer vulnerability, 338
knowledge, 273
misuse, 330–332
ownership, 129
selection, 165, 166
Product categories, 270
Product contamination, 111
Product differentiation, 38
Product enthusiasts, 97
Product involvement, 97
Production orientation, 14
Productivity orientation, 119
Product placements, 64
Product positioning, 39
Products liability, 344–345
Promotion, product, 337
Promotional conversion rates, 263
Promotion focus, 90
Prospect theory, 80
Prototype, 89
Psychoanalytic approach to personality, 114–115
Psychobiological emotion, 98
Psychographics, 124
Psychology, 8
Psychology of consumer, 27
Public criticism of marketing
deceptive advertising, 341
manipulative sales tactics, 343–344

marketing to children, 341–342
planned obsolescence, 342
pollution, 342
price gouging, 342
products liability, 344–345
stealth marketing, 344
Puffery, 341
Punishers, 69
Punitive damages, 345

Q

QR codes (quick response codes), 263
Qualitative research tools, 17, 18–19
Quality, 262
Quantitative research, 19
Quartet of institutions, 193

R

Rancorous revenge, 308
Rational decision-making perspective, 254
Reacting, in perceptual process, 58–60
Reality principle, 114
Recency effect, 149
Recycling, 302
Reference group
aspirational group, 160
authority, 161
categories of influence, 163–166
conformity, 161
defined, 158
dissociative group, 161
formal group, 160
group influence, 159
individual susceptibility, 168–170
informal group, 160
primary group, 160
secondary group, 160
social media, 166–168
social power, 162–163
value and, 164–165
Referent power, 162, 163
Regional microculture, 205
Regulatory focus theory, 94
Rehearsal, 84
Relational switching cost, 314
Relationship marketing, 11
Relationship quality, 26, 322, 323
Relativism, 326
Religious microculture, 212–213
Renquing, 188
Repetition, 83, 84
Researcher dependent, 18
Reselling, 303
Resource-advantage theory, 12
Response generation, 85
Responsibility, 311
Retail atmospherics, 241
Retail borrowing, 325
Retail outlet selection, 280
Retail personality, 237
Retail personality, 236–237
Retail store, 237

NAME INDEX

A

Aaker, David, 257
Ajzen, Icek, 135
Allport, Gordon, 116

B

Beckham, Odell, Jr., 74
Bieber, Justin, 183
Bond, James, 15
Brinker, Nancy, 348

C

Cash, Johnny, 211
Cyrus, Miley, 183

D

Davis, Sammy, Jr., 15
Dietz, Doug, 45
Dylan, Bob, 172

E

Edison, Thomas A., 44

F

Fishbein, Martin, 135
Fullerton, Ronald, 327

G

Garreau, Joel, 205

H

Hofstede, Geert, 185

K

Kant, Immanuel, 326
Kardashian, Khloé, 51
Kardashian, Kim, 51
Kardashian, Kourtney, 51
Kelley, David, 45
Knauer, Tracy, 283
Kotler, Philip, 337
Kuang, Cliff, 44

L

Levitt, Theodore, 13, 336–337

M

Manning, Peyton, 144, 145
Martin, Dean, 90

N

Nelson, Willie, 211

O

Odbert, Henry, 116

P

Pavlov, Ivan, 67
Piktelis, Judy, 283
Punj, Girish, 327

R

Roebuck, Alvah, 50
Rosecrans, Tom, 152–153

S

Sears, Richard W., 50
Sinatra, Frank, 15

T

Teng, Joe, 346–347

U

Updyke, Harvey, 350

W

Wade, Dwayne, 151

Y

Yadav, Tarun, 346–347

PRODUCTS/ORGANIZATIONS INDEX

1-1 **Understand the meaning of *consumption* and *consumer behavior*.** Consumption represents the process by which goods, services, or ideas are used and transformed into value. The basic consumer behavior process includes steps that begin with consumer needs and finish with value. Consumer behavior, or CB as it is sometimes called, can be viewed either from the standpoint of human behavior or as a field of study. In terms of human behavior, consumer behavior is the set of value-seeking activities that take place as people go about addressing realized needs. Thus, consumer behavior captures the things that we do as we try to seek out, purchase, and use goods, products, services, and ideas. Consumer behavior as a field of study represents the study of consumers as they go about the consumption process. Thus, textbooks, trade literature, and research journals all direct their subject matter toward the behavior of consumers in an effort to develop consumer behavior theory.

Exhibit 1.1

The Basic Consumption Process

Need → Want → Exchange → Costs and Benefits → Reaction → Value

iStockphoto.com/Squaredpixels

consumer behavior set of value-seeking activities that take place as people go about addressing their real needs (p. 4)

want a specific desire representing a way a consumer may go about addressing a recognized need (p. 5)

exchange acting out of the decision to give something up in return for something perceived to be of greater value (p. 5)

costs negative results of consumption experiences (p. 5)

benefits positive results of consumption experiences (p. 5)

consumption process by which consumers use and transform goods, services, or ideas into value (p. 6)

consumer behavior as a field of study study of consumers as they go about the consumption process; the science of studying how consumers seek value in an effort to address real needs (p. 6)

economics study of production and consumption (p. 6)

psychology study of human reactions to their environment (p. 8)

social psychology study that focuses on the thoughts, feelings, and behaviors that people have as they interact with other people (p. 8)

cognitive psychology study of the intricacies of mental reactions involved in information processing (p. 8)

neuroscience the study of the central nervous system including brain mechanisms associated with emotion (p. 8)

marketing multitude of value-producing seller activities that facilitate *exchanges* between buyers and sellers, including production, pricing, promotion, distribution, and retailing (p. 8)

sociology the study of groups of people within a society, with relevance for consumer behavior because a great deal of consumption takes place within group settings or is affected by group behavior (p. 9)

anthropology field of study involving interpretation of relationships between consumers and the things they purchase, the products they own, and the activities in which they participate (p. 9)

1-2 **Describe how competitive marketing environments lead to better outcomes for consumers.** Two market characteristics help explain how customers are treated: competitiveness and dependence. In a competitive market, consumers do not have to put up with poor treatment because some other business will gladly provide a better alternative. Thus, competitive markets drive organizations toward a consumer orientation as a way of surviving in the marketplace. Similarly, a business that depends on repeat business also must emphasize the creation of valuable exchange relationships with its customers, otherwise customers will simply go elsewhere the next time they desire that particular good or service. More and more firms recognize that they serve many stakeholders and, in doing so, practice stakeholder marketing.

consumer (customer) orientation way of doing business in which the actions and decision making of the institution prioritize consumer value and satisfaction above all other concerns (p. 10)

market orientation organizational culture that embodies the importance of creating value for customers among all employees (p. 11)

stakeholder marketing an orientation in which firms recognize that more than just the buyer and seller are involved in the marketing process, and a host of primary and secondary entities affect and are affected by the value creation process (p. 11)

relationship marketing activities based on the belief that the firm's performance is enhanced through repeat business (p. 11)

touchpoints direct contacts between the firm and a customer (p. 11)

1-3 **Explain the role of consumer behavior in today's business and society.** Consumer behavior is clearly an important input to business/marketing strategy. The firm can build value only with an understanding of what exactly leads to a high-value experience. In addition, consumer behavior knowledge is necessary in understanding how customers view competing firms within a market. Consumer behavior also is important because it is a force that shapes society. In fact, CB helps form society in many ways. Trends such as the decreasing acceptability of smoking, the increasing acceptability of using mobile phones in social situations, as well as changes in general marketplace etiquette are all caused by consumers. Finally, knowledge of consumer behavior is important in making responsible decisions as a consumer. An educated consumer is a more effective consumer.

resource-advantage theory theory that explains why companies succeed or fail; the firm goes about obtaining resources from consumers in return for the value the resources create (p. 12)

attribute a part, or tangible feature, of a product that potentially delivers a benefit of consumption (p. 12)

product potentially valuable bundle of benefits (p. 13)

undifferentiated marketing plan where in the same basic product is offered to all customers (p. 14)

production orientation approach where innovation is geared primarily toward making the production process as efficient and economic as possible (p. 14)

differentiated marketers firms that serve multiple market segments, each with a unique product offering (p. 14)

one-to-one marketing plan where in a different product is offered for each individual customer so that each customer is treated as a segment of one (p. 14)

niche marketing plan wherein a firm specializes in serving one market segment with particularly unique demand characteristics (p. 15)

1-4 **Be familiar with basic approaches to studying consumer behavior.** Many people with varied backgrounds study consumer behavior. Thus, consumer behavior is studied from many different perspectives involving many different research tools. An interpretative approach seeks to explain the inner meanings and motivations associated with specific consumption experiences. Interpretative research usually involves qualitative research tools such as case analyses, clinical interviews, focus group interviews, and others where data are gathered in a relatively unstructured way. Quantitative research addresses questions about consumer behavior using numerical measurement and analysis tools. The measurement is usually structured, meaning the consumer simply chooses a response from among alternatives supplied by the researcher.

interpretive research approach that seeks to explain the inner meanings and motivations associated with specific consumption experiences (p. 17)

qualitative research tools means for gathering data in a relatively unstructured way, including case analysis, clinical interviews, and focus group interviews (p. 17)

researcher dependent subjective data that requires a researcher to interpret the meaning (p. 18)

phenomenology qualitative approach to studying consumers that relies on interpretation of the lived experience associated with some aspect of consumption (p. 18)

ethnography qualitative approach to studying consumers that relies on

interpretation of artifacts to draw conclusions about consumption (p. 18)

netnography a branch of ethnography that studies the behavior of online cultures and communities (p. 18)

quantitative research approach that addresses questions about consumer behavior using numerical measurement and analysis tools (p. 19)

1-5 **Appreciate how dynamic the field of consumer behavior continues to be, particularly as CB is shaped by technological advances including big data analytics, the "internet of things" and the sharing economy.** Consumer behavior is ever changing. Several trends are shaping today's consumer climate. These include increasing internationalization of the marketplace, the rate of technological innovation, and changes in demographics that affect buying power and quality of life. Consumer research continues to evolve along with these changes.

big data term used to represent the massive amounts of data available to companies, which can potentially be used to predict customer behaviors (p. 21)

predictive analytics the application of statistical tools in an effort to discover patterns in data that allow prediction of consumer behavior (p. 21)

Internet of things the automatic recording of data from everyday products that signal consumers patterns of behavior (p. 22)

sharing economy the global consumer trend toward rental (temporary usage for hire) rather than ownership (p. 23)

collaborative consumption the term used for a rental transaction activity that is consumer to consumer, rather than business to consumer or business to business (p. 23)

2-1 Describe the consumer value framework, including its basic components. The Consumer Value Framework (CVF) represents consumer behavior theory illustrating factors that shape consumption-related behaviors and ultimately determine the value associated with consumption. Value lies at the heart of the CVF. Value results from the consumption process, which represents the decision-making process of consumers seeking value. This process is influenced directly and indirectly by external and internal influences such as culture and psychology, respectively. When high value results, consumers may become loyal and committed customers. The CVF is useful for organizing consumer behavior knowledge both in theory and in practice.

Consumer Value Framework (CVF) consumer behavior theory that illustrates factors that shape consumption-related behaviors and ultimately determine the value associated with consumption (p. 25)

Customer Relationship Management (CRM) systematic information management system that collects, maintains, and reports detailed information about customers to enable a more customer-oriented managerial approach (p. 26)

relationship quality degree of connectedness between a consumer and a retailer, brand, or service provider (p. 26)

service an organization's efforts and resources applied toward value creation (p. 26)

internal influences things that go on inside the mind and heart of the consumer or that are truly a part of the consumer psychologically (p. 27)

cognition thinking or mental processes that go on as we process and store things that can become knowledge (p. 27)

affect feelings associated with objects or activities (p. 27)

individual differences characteristic traits of individuals, including demographics, personality, and lifestyle (p. 27)

external influences social and cultural aspects of life as a consumer (p. 28)

social environment elements that specifically deal with the way other people influence consumer decision making and value (p. 28)

zero moment of truth The point when a shopper moves from passive to active and seeks out exchange alternatives (p. 28)

situational influences things unique to a time or place that can affect consumer decision making and the value received from consumption (p. 29)

2-2 Define consumer value and compare and contrast two key types of value. Value is a personal assessment of the net worth obtained from an activity. Value is what consumers ultimately pursue because valuable actions address motivations that manifest themselves in needs and desires. In this sense, value captures how much gratification a consumer receives from consumption. Activities and objects that lead to high utilitarian value do so because they help the consumer accomplish some task. Utilitarian value is how the consumer solves problems that come with being a consumer. The second type of value is hedonic value, which is the net worth obtained from the experience itself and the emotions associated with consumption. Hedonic value represents the immediate gratification that comes from some activity or experience. Hedonic value is very emotional and subjective in contrast to utilitarian value; however, the best consumption experiences offer some levels of both types of value.

$$\text{Value} = \text{What you get} - \text{What you give}$$

value a personal assessment of the net worth obtained from an activity (p. 30)

utilitarian value gratification derived because something helps a consumer solve a problem or accomplish some task (p. 31)

hedonic value value derived from the immediate gratification that comes from some activity (p. 31)

2-3 Apply the concepts of marketing strategy and marketing tactics to describe the way firms go about creating value for consumers. A marketing strategy is the way a company goes about creating value for customers. Thus, strategy and value go hand in hand. Marketing strategy is most effective when a firm adopts the total value concept. The total value concept is practiced when companies operate with the understanding that products provide value in multiple ways. Many products and brands, for instance, provide benefits that produce utilitarian value and some that provide hedonic value.

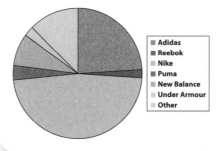

Exhibit 2.7

Market Share for Athletic Shoes

- Adidas
- Reebok
- Nike
- Puma
- New Balance
- Under Armour
- Other

understanding that products provide value in multiple ways (p. 35)

value co-creation the realization that a consumer is necessary and must play a part in order to produce value (p. 36)

strategy a planned way of doing something to accomplish some goal (p. 33)

marketing strategy way a company goes about creating value for customers (p. 33)

marketing myopia a common condition in which a shortsighted company views itself in a product business rather than in a value- or benefits-producing business (p. 33)

corporate strategy way a firm is defined and its general goals (p. 33)

marketing tactics ways marketing management is implemented; involves price, promotion, product, and distribution decisions (p. 34)

augmented product actual physical product purchased plus any services such as installation and warranties necessary to use the product and obtain its benefits (p. 35)

total value concept business practice wherein companies operate with the

2-4 **Explain the way market characteristics like market segmentation and product differentiation affect marketing strategy.** Market segmentation is the separation of a market into groups based on the different demand curves associated with each group. Product differentiation is a marketplace condition in which consumers do not view all competing products as identical to one another. Thus, if multiple segments are offered a unique product that closely matches their particular desires, all segments can receive high value. These characteristics affect the value consumers take from consumption. Individual market segments represent groups of consumers with similar tastes and thus receive value in much the same way as the other.

marketing mix combination of product, pricing, promotion, and distribution strategies used to implement a marketing strategy (p. 36)

target market identified segment or segments of a market that a company serves (p. 36)

market segmentation separation of a market into groups based on the different demand curves associated with each group (p. 36)

elasticity reflects how sensitive a consumer is to changes in some product characteristic (p. 37)

product differentiation marketplace condition in which consumers do not view all competing products as identical to one another (p. 38)

2-5 **Analyze consumer markets using elementary perceptual maps.** Positioning refers to the way a product is perceived by a consumer. This can be represented by the amount and types of characteristics perceived. A standard marketing tool is a perceptual map. A perceptual map is used to depict the positioning of competing products graphically. Consumer ideal points also can be located on a perceptual map. Perceptual mapping can help marketers identify competitors, analyze the potential effect associated with changing the marketing mix, and spot opportunities in the marketplace.

product positioning way a product is perceived by a consumer (p. 39)

perceptual map tool used to depict graphically the positioning of competing products (p. 39)

blue ocean strategy positioning a firm far away from competitors' positions so that it creates an industry of its own and, at least for a time, isolates itself from competitors (p. 39)

ideal point combination of product characteristics that provide the most value to an individual consumer or market segment (p. 39)

2-6 **Justify consumers' lifetime value as an effective focus for long-term business success.** Customer lifetime value (CLV) represents the approximate worth of a customer to a company in economic terms. Put another way, CLV is the overall profitability of an individual consumer. Thus, marketers can maximize the value they receive from exchange by concentrating their marketing efforts on consumers with high CLVs. From a business standpoint, firms that adopt the CLV as an important outcome are consumer oriented in the long term.

Customer Lifetime Value (CLV) approximate worth of a customer to a company in economic terms; overall profitability of an individual consumer (p. 42)

3-1 **Define learning and perception and how the two are connected.** Perception can be thought of as a consumer's awareness and interpretation of reality. Perception essentially represents one's subjective reality. During the perceptual process, consumers are exposed to stimuli, devote attention to stimuli, and attempt to comprehend the stimuli. Exposure refers to the process of bringing some stimulus within the proximity of a consumer so that it can be sensed by one of the five human senses. Attention is the purposeful allocation of information processing capacity toward developing an understanding of some stimulus. Comprehension occurs when the consumer attempts to derive meaning from information that is received.

learning change in behavior resulting from some interaction between a person and a stimulus (p. 52)

perception consumer's awareness and interpretation of reality (p. 53)

exposure process of bringing some stimulus within proximity of a consumer so that the consumer can sense it with one of the five human senses (p. 54)

sensation consumer's immediate response to a stimulus (p. 54)

sensory marketing actively seeking to engage customers' senses as the primary aspect of the value proposition (p. 54)

attention purposeful allocation of information-processing capacity toward developing an understanding of some stimulus (p. 55)

3-2 **List and define phases of the consumer perception process.** Consumers develop perceptions through the perceptual process. The perceptual process consists of three stages: sensing some stimuli by seeing, hearing, smelling, tasting, or touching; organizing the input from these human senses; and reacting as a result of this organization. This perceptual process allows consumers to interpret stimuli.

grounded cognition theory that suggests that bodily sensations influences thoughts and meaning independent of effortful thinking (p. 56)

cognitive organization process by which the human brain assembles sensory evidence into something recognizable (p. 57)

assimilation state that results when a stimulus has characteristics such that consumers readily recognize it as belonging to some specific category (p. 57)

accommodation state that results when a stimulus shares some but not all of the characteristics that would lead it to fit

neatly in an existing category, and consumers must process exceptions to rules about the category (p. 58)

contrast state that results when a stimulus does not share enough in common with existing categories to allow categorization (p. 58)

anthropomorphism giving humanlike characteristics to inanimate objects (p. 58)

selective exposure process of screening out certain stimuli and purposely exposing oneself to other stimuli (p. 59)

selective attention process of paying attention to only certain stimuli (p. 59)

selective distortion process by which consumers interpret information in ways that are biased by their previously held beliefs (p. 59)

subliminal processing way that the human brain deals with very low-strength stimuli, so low that the person has no conscious awareness (p. 59)

absolute threshold minimum strength of a stimulus that can be perceived (p. 59)

subliminal persuasion behavior change induced by subliminal processing (p. 60)

3-3 **Apply the concept of the just noticeable difference.** The JND (just noticeable difference) represents how much stronger one stimulus is relative to another so that someone can actually notice that the two are not the same. The key to using the JND concept is to realize that when some positive change is made to a stimulus, the best strategy is usually to make the change in a big enough increment that consumers notice something has changed. When some negative change must be made, marketers may consider small incremental changes that are less likely to be noticed.

JND just noticeable difference; condition in which one stimulus is sufficiently stronger than another so that someone can actually notice that the two are not the same (p. 60)

Weber's Law law that states that a consumer's ability to detect differences between two levels of a stimulus decreases as the intensity of the initial stimulus increases (p. 61)

JMD just meaningful difference; smallest amount of change in a stimulus that would influence consumer consumption and choice (p. 62)

3-4 **Contrast the concepts of implicit and explicit memory.** Implicit memory is memory for things that a person did not try to remember. Thus, when someone learns something after only a simple exposure to a stimulus, implicit memory is the explanation. Preattentive processes like mere exposure can produce implicit memory. Information processing and cognitive learning result in explicit memory, whereby a consumer actively tries to remember the stimuli to which he or she has been exposed.

explicit memory memory that develops when a person is exposed to, attends, and tries to remember information (p. 62)

implicit memory memory for things that a person did not try to remember (p. 62)

preattentive effects learning that occurs without attention (p. 62)

mere exposure effect effect that leads consumers to prefer a stimulus to which they've previously been exposed (p. 62)

mere association effect the transfer of meaning between objects that are similar only by accidental association (p. 64)

product placements intentional insertions of branded products within media

content not otherwise seen as advertising (p. 64)

involuntary attention attention that is autonomic, meaning beyond the conscious control of a consumer (p. 65)

orientation reflex natural reflex that occurs as a response to something threatening (p. 65)

3-5 **Know ways to help get consumers' attention in a crowded information environment.** Attention is the purposeful allocation of information processing capacity toward developing an understanding of some stimulus. Consumer attention can be enhanced in a number of ways. These include the use of stronger stimuli, contrast, movement, and surprise.

involvement the personal relevance toward, or interest in, a particular product (p. 65)

3-6 **Understand key differences between intentional and unintentional learning.** Learning is a change in behavior. Learning takes place in one of two ways. Either consumers learn things without trying to do so or they actively expend some effort. The first approach corresponds more to a behavioral theory of learning, while the second approach corresponds more closely to an information processing, or cognitive learning, perspective. Learning without trying only requires that a consumer be exposed to a stimulus. In contrast, the information processing perspective requires active learning and the ability to pay attention to information.

unintentional learning learning that occurs when behavior is modified through a consumer-stimulus interaction without any effortful allocation of cognitive processing capacity toward that stimulus (p. 66)

intentional learning process by which consumers set out to specifically learn information devoted to a certain subject (p. 66)

behaviorist approach to learning theory of learning that focuses on changes in behavior due to association without great concern for the cognitive mechanics of the learning process (p. 66)

information processing (or cognitive) perspective learning perspective that focuses on the cognitive processes associated with comprehension and how these precipitate behavioral changes (p. 67)

classical conditioning change in behavior that occurs simply through associating some stimulus with another stimulus that naturally causes some reaction; a type of unintentional learning (p. 67)

unconditioned stimulus stimulus with which a behavioral response is already associated (p. 67)

conditioned stimulus object or event that does not cause the desired response naturally but that can be conditioned to do so by pairing with an unconditioned stimulus (p. 67)

unconditioned response response that occurs naturally as a result of exposure to an unconditioned stimulus (p. 67)

conditioned response response that results from exposure to a conditioned stimulus that was originally associated with the unconditioned stimulus (p. 67)

instrumental conditioning type of learning in which a behavioral response can be conditioned through reinforcement—either punishment or rewards associated with undesirable or desirable behavior (p. 67)

positive reinforcers reinforcers that take the form of a reward (p. 68)

discriminative stimuli stimuli that occur solely in the presence of a reinforcer (p. 68)

shaping process through which a desired behavior is altered over time, in small increments (p. 68)

punishers stimuli that decrease the likelihood that a behavior will persist (p. 69)

extinction process through which behaviors cease due to lack of reinforcement (p. 69)

4-1 Identify factors that influence consumer comprehension. Comprehension refers to the interpretation or understanding that a consumer develops about some attended stimulus. From an information-processing perspective, comprehension results after a consumer is exposed to and attends some information. Several factors influence comprehension including characteristics of the message, characteristics of the receiver, and characteristics of the environment. Multiple aspects of each of these factors come together to shape what things mean in the mind of the consumer.

comprehension the way people cognitively assign meaning to (i.e., understand) things they encounter (p. 70)

signal theory explains ways in which communications convey meaning beyond the explicit or obvious interpretation (p. 72)

PMG price matching guarantee (p. 72)

physical characteristics tangible elements or the parts of a message that can be sensed (p. 73)

golden section a preferred ratio of objects, equal to 1.62 to 1.00 (p. 74)

message congruity extent to which a message is internally consistent and fits surrounding information (p. 74)

figure object that is intended to capture a person's attention, the focal part of any message (p. 75)

ground background in a message (p. 75)

figure-ground distinction notion that each message can be separated into the focal point (figure) and the background (ground) (p. 75)

figurative language use of expressions that send a nonliteral meaning (p. 75)

expertise amount of knowledge that a source is perceived to have about a subject (p. 76)

trustworthiness how honest and unbiased the source is perceived to be (p. 76)

credibility extent to which a source is considered to be both an expert in a given area and trustworthy (p. 76)

counterarguments thoughts that contradict a message (p. 76)

support arguments thoughts that further support a message (p. 76)

habituation process by which continuous exposure to a stimulus affects the comprehension of, and response to, the stimulus (p. 77)

adaptation level level of a stimulus to which a consumer has become accustomed (p. 78)

expectations beliefs about what will happen in some future situation (p. 79)

brain dominance refers to the phenomenon of *hemispheric lateralization*. Some people tend to be either right brain or left brain (p. 79)

metaphor in a consumer context, an ad claim that is not literally true but figuratively communicates a message (p. 79)

information intensity amount of information available for a consumer to process within a given environment (p. 80)

framing a phenomenon in which the meaning of something is influenced (perceived differently) by the information environment (p. 80)

prospect theory theory that suggests that a decision, or argument, can be framed in different ways and that the framing affects risk assessments consumers make (p. 80)

priming cognitive process in which context or environment activates concepts and frames thoughts and therefore affects both value and meaning (p. 80)

construal level whether or not we are thinking about something using a concrete or an abstract mindset (p. 81)

4-2 Explain how knowledge, meaning, and value are inseparable, using the multiple stores memory theory. The multiple stores theory of memory explains how processing information involves three separate storage areas: sensory, workbench (short-term), and long-term memory. Everything sensed is recorded by sensory memory, but the record lasts too short a time to develop meaning. A small portion of this information is passed to the workbench, where already known concepts are retrieved from long-term memory and attached to new stimuli in a process known as meaningful encoding. All meaning is stored in an associative network residing in long-term memory. This network of knowledge links together concepts in a way that explains why things have value. Thus, value is rooted in meaning.

memory psychological process by which knowledge is recorded (p. 81)

multiple store theory of memory theory that explains memory as utilizing three different storage areas within the human brain: sensory, workbench, and long-term (p. 81)

sensory memory area in memory where a consumer stores things exposed to one of the five senses (p. 82)

iconic storage storage of visual information in sensory memory and the idea that things are stored with a one-to-one representation with reality (p. 82)

echoic storage storage of auditory information in sensory memory (p. 82)

haptic perception interpretations created by the way some object feels (p. 82)

workbench, or working, memory storage area in the memory system where information is stored while it is being processed and encoded for later recall (p. 83)

encoding process by which information is transferred from workbench memory to long-term memory for permanent storage (p. 83)

retrieval process by which information is transferred back into workbench memory for additional processing when needed (p. 83)

4-3 **Understand how the mental associations that consumers develop are a key to learning.** Chunking is a way that multiple stimuli can become one memory unit. Chunking is related to meaningful encoding in that meaning can be used to facilitate this process. A group of randomly arranged letters is likely to be difficult to chunk. In this case, seven letters are seven memory units. Arranged into a word, however, such as "meaning," the seven become one memory unit. Marketers who aid chunking are better able to convey information to consumers. The things that become associated with a brand are the things that will shape the brand's value and meaning.

repetition simple mechanism in which a thought is kept alive in short-term memory by mentally repeating the thought (p. 83)

dual coding coding that occurs when two different sensory traces are available to remember something (p. 83)

meaningful encoding coding that occurs when information from long-term memory is placed on the workbench and attached to the information on the workbench in a way that the information can be recalled and used later (p. 84)

chunking process of grouping stimuli by meaning so that multiple stimuli can become one memory unit (p. 84)

cognitive interference notion that everything else that the consumer is exposed to while trying to remember something is also vying for processing capacity and thus interfering with memory and comprehension (p. 84)

chunk single memory unit (p. 85)

response generation reconstruction of memory traces into a formed representation of what they are trying to remember or process (p. 85)

long-term memory repository for all information that a person has encountered (p. 86)

semantic coding type of coding wherein stimuli are converted to meaning that can be expressed verbally (p. 86)

memory trace mental path by which some thought becomes active (p. 86)

spreading activation way cognitive activation spreads from one concept (or node) to another (p. 86)

tag small piece of coded information that helps with the retrieval of knowledge (p. 86)

rumination unintentional but recurrent memory of long-ago events that are spontaneously (not evoked by the environment) triggered (p. 86)

nostalgia a yearning to relive the past that can produce lingering emotions (p. 87)

elaboration extent to which a consumer continues processing a message even after an initial understanding is achieved (p. 87)

personal elaboration process by which people imagine themselves somehow associating with a stimulus that is being processed (p. 87)

4-4 **Use the concept of associative networks to map relevant consumer knowledge.** An associative network, sometimes referred to as a semantic network, is the network of mental pathways linking all knowledge within memory. Associative networks can be drawn similarly to the way a road map would be constructed. All nodes are linked to all other nodes through a series of paths. Nodes with high strength tend to become conscious together based on their high strength of association.

associative network network of mental pathways linking knowledge within memory; sometimes referred to as a semantic network (p. 87)

declarative knowledge cognitive components that represent facts (p. 87)

nodes concepts found in an associative network (p. 88)

paths representations of the association between nodes in an associative network (p. 88)

4-5 **Apply the cognitive schema concept in understanding how consumers react to products, brands, and marketing agents.** A schema is the cognitive representation of a phenomenon that provides meaning to that entity. Thus, products and brands have schemas. To the extent that a new product or brand can share the same "nodes" or characteristics with an existing brand, consumers will more easily understand what the product does. Category exemplars and prototypes often provide the comparison standard for new brands. In addition, consumers react initially to service providers based on how much they match the expected social schema for that particular category of person.

schema a portion of an associative network that represents a specific entity and thereby provides it with meaning (p. 88)

exemplar concept within a schema that is the single best representative of some category; schema for something that really exists (p. 89)

prototype schema that is the best representative of some category but that is not represented by an existing entity; conglomeration of the most associated characteristics of a category (p. 89)

script schema representing an event (p. 90)

episodic memory memory for past events in one's life (p. 90)

social schema cognitive representation that gives a specific type of person meaning (p. 90)

social stereotype another word for social schema (p. 90)

social identity the idea that one's individual identity is defined in part by the social groups to which one belongs (p. 91)

CHAPTER 5 LEARNING OBJECTIVES / KEY TERMS

5-1 **Understand what initiates human behavior.** Human behavior, meaning the actions of a consumer, is initiated by the realization that something is needed to either maintain one's current status or to improve one's life status. The concept of homeostasis captures this phenomenon. Consumer motivations are the inner reasons or driving forces behind human actions as consumers are driven to address real needs. Needs are the first stage in the consumption process which is in the center of the CVF.

sentiment analysis sometimes called conversation analysis; automatic procedures that search social networking sites like Twitter for phrases/sentences that are coded for emotional meaning (p. 92)

motivations inner reasons or driving forces behind human actions that

drive consumers to address real needs (p. 92)

homeostasis state of equilibrium wherein the body naturally reacts in a way so as to maintain a constant, normal bloodstream (p. 93)

self-improvement motivation motivations aimed at changing the current state to a level that is more ideal, not at simply maintaining the current state (p. 93)

regulatory focus theory puts forward the notion that consumers orient their behavior either through a prevention or promotion focus (p. 94)

5-2 **Classify basic consumer motivations.** Consumer motivations can be classified a number of ways. Maslow's hierarchy of needs provides a classification mechanism by which consumer needs are prioritized. The most basic needs are physical, followed by needs for safety, belongingness, esteem and status, and self-actualization, respectively. Additionally, consumer motivations can be usefully divided into two groups: utilitarian motivations drive the pursuit of utilitarian value, and hedonic motivations drive the pursuit of hedonic value.

Maslow's hierarchy of needs a theory of human motivation that describes consumers as addressing a finite set of prioritized needs (p. 94)

utilitarian motivation drive to acquire products that can be used to accomplish something (p. 95)

hedonic motivation drive to experience something emotionally gratifying (p. 95)

consumer involvement degree of personal relevance a consumer finds in pursuing value from a particular category of consumption (p. 96)

moderating variable variable that changes the nature of the relationship between two other variables (p. 96)

product involvement the personal relevance of a particular product category (p. 97)

product enthusiasts consumers with very high involvement in some product category (p. 97)

shopping involvement personal relevance of shopping activities (p. 97)

situational involvement temporary interest in some imminent purchase situation (p. 97)

enduring involvement ongoing interest in some product or opportunity (p. 97)

Exhibit 5.1

An Illustration of Consumer Motivations According to Maslow's Hierarchy

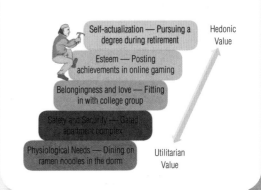

emotional involvement type of deep personal interest that evokes strongly felt feelings simply from the thoughts or behavior associated with some object or activity (p. 97)

5-3 **Describe consumer emotions and demonstrate how they help shape value.** Emotions are psychobiological reactions to human appraisals. Emotions are considered psychobiological because they involve psychological processing and physical responses.1 Emotions result from cognitive appraisals, and each emotion creates visceral responses so that they are tied to behavior in a very direct way. The close link between emotion and behavior means that marketing success is determined by the emotions that consumption creates because consumers value positive emotional experiences. Emotions are particularly closely linked to hedonic value.

emotion a specific psychobiological reaction to a human appraisal (p. 98)

psychobiological a response involving both psychological and physical human responses (p. 98)

visceral responses certain feeling states that are tied to physical reactions/behavior in a very direct way (p. 98)

cognitive appraisal theory school of thought proposing that specific types of appraisal thoughts can be linked to specific types of emotions (p. 98)

anticipation appraisal appraisal focusing on the future that can elicit anticipatory emotions like hopefulness or anxiety (p. 98)

agency appraisal reviewing responsibility for events; can evoke consequential emotions like gratefulness, frustration, guilt, or sadness (p. 99)

equity appraisal considering how fair some event is; can evoke emotions like warmth or anger (p. 99)

outcomes appraisal considering how something turned out relative to one's goals; can evoke emotions like joyfulness, satisfaction, sadness, or pride (p. 99)

mood transient and general affective state (p. 99)

mood-congruent judgments evaluations in which the value of a target is influenced in a consistent way by one's mood (p. 100)

consumer self-construal the manner in which a consumer thinks about him/herself as either an independent person or an interdependent self within a network of others (p. 100)

consumer affect feelings a consumer has about a particular product or activity, often expressed as tone or liking (p. 100)

5-4 Apply different approaches to measuring consumer emotions. Several different approaches for measuring emotion exist. Because of the visceral nature of emotion, autonomic measures can capture emotional experience by sensing changes in the body chemistry such as sweating or neurological activity. Unfortunately, such measures are usually obtrusive and interfere with the natural experience of emotion. Therefore, self-report approaches such slider scales, the PANAS, and the PAD scales are popular for assessing consumer emotion. The PANAS assumes that positive and negative emotion can be experienced separately to some extent, while the PAD scale assumes that emotions such as pleasure and displeasure are bipolar opposites.

autonomic measures means of recording responses based on either automatic visceral reactions or neurological brain activity (p. 101)

eye-tracking technology combination of hardware and software that measures precisely where one's pupils are gazing and assesses amount of pupil dilation. Eye-tracking technologies automatically record consumers' gazes. Mere milliseconds can mean the difference between success and failure. (p. 101)

PAD pleasure–arousal–dominance; a self-report measure that asks respondents to rate feelings using semantic differential items (p. 102)

bipolar situation wherein if one feels joy he or she cannot also experience sadness (p. 102)

5-5 Understand how different consumers express emotions in different ways. Several individual difference characteristics influence the way consumers react emotionally and react to emotions in a consumption situation. For example, high levels of the personality trait neuroticism tend to lead to consumers experiencing relatively high levels of negative emotion. Additionally, in any given consumption situation, consumers are likely to vary in emotional involvement. Consumers with high emotional involvement can experience intense emotions during consumption and can even reach the level of a flow experience. Furthermore, consumers have different levels of emotional expressiveness. Although men and women tend to experience the same amounts of emotion, women tend to be more emotionally expressive. Very highly involved consumers can obtain flow experiences. These experiences create a great deal of value. Computer activities such as gaming and Facebook typify these flow experiences.

flow extremely high emotional involvement in which a consumer is engrossed in an activity (p. 105)

emotional expressiveness extent to which a consumer shows outward behavioral signs and otherwise reacts obviously to emotional experiences (p. 105)

emotional intelligence awareness of the emotions experienced in a given situation and the ability to control reactions to these emotions (p. 106)

5-6 Define and apply the concepts of schema-based affect and emotional contagion. Perhaps no concept better illustrates how emotion and cognition are "wired" together than schema-based affect. Schema-based affect represents the fact that emotions become stored as part of the meaning for any category or thing. The feelings associated with a category are activated along with the activation of the schema. When a brand schema becomes associated with high levels of positive affect, the brand has high brand equity. Similarly, a brand that is associated with high levels of negative schema-based affect is probably in trouble. Negative self-conscious emotions such as embarrassment, guilt, shame, and regret can be particularly important in motivating consumer behavior.

emotional effect on memory relatively superior recall for information presented with mild affective content compared to similar information presented in an affectively neutral way (p. 107)

autobiographical memories cognitive representation of meaningful events in one's life (p. 107)

mood-congruent recall consumers will remember information better when the mood they are currently in matches the mood they were in when originally exposed to the information (p. 108)

schema-based affect emotions that become stored as part of the meaning for a category (a schema) (p. 108)

aesthetic labor effort put forth by employees in carefully managing their appearance as a requisite for performing their job well (p. 109)

emotional labor effort put forth by service workers who have to overtly manage their own emotional displays as part of the requirements of the job (p. 110)

self-conscious emotions specific emotions that result from some evaluation or reflection of one's own behavior, including pride, shame, guilt, and embarrassment (p. 110)

emotional contagion extent to which an emotional display by one person influences the emotional state of a bystander (p. 110)

product contamination refers to the diminished positive feelings someone has about a product because another consumer has handled the product (p. 111)

6-1 **Define personality and understand how various approaches to studying personality can be applied to consumer behavior.** Personality can be defined as the totality of thoughts, emotions, intentions, and behaviors that people exhibit consistently as they adapt to their environment. There are several different ways to study the human personality. Freud's psychoanalytic approach received considerable attention in the early days of consumer research. Trait theory, wherein researchers examine specific traits that relate to consumption, has also received much research attention. With this approach, consumer researchers have focused on both single- and multiple-trait perspectives. The five-factor model is a popular multiple-trait model. The personology approach combines both motivational theory and personality.

individual difference variables descriptions of how individual consumers differ according to specific trait patterns of behavior (p. 112)

personality totality of thoughts, emotions, intentions, tendencies, and behaviors that a person exhibits consistently as he or she adapts to the environment (p. 112)

aggregation approach approach to studying personality in which behavior is assessed at a number of points in time (p. 113)

psychoanalytic approach to personality approach to personality research, advocated by Sigmund Freud, that suggests personality results from a struggle between inner motives and societal pressures to follow rules and expectations (p. 114)

id the personality component in psychoanalytic theory that focuses on pleasure-seeking motives and immediate gratification (p. 114)

pleasure principle principle found in psychoanalytic theory that describes the factor that motivates pleasure-seeking behavior within the id (p. 114)

superego component in psychoanalytic theory that works against the id by motivating behavior that matches the expectations and norms of society (p. 114)

ego component in psychoanalytic theory that attempts to balance the struggle between the superego and the id (p. 114)

reality principle the principle in psychoanalytic theory under which the ego attempts to satisfy the id within societal constraints (p. 114)

motivational research era era in consumer research that focused heavily on psychoanalytic approaches (p. 114)

trait approach to personality approaches in personality research that focus on specific consumer traits as motivators of various consumer behaviors (p. 115)

trait distinguishable characteristic that describes one's tendency to act in a relatively consistent manner (p. 115)

nomothetic perspective variable-centered approach to personality that focuses on particular traits that exist across a number of people (p. 115)

idiographic perspective approach to personality that focuses on understanding the complexity of each individual consumer (p. 115)

single-trait approach approach in trait research wherein the focus is on one particular trait (p. 116)

multiple-trait approach approach in trait research wherein the focus remains on combinations of traits (p. 116)

6-2 **Discuss major traits that have been examined in consumer research.** Value consciousness refers to the tendency of consumers to be highly focused on receiving value in their purchases. Materialism refers to the extent to which material goods have importance in a consumer's life. Consumers who are relatively materialistic view possessions as a means to achieve happiness and as symbols of success. Innovativeness refers to the degree to which an individual is open to new ideas and tends to be relatively early in adopting new products, services, or experiences. Innovativeness has been shown to relate to a number of consumer behaviors, including new product adoption, novelty seeking, information seeking, and online shopping. Need for cognition refers to the degree to which consumers enjoy engaging in effortful cognitive information processing. Consumers who have a high degree of need for cognition think carefully about products, problems, and advertisements. They also tend to pay close attention to the quality of arguments in ads.

value consciousness the extent to which consumers tend to maximize what they receive from a transaction as compared to what they give (p. 116)

value consciousness the extent to which consumers tend to maximize what they receive from a transaction as compared to what they give (p. 117)

materialism extent to which material goods have importance in a consumer's life (p. 117)

innovativeness degree to which an individual is open to new ideas and tends to be relatively early in adopting new products, services, or experiences (p. 117)

need for cognition refers to the degree to which consumers enjoy engaging in effortful cognitive information processing (p. 118)

competitiveness enduring tendency to strive to be better than others (p. 118)

productivity orientation represents the tendency for consumers to focus on being productive, making progress, and accomplishing more in less time (p. 119)

five-factor model multiple-trait perspective that proposes that the human personality consists of five traits: agreeableness, extroversion, openness to experience (or creativity), conscientiousness, and neuroticism (or stability) (p. 119)

hierarchical approaches to personality approaches to personality inquiry that assume that personality traits exist at varying levels of abstraction (p. 120)

brand personality collection of human characteristics that can be associated with a brand (p. 121)

brand personality appeal a product's ability to appeal to consumers based on the human characteristics associated with it (p. 122)

Personality, Lifestyles, and the Self-Concept

6-3 **Understand why lifestyles, psychographics, and demographics are important to the study of consumer behavior.** Given that lifestyle concepts give marketers much valuable information about consumers, lifestyle studies have been popular with consumer researchers for many years. Purchase patterns are often influenced heavily by consumer lifestyles, and for this reason marketers often target consumers based on lifestyles. Psychographics, the quantitative investigation of consumer lifestyles, is well suited to help marketers in this process. Both VALS and PRIZM represent important psychographic techniques. The great advantage of lifestyles and psychographics is the ability to capture information in a specific, relevant consumer context. Demographics are observable, statistical aspects of populations including such factors as age, gender, or income. This concept is different from lifestyles and psychographics. Demographic variables can be used to help locate and understand lifestyle segments.

lifestyles distinctive modes of living, including how people spend their time and money (p. 123)

psychographics quantitative investigation of consumer lifestyles (p. 124)

AIO statements activity, interest, and opinion statements that are used in lifestyle studies (p. 124)

VALS popular psychographic method in consumer research that divides consumers into groups based on resources and consumer behavior motivations (p. 125)

geodemographic techniques techniques that combine data on consumer expenditures and socioeconomic variables with geographic information in order to identify commonalities in consumption

patterns of households in various regions (p. 125)

PRIZM popular geodemographic technique that stands for Potential Ratings Index by ZIP Market (p. 125)

demographics observable, statistical aspects of populations such as age, gender, or income (p. 125)

6-4 **Comprehend the role of the self-concept in consumer behavior.** The self-concept, defined as the totality of thoughts and feelings that an individual has about himself or herself, is another important topic in consumer behavior research. Consumers are motivated to act in accordance with their self-concepts, and for this reason, several product choices can be related to the self-concept. A consumer can hold a number of different concepts about the self, including the actual self, the ideal self, the social self, the ideal social self, the possible self, and the extended self.

self-concept totality of thoughts and feelings that an individual has about himself or herself (p. 126)

symbolic interactionism perspective that proposes that consumers live in a symbolic environment and interpret the

myriad of symbols around them, and that members of a society agree on the meanings of symbols (p. 126)

semiotics study of symbols and their meanings (p. 126)

self-esteem positivity of the self-concept that one holds (p. 127)

body esteem positivity with which people hold their body image (p. 127)

6-5 **Understand the concept of self-congruency and how it applies to consumer behavior issues.** Self-congruency theory helps to explain why consumers are motivated to purchase products that match their self-concepts. Consumers often desire to buy products that match their own self-concepts, and marketers segment markets based on the match between consumer self-concept and product attributes. When congruency becomes quite strong, consumers use brands to help promote consumer identities, and they may also form strong organizational identification for organizations or companies.

self-congruency theory theory that proposes that much of consumer behavior can be explained by the congruence of a

consumer's self-concept with the image of typical users of a focal product (p. 128)

7-1 Define attitudes and describe attitude components. Consumer attitudes are relatively enduring evaluations of objects, products, services, issues, or people. Attitudes have three components. The first component is a cognitive component. This component consists of the beliefs that consumers have about products and their features. The next component is the affective component. This component consists of the feelings that consumers have about the product and its features. The last component is a behavioral component, which describes how consumers act toward the object in question.

attitudes relatively enduring overall evaluations of objects, products, services, issues, or people (p. 131)

ABC approach to attitudes approach that suggests that attitudes encompass one's affect, behavior, and cognitions (or beliefs) toward an object (p. 132)

7-2 Describe the functions of attitudes. Several functions of attitudes are presented in this chapter, including the utilitarian, ego-defensive, value-expressive, and knowledge functions. The utilitarian function refers to the use of attitudes to gain something that is valued. The ego-defensive function refers to the use of attitudes to protect oneself from harm. The value-expressive function refers to the use of attitudes to express a consumer's core beliefs and self-image. The knowledge function refers to the use of attitudes to simplify consumer decision making.

functional theory of attitudes theory of attitudes that suggests that attitudes perform four basic functions (p. 132)

utilitarian function of attitudes function of attitudes in which consumers use attitudes as ways to maximize rewards and minimize punishment (p. 132)

knowledge function of attitudes function of attitudes whereby attitudes allow consumers to simplify decision-making processes (p. 133)

value-expressive function of attitudes function of attitudes whereby attitudes allow consumers to express their core values, self-concept, and beliefs to others (p. 133)

ego-defensive function of attitudes function of attitudes whereby attitudes work as a defense mechanism for consumers (p. 133)

7-3 Understand how the hierarchy of effects concept applies to attitude theory. The hierarchy of effects approach explains the process through which beliefs, affect, and behavior occur. These hierarchies depend upon the consumer's buying situation. In a high-involvement context, consumer beliefs are formed, followed by affect, and finally by behavior. Low-involvement, experiential, and behavioral influence hierarchies are also quite common in consumer behavior.

hierarchy of effects attitude approach that suggests that affect, behavior, and cognitions form in a sequential order (p. 133)

7-4 Comprehend the major consumer attitude models. Two major approaches to measuring consumer attitudes were presented in this chapter: the attitude-toward-the-object (ATO) and behavioral intentions models. The ATO model includes three key elements: salient beliefs, strength of beliefs, and evaluation of attributes. The behavioral intentions model includes two key elements: attitude toward a behavior and subjective norms. These models are commonly used by consumer researchers who focus on understanding the elements that comprise consumer attitudes. The approaches are also useful for marketing managers who develop marketing campaigns.

ATO Model

$$A_o = \sum_{I=1}^{N}(b_i)(e_i)$$

A_o = attitude toward the object in question (or A_{brand}),
b_i = strength of belief that the object possesses attribute i,
e_i = evaluation of the attractiveness or goodness of attribute i,
N = number of attributes and beliefs.

multiattribute attitude model a model that combines a number of pieces of information about belief and evaluations of attributes of an object (p. 135)

attitude-toward-the-object (ATO) model attitude model that considers three key elements: beliefs consumers have about salient attributes, the strength of the belief that an object possesses the attribute, and evaluation of the particular attribute (p. 135)

compensatory model attitudinal model wherein low ratings for one attribute are compensated for by higher ratings on another (p. 137)

attitude–behavior consistency extent to which a strong relationship exists between attitudes and actual behavior (p. 138)

behavioral intentions model model developed to improve on the ATO model, focusing on behavioral intentions, subjective norms, and attitude toward a particular behavior (p. 138)

theory of planned action attitudinal measurement approach that expands upon the behavioral intentions model by including a perceived control component (p. 139)

attitude tracking effort of a marketer or researcher to track changes in consumer attitudes over time (p. 140)

CHAPTER REVIEW

CHAPTER 7 LEARNING OBJECTIVES / KEY TERMS

7-5 **Describe attitude change theories and their role in persuasion.** There are a number of major approaches to changing attitudes presented in this chapter. The first approach focuses on the ATO model. According to this approach, attitudes can be changed by changing the strength of beliefs about attributes, by adding new beliefs to the attitude equation, by changing the evaluation of attributes, or by altering the schema-based affect for the brand/object. The second approach was the behavioral influence approach, which focuses on changing behaviors directly. The third approach was the schema-based affect approach. This approach focuses on changing affect found in product schemas. The fourth approach was the balance theory approach. This approach suggests that consumers seek consistency in systems that are comprised of three elements: the observer, another person, and an object. Attitudes toward an object are affected by the perceived relations found with the system. The fifth approach was the elaboration likelihood model (ELM). The ELM suggests that persuasion occurs as the result of processing within one of two routes: a central route and a peripheral route. In high-involvement situations, the central route is activated, and in low-involvement situations, the peripheral route is activated. Attitude change is usually longer lasting when persuasion occurs in the central route. The sixth and final approach to attitude change is the social judgment theory approach. This theory suggests that an incoming message is compared to an initial attitudinal position and an assimilation or contrast effect occurs depending on the perceived closeness of the incoming message to the original attitude.

persuasion attempt to change attitudes (p. 140)

elaboration likelihood model (ELM) attitudinal change model that shows attitudes are changed based on differing levels of consumer involvement through either central or peripheral processing (p. 142)

central route to persuasion path to persuasion found in ELM where the consumer has high involvement, motivation, and/or ability to process a message (p. 142)

central cues information presented in a message about the product itself, its attributes, or the consequences of its use (p. 143)

peripheral route to persuasion path to persuasion found in ELM where the consumer has low involvement, motivation, and/or ability to process a message (p. 143)

peripheral cues nonproduct-related information presented in a message (p. 144)

balance theory theory that states that consumers are motivated to maintain perceived consistency in the relations found in a system (p. 144)

consistency principle principle that states that human beings prefer consistency among their beliefs, attitudes, and behaviors (p. 144)

social judgment theory theory that proposes that consumers compare incoming information to their existing attitudes about a particular object or issue and that attitude change depends upon how consistent the information is with the initial attitude (p. 145)

7-6 **Understand how message and source effects influence persuasion.** Both source and message effects play important roles in persuasion. Message effects include issues related to the overall content and construction of the message. Sex appeals, humor appeals, and fear appeals are all used frequently by marketers. Source effects, or effects that are attributed to the spokesperson or company, are also important. Source effects include source credibility, source likeability, source attractiveness, and source meaningfulness.

message effects how the appeal of a message and its construction affect persuasiveness (p. 146)

source effects characteristics of a source that influence the persuasiveness of a message (p. 146)

serial position effect occurs when the placement of information in a message impacts recall of the information (p. 149)

primacy effect occurs when the information placed early in a message has the most impact (p. 149)

recency effect occurs when the information placed late in a message has the most impact (p. 149)

matchup hypothesis hypothesis that states that a source feature is most effective when it is matched with relevant products (p. 151)

8-1 Understand the different types of reference groups that influence consumers and how reference groups influence value perceptions. A number of different types of reference groups influence consumers. A primary group is a group that includes members who have frequent, direct contact. A secondary group is a group that has much less contact than a primary group, but these groups still influence consumer behavior. A formal group is a group in which consumers formally become members. An informal group is a group that has no membership or application requirements and codes of conduct may be nonexistent. Most online social networking groups are informal and secondary. An aspirational group is a group in which a consumer desires to become a member. A dissociative group is a group that a consumer wants to avoid being perceived as belonging to. Belonging to groups can be quite valuable for consumers. The benefits associated with membership often outweigh the costs. Also, hedonic value is often derived from belonging to groups and from participating in group activities. Group members often receive economic, or utilitarian, value from membership as well.

reference group individuals who have significant relevance for a consumer and who have an impact on the consumer's evaluations, aspirations, and behavior (p. 158)

group influence ways in which group members influence attitudes, behaviors, and opinions of others within the group (p. 159)

ingroup a group that a person identifies with as a member (p. 159)

outgroup a group with which a person does not identify (p. 159)

primary group group that includes members who have frequent, direct contact with one another (p. 160)

secondary group group to which a consumer belongs, with less frequent contact and weaker influence than that found in a primary group (p. 160)

brand community group of consumers who develop relationships based on shared interests or product usage (p. 160)

formal group group in which a consumer formally becomes a member (p. 160)

informal group group that has no membership or application requirements and that may have no code of conduct (p. 160)

aspirational group group in which a consumer desires to become a member (p. 160)

dissociative group group to which a consumer does not want to belong (p. 161)

conformity result of group influence in which an individual yields to the attitudes and behaviors of others (p. 161)

authority the ability of a person or group to enforce the obedience of others (p. 161)

peer pressure extent to which group members feel pressure to behave in accordance with group expectations (p. 161)

8-2 Describe the various types of social power that reference groups exert on members. Social power refers to the ability of an individual or a group to alter the actions of others. Social power is divided into specific categories that include referent power, legitimate power, expert power, reward power, and coercive power. Referent power exists when a consumer wishes to model his or her behaviors after a group or another person. Here, the consumer imitates the behaviors and attitudes of the referent others because of their liking or admiration for that person or group of people. Legitimate power is exerted when one's position in a group determines the level of social power he or she can hold over group members. Expert power refers to the ability of a group or individual to influence a consumer due to his or her knowledge of, or experience with, a specific subject matter. Reward power exists when groups are able to reward members for compliance with expectations. Finally, coercive power exists when groups have the ability to sanction or punish members for noncompliance with group expectations

social power ability of an individual or a group to alter the actions of others (p. 162)

8-3 Comprehend the difference between informational, utilitarian, and value-expressive reference group influence. The informational influence of groups refers to the ways in which consumers use the behaviors and attitudes of reference groups as information for making their own decisions. The utilitarian influence of groups refers to the ways in which consumers conform to group expectations in order to receive a reward or avoid punishment. The value-expressive influence of groups refers to the ways in which consumers internalize a group's values or the extent to which consumers join groups in order to express their own closely held values and beliefs.

informational influence ways in which a consumer uses the behaviors and attitudes of reference groups as information for making his or her own decisions (p. 163)

utilitarian influence ways in which a consumer conforms to group expectations in order to receive a reward or avoid punishment (p. 164)

value-expressive influence ways in which a consumer internalizes a group's values or the extent to which consumers join groups in order to express their own closely held values and beliefs (p. 164)

8-4 Understand social media's role in consumer behavior. Social media and social networking currently play major roles in consumer behavior. Consumers derive both utilitarian and hedonic value from group membership and this pertains to social media as well. Social media refers to media through which communication occurs. This term is nearly synonymous with the term *internet*. Social networks are networks of consumers that are formed based on common interest, associations, or goals. Social networking websites facilitate online social networking. Consumers may engage in social buying through social buying websites or social couponing through social couponing websites. These websites continue to grow in popularity and adoption.

social media media through which communication occurs (p. 166)

social networks consumers connecting with one another based on common interests, associations, or goals (p. 166)

social networking website website that facilitates online social networking (p. 166)

apps mobile application software that runs on devices like smartphones, tablets, and other computer-based tools (p. 166)

social gaming online or app-based game played on a social media platform (p. 168)

social buying consumer buying behavior that takes place on social networking sites (p. 168)

social couponing type of buying where consumers receive a coupon, or deal, by joining a special social networking website (p. 168)

susceptibility to interpersonal influence individual difference variable that assesses a consumer's need to enhance the image others hold of him or her by acquiring and using products, conforming to the expectations of others, and learning about products by observing others (p. 168)

attention to social comparison information (ATSCI) individual difference variable that assesses the extent to which consumers are concerned about how other people react to their behavior (p. 168)

separated self-schema self-conceptualization of the extent to which a consumer perceives himself or herself as distinct and separate from others (p. 169)

connected self-schema self-conceptualization of the extent to which a consumer perceives himself or herself as being an integral part of a group (p. 169)

8-5 **Understand the importance of word-of-mouth in influencing consumer behavior.** Word-of-mouth (WOM) refers to information about products, services, and experiences that is transmitted from consumer to consumer. WOM is influential because consumers tend to believe other consumers more than they believe advertisements and explicit marketing messages from companies. Consumers tend to place more emphasis on negative WOM than on positive WOM. It is also important because in today's information age WOM can be spread to millions of consumers very easily on the Internet via social networking websites or emailing, or even through texting.

---

word-of-mouth (WOM) information about products, services, and experiences that is transmitted from consumer to consumer (p. 170)

social media marketing the practice of using social media to generate consumer interest in a product, service, or idea (p. 171)

buzz marketing marketing efforts that focus on generating excitement among consumers and that are spread from consumer to consumer (p. 171)

guerrilla marketing marketing of a product using unconventional means (p. 171)

viral marketing marketing method that uses online technologies to facilitate WOM by having consumers spread messages through their online conversations (p. 172)

stealth marketing guerrilla marketing tactic in which consumers do not realize that they are being targeted for a marketing message (p. 172)

opinion leader consumer who has a great deal of influence on the behavior of others relating to product adoption and purchase (p. 173)

market maven consumer who spreads information about all types of products and services that are available in the marketplace (p. 173)

surrogate consumer consumer who is hired by another to provide input into a purchase decision (p. 173)

diffusion process way in which new products are adopted and spread throughout a marketplace (p. 174)

8-6 **Comprehend the role of household influence in consumer behavior.** The family unit is a very important primary reference group for consumers. Family members typically have a great deal of influence over one another's attitudes, thoughts, and behaviors. This is also true of "nonfamily" households. Because household members usually have frequent, close contact with one another, they often have much influence on the behavior of one another. The role that each household member plays in the household decision-making process depends on the beliefs and sexual orientation of each individual household

---

household decision making process by which decisions are made in household units (p. 174)

family household at least two people who are related by blood or marriage who occupy a housing unit (p. 174)

nuclear family a mother, a father, and a set of siblings (p. 175)

extended family three or more generations of family members (p. 175)

household life cycle (HLC) segmentation technique that acknowledges that changes in family composition and income alter household demand for products and services (p. 176)

boomerang kids young adults between the ages of 18 and 34 who move back home with their parents after they graduate from college (p. 176)

sandwich generation consumers who must take care of both their own children and their aging parents (p. 177)

sex role orientation (SRO) family's set of beliefs regarding the ways in which household decisions are reached (p. 178)

consumer socialization the process through which young consumers develop attitudes and learn skills that help them function in the marketplace (p. 179)

9-1 Understand how culture provides the true meaning of objects and activities. Culture is the set of commonly held societal beliefs that define what behaviors are socially gratifying among a societal group. These societal beliefs are sometimes referred to as core societal values (CSVs) or cultural values. These beliefs frame everyday life and provide a reference point with which to judge behaviors. Acceptable behaviors become norms of the society and when consumers act inconsistently with these norms, they face negative repercussions in the form of cultural sanctions. Culturally consistent behaviors are rewarded and are thus associated with greater value than culturally inconsistent behaviors.

consumer culture commonly held societal beliefs that define what is socially gratifying (p. 181)

cultural norm rule that specifies the appropriate consumer behavior in a given situation within a specific culture (p. 182)

cultural sanction penalty associated with performing a nongratifying or culturally inconsistent behavior (p. 182)

role expectations the specific expectations that are associated with each type of person within a culture or society (p. 184)

9-2 Use the key dimensions of core societal values to apply the concept of cultural distance. Five key CSV dimensions are discussed in the chapter: individualism–collectivism, power distance, masculinity–femininity, uncertainty avoidance, and long-term orientation. Societies that share similar CSV profiles, like the CANZUS nations, tend to have low cultural distance. In contrast, societies with very different profiles, such as the CANZUS nations compared to most Arab nations, have high cultural distance. Chances are that high cultural distance means consumers in those different cultures find value in significantly different behaviors. Therefore, cultural distance may be at least as important as geographic distance when a company is facing a decision about serving a foreign market. Cultural difference can be computed using a simple distance formula described in the chapter. Consumer markets that are close culturally should find value in the same sorts of products and brands.

ecological factors physical characteristics that describe the physical environment and habitat of a particular place (p. 184)

tradition customs and accepted ways of everyday behavior in a given culture (p. 185)

core societal values (CSV) commonly agreed-upon consensus about the most preferable ways of living within a society, also known as cultural values (p. 185)

individualism extent to which people are expected to take care of themselves and their immediate families (p. 185)

collectivism extent to which an individual's life is intertwined with a large cohesive group (p. 186)

masculinity sex role distinction within a group that values assertiveness and control; CSV opposite of femininity (p. 186)

femininity sex role distinction within a group that emphasizes the prioritization of relational variables such as caring, conciliation, and community; CSV opposite of masculinity (p. 186)

power distance extent to which authority and privileges are divided among different groups within society and the extent to which these facts of life are accepted by the people within the society (p. 186)

uncertainty avoidance extent to which a culture is uncomfortable with things that are ambiguous or unknown (p. 187)

long-term orientation values consistent with Confucian philosophy and a pragmatic prioritization of future rewards over short-term benefits (p. 188)

guanxi Chinese term for a way of doing business in which parties must first invest time and resources in getting to know one another and becoming comfortable with one another before consummating any important deal (p. 188)

renquing the idea that favors given to another are reciprocal and must be returned (p. 188)

indulgence-restraint a cultural value dimension distinguishing societies based on how oriented people are toward immediate fun and enjoyment versus restraining oneself from much indulgence in such things (p. 188)

BRIC acronym that refers to the collective economies of Brazil, Russia, India, and China (p. 189)

cultural distance (CD) representation of how disparate one nation is from another in terms of their CSV (p. 190)

CANZUS acronym that refers to the close similarity in values among Canada, Australia, New Zealand, and the United States (p. 192)

9-3 Define acculturation and enculturation. Acculturation and enculturation are two important consumer socialization processes. Acculturation is the process by which consumers come to learn a culture other than their natural, native culture. Enculturation is the process by which consumers learn their native culture. In both cases, the learning takes place through both formal and informal methods. Much of this learning occurs through the process of modeling. Modeling means that consumers try to mimic the behavior of others within the societal group. When the behavior is consistent with cultural norms, the rewards the consumer receives help to shape their overall pattern of behavior.

socialization learning through observation of and the active processing of information about lived, everyday experience (p. 192)

enculturation way people learn their native culture (p. 192)

acculturation process by which consumers come to learn a culture other than their natural, native culture (p. 192)

ethnic identification degree to which consumers feel a sense of belonging to the culture of their ethnic origins (p. 193)

consumer ethnocentrism belief among consumers that their ethnic group is superior to others and that the products that come from their native land are superior to other products (p. 193)

quartet of institutions four groups responsible for communicating the CSVs through both formal and informal processes: family, school, church, and media (p. 193)

modeling process of imitating others' behavior; a form of observational learning (p. 194)

9-4 **List fundamental elements of verbal and nonverbal communication.** Verbal communication refers to the transfer of information through the literal spoken or written word. One of the key elements of verbal communication is comprehension across languages. When communicating with consumers in a different language, the process of translation–back translation is important to make sure the intended message is really being communicated. Nonverbal communication refers to elements such as body language, etiquette, symbols, and the meaning of time and space, as well as the way a consumer signals agreement. High-context cultures depend heavily on nonverbal communication.

verbal communication transfer of information through either the literal spoken or written word (p. 195)

dialects variations of a common language (p. 195)

translational equivalence two phrases share the same precise meaning in two different cultures (p. 195)

metric equivalence statistical tests used to validate the way people use numbers to represent quantities across cultures (p. 197)

Globish simplified form of English that reduces the vocabulary to around 1,500 words and eliminates grammatical complications (p. 197)

nonverbal communication information passed through some nonverbal act (p. 197)

body language nonverbal communication cues signaled by somatic responses (p. 198)

etiquette customary mannerisms consumers use in common social situations (p. 198)

9-5 **Discuss current emerging consumer markets and learn to scan for opportunities.** New consumer markets have emerged over the previous few years. The fall of communism, advances in technology, and the desire for firms to obtain low-cost labor have enabled consumers in places like China and Russia to participate more fully in the free-market economy. In fact, the acronym BRIC refers to the combined market power of consumers in Brazil, Russia, India, and China. Firms can have success marketing to these emerging consumer markets but they must first understand each culture's CSV profile and the proper way to communicate with consumers in those markets.

Chindia combined market and business potential of China and India (p. 201)

glocalization idea that marketing strategy may be global but the implementation of that strategy at the marketing tactics level should be local (p. 201)

WWW.CENGAGEBRAIN.COM

10-1 **Apply the concept of microculture as it influences consumer behavior.** A microculture is a group of people who share similar values and tastes that are subsumed within a larger culture. Both culture and microculture are important influencers of consumer behavior. Ultimately, they explain the habits and idiosyncrasies of all groups of consumers. Consumers move in and out of microcultures, and their behavior is strongly influenced by membership. Microcultures bring sets of role expectations for their members. These expectations provide signals as to the behaviors that one should perform to belong to the group. Microculture membership changes the value of things. What is valued by one microculture may not be valued at all by another.

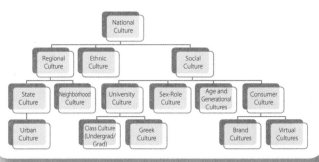

Exhibit 10.1

The Hierarchical Nature of Culture and Microculture

microculture a group of people who share similar values and tastes that are subsumed within a larger culture (p. 202)

role conflict a situation involving conflicting expectations based on cultural role expectations (p. 204)

divergence situation in which consumers choose membership in microcultures in an effort to stand out or define themselves from the crowd (p. 204)

10-2 **Know the major U.S. microcultural groups.** There are many microcultural groups in the United States. Marketers can divide the country into consumer groups along a number of these dimensions as market segmentation strategies. This chapter discusses the following microcultures that are found in the U.S. culture: regional, sex role, age-based, generation, religious, ethnic, income/social class, and street microcultures.

Exhibit 10.3

Regional Differences and Preferences among U.S. Consumers

Actual place	"Nine-nation region" (Garreau)	Geographical designation	Core societal value priority	Example preference
Birmingham, AL	Dixie	South	Security and self-respect	Watch Discovery Health Channel
Los Angeles, CA	MexAmerica	West	Warm relationships with others and self-fulfillment	In-home cosmetics
Boston, MA	New England	Northeast	Self-fulfillment, achievement	Viewing foreign movies
Chicago, IL	Breadbasket	Midwest	Security and warm relationships	Chicago pizza

sex roles societal expectations for men and women among members of a cultural group (p. 205)

cognitive structuring term that refers to the reliance on schema-based heuristics in making decisions (p. 207)

age-based microculture term that describes the concept that people of the same age end up sharing many of the same values and develop similar consumer preferences (p. 207)

world teen culture speculation that teenagers around the world are more similar to each other than to people from other generations in the same culture (p. 208)

cohort a group of people who have lived the same major experiences in their lives (p. 208)

stigmatization a situation in which consumers are marked in some way that indicates their place in society (p. 213)

bicultural used to describe immigrants as they face decisions and form preferences based on their old or new cultures (p. 214)

social class a culturally defined group to which a consumer belongs based on

resources like prestige, income, occupation, and education (p. 215)

habitus mental and cognitive structures through which individuals perceive the world based largely on their standing in a social class (p. 215)

homogamy the finding that most marriages comprise people from similar classes (p. 215)

social stratification the division of society into classes that have unequal access to scarce and valuable resources (p. 215)

status symbols products or objects that are used to signal one's place in society (p. 216)

10-3 **Realize that microculture is not a uniquely American phenomenon.** It is clear that microcultures are not merely an American phenomenon. Rather, they exist throughout the world. Countries worldwide have many bases around which microcultures are formed, and nearly all countries exhibit at least some degree of diversity. Religious, age- based, generational, ethnic, income, and street microcultures exist in nearly all nations.

10-4 **Perform a demographic analysis.** Demographics refer to relatively tangible human characteristics that describe consumers. Demographics include characteristics such as age, ethnicity, sex, occupation, income, region, religion, and gender. Demographic variables are closely related to microcultures, and demographic analyses assist the researcher in gaining a better understanding of microcultures. The information obtained becomes even more valuable when it is combined with geodemographic information. Demographic analyses develop a profile of a consumer group based on their demographics. One very important source for performing a demographic analysis is the U.S. Census Bureau's website.

demographic analysis a profile of a consumer group based on their demographics (p. 217)

10-5 **Identify major cultural and demographic trends.** One of the biggest trends in Western countries is the declining birthrate and increasing life expectancy. These trends, of course, do not hold true for every nation in the world. Nevertheless, they do attract consumer research and marketing attention. As a general statement, consumer affluence is growing in many parts of the world, particularly in the United States, India, and China. Of course, problems still remain worldwide with poverty nonetheless. Cultural and microcultural trends vary widely throughout the world. Growing cultural diversity has been witnessed throughout Europe, particularly with the growth of Islam. Cultural diversity has also increased in the United States, as evidenced especially in the borderland regions. Street microcultures continue to evolve worldwide as well.

11-1 **Understand how value varies with situations.** The value a consumer obtains from a purchase or consumption act varies based on the context in which the act takes place. These contextual effects are known as situational influences, meaning effects independent of enduring consumer, brand, or product characteristics. Contextual effects can involve things related to time, place, or antecedent conditions. They also can affect consumer information processing and shopping including purchase situations and actual consumption. Situational influences change the desirability of consuming things and therefore change the value of these things. Situational influences can also override consumer brand preferences in many product categories.

11-2 **Know the different ways that time affects consumer behavior.** The term *temporal factors* refers to situational characteristics related to time. Time can affect consumer behavior by creating time pressure. A consumer facing time pressure may not be able to process information related to making the best choice. The time of year can affect consumer behavior through seasonality. Cyclical patterns of consumption exist such as the case for many products, like champagne, that are predominantly sold during the holiday times. The time of day can also influence consumption. For instance, most consumers do not want gumbo for breakfast. But for lunch or dinner, gumbo is great! The circadian rhythm concept explains how a person's body reacts to time-of-day effects.

temporal factors situational characteristics related to time (p. 230)

time pressure urgency to act based on some real or self-imposed deadline (p. 231)

discretionary (spare) time the days, hours, or minutes that are not obligated toward some compulsory and time-consuming activity (p. 231)

seasonality regularly occurring conditions that vary with the time of year (p. 232)

circadian cycle rhythm (level of energy) of the human body that varies with the time of day (p. 232)

advertiming ad buys that include a schedule that runs the advertisement primarily at times when customers will be most receptive to the message (p. 232)

near-field communication (NFC) Wi-fi–like systems communicating with specific devices within a defined space like inside or around the perimeter of a retail unit or signage (p. 233)

11-3 **Analyze shopping as a consumer activity using the different categories of shopping activities.** Shopping can be defined as the set of value-producing consumer activities that directly increase the likelihood that something will be purchased. Shopping activities are very strongly shaped by the sense of place and therefore they are highly relevant to understanding how situations influence consumption. Shopping activities can be divided into four categories: acquisitional, epistemic, experiential, and impulsive. Each category is associated with a different orientation toward buying things and receiving shopping value.

shopping set of value-producing consumer activities that directly increase the likelihood that something will be purchased (p. 233)

smart agent software software capable of learning an Internet user's preferences and automatically searching out information in selected websites and then distributing it (p. 233)

acquisitional shopping activities oriented toward a specific, intended purchase or purchases (p. 234)

epistemic shopping activities oriented toward acquiring knowledge about products (p. 234)

experiential shopping recreationally oriented activities designed to provide interest, excitement, relaxation, fun, social interaction, or some other desired feeling (p. 234)

impulsive shopping spontaneous activities characterized by a diminished regard for consequences, spontaneity, and a desire for immediate self-fulfillment (p. 234)

outshopping shopping in a city or town to which consumers must travel rather than in their own hometowns (p. 235)

reversal theory tries to explain how environmental elements can lead to near 180-degree changes in shopping orientation (p. 236)

personal shopping value (PSV) overall subjective worth of a shopping activity considering all associated costs and benefits (p. 236)

utilitarian shopping value worth obtained because some shopping task or job is completed successfully (p. 236)

hedonic shopping value worth of a shopping activity because the time spent doing the activity itself is personally gratifying (p. 236)

functional quality retail positioning that emphasizes tangible things like a wide selection of goods, low prices, guarantees, and knowledgeable employees (p. 237)

affective quality retail positioning that emphasizes a unique environment, exciting décor, friendly employees, and, in general, the feelings experienced in a retail place (p. 237)

retail personality way a retail store is defined in the mind of a shopper based on the combination of functional and affective qualities (p. 237)

11-4 **Distinguish the concepts of unplanned, impulse, and compulsive consumer behavior.** The line between unplanned and impulse behavior is not always clear because some unplanned acts are impulsive and many impulsive acts are unplanned. Simple unplanned purchases usually lack any real emotional involvement or significant amounts of self-gratification. Additionally, unplanned purchases often involve only minimal negative consequences and thus fail to really qualify as having negative consequences at all. Compulsive acts are distinguished from impulsive acts by the relative degree of harmfulness associated with them. Impulsive acts are relatively harmless and in fact can have significant positive outcomes in terms of a consumer's emotional well-being. Compulsive acts, however, are associated with a consumer whose behavior is either self-detrimental or truly harmful to another consumer.

impulsive consumption consumption acts characterized by spontaneity, a diminished regard for consequences, and a need for self-fulfillment (p. 237)

unplanned shopping shopping activity that shares some, but not all, characteristics of truly impulsive consumer behavior; being characterized by situational memory,

a utilitarian orientation, and feelings of spontaneity (p. 237)

impulsivity personality trait that represents how sensitive a consumer is to immediate rewards (p. 239)

consumer self-regulation tendency for consumers to inhibit outside, or

situational, influences from interfering with shopping intentions (p. 239)

action-oriented consumers with a high capacity to self-regulate their behavior (p. 239)

state-oriented consumers with a low capacity to self-regulate their behavior (p. 239)

11-5 **Use the concept of atmospherics to create consumer value** A store's atmosphere can create value either through facilitating the task of shopping or through the gratification of the shopping experience itself. Each retail or service place is characterized by a particular atmosphere. An atmosphere can be designed that greatly facilitates the shopping task. Convenience stores have redesigned their sales floors and taken out

substantial numbers of product offerings. The result is that the consumer can complete the task of getting a needed product in less time. An atmosphere can also simply be more emotionally pleasant and therefore gratifying to be in. People make up a big part of the atmosphere and create social factors. One result is social comparison. Shopping companions influence shopping outcomes.

---

atmospherics emotional nature of an environment or the feelings created by the total aura of physical attributes that comprise a physical environment (p. 241)

servicescape physical environment in which consumer services are performed (p. 241)

fit how appropriate the elements of a given environment are (p. 242)

congruity how consistent the elements of an environment are with one another (p. 242)

olfactory refers to humans' physical and psychological processing of smells (p. 242)

foreground music music that becomes the focal point of attention and can have strong effects on a consumer's willingness to approach or avoid an environment (p. 243)

background music music played below the audible threshold that would make it the center of attention (p. 243)

crowding density of people and objects within a given space (p. 245)

nonlinear effect a plot of an effect that does not make a straight line (p. 246)

source attractiveness the degree to which a source's physical appearance matches

a prototype for beauty and elicits a favorable or desirous response (p. 246)

emotional ability capability of a salesperson to convey emotional information to shape a more valuable outcome for consumers (p. 246)

social comparison a naturally occurring mental personal comparison of the self with a target individual within the environment (p. 246)

11-6 **Understand what is meant by antecedent conditions.** Antecedent conditions refer to situational characteristics that a consumer brings to a particular information processing, purchase, or consumption environment. Antecedent conditions include things like economic resources, orientation, mood, and other emotional perceptions such as fear. They can shape the value in a situation by framing the events that take place. A consumer in a good mood, for example, tends to look at things more favorably than a consumer in a bad mood.

antecedent conditions situational characteristics that a consumer brings to information processing (p. 247)

mental budgeting memory accounting for recent spending (p. 248)

Exhibit 11.6

The Qualities of an Environment

- Knowledgeable Employees
- Low Prices
- Wide Selection
- Convenient
  - Shopping
  - Parking
  - Payment
  - Hours
  - Location

→ Functional Quality

- Friendly Employees
- Colors
- Lights
- Music
- Odors
- Prestigious Brands
- Other Shoppers
  - Crowds
  - Ease of Movement

→ Affective Quality

ATMOSPHERE

CHAPTER 12 LEARNING OBJECTIVES / KEY TERMS

12-1 **Understand the activities involved in the consumer decision making process.** The consumer decision-making process consists of five activities: (1) need recognition, (2) search for information, (3) evaluation of alternatives, (4) choice, and (5) postchoice evaluation. Consumers recognize needs when discrepancies are realized between actual and desired states. Consumers search for information from both internal and external sources. With internal search, consumers search their memories for appropriate solutions to problems. External searches consist of information-gathering activities that focus on friends, family, salespeople, advertising, and Internet-based information. Consumers evaluate alternatives based on the information that has been gathered and eventually make a decision.

12-2 **Describe the three major decision-making research perspectives.** The three major decision-making research perspectives are the rational decision-making perspective, the experiential decision-making perspective, and the behavioral influence decision-making perspective. The rational perspective assumes that consumers diligently gather information about purchases, carefully compare various brands of products on salient attributes, and make informed decisions regarding what brand to buy. This approach centers around the assumption that human beings are rational creatures who are careful with their decision making and behavior. The experiential decision-making perspective assumes that consumers often make purchases and reach decisions based on the affect, or feeling, attached to the product or behavior under consideration. The behavioral influence decision-making perspective assumes that consumer decisions are learned responses to environmental influences.

Exhibit 12.3

Perspectives on Consumer Decision Making

Perspective	Description	Example
Rational Perspective	Consumers are rational and they carefully arrive at decisions.	Jamal carefully considers the various features of apartment complexes.
Experiential Perspective	Decision making is often influenced by the feelings associated with consumption.	Riley goes longboarding just for the fun of it.
Behavioral Influence Perspective	Decisions are responses to environmental influences.	A product display leads Karissa to buy a snack.

rational decision-making perspective assumes consumers diligently gather information about purchases, carefully compare various brands of products on salient attributes, and make informed decisions regarding what brand to buy (p. 254)

experiential decision-making perspective assumes consumers often make purchases and reach decisions based on the affect, or feeling, attached to the product or behavior under consideration (p. 254)

variety-seeking behavior seeking new brands or products as a response to boredom or to satisfy a perceived need for change (p. 254)

behavioral influence decision-making perspective assumes many consumer decisions are actually learned responses to environmental influences (p. 254)

12-3 **Explain the three major types of decision-making approaches.** Decision-making approaches can be classified into extended decision making, limited decision making, and habitual (or "routine") decision making categories. With extended decision making, consumers search diligently for the best information that will help them reach a decision. They then assimilate the information that they have gathered and evaluate each alternative based on its potential to solve their problem. This process is usually lengthy and generally occurs when involvement is high and when there is a significant amount of purchase risk involved with the decision. With limited decision making, consumers spend little time searching for information and often reach decisions based largely on prior beliefs about products and their attributes. There is also little comparison between brands. Choice strategies are often based on simple decision rules that consumers develop. With habitual decision making, practically no information search takes place, and decisions are reached via habit.

perceived risk perception of the negative consequences that are likely to result from a course of action and the uncertainty of which course of action is best to take (p. 255)

extended decision making consumers move diligently through various problem-solving activities in search of the best information that will help them reach a decision (p. 256)

limited decision making consumers search very little for information and often reach decisions based largely on prior beliefs about products and their attributes (p. 256)

habitual decision making consumers generally do not seek information at all when a problem is recognized and select a product based on habit (p. 256)

brand loyalty deeply held commitment to rebuy a product or service regardless of situational influences that could lead to switching behavior (p. 256)

brand inertia occurs when a consumer simply buys a product repeatedly without any real attachment (p. 256)

satisficing practice of using decision-making shortcuts to arrive at satisfactory, rather than optimal, decisions (p. 257)

12-4 **Understand the importance of the consideration set in the decision-making process.** The consideration set is valuable because brands are placed in the set as consumers proceed through the decision-making process. For this reason, marketers find it valuable to understand the consideration set of their customers. Although the total universe of alternatives available for potentially satisfying a need may be quite large, only a small fraction of these options are generally included in the consideration set.

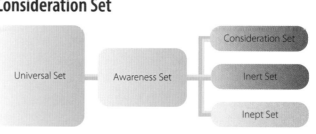

Exhibit 12.5

Consideration Set

Universal Set — Awareness Set — Consideration Set / Inert Set / Inept Set

actual state consumer's perceived current state (p. 258)

desired state perceived state for which a consumer strives (p. 258)

consumer search behavior behaviors that consumers engage in as they seek information that can be used to satisfy needs (p. 259)

ongoing search search effort that is not necessarily focused on an upcoming purchase or decision but rather on staying up to date on the topic (p. 259)

prepurchase search search effort aimed at finding information to solve an immediate problem (p. 259)

information overload situation in which consumers are presented with so much information that they cannot assimilate the variety of information presented (p. 260)

internal search retrieval of knowledge stored in memory about products, services, and experiences (p. 260)

consideration set alternatives that are considered acceptable for further consideration in decision making (p. 260)

universal set total collection of all possible solutions to a consumer problem (p. 260)

awareness set set of alternatives of which a consumer is aware (p. 260)

inept set alternatives in the awareness set that are deemed to be unacceptable for further consideration (p. 261)

inert set alternatives in the awareness set about which consumers are indifferent or do not hold strong feelings (p. 261)

12-5 **Understand the factors that influence the type and amount of search performed by consumers.** Several factors influence the amount of search that consumers actually perform. Factors such as previous experience with a product, purchase involvement, perceived risk, time availability, attitudes toward shopping, personal factors, and situational pressures all have an impact on the information search effort.

external search gathering of information from sources external to the consumer such as friends, family, salespeople, advertising, independent research reports, and the internet (p. 261)

price information that signals the amount of potential value contained in a product (p. 261)

quality perceived overall goodness or badness of some product (p. 262)

search regret negative emotions that come from failed search processes (p. 265)

CHAPTER 13 LEARNING OBJECTIVES / KEY TERMS

13-1 **Understand the difference between evaluative criteria and determinant criteria.** The attributes that consumers consider when evaluating alternative solutions to a problem are evaluative criteria. These criteria include features or benefits associated with a potential solution. Determinant criteria are the factors that have the biggest impact on actual consumer choice. Both evaluative and determinant criteria influence decision making.

evaluative criteria attributes that consumers consider when reviewing alternative solutions to a problem (p. 267)

feature performance characteristic of an object (p. 267)

benefit perceived favorable results derived from a particular feature (p. 267)

determinant criteria criteria that are most carefully considered and directly related to the actual choice that is made (p. 268)

13-2 **Comprehend how value affects the evaluation of alternatives.** Value is at the heart of the alternative evaluation process. Consumers seek benefits that are associated with a potential solution to a problem. Benefits come from the features or characteristics of the alternatives under consideration. From the value perspective, consumers seek solutions that will deliver benefits while minimizing associated costs.

bounded rationality idea that consumers attempt to act rationally within their information-processing constraints (p. 269)

affect-based evaluation evaluative process wherein consumers evaluate products based on the overall feeling that is evoked by the alternative (p. 269)

attribute-based evaluation evaluative process wherein alternatives are evaluated across a set of attributes that are considered relevant to the purchase situation (p. 270)

13-3 **Explain the importance of product categorization in the evaluation of alternatives process.** Categorization is important because product categories provide the framework from which consumers evaluate alternative solutions to a problem. When new information about a viable alternative is presented, this information is compared to information that is stored as knowledge in a consumer's perceived product category. This information allows the consumer to make better inferences about the alternative solution.

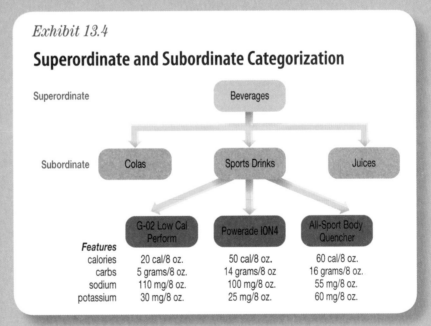

Exhibit 13.4

Superordinate and Subordinate Categorization

	Superordinate	Beverages	
Subordinate	Colas	Sports Drinks	Juices

Features	G-02 Low Cal Perform	Powerade ION4	All-Sport Body Quencher
calories	20 cal/8 oz.	50 cal/8 oz.	60 cal/8 oz.
carbs	5 grams/8 oz.	14 grams/8 oz	16 grams/8 oz.
sodium	110 mg/8 oz.	100 mg/8 oz.	55 mg/8 oz.
potassium	30 mg/8 oz.	25 mg/8 oz.	60 mg/8 oz.

product categories mental representations of stored knowledge about groups of products (p. 270)

perceptual attributes attributes that are visually apparent and easily recognizable (p. 272)

underlying attributes attributes that are not readily apparent and can be learned only through experience or contact with the product (p. 272)

signal attribute that consumers use to infer something about another attribute (p. 272)

judgments mental assessments of the presence of attributes and the benefits associated with those attributes. (p. 273)

attribute correlation perceived relationship between product features (p. 274)

conjoint analysis technique used to develop an understanding of the attributes that guide consumer preferences by having consumers compare product preferences across varying levels of evaluative criteria and expected utility (p. 276)

13-4 **Distinguish between compensatory and noncompensatory rules that guide consumer choice.** The attitude-toward-the-object model is a compensatory model. This type of model allows an alternative to be selected even if it performs poorly on a specific attribute. Noncompensatory models focus on strict guidelines that are set before alternative evaluation. The major noncompensatory rules are the conjunctive, disjunctive, lexicographic, and elimination-by-aspects rule. The conjunctive rule is a rule in which an option that is selected must surpass a minimum cutoff across all relevant attributes.

The disjunctive rule is used when an option that surpasses a relatively high cutoff point on any attribute is selected. The lexicographic rule leads the consumer to select the option that performs best on the most important attribute. The elimination-by-aspects rule is used when the consumer begins evaluating options by first looking at the most important attribute and eliminating any option that does not meet a minimum cutoff point for that attribute. The process continues as the consumer considers the next most important attribute, and so on, until only one option is left to be chosen.

compensatory rule decision rule that allows consumers to select products that may perform poorly on one criterion by compensating for the poor performance by good performance on another (p. 276)

noncompensatory rule decision rule in which strict guidelines are set prior to selection and any option that does not meet the guidelines is eliminated from consideration (p. 276)

conjunctive rule noncompensatory decision rule where the option selected must surpass a minimum cutoff across all relevant attributes (p. 278)

disjunctive rule noncompensatory decision rule where the option selected surpasses a relatively high cutoff point on any attribute (p. 278)

lexicographic rule noncompensatory decision rule where the option selected

is thought to perform best on the most important attribute (p. 278)

elimination-by-aspects rule (EBA) noncompensatory decision rule where the consumer begins evaluating options by first looking at the most important attribute and eliminating any option that does not meet a minimum cutoff point for that attribute, and where subsequent evaluations proceed in order of importance until only one option remains (p. 278)

14-1 Know the connections among consumption, value, and satisfaction. Consumers receive value from marketing efforts through consumption. Consumers consume products, services, and experiences and receive value in return. The value that they receive helps create overall satisfaction, as consumers tend to be more satisfied with exchanges they find valuable. Meaning plays a key role in consumption and the meaning of products, which can change over different situations, transfers itself into the experience and adds value

potential value benefits not yet realized from a service because they have yet to be consumed (p. 287)

durable goods goods that are typically expensive and usually consumed over a long period of time (p. 287)

nondurable goods goods that are typically inexpensive and usually consumed quickly (p. 288)

consumption frequency number of times a product or service is consumed in a given period of time (p. 288)

authenticity the degree to which an object, person, or experience seems real, genuine, unique, and part of history or tradition (p. 288)

meaning transference process through which cultural meaning is transferred to a product and onto the consumer (p. 289)

14-2 Discuss the relative importance of satisfaction and value in marketing and consumer behavior. Many companies go out of their way to emphasize how hard they work to create customer satisfaction. Consumer satisfaction itself is a mild, positive emotional state resulting from a favorable appraisal of a consumption outcome—i.e., a favorable satisfaction judgment. Satisfaction, in turn, correlates with a number of postconsumption behaviors such as word-of-mouth intentions, loyalty, and repeat purchase behavior. Satisfaction and value relate to one another, but not perfectly. In fact, some marketers provide customers with low satisfaction but still do remarkably well in the marketplace because they provide high value. Walmart is perhaps one of the best companies to illustrate this phenomenon. For this reason, while satisfaction is important, value remains even more important as the key outcome for consumer behavior.

top-line performance a business term referring to sales growth (sales being at the top of an earnings statement) (p. 291)

consumer satisfaction mild, positive emotion resulting from a favorable appraisal of a consumption outcome (p. 292)

consumer dissatisfaction mild, negative affective reaction resulting from an unfavorable appraisal of a consumption outcome (p. 293)

14-3 Understand how emotions other than satisfaction can affect post-consumption behavior. Emotions other than satisfaction result from appraisals of consumption outcomes. Some, like anger, are both negative and much stronger in motivating behavior following consumption. Others, like warmth, are controlling and can help build relationships. While satisfaction receives considerable attention, a fuller range of emotion is needed to fully account for consumption outcomes.

14-4 Use expectancy disconfirmation, equity, and attribution theory approaches to explain consumers' post-consumption reactions. The expectancy disconfirmation model proposes that consumers use expectations as benchmarks against which performance perceptions are judged. When performance perceptions are more positive than what was expected, *positive disconfirmation* is said to occur. When performance perceptions fall below expectations, *negative disconfirmation* occurs. The expectancy disconfirmation approach remains the dominant theory of viewing satisfaction processes today. Equity theory proposes that consumers consider the fairness of transactions by comparing their own outcomes and inputs to the outcomes and inputs of another party in the transaction. As long as the ratio of outcomes to inputs of each party is approximately equal or favors the consumer, satisfaction is likely to result. Attribution theory proposes that consumers consider the cause of events when making satisfaction judgments. When consumers make external attributions, they tend to be more dissatisfied with unpleasant experiences than when they make internal attributions. Taken together, disconfirmation, attributions, and equity judgments make up the primary cognitive bases for consumer satisfaction/dissatisfaction.

expectancy/disconfirmation theory satisfaction formation theory that proposes that consumers use expectations as a benchmark against which performance perceptions are judged (p. 294)

positive disconfirmation according to the expectancy/disconfirmation approach, a perceived state wherein performance perceptions exceed expectations (p. 294)

negative disconfirmation according to the expectancy/disconfirmation approach, a perceived state wherein performance perceptions fall short of expectations (p. 294)

expectations pre-consumption beliefs of what will occur during an exchange and consumption of a product (p. 294)

hope a fundamental emotion evoked by positive, anticipatory appraisals that signal uncertainty about a potentially positive outcome (p. 295)

confirmatory bias tendency for expectations to guide performance perceptions (p. 296)

self-perception theory theory that states that consumers are motivated to act in accordance with their attitudes and behaviors (p. 296)

service quality overall goodness or badness of a service experience, which is often measured by SERVQUAL (p. 297)

SERVQUAL way of measuring service quality that captures consumers' disconfirmation of service expectations (p. 297)

desire level of a particular benefit that will lead to a valued end state (p. 297)

equity theory theory that proposes that people compare their own level of inputs

(continued)

and outcomes to those of another party in an exchange (p. 297)

distributive fairness refers to the way a consumer judges the outcomes of an exchange (p. 297)

interactional fairness captures how fairly a consumer believes he or she was treated when dealing with service personnel in resolving some issue (p. 298)

attribution theory theory that proposes that consumers look for the cause of

particular consumption experiences when arriving at satisfaction judgments (p. 298)

cognitive dissonance an uncomfortable feeling that occurs when a consumer has lingering doubts about a decision that has occurred (p. 299)

14-5 **Avoid problems associated with typical satisfaction measures.** Marketers often express frustration with measuring satisfaction because the results may not be as useful or diagnostic as they may have hoped. One problem is that the typical ways of measuring, such as a four-item check box, end up providing very little information because consumers overwhelmingly report satisfaction. The result is left-skewed data, in this instance meaning that the bulk of consumers have indicated that they are satisfied or very satisfied. A better way of measuring satisfaction is to ask the question several different ways with at least some of those ways providing a wider range of possible responses.

left skewed distribution of responses consistent with most respondents choosing responses so the distribution is clustered toward the positive end of the scale (p. 301)

14-6 **Describe ways that consumers dispose of products.** Disposal represents the final process in consumption. In this stage of the consumption process, consumers either permanently or temporarily get rid of products. There are many alternatives available to consumers to do this, including trashing, recycling, trading, donating, or reselling

consumer refuse any packaging that is no longer necessary for consumption to take place or, in some cases, the actual good that is no longer providing value to the consumer (p. 301)

e-waste the mass of discarded electronics such as cell phones, old computers, tablets, etc. (p. 302)

packrats consumers possessing high levels of a lifestyle trait leading to a strong tendency toward retaining consumption-related possessions (p. 303)

15-1 List and define the behavioral outcomes of consumption. Complaining behavior occurs when a consumer actively seeks out someone to share an opinion with regarding a negative consumption event. WOM (word-of-mouth) behavior occurs when a consumer decides to complain or state an opinion publicly to other consumers about something that happened during a consumption experience with a specific company. When negative WOM reaches a large scale, such as when public media get involved, negative WOM becomes negative publicity. Switching behavior refers to times when a consumer chooses a competing choice, rather than repeating the previous purchase behavior in a given product category. Consumers can also exhibit loyalty-related behaviors. Loyal consumers tend to repeat consumption behavior repeatedly.

procedural justice an equity-based cognition representing the extent that consumers believe the processes involved in processing a transaction, performing a service, or handling any complaint are fair (p. 305)

critical incident exchange between consumers and businesses that the consumer views as unusually negative with implications for the relationship (p. 305)

15-2 Know why and how consumers complain and spread word-of-mouth, and know how word-of-mouth helps and hurts marketers. Emotions influence whether or not a consumer complains, and negative approach emotions, like anger, are more likely to precede complaining behavior than are avoidance emotions, like disgust, or even milder negative emotions, like dissatisfaction. Complaining should actually be encouraged because when a customer complains, the firm has a chance to recover and convert the complaining customer into a satisfied customer. Aside from this, complaints are an extremely valuable source of feedback for improving the product offering. In the extreme, though, complaining can go beyond just verbal behavior and can even end up in revenge-oriented behaviors.

complaining behavior action that occurs when a consumer actively seeks out someone (supervisor, service provider, etc.) with whom to share an opinion regarding a negative consumption event (p. 306)

rancorous revenge is when a consumer yells insults and makes a public scene in an effort to harm the business in response to an unsatisfactory experience (p. 308)

retaliatory revenge consumer becomes violent with employees and/or tries to vandalize a business in response to an unsatisfactory experience (p. 308)

negative word-of-mouth (negative WOM); action that takes place when consumers pass on negative information about a company from one to another (p. 309)

positive WOM action that occurs when consumers spread information from one to another about positive consumption experiences with companies (p. 309)

negative public publicity action that occurs when negative WOM spreads on a relatively large scale, possibly even involving media coverage (p. 310)

third-party endorsement one form of publicity in which an ostensibly objective outsider (neither the customer nor the business) provides publicly available purchase recommendations or evaluations (p. 313)

15-3 Use the concept of switching costs to understand why consumers do or do not continue to do business with a company. Switching costs involve the cost of changing from one brand/retailer/service provider to another. Switching costs can be procedural, financial, or relational. Any of these can motivate a consumer to continue making the same purchase decisions as in the past. This can occur even if the consumer is dissatisfied with this behavior. When switching costs are high and few competitors are available to consumers, they can end up feeling captive and forced to continue to do business with a company even when they believe service is bad and they are dissatisfied. Some types of procedural switching costs in particular, such as loyalty cards or incompatible features, can alienate consumers.

switching times when a consumer chooses a competing choice, rather than the previously purchased choice, on the next purchase occasion (p. 313)

switching costs costs associated with changing from one choice (brand/retailer/service provider) to another (p. 314)

procedural switching costs lost time and extended effort spent in learning ways of using some product offering (p. 314)

financial switching costs total economic resources that must be spent or invested as a consumer learns how to obtain value from a new product choice (p. 314)

relational switching cost emotional and psychological consequences of changing from one brand/retailer/service provider to another (p. 314)

competitive intensity number of firms competing for business within a specific category (p. 316)

15-4 Describe each component of true consumer loyalty. True consumer loyalty is more than just repeated behavior. Consumer loyalty can be described behaviorally by the concept of customer share, sometimes known as share of wallet. This is the percent of resources allocated to one from among a set of competing marketers. Over time, consumers may also begin to identify strongly with a brand and develop customer commitment. Committed customers will go out of their way and even pay more to continue doing business with a preferred brand, retailer, or service provider.

Exhibit 15.4

Vulnerability to Defections Based on CS/D

Customers are relatively:	High competitive intensity		Low competitive intensity	
	Switching costs		Switching costs	
	Low	High	Low	High
Satisfied	Vulnerable	Low vulnerability	Low vulnerability	No vulnerability
Dissatisfied	High vulnerabilty	Vulnerable	Vulnerable	Low vulnerability

customer share portion of resources allocated to one brand from among the set of competing brands (p. 316)

share of wallet customer share (p. 316)

consumer inertia situation in which a consumer tends to continue a pattern of behavior until some stronger force motivates him or her to change (p. 317)

loyalty card/program device that encourages repeated purchasing and keeps track of the amount of purchasing a consumer has had with a given marketer once some level is reached (p. 317)

customer commitment sense of attachment, dedication, and identification (p. 318)

antiloyal consumers consumers who will do everything possible to avoid doing business with a particular marketer (p. 319)

15-5 Link the concept of consumer co-creation of value to consumption outcomes. Value is the result of consumption and as such plays a key role in determining how the consumer behaves following consumption. For functional goods and services, such as banking or auto repair, utilitarian value is particularly important in bringing consumers back and creating loyalty. For experiential goods and services, such as fine dining, hedonic value is relatively important in bringing consumers back and creating loyalty.

relationship quality degree of connectedness between a consumer and a retailer (p. 322)

16-1 Understand the consumer misbehavior phenomenon and how it affects the exchange process. Consumer misbehavior does indeed affect the exchange process. For fair exchanges to occur, the consumer, the marketer, and other consumers must trust each other. Abusive or threatening consumers can harm employees, other consumers, and even themselves. Consumers who misbehave also cause monetary harm to the entire marketing system. Insurance costs escalate, prices of consumer products soar, employees must be counseled, and new technologies must be added to retail outlets all because of consumer misbehavior. Computer mediated misbehavior also causes disruptions in electronic commerce.

consumer misbehavior behaviors that are in some way unethical and that potentially harm the self or others (p. 325)

moral beliefs beliefs about the perceived ethicality or morality of behaviors (p. 326)

moral equity beliefs regarding an act's fairness or justness (p. 326)

contractualism beliefs about the violation of written (or unwritten) laws (p. 326)

relativism beliefs about the social acceptability of an act in a culture (p. 326)

deontological evaluations evaluations regarding the inherent rightness or wrongness of specific actions (p. 326)

teleological evaluations consumers' assessment of the goodness or badness of the consequences of actions (p. 326)

16-2 Distinguish between consumer misbehavior and consumer problem behavior. Consumer misbehavior can be distinguished from consumer problem behavior in terms of self-control. In most situations, a consumer can control consumer misbehavior; however, a consumer will experience great difficulty controlling problem behavior. This is particularly the case for addictive consumer behavior when a consumer becomes physically dependent on the consumption of a product.

consumer problem behavior consumer behavior that is deemed to be unacceptable but that is seemingly beyond the control of the consumer (p. 327)

compulsive consumption repetitive, excessive, and purposeful consumer behaviors that are performed as a response to tension, anxiety, or obtrusive thoughts (p. 332)

addictive consumption physiological dependency on the consumption of a consumer product (p. 332)

compulsive buying chronic, repetitive purchasing that is a response to negative events or feelings (p. 332)

compulsive shopping repetitive shopping behaviors (p. 332)

binge eating consumption of large amounts of food while feeling a general loss of control over food intake (p. 333)

binge drinking consumption of five or more drinks in a single drinking session for

men and four or more drinks for women (p. 333)

problem gambling obsession over the thought of gambling and the loss of control over gambling behavior and its consequences (p. 333)

16-3 Discuss marketing ethics and how marketing ethics guide the development of marketing programs. Marketing ethics are societal and professional standards of right and fair practices that are expected of marketing managers. Marketing programs must be planned in ways that adhere to marketing ethics. Most firms have explicitly stated rules and codes of conduct for their employees and their activities in the marketplace. Most professional organizations also have these codes. These ethics provide a framework from which marketing decisions can be made.

ethics standards or moral codes of conduct to which a person, group, or organization adheres (p. 334)

marketing ethics societal and professional standards of right and fair practices that are expected of marketing managers as they develop and implement marketing strategies (p. 334)

marketing concept states a firm should focus on consumer needs as a means of achieving long-term success (p. 336)

consumerism activities of various groups to voice concern for, and to protect, basic consumer rights (p. 336)

Consumer Bill of Rights introduced by President John F. Kennedy in 1962, list of rights that include the right to safety, the right to be informed, the right to redress and to be heard, and the right to choice (p. 336)

morals personal standards and beliefs used to guide individual action (p. 339)

16-4 Comprehend the role of corporate social responsibility in the field of marketing. It is important for businesses today to focus on "doing well by doing good." Being socially responsible is one way in which businesses attempt to do well by doing the right things. Corporate social responsibility (CSR) refers to an organization's activities and status related to its societal obligations. Due to increased pressure from various consumer and media groups, companies are finding that they must be socially responsible with their marketing programs.

corporate social responsibility (CSR) organization's activities and status related to its societal obligations (p. 339)

societal marketing concept marketing concept that states that marketers should consider not only the wants and

needs of consumers but also the needs of society (p. 339)

16-5 Understand the various forms of regulation that affect marketing practice. Federal, state, and local laws are in place to protect consumers from many forms of marketer misbehavior. Federal bodies, such as the Federal Trade Commission and the Food and Drug Administration, exist to monitor exchanges that take place between consumers and marketing organizations. Other groups, such as the Better Business Bureau, the American Association of Advertising Agencies, and the American Marketing Association, also play important roles in monitoring marketing activities. Although these groups attempt to bring fairness to the marketplace, ultimately it is up to the decision makers to ensure that their own actions, and the actions of their firms, fall within generally accepted business guidelines.

16-6 Comprehend the major areas of criticism to which marketers are subjected. Several issues in marketing receive criticism from various groups. Issues such as deceptive advertising, marketing to children, pollution, planning the obsolescence of current products, price gouging, using manipulative sales tactics, and practicing stealth marketing campaigns are all considered questionable by various groups.

deceptive advertising message that omits information that is important in influencing a consumer's buying behavior and is likely to mislead consumers acting reasonably (p. 341)

puffery practice of making exaggerated claims about a product and its superiority (p. 341)

planned obsolescence act of planning the premature discontinuance of product models that perform adequately (p. 342)

sales orientation practice of using sales techniques that are aimed at satisfying the salesperson's own needs and motives for short-term sales success (p. 343)

customer orientation practice of using sales techniques that focus on customer needs (p. 343)

foot-in-the-door technique ingratiation technique used in personal selling in which a salesperson begins with a small request and slowly leads up to one major request (p. 343)

door-in-the-face technique ingratiation technique used in personal selling in which a salesperson begins with a major request and then follows with a series of smaller requests (p. 343)

even-a-penny-will-help technique ingratiation technique in which a marketing message is sent that suggests that even the smallest donation, such as a penny or a dollar, will help a cause (p. 343)

"I'm working for you!" technique technique used by salespeople to create the perception that they are working as hard as possible to close a sale when they really are not doing so (p. 344)

products liability extent to which businesses are held responsible for product-related injuries (p. 344)

strict liability legal action against a firm whereby a consumer demonstrates in court that an injury occurred and that the product associated with the injury was faulty in some way (p. 344)

negligence situation whereby an injured consumer attempts to show that a firm could foresee a potential injury might occur and then decided not to act on that knowledge (p. 344)

punitive damages damages that are sought to punish a company for behavior associated with an injury (p. 345)

compensatory damages damages that are intended to cover costs incurred by a consumer due to an injury (p. 345)